LONDON LABOUR AND THE LONDON POOR

HENRY MAYHEW (1812–87), journalist, novelist, dramatist, and social investigator, was born in London on 25 November 1812. He was educated at Westminster School, but ran away in 1827 after refusing to accept a flogging, and travelled as a midshipman to India. After returning to London, he spent an unhappy period in the office of his father, a prominent solicitor, before abandoning the law to pursue a career as a freelance journalist and writer. Following the launch of the satirical weekly newspaper *Figaro in London* in 1831, and successful ventures into writing for the theatre, in 1841 he was one of the founding editors of *Punch*. His marriage in 1844 to the daughter of Douglas Jerrold was not a success (they separated in the 1860s), and his career threatened to splutter to a halt with a series of incomplete projects. The failure of a journal established to take advantage of the railway boom (*Iron Times*) led to his bankruptcy in 1846. However, despite these personal and professional disappointments, Mayhew went on to produce some of the most important journalism of the nineteenth century. As the metropolitan correspondent of the *Morning Chronicle*, between October 1849 and December 1850 he contributed a series of eighty-two articles on 'Labour and the Poor' that attracted wide notice for their sympathetic yet unsentimental depiction of the 'London street-folk'. In 1850 he left the *Chronicle*, but continued to publish his articles in a new weekly serial, *London Labour and the London Poor*, between December 1850 and February 1852. The work was abandoned after a dispute with his printer, and was only completed with the assistance of others in 1861–2. The rest of Mayhew's life was spent travelling and writing, but although he published widely in genres as diverse as travel books, children's stories, and comic novels, he never recaptured his earlier success. When he died in Holborn on 25 July 1887 his pioneering work as a social investigator had largely been superseded or forgotten. He is buried in Kensal Green cemetery.

ROBERT DOUGLAS-FAIRHURST is Fellow and Tutor in English at Magdalen College, University of Oxford. He is the author of *Victorian Afterlives: The Shaping of Influence in Nineteenth-Century Literature* (2002) and has edited Charles Dickens's *A Christmas Carol and Other Christmas Books* for Oxford World's Classics.

OXFORD WORLD'S CLASSICS

For over 100 years Oxford World's Classics have brought readers closer to the world's great literature. Now with over 700 titles—from the 4,000-year-old myths of Mesopotamia to the twentieth century's greatest novels—the series makes available lesser-known as well as celebrated writing.

The pocket-sized hardbacks of the early years contained introductions by Virginia Woolf, T. S. Eliot, Graham Greene, and other literary figures which enriched the experience of reading. Today the series is recognized for its fine scholarship and reliability in texts that span world literature, drama and poetry, religion, philosophy, and politics. Each edition includes perceptive commentary and essential background information to meet the changing needs of readers.

OXFORD WORLD'S CLASSICS

HENRY MAYHEW

London Labour and the London Poor

A Selected Edition

Edited with an Introduction and Notes by
ROBERT DOUGLAS-FAIRHURST

UNIVERSITY PRESS

OXFORD
UNIVERSITY PRESS

Great Clarendon Street, Oxford OX2 6DP
Oxford University Press is a department of the University of Oxford.
It furthers the University's objective of excellence in research, scholarship,
and education by publishing worldwide in

Oxford New York

Auckland Cape Town Dar es Salaam Hong Kong Karachi
Kuala Lumpur Madrid Melbourne Mexico City Nairobi
New Delhi Shanghai Taipei Toronto

With offices in

Argentina Austria Brazil Chile Czech Republic France Greece
Guatemala Hungary Italy Japan Poland Portugal Singapore
South Korea Switzerland Thailand Turkey Ukraine Vietnam

Oxford is a registered trade mark of Oxford University Press
in the UK and in certain other countries

Published in the United States
by Oxford University Press Inc., New York

First published 2010
First published as an Oxford World's Classics paperback 2012

British Library Cataloguing in Publication Data
Data available

Library of Congress Cataloging in Publication Data
Library of Congress Control Number: 2011945244

Typeset by Glyph International, Bangalore, India

Printed and bound in Great Britain by Clays Ltd, Elcograf S.p.A.

ISBN 978–0–19–969757–1

10

CONTENTS

List of Illustrations xi
Introduction xiii
Note on the Text and Illustrations xliv
Select Bibliography xlvi
A Chronology of Henry Mayhew xlix

LONDON LABOUR AND THE LONDON POOR

Preface 3

VOLUME I: THE LONDON STREET-FOLK

Of the London Street-Folk 9
Costermongers 14
The London Street Markets on a Saturday Night 14
Habits and Amusements of Costermongers 16
'Vic. Gallery' 24
Of the Uneducated State of Costermongers 28
Language of Costermongers 30
Of the Nicknames of Costermongers 34
Of the Homes of the Costermongers 34
Of the Cries, Rounds, and Days of Costermongers 39
Of the Tricks of Costermongers 41
Street-Sellers of Fruit and Vegetables 43
Of Covent Garden Market 43
Watercress Girl 47
Street-Sellers of Eatables and Drinkables 51
Of the Street-Sellers of Eatables and Drinkables 51

Of the Experience of a Fried Fish-Seller, and of the Class of Customers 53
Of the Street-Sellers of Ham-Sandwiches 55
Of the Experience of a Ham Sandwich-Seller 56
Of Cats' and Dogs'-Meat Dealers 58
Of Coffee-Stall Keepers 60
Of Milk Selling in St James's Park 64
Of Street Piemen 66
Of the Street-Sellers of Gingerbread-Nuts 67
Of the Street Sale of Sweet-Stuff 70
Of the Street-Sellers of Ices and of Ice Creams 71
Street-Sellers of Stationery, Literature, and the Fine Arts 74
Of the Street-Sellers of Stationery, Literature, and the Fine Arts 74
Of Running Patterers 76
Experience of a Running Patterer 77
Of the Death and Fire Hunters 81
Of the Sham Indecent Street-Trade 85
Of Ancient and Modern Street Ballad Minstrelsy 89
Of the 'Gallows' Literature of the Streets 92
Of the Street-Sellers of Conundrums 99
Of the Street-Sellers of Engravings, etc., in Umbrellas, etc. 102
Street-Sellers of Manufactured Articles 105
Of the Street-Sellers of Manufactured Articles 105
Of the Cheap Johns, or Street Hansellers 106
The Crippled Street-Seller of Nutmeg-Graters 109
Of the Life of a Street-Seller of Dog-Collars 112
Of the Tally Packman 116

Of the 'Duffers' or Hawkers of Pretended Smuggled Goods 120
The Blind Street-Seller of Boot-Laces 123
Of the Street-Sellers of Corn-Salve 130
Of the Street-Seller of Crackers and Detonating Balls 132
Of the Street-Sellers of Dolls 134
Of the Street-Sellers of Poison for Rats 136
Of the Hawking of Tea 139
Children Street-Sellers 141
Of the Children Street-Sellers of London 141

VOLUME II: THE LONDON STREET-FOLK (CONTINUED)

Street-Sellers of Second-Hand Articles 149
Of the Street-Sellers of Second-Hand Articles 149
Of the Uses of Second-Hand Garments 149
Of the Street-Sellers of Petticoat and Rosemary-Lanes 152
Street-Sellers of Mineral Productions and Natural Curiosities 157
Of the Street-Sellers of Coals 157
Street-Buyers 162
Of the Street-Buyers 162
Of the Street-Buyers of Rags, Broken Metal, Bottles, Glass, and Bones 163
Of the 'Rag-and-Bottle', and the 'Marine-Store' Shops 165
Of the Street-Buyers of Waste (Paper) 170
Of the Street-Buyers of Umbrellas and Parasols 173
Street-Finders or Collectors 175
Of the Street-Finders or Collectors 175
Bone-Grubbers and Rag-Gatherers 175

Of the Cigar-End Finders 180
Of the Sewer-Hunters 182
Of the Mud-Larks 189
Of the Dustmen of London 193
Chimney-Sweepers 198
Of the General Characteristics of the Working Chimney-Sweepers 198
The Quantity of Refuse Bought, Collected, or Found, in the Streets of London 206
Crossing-Sweepers 208
The Negro Crossing-Sweeper, who had lost both his Legs 209
Boy Crossing-Sweepers and Tumblers 214
The 'King' of the Tumbling-Boy Crossing-Sweepers 218

VOLUME III: THE LONDON STREET-FOLK (CONCLUDED)

Destroyers of Vermin 225
The Rat-Killer 225
A Night at Rat-Killing 226
'Catch-'em-Alive' Sellers 236
Street Exhibitors 239
Punch 239
Exhibitor of Mechanical Figures 243
Exhibitor of the Microscope 245
The Strong Man 249
The Street Fire-King, or Salamander 253
The Snake, Sword, and Knife-Swallower 257
Street Clown 261
Strolling Actors 265
Gun-Exercise Exhibitor—One-Legged Italian 269

Street Musicians 273
'Old Sarah' 274
'Farm-Yard' Player 278
The Dancing Dogs 279
Street Artists 283
Street Photography 283
Statement of a Photographic Man 287
Exhibitors of Trained Animals 293
The Happy Family Exhibitor 293
Skilled and Unskilled Labour 295
The Doll's-Eye Maker 295
Cheap Lodging-Houses 299
London Omnibus-Drivers and Conductors 306
Omnibus Drivers 306
London Vagrants 309
Statements of Vagrants 311
Statement of a Returned Convict 318
Description of the Asylum for the Houseless 323

VOLUME IV: THOSE THAT WILL NOT WORK

Introduction and Classification [Henry Mayhew] 329
Of the Workers and Non-Workers 329
Prostitution in London [Bracebridge Hemyng] 332
Seclusives, or Those that Live in Private Houses and Apartments 332
Board Lodgers 334
Thieves' Women 336
Thieves and Swindlers [John Binny] 341
The Sneaks, or Common Thieves 341
A Visit to the Rookery of St Giles and its Neighbourhood 348

Pickpockets and Shoplifters 357
Statement of a Young Pickpocket [Henry Mayhew] 363
Housebreakers and Burglars 366
Narrative of a Burglar 373
Swindlers 381
Beggars and Cheats [Andrew Halliday] 389
Begging-Letter Writers 389
Ashamed Beggars 394
Naval and Military Beggars 396
Turnpike Sailor 396
Street Campaigners 400
Disaster Beggars 404
A Shipwrecked Mariner 404
Lucifer Droppers 406
Bodily Afflicted Beggars 407
Seventy Years a Beggar 408
Beggars Subject to Fits 410
Petty Trading Beggars 411

Appendix 1: Money and the Cost of Living 417
Appendix 2: Map: London c.1848 423
Appendix 3: 'A Table Showing the Quantity of Refuse Bought, Collected, or Found, in the Streets of London' 427
Appendix 4: 'A Visit to the Cholera Districts of Bermondsey' 430
Explanatory Notes 439

LIST OF ILLUSTRATIONS

Henry Mayhew (frontispiece to vol. I of the first edition) liv

Title page to vol. I of the first edition 1

The London Costermonger 19

The London Coffee-Stall 63

The Coster Boy and Girl Tossing the Pieman 68

Illustrations of Street-Art, No. 1 79

The Street-Seller of Nutmeg-Graters 110

The Street-Seller of Dog's Collars 114

Scene in Petticoat-Lane 153

The Bone-Grubber 176

The Sewer-Hunter 183

The Mud-Lark 190

View of a Dust Yard 196

The London Sweep 204

The Boy Crossing-Sweepers 216

Ratting—'The Graham Arms', Graham Street 234

Punch's Showmen 242

Circus Clown at Fair 263

'Old Sarah', the well-known hurdy-gurdy player 275

Photographic Saloon, East End of London 291

Vagrant from the Refuge in Playhouse Yard, Cripplegate 312

The Haymarket—Midnight 337

Boys Exercising at Tothill Fields' Prison 349

INTRODUCTION

'The Great World of London'

HENRY MAYHEW did not lack ambition. In 1856 he launched a new periodical, to be published in weekly parts, that boasted the title *The Great World of London*. It reflected his recognition that London was becoming more than just another literary market; by the mid-nineteenth century this restless, tangled, relentlessly surprising city had also emerged as one of the most important subjects confronting the modern writer. As London continued to expand—the heart of the Empire growing larger and stronger the harder it worked—more people than ever before wanted to read about each other and themselves, and the books and journals that set out to meet this need were at once mirrors of contemporary life and barriers against its worst excesses. But as the introduction to *The Great World of London* develops, and editorial throat-clearing is replaced by the first extended description of London as a whole, it quickly becomes clear that Mayhew was not content merely to analyse the city from the outside. He wanted his writing to inhabit it, to become a sounding board for the world around him. Climbing the 500-odd steps to the gallery of St Paul's Cathedral, and gazing down at the streets below, Mayhew discovers a world that is both familiar and strange. A landscape of fact repeatedly knocks up against one of fairy-tale transformations: long lines of omnibuses are 'no bigger than tin toys, and crowded with pigmies on the roof'; brewers' drays are distinguished by the round backs of their horses, 'looking like plump mice'; the pavements are darkened 'with dense streams of busy little men, that looked almost like ants, hurrying along in opposite directions'. Yet Mayhew's sense of wonder at a world usually hidden from us does not altogether muffle his awareness of the potentially deadly competition going on beneath his feet: 'what with the closely-packed throng of carts, cabs, and omnibuses, the earth seemed all alive with tiny creeping things, as when one looks into the grass on a warm summer's day.'[1]

[1] *The Great World of London*, 1 (March 1856), 24.

Three years after the publication of *The Great World of London*, Darwin reminded his readers that similar tussles went on at every level of existence. The *Origin of Species* (1859) concludes with the famous image of 'an entangled bank, clothed with many plants of many kinds, with birds singing on the bushes, with various insects flitting about, and with worms crawling through the damp earth': an attractive sight, but also proof of 'a Struggle for Life' producing 'Divergence of Character and the Extinction of less-improved forms'.[2] By the time he came to write *The Great World of London*, Mayhew already had plenty of evidence that human society worked according to a more deliberate version of the same principle. Individuals had to find a niche for themselves within the city's complex and ever-changing economy. Costermongers, in particular, the street hawkers who sold everything from fruit to fireworks, needed to get themselves noticed if they wanted to win customers; like a bird asserting its territory in the branches of a tree, their street-cries were defiant signatures of selfhood, a means of asserting their individuality against the anonymous roar of the city. Accordingly, as Mayhew continues his description, he passes over the groups that huddle together in the chilly morning air before zooming in on an individual:

as the streets grow blue with the coming light, and the church spires and roof-tops stand out against the clear sky with a sharpness of outline that is seen only in London before its million chimneys cover the town with their smoke—then come sauntering forth the unwashed poor; some with greasy wallets on their backs to hunt over each dust-heap, and eke out life by seeking refuse bones, or stray rags and pieces of old iron; others, whilst on their way to their work, are gathered at the corner of some street round the early breakfast-stall, and blowing saucers of steaming coffee, drawn from tall tin cans that have the red-hot charcoal shining crimson through the holes in the fire-pan beneath them; whilst already the little slattern girl, with her basket slung before her, screams, 'Water-*creases*!' through the sleeping streets.[3]

The present tense of this passage is carefully judged, dramatizing how the lives of these specimens in the 'huge human "vivarium" ' of London have hardened into routines that go on in the same way

[2] *On the Origin of Species* [1859], ed. Gillian Beer (Oxford: Oxford World's Classics, 1996), 360.

[3] *Great World of London*, 29.

whether they are aware of being observed or not.[4] Every day the same search for scraps to eat; every day the same rounds to make, as unvarying as a goldfish circling its bowl. Several times the sentence shifts focus, as the observer's attention is distracted by new sights and sounds, before it settles on the watercress girl, at which point she marks out her pitch with the cry 'Water-*creases*!' (watercresses), a jabbing emphasis that is the aural equivalent of someone using her elbow in a crowd. In showing how this figure tries to make herself heard with those 'screams', no other social investigator of the period comes close to bringing alive what *The Great World of London* describes as 'the riot, the struggle, and the scramble for a living'.[5]

Mayhew's readers would have encountered the watercress girl before, on the page if not in person, because her life-story featured in the work that had made his reputation: *London Labour and the London Poor*. This set of interviews and statistical surveys was first published as a periodical in 1850–2, and later collected and revised as a set of four volumes in 1861–2. It was a development of an earlier set of letters on 'Labour and the Poor' Mayhew had contributed to the *Morning Chronicle* in 1849–50, one of which had dealt with 'the great watercress mart' in Farringdon, with its 'poor shivering, half-clad boys and girls surrounding the dealers' stands'.[6] And this was the key to Mayhew's success. Other writers may have noticed these scrawny children before, but none had elevated them to the dignity of print, certainly not with Mayhew's ability to reconcile objectivity with compassion. (These are 'poor' children in more than just a financial sense.) Though they and the other 'London Street-Folk' could be numbered in their thousands—Mayhew reckoned there were 30,000 costermongers alone—in terms of cultural representation they were invisible, silent, secret. Their world was like a shadowy twin of the London most of his readers knew, one that occasionally bumped into middle-class society but until now had largely been avoided. Not any more. Economic and social problems that had mostly been written about in abstract terms of 'labour' and 'capital' were suddenly individualized and brought vividly to life. Working-class figures who might only have featured as walk-on extras in a novel were thrust

[4] The 'vivarium' was a newly fashionable way of studying fish and other life forms under the controlled conditions of a glass tank.

[5] *Great World of London*, 63.

[6] Letter CXXXI, *Morning Chronicle* (5 December 1850).

centre-stage and asked to talk about themselves at length. Given the time to speak, and the promise that people would listen, many found voices of surprising subtlety and power. Indeed, as Mayhew prompted and probed, and the street folk responded by talking about everything from their wages to their histories, diets, families, pets, hopes, and fears, his readers discovered that these previously anonymous figures were just as surprising as themselves.

London Labour and the London Poor was originally advertised as a 'cyclopaedia' of street life, implying that the finished work would be a compendium of facts for dipping into rather than a book to be read from cover to cover, and it certainly lived up to its billing. In its 2,000-odd cramped pages, totalling close to 2 million words, there is scarcely a paragraph that does not contain an eye-opening or ear-catching piece of information. Conmen routinely sold greenfinches they had painted to resemble more exotic species of singing birds (ii.70).[7] The popularity of oysters in London meant that 'in round numbers' there were 500 million shells to be disposed of every year (ii.285). An old showman who travelled with performing animals 'sometimes had trouble to get lodgings for the bear', even though 'Bears is well-behaved enough if they ain't aggravated' (iii.73). In its teasing, testing combination of authorial overview and individual insights, humour and horror, models of conduct and examples of actual behaviour, *London Labour and the London Poor* was not only the first major work of sociology (a word first coined in the 1840s). It was also the greatest Victorian novel never written.

The Wandering Minstrel

London Labour and the London Poor would have been an extraordinary achievement no matter who had written it. Coming from Mayhew it was close to a miracle. Nothing in his previous history had indicated that he had the dedication required to produce such an ambitious work. Although reasonably well known as a writer before he started his research, nothing he produced seemed to be of any lasting interest, and when his contemporaries spoke of him it was usually with an

[7] All references to *London Labour and the London Poor* (hereafter abbreviated to *LLLP*) are to the four-volume edition published in 1861–2: see the Note on the Text and Illustrations, p. xliv, for more details; additional page references are given where the passages are reprinted in the present edition.

amused tolerance that bordered on contempt. The journalist and publisher Henry Vizetelly, who knew him in his later years, concluded that Mayhew was a man of 'multifarious schemes and singularly original ideas, but of torpid energy'.[8]

> Mayhew . . . was constantly planning some new publication or broaching novel ideas on the most out-of-the-way subjects. He would scheme and ponder all the day long, but he abominated the labour of putting his ideas into tangible shape. He would talk like a book on any subject for hours together if he could only find listeners, but could with difficulty be brought to put pen to paper.[9]

When Mayhew did try to put his ideas into a tangible shape the results could be explosive. At one stage he seems to have attempted to create artificial diamonds, almost blowing up his house in the process, while other get-rich-quick schemes included the manufacture of a new kind of artificial dye—equally far-fetched and equally unsuccessful. In the literary world, too, he seemed much better at coming up with ideas than seeing them through. In the 1830s and 1840s he is a fitful, flickering presence: there are glimpses of him here and there, enthusiastically talking and drinking, 'with an extraordinary mop of dark hair that sadly wanted trimming',[10] but none of his efforts to make a name for himself worked much better than the diamonds or the dye, and the patchy record of his movements in this period indicates how close he was to swelling the ranks of London's anonymous poor. The closest he came to a success was with a theatrical farce entitled *The Wandering Minstrel* (1834), and this may have had something to do with his own affinity for the subject. Few writers of the early Victorian period so perfectly sum up its atmosphere of nervous ambition, in which clever young men (and, more rarely, women) turned themselves into pens for hire, roaming the streets of literary London in search of the right formula to bring them money and fame. Mayhew tried almost everything. From 1835 he edited *Figaro in London*, a satirical journal that sought to address weighty social concerns with a light touch; it collapsed in 1839. In 1841 he helped to found *Punch*, another journal that tried to combine serious campaigning with jokes: it went from strength to strength, but Mayhew was ousted as editor

[8] Henry Vizetelly, *Glances Back Through Seventy Years* (London, 1893), i.408.

[9] Reported in M. H. Spielmann, *The History of 'Punch'* (London: Cassell, 1895), 268.

[10] Athol Mayhew, *A Jorum of 'Punch' with those who helped to brew it* (London, 1895), 94.

after less than a year. He seemed doomed to be the nearly man of Victorian letters. His theatrical follow-ups to *The Wandering Minstrel* failed to hit the mark: 'coarse, loud, and clumsy' is the brisk summary of one modern critic.[11] His novels, too, were quickly written and just as quickly forgotten, each one a limp comedy of manners that set out to chime with some fashionable debate or other and was destined not to outlast it. *The Greatest Plague in Life* (1847) dealt with the problem of how to attract and retain servants; *Whom to Marry and How to Get Married!* (1848) offered a genial but blunt satire on middle-class sexual morality. Neither created more than a ripple in the market-place, and both may have been attempts at self-therapy as much as dispassionate pieces of social diagnosis. Mayhew's own marriage was an unhappy one, largely because of his irrepressible over-spending, and in 1847 he was declared bankrupt in a court case that saw even his own defence counsel admit that his client was 'somewhat irregular in his accounts' and 'too sanguine in his hopes'.[12] In effect he was a real-life Mr Micawber, living beyond his means while waiting for something to turn up.

Fortunately it did. In September 1849 he was invited to contribute a piece to the *Morning Chronicle*, a liberal newspaper with a tradition of depicting ordinary London life (in the 1830s it had published the first of Dickens's *Sketches by Boz*) and campaigning to improve miserable social conditions.[13] The request came exactly halfway through Mayhew's life, and although he did not know it at the time, 'A Visit to the Cholera Districts of Bermondsey' (reprinted here as Appendix 4) turned out to be the pivot on which his career turned. In many ways it was a standard assignment: concern over the spread of cholera had been simmering away in the press for several years, and by the summer of 1849 matters had reached crisis point. In London alone, around 13,000 people had died of cholera within three months, and on

[11] John L. Bradley (ed.), Selections from 'London Labour and the London Poor' (London: Oxford University Press, 1965), p. xi.

[12] Ibid., p. xxii.

[13] E. P. Thompson points out that the *Morning Chronicle* had been sold in February 1848 to a consortium with broadly liberal views: 'The paper had, decidedly, a philanthropic and evangelical conscience; and its columns, in the summer and autumn of 1849, do not make pleasant reading. Column after column deals in detail with the causes of sanitary reform: sewerage, water supplies, the choked burial grounds of the metropolis.' See E. P. Thompson and Eileen Yeo (eds.), *The Unknown Mayhew* (New York: Pantheon, 1971), 20.

10 September public fears peaked with the confirmation of 432 victims in a single day. Such fears were closely bound up with uncertainty over how cholera spread (noxious air or water seemed to be the likeliest explanation), and the recognition that London's teeming slums created conditions in which the disease could thrive—a disease that was no respecter of geographical or social boundaries. In this context, Mayhew's readers would probably not have been surprised by the appearance of his article, nor by the way he chose to introduce it: 'So well known are the localities of fever and disease, that London would almost admit of being mapped out pathologically.' So far, so familiar; but as the article develops by describing the notorious slum Jacob's Island ('the very capital of cholera . . . the Venice of drains'), Mayhew's writing takes on a new edge:

> We crossed the bridge, and spoke to one of the inmates. In answer to our questions, she told us she was never well. Indeed, the signs of the deadly influence of the place were painted in the earthy complexion of the poor woman. 'Neither I nor my children know what health is,' said she. 'But what is one to do? We must live where our bread is. I've tried to let the house, and put a bill up, but cannot get any one to take it.' From this spot we were led to narrow close courts, where the sun never shone, and the air seemed almost as stagnant and putrid as the ditch we had left. The blanched cheeks of the people that now came out to stare at us, were white as vegetables grown in the dark, and as we stopped to look down the alley, our informant told us that the place teemed with children, and that if a horn was blown they would swarm like bees at the sound of a gong.

It is a remarkable piece of writing. Jacob's Island was no stranger to print: in *Oliver Twist* (1838), Dickens had given a lingering and appalled description of its 'dirt-besmeared walls and decaying foundations; every repulsive lineament of poverty, every loathsome indication of filth, rot and garbage' (ch. 50). Mayhew's account seems similarly torn between fascination and disgust, or what Dickens's biographer John Forster acutely described as 'the attraction of repulsion'.[14] (Mayhew himself would later echo the phrase when referring to the 'attractively-repulsive' details of street art; *LLLP*, i.215.) Facts start to drift into metaphor before being jerked back to the reality of stink and ooze, and as Mayhew continues from 'The Folly' to

[14] John Forster, *The Life of Charles Dickens*, ed. J. W. T. Ley (London: C. Palmer, 1928), 11.

'Providence-buildings', his account starts to resemble a modern reworking of Bunyan's *Pilgrim's Progress*, a voyage through an allegorical landscape in which wasted bodies are the physical manifestation of wasted lives. In this stagnant world, having an 'earthy' complexion starts to look ominously like a death sentence, just as the little dabs of blank verse that come into the speaker's voice ('But what is one to do? . . . I've tried to let the house') give her story the sort of tragic inevitability made familiar by poems like Wordsworth's *The Ruined Cottage*. Even the most ordinary words ask us to look again at what we thought we knew—not only 'poor' ('the poor woman'), but also 'spot', which seems determinedly chatty until we remember that in his introduction Mayhew characterized such areas as 'plague-spots'.

Such double takes, in which ordinary life suddenly reveals itself in unexpected ways, were to become a standard feature of Mayhew's writing. In a sense this was a natural development of his earlier career as a satirist, which also depended on refusing to take received wisdom for granted, but in his new venture the comic potential of the everyday was subdued to other ways of looking at it: through statistics, first-hand testimony, and measured calls for reform. For the success of Mayhew's visit to Jacob's Island quickly prompted the *Morning Chronicle*'s editors into action: by October 1849 they had announced a new series of articles to provide 'a full and detailed description of the moral, intellectual, material, and physical condition of the industrial poor throughout England'. Special correspondents were to report on the industrial towns and the rural districts, while Mayhew was to be the *Chronicle*'s 'Metropolitan Correspondent', reporting from areas of London that might as well have been on the moon for all the notice many people took of them. The series may have been Mayhew's idea, as he later claimed, but in any case he quickly made it his own, as he set about interviewing costermongers, tramps, dock workers, slop tailors, entertainers, and all the rest of the human flotsam and jetsam that had washed up in the capital.

Two or three letters per week, averaging around 3,500 words each, appeared over the course of the next year, although the number and variety of Mayhew's subjects sometimes disguise the fact that he tended to target the most desperate and, in many cases, oddest examples that came under the series heading 'Labour and the Poor'. There was little on skilled craftsmen, and nothing at all on servants, who by the time of the 1851 census amounted to 1 in 18 of the population as a whole. But Mayhew's combination of statistics and interviews proved compelling, and his trick of introducing local details that only revealed their true significance retrospectively was repeated on a much larger scale in the reactions of his readers. Widely admired for his bravery in undertaking potentially dangerous research—he later described how a missionary, sent into the East End to convert the heathen, ended up in a water-butt, his mouth filled with mustard and his 'nether garments' torn 'in a way I must not describe' (*LLLP*, i.249)—he was also praised as a voyager into the unknown: part pioneer, part anthropologist, part diplomatic envoy. Thackeray's response was typical:

> What a confession it is that we have almost all of us been obliged to make! A clever and earnest writer . . . goes amongst labouring people and poor of all kinds—and brings back what? A picture of human life so wonderful, so awful, so piteous and pathetic, so exciting and terrible, that readers of romances own they never read anything like it; and that the griefs, struggles, strange adventures here depicted exceed anything that any of us could imagine. Yes; and these wonders and terrors have been lying by your door and mine ever since we had a door of our own. We had to go but a hundred yards off and see for ourselves, but we never did.[15]

Of course Mayhew was not the first writer to describe the lives of London's poor. Engels's great work *The Condition of the Working Class in England in 1844*, while it analysed poverty in more abstract terms, and drew most of its examples from Manchester, quoted a report from *The Times* (12 October 1843) declaring that 'within the most courtly precincts of the richest city on God's earth' may be found the 'outcasts of society—ROTTING FROM FAMINE, FILTH, AND DISEASE'. Closer to the time, if not the tone, of Mayhew's reports, in 1846 an article had noted that although most people's lives were governed by the need for regular employment, there was also 'a class of irregular industrials' whose occupations 'have a smack of the bizarre about them': 'They sweep crossings, rake for lost trifles in cinder heaps, or in the sludge of the Thames; vend oranges, penknives, and last week's morning papers at omnibus stations; distribute hand-bills, and bear placards on their backs or their vans . . . it

[15] 'Waiting at the Station' (1850), repr. in *Miscellanies: Prose and Verse* (London: Bradbury & Evans, 1856).

must be admitted that when one is in a hurry they are continually in the way.'[16] Parliamentary inquiries, religious tracts, the stinging essays of Thomas Carlyle: all had dealt with the poor in one form or another, although without much agreement over which of the various factors singled out by the *Morning Chronicle* ('moral, intellectual, material, and physical') deserved most attention, or whether poverty was the sort of problem that admitted of any solutions at all. But as Thackeray's remark about 'romances' suggests, this social underworld or parallel world was probably most familiar to Mayhew's readers from the pages of fiction: either the picaresque caperings of works such as Pierce Egan's *Life in London* (1821), or the darker, Chartist-inspired reflections of G. M. W. Reynolds's best-selling series *The Mysteries of London* (1845–8).

Egan's novel centres on two Regency bucks, Tom and Jerry, whose rambles through the streets of London feature a number of low-life characters, including 'Chaffing Peter' the dustman and a costermonger with his donkey, who wink and leer their way through episodes such as a visit to the docks, a dance with prostitutes, and an initiation into the ways of 'Cadgers'. Far from being a serious piece of investigative journalism, Tom and Jerry's adventures are meant to demonstrate a simple moral: 'It is . . . the LOWER ORDERS of society who really ENJOY themselves.'[17] Not so the lower orders who slink out of the shadows in *The Mysteries of London*. According to Mayhew, Reynolds was the most popular author among the costermongers, and the gaudy horrors in his tales make it easy to imagine why: a corpse is left to rot in the room occupied by the rest of the family; a pig eats a dead child's face; a mother plans to blind her own daughter to make her a more convincing beggar. Reynolds may well have been one of Mayhew's inspirations: *The Mysteries of London* incorporated first-person 'histories' of various scoundrels, its rolling narrative was frequently interrupted with charts of statistics and digressions on topics such as 'The Treatment of the Workhouse', and when the weekly numbers were published together the book was advertised as

[16] 'A Plea for Advertising Vans', *Our Own Time* (July 1846), 123.

[17] *Life in London, or the day and night scenes of Jerry Hawthorn and Corinthian Tom* (1820), ed. John Camden Hotten (London, 1869), 320. Egan's novel is helpfully put into the context of other early nineteenth-century writings about the poor in P. J. Keating, *The Working Classes in Victorian Fiction* (New York: Barnes & Noble, 1971).

an 'Encyclopaedia'.[18] But Mayhew did not need to resort to fiction in order to make his readers' flesh creep. When he described how the frostbitten legs of a beggar burst after being put into an oven to thaw (*LLLP*, ii.490–3; pp. 209–13), it was simply what he had been told by the victim himself. Unlike the sketches of Egan or Reynolds, the class of his subjects was not the most interesting thing about them. Nor were they introduced merely as splashes of local colour, as they are in *Dombey and Son*'s description of 'the water-carts and the old-clothes men, and the people with geraniums, and the umbrella-mender, and the man who trilled the little bell of the Dutch clock as he went along' (ch. 3). Instead, Mayhew set out 'to deal with human nature as a natural philosopher or a chemist deals with any material object'—that is, to employ a deductive method in which detailed factual information needed to be gathered before any general laws or principles could be abstracted from it.[19] What his interview subjects said would be the foundations of his argument rather than a set of footnotes to it. In a dizzying shift of perspective, the publication of the *Morning Chronicle* letters thrust the background into the foreground, and for readers like Thackeray the effect was as astonishing as it would have been if pieces of theatrical scenery had come to the front of the stage and introduced themselves to the audience.

The impact of Mayhew's investigations was immediate and far-reaching. Charles Kingsley's pamphlet *Cheap Clothes and Nasty* and his novel *Alton Locke* (1850) both borrowed heavily from Mayhew, the former through generous quotation and the latter in hard-hitting descriptions of sweatshop labour and the hovels of Jacob's Island. There is also evidence that Elizabeth Gaskell's social criticism was sharpened between *Mary Barton* (1848) and *Ruth* (1853) by Mayhew's revelation of the appalling working conditions of dressmakers.[20] But the *Morning Chronicle* articles did more than raise awareness; they also raised money. The Female Emigration Society, established to send unemployed seamstresses out to the colonies, quickly attracted

[18] See G. W. M. Reynolds, *The Mysteries of London*, ed. Trefor Thomas (Keele: Keele University Press, 1996).

[19] Letter to the editor of the *Morning Chronicle*, quoted in Peter Razzell's introduction to *The Morning Chronicle Survey of Labour and the Poor: The Metropolitan Districts*, 6 vols. (Firle, Sussex: Caliban Books, 1980), i.5.

[20] See Aina Rubenius, *The Woman Question in Mrs Gaskell's Life and Works* (Cambridge, Mass.: Harvard University Press, 1950), 159–74.

contributions totalling £17,000, and by the time the last ship sailed in 1852 had resettled over 700 women. Many of the saddest individual cases reported also led to charitable donations, although these did not always provide their stories with happy endings. The account of a paralysed seller of groundsel and chickweed and his family, most of whose clothes had been pawned to buy food, generated several donations sent to the *Morning Chronicle* offices, which 'were the means of removing them to a more comfortable home' (*LLLP*, i.155). Equally fortunate was 'the poor half-witted and very persecuted harp-player, so well-known in the streets of London', whose direct petition to the public—

Your humble Partitionar as been obtaining a lively hood the last 4 years by playing an harp in the streets and is desirous of doing so but from the delapedated condition of my present instrument I only produce ridicule instead of a living Trusting you will be kind anough to asist me in getting another I beg to remain your humble Partitionar, FOSTER.

—resulted in donations of £2 10*s.* to buy himself a new harp.[21] Less heart-warming, and probably the most desperate case reported, the crippled nutmeg-grater seller (see pp. 109–12) seems to have become even unhappier as a result of Mayhew's well-intentioned intervention. 'I am gazed at in the street,' he reported after the publication of his story with its accompanying illustration, 'and observations made within my hearing with respect to the Exact likeness of the portrait.' Worse still, after a total of £9 was advanced to him to buy a donkey and order a cart, he was hit by new disasters: the donkey fell ill, and the carpenter absconded with his money.[22]

Like most of Mayhew's subjects, the crippled nutmeg-grater seller was only briefly centre-stage, and soon disappeared back into the wings of history. Other subjects seem to have migrated into the pages of fiction. Dickens certainly knew Mayhew earlier in his career (Mayhew played Knowell in Dickens's 1845 amateur theatrical production of *Every Man in His Humour*), and occasional textual overlaps suggest that they continued to be aware of each other's work. While Dickens's novels showed Mayhew how to strike a balance between London's sprawl of contingent details and the promise of an

[21] See Thompson and Yeo (eds.), *The Unknown Mayhew*, 47.
[22] Ibid.

underlying pattern, Mayhew's interviews gave factual support to ideas that Dickens was attempting to work through in his fiction. Indeed, Mayhew's account of the clown who cracks jokes even though he is starving (*LLLP*, iii.119–21; pp. 261–5) is so close to one of the interpolated stories in *The Pickwick Papers* (1836–7)—later reworked in a factual vein by Dickens's biography of Grimaldi (1838)—that one wonders if Mayhew sometimes deliberately sought out figures who appeared to have sprung off the page into real life.[23] Not that he was always complimentary about Dickens: he dismissed the sentimental depictions of working-class life in *The Chimes* as 'profound rubbish'.[24] But it is hard to avoid feeling, when we start to listen to Mayhew's speakers, that we have heard them somewhere before, or that the accompanying engravings are on the verge of twisting themselves into the grotesque illustrations of Cruikshank or Phiz. The rag-and-bottle shop owner who 'can't read very much' is only one layer of grime away from becoming *Bleak House*'s illiterate Krook, while the 'pure-finder' (i.e. collector of dogs' dung) who would 'sooner die in the street' than go into the workhouse gets her wish as Betty Higden in *Our Mutual Friend*, a novel which also contains the ballad-seller Silas Wegg and scavenger Gaffer Hexam, both of whom have close relations in Mayhew.[25] Even the nameless dead in Mayhew seem reluctant to stay put, drifting into Dickens's writing as some of his most restless ghosts. The pure-finder mentions a 'very quiet man' who also used to pick up dung for a living and was known as 'Mr Brown'; only when he died was it discovered that 'Mr Brown was a real gentleman all the time', and 'his name was not Brown; he had taken that name to hide his real one, which, of course, he did not want any one to know' (*LLLP*, ii.145). It sounds like an urban legend or the stuff of romance: the man with a secret who becomes a dung-collector and renames himself 'Brown', like a playful reimagining of finding oneself in the shit, and perhaps also recalling that to be 'done brown' was a slang expression meaning to be deceived or taken in.

[23] *Memoirs of Joseph Grimaldi* [1838], ed. Richard Findlater (London: MacGibbon & Kee, 1968), 112; in ch. 3 of *The Pickwick Papers*, Dickens tells the story of a clown rising from his deathbed to entertain his audience.

[24] *Young Benjamin Franklin; or, The right road through life* (London, 1861), 250 n.

[25] *LLLP*, ii.110 (p. 169); ii.145; i.272; ii.226. These examples are discussed in Anne Humpherys, *Travels into the Poor Man's Country: The Work of Henry Mayhew* (Athens: University of Georgia Press, 1977), 178–94, and Richard J. Dunn, 'Dickens and Mayhew Once More', *Nineteenth-Century Fiction*, 25 (1970), 348–53.

But Mr Brown's story is also very close to the plot of *Bleak House*, which centres on a man called 'Nemo' ('Nobody') who dies in squalor and is revealed retrospectively to be the father of the heroine Esther Summerson. It is not quite that truth is stranger than fiction, rather that in Mayhew's work, as in Dickens's, truth and fiction keep swapping places until, like Mrs Flintwich in *Little Dorrit*, we 'don't know which is which, or what is what' (ch. 15).

The resemblance to Dickens was noticed by some of Mayhew's early reviewers, but by that stage his investigations had started to outgrow their original home in the *Morning Chronicle.* Local disputes over editorial interference quickly escalated, and by October 1850 the relationship with the newspaper's owners had irrevocably broken down. Like so many of Mayhew's projects, it seemed that his research into poverty was doomed to end with an interruption rather than a proper conclusion, but in the months that followed he set about turning the breakdown into a breakthrough. By December he had established his own London office and published the first number of *London Labour and the London Poor*, at the same time promising that this was merely the introduction to an even more ambitious work, 'which it is hoped will form, when complete, a cyclopaedia of the industry, the want, and the vice of the great Metropolis' (p. 3). Nothing could be more characteristic of Mayhew than that sudden switch from the caution of 'it is hoped' to the confidence of 'when complete'. Perhaps inevitably, this dream was never to be realized; indeed, much of the new publication consisted of expanded and reshaped versions of the articles he had already published in the *Chronicle*, Mayhew's usual way of developing an idea being to delve more deeply into it. But for several months, as his new work continued to grow in size and influence, he seemed finally to have discovered a form equal to his ambitions.

Statistics and Style

Exactly how Mayhew set about the task of gathering his data has long been a matter of conjecture. His own notebooks have not survived, and nor has the standard questionnaire he seems to have used as the basis of his interviews. While there are some contemporary accounts of his activities, they tend to be unhelpfully partial, at once limited in scope and blinkered by the writer's particular agenda.

H. Sutherland Edwards was typically catty in recalling the *Morning Chronicle* period as one when Mayhew was 'in his glory':

> He was largely paid, and the greatest joy of all, had an army of assistant writers, stenographers, and hansom cabmen constantly at his call. London labourers . . . were brought to the *Chronicle* offices, where they told their tales to Mayhew, who redictated them, with an added colour of his own, to the shorthand writer . . . Augustus helped him in his vivid descriptions, and an authority on political economy controlled his gay statistics.[26]

It is wonderfully brazen of Edwards to claim that Mayhew 'added colour' to the truth, given how often memoirs like these teeter between recalling the past and rewriting it. But although Mayhew undoubtedly relied on a team to assist him in gathering bits of information, hunting out potential interview subjects, cross-checking statements, and so on, there is no proof that he tampered with the evidence. His aim, he explained, was to give 'a literal description of [the people's] labour, their earnings, their trials, and their sufferings, in their own "unvarnished" language' (*LLLP*, vol. i, p. xv), and he fleshed out his reasons when discussing the alternative route taken by his contemporaries: 'This disposition to cant, and varnish matters over with a sickly sentimentality, angelizing or canonizing the whole body of operatives of this country, instead of speaking to them as possessing the ordinary vices and virtues of human nature . . . is the besetting sin of the age.'[27] An exasperation with this tendency, or possibly a private joke, may have influenced Mayhew's final classification of 'Authors, Editors and Reporters' under Sub-Group D, 'Makers or Artificers', category 3, alongside 'Dyers, Bleachers, Scourers . . . Fancy Workers'.[28] What Mayhew did not point out is that ordinary human nature also includes a powerful tendency to reshape the awkward facts of real life until they fit the more compliant patterns of narrative. 'In order to make you understand, to give you my life, I must tell you a story', remarks one of Virginia Woolf's characters in *The Waves*.[29] But what kind of story best fits the facts of a particular life? And what kind is

[26] H. Sutherland Edwards, *Personal Recollections* (London, 1900), 60.

[27] Henry Mayhew and George Cruikshank, *1851; or the Adventures of Mr and Mrs Sandboys* (London, 1851), 154.

[28] *LLLP*, iv.14; W. H. Auden points out that this classification does not place authors among the 'Benefactors' such as teachers and physicians, 'A Very Inquisitive Old Party', *New Yorker* (24 February 1968), 121–33 (p. 122).

[29] *The Waves* [1931], ed. Gillian Beer (Oxford: Oxford World's Classics, 1992), 199.

appropriate for a life that in most historical surveys would not register as more than a statistical blip? Mayhew never asks these questions explicitly, but they continue to bubble away under the surface of his work. Different interview-subjects seem to have understood the experience of talking to him in different ways, as confession, therapy, or interrogation, and this uncertainty is reflected in the mobility of the terms he uses to describe their testimony: 'statements', 'accounts', 'experiences', 'street-biography'. His own identity is equally unstable: at different times he was mistaken for a truant officer and a dog-tax collector, which suggests the potential theatricality of the project as a whole, and just as he took on the role of serious investigator, so his subjects could reinvent themselves, shaping their life-stories through the reciprocal pressures exerted by a commitment to fact and the more playful possibilities of fiction.

One of the longest accounts Mayhew printed was the 'Statement of a Returned Convict', to which he added a reassuring note that he had 'confirmations' it 'was altogether truthful' (iii.388; p. 322). Actually, it has been pointed out that many of the details given by 'D——' are probably incorrect, from the seriousness of his crimes to the length of the thongs on the cat-o'-nine-tails used to flog him: discrepancies that, in the judgement of one modern critic, make Mayhew nothing less than 'an accomplice in falsehood'.[30] But this is to assume that 'D——' was knowingly warping the truth, whereas it seems just as likely that while telling his story he found the truth starting to slip into one of the popular narrative models available to him, such as an episode in the *Newgate Calendar* or the tall tale of a street patterer. The same is true of the sewer-hunters' relish for stories about the rats that prowled the sewers, supposedly ready to strip the flesh of any body unfortunate enough to fall into their furry clutches. Such nightmarish images are consistent with other accounts from the period: an article on 'The Natural History of Rats' tells of a watchdog wandering off, and its skeleton being discovered later in the sewers, licked clean by 'the insatiable rats',[31] while the contents page of James Rodwell's *The Rat: Its History and Destructive Character* (1858) moves smoothly from 'A Child's Fingers eaten off by a Rat' and 'A Child's Toe gnawed by a Rat' to 'A Bishop eaten by Rats' and 'Death of a

[30] F. B. Smith, 'Mayhew's Convict', *Victorian Studies*, 22 (1979), 431–48 (p. 438).
[31] *Chamber's Edinburgh Journal*, 3/105 (1835), 10.

British Officer by Rats'. But although such stories might tell us something about the viciousness of Victorian sewer-rats, they tell us something even more important about how much of ordinary life in the period occupied an indeterminate borderland between fact and folklore. No work demonstrates this better than *London Labour and the London Poor*, which is at once a towering historical record and a suggestive inquiry into cultural myth-making. Each of Mayhew's test cases revealed a self that was both moulded by experience and haunted by all the alternative selves that circumstances had not allowed to flourish. Repeatedly, we see these speakers casting around for a genre suitable for their stories, but the genre that dominates throughout is elegy, in which what shocks us is not just the fate of particular individuals, or even the gradual extinction of a whole way of life, but something more like the death of possibility itself. Although *London Labour and the London Poor* celebrates the ingenuity and comic resilience of ordinary working people, it also offers a long lament over the fate of those who, like many costermongers, found their options gradually narrowing until the only way of life open to them was to follow the same rounds and repeat the same cries as their ancestors, like the needle skipping on an old record.

In mapping out this world, Mayhew sometimes found himself pushing truth to its limits. There were precedents for this: the published results of official government inquiries ('blue books') provided many examples of interviewers asking questions with built-in answers, and Mayhew too can sometimes be heard forcing the hands or tongues of his witnesses. (It is hard to believe that a vagrant would say 'To tell you the truth, I loved a roving, idle life' (iii.38) unless he heard the coins chinking in his interviewer's pocket.) But Mayhew's presence in his interviews is usually more elusive than this. Although he preferred to melt into the background, only occasionally employing an authorial voice-over, as when he observes that one girl crossing-sweeper, 'each time she was asked a question frowned, like a baby in its sleep' (ii.506), he never entirely succeeds in removing himself from the scene, as he shapes fragments of testimony into coherent stories, tiptoes around what he primly refers to as 'certain gross acts', and edits out the more offensive examples of 'oaths and slang' (i.22; p. 29). His writing may not varnish the truth, but it does varnish some parts of it. This in itself was not an unusual way of going about things, given how often the period's writers were obliged to seek a compromise between truthfulness and decorum: even Reynolds felt the need, in *The Mysteries of London*, to explain that he had taken the liberty of 'altering and improving' the language of one character, correcting his 'grammatical solecisms', and putting his 'random observations into a tangible shape'.[32] Mayhew's authorial presence is more complicated, though, because often it is neither fully visible nor fully invisible, like someone trying to stay out of sight while occasionally straying into the reader's peripheral vision. And it is at these moments that his writing comes most vividly to life, as, like any properly self-aware anthropologist, he is forced to consider how far the observer and the observed affect each other's activities. To borrow the distinction he was to make in the preface to *The Upper Rhine and its Picturesque Scenery* (1858), this is where the standard kind of descriptive writing (rendering the exact properties of a scene) starts to shade into another kind, 'the highest and most artistic of all', in which the scene is filtered through 'the effects or feelings produced'.[33]

Take his description of the London street markets on a Saturday night, when the scene 'has more of the character of a fair than a market':

> One man stands with his red-edged mats hanging over his back and chest, like a herald's coat; and the girl with her basket of walnuts lifts her brown-stained fingers to her mouth, as she screams, 'Fine warnuts! sixteen a penny, fine war-r-nuts.' A bootmaker, to 'ensure custom', has illuminated his shop-front with a line of gas, and in its full glare stands a blind beggar, his eyes turned up so as to show only 'the whites', and mumbling some begging rhymes, that are drowned in the shrill notes of the bamboo-flute-player next to him. The boy's sharp cry, the woman's cracked voice, the gruff, hoarse shout of the man, are all mingled together. . . . Then the sights, as you elbow your way through the crowd, are equally multifarious. Here is a stall glittering with new tin saucepans; there another, bright with its blue and yellow crockery, and sparkling with white glass. . . . One minute you pass a man with an umbrella turned inside up and full of prints; the next, you hear one with a peepshow of Mazeppa, and Paul Jones the pirate, describing the pictures to the boys looking in at the little round windows. (i.9–10; pp. 15–16)

Mayhew's description is itself a kind of peepshow, in which the

[32] *Mysteries of London*, i.303–10.

[33] *The Upper Rhine and its Picturesque Scenery* (London, 1858), pp. vi–vii.

'confusion and uproar' of the market is tamed by his skill in isolating and framing different parts of it. As he travels through the street, his attention is repeatedly snagged by details—the walnut-girl's brown-stained fingers, or the beggar who displays himself in front of the shop's gas jets like an actor in the footlights—before they are lost again in the crowd. Such a scene, he goes on to claim, has 'a bewildering and saddening effect upon the thoughtful mind', but his writing is also excited by its variety, its energy, its sheer challenge to sense and to the senses. It is a world of brute facts and magical transformations, enchantment and disenchantment, which suspends moral judgements but remains conscious of the quiet desperation of the beggar's 'mumbling', the urgency of the flute-player's 'shrill notes'.

The flexibility of this description reflects Mayhew's control of his material, but also some of his uncertainty over how to account for, or even write an account of, people whose lives were so alien to his own; hence his frequent recourse to words such as 'peculiar', 'odd', 'strange', and 'distinct' when referring to activities that for the people themselves were usually too ordinary to be worth noticing.[34] One response against which Mayhew constantly had to guard was simple revulsion, of a sort characterized by Charles Kinglsey's nose-wrinkling description of 'foul' street-markets in *Alton Locke* (ch. 8), although when it came to certain groups he seems to have been all too ready to let his guard down. Long sections on London's Jews and Irish rarely rise above the period's standard stereotypes, and he cannot always resist the temptation to massage the speech of his Cockney costermongers until it slips into a familiar form of comic patter. Still, Mayhew's occasional flashes of prejudice are mild when compared to the more venomous rhetoric of his collaborators in volume IV, which reaches a peak, or a nadir, of anxieties about class, race, and sex in the account of a 'base coloured woman' who is paid by other prostitutes to go away, as 'gentlemen are often scared away from them by the intrusion of this shameless hag, with her thick lips, sable black skin, leering countenance and obscene disgusting tongue, resembling a lewd spirit of darkness from the nether world' (iv.359). Such spittle-flecked prose is not Mayhew's style, and although it can be disquieting to read his lazy approximation of some accents

[34] See Gertrude Himmelfarb, *The Idea of Poverty: England in the Early Industrial Age* (London: Faber & Faber, 1984), 334.

('in Ireland . . . things is bhutiful and chape', ii.337), he is usually too good a writer to be bound by his own prejudices. More often, his assumptions and his conclusions move in different directions, and his prose registers the resulting strain, as when he observes the 'apparent listlessness and lazy appearance' of the 'Street-Irish' on a visit to their homes, and the word 'apparent' continues to smoulder under the next paragraph before it blows up in a complacent reader's face: 'And yet it is curious that these people . . . will perform the severest bodily labour, undertaking tasks that the English are almost unfitted for' (i.111). At such moments Mayhew's style starts to reach towards the sort of social understanding that his argument might seem to discount. Indeed, in its generosity, diversity, and willingness to think from the point of view of other people, *London Labour and the London Poor* comes close to offering itself as a working alternative to the society it describes. The 'Happy Family' exhibitor, who shows off 'animals of diverse habits and propensities living amicably, or at least quietly, in one cage' (iii.214; p. 293), provides at once a utopian dream of city life and a model of Mayhew's writing.

Never before had Mayhew succeeded in producing such a searching piece of work, and he would not do so again. His later publications have an easy, breezy confidence to them, as if the only matter still to be decided was how he would spend the royalties, but for the most part they are a betrayal of the puzzled questions that lay at the heart of *London Labour and the London Poor*. Was character fixed by birth or determined by circumstances? Was poverty a function of class or simply a matter of luck? Were 'street-folk' central to the life of the nation, like the Germanic *Volk*, or as marginal as folk-dancing? (Mayhew's work came at the end of a decade that had already produced other 'folk' compounds in response to the growing interest in oral history, including 'folklore' in 1846 and 'folk-song' in 1847.) Whenever such awkward questions raise their heads in Mayhew's later works they are quickly slapped down again. By 1865 he was happy to publish *The Shops and Companies of London*, which was effectively assembled from long advertising puffs for various branches of manufacture and commerce, without any reference to the workers whose appalling conditions he had exposed only a few years earlier. Even *Young Benjamin Franklin*, published in the same year as the final version of *London Labour and the London Poor* (1861), shows Mayhew moving towards, or perhaps moving back to, a more complacent political position, as he describes the 'comfortless homes' and 'aching limbs' of the poor, but ends his chapter on 'the law of human suffering' by making young Benjamin's uncle explain that 'it was for the development of the finest feelings of our soul, that some have been born to want and suffering, and some, on the other hand, endowed with the power to commiserate and relieve'—a curiously topsy-turvy conclusion in which starving beggars exist in order for us to exercise our compassion on them.[35] Nor were his reserves of social tolerance greatly enhanced by age: the occasional glimmers of xenophobia detectable in *London Labour and the London Poor* burst into dazzling life in *German Life and Manners* (1864), which devotes hundreds of testy pages to proving that, in their appearance, diet, language, personal hygiene, and so on, the Germans are unmistakably not English.

Further clues as to how differently *London Labour and the London Poor* might have turned out are provided by popular theatrical adaptations. The thinly written melodrama of works such as J. Elphinstone's *London Labour and the London Poor; or, Want and Vice* (1854), J. B. Johnstone's *How We Live in the World of London* (1856), or William Travers's *The Watercress Girl* (1865), shows how easily the attitudes of Mayhew's speakers could have stiffened into poses, their testimony pumped up into speeches. However, the nineteenth-century genre that Mayhew's writing probably resembles most closely is one carefully situated between theatrical speech and the quieter reflections of print: the dramatic monologue. The origins of this form have been much debated, but in the work of poets such as Tennyson and Browning it had a number of common features. A speaker tells his or her story to an interlocutor whose presence is detectable only by the movements and tone of the speaker's voice. Often, we come to eavesdrop on this one-sided conversation at a moment of crisis: something has happened, or is about to happen, which demands explanation, or justification, or acceptance of some kind. Because the speaker is usually at a remove from us, in time, space, or understanding—an Italian nobleman who has murdered his wife, or a hermit on the cusp of sainthood—the dramatic monologue pushes us to the limits of our sympathy, and in doing so it discovers where those limits are. One way in which the dramatic monologue encourages us to judge

[35] *Young Benjamin Franklin*, 517.

the speaker's behaviour is through its own form. The rhythm of a poem like Browning's 'My Last Duchess' or Tennyson's 'St Simeon Stylites' allows us to hear the speaker's voice falling in and out of step with the regular march of verse, and in this way it dramatizes some of the most important questions he is trying to puzzle out: how far individual people can represent social types; what overlap there can be between ideals of conduct and more unpredictable human behaviour; whether people can avoid falling into certain habits over time. These are also key concerns of *London Labour and the London Poor*, and here too Mayhew measures the wandering tendencies of his speakers against the underlying patterns of his own style.

One example that stretches across Mayhew's career is his attraction to lists, which bring together his respect for order and the thrill generated by clutter in ever more elaborate forms. A list like the one that records the first items ever stolen by a group of young thieves offers both the reassuring solidity of a police charge sheet, and an invitation to rummage through the literary equivalent of a bag marked 'swag':

> Six rabbits, silk shawls from home, a pair of shoes, a Dutch cheese, a few shillings from home, a coat and trousers, a bullock's heart, four 'tiles' of copper, fifteen and sixpence from master, two handkerchiefs, half a quartern loaf, a set of tools worth 3*l*., clothes from a warehouse, worth 22*l*., a Cheshire cheese, a pair of carriage lamps, some handkerchiefs, five shillings, some turnips, watch-chain and seals, a sheep, three and sixpence, and an invalid's chair.[36]

These are not just stray objects, like the ones picked up by the bone-grubbers and mud-larks, but the props in a series of personal dramas, and the attention Mayhew lavishes on them makes it clear that each one has a history and meaning that goes far beyond its material existence. Few Victorian writers are as good at revealing the texture of everyday life, and the acquisitiveness of a developing economy, that are present in ordinary piles of things, such as the wares which '*crowd* the window' (Mayhew's emphasis) of London's swag-shops:

> egg-boilers, tapers, flat and box irons, Italian irons and heaters, earthenware jugs, metal covers, tea-pots, plaited straw baskets, sieves, wood pails, camera-obscuras, medals, amulets, perfumery and fancy soaps of all kinds,

[36] Letter V, *Morning Chronicle* (2 November 1849).

mathematical instruments, steel pens, silver and German silver patent pencil-cases and leads, snuff-boxes 'in great variety', strops, ink, slates, metal eyelet-holes and machines, padlocks, braces, belts, Congreves, lucifers, fuzees, pocket-books, bill-cases, bed-keys, and a great variety of articles too numerous to mention. (i.335)

With its stock catalogued, and each item ready to be lingered over, the shop starts to resemble a working-class version of the Great Exhibition, a glass-fronted temple to consumerism where even the most humdrum of objects acquires a sudden new glamour. It is only a short step from this to the scene in *Oliver Twist* when Mr Bumble is left alone in Mrs Corney's front room: 'He opened the closet, counted the teaspoons, weighed the sugar-tongs, closely inspected a silver milk-pot to ascertain that it was of the genuine metal, and, having satisfied his curiosity on these points, put on his cocked hat corner-wise, and danced with much gravity four distinct times round the table' (ch. 23). A similar mixture of pleasure and gravity characterizes Mayhew's visits to other people's houses, such as those of the street Irish: 'The cupboard fastened in the corner of the room, and stocked with mugs and cups, the mantelpiece with its images, and the walls covered with showy-coloured prints of saints and martyrs, gave an air of comfort' (i.110). It is not clear who is more comforted by such scenes of neat domesticity: the inhabitants or Mayhew himself.

Mayhew's statistics, similarly, can reveal less about his subjects than they do about his own obsessions. Sober tables of research are regularly interrupted by facts of the strange-but-true variety. 'Total quantity of rain falling yearly in the metropolis, 10,686,132,230,400 cubic inches' (ii.203). 'The drainage of London is about equal in length to the diameter of the earth itself!' (ii.401). '[T]he grand aggregate of travel by all the rail passengers of the kingdom [is] 1,052,327,632½ miles, or nearly eleven times the distance between the earth and the sun every year' (iii.324). That mixture of fussy exactness (going the extra half mile in his calculations) and awed vagueness is a standard feature of Mayhew's statistical manoeuvrings, as is the exclamation mark that follows a conclusion about drains, one of the moments in *London Labour and the London Poor* when we catch a glimpse of the excited schoolboy who needed to be kept in check by the solid establishment man. Also just visible is the period's development of statistical analysis into one of the key tools for mastering the otherwise terrifying plenitude of life. By 1834, statistical societies had been founded in Manchester and London, their declared aim being to gather and explain 'facts calculated to illustrate the condition and prospects of society', which included statistics about industry and commerce as well as 'moral and social statistics' from areas such as housing, sanitation, education, crime, and pauperism.[37] Mayhew offered something different. While he shared the professional statistician's desire to shuffle teeming human life into some kind of order, he was always more interested in quirky individuals than representative cases, and always happy to distract himself with the sort of characterful odds and ends that a more rigorous mind would have dismissed as statistically insignificant: the people who 'strengthen a sickly child's back' by rubbing it with snails (ii.74), or the footman who considered enlisting in the army but 'knew I should be rejected because I was getting bald' (ii.79). He was equally unafraid to supplement standard ways of dividing up labour with eccentric categories of his own:

> The *cheap workmen* in all trades, I find, are divisible into three classes:
>
> 1. The unskilful.
> 2. The untrustworthy.
> 3. The inexpensive. (ii.333)

It is not clear how one might *measure* a category such as 'untrustworthy'; he might just as well have divided them up according to whether or not he liked the cut of their trousers. Even when Mayhew sticks closely to facts they can take on a strange fairy-tale quality. Like a Pre-Raphaelite painter, the further he goes to demonstrate painstaking accuracy, the more tempted he is to retreat into the consolations of romance. Not content with calculating the number of cigar-ends thrown away each week (30,000) and guessing at the proportion picked up by the cigar-end finders (a sixth), he continues by explaining how this 'refuse tobacco' is made into new cigars; 'or, in other words, they are worked up again to be again cast away, and again collected by the finders, and so on perhaps, till the millennium comes' (ii.146; p. 182). It is a good example of what an early review meant by Mayhew's 'wonderful series of revelations suddenly disclosed in our

[37] See Himmelfarb, *The Idea of Poverty*, 348 n.

own country, existing as it were, under our very feet'.[38] Like much of the best Victorian writing, his work sets out to find a compromise between realism and romance, and at moments like this the sheer ordinariness of working-class life combines to unsettling effect with the unexpected wonder of the everyday.

Mayhew's finicky calculations are easy to satirize. He may have recognized as much himself: a hint of self-parody lurks in the way he halts one particularly Gothic piece of arithmetical construction by admitting that 'What is the amount of atmospherical granite, dung, and refuse-dust received in a given period into the human lungs, has never, I am informed, been ascertained even by approximation; but according to the above facts it must be something fearful to contemplate' (ii.188). Fearful? The sentence practically hugs itself with pleasure. However, what prevents Mayhew from slipping too far in this direction is his unwillingness to ignore the human figures that lie behind his mathematical figures. Throughout *London Labour and the London Poor*, the pressure to extrapolate and expand is met by an equal and opposite pressure to individuate and concentrate. Whenever idiosyncrasy beckons, Mayhew is there to point the larger moral or engage the wider context; whenever a story starts to sag into platitudes, he notices something to restore the uniqueness of his subject. Part of a class, yet often lost or lonely; caught up in a shared way of life, yet full of private dodges and mannerisms: each speaker is, in both senses, one of a kind.

The Undiscovered Country

Mayhew's contemporaries were not slow to exploit the city's blurring of individuals and types. Genres such as comedy and melodrama were particularly fertile ground for the snapshot judgements that seemed to be an inevitable result of the speed and crowds of urban life.[39] Consider Thomas Rowlandson's 'Characteristic Sketches of the Lower Orders', originally commissioned to accompany *The New Picture of London* (1820), or the comic labourers and servants who throng the pages of *Punch*. Both works carefully whittle people away until they are reduced to cartoon outlines, lacking any

[38] *British Quarterly Review* (May 1850), 491.

[39] The 'city hunger for quick ways of classifying people' is brilliantly discussed in Jonathan Raban, *Soft City* (London: Picador, 1974), 27.

discernible inner life beneath their comic catchphrases. A similar drive can be detected in other Victorian works of social investigation, even when they aim at a more subtle form of analysis than the crowd-pleasing simplicities of comedy or melodrama. John Thomson's *Street Life in London* (1877) claimed to present 'true types of the London poor' with 'unquestionable accuracy', and in one sense this was true: advances in printing technology meant that he could reproduce photographs of Covent Garden labourers as if his readers were looking through a window. But this window was not altogether transparent: the carefully posed spontaneity of his subjects was modelled on the photographs he took for several earlier works of travel literature, such as *Illustrations of China and its People* (1873–4),[40] so that when he came to photograph the London poor he could keep 'street life' as safely out of reach as a naturalist examining 'pond life'. Looked at through his eyes, the East End becomes as exotic, as untouchable, as the Far East. Indeed, set between himself and his subjects, the camera lens becomes just one more example of the barrier that, according to G. M. W. Reynolds, separated London into two distinct classes:

> There are but two words known in the moral alphabet of this great city; for all virtues are summed up in the one, and all vices in the other: and those words are
>
> WEALTH. | POVERTY.[41]

Mayhew himself was not beyond viewing the poor in this way; indeed, Thomson's comparison of Mongolians to the 'London Nomades' who form the subject of *Street Life in London*'s first plate (pp. 15–16) echoes the strange introduction Mayhew attached to the first edition of *London Labour and the London Poor*, which argued that beggars and costermongers were part of the 'nomade tribes', a distinct race who opposed themselves to a settled way of life and were 'all more or less distinguished for their high cheek-bones and protruding jaws' (i.1–3). Little that followed gave support to this crackpot racial theory, although one might think of Mayhew's statistical tables as a form of social control analogous to Thomson's

[40] The connection is made by Richard L. Stein, 'Street Figures: Victorian Urban Iconography', in Carol T. Christ and John O. Jordan (eds.), *Victorian Literature and the Victorian Visual Imagination* (Berkeley: University of California Press, 1995), 233–63.

[41] *Mysteries of London*, i.4.

photographs, an alternative way of pinning down this disturbingly rootless group of people. Mayhew certainly liked to think of himself as an anthropologist or ethnologist: Thackeray's admiration for his voyages into the world of the costermongers merely echoed Mayhew's own characterization of himself as a 'traveller in the undiscovered country of the poor', who brought back extraordinary but everyday stories about people 'of whom the public had less knowledge than of the most distant tribes of the earth' (i.xv; p. 3). The chief danger of viewing the poor in this way, of course, was that their condition might be wondered at but left unaltered. All those calculations seemed to show that an alien culture had been mastered, but only at the risk of assuming that its workings were as inevitable as a piece of arithmetic.

Mayhew's success in guarding against this danger can largely be put down to the self-revising, improvisatory quality of his investigation, which meant that the usual stereotypes of urban writing were repeatedly put under pressure by a new case study here or unexpected piece of data there. It would be only slightly unfair to say that he made his categories up as he went along: it is remarkable, for example, that in the first three volumes he divided the population up into 'Those That Will Work', 'Those That Cannot Work', and 'Those That Will Not Work', but then added a wholly separate category to the fourth volume almost as an afterthought: 'Those Who Need Not Work'. As his own work grew, and his categories swelled or mutated under his pen, such complex classificatory schemes started to look increasingly like a bluffer's charter; his confidence was sometimes indistinguishable from that of a showman, as he manipulated his data like a pack of cards. The excitement, and the frustration, of this for Mayhew's readers was that they could never be altogether sure what they were going to get from him, probably because he was not always sure himself. In his hands, *London Labour and the London Poor* gradually transformed itself from a statistical survey into an epic struggle between the centripetal forces of structure and containment, and the centrifugal forces of expansion and collapse. Put another way, what had begun as an investigation into how London worked started to look increasingly like a reflection of the city itself. In this context, perhaps it is not surprising that Mayhew never finished his book. It was unfinishable. He might just as well have volunteered to draw a map of London on a scale of 1:1.

Mayhew's capacity to surprise was not always echoed in the works that tried to follow his example. A number of later writers set out to poke around in the seamier corners of the East End, and it became something of a cliché to describe these areas as the 'dark continent' lurking on our doorstep, as George Sims's *How the Poor Live* (1883) promised a 'voyage of discovery' into 'a dark continent that was within easy walking distance of the General Post Office'.[42] Novels such as William Green's *The Life and Adventures of a Cheap Jack, by One of the Fraternity* (1876) also attempted to tap this growing market, although they rarely troubled the bestseller lists. Such works were largely sequels and supplements to Mayhew's investigations, and although some liberally wrung their hands over what they discovered, like Prospero taking responsibility for Caliban ('This thing of darkness I acknowledge mine'), most offered their readers little more than a kind of class tourism, in which the thrill of uncovering shameful secrets in the lives of the poor (promiscuity, cruelty, violence) was tempered either by syrupy sentimentality or a lofty moral tone designed to keep these horrors safely in their place. However, by the time of William Booth's *In Darkest England and the Way Out* (1890), which asked 'As there is a darkest Africa, is there not a darkest England?', Mayhew's influence was on the wane. One of Mayhew's most important modern critics has described *London Labour and the London Poor* as a 'transient form',[43] the revelations of which were already out of date when they were finally published as a whole in 1861–2, and her phrase nicely catches at the work's central paradox. Like the 'transients' it described—the tramps, beggars, and other wanderers who crowd its pages—*London Labour and the London Poor* is easy to ignore as a local distraction in the period, even a mild embarrassment when compared to more obviously influential studies such as Charles Booth's *Life and Labour of the People of London*, which eventually swelled to seventeen volumes (1902–3) and was instrumental in establishing the Old Age Pensions Act (1908) and the

[42] See Raymond A. Kent, *A History of British Empirical Sociology* (Aldershot: Gower, 1981), 52. Other works that combined anthropology and travel writing include C. M. Smith, *Curiosities of London Life* (1853); John Garwood, *The Million Peopled City: Or, One-Half of the People of London Made Known to the Other Half* (1853); George Godwin, *London's Shadows* (1854); Watts Phillips, *The Wild Tribes of London* (1855); M. A. S. Barber, *The Sorrows of the Streets* (1855); John Hollingshead, *Ragged London* (1861).

[43] Humpherys, *Travels into the Poor Man's Country*, 165.

National Insurance Act (1911). Yet Mayhew's work is also like his transients in its resistance to staying in one place. And it is still on the move. In part this is because so much of what he described is still current: his account of cheap goods sold on the street 'set off with gaudy labels bearing sometimes the name of a well-known firm, but altered in spelling or otherwise' (i.376) will be familiar to anyone who has been tempted to buy a 'Louis Viton' handbag or 'Guchi' watch, just as the swindler who poses as a 'Decayed Gentleman' and sends out begging-letters (iv.404) will strike a chord with anyone stung by emails purporting to come from formerly high-ranking officials needing nothing more than a hospitable bank account to get them back on their feet. To borrow Ezra Pound's definition of literature, Mayhew's inquiry into poverty, for all its idiosyncratic, even eccentric way of going about things, produced the sort of news that has stayed news.

Mayhew's influence can also be traced in more specific ways. The revival of interest in the 1950s sparked by Peter Quennell's selections from *London Labour and the London Poor* produced responses as diverse as Philip Larkin's poem 'Deceptions', a reimagining of Mayhew's harrowing story about a young girl who is drugged and raped, and Ronald Searle's *The Big City, or The New Mayhew* (1958), an illustrated series of character sketches ('A Night at Wrestling', 'An Actress of Advancing Years', 'Television Man') that had originally been published, appropriately enough, in *Punch*. More recently, novels such as Charles Palliser's *The Quincunx* (1989), Matthew Kneale's *Sweet Thames* (1992), Michel Faber's *The Crimson Petal and the White* (2002), and Louis Bayard's *Mr Timothy* (2003) have all used Mayhew as source material or a sounding-board for their own concerns,[44] while John Seed's *Pictures from Mayhew* (2005) offers a startling revision or rehearing of *London Labour and the London Poor* by putting fragments of it into verse:

that May we had neither
bite nor sup the water
was too bad to drink
cold they were afraid of
their lives he knocked them
about so drink made him

[44] See Chris Louttit, 'The Novelistic Afterlife of Henry Mayhew', *Philological Quarterly*, 85/3–4 (Summer–Fall 2006), 315–42.

a savage took the father
out of him his children
was starving but I durstn't
say that aloud when
his mates were by . . .[45]

Here the layout of the speaker's voice captures everything Mayhew hints at but does not state out loud, such as the gaps of mistrust and fear that could exist between different members of the same class, or the sudden relieved outpouring that could result when neglected voices were asked to speak.

Other modern reworkings of Victorian street-life are less directly indebted to Mayhew, but even the slightest of them can carry a heavy cultural punch. A famous scene in the film version of Lionel Bart's musical *Oliver!* begins with the young hero waking up in the house of his benefactor Mr Brownlow to the sounds of street-criers: a rose-seller offering 'two blooms for a penny'; a gruff knife-grinder; a quintet of pert milkmaids. As the cherubic Oliver starts to sing, the scene rapidly transforms itself into a spectacular dance routine. Window-cleaners make sychronized dashes up and down ladders. Pastry-sellers leap and pirouette. A street musician jovially plays the flute as troupes of schoolchildren engage in some carefully choreographed fun. It comes as something of a shock to realize that by the end of a song called 'Who will buy?' nobody has bought anything. The well-fed and well-scrubbed Cockneys seem happy to sing for the sake of it, rather than because they are trying to attract customers, and even happier to ignore the hard facts of competition by letting their voices blend into a rousing chorus. It is hard to be severe about a scene that is about as substantial as a handful of soapsuds, but in many ways these film extras are the relics of a tradition that preferred street-folk when they remained in the background, too busy being picturesque to make any practical demands on the people observing them. Mayhew was different, not least because what he most loved about his subjects was that they were so different from each other as well as from him. Whenever his writing threatens to descend into the period's standard responses of disdain or whimsy, his ear catches the unique accent of an individual and affords it the same respect as a shorthand reporter taking down the latest proceedings in Parliament. The realism of the

[45] *Pictures from Mayhew* (Exeter: Shearsman, 2005), 18.

Italian showman who lost his monkey: 'I did cry!—I cry because I have no money to go and buy anoder monkey!' (iii.180). The humour of the man who hawks fly-papers: 'it ain't a purfession and it ain't a trade, I suppose it's a calling' (iii.33). The strange poetry of the street-seller of gingerbread-nuts: 'the streets saved me: my nuts was my bread' (i.200; p. 70).

Open the pages of this extraordinary work, and once again the voices of Victorian London stir into life: 'I ain't a child, and I shan't be a woman till I'm twenty, but I'm past eight, I am' (i.152; p. 50)...'It was the best trotter night I ever had' (i.172) . . . 'Ain't it curious now, sir, that wot a man larns in his fingers he never forgets?' (i.360; p. 115). Once again the clatter and clamour of the streets rise into the air until, like the evening scene Dickens describes in *Bleak House*, 'every noise is merged . . . into a distant ringing hum, as if the city were a vast glass, vibrating' (ch. 48).

NOTE ON THE TEXT AND ILLUSTRATIONS

London Labour and the London Poor has a long and tangled textual history. The original series was published in weekly numbers, priced at twopence, between December 1850 and February 1852, although some of the material had previously appeared in Mayhew's weekly articles in the *Morning Chronicle* under the title 'Labour and the Poor' (19 October 1849–12 December 1850). Publication of Mayhew's new journal ceased abruptly with the issue of 12 February 1852, following a lawsuit by the printer George Woodfall, although Mayhew recycled some of the previously published material in later works, including the short-lived journal *The Great World of London* (March–December 1856) and the novel *Paved with Gold* (1857) which was co-authored with his brother Augustus. In 1861 Mayhew brought together the weekly numbers of *London Labour and the London Poor*, added extra material that had previously appeared in the *Morning Chronicle*, and, with editorial assistance from Augustus, published it as a single work in three volumes; a fourth volume, compiled from reports on London's criminal underworld contributed mostly by other hands, was published in 1862. All four volumes were reprinted, with different pagination, in 1865 by Charles Griffin & Co.

This selection uses the original 1861–2 edition, published by Griffin, Bohn & Co., as its copy-text; errors reported in the list of 'Errata' at the end of vol. I, together with other misprints, have been silently corrected, except where a mistake may be deliberate (as when one of Mayhew's patterers offers lightly garbled versions of names in the public eye on p. 78), in which case the original spelling is retained and the speaker's slip explained in a note. This edition preserves Mayhew's original volume divisions and ordering of his material, together with his complex and somewhat haphazard categories, although reducing a work to around one-tenth of its original size has inevitably meant the loss of some of his more byzantine distinctions. The only exception to this rule is the 'Statement of a Young Pickpocket' (p. 363), which originally appeared as part of a long digression on 'Low Lodging Houses' in vol. I, and has been moved to the section on thieves and swindlers to replace the less interesting 'Narrative of a Pickpocket' contributed to vol. IV by one of Mayhew's collaborators. Most of the exhaustive tables detailing quantities of material sold, consumed, and so on, have been cut to leave more space for the testimonies of Mayhew's subjects, but a representative example is given in Appendix 3: 'A Table Showing the Quantity of Refuse Bought, Collected, or Found, in the Streets of London'. For ease of reading, omissions have not been indicated in the text.

The illustrations in this edition are selected from the woodcuts printed at the start of each number of *London Labour and the London Poor*. Most were engraved from daguerreotypes taken by Richard Beard, a London photographer who opened the first portrait studio in Europe in 1841 and, according to the 1851 census, by the time of his engagement by Mayhew was one of only fifty-one professional photographers in Great Britain. Printing technology did not yet allow photographs to be reproduced, and Beard's original daguerreotypes have been lost, but the woodcuts represent some of the most accurate representations we have of working-class Victorians: their faces, clothes, belongings, and sense of personal identity.

SELECT BIBLIOGRAPHY

Editions

London Labour and the London Poor, with an introduction by John D. Rosenberg, 4 vols. (New York: Dover Publications, 1968).

John L. Bradley (ed.), *Selections from 'London Labour and the London Poor'* (London: Oxford University Press, 1965).

Peter Quennell (ed.), *London's Underworld* (London: William Kimber, 1950) [selections from vol. 4 of *LLLP*].

—— (ed.), *Mayhew's London* (London: William Kimber, 1951) [selections from vols. 1–3 of *LLLP*].

—— (ed.), *Mayhew's Characters* (London: William Kimber, 1951) [further selections from *LLLP*].

London Labour and the London Poor, selected and introduced by Victor Neuburg (London: Penguin, 1985).

London Labour and the London Poor (extracts), introduced by Rosemary O'Day (Ware: Wordsworth Classics, 2008).

Related Writings by Mayhew

The Morning Chronicle Survey of Labour and the Poor: The Metropolitan Districts, 6 vols. (Firle, Sussex: Caliban Books, 1980).

Anne Humpherys (ed.), *Voices of the Poor* (London: Frank Cass, 1971) [selections from Mayhew's letters to the *Morning Chronicle*].

—— (ed.), Henry and Augustus Mayhew, *Paved with Gold* (London: Frank Cass, 1971).

Bartrand Taithe, *The Essential Mayhew: Representing and Communicating the Poor* (London: Rivers Oram Press, 1996) [reprints Mayhew's correspondence with his readers].

E. P. Thompson and Eileen Yeo (eds.), *The Unknown Mayhew* (New York: Pantheon, 1971) [selections from Mayhew's letters to the *Morning Chronicle* together with his pamphlet *Low Wages*].

Critical Studies

W. H. Auden, 'A Very Inquisitive Old Party', *New Yorker* (24 February 1968), 121–33 [a review of the Dover Press reissue of *LLLP*].

Gillian Beer, *Open Fields: Science in Cultural Encounter* (Oxford: Clarendon Press, 1996), ch. 4: 'Speaking for the Others'.

James Bennett, *Oral History and Delinquency: The Rhetoric of Criminality* (Chicago and London: University of Chicago Press, 1981).

John L. Bradley, Introduction to *Selections from 'London Labour and the London Poor'* (London: Oxford University Press, 1965).

Kellow Chesney, *The Victorian Underworld* (1970; repr. New York: Schocken, 1972).

Peter Conrad, *The Victorian Treasure-House* (London: Collins, 1973).

Richard J. Dunn, 'Dickens and Mayhew Once More', *Nineteenth-Century Fiction,* 25 (1970), 348–53.

Catherine Gallagher, 'The Body Versus the Social Body in the Works of Thomas Malthus and Henry Mayhew', *Representations*, 14 (Spring 1986), 83–106.

Gertrude Himmelfarb, *The Idea of Poverty: England in the Early Industrial Age* (London: Faber & Faber, 1984).

Anne Humpherys, *Travels into the Poor Man's Country: The Work of Henry Mayhew* (Athens: University of Georgia Press, 1977).

—— *Henry Mayhew* (Boston: Twayne Publishers, 1984).

Gareth Stedman Jones, *Outcast London* (Oxford: Clarendon Press, 1971).

P. J. Keating, *The Working Classes in Victorian Fiction* (New York: Barnes & Noble, 1971).

Raymond A. Kent, *A History of British Empirical Sociology* (Aldershot: Gower, 1981).

Chris Louttit, 'The Novelistic Afterlife of Henry Mayhew', *Philological Quarterly,* 85/3–4 (Summer–Fall 2006), 315–42.

Richard Maxwell, 'Henry Mayhew and the Life of the Streets', *Journal of British Studies,* 17/2 (1977–8), 87–105.

Harland S. Nelson, 'Dickens's *Our Mutual Friend* and Henry Mayhew's *London Labour and the London Poor*', *Nineteenth-Century Fiction*, 20 (1965), 207–22.

V. S. Pritchett, 'True to Life', *New York Review of Books* (17 March 1966), 5–6 [a review of the Dover Press reissue of *LLLP*].

Jonathan Raban, 'The Invisible Mayhew: London Secrecies', *Encounter* (August 1973), 64–70.

—— *Soft City* (London: Picador, 1974).

F. B. Smith, 'Mayhew's Convict', *Victorian Studies,* 22 (1979), 431–48.

Sheila M. Smith, *The Other Nation: The Poor in English Novels of the 1840s and 1850s* (Oxford: Oxford University Press, 1980).

Richard L. Stein, 'Street Figures: Victorian Urban Iconography', in Carol T. Christ and John O. Jordan (eds.), *Victorian Literature and the Victorian Visual Imagination* (Berkeley: University of California Press, 1995), 233–63.

Harvey Peter Sucksmith, 'Dickens and Mayhew: A Further Note', *Nineteenth-Century Fiction,* 24 (1969), 345–9.

E. P. Thompson, 'The Political Education of Henry Mayhew', *Victorian Studies*, 11 (September 1967), 41–67.

Jerry White, *London in the Nineteenth Century* (London: Jonathan Cape, 2007).

George Woodcock, 'Henry Mayhew and the Undiscovered Country of the Poor', *Sewanee Review*, 92 (Fall 1984), 556–73.

Eileen Yeo, 'Mayhew as a Social Investigator', in E. P. Thompson & Eileen Yeo (eds.), *The Unknown Mayhew* (New York: Pantheon, 1971).

Further Reading in Oxford World's Classics

Charles Dickens, *Bleak House*, ed. Stephen Gill.

—— *Oliver Twist*, ed. Stephen Gill.

—— *The Old Curiosity Shop*, ed. Elizabeth M. Brennan.

Benjamin Disraeli, *Sybil, or the Two Nations*, ed. Sheila Smith.

George Gissing, *The Nether World*, ed. Stephen Gill.

Émile Zola, *Germinal*, trans. Peter Collier, with an introduction by Robert Lethbridge.

—— *L'Assommoir*, ed. Robert Lethbridge.

A CHRONOLOGY OF HENRY MAYHEW

	Life and Works	*Historical and Cultural Background*
1812	Born on 25 November, the fourth son of Joshua Mayhew, a successful solicitor, and Mary Ann Fenn.	Luddite riots.
1827	Runs away from Westminster School and is sent to India as a midshipman.	Dickens starts work in London as a solicitor's clerk.
1831–9	Freelance journalist and writer in London.	
1831		Reform Bill. Major cholera epidemic.
1833		Factory Act forbids employment of children under 9.
1834	*The Wandering Minstrel* is staged in London.	Robert Owen's Grand National Trades Union. Workhouses established under the Poor Law Amendment Act.
1835	Becomes editor of *Figaro in London* (until 1839).	
1836		Beginning of Chartism. Dickens, *Sketches by Boz*.
1837		Queen Victoria succeeds William IV. Carlyle, *The French Revolution*. Dickens begins *Oliver Twist*.
1838		Irish Poor Law. People's Charter advocates universal suffrage.
1839		Chartist riots; Carlyle, *Chartism*.
1841	Editor of *Punch* (first issue 17 July); Mayhew leaves his post in 1842, but continues as a contributor until 1845.	Peel becomes Prime Minister.
1842	*What to Teach and How to Teach It.*	Chartist riots. Chadwick, *Report on the Sanitary Condition of the Labouring Population of Great Britain*.
1843		Thomas Hood, 'Song of the Shirt'; Dickens, 'A Christmas Carol'.

	Life and Works	*Historical and Cultural Background*
1844	*The Prince of Wales's Library*; marries Jane Jerrold, daughter of the journalist Douglas Jerrold (1803–57).	Factory Act restricts the working hours of women and children. Ragged School Union.
1845		Irish potato famine: 1 million die and 8 million emigrate. Disraeli, *Sybil*; Engels, *Condition of the Working Class in England*.
1846	Declared bankrupt.	Corn Laws repealed.
1847	*The Greatest Plague in Life* and *The Good Genius Who Turned Everything into Gold* published by the Brothers Mayhew.	Factory Act limits working day for women and children to 10 hours. Dickens helps to found Urania Cottage, a 'Home for Homeless Women' in London.
1848	*Whom to Marry and How to Get Married!* and *The Image of His Father* (the Brothers Mayhew).	Cholera outbreak in London. Public Health Act. 'The Year of Revolutions' in Europe. Marx and Engels, *Communist Manifesto*; J. S. Mill, *Principles of Political Economy*.
1849	*The Magic of Kindness* (the Brothers Mayhew). The first letter by Mayhew as the *Morning Chronicle*'s metropolitan correspondent appears on 19 October under the heading 'Labour and the Poor'.	Suppression of Communist riots in Paris. Charlotte Brontë, *Shirley*.
1850	*Fear of the World* and *Acting Charades* (the Brothers Mayhew). Henry Mayhew becomes editor of the *Comic Almanac*. On 12 December the *Morning Chronicle* publishes the last letter from its metropolitan correspondent. The first number of *London Labour and the London Poor* is published later in the same month.	Factory Act limits the working week to 60 hours for women and young people.
1851	*London Labour and the London Poor* continues in weekly numbers. Mayhew publishes *1851; or the Adventures of Mr and Mrs Sandboys* (with George Cruikshank) and *Low Wages*.	Great Exhibition in the Crystal Palace, Hyde Park.

	Life and Works	*Historical and Cultural Background*
1852	Publication of *London Labour and the London Poor* is halted by a lawsuit by the printer, George Woodfall. The last number appears on 21 February.	Harriet Beecher Stowe, *Uncle Tom's Cabin*; Dickens begins *Bleak House*.
1854	Mayhew in Germany; *The Story of the Peasant-Boy Philosopher*.	Crimean War begins. Dickens, *Hard Times*.
1855	*The Wonders of Science, or Young Humphry Davy*.	Gaskell, *North and South*.
1856	Begins a new journal: *The Great World of London* appears March–December. Mayhew also publishes *The Rhine and its Picturesque Scenery*.	End of Crimean War. Mulock, *John Halifax, Gentleman*; Flaubert, *Madame Bovary*.
1857	Begins *Paved with Gold* with his brother Augustus; leaves the project after the fifth number.	E. B. Browning, *Aurora Leigh*; Dickens, *Little Dorrit*; Livingstone, *Missionary Travels*.
1858	Death of Mayhew's father; *The Upper Rhine and its Picturesque Scenery*.	Indian Mutiny suppressed. Clough, *Amours de Voyage*.
1859	Editor of the *Morning News* in January, after which the newspaper folds.	Darwin, *On the Origin of Species*; J. S. Mill, *On Liberty*; Samuel Smiles, *Self-Help*.
1861	Vols. I–III of *London Labour and the London Poor*. Mayhew also publishes *Young Benjamin Franklin*, and returns to Germany to research a book on Martin Luther.	Outbreak of American Civil War. Serfdom abolished in Russia. Mrs Beeton, *Book of Household Management*; Eliot, *Silas Marner*.
1862	Vol. IV of *London Labour and the London Poor*. Mayhew also publishes *The Criminal Prisons of London*.	Famine among Lancashire cotton workers. Hugo, *Les Misérables*; C. G. Rossetti, *Goblin Market*.
1863	*The Boyhood of Martin Luther*.	Beginning of work on London underground railway. Emancipation of US slaves.
1864	*German Life and Manners as Seen in Saxony at the Present Day*.	Marx organizes first Socialist International in London.
1865	Second printing of the four-volume edition of *London Labour and the London Poor*. Edits *The Shops and Companies of London*.	William Booth founds Christian Mission in Whitechapel, known from 1878 as the Salvation Army. Dickens, *Our Mutual Friend*; Lewis Carroll, *Alice's Adventures in Wonderland*.

	Life and Works	Historical and Cultural Background
1866		Second Reform Bill. Dr Barnado opens home for destitute children in London's East End. Eliot, *Felix Holt, the Radical*. Hyde Park riots.
1867		Factory Act. Marx, *Das Kapital*.
1868		Trades Union Congress founded.
1869		Arnold, *Culture and Anarchy*; J. S. Mill, *On the Subjection of Women*.
1870	Edits *Only Once a Year* and joins his son Athol as a correspondent in Metz.	Elementary Education Act. Death of Dickens.
1871	Writes a report on Working Men's Clubs for the Licensed Victuallers.	Legalization of Trade Unions. Eliot begins *Middlemarch*.
1872		Licensing Act.
1874	*London Characters* (2nd edn.) is published under Mayhew's name; his play *Mont Blanc* (co-authored with his son) flops.	Factory Act establishes a 56-hour working week. Strike of agricultural workers.
1875		Public Health Act. Trollope, *The Way We Live Now*.
1880	Mayhew's estranged wife dies on 26 February.	Greenwich Mean Time adopted across Britain.
1887	Mayhew dies of bronchitis on 25 July.	Bloody Sunday: protesters and police clash in Hyde Park.

HENRY MAYHEW.

[*From a Daguerreotype* by BEARD.]

LONDON LABOUR

AND THE

LONDON POOR;

A

CYCLOPÆDIA OF THE CONDITION AND EARNINGS

OF

THOSE THAT *WILL* WORK,
THOSE THAT *CANNOT* WORK, AND
THOSE THAT *WILL NOT* WORK.

BY

HENRY MAYHEW.

THE LONDON STREET-FOLK;

COMPRISING,

STREET SELLERS.	STREET PERFORMERS.
STREET BUYERS.	STREET ARTIZANS.
STREET FINDERS.	STREET LABOURERS.

WITH NUMEROUS ILLUSTRATIONS FROM PHOTOGRAPHS.

VOLUME I.

LONDON:
GRIFFIN, BOHN, AND COMPANY,
STATIONERS' HALL COURT.
1861.

PREFACE

THE present volume is the first of an intended series, which it is hoped will form, when complete, a cyclopaedia of the industry, the want, and the vice of the great Metropolis.

It is believed that the book is curious for many reasons:

It surely may be considered curious as being the first attempt to publish the history of a people, from the lips of the people themselves—giving a literal description of their labour, their earnings, their trials, and their sufferings, in their own 'unvarnished' language; and to pourtray the condition of their homes and their families by personal observation of the places, and direct communion with the individuals.

It may be considered curious also as being the first commission of inquiry into the state of the people, undertaken by a private individual, and the first 'blue book'* ever published in twopenny numbers.

It is curious, moreover, as supplying information concerning a large body of persons, of whom the public had less knowledge than of the most distant tribes of the earth—the government population returns not even numbering them among the inhabitants of the kingdom; and as adducing facts so extraordinary, that the traveller in the undiscovered country of the poor must, like Bruce,* until his stories are corroborated by after investigators, be content to lie under the imputation of telling such tales, as travellers are generally supposed to delight in.

Be the faults of the present volume what they may, assuredly they are rather short-comings than exaggerations, for in every instance the author and his coadjutors have sought to understate, and most assuredly never to exceed the truth. For the omissions, the author would merely remind the reader of the entire novelty of the task—there being no other similar work in the language by which to guide or check his inquiries. When the following leaves are turned over, and the two or three pages of information derived from books contrasted with the hundreds of pages of facts obtained by positive observation and investigation, surely some allowance will be made for the details which may still be left for others to supply. Within the last two years some thousands of the humbler classes of society must have been seen and visited with the especial view of noticing their condition and learning their histories; and it is but right that the truthfulness of the poor generally should be made known; for though checks have been usually adopted, the people have been mostly found to be astonishingly correct in their statements,—so much so indeed, that the attempts at deception are certainly the exceptions rather than the rule. Those persons who, from an ignorance of the simplicity of the honest poor, might be inclined to think otherwise, have, in order to be convinced of the justice of the above remarks, only to consult the details given in the present volume, and to perceive the extraordinary agreement in the statements of all the vast number of individuals who have been seen at different times, and who cannot possibly have been supposed to have been acting in concert.

The larger statistics, such as those of the quantities of fish and fruit, &c., sold in London, have been collected from tradesmen connected with the several markets, or from the wholesale merchants belonging to the trade specified—gentlemen to whose courtesy and co-operation I am indebted for much valuable information, and whose names, were I at liberty to publish them, would be an indisputable guarantee for the facts advanced. The other statistics have been obtained in the same manner—the best authorities having been invariably consulted on the subject treated of.

It is right that I should make special mention of the assistance I have received in the compilation of the present volume from Mr HENRY WOOD and Mr RICHARD KNIGHT* (late of the City Mission), gentlemen who have been engaged with me from nearly the commencement of my inquiries, and to whose hearty co-operation both myself and the public are indebted for a large increase of knowledge. Mr Wood, indeed, has contributed so large a proportion of the contents of the present volume that he may fairly be considered as one of its authors.

The subject of the Street-Folk will still require another volume, in order to complete it in that comprehensive manner in which I am desirous of executing the modern history of this and every other portion of the people. There still remain—the *Street-Buyers*, the *Street-Finders*, the *Street-Performers*, the *Street-Artizans*, and the *Street-Labourers*, to be done, among the several classes of street-people; and the *Street Jews*, the *Street Italians* and *Foreigners*, and the *Street Mechanics*, to be treated of as varieties of the order. The present volume refers more particularly to the *Street-Sellers*, and includes special accounts of the *Costermongers** and the *Patterers** (the two broadly-marked varieties of street tradesmen), the *Street Irish*, the *Female Street-Sellers*, and the *Children Street-Sellers* of the metropolis.

My earnest hope is that the book may serve to give the rich a more intimate knowledge of the sufferings, and the frequent heroism under those sufferings, of the poor—that it may teach those who are beyond temptation to look with charity on the frailties of their less fortunate brethren—and cause those who are in 'high places', and those of whom much is expected, to bestir themselves to improve the condition of a class of people whose misery, ignorance, and vice, amidst all the immense wealth and great knowledge of 'the first city in the world', is, to say the very least, a national disgrace to us.

VOLUME I

THE LONDON STREET-FOLK

OF THE LONDON STREET-FOLK

THOSE who obtain their living in the streets of the metropolis are a very large and varied class; indeed, the means resorted to in order 'to pick up a crust', as the people call it, in the public thoroughfares (and such in many instances it *literally* is), are so multifarious that the mind is long baffled in its attempts to reduce them to scientific order or classification.

It would appear, however, that the street-people may be all arranged under six distinct genera or kinds.

These are severally:

I. STREET-SELLERS.
II. STREET-BUYERS.
III. STREET-FINDERS.
IV. STREET-PERFORMERS, ARTISTS, AND SHOWMEN.
V. STREET-ARTIZANS, OR WORKING PEDLARS; and
VI. STREET-LABOURERS.

The first of these divisions—the STREET-SELLERS—includes many varieties; viz.—

1. *The Street-sellers of Fish, &c.*—'wet', 'dry', and shell-fish—and poultry, game, and cheese.

2. *The Street-sellers of Vegetables*, fruit (both 'green' and 'dry'), flowers, trees, shrubs, seeds, and roots, and 'green stuff' (as water-cresses, chickweed and grun'sel,* and turf).

3. *The Street-sellers of Eatables and Drinkables*,—including the vendors of fried fish, hot eels, pickled whelks, sheep's trotters, ham sandwiches, peas'-soup, hot green peas, penny pies, plum 'duff',* meat-puddings, baked potatoes, spice-cakes, muffins and crumpets, Chelsea buns, sweetmeats, brandy-balls, cough drops, and cat and dog's meat—such constituting the principal eatables sold in the street; while under the head of street-drinkables may be specified tea and coffee, ginger-beer, lemonade, hot wine, new milk from the cow, asses milk, curds and whey, and occasionally water.

4. *The Street-sellers of Stationery, Literature, and the Fine Arts*—among whom are comprised the flying stationers, or standing and running patterers; the long-song-sellers; the wall-song-sellers (or 'pinners-up', as they are technically termed); the ballad sellers; the vendors of playbills, second editions of newspapers, back numbers of periodicals and old books, almanacks, pocket books, memorandum books, note paper, sealing-wax, pens, pencils, stenographic cards, valentines, engravings, manuscript music, images, and gelatine poetry cards.*

5. *The Street-sellers of Manufactured Articles*, which class comprises a large number of individuals, as, (*a*) the vendors of chemical articles of manufacture—viz., blacking, lucifers,* corn-salves,* grease-removing compositions, plating-balls,* poison for rats, crackers, detonating-balls,* and cigar-lights.* (*b*) The vendors of metal articles of manufacture—razors and pen-knives, tea-trays, dog-collars, and key-rings, hardware, bird-cages, small coins, medals, jewellery, tin-ware, tools, card-counters, red-herring-toasters, trivets, gridirons, and Dutch ovens.* (*c*) The vendors of china and stone articles of manufacture—as cups and saucers, jugs, vases, chimney ornaments, and stone fruit, (*d*) The vendors of linen, cotton, and silken articles of manufacture—as sheeting, table-covers, cotton, tapes and thread, boot and stay-laces,* haberdashery, pretended smuggled goods, shirt-buttons, etc., etc.; and (*e*) the vendors of miscellaneous articles of manufacture—as cigars, pipes, and snuff-boxes, spectacles, combs, 'lots',* rhubarb, sponges, wash-leather,* paper-hangings, dolls, Bristol toys,* sawdust, and pin-cushions.

6. *The Street-sellers of Second-hand Articles*, of whom there are again four separate classes; as (*a*) those who sell old metal articles—viz. old knives and forks, keys, tin-ware, tools, and marine stores generally; (*b*) those who sell old linen articles—as old sheeting for towels; (*c*) those who sell old glass and crockery—including bottles, old pans and pitchers, old looking glasses, &c.; and (*d*) those who sell old miscellaneous articles—as old shoes, old clothes, old saucepan lids, &c., &c.

7. *The Street-sellers of Live Animals*—including the dealers in dogs, squirrels, birds, gold and silver fish, and tortoises.

8. *The Street-sellers of Mineral Productions and Curiosities*—as red and white sand, silver sand, coals, coke, salt, spar ornaments,* and shells.

These, so far as my experience goes, exhaust the whole class of street-sellers, and they appear to constitute nearly three-fourths of the entire number of individuals obtaining a subsistence in the streets of London.

The next class are the STREET-BUYERS, under which denomination come the purchasers of hare-skins, old clothes, old umbrellas, bottles, glass, broken metal, rags, waste paper, and dripping.

After these we have the STREET-FINDERS, or those who, as I said before, literally 'pick up' their living in the public thoroughfares. They are the 'pure' pickers, or those who live by gathering dogs'-dung; the cigar-end finders, or 'hard-ups', as they are called, who collect the refuse pieces of smoked cigars from the gutters, and having dried them, sell them as tobacco to the very poor; the dredgermen or coal-finders; the mud-larks, the bone-grubbers; and the sewer-hunters.

Under the fourth division, or that of the STREET-PERFORMERS, ARTISTS, AND SHOWMEN, are likewise many distinct callings.

1. *The Street-Performers*, who admit of being classified into (*a*) mountebanks—or those who enact puppet-shows, as Punch and Judy, the fantoccini,* and the Chinese shades.* (*b*) The street-performers of feats of strength and dexterity—as 'acrobats' or posturers, 'equilibrists' or balancers, stiff and bending tumblers, jugglers, conjurors, sword-swallowers, 'salamanders' or fire-eaters, swordsmen, etc. (*c*) The street-performers with trained animals—as dancing dogs, performing monkeys, trained birds and mice, cats and hares, sapient pigs,* dancing bears, and tame camels. (*d*) The street-actors—as clowns, 'Billy Barlows',* 'Jim Crows',* and others.

2. *The Street Showmen*, including shows of (*a*) extraordinary persons—as giants, dwarfs, Albinoes, spotted boys, and pig-faced ladies. (*b*) Extraordinary animals—as alligators, calves, horses and pigs with six legs or two heads, industrious fleas, and happy families.* (*c*) Philosophic instruments—as the microscope, telescope, thaumascope.* (*d*) Measuring-machines—as weighing, lifting, measuring, and striking machines; and (*e*) miscellaneous shows—such as peep-shows, glass ships, mechanical figures, wax-work shows, pugilistic shows, and fortune-telling apparatus.

3. *The Street-Artists*—as black profile-cutters, blind paper-cutters, 'screevers' or draughtsmen in coloured chalks on the pavement, writers without hands, and readers without eyes.

4. *The Street Dancers*—as street Scotch girls, sailors, slack and tight rope dancers, dancers on stilts, and comic dancers.

5. *The Street Musicians*—as the street bands (English and German), players of the guitar, harp, bagpipes, hurdy-gurdy, dulcimer, musical bells, cornet, tom-tom, &c.

6. *The Street Singers*, as the singers of glees, ballads, comic songs, nigger melodies, psalms, serenaders, reciters, and improvisatori.*

7. *The Proprietors of Street Games*, as swings, highflyers, roundabouts, puff-and-darts, rifle shooting, down the dolly, spin-'em-rounds, prick the garter, thimble-rig, etc.

Then comes the Fifth Division of the Street-Folk, viz., the STREET-ARTIZANS, or WORKING PEDLARS;

These may be severally arranged into three distinct groups—(1) Those who *make* things in the streets; (2) Those who *mend* things in the streets; and (3) Those who *make* things *at home* and *sell* them in the *streets*.

1. Of *those who make things in the streets* there are the following varieties: (*a*) the metal workers—such as toasting-fork makers, pin makers, engravers, tobacco-stopper makers. (*b*) The textile-workers—stocking-weavers, cabbage-net makers, night-cap knitters, doll-dress knitters. (*c*) The miscellaneous workers,—the wooden spoon makers, the leather brace and garter makers, the printers, and the glass-blowers.

2. *Those who mend things in the streets*, consist of broken china and glass menders, clock menders, umbrella menders, kettle menders, chair menders, grease removers, hat cleaners, razor and knife grinders, glaziers, travelling bell hangers, and knife cleaners.

3. *Those who make things at home and sell them in the streets*, are (*a*) the wood workers—as the makers of clothes-pegs, clothes-props, skewers, needle-cases, foot-stools and clothes-horses, chairs and tables, tea-caddies, writing-desks, drawers, work-boxes, dressing-cases, pails and tubs. (*b*) The trunk, hat, and bonnet-box makers, and the cane and rush basket makers. (*c*) The toy makers—such as Chinese roarers,* children's windmills, flying birds and fishes, feathered cocks, black velvet cats and sweeps, paper houses, cardboard carriages, little copper pans and kettles, tiny tin fireplaces, children's watches, Dutch dolls,* buy-a-brooms,* and gutta-percha heads.* (*d*) The apparel makers—viz., the makers of women's caps, boys and men's cloth

caps, night-caps, straw bonnets, children's dresses, watch-pockets, bonnet shapes, silk bonnets, and gaiters, (*e*) The metal workers,—as the makers of fire-guards, bird-cages, the wire workers. (*f*) The miscellaneous workers—or makers of ornaments for stoves, chimney ornaments, artificial flowers in pots and in nosegays, plaster-of-Paris night-shades,* brooms, brushes, mats, rugs, hearthstones, firewood, rush matting, and hassocks.*

Of the last division, or STREET-LABOURERS, there are four classes:

1. *The Cleansers*—such as scavengers, nightmen, flushermen,* chimney-sweeps, dustmen, crossing-sweepers, 'street-orderlies',* labourers to sweeping-machines and to watering-carts.*

2. *The Lighters and Waterers*—or the turn-cocks* and the lamp-lighters.

3. *The Street-Advertisers*—viz., the bill-stickers, bill-deliverers, boardmen, men to advertising vans, and wall and pavement sten-cillers.

4. *The Street-Servants*—as horse holders, link-men,* coach-hirers, street-porters, shoe-blacks.

COSTERMONGERS

The London Street Markets on a Saturday Night

The street sellers are to be seen in the greatest numbers at the London street markets on a Saturday night. Here, and in the shops immediately adjoining, the working-classes generally purchase their Sunday's dinner; and after pay-time on Saturday night, or early on Sunday morning, the crowd in the New-cut, and the Brill* in particular, is almost impassable. Indeed, the scene in these parts has more of the character of a fair than a market. There are hundreds of stalls, and every stall has its one or two lights; either it is illuminated by the intense white light of the new self-generating gas-lamp,* or else it is brightened up by the red smoky flame of the old-fashioned grease lamp. One man shows off his yellow haddock with a candle stuck in a bundle of firewood; his neighbour makes a candlestick of a huge turnip, and the tallow gutters over its sides; whilst the boy shouting 'Eight a penny, stunning pears!' has rolled his dip in a thick coat of brown paper, that flares away with the candle. Some stalls are crimson with the fire shining through the holes beneath the baked chestnut stove; others have handsome octohedral lamps, while a few have a candle shining through a sieve: these, with the sparkling ground-glass globes of the tea-dealers' shops, and the butchers' gaslights streaming and fluttering in the wind, like flags of flame, pour forth such a flood of light, that at a distance the atmosphere immediately above the spot is as lurid as if the street were on fire.

The pavement and the road are crowded with purchasers and street-sellers. The housewife in her thick shawl, with the market-basket on her arm, walks slowly on, stopping now to look at the stall of caps, and now to cheapen* a bunch of greens. Little boys, holding three or four onions in their hand, creep between the people, wriggling their way through every interstice, and asking for custom in whining tones, as if seeking charity. Then the tumult of the thousand different cries of the eager dealers, all shouting at the top of their voices, at one and the same time, is almost bewildering. 'So-old again,' roars one. 'Chestnuts all 'ot, a penny a score,' bawls another. 'An 'aypenny a skin, blacking,'* squeaks a boy. 'Buy, buy, buy, buy, buy—bu-u-uy!' cries the butcher. 'Half-quire* of paper for a penny,' bellows the street stationer. 'An 'aypenny a lot ing-uns.' 'Twopence a pound grapes.' 'Three a penny Yarmouth bloaters.' 'Who'll buy a bonnet for fourpence?' 'Pick 'em out cheap here! three pair for a halfpenny, bootlaces.' 'Now's your time! beautiful whelks, a penny a lot.' 'Here's ha'p'orths,'* shouts the perambulating confectioner. 'Come and look at 'em! here's toasters!'* bellows one with a Yarmouth bloater stuck on a toasting-fork. 'Penny a lot, fine russets,' calls the apple woman: and so the Babel goes on.

One man stands with his red-edged mats hanging over his back and chest, like a herald's coat; and the girl with her basket of walnuts lifts her brown-stained fingers to her mouth, as she screams, 'Fine warnuts! sixteen a penny, fine war-r-nuts.' A bootmaker, to 'ensure custom', has illuminated his shop-front with a line of gas, and in its full glare stands a blind beggar, his eyes turned up so as to show only 'the whites', and mumbling some begging rhymes, that are drowned in the shrill notes of the bamboo-flute-player next to him. The boy's sharp cry, the woman's cracked voice, the gruff, hoarse shout of the man, are all mingled together. Sometimes an Irishman is heard with his 'fine ating apples'; or else the jingling music of an unseen organ breaks out, as the trio of street singers rest between the verses.

Then the sights, as you elbow your way through the crowd, are equally multifarious. Here is a stall glittering with new tin saucepans; there another, bright with its blue and yellow crockery, and sparkling with white glass. Now you come to a row of old shoes arranged along the pavement; now to a stand of gaudy tea-trays; then to a shop with red handkerchiefs and blue checked shirts, fluttering backwards and forwards, and a counter built up outside on the kerb, behind which are boys beseeching custom. At the door of a tea-shop, with its hundred white globes of light, stands a man delivering bills, thanking the public for past favours, and 'defying competition'. Here, alongside the road, are some half-dozen headless tailors' dummies, dressed in Chesterfields* and fustian jackets,* each labelled, 'Look at the prices', or 'Observe the quality'. After this is a butcher's shop, crimson and white with meat piled up to the first-floor, in front of which the butcher himself, in his blue coat, walks up and down, sharpening his knife on the steel that hangs to his waist. A little further on stands the clean family, begging; the father with his head down as if in shame, and a box of lucifers held forth in his hand—the boys in newly-washed pinafores, and the tidily got-up mother with a child at her breast. This stall is green and white with bunches of turnips—that red with apples, the next yellow with onions, and another purple with pickling cabbages. One minute you pass a man with an umbrella turned inside up and full of prints; the next, you hear one with a peepshow of Mazeppa,* and Paul Jones the pirate,* describing the pictures to the boys looking in at the little round windows. Then is heard the sharp snap of the percussion-cap from the crowd of lads firing at the target for nuts; and the moment afterwards, you see either a black man half-clad in white, and shivering in the cold with tracts in his hand, or else you hear the sounds of musk from 'Frazier's Circus', on the other side of the road, and the man outside the door of the penny concert, beseeching you to 'Be in time—be in time!' as Mr Somebody is just about to sing his favourite song of the 'Knife Grinder'. Such, indeed, is the riot, the struggle, and the scramble for a living, that the confusion and uproar of the New-cut on Saturday night have a bewildering and saddening effect upon the thoughtful mind.

Each salesman tries his utmost to sell his wares, tempting the passers-by with his bargain. The boy with his stock of herbs offers 'a double 'andful of fine parsley for a penny'; the man with the donkey-cart filled with turnips has three lads to shout for him to their utmost, with their 'Ho! ho! hi-i-i! What do you think of this here? A penny a bunch—hurrah for free trade! *Here's* your turnips!' Until it is seen and heard, we have no sense of the scramble that is going on throughout London for a living. The same scene takes place at the Brill—the same in Leather-lane—the same in Tottenham-court-road—the same in Whitecross-street;* go to whatever corner of the metropolis you please, either on a Saturday night or a Sunday morning, and there is the same shouting and the same struggling to get the penny profit out of the poor man's Sunday's dinner.

Habits and Amusements of Costermongers

I find it impossible to separate these two headings; for the habits of the costermonger are not domestic. His busy life is past in the markets or the streets, and as his leisure is devoted to the beer-shop, the dancing-room, or the theatre, we must look for his habits to his demeanour at those places. Home has few attractions to a man whose life is a street-life. Even those who are influenced by family ties and affections, prefer to 'home'—indeed that word is rarely mentioned among them—the conversation, warmth, and merriment of the beer-shop, where they can take their ease among their 'mates'. Excitement or amusement are indispensable to uneducated men. Of beer-shops resorted to by costermongers, and principally supported by them, it is computed that there are 400 in London.

Those who meet first in the beer-shop talk over the state of trade and of the markets, while the later comers enter at once into what may be styled the serious business of the evening—amusement.

Business topics are discussed in a most peculiar style. One man takes the pipe from his mouth and says, 'Bill made a doogheno hit this morning.' 'Jem,' says another, to a man just entering, 'you'll stand a top o' reeb?' 'On,' answers Jem, 'I've had a trosseno tol, and have been doing dab.' For an explanation of what may be obscure in this dialogue, I must refer my readers to my remarks concerning the language of the class.* If any strangers are present, the conversation is still further clothed in slang, so as to be unintelligible even to the partially initiated. The evident puzzlement of any listener is of course gratifying to the costermonger's vanity, for he feels that he possesses a knowledge peculiarly his own.

Among the in-door amusements of the costermonger is card-playing, at which many of them are adepts. The usual games* are all-fours, all-fives, cribbage, and put. Whist is known to a few, but is never played, being considered dull and slow. Of short whist they have not heard; 'but,' said one, whom I questioned on the subject, 'if it's come into fashion, it'll soon be among us.' The play is usually for beer, but the game is rendered exciting by bets both among the players and the lookers-on. 'I'll back Jem for a yanepatine,' says one. 'Jack for a gen,' cries another. A penny is the lowest sum laid, and five shillings generally the highest, but a shilling is not often exceeded. 'We play fair among ourselves,' said a costermonger to me—'aye, fairer than the aristocrats—but we'll take in anybody else.' Where it is known that the landlord will not supply cards, 'a sporting coster' carries a pack or two with him. The cards played with have rarely been stamped; they are generally dirty, and sometimes almost illegible, from long handling and spilled beer. Some men will sit patiently for hours at these games, and they watch the dealing round of the dingy cards intently, and without the attempt—common among politer gamesters—to appear indifferent, though they bear their losses well. In a full room of card-players, the groups are all shrouded in tobacco-smoke, and from them are heard constant sounds—according to the games they are engaged in—of 'I'm low, and Ped's high.' 'Tip and me's game.' 'Fifteen four and a flush of five.' I may remark it is curious that costermongers, who can neither read nor write, and who have no knowledge of the multiplication table, are skilful in all the intricacies and calculations of cribbage. There is not much quarrelling over the cards, unless strangers play with them, and then the costermongers all take part one with another, fairly or unfairly.

It has been said that there is a close resemblance between many of the characteristics of a very high class, socially, and a very low class. Those who remember the disclosures on a trial a few years back, as to how men of rank and wealth passed their leisure in card-playing—many of their lives being one continued leisure—can judge how far the analogy holds when the card-passion of the costermongers is described.

'Shove-halfpenny' is another game played by them; so is 'Three up'. Three halfpennies are thrown up, and when they fall all 'heads' or all 'tails', it is a mark; and the man who gets the greatest number of marks out of a given amount—three, or five, or more—wins. 'Three-up' is played fairly among the costermongers; but is most frequently resorted to when strangers are present to 'make a pitch',—which is, in plain words, to cheat any stranger who is rash enough to bet upon them. 'This is the way, sir,' said an adept to me; 'bless you, I can make them fall as I please. If I'm playing with Jo, and a stranger bets with Jo, why, of course, I make Jo win.' This adept illustrated his skill to me by throwing up three halfpennies, and, five times out of six, they fell upon the floor, whether he threw them nearly to the ceiling or merely to his shoulder, all heads or all tails. The halfpence were the proper current coins—indeed, they were my own; and the result is gained by a peculiar position of the coins on the fingers, and a peculiar jerk in the throwing. There was an amusing manifestation of the pride of art in the way in which my obliging informant displayed his skill.

'Skittles'* is another favourite amusement, and the costermongers class themselves among the best players in London. The game is always for beer, but betting goes on.

THE LONDON COSTERMONGER.

"Here Pertaters! Kearots and Turnups! fine Brockello-o-o!"

[*From a Daguerreotype by* BEARD.]

A fondness for 'sparring' and 'boxing' lingers among the rude members of some classes of the working men, such as the tanners.* With the great majority of the costermongers this fondness is still as dominant as it was among the 'higher classes', when boxers were the pets of princes and nobles. The sparring among the costers is not for money, but for beer and 'a lark'*—a convenient word covering much mischief. Two out of every ten landlords, whose houses are patronised by these lovers of 'the art of self-defence',* supply gloves. Some charge 2*d.* a night for their use; others only 1*d.* The sparring seldom continues long, sometimes not above a quarter of an hour; for the costermongers, though excited for a while, weary of sports in which they cannot personally participate, and in the beer-shops only two spar at a time, though fifty or sixty may be present. The shortness of the duration of this pastime may be one reason why it seldom leads to quarrelling. The stake is usually a 'top of reeb', and the winner is the man who gives the first 'noser'; a *bloody* nose however is required to show that the blow was veritably a noser. The costermongers boast of their skill in pugilism as well as at skittles. 'We are all handy with our fists,' said one man, 'and are matches, aye, and more than matches, for anybody but reg'lar boxers. We've stuck to the ring, too, and gone reg'lar to the fights, more than any other men.'

'Twopenny-hops'* are much resorted to by the costermongers, men and women, boys and girls. At these dances decorum is sometimes, but not often, violated. 'The women,' I was told by one man, 'doesn't show their necks as I've seen the ladies do in them there pictures of high life in the shop-winders, or on the stage. Their Sunday gowns, which is their dancing gowns, ain't made that way.' At these 'hops' the clog-hornpipe is often danced, and sometimes a collection is made to ensure the performance of a first-rate professor* of that dance; sometimes, and more frequently, it is volunteered gratuitously. The other dances are jigs, 'flash jigs'—hornpipes in fetters—a dance rendered popular by the success of the acted 'Jack Sheppard'*—polkas, and country-dances, the last-mentioned being generally demanded by the women. Waltzes are as yet unknown to them. Sometimes they do the 'pipe-dance'. For this a number of tobacco-pipes, about a dozen, are laid close together on the floor, and the dancer places the toe of his boot between the different pipes, keeping time with the music. Two of the pipes are arranged as a cross, and the toe has to be inserted between each of the angles, without breaking them. The numbers present at these 'hops' vary from 30 to 100 of both sexes, their ages being from 14 to 45, and the female sex being slightly predominant as to the proportion of those in attendance. At these 'hops' there is nothing of the leisurely style of dancing —half a glide and half a skip—but vigorous, laborious capering. The hours are from half-past eight to twelve, sometimes to one or two in the morning, and never later than two, as the costermongers are early risers. There is sometimes a good deal of drinking; some of the young girls being often pressed to drink, and frequently yielding to the temptation. From 1*l.* to 7*l.* is spent in drink at a hop; the youngest men or lads present spend the most, especially in that act of costermonger politeness—'treating the gals'. The music is always a fiddle, sometimes with the addition of a harp and a cornopean.* The band is provided by the costermongers, to whom the assembly is confined; but during the present and the last year, when the costers' earnings have been less than the average, the landlord has provided the harp, whenever that instrument has added to the charms of the fiddle.

The other amusements of this class of the community are the theatre and the penny concert, and their visits are almost entirely confined to the galleries of the theatres on the Surrey-side*—the Surrey, the Victoria, the Bower Saloon, and (but less frequently) Astley's. Three times a week is an average attendance at theatres and dances by the more prosperous costermongers. The most intelligent man I met with among them gave me the following account. He classes himself with the many, but his tastes are really those of an educated man: —'Love and murder suits us best, sir; but within these few years I think there's a great deal more liking for deep tragedies among us. They set men a thinking; but then we all consider them too long. Of *Hamlet* we can make neither end nor side;* and nine out of ten of us—ay, far more than that—would like it to be confined to the ghost scenes, and the funeral, and the killing off at the last. *Macbeth* would be better liked, if it was only the witches and the fighting. The high words in a tragedy we call jaw-breakers, and say we can't tumble to that barrikin.* We always stay to the last, because we've paid for it all, or very few costers would see a tragedy out if any money was returned to those leaving after two or three acts. We are fond of music. Nigger music was very much liked among us, but it's stale now. Flash* songs are liked, and sailors' songs, and patriotic songs. Most costers—indeed, I can't call to mind an exception—listen very quietly to songs that they don't in the least understand. We have among us translations of the patriotic French songs. "Mourir pour la patrie" is very popular, and so is the "Marseillaise". A song to take hold of us must have a good chorus.' 'They like something, sir, that is worth hearing,' said one of my informants, 'such as the "Soldier's Dream", "The Dream of Napoleon", or "I 'ad a dream—an 'appy dream".'

The songs in ridicule of Marshal Haynau,* and in laudation of Barclay and Perkin's draymen, were and are very popular among the costers; but none are more popular than Paul Jones—'A noble commander, Paul Jones was his name'. Among them the chorus of 'Britons never shall be slaves',* is often rendered 'Britons always shall be slaves'. The most popular of all songs with the class, however, is 'Duck-legged Dick', of which I give the first verse.

'Duck-legged Dick had a donkey,
    And his lush loved much for to swill,
One day he got rather lumpy,
    And got sent seven days to the mill.
His donkey was taken to the green-yard,
    A fate which he never deserved.
Oh! it was such a regular mean yard,
    That alas! the poor moke got starved.
Oh! bad luck can't be prevented,
    Fortune she smiles or she frowns,
He's best off that's contented,
    To mix, sirs, the ups and the downs.'

Their sports are enjoyed the more, if they are dangerous and require both courage and dexterity to succeed in them. They prefer, if crossing a bridge, to climb over the parapet, and walk along on the stone coping. When a house is building, rows of coster lads will climb up the long ladders, leaning against the unsalted roof, and then slide down again, each one resting on the other's shoulders. A peep show with a battle scene is sure of its coster audience, and a favourite pastime is fighting with cheap theatrical swords. They are, however, true to each other, and should a coster, who is the hero of his court* fall ill and go to a hospital, the whole of the inhabitants of his quarter will visit him on the Sunday, and take him presents of various articles so that 'he may live well'.

Among the men, rat-killing is a favourite sport. They will enter an old stable, fasten the door and then turn out the rats. Or they will find out some unfrequented yard, and at night time build up a pit with apple-case boards, and lighting up their lamps, enjoy the sport. Nearly every coster is fond of dogs. Some fancy them greatly, and are proud of making them fight. If when out working, they see a handsome stray, whether he is a 'toy' or 'sporting' dog, they whip him up—many of the class not being *very* particular whether the animals are stray or not.

Their dog fights are both cruel and frequent. It is not uncommon to see a lad walking with the trembling legs of a dog shivering under a bloody handkerchief, that covers the bitten and wounded body of an animal that has been figuring at some 'match'. These fights take place on the sly—the tap-room or back-yard of a beer-shop, being generally chosen for the purpose. A few men are let into the secret, and they attend to bet upon the winner, the police being carefully kept from the spot.

Pigeons are 'fancied' to a large extent, and are kept in lath cages on the roofs of the houses. The lads look upon a visit to the Red-house,* Battersea, where the pigeon-shooting takes place, as a great treat. They stand without the hoarding that encloses the ground, and watch for the wounded pigeons to fall, when a violent scramble takes place among them, each bird being valued at 3*d.* or 4*d.* So popular has this sport become, that some boys take dogs with them trained to retrieve the birds, and two Lambeth costers attend regularly after their morning's work with their guns, to shoot those that escape the 'shots' within.

A good pugilist is looked up to with great admiration by the costers, and fighting is considered to be a necessary part of a boy's education. Among them cowardice in any shape is despised as being degrading and loathsome, indeed the man who would avoid a fight, is scouted by the whole of the court he lives in. Hence it is important for a lad and even a girl to know how to 'work their fists well'—as expert boxing is called among them. If a coster man or woman is struck they are obliged to fight. When a quarrel takes place between two boys, a ring is formed, and the men urge them on to have it out, for they hold that it is a wrong thing to stop a battle, as it causes bad blood for life; whereas, if the lads fight it out they shake hands and forget all about it. Everybody practises fighting, and the man who has the largest and hardest muscle is spoken of in terms of the highest commendation. It is often said in admiration of such a man that 'he could muzzle half a dozen bobbies* before breakfast'.

To serve out a policeman is the bravest act by which a costermonger can distinguish himself. Some lads have been imprisoned upwards of a dozen times for this offence; and are consequently looked upon by their companions as martyrs. When they leave prison for such an act, a subscription is often got up for their benefit. In their continual warfare with the force, they resemble many savage nations, from the cunning and treachery they use. The lads endeavour to take the unsuspecting 'crusher' by surprise, and often crouch at the entrance of a court until a policeman passes, when a stone or a brick is hurled at him, and the youngster immediately disappears. Their love of revenge too, is extreme—their hatred being in no way mitigated by time; they will wait for months, following a policeman who has offended or wronged them, anxiously looking out for an opportunity of paying back the injury. One boy, I was told, vowed vengeance against a member of the force, and for six months never allowed the man to escape his notice. At length, one night, he saw the policeman in a row outside a public-house, and running into the crowd kicked him savagely, shouting at the same time: 'Now, you b——, I've got you at last.' When the boy heard that his persecutor was injured for life, his joy was very great, and he declared the twelvemonth's imprisonment he was sentenced to for the offence to be 'dirt cheap'. The whole of the court where the lad resided sympathized with the boy, and vowed to a man, that had he escaped, they would have subscribed a pad* or two of dry herrings, to send him into the country until the affair had blown over, for he had shown himself a 'plucky one'.

It is called 'plucky' to bear pain without complaining. To flinch from expected suffering is scorned, and he who does so is sneered at and told to wear a gown, as being more fit to be a woman. To show a disregard for pain, a lad, when without money, will say to his pal, 'Give us a penny, and you may have a punch at my nose.' They also delight in tattooing their chests and arms with anchors, and figures of different kinds. During the whole of this painful operation, the boy will not flinch, but laugh and joke with his admiring companions, as if perfectly at ease.

'Vic. Gallery'

On a good attractive night, the rush of costers to the threepenny gallery of the Coburg* (better known as 'the Vic') is peculiar and almost awful.

The long zig-zag staircase that leads to the pay box is crowded to suffocation at least an hour before the theatre is opened; but, on the occasion of a piece with a good murder in it, the crowd will frequently collect as early as three o'clock in the afternoon. Lads stand upon the broad wooden bannisters about 50 feet from the ground, and jump on each others' backs, or adopt any expedient they can think of to obtain a good place.

The walls of the well-staircase having a remarkably fine echo, and the wooden floor of the steps serving as a sounding board, the shouting, whistling, and quarrelling of the impatient young costers is increased tenfold. If, as sometimes happens, a song with a chorus is started, the ears positively ache with the din, and when the chant has finished it seems as though a sudden silence had fallen on the people. To the centre of the road, and all round the door, the mob is in a ferment of excitement, and no sooner is the money-taker at his post than the most frightful rush takes place, every one heaving with his shoulder at the back of the person immediately in front of him. The girls shriek, men shout, and a nervous fear is felt lest the massive staircase should fall in with the weight of the throng, as it lately did with the most terrible results.* If a hat tumbles from the top of the staircase, a hundred hands snatch at it as it descends. When it is caught a voice roars above the tumult, 'All right, Bill, I've got it'—for they all seem to know one another—'Keep us a pitch and I'll bring it.'

To any one unaccustomed to be pressed flat it would be impossible to enter with the mob. To see the sight in the gallery it is better to wait until the first piece is over. The ham-sandwich men and pig-trotter women will give you notice when the time is come, for with the first clatter of the descending footsteps they commence their cries.

There are few grown-up men that go to the 'Vic' gallery. The generality of the visitors are lads from about twelve to three-and-twenty, and though a few black-faced sweeps or whitey-brown dustmen may be among the throng, the gallery audience consists mainly of costermongers. Young girls, too, are very plentiful, only one-third of whom now take their babies, owing to the new regulation of charging half-price for infants. At the foot of the staircase stands a group of boys begging for the return checks,* which they sell again for 1½*d.* or 1*d.*, according to the lateness of the hour.

At each step up the well-staircase the warmth and stench increase, until by the time one reaches the gallery doorway, a furnace-heat rushes out through the entrance that seems to force you backwards, whilst the odour positively prevents respiration. The mob on the landing, standing on tiptoe and closely wedged together, resists any civil attempt at gaining a glimpse of the stage, and yet a coster lad will rush up, elbow his way into the crowd, then jump up on to the shoulders of those before him, and suddenly disappear into the body of the gallery.

The gallery at 'the Vic' is one of the largest in London. It will hold from 1,500 to 2,000 people, and runs back to so great a distance, that the end of it is lost in shadow, excepting where the little gas-jets, against the wall, light up the two or three faces around them. When the gallery is well packed, it is usual to see piles of boys on each others' shoulders at the back, while on the partition boards, dividing off the slips, lads will pitch themselves, despite the spikes.

As you look up the vast slanting mass of heads from the upper boxes, each one appears on the move. The huge black heap, dotted with faces, and spotted with white shirt sleeves, almost pains the eye to look at, and should a clapping of hands commence, the twinkling nearly blinds you. It is the fashion with the mob to take off their coats; and the cross-braces on the backs of some, and the bare shoulders peeping out of the ragged shirts of others, are the only variety to be found. The bonnets of the 'ladies' are hung over the iron railing in front, their numbers nearly hiding the panels, and one of the amusements of the lads in the back seats consists in pitching orange peel or nutshells into them, a good aim being rewarded with a shout of laughter.

When the orchestra begins playing, before 'the gods'* have settled into their seats, it is impossible to hear a note of music. The puffed-out cheeks of the trumpeters, and the raised drumsticks tell you that the overture has commenced, but no tune is to be heard. An occasional burst of the full band being caught by gushes, as if a high wind were raging. Recognitions take place every moment, and 'Bill Smith' is called to in a loud voice from one side, and a shout in answer from the other asks 'What's up?' Or family secrets are revealed, and 'Bob Triller' is asked where 'Sal' is, and replies amid a roar of laughter, that she is 'a-larning the pynanney'.*

By-and-by a youngster, who has come in late, jumps up over the shoulders at the door, and doubling himself into a ball, rolls down over the heads in front, leaving a trail of commotion for each one as he passes aims a blow at the fellow. Presently a fight is sure to begin, and then every one rises from his seat whistling and shouting; three or four pairs of arms fall to, the audience waving their hands till the moving mass seems like microscopic eels in paste.* But the commotion ceases suddenly on the rising of the curtain, and then the cries of 'Silence!' 'Ord-a-a-r!' 'Ord-a-a-r!' make more noise than ever.

The 'Vic' gallery is not to be moved by touching sentiment. They prefer vigorous exercise to any emotional speech. 'The Child of the Storm's' declaration* that she would share her father's 'death or imprisonment as her duty', had no effect at all, compared with the split in the hornpipe.* The shrill whistling and brayvos that followed the tar's performance showed how highly it was relished, and one 'god' went so far as to ask 'how it was done'. The comic actor kicking a dozen Polish peasants was encored, but the grand banquet of the Czar of all the Russias only produced merriment, and a request that he would 'give them a bit' was made directly the Emperor took the willow-patterned plate in his hand. All affecting situations were sure to be interrupted by cries of 'orda-a-r'; and the lady begging for her father's life was told to 'speak up old gal'; though when the heroine of the 'dummestic dreamer'* (as they call it) told the general of all the Cossack forces 'not to be a fool', the uproar of approbation grew greater than ever,—and when the lady turned up her swan's-down cuffs, and seizing four Russian soldiers shook them successively by the collar, then the enthusiasm knew no bounds, and the cries of 'Bray-vo Vincent! Go it my tulip!' resounded from every throat.

Altogether the gallery audience do not seem to be of a gentle nature. One poor little lad shouted out in a crying tone, 'that he couldn't see', and instantly a dozen voices demanded 'that he should be thrown over'.

Whilst the pieces are going on, brown, flat bottles are frequently raised to the mouth, and between the acts a man with a tin can, glittering in the gas-light, goes round crying, 'Port-a-a-a-r!* who's for port-a-a-a-r.' As the heat increased the faces grew bright red, every bonnet was taken off and ladies could be seen wiping the perspiration from their cheeks with the play-bills.

No delay between the pieces will be allowed, and should the interval appear too long, some one will shout out—referring to the curtain—'Pull up that there winder blind!' or they will call to the orchestra, saying, 'Now then you catgut-scrapers! Let's have a ha'purth of liveliness.' Neither will they suffer a play to proceed until they have a good view of the stage, and 'Higher the blue,' is constantly shouted, when the sky is too low, or 'Light up the moon', when the transparency is rather dim.

The dances and comic songs, between the pieces, are liked better than anything else. A highland fling is certain to be repeated, and a stamping of feet will accompany the tune, and a shrill whistling, keep time through the entire performance.

But the grand hit of the evening is always when a song is sung to which the entire gallery can join in chorus. Then a deep silence prevails all through the stanzas. Should any burst in before his time, a shout of 'orda-a-r' is raised, and the intruder put down by a thousand indignant cries. At the proper time, however, the throats of the mob burst forth in all their strength. The most deafening noise breaks out suddenly, while the cat-calls keep up the tune, and an imitation of a dozen Mr Punches squeak out the words. Some actors at the minor theatres make a great point of this, and in the bill upon the night of my visit, under the title of 'There's a good time coming, boys', there was printed, 'assisted by the most numerous and effective chorus in the metropolis—' meaning the whole of the gallery. The singer himself started the mob, saying, 'Now then, the Exeter Hall* touch if you please gentlemen,' and beat time with his hand, parodying M. Jullien with his *baton*. An 'angcore'* on such occasions is always demanded, and, despite a few murmurs of 'change it to "Duck-legged Dick" ',* invariably insisted on.

Of the Uneducated State of Costermongers

I have stated elsewhere, that only about one in ten of the regular costermongers is able to read. The want of education among both men and women is deplorable, and I tested it in several instances. The following statement, however, from one of the body, is no more to be taken as representing the ignorance of the class generally, than are the clear and discriminating accounts I received from intelligent costermongers to be taken as representing the intelligence of the body.

The man with whom I conversed, and from whom I received the following statement, seemed about thirty. He was certainly not ill-looking, but with a heavy cast of countenance, his light blue eyes having little expression. His statements, or opinions, I need hardly explain, were given both spontaneously in the course of conversation, and in answer to my questions. I give them almost verbatim, omitting oaths and slang:

'Well, times is bad, sir,' he said, 'but it's a deadish time. I don't do so well at present as in middlish times, I think. When I served the Prince of Naples, not far from here (I presume that he alluded to the Prince of Capua), I did better and times was better. That was five years ago, but I can't say to a year or two. He was a good customer, and was wery fond of peaches. I used to sell them to him, at *12s.* the plasket* when they was new. The plasket held a dozen, and cost me *6s.* at Covent-garden—more sometimes; but I didn't charge him more when they did. His footman was a black man, and a ignorant man quite, and his housekeeper was a Englishwoman. He was the Prince o' Naples, was my customer; but I don't know what he was like, for I never saw him. I've heard that he was the brother of the king of Naples. I can't say where Naples is, but if you was to ask at Euston-square;* they'll tell you the fare there and the time to go it in. It may be in France for anything I know may Naples, or in Ireland. Why don't you ask at the square? I went to Croydon once by rail, and slept all the way without stirring, and so you may to Naples for anything I know. I never heard of the Pope being a neighbour of the King of Naples. Do you mean living next door to him? But I don't know nothing of the King of Naples, only the prince. I don't know what the Pope is. Is he any trade? It's nothing to me, when he's no customer of mine. I have nothing to say about nobody that ain't no customers. My crabs is caught in the sea, in course. I gets them at Billingsgate.* I never saw the sea, but it's salt-water, I know. I can't say whereabouts it lays. I believe it's in the hands of the Billingsgate salesmen—all of it? I've heard of shipwrecks at sea, caused by drownding, in course. I never heard that the Prince of Naples was ever at sea. I like to talk about him, he was such a customer when he lived near here.' (Here he repeated his account of the supply of peaches to his Royal Highness.) 'I never was in France, no, sir, never. I don't know the way. Do you think I could do better there? I never was in the Republic there. What's it like? Bonaparte? O, yes; I've heard of him. He was at Waterloo. I didn't know he'd been alive now and in France, as you ask me about him. I don't think you're larking, sir. Did I hear of the French taking possession of Naples, and Bonaparte making his brother-in-law king? Well, I didn't, but it may be true, because I served the Prince of Naples, what *was* the brother of the king. I never heard whether the Prince was the king's older brother or his younger. I wish he may turn out his older if there's property coming to him, as the oldest has the first turn; at least so I've heard—first come, first served. I've worked the streets and the courts at all times. I've worked them by moonlight, but you couldn't see the moonlight where it was busy. I can't say how far the moon's off us. It's nothing to me, but I've seen it a good bit higher than St Paul's. I don't know nothing about the sun. Why do you ask? It must be nearer than the moon for it's warmer,—and if they're both fire, that shows it. It's like the tap-room* grate and that bit of a gas-light; to compare the two is. What was St Paul's that the moon was above? A church, sir; so I've heard. I never was in a church. O, yes, I've heard of God; he made heaven and earth; I never heard of his making the sea; that's another thing, and you can best learn about that at Billingsgate. (He seemed to think that the sea was an appurtenance of Billingsgate.) Jesus Christ? Yes. I've heard of him. Our Redeemer? Well, I only wish I could redeem my Sunday togs from my uncle's.'*

Another costermonger, in answer to inquiries, said: 'I 'spose you think us 'riginal coves that you ask. We're not like Methusalem, or some such swell's name, (I presume that Malthus* was meant) as wanted to murder children afore they was born, as I once heerd lectured about—we're nothing like that.'

Another on being questioned, and on being told that the information was wanted for the press, replied: 'The press? I'll have nothing to say to it. We are oppressed enough already.'

That a class numbering 30,000 should be permitted to remain in a state of almost brutish ignorance is a national disgrace. If the London costers belong especially to the 'dangerous classes', the danger of such a body is assuredly an evil of our own creation; for the gratitude of the poor creatures to any one who seeks to give them the least knowledge is almost pathetic.

Language of Costermongers

The slang language of the costermongers is not very remarkable for originality of construction; it possesses no humour: but they boast that it is known only to themselves; it is far beyond the Irish, they say, and puzzles the Jews. The *root* of the costermonger tongue, so to speak, is to give the words spelt backward, or rather pronounced rudely backward,—for in my present chapter the language has,

I believe, been reduced to orthography for the first time. With this backward pronunciation, which is very arbitrary, are mixed words reducible to no rule and seldom referrable to any origin, thus complicating the mystery of this unwritten tongue; while any syllable is added to a proper slang word, at the discretion of the speaker.

Slang is acquired very rapidly, and some costermongers will converse in it by the hour. The women use it sparingly; the girls more than the women; the men more than the girls; and the boys most of all. The most ignorant of all these classes deal most in slang and boast of their cleverness and proficiency in it. In their conversations among themselves, the following are invariably the terms used in money matters. A rude back-spelling may generally be traced:

Flatch	Halfpenny.
Yenep.	Penny.
Owt-yenep	Twopence.
Erth-yenep	Threepence.
Rouf-yenep	Fourpence.
Ewif-yenep	Fivepence.
Exis-yenep	Sixpence.
Neves-yenep	Sevenpence.
Teaich-yenep	Eightpence.
Enine-yenep	Ninepence.
Net-yenep	Tenpence.
Leven	Elevenpence.
Gen	Twelvepence.
Yenep-flatch	Three half-pence.

and so on through the penny-halfpennies.

Speaking of this language, a costermonger said to me: 'The Irish can't tumble to it anyhow; the Jews can tumble better, but we're *their* masters. Some of the young salesmen at Billingsgate understand us,—but only at Billingsgate; and they think they're uncommon clever, but they're not quite up to the mark. The police don't understand us at all. It would be a pity if they did.'

I give a few more phrases:

A doogheno or dabheno?	Is it a good or bad market?
A regular trosseno	A regular bad one.
On	No.

Say	Yes.
Tumble to your barrikin	Understand you.
Top o' reeb	Pot of beer.
Doing dab	Doing badly.
Cool him.	Look at him.

The latter phrase is used when one costermonger warns another of the approach of a policeman 'who might order him to move on, or be otherwise unpleasant'. 'Cool' (look) is exclaimed, or 'Cool him' (look at him). One costermonger told me as a great joke that a very stout policeman, who was then new to the duty, was when in a violent state of perspiration, much offended by a costermonger saying 'Cool him.'

Cool the esclop	Look at the police.
Cool the namesclop.	Look at the policeman.
Cool ta the dillo nemo.	Look at the old woman;

said of any woman, young or old, who, according to costermonger notions, is 'giving herself airs'.

This language seems confined, in its general use, to the immediate objects of the costermonger's care; but is, among the more acute members of the fraternity, greatly extended, and is capable of indefinite extension.

The costermongers' oaths, I may conclude, are all in the vernacular; nor are any of the common salutes, such as 'How d'you do?' or 'Good-night' known to their slang.

Kennetseeno.	Stinking;
(applied principally to the quality of fish.)	
Flatch kanurd	Half-drunk.
Flash it.	Show it;
(in cases of bargains offered.)	
On doog.	No good.
Cross chap	A thief.
Showfulls	Bad money;
(seldom in the hands of costermongers.)	
I'm on to the deb	I'm going to bed.
Do the tightner	Go to dinner.

Nommus.	Be off.
Tol.	Lot, Stock, or Share.

Many costermongers, 'but principally—perhaps entirely,'—I was told, 'those who had not been regular born and bred to the trade, but had taken to it when cracked up in their own', do not trouble themselves to acquire any knowledge of slang. It is not indispensable for the carrying on of their business; the grand object, however, seems to be, to shield their bargainings at market, or their conversation among themselves touching their day's work and profits, from the knowledge of any Irish or uninitiated fellow-traders.

The simple principle of costermonger slang—that of pronouncing backward, may cause its acquirement to be regarded by the educated as a matter of ease. But it is a curious fact that lads who become costermongers' boys, without previous association with the class, acquire a very ready command of the language, and this though they are not only unable to spell, but don't 'know a letter in a book'. I saw one lad, whose parents had, until five or six months back, resided in the country. The lad himself was fourteen; he told me he had not been 'a costermongering' more than three months, and prided himself on his mastery over slang. To test his ability, I asked him the coster's word for 'hippopotamus'; he answered, with tolerable readiness, 'musatoppop'. I then asked him for the like rendering of 'equestrian' (one of Astley's bills having caught my eye). He replied, but not quite so readily, 'nirtseque'. The last test to which I subjected him was 'good-naturedly', and though I induced him to repeat the word twice, I could not, on any of the three renderings, distinguish any precise sound beyond an indistinct gabbling, concluded emphatically with 'doog':—'good' being a word with which all these traders are familiar. It must be remembered, that the words I demanded were remote from the young costermonger's vocabulary, if not from his understanding.

Before I left this boy, he poured forth a minute or more's gibberish, of which, from its rapid utterance, I could distinguish nothing; but I found from his after explanation, that it was a request to me to make a further purchase of his walnuts.

This slang is utterly devoid of any applicability to humour. It gives no new fact, or approach to a fact, for philologists. One superior genius among the costers, who has invented words for them, told me that he had no system for coining his term. He gave to the known words some terminating syllable, or, as he called it, 'a new turn, just', to use his own words, 'as if he chorussed them, with a tol-de-rol'.* The intelligence communicated in this slang is, in a great measure, communicated, as in other slang, as much by the inflection of the voice, the emphasis, the tone, the look, the shrug, the nod, the wink, as by the words spoken.

Of the Nicknames of Costermongers

Like many rude, and almost all wandering communities, the costermongers, like the cabmen and pickpockets, are hardly ever known by their real names; even the honest men among them are distinguished by some strange appellation. Indeed, they are all known one to another by nicknames, which they acquire either by some mode of dress, some remark that has ensured costermonger applause, some peculiarity in trading, or some defect or singularity in personal appearance. Men are known as 'Rotten Herrings', 'Spuddy' (a seller of bad potatoes, until beaten by the Irish for his bad wares), 'Curly' (a man with a curly head), 'Foreigner' (a man who had been in the Spanish-Legion), 'Brassy' (a very saucy person), 'Gaffy'* (once a performer), 'The One-eyed Buffer', 'Jawbreaker', 'Pine-apple Jack', 'Cast-iron Poll' (her head having been struck with a pot without injury to her), 'Whilky', 'Blackwall Poll' (a woman generally having two black eyes), 'Lushy Bet', 'Dirty Sall' (the costermongers generally objecting to dirty women), and 'Dancing Sue'.

Of the Homes of the Costermongers

The costermongers usually reside in the courts and alleys in the neighbourhood of the different street-markets. They themselves designate the locality where, so to speak, a colony of their people has been established, a 'coster district', and the entire metropolis is thus parcelled out, almost as systematically as if for the purposes of registration. These costermonger districts are as follows, and are here placed in the order of the numerical importance of the residents:

The New Cut (Lambeth).
Whitecross-street.
Petticoat and Rosemary-lane.
Marylebone-lane.

Leather-lane.	Ratcliffe Highway.
The Brill, Somers' Town.	Lisson-grove.
Whitechapel.	Oxford-street.
Camberwell.	Rotherhithe.
Walworth.	Deptford.
Peckham.	Dockhead.
Bermondsey.	Greenwich.
The Broadway, Westminster.	Commercial-road (East).
Shoreditch.	Poplar.
Paddington and Edgeware Road.	Limehouse.
Tottenham-court Road.	Bethnal-green.
Drury-lane.	Hackney-road.
Old-street Road.	Kingsland.
Clare Market	Camden Town.

The homes of the costermongers in these places, may be divided into three classes; firstly, those who, by having a regular trade or by prudent economy, are enabled to live in comparative ease and plenty; secondly, those who, from having a large family or by imprudent expenditure, are, as it were, struggling with the world; and thirdly, those who for want of stock-money, or ill success in trade are nearly destitute.

The first home I visited was that of an old woman, who with the assistance of her son and girls, contrived to live in a most praiseworthy and comfortable manner. She and all her family were teetotallers, and may be taken as a fair type of the thriving costermonger.

As I ascended a dark flight of stairs, a savory smell of stew grew stronger at each step I mounted. The woman lived in a large airy room on the first floor ('the drawing-room', as she told me laughing at her own joke), well lighted by a clean window, and I found her laying out the savory smelling dinner looking most temptingly clean. The floor was as white as if it had been newly planed, the coke fire was bright and warm, making the lid of the tin saucepan on it rattle up and down as the steam rushed out. The wall over the fire-place was patched up to the ceiling with little square pictures of saints, and on the mantel-piece, between a row of bright tumblers and wine glasses filled with odds and ends, stood glazed crockeryware images of Prince Albert and M. Jullien.* Against the walls, which were papered with 'hangings' of four different patterns and colours, were hung several warm shawls, and in the band-box, which stood on the stained chest of drawers, you could tell that the Sunday bonnet was stowed safely away from the dust. A turn-up bedstead thrown back, and covered with a many-coloured patch-work quilt, stood opposite to a long dresser with its mugs and cups dangling from the hooks, and the clean blue plates and dishes ranged in order at the back. There were a few bushel baskets piled up in one corner, 'but the apples smelt so,' she said, 'they left them in a stable at night.'

By the fire sat the woman's daughter, a pretty meek-faced gray-eyed girl of sixteen, who 'was home nursing' for a cold. 'Steve' (her boy) I was informed, was out working. With his help, the woman assured me, she could live very comfortably—'God be praised!' and when he got the barrow he was promised, she gave me to understand, that their riches were to increase past reckoning. Her girl too was to be off at work as soon as sprats came in. 'It's on Lord Mayor's-day they comes in,' said a neighbour who had rushed up to see the strange gentleman, 'they says he has 'em on his table, but I never seed 'em. They never gives us the pieces, no not even the heads,' and every one laughed to their utmost. The good old dame was in high spirits, her dark eyes sparkling as she spoke about her 'Steve'. The daughter in a little time lost her bashfulness, and informed me 'that one of the Polish refugees was a-courting Mrs M——, who had given him a pair of black eyes'.

On taking my leave I was told by the mother that their silver gilt Dutch clock*—with its glass face and blackleaded weights—'was the best one in London, and might be relied on with the greatest safety'.

As a specimen of the dwellings of the struggling costers, the following may be cited:

The man, a tall, thick-built, almost good-looking fellow, with a large fur cap on his head, lived with his family in a front kitchen, and as there were, with his mother-in-law, five persons, and only one bed, I was somewhat puzzled to know where they could *all* sleep. The barrow standing on the railings over the window, half shut out the light, and when any one passed there was a momentary shadow thrown over the room, and a loud rattling of the iron gratings above that completely prevented all conversation. When I entered, the mother-in-law was reading aloud one of the threepenny-papers to her son, who lolled on the bed, that with its curtains nearly filled the room. There was the usual attempt to make the fireside comfortable.

The stone sides had been well whitened, and the mantel-piece decorated with its small tin trays, tumblers, and a piece of looking-glass. A cat with a kitten were seated on the hearthrug in front. 'They keeps the varmint away,' said the woman, stroking the 'puss', 'and gives a look of home.' By the drawers were piled up four bushel baskets, and in a dark corner near the bed stood a tall measure full of apples that scented the room. Over the head, on a string that stretched from wall to wall, dangled a couple of newly-washed shirts, and by the window were two stone barrels, for lemonade, when the coster visited the fairs and races.

Whilst we were talking, the man's little girl came home. For a poor man's child she was dressed to perfection; her pinafore was clean, her face shone with soap, and her tidy cotton print gown had clearly been newly put on that morning. She brought news that 'Janey' was coming home from auntey's, and instantly a pink cotton dress was placed by the mother-in-law before the fire to air. (It appeared that Janey was out at service, and came home once a week to see her parents and take back a clean frock.) Although these people were living, so to speak, in a cellar, still every endeavour had been made to give the home a look of comfort. The window, with its paper-patched panes, had a clean calico blind. The side-table was dressed up with yellow jugs and cups and saucers, and the band-boxes* had been stowed away on the flat top of the bedstead. All the chairs, which were old fashioned mahogany ones, had sound backs and bottoms.

Of the third class, or the very poor, I chose the following 'type' out of the many others that presented themselves. The family here lived in a small slanting-roofed house, partly stripped of its tiles. More than one half of the small leaden squares of the first-floor window were covered with brown paper, puffing out and crackling in the wind, while through the greater part of the others were thrust out ball-shaped bundles of rags, to keep out the breeze. The panes that did remain were of all shapes and sizes, and at a distance had the appearance of yellow glass, they were so stained with dirt. I opened a door with a number chalked on it, and groped my way up a broken tottering staircase.

It took me some time after I had entered the apartment before I could get accustomed to the smoke, that came pouring into the room from the chimney. The place was filled with it, curling in the light, and making every thing so indistinct that I could with difficulty see the white mugs ranged in the corner-cupboard, not three yards from me. When the wind was in the north, or when it rained, it was always that way, I was told, 'but otherwise,' said an old dame about sixty, with long grisly hair spreading over her black shawl, 'it is pretty good for that'.

On a mattrass, on the floor, lay a pale-faced girl—'eighteen years old last twelfth-cake day'*—her drawn-up form showing in the patch-work counterpane that covered her. She had just been confined, and the child had died! A little straw, stuffed into an old tick,* was all she had to lie upon, and even that had been given up to her by the mother until she was well enough to work again. To shield her from the light of the window, a cloak had been fastened up slantingly across the panes; and on a string that ran along the wall was tied, amongst the bonnets, a clean nightcap—'against the doctor came', as the mother, curtsying, informed me. By the side of the bed, almost hidden in the dark shade, was a pile of sieve baskets, crowned by the flat shallow that the mother 'worked' with.

The room was about nine feet square, and furnished a home for three women. The ceiling slanted like that of a garret, and was the colour of old leather, excepting a few rough white patches, where the tenants had rudely mended it. The white light was easily seen through the laths, and in one corner a large patch of the paper looped down from the wall. One night the family had been startled from their sleep by a large mass of mortar—just where the roof bulged in—falling into the room. 'We never want rain water,' the woman told me, 'for we can catch plenty just over the chimney-place.'

They had made a carpet out of three or four old mats. They were 'obligated to it, for fear of dropping anything through the boards into the donkey stables in the parlour underneath. But we only pay ninepence a week rent,' said the old woman, 'and mustn't grumble.'

The only ornament in the place was on the mantel-piece—an old earthenware sugar-basin, well silvered over, that had been given by the eldest girl when she died, as a remembrance to her mother. Two cracked tea-cups, on their inverted saucers, stood on each side, and dressed up the fire-side into something like tidiness. The chair I sat on was by far the best out of the three in the room, and that had no back, and only half its quantity of straw.

The parish, the old woman told me, allowed her 1*s*. a week and two loaves. But the doctor ordered her girl to take sago and milk, and she was many a time sorely puzzled to get it. The neighbours helped her a good deal, and often sent her part of their unsold greens;—even if it was only the outer leaves of the cabbages, she was thankful for them. Her other girl—a big-boned wench, with a red shawl crossed over her bosom, and her black hair parted on one side—did all she could, and so they lived on. 'As long as they kept out of the "big house" (the workhouse) she would not complain.'

I never yet beheld so much destitution borne with so much content. Verily the acted philosophy of the poor is a thing to make those who write and preach about it hide their heads.

Of the Cries, Rounds, and Days of Costermongers

I shall now proceed to treat of the London costermongers' mode of doing business.

In the first place all the goods they sell are cried or 'hawked', and the cries of the costermongers in the present day are as varied as the articles they sell. The principal ones, uttered in a sort of cadence, are now, 'Ni-ew mackerel, 6 a shilling.' ('I've got a good jacketing* many a Sunday morning,' said one dealer, 'for waking people up with crying mackerel, but I've said, "I must live while you sleep." ') 'Buy a pair of live soles, 3 pair for 6*d.*'—or, with a barrow, 'Soles, 1*d.* a pair, 1*d.* a pair'; 'Plaice alive, alive, cheap'; 'Buy a pound crab, cheap'; 'Pine-apples, ½*d.* a slice'; 'Mussels a penny a quart'; 'Oysters, a penny a lot'; 'Salmon alive, 6*d.* a pound'; 'Cod alive, 2*d.* a pound'; 'Real Yarmouth bloaters, 2 a penny'; 'New herrings alive, 16 a groat' (this is the loudest cry of any); 'Penny a bunch turnips' (the same with greens, cabbages, &c.); 'All new nuts, 1*d.* half-pint'; 'Oranges, 2 a penny'; 'All large and alive-O, new sprats, O, 1*d.* a plate'; 'Wi-ild Hampshire rabbits, 2 a shilling'; 'Cherry ripe, 2*d.* a pound'; 'Fine ripe plums, 1*d.* a pint'; 'Ing-uns,* a penny a quart'; 'Eels, 3lbs. a shilling—large live eels 3lbs. a shilling'.

The continual calling in the streets is very distressing to the voice. One man told me that it had broken his, and that very often while out he lost his voice altogether. 'They seem to have no breath,' the men say, 'after calling for a little while.' The repeated shouting brings on a hoarseness, which is one of the peculiar characteristics of hawkers in general. The costers mostly go out with a boy to cry their goods for them. If they have two or three hallooing together, it makes more noise than one, and the boys can shout better and louder than the men. The more noise they can make in a place the better they find their trade. Street-selling has been so bad lately that many have been obliged to have a drum for their bloaters, 'to drum the fish off', as they call it.

In the second place, the costermongers, as I said before, have mostly their little bit of a 'round'; that is, they go only to certain places; and if they don't sell their goods they 'work back' the same way again. If they visit a respectable quarter, they confine themselves to the mews near the gentlemen's houses. They generally prefer the poorer neighbourhoods. They go down or through almost all the courts and alleys—and avoid the better kind of streets, unless with lobsters, rabbits, or onions. If they have anything inferior, they visit the low Irish districts—for the Irish people, they say, want only quantity, and care nothing about quality—*that* they don't study. But if they have anything they wish to make a price of, they seek out the mews, and try to get it off among the gentlemen's coachmen, for *they* will have what is good; or else they go among the residences of mechanics,—for their wives, they say, like good-living as well as the coachmen. Some costers, on the other hand, go chance rounds.

Concerning the busiest days of the week for the coster's trade, they say Wednesdays and Fridays are the best, because they are regular fish days. These two days are considered to be those on which the poorer classes generally run short of money. Wednesday night is called 'draw night' among some mechanics and labourers—that is, they then get a portion of their wages in advance, and on Friday they run short as well as on the Wednesday, and have to make shift for their dinners. With the few halfpence they have left, they are glad to pick up anything cheap, and the street-fishmonger never refuses an offer. Besides, he can supply them with a cheaper dinner than any other person. In the season the poor generally dine upon herrings. The poorer classes live mostly on fish, and the 'dropped' and 'rough' fish is bought chiefly for the poor. The fish-huckster has no respect for persons, however; one assured me that if Prince Halbert* was to stop him in the street to buy a pair of soles of him, he'd as soon sell him a 'rough pair as any other man—indeed, I'd take in my own father,' he added, 'if he wanted to deal with me'. Saturday is the worst day of all for fish, for then the poor people have scarcely anything at all to spend; Saturday night, however, the street-seller takes more money than at any other time in the week.

Of the Tricks of Costermongers

I shall now treat of the tricks of trade practised by the London costermongers. Of these the costers speak with as little reserve and as little shame as a fine gentleman of his peccadilloes. 'I've boiled lots of oranges,' chuckled one man, 'and sold them to Irish hawkers, as wasn't wide awake, for stunning big uns. The boiling swells the oranges and so makes 'em look finer ones, but it spoils them, for it takes out the juice. People can't find that out though until it's too late. I boiled the oranges only a few minutes, and three or four dozen at a time.' Oranges thus prepared will not keep, and any unfortunate Irishwoman, tricked as were my informant's customers, is astonished to find her stock of oranges turn dark-coloured and worthless in forty-eight hours. The fruit is 'cooked' in this way for Saturday night and Sunday sale—times at which the demand is the briskest. Some prick the oranges and express the juice, which they sell to the British wine-makers.

Apples cannot be dealt with like oranges, but they are mixed. A cheap red-skinned fruit, known to costers as 'gawfs', is rubbed hard, to look bright and feel soft, and is mixed with apples of a superior description. 'Gawfs are sweet and sour at once,' I was told, 'and fit for nothing but mixing.' Some foreign apples, from Holland and Belgium, were bought very cheap last March, at no more than 16*d*. a bushel, and on a fine morning as many as fifty boys might be seen rubbing these apples, in Hooper-street, Lambeth. 'I've made a crown out of a bushel of 'em on a fine day,' said one sharp youth. The larger apples are rubbed sometimes with a piece of woollen cloth, or on the coat skirt, if that appendage form part of the dress of the person applying the friction, but most frequently they are rolled in the palms of the hand. The smaller apples are thrown to and fro in a sack, a lad holding each end. 'I wish I knew how the shopkeepers manages *their* fruit,' said one youth to me; 'I should like to be up to some of their moves; they do manage their things so plummy.'

Cherries are capital for mixing, I was assured by practical men. They purchase three sieves of indifferent Dutch, and one sieve of good English cherries, spread the English fruit over the inferior quality, and sell them as the best. Strawberry pottles* are often half cabbage leaves, a few tempting strawberries being displayed on the top of the pottle. 'Topping up', said a fruit dealer to me, 'is the principal thing, and we are perfectly justified in it. You ask any coster that knows the world, and he'll tell you that all the salesmen in the markets tops up. It's only making the best of it.' Filberts they bake to make them look brown and ripe. Prunes they boil to give them a plumper and finer appearance. The latter trick, however, is not unusual in the shops.

The more honest costermongers will throw away fish when it is unfit for consumption, less scrupulous dealers, however, only throw away what is utterly unsaleable; but none of them fling away the dead eels, though their prejudice against such dead fish prevents their indulging in eel-pies. The dead eels are mixed with the living, often in the proportion of 20 lb. dead to 5 lb. alive, equal quantities of each being accounted very fair dealing. 'And after all,' said a street fish dealer to me, 'I don't know why dead eels should be objected to; the aristocrats don't object to them. Nearly all fish is dead before it's cooked, and why not eels? Why not eat them when they're sweet, if they're ever so dead, just as you eat fresh herrings? I believe it's only among the poor and among our chaps, that there's this prejudice. Eels die quickly if they're exposed to the sun.'

Herrings are made to look fresh and bright by candle-light, by the lights being so disposed 'as to give them', I was told, 'a good reflection. Why I can make them look splendid; quite a pictur. I can do the same with mackerel, but not so prime as herrings.'

There are many other tricks of a similar kind detailed in the course of my narrative. We should remember, however, that *shopkeepers* are not immaculate in this respect.

STREET-SELLERS OF FRUIT AND VEGETABLES

Of Covent Garden Market

On a Saturday—the coster's business day—it is computed that as many as 2,000 donkey-barrows, and upwards of 3,000 women with shallows and head-baskets visit this market during the forenoon. About six o'clock in the morning is the best time for viewing the wonderful restlessness of the place, for then not only is the 'Garden' itself all bustle and activity, but the buyers and sellers stream to and from it in all directions, filling every street in the vicinity. From Long Acre to the Strand on the one side, and from Bow-street to Bedford-street on the other, the ground has been seized upon by the market-goers. As you glance down any one of the neighbouring streets, the long rows of carts and donkey-barrows seem interminable in the distance. They are of all kinds, from the greengrocer's taxed cart to the coster's barrow—from the showy excursion-van* to the rude square donkey-cart and bricklayer's truck. In every street they are ranged down the middle and by the kerb-stones. Along each approach to the market, too, nothing is to be seen, on all sides, but vegetables; the pavement is covered with heaps of them waiting to be carted; the flagstones are stained green with the leaves trodden under foot; sieves and sacks full of apples and potatoes, and bundles of brocoli and rhubarb, are left unwatched upon almost every door-step; the steps of Covent Garden Theatre are covered with fruit and vegetables; the road is blocked up with mountains of cabbages and turnips; and men and women push past with their arms bowed out by the cauliflowers under them, or the red tips of carrots pointing from their crammed aprons, or else their faces are red with the weight of the loaded head-basket.

The donkey-barrows, from their number and singularity, force you to stop and notice them. Every kind of ingenuity has been exercised to construct harness for the costers' steeds; where a buckle is wanting, tape or string make the fastening secure; traces are made of rope and old chain, and an old sack or cotton handkerchief is folded up as a saddle-pad. Some few of the barrows make a magnificent exception, and are gay with bright brass; while one of the donkeys may be seen dressed in a suit of old plated carriage-harness, decorated with coronets in all directions. At some one of the coster conveyances stands the proprietor, arranging his goods, the dozing animal starting up from its sleep each time a heavy basket is hoisted on the tray. Others, with their green and white and red load neatly arranged, are ready for starting, but the coster is finishing his breakfast at the coffee-stall. On one barrow there may occasionally be seen a solitary sieve of apples, with the horse of some neighbouring cart helping himself to the pippins while the owner is away. The men that take charge of the trucks, whilst the costers visit the market, walk about, with their arms full of whips and sticks. At one corner a donkey has slipped down, and lies on the stones covered with the cabbages and apples that have fallen from the cart.

The market itself presents a beautiful scene. In the clear morning air of an autumn day the whole of the vast square is distinctly seen from one end to the other. The sky is red and golden with the newly-risen sun, and the rays falling on the fresh and vivid colours of the fruit and vegetables, brightens up the picture as with a coat of varnish. There is no shouting, as at other markets, but a low murmuring hum is heard, like the sound of the sea at a distance, and through each entrance to the market the crowd sweeps by. Under the dark Piazza little bright dots of gas-lights are seen burning in the shops; and in the paved square the people pass and cross each other in all directions, hampers clash together, and excepting the carters from the country, every one is on the move. Sometimes a huge column of baskets is seen in the air, and walks away in a marvellously steady manner, or a monster railway van, laden with sieves of fruit, and with the driver perched up on his high seat, jolts heavily over the stones. Cabbages are piled up into stacks as it were. Carts are heaped high with turnips, and bunches of carrots like huge red fingers, are seen in all directions. Flower-girls, with large bundles of violets under their arms, run past, leaving a trail of perfume behind them. Wagons, with their shafts sticking up in the air, are ranged before the salesmen's shops, the high green load railed in with hurdles, and every here and there bunches of turnips are seen flying in the air over the heads of the people. Groups of apple-women, with straw pads on their crushed bonnets, and coarse shawls crossing their bosoms, sit on their porter's knots, chatting in Irish, and smoking short pipes; every passer-by is hailed with the cry of, 'Want a baskit, yer honor?' The porter, trembling under the piled-up hamper, trots along the street, with his teeth clenched and shirt wet with the weight, and staggering at every step he takes.

Inside the market all is bustle and confusion. The people walk along with their eyes fixed on the goods, and frowning with thought. Men in all costumes, from the coster in his corduroy suit to the greengrocer in his blue apron, sweep past. A countryman, in an old straw hat and dusty boots, occasionally draws down the anger of a woman for walking about with his hands in the pockets of his smock-frock, and is asked, 'if that is the way to behave on a market-day?' Even the granite pillars cannot stop the crowd, for it separates and rushes past them, like the tide by a bridge pier. At every turn there is a fresh odour to sniff at; either the bitter aromatic perfume of the herbalists' shops breaks upon you, or the scent of oranges, then of apples, and then of onions is caught for an instant as you move along. The brocoli tied up in square packets, the white heads tinged slightly red, as it were, with the sunshine,—the sieves of crimson love-apples, polished like china,—the bundles of white glossy leeks, their roots dangling like fringe,—the celery, with its pinky stalks and bright green tops,—the dark purple pickling-cabbages,—the scarlet carrots,—the white knobs of turnips,—the bright yellow balls of oranges, and the rich brown coats of the chestnuts—attract the eye on every side. Then there are the apple-merchants, with their fruit of all colours, from the pale yellow green to the bright crimson, and the baskets ranged in rows on the pavement before the little shops. Round these the customers stand examining the stock, then whispering together over their bargain, and counting their money. 'Give you four shillings for this here lot, master,' says a coster, speaking for his three companions. 'Four and six is my price,' answers the salesman. 'Say four, and it's a bargain,' continues the man. 'I said my price,' returns the dealer; 'go and look round, and see if you can get 'em cheaper; if not, come back. I only wants what's fair.' The men, taking the salesman's advice, move on. The walnut merchant, with the group of women before his shop, peeling the fruit, their fingers stained deep brown, is busy with the Irish purchasers. The onion stores, too, are surrounded by Hibernians,* feeling and pressing the gold-coloured roots, whose dry skins crackle as they are handled. Cases of lemons in their white paper jackets, and blue grapes, just seen above the sawdust are ranged about, and in some places the ground is slippery as ice from the refuse leaves and walnut husks scattered over the pavement.

Against the railings of St Paul's Church are hung baskets and slippers for sale, and near the public-house is a party of countrymen preparing their bunches of pretty coloured grass—brown and glittering, as if it had been bronzed. Between the spikes of the railing are piled up square cakes of green turf for larks; and at the pump, boys, who probably have passed the previous night in the baskets about the market, are washing, and the water dripping from their hair that hangs in points over the face. The kerb-stone is blocked up by a crowd of admiring lads, gathered round the bird-catcher's green stand, and gazing at the larks beating their breasts against their cages. The owner, whose boots are red with the soil of the brick-field, shouts, as he looks carelessly around, 'A cock linnet for tuppence,' and then hits at the youths who are poking through the bars at the fluttering birds.

Under the Piazza the costers purchase their flowers (in pots) which they exchange in the streets for old clothes. Here is ranged a small garden of flower-pots, the musk and mignonette smelling sweetly, and the scarlet geraniums, with a perfect glow of coloured air about the flowers, standing out in rich contrast with the dark green leaves of the evergreens behind them. 'There's myrtles, and larels, and boxes,' says one of the men selling them, 'and there's a harbora witus, and lauristiners, and that bushy shrub with pink spots is heath.' Men and women, selling different articles, walk about under the cover of the colonnade. One has seedcake, another small-tooth and other combs, others old caps, or pig's feet, and one hawker of knives, razors, and short hatchets, may occasionally be seen driving a bargain with a countryman, who stands passing his thumb over the blade to test its keenness. Between the pillars are the coffee-stalls, with their large tin cans and piles of bread and butter, and protected from the wind by paper screens and sheets thrown over clothes-horses; inside these little parlours, as it were, sit the coffee-drinkers on chairs and benches, some with a bunch of cabbages on their laps, blowing the steam from their saucers, others, with their mouths full, munching away at their slices, as if not a moment could be lost. One or two porters are there besides, seated on their baskets, breakfasting with their knots on their heads.

As you walk away from this busy scene, you meet in every street barrows and costers hurrying home. The pump in the market is now surrounded by a cluster of chattering wenches quarrelling over whose turn it is to water their drooping violets, and on the steps of Covent Garden Theatre are seated the shoeless girls, tying up the halfpenny and penny bundles.

Watercress Girl

The little watercress girl who gave me the following statement, although only eight years of age, had entirely lost all childish ways, and was, indeed, in thoughts and manner, a woman. There was something cruelly pathetic in hearing this infant, so young that her features had scarcely formed themselves, talking of the bitterest struggles of life, with the calm earnestness of one who had endured them all. I did not know how to talk with her. At first I treated her as a child, speaking on childish subjects; so that I might, by being familiar with her, remove all shyness, and get her to narrate her life freely. I asked her about her toys and her games with her companions; but the look of amazement that answered me soon put an end to any attempt at fun on my part. I then talked to her about the parks, and whether she ever went to them. 'The parks!' she replied in wonder, 'where are they?' I explained to her, telling her that they were large open places with green grass and tall trees, where beautiful carriages drove about, and people walked for pleasure, and children played. Her eyes brightened up a little as I spoke; and she asked, half doubtingly, 'Would they let such as me go there—just to look?' All her knowledge seemed to begin and end with watercresses, and what they fetched. She knew no more of London than that part she had seen on her rounds, and believed that no quarter of the town was handsomer or pleasanter than it was at Farringdon-market or at Clerkenwell, where she lived. Her little face, pale and thin with privation, was wrinkled where the dimples ought to have been, and she would sigh frequently. When some hot dinner was offered to her, she would not touch it, because, if she eat too much, 'it made her sick,' she said; 'and she wasn't used to meat, only on a Sunday.'

The poor child, although the weather was severe, was dressed in a thin cotton gown, with a threadbare shawl wrapped round her shoulders. She wore no covering to her head, and the long rusty hair stood out in all directions. When she walked she shuffled along, for fear that the large carpet slippers that served her for shoes should slip off her feet.

'I go about the streets with water-creases crying, "Four bunches a penny, water-creases." I am just eight years old—that's all, and I've a big sister, and a brother and a sister younger than I am. On and off, I've been very near twelvemonth in the streets. Before that, I had to take care of a baby for my aunt. No, it wasn't heavy—it was only two months old; but I minded it for ever such a time—till it could walk. It was a very nice little baby, not a very pretty one; but, if I touched it under the chin, it would laugh. Before I had the baby, I used to help mother, who was in the fur trade; and, if there was any slits in the fur, I'd sew them up. My mother learned me to needle-work and to knit when I was about five. I used to go to school, too; but I wasn't there long. I've forgot all about it now, it's such a time ago; and mother took me away because the master whacked me, though the missus use'n't to never touch me. I didn't like him at all. What do you think? he hit me three times, ever so hard, across the face with his cane, and made me go dancing down stairs; and when mother saw the marks on my cheek, she went to blow him up, but she couldn't see him—he was afraid. That's why I left school.

'The creases is so bad now, that I haven't been out with 'em for three days. They're so cold, people won't buy 'em; for when I goes up them, they say, "They'll freeze our bellies." Besides, in the market, they won't sell a ha'penny handful now—they're ris to a penny and tuppence. In summer there's lots, and 'most as cheap as dirt; but I have to be down at Farringdon-market between four and five, or else I can't get any creases, because everyone almost—especially the Irish—is selling them, and they're picked up so quick. Some of the saleswomen—we never calls 'em ladies—is very kind to us children, and some of them altogether spiteful. The good one will give you a bunch for nothing, when they're cheap; but the others, cruel ones, if you try to bate them a farden less than they ask you, will say, "Go along with you, you're no good." I used to go down to market along with another girl, as must be about fourteen, 'cos she does her back hair up. When we've bought a lot, we sits down on a door-step, and ties up the bunches. We never goes home to breakfast till we've sold out; but, if it's very late, then I buys a penn'orth of pudden, which is very nice with gravy. I don't know hardly one of the people, as goes to Farringdon, to talk to; they never speaks to me, so I don't speak to them. We children never play down there, 'cos we're thinking of our living. No; people never pities me in the street—excepting one gentleman, and he says, says he, "What do you do out so soon in the morning?" but he gave me nothink—he only walked away.

'It's very cold before winter comes on reg'lar—specially getting up of a morning. I gets up in the dark by the light of the lamp in the court. When the snow is on the ground, there's no creases. I bears the cold—you must; so I puts my hands under my shawl, though it hurts 'em to take hold of the creases, especially when we takes 'em to the pump to wash 'em. No; I never see any children crying—it's no use.

'Sometimes I make a great deal of money. One day I took 1*s*. 6*d*., and the creases cost 6*d*.; but it isn't often I get such luck as that. I oftener makes 3*d*. or 4*d*. than 1*s*.; and then I'm at work, crying, "Creases, four bunches a penny, creases!" from six in the morning to about ten. What do you mean by mechanics?*—I don't know what they are. The shops buys most of me. Some of 'em says, "Oh! I ain't a-goin' to give a penny for these"; and they want 'em at the same price as I buys 'em at.

'I always give mother my money, she's so very good to me. She don't often beat me; but, when she do, she don't play with me. She's very poor, and goes out cleaning rooms sometimes, now she don't work at the fur. I ain't got no father, he's a father-in-law. No; mother ain't married again—he's a father-in-law. He grinds scissors, and he's very good to me. No; I don't mean by that that he says kind things to me, for he never hardly speaks. When I gets home, after selling creases, I stops at home. I puts the room to rights: mother don't make me do it, I does it myself. I cleans the chairs, though there's only two to clean. I takes a tub and scrubbing-brush and flannel, and scrubs the floor—that's what I do three or four times a week.

'I don't have no dinner. Mother gives me two slices of bread-and-butter and a cup of tea for breakfast, and then I go till tea, and has the same. We has meat of a Sunday, and, of course, I should like to have it every day. Mother has just the same to eat as we has, but she takes more tea—three cups, sometimes. No; I never has no sweet-stuff; I never buy none—I don't like it. Sometimes we has a game of "honey-pots" with the girls in the court, but not often. Me and Carry H—— carries the little 'uns. We plays, too, at "kiss-in-the-ring". I knows a good many games, but I don't play at 'em, 'cos going out with creases tires me. On a Friday night, too, I goes to a Jew's house till eleven o'clock on Saturday night. All I has to do is to snuff the candles and poke the fire. You see they keep their Sabbath then, and they won't touch anything; so they gives me my wittals and 1½*d*., and I does it for 'em. I have a reg'lar good lot to eat. Supper of Friday night, and tea after that, and fried fish of a Saturday morning, and meat for dinner, and tea, and supper, and I like it very well.

'Oh, yes; I've got some toys at home. I've a fire-place, and a box of toys, and a knife and fork, and two little chairs. The Jews gave 'em to me where I go to on a Friday, and that's why I said they was very kind to me. I never had no doll; but I misses little sister—she's only two years old. We don't sleep in the same room; for father and mother sleeps with little sister in the one pair, and me and brother and other sister sleeps in the top room. I always goes to bed at seven, 'cos I has to be up so early.

'I am a capital hand at bargaining—but only at buying watercreases. They can't take me in. If the woman tries to give me a small handful of creases, I says, "I ain't a goin' to have that for a ha'porth," and I go to the next basket, and so on, all round. I know the quantities very well. For a penny I ought to have a full market hand, or as much as I could carry in my arms at one time, without spilling. For 3*d*. I has a lap full, enough to earn about a shilling; and for 6*d*. I gets as many as crams my basket. I can't read or write, but I knows how many pennies goes to a shilling, why, twelve, of course, but I don't know how many ha'pence there is, though there's two to a penny. When I've bought 3*d*. of creases, I ties 'em up into as many little bundles as I can. They must look biggish, or the people won't buy them, some puffs them out as much as they'll go. All my money I earns I puts in a club and draws it out to buy clothes with. It's better than spending it in sweet-stuff, for them as has a living to earn. Besides it's like a child to care for sugar-sticks, and not like one who's got a living and vittals to earn. I ain't a child, and I shan't be a woman till I'm twenty, but I'm past eight, I am. I don't know nothing about what I earns during the year, I only know how many pennies goes to a shilling, and two ha'pence goes to a penny, and four fardens goes to a penny. I knows, too, how many fardens goes to tuppence—eight. That's as much as I wants to know for the markets.'

STREET-SELLERS OF EATABLES AND DRINKABLES

Of the Street-Sellers of Eatables and Drinkables

The class engaged in the manufacture, or in the sale, of these articles, are a more intelligent people than the generality of street-sellers. They have nearly all been mechanics who, from inability to procure employment at their several crafts—from dislike to an irksome and, perhaps, sedentary confinement—or from an overpowering desire 'to be their own masters', have sought a livelihood in the streets. The purchase and sale of fish, fruit, or vegetables require no great training or deftness; but to make the dainties, in which street-people are critical, and to sell them at the lowest possible price, certainly requires some previous discipline to produce the skill to combine and the taste to please.

I may here observe, that I found it common enough among these street-sellers to describe themselves and their fraternity not by their names or callings, but by the article in which they deal. This is sometimes ludicrous enough: 'Is the man you're asking about a pickled whelk, sir?' was said to me. In answer to another inquiry, I was told, 'Oh, yes, I know him—he's a sweet-stuff'. Such ellipses, or abbreviations, are common in all mechanical or commercial callings.

Men and women, and most especially boys, purchase their meals day after day in the streets. The coffee-stall supplies a warm breakfast; shell-fish of many kinds tempt to a luncheon; hot-eels or pea-soup, flanked by a potato 'all hot', serve for a dinner; and cakes and tarts, or nuts and oranges, with many varieties of pastry, confectionary, and fruit, woo to indulgence in a dessert; while for supper there is a sandwich, a meat pudding, or a 'trotter'.

The street provisions consist of cooked or prepared victuals, which may be divided into solids, pastry, confectionary, and drinkables.

The 'solids' however, of these three divisions, are such as only regular street-buyers consider to be sufficing for a substantial meal, for it will be seen that the comestibles accounted 'good for dinner', are all of a *dainty*, rather than a solid character. Men whose lives, as I have before stated, are alternations of starvation and surfeit, love some easily-swallowed and comfortable food, better than the most approved substantiality of a dinner-table. I was told by a man, who was once foodless for thirty-eight hours, that in looking into the window of a cook-shop—he longed far more for a basin of soup than for a cut from the boiled round, or the roasted ribs, of beef. He felt a gnawing rather than a ravenous desire, and some tasty semi-liquid was the incessant object of his desires.

The solids then, according to street estimation, consist of hot-eels, pickled whelks, oysters, sheep's-trotters, pea-soup, fried fish, ham-sandwiches, hot green peas, kidney puddings, boiled meat puddings, beef, mutton, kidney, and eel pies, and baked potatos. In each of these provisions the street poor find a mid-day or mid-night meal.

The pastry and confectionary which tempt the street eaters are tarts of rhubarb, currant, gooseberry, cherry, apple, damson, cranberry, and (so called) mince pies; plum dough and plum-cake; lard, currant, almond and many other varieties of cakes, as well as of tarts; gingerbread-nuts and heart-cakes,* Chelsea buns; muffins and crumpets; 'sweet stuff' includes the several kinds of rocks, sticks, lozenges, candies, and hard-bakes;* the medicinal confectionary of cough-drops and horehound;* and, lastly, the more novel and aristocratic luxury of street-ices; and strawberry cream, at 1*d.* a glass (in Greenwich Park).

The drinkables are tea, coffee, and cocoa; ginger-beer, lemonade, Persian sherbet,* and some highly-coloured beverages which have no specific name, but are introduced to the public as 'cooling' drinks; hot elder cordial or wine; peppermint water; curds and whey; water (as at Hampstead); rice milk; and milk in the parks.

At different periods there have been attempts to introduce more substantial viands into the street provision trade, but all within these twenty years have been exceptional and unsuccessful. One man a few years back established a portable cook-shop in Leather-lane, cutting out portions of the joints to be carried away or eaten on the spot, at the buyer's option. But the speculation was a failure. Black puddings used to be sold, until a few years back, smoking from cans, not unlike potato cans, in such places as the New Cut; but the trade in these rather suspicious articles gradually disappeared.

Of the Experience of a Fried Fish-Seller, and of the Class of Customers

The man who gave me the following information was well-looking, and might be about 45 or 50. He was poorly dressed, but his old brown surtout* fitted him close and well, was jauntily buttoned up to his black satin stock, worn, but of good quality; and, altogether, he had what is understood among a class as 'a *betterly* appearance about him'. His statement, as well as those of the other vendors of provisions, is curious in its details of public-house vagaries:

'I've been in the trade,' he said, 'seventeen years. Before that, I was a gentleman's servant, and I married a servant-maid, and we had a family, and, on that account, couldn't, either of us, get a situation, though we'd good characters. I was out of employ for seven or eight months, and things was beginning to go to the pawn for a living; but at last, when I gave up any hope of getting into a gentleman's service, I raised 10*s*., and determined to try something else. I was persuaded, by a friend who kept a beer-shop, to sell oysters at his door, I took his advice, and went to Billingsgate for the first time in my life, and bought a peck* of oysters for 2*s*. 6*d*. I was dressed respectable then—nothing like the mess and dirt I'm in now' [I may observe, that there was no dirt about him]; 'and so the salesman laid it on, but I gave him all he asked. I know a deal better now. I'd never been used to open oysters, and I couldn't do it. I cut my fingers with the knife slipping all over them, and had to hire a man to open for me, or the blood from my cut fingers would have run upon the oysters. For all that, I cleared 2*s*. 6*d*. on that peck, and I soon got up to the trade, and did well; till, in two or three months, the season got over, and I was advised, by the same friend, to try fried fish. That suited me. I've lived in good families, where there was first-rate men-cooks, and I know what good cooking means. I bought a dozen plaice; I forget what I gave for them, but they were dearer then than now. For all that, I took between 11*s*. and 12*s*. the first night—it was Saturday—that I started; and I stuck to it, and took from 7*s*. to 10*s*. every night, with more, of course, on Saturday, and it was half of it profit then. I cleared a good mechanic's earnings at that time—30*s*. a week and more. Soon after, I was told that, if agreeable, my wife could have a stall with fried fish, opposite a wine-vaults just opened, and she made nearly half as much as I did on my rounds. I served the public-houses, and soon got known.

With some landlords I had the privilege of the parlour, and tap-room, and bar, when other tradesmen have been kept out. The landlords will say to me still: "*You* can go in, Fishy." Somehow, I got the name of "Fishy" then, and I've kept it ever since. There was hospitality in those days. I've gone into a room in a public-house, used by mechanics, and one of them has said: "I'll stand fish round, gentlemen"; and I've supplied fifteen penn'orths. Perhaps he was a stranger, such a sort of customer, that wanted to be agreeable. Now, it's more likely I hear: "Jack, lend us a penny to buy a bit of fried"; and then Jack says: "You be d——d! here, lass, let's have another pint." The insults and difficulties I've had in the public-house trade is dreadful. I once sold 16*d*. worth to three rough-looking fellows I'd never seen before, and they seemed hearty, and asked me to drink with them, so I took a pull; but they wouldn't pay me when I asked, and I waited a goodish bit before I did ask. I thought, at first, it was their fun, but I waited from four to seven, and I found it was no fun. I felt upset, and ran out and told the policeman, but he said it was only a debt, and he couldn't interfere. So I ran to the station, but the head man there said the same, and told me I should hand over the fish with one hand, and hold out the other hand for my money. So I went back to the public-house, and asked for my money—and there was some mechanics that knew me there then—but I got nothing but "—— you's!" and one of 'em used most dreadful language. At last, one of the mechanics said: "Muzzle him, Fishy, if he won't pay." He was far bigger than me, him that was one in debt; but my spirit was up, and I let go at him and gave him a bloody nose, and the next hit I knocked him backwards, I'm sure I don't know how, on to a table; but I fell on him, and he clutched me by the coat-collar—I was respectable dressed then—and half smothered me. He tore the back of my coat, too, and I went home like Jim Crow.* The pot-man and the others parted us, and they made the man give me 1*s*., and the waiter paid me the other 4*d*., and said he'd take his chance to get it—but he never got it. Another time I went into a bar, and there was a ball in the house, and one of the ball gents came down and gave my basket a kick without ever a word, and started the fish; and in a scuffle—he was a little fellow, but my master—I had this finger put out of joint—you can see that, sir, still—and was in the hospital a week from an injury to my leg; the tiblin bone was hurt, the doctors said' [the tibia.] 'I've had my tray kicked over for a lark in a public-house, and a scramble for my fish, and all gone, and no help and no money for me. The landlords always prevent such things, when they can, and interfere for a poor man; but then it's done sudden, and over in an instant. That sort of thing wasn't the worst. I once had some powdery stuff flung sudden over me at a parlour door. My fish fell off, for I jumped, because I felt blinded, and what became of them I don't know; but I aimed at once for home—it was very late—and had to feel my way almost like a blind man. I can't tell what I suffered. I found it was something black, for I kept rubbing my face with my apron, and could just tell it came away black. I let myself in with my latch, and my wife was in bed, and I told her to get up and look at my face and get some water, and she thought I was joking, as she was half asleep; but when she got up and got a light, and a glass, she screamed, and said I looked such a shiny image; and so I did, as well as I could see, for it was black lead—such as they use for grates—that was flung on me. I washed it off, but it wasn't easy, and my face was sore days after. I had a respectable coat on then, too, which was greatly spoiled, and no remedy at all. I don't know who did it to me. I heard some one say: "You're served out beautiful." It's men that calls themselves gentlemen that does such things. I know the style of them then—it was eight or ten years ago; they'd heard of Lord ——, and his goings on. That way it's better now, but worse, far, in the way of getting a living. I dare say, if I had dressed in rough corderoys, I shouldn't have been larked at so much, because they might have thought I was a regular coster, and a fighter; but I don't like that sort of thing—I like to be decent and respectable, if I can.'

Of the Street-Sellers of Ham-Sandwiches

The ham-sandwich-seller carries his sandwiches on a tray or flat basket, covered with a clean white cloth; he also wears a white apron, and white sleeves. His usual stand is at the doors of the theatres.

The trade was unknown until eleven years ago, when a man who had been unsuccessful in keeping a coffee-shop in Westminster, found it necessary to look out for some mode of living, and he hit upon the plan of vending sandwiches, precisely in the present style, at the theatre doors. The attempt was successful; the man soon took 10*s*. a night, half of which was profit. He 'attended' both the great theatres,* and was 'doing well'; but at five or six weeks' end, competitors appeared in the field, and increased rapidly, and so his sale was affected, people being regardless of his urging that he 'was the original ham-sandwich'.

'There are now, sir, at the theatres this (the Strand) side the water, and at Ashley's, the Surrey, and the Vic.,* two dozen and nine sandwiches.' So said one of the trade, who counted up his brethren for me. This man calculated also that at the Standard,* the saloons, the concert-rooms, and at Limehouse, Mile-end, Bethnal-green-road, and elsewhere, there might be more than as many again as those 'working' the theatres—or 70 in all. They are nearly all men, and no boys or girls are now in the trade. The number of these people, when the large theatres were open with the others, was about double what it is now.

The information collected shows that the expenditure in ham-sandwiches, supplied by street-sellers, is 1,820*l.* yearly, and a consumption of 436,800 sandwiches.

Of the Experience of a Ham Sandwich-Seller

A young man gave me the following account. His look and manners were subdued; and, though his dress was old and worn, it was clean and unpatched:

'I hardly remember my father, sir,' he said; 'but I believe, if he'd lived, I should have been better off. My mother couldn't keep my brother and me—he's older than me—when we grew to be twelve or thirteen, and we had to shift for ourselves. She works at the stays,* and now makes only 3*s.* a week, and we can't help her. I was first in place as a sort of errand-boy, then I was a stationer's boy, and then a news agent's boy. I wasn't wanted any longer, but left with a good character. My brother had gone into the sandwich trade—I hardly know what made him—and he advised me to be a ham sandwich-man, and so I started as one. At first, I made 10*s.*, and 7*s.*, and 8*s.* a week—that's seven years, or so—but things are worse now, and I make 3*s.* 6*d.* some weeks, and 5*s.* others, and 6*s.* is an out-and-outer. My rent's 2*s.* a week, but I haven't my own things. I am so sick of this life, I'd do anything to get out of it; but I don't see a way. Perhaps I might have been more careful when I was first in it; but, really, if you do make 10*s.* a week, you want shoes, or a shirt—so what is 10*s.* after all? I wish I had it now, though. I used to buy my sandwiches at 6*d.* a dozen, but I found that wouldn't do; and now I buy and boil the stuff, and make them myself. What *did* cost 6*d.*, now only costs me 4*d.* or 4½*d.*

I work the theatres this side of the water, chiefly the 'Lympic and the 'Delphi.* The best theatre I ever had was the Garding, when it had two galleries, and was dramatic—the operas there wasn't the least good to me. The Lyceum was good, when it was Mr Keeley's. I hardly know what sort my customers are, but they're those that go to the-aytres: shopkeepers and clerks, I think. Gentlemen don't often buy of me. They *have* bought, though. Oh, no, they never give a farthing over; they're more likely to want seven for 6*d*. The women of the town buy of me, when it gets late, for themselves and their fancy men. They're liberal enough when they've money. They sometimes treat a poor fellow in a public-house. In summer I'm often out 'till four in the morning, and then must lie in bed half next day. The 'Delphi was better than it is. I've taken 3*s*. at the first "turn out" (the leaving the theatre for a short time after the first piece), but the turn-outs at the Garding was better than that. A penny pie-shop has spoiled us at the 'Delphi and at Ashley's. I go out between eight and nine in the evening. People often want more in my sandwiches, though I'm starv-ing on them. "Oh," they'll say, "you've been 'prenticed to Vauxhall* you have." "They're 1*s*. there," says I, "and no bigger. I haven't Vauxhall prices." I stand by the night-houses when it's late—not the fashionables. Their customers wouldn't look at me; but I've known women, that carried their heads very high, glad to get a sandwich afterwards. Six times I've been upset by drunken fellows, on purpose, I've no doubt, and lost all my stock. Once, a gent kicked my basket into the dirt, and he was going off—for it was late—but some people by began to make remarks about using a poor fellow that way, so he paid for all, after he had them counted. I am *so* sick of this life, sir. I *do* dread the winter so. I've stood up to the ankles in snow till after midnight, and till I've wished I was snow myself, and could melt like it and have an end. I'd do anything to get away from this, but I can't. Passion Week's another dreadful time. It drives us to starve, just when we want to get up a little stock-money for Easter. I've been bilked by cabmen, who've taken a sandwich; but, instead of paying for it, have offered to fight me. There's no help. We're knocked about sadly by the police. Time's very heavy on my hands, sometimes, and that's where you feel it. I read a bit if I can get anything to read, for I was at St Clement's school; or I walk out to look for a job. On summer-days I sell a trotter or two. But mine's a wretched life, and so is most ham sandwich-men. I've no enjoyment of my youth and no comfort.

'Ah, sir! I live very poorly. A ha'porth or a penn'orth of cheap fish, which I cook myself, is one of my treats—either herrings or plaice—with a 'tatur, perhaps. Then there's a sort of meal, now and then, off the odds and ends of the ham, such as isn't quite viewy enough for the public, along with the odds and ends of the loaves. I can't boil a bit of greens with my ham, 'cause I'm afraid it might rather spoil the colour. I don't slice the ham till it's cold—it cuts easier, and is a better colour then, I think. I wash my aprons, and sleeves, and cloths myself, and iron them too. A man that sometimes makes only 3*s.* 6*d.* a week, and sometimes less, and must pay 2*s.* rent out of that, must look after every farthing. I've often walked eight miles to see if I could find ham a halfpenny a pound cheaper anywhere. If it was tainted, I know it would be flung in my face. If I was sick there's only the parish* for me.'

Of Cats' and Dogs'-Meat Dealers

The supply of food for cats and dogs is far greater than may be generally thought. 'Vy, sir,' said one of the dealers to me, 'can you tell me 'ow many people's in London?' On my replying, upwards of two millions; 'I don't know nothing vatever,' said my informant, 'about millions, but I think there's a cat to every ten people, aye, and more than that; and so, sir, you can reckon.' [I told him this gave a total of 200,000 cats in London; but the number of inhabited houses in the metropolis was 100,000 more than this, and though there was not a cat to every house, still, as many lodgers as well as householders kept cats, I added that I thought the total number of cats in London might be taken at the same number as the inhabited houses, or 300,000 in all.] 'There's not near half so many dogs as cats. I must know, for they all knows me, and I sarves about 200 cats and 70 dogs. Mine's a middling trade, but some does far better. Some cats has a hap'orth a day, some every other day; werry few can afford a penn'orth, but times is inferior. Dogs is better pay when you've a connection among 'em.'

The cat and dogs'-meat dealers, or 'carriers', as they call themselves, generally purchase the meat at the knackers' (horse-slaughterers') yards. There are upwards of twenty of such yards in London; three or four are in White-chapel, one in Wandsworth, two in Cow-cross—one of the two last mentioned is the largest establishment in London—and there are two about Bermondsey. The proprietors of these yards purchase live and dead horses. They contract for them with large firms, such as brewers, coal-merchants, and large cab and 'bus yards, giving so much per head for their old live and dead horses through the year. The price varies from 2*l.* to 50*s.* the carcass. The knackers also have contractors in the country (harness-makers and others), who bring or send up to town for them the live and dead stock of those parts. The dead horses are brought to the yard—two or three upon one cart, and sometimes five. The live ones are tied to the tail of these carts, and behind the tail of each other. Occasionally a string of fourteen or fifteen are brought up, head to tail, at one time. The live horses are purchased merely for slaughtering. If among the lot bought there should chance to be one that is young, but in bad condition, it is placed in the stable, fed up, and then put into the knackers' carts, or sold by them, or let on hire. Occasionally a fine horse has been rescued from death in this manner. One person is known to have bought an animal for 15*s.*, for which he afterwards got 150*l.* Frequently young horses that will not work in cabs—such as 'jibs'—are sold to the horse-slaughterers as useless. They are kept in the yard, and after being well fed, often turn out good horses. The live horses are slaughtered by the persons called 'knackers'. These men get upon an average 4*s.* a day. They begin work at twelve at night, because some of the flesh is required to be boiled before six in the morning; indeed, a great part of the meat is delivered to the carriers before that hour. The horse to be slaughtered has his mane clipped as short as possible (on account of the hair, which is valuable). It is then blinded with a piece of old apron smothered in blood, so that it may not see the slaughterman when about to strike. A pole-axe is used, and a cane, to put an immediate end to the animal's sufferings. After the animal is slaughtered, the hide is taken off, and the flesh cut from the bones in large pieces. These pieces are termed, according to the part from which they are cut, hind-quarters, fore-quarters, cram-bones,* throats, necks, briskets, backs, ribs, kidney pieces, hearts, tongues, liver and lights.* The bones (called 'racks' by the knackers) are chopped up and boiled, in order to extract the fat, which is used for greasing common harness, and the wheels of carts and drags, &c. The bones themselves are sold for manure. The pieces of flesh are thrown into large coppers or pans, about nine feet in diameter and four feet deep. Each of these pans will hold about three good-sized horses. Sometimes two large brewers' horses will fill them, and sometimes as many as four 'poor' cab-horses may be put into them. The flesh is boiled about an hour and 20 minutes for a 'killed' horse, and from two hours to two hours and 20 minutes for a dead horse (a horse dying from age or disease). The flesh, when boiled, is taken from the coppers, laid on the stones, and sprinkled with water to cool it. It is then weighed out in pieces of 112, 56, 28, 21, 14, 7, and 3½ lbs. weight. These are either taken round in a cart to the 'carriers', or, at about five, the carriers call at the yard to purchase, and continue doing so till twelve in the day. The price is 14*s*. per cwt. in winter, and 16*s*. in summer. The tripe is served out at 12 lb. for 6*d*. All this is for cats and dogs. The carriers then take the meat round town, wherever their 'walk' may lie. They sell it to the public at the rate of 2½*d*. per lb., and in small pieces, on skewers, at a farthing, a halfpenny, and a penny each.

The carriers frequently serve as much as ten pennyworths to one person in a day. One gentleman has as much as 4 lbs. of meat each morning for two Newfoundland dogs; and there was one woman—a black—who used to have as much as 16 pennyworth every day. This person used to get out on the roof of the house and throw it to the cats on the tiles. By this she brought so many stray cats round about the neighbourhood, that the parties in the vicinity complained; it was quite a nuisance. She *would* have the meat always brought to her before ten in the morning, or else she would send to a shop for it, and between ten and eleven in the morning the noise and cries of the hundreds of stray cats attracted to the spot was 'terrible to hear'. When the meat was thrown to the cats on the roof, the riot, and confusion, and fighting, was beyond description. 'A beer-shop man', I was told, 'was obliged to keep five or six dogs to drive the cats from his walls.' There was also a mad woman in Islington, who used to have 14 lbs. of meat a day. The party who supplied her had his money often at 2*l*. and 3*l*. at a time. She had as many as thirty cats at times in her house. Every stray one that came she would take in and support. The stench was so great that she was obliged to be ejected.

Of Coffee-Stall Keepers

The vending of tea and coffee, in the streets, was little if at all known twenty years ago, saloop* being then the beverage supplied from stalls to the late and early wayfarers. Nor was it until after 1842 that the stalls approached to anything like their present number, which is said to be upwards of 300—the majority of the proprietors being women. Prior to 1824, coffee was in little demand, even among the smaller tradesmen or farmers, but in that year the duty having been reduced from 1*s*. to 6*d*. per lb., the consumption throughout the kingdom in the next seven years was nearly trebled, the increase being from 7,933,041 lbs., in 1824, to 22,745,627 lbs., in 1831. In 1842, the duty on coffee was fixed at 4*d*., from British possessions, and from foreign countries at 6*d*.

But it was not owing solely to the reduced price of coffee, that the street-vendors of it increased in the year or two subsequent to 1842, at least 100 per cent. The great facilities then offered for a cheap adulteration,* by mixing ground chicory with the ground coffee, was an enhancement of the profits, and a greater temptation to embark in the business, as a smaller amount of capital would suffice. Within these two or three years, this cheapness has been still further promoted, by the medium of adulteration, the chicory itself being, in its turn, adulterated by the admixture of baked carrots, and the like saccharine roots, which, of course, are not subjected to any duty, while foreign chicory is charged 6*d*. per lb. English chicory is not chargeable with duty, and is now cultivated, I am assured, to the yield of between 4,000 and 5,000 tons yearly, and this nearly all used in the adulteration of coffee. Nor is there greater culpability in this trade among street-venders, than among 'respectable' shopkeepers; for I was assured, by a leading grocer, that he could not mention twenty shops in the city, of which he could say: 'You can go and buy a pound of ground coffee there, and it will not be adulterated.' The revelations recently made on this subject by the *Lancet* are a still more convincing proof of the *general* dishonesty of grocers.

The coffee-stall keepers generally stand at the corner of a street. In the fruit and meat markets there are usually two or three coffee-stalls, and one or two in the streets leading to them; in Covent-garden there are no less than four coffee-stalls. Indeed, the stalls abound in all the great thoroughfares, and the most in those not accounted 'fashionable' and great 'business' routes, but such as are frequented by working people, on their way to their day's labour. The best 'pitch' in London is supposed to be at the corner of Duke-street, Oxford-street. The proprietor of that stall is said to take full 30*s*. of a morning, in halfpence. One stall-keeper, I was informed, when 'upon the drink' thinks nothing of spending his 10*l*. or 15*l*. in a week. A party assured me that once, when the stall-keeper above mentioned was away 'on the spree', he took up his stand there, and got from 4*s*. to 5*s*. in the course of ten minutes, at the busy time of the morning.

The coffee-stall usually consists of a spring-barrow, with two, and occasionally four, wheels. Some are made up of tables, and some have a tressel and board. On the top of this are placed two or three, and sometimes four, large tin cans, holding upon an average five gallons each. Beneath each of these cans is a small iron fire-pot, perforated like a rushlight* shade, and here charcoal is continually burning, so as to keep the coffee or tea, with which the cans are filled, hot throughout the early part of the morning. The board of the stall has mostly a compartment for bread and butter, cake, and ham sandwiches, and another for the coffee mugs. There is generally a small tub under each of the stalls, in which the mugs and saucers are washed.

The class of persons usually belonging to the business have been either cab-men, policemen, labourers, or artisans. Many have been bred to dealing in the streets, and brought up to no other employment, but many have taken to the business owing to the difficulty of obtaining work at their own trade. The generality of them are opposed to one another.

They are half too many, they say. 'Two of us', to use their own words, 'are eating one man's bread.' 'When coffee in the streets first came up, a man could go and earn', I am told, 'his 8*s*. a night at the very lowest; but now the same class of men cannot earn more than 3*s*.' Some men may earn comparatively a large sum, as much as 38*s*. or 2*l*., but the generality of the trade cannot make more than 1*l*. per week, if so much. The following is the statement of one of the class:

'I was a mason's labourer, a smith's labourer, a plasterer's labourer, or a bricklayer's labourer. I was, indeed, a labouring man. I could not get employment. I was for six months without any employment. I did not know which way to support my wife and child (I have only one child). Being so long out of employment, I saw no other means of getting a living but out of the streets. I was almost starving before I took to it—that I certainly was. I'm not ashamed of telling anybody that, because it's true, and I sought for a livelihood wherever I could. Many said they wouldn't do such a thing as keep a coffee-stall, but I said I'd do anything to get a bit of bread honestly. Years ago, when I was a boy, I used to go out selling water-cresses, and apples, oranges, and radishes, with a barrow, for my landlord; so I thought, when I was

THE LONDON COFFEE-STALL.

[*From a Daguerreotype by* BEARD.]

thrown out of employment, I would take to selling coffee in the streets. I went to a tinman, and paid him 10*s.* 6*d.* (the last of my savings, after I'd been four or five months out of work) for a can, I didn't care how I got my living so long as I could turn an honest penny. Well; I went on, and knocked about, and couldn't get a pitch anywhere; but at last I heard that an old man, who had been in the habit of standing for many years at the entrance of one of the markets, had fell ill; so, what did I do, but I goes and pops into his pitch, and there I've done better than ever I did afore. I get 20*s.* now where I got 10*s.* one time; and if I only had such a thing as 5*l.* or 10*l.*, I might get a good living for life. I cannot do half as much as the man that was there before me. He used to make his coffee down there, and had a can for hot water as well; but I have but one can to keep coffee and all in; and I have to borrow my barrow, and pay 1*s.* a week for it. If I sell my can out, I can't do any more. The struggle to get a living is so great, that, what with one and another in the coffee-trade, it's only those as can get good "pitches" that can get a crust at it.'

Of Milk Selling in St James's Park

The principal sale of milk from the cow is in St James's Park. The once fashionable drink known as syllabubs—the milk being drawn warm from the cow's udder, upon a portion of wine, sugar, spice, &c.—is now unknown. As the sellers of milk in the park are merely the servants of cow-keepers, and attend to the sale as a part of their business, no lengthened notice is required.

The milk-sellers obtain leave from the Home Secretary, to ply their trade in the park. There are eight stands in the summer, and as many cows, but in the winter there are only four cows. The milk-vendors sell upon an average, in the summer, from eighteen to twenty quarts per day; in the winter, not more than a third of that quantity. The interrupted milking of the cows, as practised in the Park, often causes them to give less milk, than they would in the ordinary way. The chief customers are infants, and adults, and others, of a delicate constitution, who have been recommended to take new milk. On a wet day scarcely any milk can be disposed of. Soldiers are occasional customers.

A somewhat sour-tempered old woman, speaking as if she had been crossed in love, but experienced in this trade, gave me the following account:

'It's not at all a lively sort of life, selling milk from the cows, though some thinks it's a gay time in the Park! I've often been dull enough, and could see nothing to interest one, sitting alongside a cow. People drink new milk for their health, and I've served a good many such. They're mostly young women, I think, that's delicate, and makes the most of it. There's twenty women, and more, to one man what drinks new milk. If they was set to some good hard work, it would do them more good than new milk, or ass's milk either, I think. Let them go on a milk-walk to cure them—that's what I say. Some children come pretty regularly with their nurses to drink new milk. Some bring their own china mugs to drink it out of; nothing less was good enough for them. I've seen the nurse-girls frightened to death about the mugs. I've heard one young child say to another: "I shall tell mama that Caroline spoke to a mechanic, who came and shook hands with her." The girl was as red as fire, and said it was her brother. Oh, yes, there's a deal of brothers comes to look for their sisters in the Park. The greatest fools I've sold milk to is servant-gals out for the day. Some must have a day, or half a day, in the month. Their mistresses ought to keep them at home, I say, and not let them out to spend their money, and get into nobody knows what company for a holiday; mistresses is too easy that way. It's such gals as makes fools of themselves in liking a soldier to run after them. I've seen one of them—yes, some would call her pretty, and the prettiest is the silliest and easiest tricked out of money, that's my opinion, anyhow—I've seen one of them, and more than one, walk with a soldier, and they've stopped a minute, and she's taken something out of her glove and given it to him. Then they've come up to me, and he's said to her, "Mayn't I treat you with a little new milk, my dear?" and he's changed a shilling. Why, of course, the silly fool of a gal had given him that there shilling. I thought, when Annette Myers* shot the soldier, it would be a warning, but nothing's a warning to some gals. *She* was one of those fools. It was a good deal talked about at the stand, but I think none of us know'd her. Indeed, we don't know our customers but by sight. Yes, there's now and then some oldish gentlemen—I suppose they're gentlemen, anyhow, they're idle men—lounging about the stand: but there's no nonsense there. They tell me, too, that there's not so much lounging about as there was; those that's known the trade longer than me thinks so. Them children's a great check on the nusses, and they can't be such fools as the servant-maids. I don't know how many of them I've served with milk along with soldiers: I never counted them. They're nothing to me. Very few elderly people drink new milk. It's mostly the young. I've been asked by strangers when the Duke of Wellington would pass to the Horse-Guards or to the House of Lords. He's pretty regular. I've had 6*d*. given me—but not above once or twice a year—to tell strangers where was the best place to see him from as he passed. I don't understand about this Great Exhibition,* but, no doubt, more new milk will be sold when it's opened, and that's all I cares about.'

Of Street Piemen

The itinerant trade in pies is one of the most ancient of the street callings of London. The meat pies are made of beef or mutton; the fish pies of eels; the fruit of apples, currants, gooseberries, plums, damsons, cherries, raspberries, or rhubarb, according to the season—and occasionally of mince-meat. A few years ago the street pie-trade was very profitable, but it has been almost destroyed by the 'pie-shops', and further, the few remaining street-dealers say 'the people now haven't the pennies to spare.' Summer fairs and races are the best places for the piemen. In London the best times are during any grand sight or holiday-making, such as a review in Hyde-park, the Lord Mayor's show, the opening of Parliament, Greenwich fair, &c. Nearly all the men of this class, whom I saw, were fond of speculating as to whether the Great Exposition would be 'any good' to them, or not.

The London piemen, who may number about forty in winter, and twice that number in summer, are seldom stationary. They go along with their pie-cans on their arms, crying, 'Pies all 'ot! eel, beef, or mutton pies! Penny pies, all 'ot—all 'ot!'

The pie-dealers usually make the pies themselves. The meat is bought in 'pieces', of the same part as the sausage-makers' purchase —the 'stickings'—at about 3*d*. the pound. 'People, when I go into houses,' said one man, 'often begin crying, "Mee-yow," or "Bow-wow-wow!" at me; but there's nothing of that kind now. Meat, you see, is so cheap.'

The penny pie-shops, the street men say, have done their trade a great deal of harm. These shops have now got mostly all the custom, as they make the pies much larger for the money than those sold in the streets. The pies in Tottenham-court-road are very highly seasoned. 'I bought one there the other day, and it nearly took the skin off my mouth; it was full of pepper,' said a street-pieman, with considerable bitterness, to me. The reason why so large a quantity of pepper is put in is, because persons can't exactly tell the flavour of the meat with it. Piemen generally are not very particular about the flavour of the meat they buy, as they can season it up into anything.

To 'toss the pieman' is a favourite pastime with costermongers' boys and all that class; some of whom aspire to the repute of being gourmands, and are critical on the quality of the comestible. If the pieman win the toss, he receives 1*d.* without giving a pie; if he lose, he hands it over for nothing. The pieman himself never 'tosses', but always calls head or tail to his customer. At the week's end it comes to the same thing, they say, whether they toss or not, or rather whether they win or lose the toss: 'I've taken as much as 2*s.* 6*d.* at tossing, which I shouldn't have had if I hadn't done so. Very few people buy without tossing, and the boys in particular. Gentlemen "out on the spree" at the late public-houses will frequently toss when they don't want the pies, and when they win they will amuse themselves by throwing the pies at one another, or at me. Sometimes I have taken as much as half-a-crown, and the people of whom I had the money has never eaten a pie. The boys has the greatest love of gambling, and they seldom, if ever, buys without tossing.'

Of the Street-Sellers of Gingerbread-Nuts

There are now only two men in London who make their own gingerbread-nuts for sale in the streets. This preparation of gingerbread is called by the street-sellers, after a common elliptical fashion, merely 'nuts'. From the most experienced man in the street trade I had the following account: he was an intelligent, well-mannered, and well-spoken man, and when he laughed or smiled, had what may be best described as a pleasant look. After he had initiated me into the art and mystery of gingerbread making, he said,

'I've been in the "nut" trade 25 years, or thereabouts, and have made my own nuts for 20 years of that time. I bought of a gingerbread baker at first—there was plenty of them in them days—and the profit a living profit, too. Certainly it was, for what I bought for 5*s.* I could sell for 16*s.* I was brought up a baker, but the moment I was out of my time I started in the street nut trade for myself. I knew the profits of it, and thought it better than the slavery of a journeyman

THE COSTER BOY AND GIRL TOSSING THE PIEMAN.

[*From a Daguerreotype by* BEARD.]

baker's life. You've mentioned, sir, in your work, a musical sort of a street-crier of gingerbread,* and I think, and indeed I'm pretty certain, that it's the same man as was my partner 20 years back; aye, more than 20, but I can't tell about years.' [The reader will have remarked how frequently this oblivion as to dates and periods characterises the statements of street-sellers. Perhaps no men take less note of time.] 'At that time he was my partner in the pig trade. Dairy-fed, d'you say, sir? Not in the slightest. The outsides of the hanimals was paste, and the insides on 'em was all mince-meat. Their eyes was currants. We two was the original pigs, and, I believe, the only two pigs in the streets. We often made 15*s.* between us, in a day, in pigs alone. The musical man, as you call him—poor fellow, he dropped down dead in the street one day as he was crying; he was regular worn out—cried himself into his grave you *may* say—poor fellow, he used to sing out

"Here's a long-tailed pig, and a short-tailed pig,
  And a pig with a curly tail:
Here's a Yorkshire pig, and a Hampshire pig,
  And a pig without e'er a tail."

'When I was first in the trade, I sold twice as many nuts as I do now, though my nuts was only 12 a penny then, and they're now 40. A little larger the 12 were, but not very much. I have taken 20*s.* and 24*s.* many and many a Saturday. I then made from 2*l.* to 2*l.* 10*s.* a week by sticking to it, and money might have been saved. I've taken between 7*l.* and 8*l.* at a Greenwich Fair* in the three days, in them times, by myself. Indeed, last Easter, my wife and me—for she works as well as I do, and sells almost as much—took 5*l.* But gingerbread was money in the old times, and I sold "lumps" as well as "nuts"; but now lumps won't go off—not in a fair, no how. I've been in the trade ever since I started in it, but I've had turns at other things. I was in the service of a Custom-house agency firm; but they got into bother about contrabands, and the revenue, and cut off to America—I believe they took money with them, a good bit of it—and I was indicted, or whatever they call it, in the Court of Exchequer—I never was in the Court in my life—and was called upon, one fine day, to pay to the Crown 1,580*l.*, and some odd pounds and shillings besides! I never understood the rights of it, but it was about smuggling. I was indicted by myself, I believe. When Mr Candy, and other great houses in the City, were found out that way, *they* made it all right; paid something, as I've heard, and sacked the profits. Well; when *I* was called on, it wasn't, I assure you, sir—ha, ha, ha!—at all convenient for a servant—and I was only that—to pay the fifteen hundred and odd; so I served 12 months and 2 days in prison for it. I'd saved a little money, and wasn't so uncomfortable in prison. I could get a dinner, and give a dinner. When I came out, I took to the nuts. It was lucky for me that I had a trade to turn to; for, even if I could have shown I wasn't at all to blame about the Exchequer, I could never have got another situation—never. So the streets saved me: my nuts was my bread.'

Of the Street Sale of Sweet-Stuff

A very intelligent man, who had succeeded his father and mother in the 'sweet-stuff' business—his father's drunkenness having kept them in continual poverty—showed me his apparatus, and explained his mode of work. His room, which was on the second-floor of a house in a busy thoroughfare, had what I have frequently noticed in the abodes of the working classes—the decency of a turn-up bedstead. It was a large apartment, the rent being 3*s.* 6*d.* a week, unfurnished. The room was cheerful with birds, of which there were ten or twelve. A remarkably fine thrush was hopping in a large wicker cage, while linnets and bullfinches showed their quick bright eyes from smaller cages on all sides. These were not kept for sale but for amusement, their owner being seldom able to leave his room.

Treacle and sugar are the ground-work of the manufacture of all kinds of sweet-stuff. 'Hardbake', 'almond tony', 'halfpenny lollipops', 'black balls', the cheaper 'bulls eyes', and 'squibs' are all made of treacle. One informant sold more of treacle rock than of anything else, as it was dispensed in larger halfpennyworths, and no one else made it in the same way. Of peppermint rock and sticks he made a good quantity. Half-a-crown's worth, as retailed in the streets, requires 4 lbs. of rough raw sugar at 4¼*d.* per lb., 1½*d.* for scent (essence of peppermint), 1½*d.* for firing, and ½*d.* for paper—in all 1*s.* 8½*d.* calculating nothing for the labour and time expended in boiling and making it. The profit on the other things was proportionate, except on almond rock, which does not leave 2½*d.* in a shilling—almonds being dear. Brandy balls are made of sugar, water, peppermint, and a little cinnamon. Rose acid, which is a 'transparent' sweet, is composed of loaf sugar at 6½*d.* per lb., coloured with cochineal. The articles sold in 'sticks' are pulled into form along a hook until they present the whitish, or speckled colour desired. A quarter of a stone of materials will, for instance, be boiled for forty minutes, and then pulled a quarter of an hour, until it is sufficiently crisp and will 'set' without waste. The flavouring—or 'scent' as I heard it called in the trade—now most in demand is peppermint. Gibraltar rock and Wellington pillars used to be flavoured with ginger, but these 'sweeties' are exploded.

One of the appliances of the street sweet-stuff trade which I saw in the room of the seller before mentioned was—Acts of Parliament. A pile of these, a foot or more deep, lay on a shelf. They are used to wrap up the rock, &c., sold. The sweet-stuff maker (I never heard them called confectioners) bought his 'paper' of the stationers, or at the old book-shops. Sometimes, he said, he got works in this way in sheets which had never been cut (some he feared were stolen), and which he retained to read at his short intervals of leisure, and then used to wrap his goods in. In this way he had read through two Histories of England! He maintained a wife, two young children, and a young sister, who could attend to the stall; his wife assisted him in his manufactures. He used 1 cwt. of sugar a week on the year's average, ½ cwt. of treacle, and 5 oz. of scents, each 8*d*. an oz.

The man who has the best trade in London streets, is one who, about two years ago, introduced—after much study, I was told—short sentences into his 'sticks'. He boasts of his secret. When snapped asunder, in any part, the stick presents a sort of coloured inscription. The four I saw were: 'Do you love me?' The next was of less touching character, 'Do you love sprats?' The others were, 'Lord Mayor's Day', and 'Sir Robert Peel'.* This man's profits are twice those of my respectable informant's.

Of the Street-Sellers of Ices and of Ice Creams

A quick-witted street-seller—but not in the 'provision' line—conversing with me upon this subject, said: 'Ices in the streets! Aye, and there'll be jellies next, and then mock turtle,* and then the real ticket, sir. I don't know nothing of the difference between the real thing and the mock, but I once had some cheap mock in an eating-house, and it tasted like stewed tripe with a little glue. You'll keep your eyes open, sir, at the Great Exhibition; and you'll see a new move or two in the streets, take my word for it. Penny glasses of champagne, I shouldn't wonder.'

Notwithstanding the sanguine anticipations of my street friend, the sale of ices in the streets has not been such as to offer any great encouragement to a perseverance in the traffic.

The sale of ice-creams was unknown in the streets until last summer, and was first introduced, as a matter of speculation, by a man who was acquainted with the confectionary business, and who purchased his ices of a confectioner in Holborn. He resold these luxuries daily to street-sellers, sometimes to twenty of them, but more frequently to twelve. The sale, however, was not remunerative, and had it not been generally united with other things, such as ginger-beer, could not have been carried on as a means of subsistence. The supplier of the street-traders sometimes went himself, and sometimes sent another to sell ice-cream in Greenwich Park on fine summer days, but the sale was sometimes insufficient to pay his railway expenses. After three or four weeks' trial, this man abandoned the trade, and soon afterwards emigrated to America.

Not many weeks subsequent to 'the first start', I was informed, the trade was entered into by a street-seller in Petticoat-lane, who had become possessed, it was said, of Masters's Freezing Apparatus. He did not vend the ices himself for more than two or three weeks, and moreover confined his sale to Sunday mornings; after a while he employed himself for a short time in making ices for four or five street-sellers, some of whom looked upon the preparation as a wonderful discovery of his own, and he then discontinued the trade.

There were many difficulties attending the introduction of ices into street-traffic. The buyers had but a confused notion how the ice was to be swallowed. The trade, therefore, spread only very gradually, but some of the more enterprising sellers purchased stale ices from the confectioners. So little, however, were the street-people skilled in the trade, that a confectioner told me they sometimes offered ice to their customers in the streets, and could supply only water! Ices were sold by the street-vendors generally at 1*d.* each, and the trade left them a profit of 4*d.* in 1*s.*, when they served them 'without waste', and some of the sellers contrived, by giving smaller modicums, to enhance the 4*d.* into 5*d.*; the profit, however, was sometimes what is expressively called 'nil'. Cent. per cent.—the favourite and simple rate known in the streets as 'half-profits' was rarely attained.

From a street-dealer I received the following account:

'Yes, sir, I mind very well the first time as I ever sold ices. I don't think they'll ever take greatly in the streets, but there's no saying. Lord! how I've seen the people splutter when they've tasted them for the first time. I did as much myself. They get among the teeth and make you feel as if you tooth-ached all over. I sold mostly strawberry ices. I haven't an idea how they're made, but it's a most wonderful thing in summer—freezing fruits in that way. One young Irish fellow—I think from his look and cap he was a printer's or stationer's boy—he bought an ice of me, and when he had scraped it all together with the spoon, he made a pull at it as if he was a drinking beer. In course it was all among his teeth in less than no time, and he stood like a stattey for a instant, and then he roared out,—"Jasus! I'm kilt. The could shivers is on to me!" But I said, "O, you're all right, you are"; and he says, "What d'you mane, you horrid horn,* by selling such stuff as that. An' you must have the money first, bad scran* to the likes o' you!"

'The persons what enjoyed their ices most', the man went on, 'was, I think, servant maids that gulped them on the sly. Pr'aps they'd been used, some on 'em, to get a taste of ices on the sly before, in their services. We sees a many dodges in the streets, sir—a many. I knew one smart servant maid, treated to an ice by her young man—they seemed as if they was keeping company—and he soon was stamping, with the ice among his teeth, but she knew how to take them, put the spoon right into the middle of her mouth, and when she'd had a clean swallow she says: "O, Joseph, why didn't you ask *me* to tell you how to eat your ice?" The conceit of sarvant gals is ridiculous. Don't you think so, sir? But it goes out of them when they gets married and has to think of how to get broth before how to eat ices.'

STREET-SELLERS OF STATIONERY, LITERATURE, AND THE FINE ARTS

Of the Street-Sellers of Stationery, Literature, and the Fine Arts

We now come to a class of street-folk wholly distinct from any before treated of. As yet we have been dealing principally with the uneducated portion of the street-people—men whom, for the most part, are allowed to remain in nearly the same primitive and brutish state as the savage—creatures with nothing but their appetites, instincts, and passions to move them, and made up of the same crude combination of virtue and vice—the same generosity combined with the same predatory tendencies as the Bedouins of the desert—the same love of revenge and disregard of pain, and often the same gratitude and susceptibility to kindness as the Red Indian—and, furthermore, the same insensibility to female honour and abuse of female weakness, and the same utter ignorance of the Divine nature of the Godhead as marks either Bosjesman, Carib, or Thug.*

The street-sellers of stationery, literature, and the fine arts, however, differ from all before treated of in the *general*, though far from universal, education of the sect. They constitute principally the class of street-orators, known in these days as 'patterers', and formerly termed 'mountebanks',—people who, in the words of Strutt, strive to 'help off their wares by pompous speeches, in which little regard is paid either to truth or propriety'. To patter, is a slang term, meaning to speak. To indulge in this kind of oral puffery, of course, requires a certain exercise of the intellect, and it is the consciousness of their mental superiority which makes the patterers look down upon the costermongers as an inferior body, with whom they object either to be classed or to associate. The scorn of some of the 'patterers' for the mere costers is as profound as the contempt of the pickpocket for the pure beggar. Those who have not witnessed this pride of class among even the most degraded, can form no adequate idea of the arrogance with which the skilled man, no matter how base the art, looks upon the unskilled. 'We are the haristocracy of the streets,' was said to me by one of the street-folks, who told penny fortunes with a bottle. 'People don't pay us for what we gives 'em, but only to hear us talk. We live like yourself, sir, by the hexercise of our hintellects—we by talking, and you by writing.'

It would be a mistake to suppose that the patterers, although a vagrant, are a disorganized class. There is a telegraphic dispatch* between them, through the length and breadth of the land. If two patterers (previously unacquainted) meet in the provinces, the following, or something like it, will be their conversation:—'Can you "voker romeny" (can you speak cant)? What is your "monekeer" (name)?'—Perhaps it turns out that one is 'White-headed Bob', and the other 'Plymouth Ned'. They have a 'shant of gatter' (pot of beer) at the nearest 'boozing ken' (ale-house), and swear eternal friendship to each other. The old saying, that 'When the liquor is in, the wit is out,' is remarkably fulfilled on these occasions, for they betray to the 'flatties' (natives) all their profits and proceedings.

It is to be supposed that, in country districts, where there are no streets, the patterer is obliged to call at the houses. As they are mostly without the hawker's licence, and sometimes find wet linen before it is lost, the rural districts are not fond of their visits; and there are generally two or three persons in a village reported to be 'gammy', (that is unfavourable). If a patterer has been 'crabbed', (that is offended) at any of the 'cribbs' (houses), he mostly chalks a signal on or near the door. I give one or two instances:

◊ 'Bone', meaning good.
▽ 'Cooper'd', spoiled by the imprudence of some other patterer.
□ 'Gammy', likely to have you taken up.
⊙ 'Flummut', sure of a month in quod.*

In most lodging-houses there is an old man who is the guide to every 'walk' in the vicinity, and who can tell every house, on every round, that is 'good for a cold 'tater'. In many cases there is over the kitchen mantle-piece a map of the district, dotted here and there with memorandums of failure or success.

Patterers are fond of carving their names and avocations about the houses they visit. The old jail at Dartford has been some years a 'padding-ken'. In one of the rooms appears the following autographs:

Jemmy, the Rake, bound to Bristol; bad beds, but no bugs. Thank God for all things.

Razor George and his moll slept here the day afore Christmas; just out of 'stir' (jail), for 'muzzling a peeler'.

Scotch Mary, with 'driz' (lace), bound to Dover and back, please God.

Sometimes these inscriptions are coarse and obscene; sometimes very well written and orderly. Nor do they want illustrations.

At the old factory, Lincoln, is a portrait of the town beadle, formerly a soldier; it is drawn with different-coloured chalks, and ends with the following couplet:

'You are a B for false swearing,
In hell they'll roast you like a herring.'

Of Running Patterers

Few of the residents in London—but chiefly those in the quieter streets—have not been aroused, and most frequently in the evening, by a hurly-burly on each side of the street. An attentive listening will not lead any one to an accurate knowledge of what the clamour is about. It is from a 'mob' or 'school' of the running patterers (for both those words are used), and consists of two, three, or four men. All these men state that the greater the noise they make, the better is the chance of sale, and better still when the noise is on each side of a street, for it appears as if the vendors were proclaiming such interesting or important intelligence, that they were vying with one another who should supply the demand which must ensue. It is not possible to ascertain with any certitude *what* the patterers are so anxious to sell, for only a few leading words are audible. One of the cleverest of running patterers repeated to me, in a subdued tone, his announcements of murders. The words 'Murder', 'Horrible', 'Barbarous', 'Love', 'Mysterious', 'Former Crimes', and the like, could only be caught by the ear, but there was no announcement of anything like 'particulars'. If, however, the 'paper' relate to any well-known criminal, such as Rush,* the name is given distinctly enough, and so is any new or pretended fact. The running patterers describe, or profess to describe, the contents of their papers as they go rapidly along, and they seldom or ever stand still. They usually deal in murders, seductions, crim.-cons.,* explosions, alarming accidents, 'assassinations', deaths of public characters, duels, and love-letters. But popular, or notorious, murders are the 'great goes'.

Experience of a Running Patterer

From a running patterer, who has been familiar with the trade for many years, I received, upwards of a twelvemonth ago, the following statement. He is well known for his humour, and is a leading man in his fraternity. After some conversation about 'cocks',* the most popular of which, my informant said, was the murder at Chigwell-row, he continued:

'That's a trump, to the present day. Why, I'd go out now, sir, with a dozen of Chigwell-rows, and earn my supper in half an hour off of 'em. The murder of Sarah Holmes at Lincoln is good, too—that there has been worked for the last five year successively every winter. Poor Sarah Holmes! Bless her! she has saved me from walking the streets all night many a time. Some of the best of these have been in work twenty years—the Scarborough murder has full twenty years. It's called "The Scarborough Tragedy". I've worked it myself. It's about a noble and rich young naval officer seducing a poor clergyman's daughter. She is confined in a ditch, and destroys the child. She is taken up for it, tried, and executed. This has had a great run. It sells all round the country places, and would sell now if they had it out. Mostly all our customers is females. They are the chief dependence we have. The Scarborough Tragedy is very attractive. It draws tears to the women's eyes to think that a poor clergyman's daughter, who is remarkably beautiful, should murder her own child; it's very touching to every feeling heart. There's a copy of verses with it, too. Then there's the Liverpool Tragedy—that's very attractive. It's a mother murdering her own son, through gold. He had come from the East Indies, and married a rich planter's daughter. He came back to England to see his parents after an absence of thirty years. They kept a lodging-house in Liverpool for sailors; the son went there to lodge, and meant to tell his parents who he was in the morning. His mother saw the gold he had got in his boxes, and cut his throat—severed his head from his body; the old man, upwards of seventy years of age, holding the candle. They had put a washing-tub under the bed to catch his blood. The morning after the murder, the old man's daughter calls and inquires for a young man. The old man denies that they have had any such person in the house. She says he had a mole on his arm, in the shape of a strawberry. The old couple go up-stairs to examine the corpse, and find they have murdered their own son, and then they both put an end to their existence. This is a deeper tragedy than the Scarborough Murder. That suits young people better; they like to hear about the young woman being seduced by the naval officer; but the mothers take more to the Liverpool Tragedy—it suits them better. Some of the "cocks" were in existence long before ever I was born or thought of. The "Great and important battle between the two young ladies of fortune", is what we calls "a ripper". I should like to have that there put down correct,' he added, ' 'cause I've taken a tidy lot of money out of it.'

My informant, who had been upwards of 20 years in the running patter line, told me that he commenced his career with the 'Last Dying Speech and Full Confession of William Corder'.* He was sixteen years of age, and had run away from his parents. 'I worked that there,' he said, 'down in the very town (at Bury) where he was executed. I got a whole hatful of halfpence at that. Why, I wouldn't even give 'em seven for sixpence—no, that I wouldn't. A gentleman's servant come out and wanted half a dozen for his master and one for himself in, and I wouldn't let him have no such thing. We often sells more than that at once. Why, I sold six at one go to the railway clerks at Norwich about the Manning affair, only a fortnight back. But Steinburgh's little job*—you know he murdered his wife and family, and committed suicide after—that sold as well as any "die". Pegsworth* was an out-and-out lot. I did tremendous with him, because it happened in London, down Ratcliff-highway—that's a splendid quarter for working—there's plenty of feelings—but, bless you, some places you go to you can't move no how, they've hearts like paving-stones. They wouldn't have "the papers" if you'd give them to 'em—especially when they knows you. Greenacre* didn't sell so well as might have been expected, for such a diabolical out-and-out crime as he committed; but you see he came close after Pegsworth, and that took the beauty off him. Two murderers together is never no good to nobody. Why there was Wilson Gleeson,* as great a villain as ever lived—went and murdered a whole family at noon-day—but Rush

ILLUSTRATIONS OF STREET-ART—No. I.

Horrible and Bar-bari-ous Murder of Poor
JAEL DENNY,
THE ILL-FATED VICTIM OF THOMAS DRORY.

coopered him—and likewise that girl at Bristol—made it no draw to any one. Daniel Good, though, was a first-rater; and would have been much better if it hadn't been for that there Madam Toosow.* You see, she went down to Roehampton, and guv *2l.* for the werry clogs as he used to wash his master's carriage in; so, in course, when the harristocracy could go and see the real things—the werry identical clogs—in the Chamber of 'Orrors, why the people wouldn't look at our authentic portraits of the fiend in human form. Hocker* wasn't any particular great shakes. There was a deal expected from him, but he didn't turn out well. Courvoisier* was much better; he sold wery well, but nothing to Blakesley. Why I worked him for six weeks. The wife of the murdered man kept the King's Head that he was landlord on open on the morning of the execution, and the place was like a fair. I even went and sold papers outside the door myself. I thought if she war'n't ashamed, why should I be? After that we had a fine "fake"—that was the fire of the Tower of London—it sold rattling. Why we had about forty apprehended for that—first we said two soldiers was taken up that couldn't obtain their discharge, and then we declared it was a well-known sporting nobleman who did it for a spree. The boy Jones in the Palace* wasn't much of an affair for the running patterers; the ballad singers—or street screamers, as we calls 'em—had the pull out of that. The patter wouldn't take; they had read it all in the newspapers before. Oxford,* and Francis,* and Bean* were a little better, but nothing to crack about. The people doesn't care about such things as them. There's nothing beats a stunning good murder, after all. Why there was Rush—I lived on him for a month or more. When I commenced with Rush, I was 14*s.* in debt for rent, and in less than fourteen days I astonished the wise men in the east by paying my landlord all I owed him. Since Dan'el Good there had been little or nothing doing in the murder line—no one could cap him—till Rush turned up a regular trump for us. Why I went down to Norwich expressly to work the execution. I worked my way down there with "*a sorrowful lamentation*" of his own composing, which I'd got written by the blind man expressly for the occasion. On the morning of the execution we beat all the regular newspapers out of the field; for we had the full, true, and particular account down, you see, by our own express, and that can beat anything that ever they can publish; for we gets it printed several days afore it comes off, and goes and stands with it right under the drop; and many's the penny I've turned away when I've been asked for an account of the whole business *before* it happened. So you see, for herly and correct hinformation, we can beat the *Sun**—aye, or the moon either, for the matter of that. Irish Jem, the Ambassador, never goes to bed but he blesses Rush the farmer; and many's the time he's told me we should never have such another windfall as that. But I told him not to despair; there's a good time coming, boys, says I, and, sure enough, up comes the Bermondsey tragedy. We might have done very well, indeed, out of the Mannings, but there was too many examinations for it to be any great account to us. I've been away with the Mannings in the country ever since. I've been through Hertfordshire, Cambridgeshire, and Suffolk, along with George Frederick Manning and his wife—travelled from 800 to 1,000 miles with 'em, but I could have done much better if I had stopped in London. Every day I was anxiously looking for a confession from Mrs Manning. All I wanted was for her to clear her conscience afore she left this here whale of tears* (that's what I always calls it in the patter), and when I read in the papers (mind they was none of my own) that her last words on the brink of heternity was, "I've nothing to say to you, Mr Rowe, but to thank you for your kindness," I guv her up entirely—had completely done with her. In course the public looks to us for the last words of all monsters in human form, and as for Mrs Manning's, they were not worth the printing.'

Of the Death and Fire Hunters

I have described the particular business of the running patterer, who is known by another and a very expressive cognomen—as a 'Death Hunter'. This title refers not only to his vending accounts of all the murders that become topics of public conversation, but to his being a 'murderer' on his own account, as in the sale of 'cocks' mentioned incidentally in this narrative. If the truth be saleable, a running patterer prefers selling the truth, for then—as one man told me—he can 'go the same round comfortably another day'. If there be no truths for sale—no stories of criminals' lives and loves to be condensed from the diffusive biographies in the newspapers—no 'helegy' for a great man gone—no prophecy and no crim. con.—the death hunter invents, or rather announces, them. He puts some one to death for the occasion, which is called 'a cock'. The paper he sells may give the dreadful details, or it may be a religious tract, 'brought out in mistake', should the vendor be questioned on the subject; or else the poor fellow puts on a bewildered look and murmurs, 'O, it's shocking to be done this way—but I can't read.' The patterers pass along so rapidly that this detection rarely happens.

One man told me that in the last eight or ten years, he, either singly or with his 'mob', had twice put the Duke of Wellington* to death, once by a fall from his horse, and the other time by a 'sudden and myst-*erious*' death, without any condescension to particulars. He had twice performed the same mortal office for Louis Phillipe,* before that potentate's departure from France; each death was by the hands of an assassin; 'one was stabbing, and the other a shot from a distance.' He once thought of poisoning the Pope, but was afraid of the street Irish. He broke Prince Albert's leg, or arm, (he was not sure which), when his royal highness was out with his harriers. He never had much to say about the Queen; 'it wouldn't go down,' he thought, and perhaps nothing had lately been said. 'Stop, there, sir,' said another patterer, of whom I inquired as to the correctness of those statements (after my constant custom in sifting each subject thoroughly), 'stop, stop, sir. I *have* had to say about the Queen lately. In coorse, nothing can be said against her, and nothing ought to; that's true enough, but the last time she was confined, I cried her *accouchement* (the word was pronounced as spelt to a merely English reader, or rather more broadly) of *three!* Lord love you, sir, it would have been no use crying *one*; people's so used to that; but a Bobby came up and he stops me, and said it was some impudence about the Queen's *coachman!* Why look at it, says I, fat-head—I knew I was safe—and see if there's anything in it about the Queen or her coachman! And he looked, and in coorse there was nothing. I forget just now what the paper *was* about.' My first-mentioned informant had apprehended Feargus O'Connor* on a charge of high treason. He assassinated Louis Napoleon, 'from a *fourth* edition of the *Times*', which 'did well'. He caused Marshal Haynau* to die of the assault by the draymen. He made Rush hang himself in prison. He killed Jane Wilbred,* and put Mrs Sloane* to death; and he announced the discovery that Jane Wilbred was Mrs Sloane's daughter.

This informant did not represent that he had originated these little pieces of intelligence, only that he had been a party to their sale, and a party to originating one or two. Another patterer—and of a higher order of genius—told me that all which was stated was undoubtedly correct, 'but me and my mates, sir,' he said, 'did Haynau in another style.

A splendid slum, sir! Capital! We assassinated him—*mys*-te-rious. Then about Rush. His hanging hisself in prison was a fake, I know; but we've had him lately. His ghost appeared—as is shown in the Australian papers—to Emily Sandford,* and threatened her; and took her by the neck, and there's the red marks of his fingers to be seen on her neck to this day!' The same informant was so loud in his praise of the 'Ass-sass-sina-tion' of Haynau that I give the account. I have little doubt it was his own writing. It is confused in passages, and has a blending of the 'I' and the 'we':

'We have just received upon undisputed authority, that, that savage and unmanly tyrant, that enemy to civil and religious liberty, the inhuman Haynau has at last finished his career of guilt by the hand of an assassin, the term assassin I have no doubt will greet harshly upon the ears of some of our readers, yet never the less I am compelled to use it although I would gladly say the *average* of outraged innocence, which would be a name more suitable to one who has been the means of ridden the world of such a despicable monster.'

[My informant complained bitterly, and not without reason, of the printer. 'Average', for instance (which I have *italicised*), should be 'avenger'. The 'average of outraged innocence!']

'It appears by the Columns of the Corour le Constituonal of Brussels,' runs the paper, 'that the evening before last, three men one of which is supposed to be the miscreant, Haynau entered a Café in the Neighbourhood of Brussels kept by a man in the name of Priduex, and after partaking of some refreshments which were ordered by his two companions they desired to be shown to their chambers, during their stay in the public or Travellers Room, they spoke but little and seemed to be very cautious as to joining in the conversations which was passing briskly round the festive board, which to use the landlord's own words was rather strange, as his Café was mostly frequented by a set of jovial fellows, M. Priduex goes on to state that after the three strangers had retired to rest some time a tall and rather noble looking man enveloped in a large cloak entered and asked for a bed, and after calling for some wine he took up a paper and appeared to be reading it very attentively, in due time he was shown to bed and all passed on without any appearance of anything wrong until about 6 o'clock in the morning, when the landlord and his family, were roused by a noise over head and cries of murder, and upon going up stairs to ascertain the cause, he discovered the person who was [known] to be Marshal Haynau, lying on his bed with his throat cut in a frightful manner, and his two companions standing by his bed side bewailing his loss. On the table was discovered a card, on which was written these words "Monster, I am avenged at last." Suspicion went upon the tall stranger, who was not anywhere to be found, the Garde arms instantly were on the alert, and are now in active persuit of him but up to the time of our going to press nothing further has transpired.'

It is very easy to stigmatise the death-hunter when he sets off all the attractions of a real or pretended murder,—when he displays on a board, as does the standing patterer, 'illustrations' of 'the 'dentical pick-axe' of Manning, or the stable of Good,*—or when he invents or embellishes atrocities which excite the public mind. He does, however, but follow in the path of those who are looked up to as 'the press',—as the 'fourth estate'. The conductors of the *Lady's Newspaper* sent an artist to Paris to give drawings of the scene of the murder by the Duc de Praslin,*—to 'illustrate' the bloodstains in the duchess's bed-chamber. The *Illustrated London News* is prompt in depicting the locality of any atrocity over which the curious in crime may gloat. The *Observer*, in costly advertisements, boasts of its 20 columns (sometimes with a supplement) of details of some vulgar and mercenary bloodshed,—the details being written in a most honest deprecation of the morbid and savage tastes to which the writer is pandering. Other weekly papers have engravings—and only concerning murder—of any wretch whom vice has made notorious. Many weekly papers had expensive telegraphic despatches of Rush's having been hung at Norwich, which event, happily for the interest of Sunday newspapers, took place in Norwich at noon on a Saturday. [I may here remark, that the patterers laugh at telegraphs and express trains for rapidity of communication, boasting that the press strives in vain to rival *them*,—as at a 'hanging match', for instance, the patterer has the full particulars, dying speech, and confession included—if a confession be feasible—ready for his customers the moment the drop falls, and while the criminal may still be struggling, at the very scene of the hanging. At a distance he sells it before the hanging. 'If the *Times* was cross-examined about it,' observed one patterer, 'he must confess he's outdone, though he's a rich *Times*, and we is poor fellows.' But to resume—]

A penny-a-liner is reported, and without contradiction, to have made a large sum by having hurried to Jersey in Manning's business, and by being allowed to accompany the officers when they conducted that paltry tool of a vindictive woman from Jersey to Southampton by steamer, and from Southampton to London by 'special engine', as beseemed the popularity of so distinguished a rascal and homicide; and next morning the daily papers, in all the typographical honour of 'leads' and 'a good place', gave details of this fellow's—this Manning's—conversation, looks, and demeanour. Until the 'respectable' press become a more healthful public instructor, we have no right to blame the death-hunter, who is but an imitator—a follower—and that for a meal. So strong has this morbid feeling about criminals become, that an earl's daughter, who had 'an order' to see Bedlam, would not leave the place until she had obtained Oxford's autograph for her album! The rich vulgar are but the poor vulgar—without an excuse for their vulgarity.

Of the Sham Indecent Street-Trade

This is one of those callings which are at once repulsive and ludicrous; repulsive, when it is considered under what pretences the papers are sold, and ludicrous, when the disappointment of the gulled purchaser is contemplated.

I have mentioned that one of the allurements held out by the strawer was that his paper—the words used by Jack Straw*—could 'not be admitted into families'. Those following the 'sham indecent trade' for a time followed his example, and professed to sell straws and give away papers; but the London police became very observant of the sale of straws—more especially under the pretences alluded to—and it has, for the last ten years, been rarely pursued in the streets.

The plan now adopted is to sell the sealed packet itself, which the 'patter' of the street-seller leads his auditors to believe to he some improper or scandalous publication. The packet is some coloured paper, in which is placed a portion of an old newspaper, a Christmas carol, a religious tract, or a slop-tailor's puff (given away in the streets for the behoof of another class of gulls). The enclosed paper is, however, never indecent.

From a man who had, not long ago, been in this trade, I had the following account. He was very anxious that nothing should be said which would lead to a knowledge that he was my informant. After having expressed his sorrow that he had ever been driven to this trade from distress, he proceeded to justify himself. He argued—and he was not an ignorant man—that there was neither common sense nor common justice in interfering with a man like him, who, 'to earn a crust, pretended to sell what *shop-keepers*, that must pay church and all sorts of rates, sold without being molested'. The word 'shopkeepers' was uttered with a bitter emphasis. There are, or were, he continued, shops—for he seemed to know them all—and some of them had been carried on for years, in which shameless publications were not only sold, but exposed in the windows; and why should he be considered a greater offender than a shopkeeper, and be knocked about by the police? There are, or lately were, he said, such shops in the Strand, Fleet-street, a court off Ludgate-hill, Holborn, Drury-lane, Wych-street, the courts near Drury-lane Theatre, Haymarket, High-street, Bloomsbury, St Martin's-court, May's buildings, and elsewhere, to say nothing of Holywell-street!* Yet *he* must be interfered with!

[I may here remark, that I met with no street-sellers who did not disbelieve, or affect to disbelieve, that they were really meddled with by the police for obstructing the thoroughfare. They either hint, or plainly state, that they are removed solely to please the shop-keepers. Such was the reiterated opinion, real or pretended, of my present informant.]

I took a statement from this man, but do not care to dwell upon the subject. The trade, in the form I have described, had been carried on, he thought, for the last six years. At one time, 20 men followed it; at present, he believed there were only 6, and they worked only at intervals, and as opportunities offered: some going out, for instance, to sell almanacs or memorandum books, and, when they met with a favourable chance, offering their sealed packets. My informant's customers were principally boys, young men, and old gentlemen; but old gentlemen chiefly when the trade was new. This street-seller's 'great gun', as he called it, was to make up packets, as closely resembling as he could accomplish it, those which were displayed in the windows of any of the shops I have alluded to. He would then station himself at some little distance from one of those shops, and, if possible, so as to encounter those who had stopped to study the contents of the window, and would represent—broadly enough, he admitted, when he dared—that he could sell for 6*d*. what was charged 5*s*., or 2*s*. 6*d*., or whatever price he had seen announced, 'in that very neighbourhood'.

He sometimes ventured, also, to mutter something, unintelligibly, about the public being imposed upon! On one occasion, he took 6*s.* in the street in about two hours. On another evening he took 4*s.* 8*d.* in the street and was called aside by two old gentlemen, each of whom told him to come to an address given (at the West-end), and ask for such and such initials. To one he sold two packets for 2*s.*; to the other, five packets, each 1*s.*—or 11*s.* 8*d.* in one evening. The packets were in different coloured papers, and had the impressions of a large seal on red wax at the back; and he assured the old gents., as he called them, one of whom, he thought, was 'silly', that they were all different. 'And very likely,' he said, chucklingly, 'they were different; for they were made out of a lot of missionary tracts and old newspapers that I got dirt cheap at a "waste" shop. I should like to have seen the old gent.'s face, as he opened his 5*s.* worth, one after another!' This trade, however, among old gentlemen, was prosperous for barely a month: 'It got blown then, sir, and they wouldn't buy any more, except a very odd one.'

This man—and he believed it was the same with all the others in the trade—never visited the public-houses, for a packet would soon have been opened and torn there, which, he said, people was ashamed to do in the public streets. As well as he could recollect, he had never sold a single packet to a girl or a woman. Drunken women of the town had occasionally made loud comments on his calling, and offered to purchase; but on such occasions, fearful of a disturbance, he always hurried away.

I have said that the straw trade is now confined to the country, and I give a specimen of the article vended there, by the patterer in the sham indecent trade. It was purchased of a man, who sold it folded in the form of a letter, and is addressed, 'On Royal Service. By Express. Private. To Her Royal Highness, Victoria, Princess Royal. Kensington Palace, London. Entered at Stationer's Hall.' The man who sold it had a wisp of straw round his neck, and introduced his wares with the following patter:

'I am well aware that many persons here present will say what an absurd idea—the idea of selling straws for a halfpenny each, when there are so many lying about the street; but the reason is simply this: I am not allowed by the authorities to sell these papers, so I give them away and sell my straws. There are a variety of figures in these papers for gentlemen; some in the bed, some on the bed, some under the bed.'

The following is a copy of the document thus sold:

"Bachelors or Maidens, Husbands and Wives,
Will love each other and lead happy lives;
If both these Letters to read are inclined,
Secrets worth knowing therein they will find.

"Dated from the Duchy of Coburg.

"MY DEAREST VICTORIA,
Hiȣhuessəs' ɐnsʍeɹ, Ibəȣ ləɐʌe ʇosnbscɹiqe ɯyseIf
plepgəsof aɟɟeɔʇiou — ɐuxiouslyɐʍɐiʇiug ʎour royal-
ɹoʎalqɹipe aud fnʇnɹəsovəɹəign, ʌeɹy mɐuʎaud ɪiʌiug
snɹəd ou mʎpɹinɔeɪy qouour, ʇqaʇI ʍiɪl aʍaɹdʇo ɯy
ɯeʇo ʇhɐt euʌiepstɐʇion oɟqeiuȣʇqy hnsqaud, ɹəsʇas-
ɪnəhɹisʇeudoɯ; aud ʍhəuʇhon qast dəiȣnədʇo əxqalt
bəudep kueəs, ʇo ɟaʌonr ɯʎsnit, aqoʌe ɐnyoʇqer dɹince
oɟ aɪl qeirsʇo ɐbɹiʇisqdiadəm — I iɯpɪoɹeʇhəe ou uʎ
amiɐbɪe oɟ Eugɪaup'sdɹiuɔessəs—ɐnd tqə ɯosʇ ʌiɹʇuons
quɹyqiɯsəɪɟ ʍiʇhiu tqy oʍndoʍuʎ dlnmɐȣe! Mosʇ
ɔhɐɹuiug uoʇes, audʍiʇh ɟɪnʇʇeɹiug ʍiugswisqes ʇo
ʍqo ɪike ɐbirpoɟ pɐrɐdise, isoaɪɪiüȣʇqeəto ɪisʇeu ʇo his
ɔome ʇo ɯyɪougiuȣ aɹaɯs—iʇ is ouɪʎtqʎ peɐr Aɪqəɹt,
ɐmiaqlə Vicʇoɹiɐ, theɯosʇ duɹe ɐnp sdoʇləss oɟ virȣius,
fnʇnɹitʎ,audɔoutiuue ʇo prəaɯoɟ loʌə ɐnptqeə! Wʎ
sqalqe əncqanʇep wiʇqtqe mosʇ bəantiful visiousoɟ
nıənt oɟ ʇhɐt qalmʎsɪeəd I hɐvəbeen ɪouȣ ʍɐntiuȣ, I
nom sɪeəpɪess ɔouch,aud resiuiuȣ ɯysouɪ ʇo tqeenjoʎ-
wonnps—Ʇqenʍiɪl I dɪeasɐnʇɪʎ rədose ɯysəɪɟ ou ɯʎ
bnʇcoɯe ɐnp ponr tqy qeɐliuȣ bəlsɐɯiuʇo ɯʎ sɯaɹtiug
ʌənɪysɐmɐriʇɐn, pass uoʇaʍaʎ ɟɹoɯ ʇqyɐdoɹiug ɐlqeɹʇ;
iugɪovə! Ʇhənqasʇeu ɯy ȣɪoɹionsəhərnb—ʇhon həa-
wqoɪeqopy is qeiuȣcousnmepin tqeɟnɹnɐsə oɟ eʌeɹlɐsʇ-
ʇɐɪisəd ʍiʇhʌɐriəd aud ɔouɟɪiɔtiuȣ eɯoʇious, aud mʎ
ɟusəto po ʇhəiɹoɟɟicə; əʌəɹʎ oueoɟ ɯy ɯeɯbəɹsɐɹə ʇɐn-
fiɹə, ɯyɟeəʇ sʇuɯbɪes—ʎeɐ, mʎ ɐɹɯs audɯy ləgs ɹe-
ɯy sənsəsʍaudəɹ, ɯy qaiɹsʇauds ou eup, mʎ qeɐd isou
ɔlɐsdtqeəiu ɯyaɹms—Mʎ qosomqeɐvəs, ɯy qeaɹʇpɐnʇs,
tqylovəlʎ foɹɯ, audɪoug for ʇhəhɐpdy qonr wqeuI sqall
royɐlqiȣhuess—ɯy sʍeeʇestauȣeɪ, oq! qow I po apore
doʍnʇo tqe pəɪiȣhʇfuɪtɐsk oɟ ʍriʇiuȣa loʌe ɪəʇʇeɹto ʇhʎ
— — nəvərpip I eujoʎgɹeɐtər qɪiss, ʇhauwqeuI sɐʇ

"Your adored Lover,
"ALBERT,
"PRINCE OF COBURG."

On the back of this page is the following cool initiation of the purchaser into the mysteries of the epistle:

'Directions for the purchasers to understand the *Royal Love Letters*, and showing them how to practise the art of Secret Letter Writing:

'Proceed to lay open "Albert's Letter" by the side of "Victoria's", and having done so, then look carefully down them until you have come to a word at the left hand corner, near the end of each Letter, having two marks thus ——, when you must commence with that word, and read from left to right after you have turned them bottom upwards before a looking glass so that you may peruse the copy reflected therein. But you must notice, throughout all the words every other letter is upside down, also every other word single; but the next two words being purposely joined together, therefore they are double; and in addition to those letters placed upside down, makes it more mysterious in the reading. The reader is recommended to copy each word in writing, when he will be able to read the letters forward, and after a little practice he can soon learn to form all his words in the same curious manner, when he wants to write a "secret letter".

'Be sure when holding it up side down before a looking-glass, that the light of a candle, is placed between then by the reflection it will show much plainer, and be sooner discovered.

'If you intend to practise a *Joke* and make it answer the purpose of a Valentine, write what you think necessary on the adjoining *blank page*; then post it, with the superscription filled up in this manner: After the word To, *write the name and address of the party* also place the word FROM *before* 'VICTORIA'S' name: then the address on the outside of this letter will read somewhat after the following fashion:—To Mr or Mrs so and so (with the number if any), in such and such a street: at the same time your letter will appear as if it came from Royalty.

'N.B. You must first buy both the letters, as the other letter is an answer to this one; and because, without the reader has got both letters, he will not have the secrets perfect.'

Notwithstanding the injunction to buy *both* letters, and the seeming necessity of having both to understand the 'directions', the patterer was selling only the one I have given.

Of Ancient and Modern Street Ballad Ministrelsy

The ballad-singer and seller of to-day is the sole descendant, or remains, of the minstrel of old, as regards the business of the streets; he is, indeed, the minstrel having lost caste, and being driven to play cheap.

The themes of the minstrels were wars, and victories, and revolutions; so of the modern man of street ballads. If the minstrel celebrated with harp and voice the unhorsings, the broken bones, the deaths, the dust, the blood, and all the glory and circumstance of a tournament, —so does the ballad-seller, with voice and fiddle, glorify the feelings, the broken bones, the blood, the deaths, and all the glory and circumstance of a prize-fight. The minstrel did not scoff at the madness which prevailed in the lists, nor does the ballad-singer at the brutality which rules in the ring. The minstrels had their dirges for departed greatness; the ballad-singer, like old Allan Bane,* also 'pours his wailing o'er the dead'—for are there not the street 'helegies' on all departed greatness? In the bestowal of flattery or even of praise the modern minstrel is far less liberal than was his prototype; but the laudation was, in the good old times, very often 'paid for' by the person whom it was sung to honour. Were the same measure applied to the ballad-singer and writer of today, there can be no reason to doubt that it would be attended with the same result. In his satire the modern has somewhat of an advantage over his predecessor. The minstrel not rarely received a 'largesse' to satirize some one obnoxious to a rival, or to a disappointed man. The ballad-singer (or chaunter, for these remarks apply with equal force to both of these street-professionals), is seldom hired to abuse. I was told, indeed, by a clever chaunter, that he had been sent lately by a strange gentleman to sing a song—which he and his mate (a patterer) happened at the time to be working—in front of a neighbouring house. The song was on the rogueries of the turf; and the 'move' had a doubly advantageous effect. 'One gentleman, you see, sir, gave us 1*s.* to go and sing; and afore we'd well finished the chorus, somebody sent us from the house another 1*s.* to go away agin.' I believe this to be the only way in which the satire of a ballad-singer is rewarded, otherwise than by sale to his usual class of customers in the streets or the public-houses. The ancient professors of street minstrelsy unquestionably played and sung satirical lays, depending for their remuneration on the liberality of their out-of-door audience; so is it precisely with the modern. The minstrel played both singly and with his fellows; the ballad-singer 'works' both alone (but not frequently) and with his 'mates' or his 'school'.

The license enjoyed by the court jesters, and, in some respects, by the minstrels of old, is certainly enjoyed, undiminished, by the street-writers and singers of ballads on a subject. They are unsparing satirists, who, with a rare impartiality, lash all classes and all creeds, as well as any individual. One man, upon whose information I can rely, told me that, eleven years ago, he himself had 'worked', in town and country, 23 different songs at the same period and on the same subject—the marriage of the Queen.* They all 'sold',—but the most profitable was one 'as sung by Prince Albert in character'. It was to the air of the 'Dusty Miller'; and 'it was good,' said the ballad-man, 'because we could easily dress up to the character given to Albert.' I quote a verse:

'Here I am in rags
  From the land of All-dirt,
To marry England's Queen,
  And my name it is Prince Albert.'

'And what's more, sir,' continued my informant, 'not very long after the honeymoon, the Duchess of L—— drove up in her carriage to the printer's, and bought all the songs in honour of Victoria's wedding, and gave a sovereign for them and wouldn't take the change. It was a duchess. Why I'm sure about it—though I can't say whether it were the Duchess of L—— or S——; for didn't the printer, like an honest man, when he'd stopped the price of the papers, hand over to us chaps the balance to drink, and *didn't* we drink it! There can't be a mistake about *that*.

'I have written all sorts of things—ballads on a subject, and copies of verses, and anything ordered of me, or on anything I thought would be accepted, but now I can't get about. I've been asked to write indecent songs, but I refused. One man offered me 5*s*. for six such songs.—"Why, that's less than the common price," said I, "instead of something over to pay for the wickedness."—All those sort of songs come now to the streets, I believe all do, from the concert-rooms. I can imitate any poetry. I don't recollect any poet I've imitated. No, sir, not Scott or Moore,* that I know of, but if they've written popular songs, then I dare say I have imitated them. Writing poetry is no comfort to me in my sickness. It might if I could write just what I please. The printers like hanging subjects best, and I don't. But when any of them sends to order a copy of verses for a "Sorrowful Lamentation" of course I must supply them. I don't think much of what I've done that way. If I'd my own fancy, I'd keep writing acrostics, such as one I wrote on our rector.' 'God bless him,' interrupted the wife, 'he's a good man.' 'That he is,' said the poet, 'but he's never seen what I wrote about him, and perhaps never will.' He then desired his wife to reach him his big Bible, and out of it he handed me a piece of paper, with the following lines written on it, in a small neat hand enough:

'C elestial blessings hover round his head,
H undreds of poor, by his kindness were fed,
A nd precepts taught which he himself obeyed.
M an, erring man, brought to the fold of God,
P reaching pardon through a Saviour's blood.
N o lukewarm priest, but firm to Heaven's cause;
E xamples showed how much he loved its laws.
Y outh and age, he to their wants attends,
S teward of Christ—the poor man's sterling friend.'

'There would be some comfort, sir,' he continued, 'if one could go on writing at will like that. As it is, I sometimes write verses all over a slate, and rub them out again. Live hard! yes, indeed, we do live hard. I hardly know the taste of meat. We live on bread and butter, and tea; no, not any fish. As you see, sir, I work at tinning. I put new bottoms into old tin tea-pots, and such like. Here's my sort of bench, by my poor bit of a bed. In the best weeks I earn 4*s*. by tinning, never higher. In bad weeks I earn only 1*s*. by it, and sometimes not that,—and there are more shilling than four shilling weeks by three to one. As to my poetry, a good week is 3*s*., and a poor week is 1*s*.—and sometimes I make nothing at all that way. So I leave you to judge, sir, whether we live hard; for the comings in, and what we have from the parish, must keep six of us—myself, my wife, and four children. It's a long, hard struggle.' 'Yes, indeed,' said the wife, 'it's just as you've heard my husband tell, sir. We've 2*s*. a week and four loaves of bread from the parish, and the rent's 2*s*. 6*d*., and the landlord every week has 2*s*., —and 6*d*. he has done for him in tinning work. Oh, we do live hard, indeed.'

As I was taking my leave, the poor man expressed a desire that I would take a copy of an epitaph which he had written for himself. 'If ever', he said, 'I am rich enough to provide for a tomb-stone, or my family is rich enough to give me one, this shall be my epitaph' [I copied it from a blank page in his Bible:]

'Stranger, pause, a moment stay,
Tread lightly o'er this mound of clay.
Here lies J—— H——, in hopes to rise,
And meet his Saviour in the skies.
Christ his refuge, Heaven his home,
Where pain and sorrow never come,

His journey's done, his trouble's past,
With God he sleeps in peace at last.'

Of the 'Gallows' Literature of the Streets

Under this head I class all the street-sold publications which relate to the hanging of malefactors. That the question is not of any minor importance must be at once admitted, when it is seen how very extensive a portion of the reading of the poor is supplied by the 'Sorrowful Lamentations' and 'Last Dying Speech, Confession, and Execution' of criminals.* One paper-worker told me, that in some small and obscure villages in Norfolk, which, he believed, were visited only by himself in his line, it was not very uncommon for two poor families to *club* for 1*d*. to purchase an execution broadsheet! Not long after Rush was hung, he saw, one evening after dark, through the uncurtained cottage window, eleven persons, young and old, gathered round a scanty fire, which was made to blaze by being fed with a few sticks. An old man was reading, to an attentive audience, a broad-sheet of Rush's execution, which my informant had sold to him; he read by the fire-light; for the very poor in those villages, I was told, rarely lighted a candle on a spring evening, saying that 'a bit o' fire was good enough to talk by'. The scene must have been impressive, for it had evidently somewhat impressed the perhaps not very susceptible mind of my informant.

The procedure on the occasion of a 'good' murder, or of a murder expected to 'turn out well', is systematic. First appears a quarter-sheet (a hand-bill, 9½ in. by 7½ in.) containing the earliest report of the matter. Next come half-sheets (twice the size) of later particulars, or discoveries, or—if the supposed murderer be in custody—of further examinations. The sale of these bills is confined almost entirely to London, and in their production the newspapers are for the most part followed closely enough. Then are produced the whole, or broad-sheets (twice the size of the half-sheets), and, lastly, but only on great occasions, the *double* broad-sheet. [I have used the least technical terms that I might not puzzle the reader with accounts of 'crowns', 'double-crowns', &c.]

The most important of all the broad-sheets of executions, according to concurrent, and indeed unanimous, testimony is the case of Rush. I speak of the testimony of the street-folk concerned, who all represent the sale of the papers relative to Rush, both in town and country, as the best in their experience of late years.

The sheet bears the title of 'The Sorrowful Lamentation and Last Farewell of J. B. Rush, who is ordered for Execution on Saturday next, at Norwich Castle'. There are three illustrations. The largest represents Rush, cloaked and masked, 'shooting Mr Jermy, Sen.'. Another is of 'Rush shooting Mrs Jermy'. A prostrate body is at her feet, and the lady herself is depicted as having a very small waist and great amplitude of gown-skirts. The third is a portrait of Rush,—a correct copy, I was assured, and have no reason to question the assurance,—from one in the *Norwich Mercury*. The account of the trial and biography of Rush, his conduct in prison, &c., is a concise and clear enough condensation from the newspapers. Indeed, Rush's Sorrowful Lamentation is the best, in all respects, of any execution broad-sheet I have seen; even the 'copy of verses' which, according to the established custom, the criminal composes in the condemned cell—his being unable, in some instances, to read or write being no obstacle to the composition—seems, in a literary point of view, of a superior strain to the run of such things. The matters of fact, however, are introduced in the same peculiar manner. The worst part is the morbid sympathy and intended apology for the criminal. I give the verses entire:

'This vain world I soon shall leave,
Dear friends in sorrow do not grieve;
Mourn not my end, though 'tis severe,
For death awaits the murderer.

Now in a dismal cell I lie,
For murder I'm condemn'd to die;
Some may pity when they read,
Oppression drove me to the deed.

My friends and home to me were dear,
The trees and flowers that blossom'd near;
The sweet loved spot where youth began
Is dear to every Englishman.

I once was happy—that is past,
Distress and crosses came at last;
False friendship smiled on wealth and me,
But shunned me in adversity.

The scaffold is awaiting me,
For Jermy I have murdered thee;
Thy hope and joys—thy son I slew,
Thy wife and servant wounded too.

I think I hear the world to say—
"Oh, Rush, why didst thou Jermy slay?
His dear loved son why didst thou kill,
For he had done to thee no ill."

If Jenny had but kindness shown,
And not have trod misfortune down,
I ne'er had fired the fatal ball
That caus'd his son and him to fall.

My cause I did defend alone,
For learned counsel I had none;
I pleaded hard and questions gave,
In hopes my wretched life to save.

The witness to confound did try,
But God ordained that I should die;
Eliza Chestney she was there,—
I'm sorry I have injured her.

Oh, Emily Sandford, was it due
That I should meet my death through you?
If you had wish'd me well indeed,
How could you thus against me plead?

I've used thee kind, though not my wife:
Your evidence has cost my life;
A child by me you have had born,
Though hard against me you have sworn.

The scaffold is, alas! my doom,—
I soon shall wither in the tomb:
God pardon me—no mercy's here
For Rush—the wretched murderer!'

Although the execution broad-sheet I have cited may be the best, taken altogether, which has fallen under my observation, nearly all I have seen have one characteristic—the facts can be plainly understood. The narrative, embracing trial, biography, &c., is usually prepared by the printer, being a condensation from the accounts in the newspapers, and is perhaps intelligible, simply because it *is* a condensation. It is so, moreover, in spite of bad grammar, and sometimes perhaps from an unskilful connection of the different eras of the trial.

When the circumstances of the case permit, or can be at all constrained to do so, the Last Sorrowful Lamentation contains a 'Love Letter', written—as one patterer told me he had occasionally expressed it, when he thought his audience suitable—'from the depths of the condemned cell, with the condemned pen, ink, and paper'. The style is stereotyped, and usually after this fashion:

'Dear ——, —Shrink not from receiving a letter from one who is condemned to die as a murderer. Here, in my miserable cell, I write to one whom I have from my first acquaintanceship, held in the highest esteem, and whom, I believe, has also had the same kindly feeling towards myself. Believe me, I forgive all my enemies and hear no malice. O, my dear ——, guard against giving way to evil passions, and a fondness for drink. Be warned by my sad and pitiful fate.'

If it be not feasible to have a love-letter—which can be addressed to either wife or sweetheart—in the foregoing style, a 'last letter' is given, and this can be written to father, mother, son, daughter, or friend; and is usually to the following purport:

'Condemned Cell, ——

'My Dear ——, —By the time you receive this my hours, in this world, will indeed be short. It is an old and true saying, that murderers will one day meet their proper reward. No one can imagine the dreadful nights of anguish passed by me since the commital of the crime on poor ——. All my previous victims have appeared before me in a thousand different shapes and forms. My sufferings have been more than I can possibly describe. Let me entreat you to turn from your evil ways and lead a honest and sober life. I am suffering so much at the present moment both from mind and body that I can write no longer. Farewell! farewell!

'Your affectionate ——.'

I have hitherto spoken of the Last Sorrowful Lamentation sheets. The next broad-sheet is the 'Life, Trial, Confession, and Execution'. This presents the same matter as the 'Lamentation', except that a part—perhaps the judge's charge at the trial, or perhaps the biography —is removed to make room for the 'Execution', and occasionally for a portion of the 'Condemned Sermon'. To judge by the productions

I treat of, both subjects are marvelously similar on all occasions. I cite a specimen of the Condemned Sermon, as preached, according to the broad-sheet, before Hewson, condemned for the murder of a turnkey. It will be seen that it is of a character to fit *any* condemned sermon whatever:

'The rev. gent. then turned his discourse particularly to the unhappy prisoner doomed to die on the morrow, and told him to call on Him who alone had the power of forgiveness; who had said, "though his sins were red as scarlet," he would "make them, white as snow,"* though he had been guilty of many heinous crimes, there was yet an opportunity of forgiveness.—During the delivery of this address, the prisoner was in a very desponding state, and at its conclusion was helped out of the chapel by the turnkeys.'

The 'Execution' is detailed generally in this manner. I cite the 'Life, Trial, Confession, and Execution of Mary May, for the Murder of W. Constable, her Half-brother, by Poison, at Wix, near Manningtree':

'At an early hour this morning the space before the prison was very much crowded by persons anxious to witness the execution of Mary May, for the murder of William Constable, her half-brother, by poison, at Wix, Manningtree, which gradually increased to such a degree, that a great number of persons suffered extremely from the pressure, and gladly gave up their places on the first opportunity to escape from the crowd. The sheriffs and their attendants arrived at the prison early this morning and proceeded to the condemn cell, were they found the reverend ordinary engaged in prayer with the miserable woman. After the usual formalities had been observed of demanding the body of the prisoner into their custody she was then conducted to the press-room. The executioner with his assistants then commenced pinioning her arms, which opporation they skillfully and quickly dispatched. During these awful preparations the unhappy woman appeared mently to suffer severely, but uttered not a word when the hour arrived and all the arrangements having been completed, the bell commenced tolling, and then a change was observed, to come over the face of the prisoner, who trembling violently, walked with the melancholy procession, proceeded by the reverend ordinary, who read aloud the funeral service for the dead. When the bell commenced tolling a moment was heard from without, and the words 'Hats off', and 'Silence', were distinctly heard, from which time nothing but a continual sobbing was heard. On arriving at the foot of the steps leading to the scaffold she thanked the sheriffs and the worthy governor of the prison, for their kind attentions to her during her confinement; & then the unfortunate woman was seen on the scaffold, there was a death like silence prevailed among the vast multitude of people assembled. In a few seconds the bolt was drawn, and, after a few convulsive struggles, the unhappy woman ceased to exist.'

This mode of procedure in 'gallows' literature, and this style of composition, have prevailed for from twenty to thirty years. I find my usual impossibility to *fix* a date among these street-folk; but the Sorrowful Lamentation sheet was unknown until the law for prolonging the term of existence between the trial and death of the capitally-convicted, was passed.* 'Before that, sir,' I was told, 'there wasn't no time for a Lamentation; sentence o' Friday, and scragging o' Monday. So we had only the Life, Trial, and Execution.'

In the most 'popular' murders, the street 'papers' are a mere recital from the newspapers, but somewhat more brief, when the suspected murderer is in custody; but when the murderer has not been apprehended, or is unknown, 'then,' said one Death-hunter, 'we has our fling, and I've hit the mark a few chances that way. We had, at the werry least, half-a-dozen coves pulled up in the slums that we printed for the murder of "The Beautiful Eliza Grimwood,* in the Waterloo-road". I did best on Thomas Hopkins,* being the guilty man—I think he was Thomas Hopkins—'cause a strong case was made out again him.'

The last publication to which the trade has recourse is 'the hook'. This is usually eight pages, but sometimes only four of a larger size. In authorship, matter, or compilation, it differs little from the narratives I have described. The majority of these books are prepared by one man. They are in a better form for being preserved as a record than is a broad-sheet, and are frequently sold, and almost always offered by the patterers when they cry a new case on a sheet, as 'people that loves such reading likes to keep a good account of the best by them; and so, when I've sold Manning's bills, I've often shoved off Rush's books.' The books, like the bills, have generally the letters and the copy of verses.

Some of these books have the title-page set forth in full display, —for example: '*Horrible Murder and Mutilation of Lucy Game, aged* 15, *by her Cruel Brother, William Game,* aged* 9, *at Westmill, Hertfordshire. His Committal and Confession. With a Copy of Letter. Also, Full Particulars of the Poisonings in Essex.*' Here, as there was no execution, the matter was extended, to include the poisonings in Essex. The title I have quoted is expanded into thirteen lines. Sometimes the title-page is adorned with a portrait. One, I was told, which was last employed as a portrait of Calcraft,* had done severe service since Courvoisier's* time,—for my informant thought that Courvoisier was the original. It is the bust of an ill-looking man, with coat and waistcoat fitting with that unwrinkled closeness which characterises the figures in tailors' 'fashions'.

The above style of work is known in the trade as 'the book'; but other publications, in the book or pamphlet form, are common enough. In some I have seen, the title-page is a history in little. I cite one of these: '*Founded on Facts. The Whitby Tragedy; or, the Gambler's Fate. Containing the Lives of Joseph Carr,* aged* 21, *and his sweetheart, Maria Leslie, aged* 19, *who were found Dead, lying by each other, on the morning of the* 23rd *of May. Maria was on her road to Town to buy some Ribbon, &c., for her Wedding Day, when her lover in a state of intoxication fired at her, and then run to rob his prey, but finding it to be his Sweetheart, reloaded his Gun, placed the Muzzle to his Mouth, and blew out his Brains, all through cursed Cards, Drink, &c. Also, an affectionate Copy of Verses.*'

To show the extent of the trade in execution broad-sheets. I obtained returns of the number of copies relating to the principal executions of late, that had been sold:

Of Rush	2,500,000 copies.
" the Mannings	2,500,000 "
" Courvoisier	1,666,000 "
" Good.	1,650,000 "
" Corder	1,650,000 "
" Greenacre.	1,666,000 "

Of the Street-Sellers of Conundrums

Among the more modern street sales are 'conundrums', generally vended, both in the shops and the streets, as 'Nuts to Crack', when not in the form of books. This is another of the 'broad-sheets', and is sufficiently clever and curious in its way.

In the centre, at the top, is the 'Wonderful Picture',* with the following description: 'This Picture when looked at from a particular point of view, will not only appear perfect in all respects and free from distortion, but the figures will actually appear to stand out in relief from the paper.' The wonderful picture, which is a rude imitation of a similar toy picture sold in a box, 'with eye-piece complete', at the shops, presents a distorted view of a church-spire, a light-house, a donjon-keep, castellated buildings backed by mountains, a moat on which are two vessels, an arch surmounted by a Britannia, a palm-tree (I presume), and a rampart, or pier, or something that way, on which are depicted two figures, with the gestures of elocutionists. The buildings are elongated, like shadows at sunset or sunrise. What may be the 'particular point of view' announced in the description of the Wonderful Picture, is not described in the 'Nuts', but the following explanation is given in a little book, published simultaneously, and entitled, 'The Nutcrackers, a Key to Nuts to Crack, or Enigmatical Repository':

'THE WONDERFUL PICTURE.—Cut out a piece of cardboard 2½ inches long, make a round hole about the size of a pea in the top of it; place this level with the right-hand side of the Engraving and just 1½ inches distant from it, then apply your eye to the little hole and look at the picture, and you will find that a beautiful symmetry pervades the landscape, there is not the slightest appearance of distortion, and the different parts appear actually to stand up in relief on the paper.'

Below the 'Wonderful Picture' are other illustrations; and the border of the broad-sheet presents a series of what may be called pictorial engravings. The first is,

D I O
C C

1.—Lately presented to a 'Wise man' by a usurper.

The answer being evidently 'Diocese'. No. 26 is

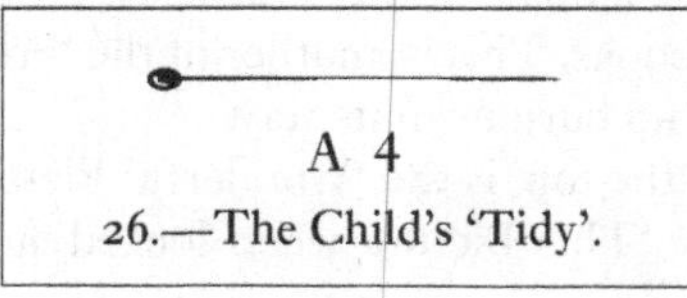

26.—The Child's 'Tidy'.

'Pinafore' is the solution. Of the next 'hieroglyphic'—for a second title to the 'Nuts' tells of '200 Hieroglyphics, Enigmas, Conundrums, Curious Puzzles, and other Ingenious Devices',—I cannot speak very highly. It consists of 'AIMER', (a figure of a hare at full speed), and 'EKA'. Answer.—'America'.

In the body of the broad-sheet are the Enigmas, &c., announced; of each of which I give a specimen, to show the nature of this street performance or entertainment. Enigma 107 is—

'I've got no wings, yet in the air
I often rise and fall;
I've got no feet, yet clogs I wear,
And shoes, and boots, and all.'

As the answer is foot-ball, the two last lines should manifestly have been placed first.

The 'Conundrums'* are next in the arrangement, and I cite one of them:

'Why are there, strictly speaking, only 325 days in the year?'

'Because,' is the reply, 'forty of them are lent and never returned.' The 'Riddles' follow in this portion of the 'Nuts to Crack'. Of these, one is not very difficult to be solved, though it is distinguished for the usual grammatical confusion of tenses:

'A man has three daughters, and each of these have a brother. How many children had he?'

The 'Charades' complete the series. Of these I select one of the best:

'I am a word of letters seven,
I'm sinful in the sight of heaven,
To every virtue I'm opposed,
Man's weary life I've often closed.
If to me you prefix two letters more,
I mean exactly what I meant before.'

The other parts of the letter-press consist of 'Anagrams', 'Transpositions', &c.

When a clever patterer 'works conundrums'—for the trade is in the hands of the pattering class—he selects what he may consider the best, and reads or repeats them in the street, sometimes with and sometimes without the answer. But he does not cripple the probable quickness of his sale by a slavish adherence to what is in type. He puts the matter, as it were, personally. 'What gentleman is it,' one man told me he would ask, 'in this street, that has—

> "Eyes like saucers, a back like a box,
> A nose like a pen-knife, and a voice like a fox?"

You can learn for a penny. Or sometimes I'll go on with the patter, thus,' he continued, 'What lady is it that we have all seen, and who can say truly—

> "I am brighter than day, I am swifter than light,
> And stronger than all the momentum of might?"

More than once people have sung out "the Queen", for they seem to think that the momentum of might couldn't fit any one else. It's "thought" as is the answer, but it wouldn't do to let people think it's anything of the sort. It must seem to fit *somebody*. If I see a tailor's name on a door, as soon as I've passed the corner of the street, and sometimes in the same street, I've asked—

"Why is Mr So-and-so, the busy tailor of this (or the next street) never at home?"

"Because he's always cutting out." I have the same questions for other tradesmen, and for gentlemen and ladies in this neighbourhood, and no gammon. All for a penny. Nuts to Crack, a penny. A pair of Nutcrackers to crack 'em, only one penny.'

Of the Street-Sellers of Engravings, etc., in Umbrellas, etc.

The sale of 'prints', 'pictures', and 'engravings'—I heard them designated by each term—in umbrellas in the streets, has been known, as far as I could learn from the street-folk for some fifteen years, and has been general from ten to twelve years. In this traffic the umbrella is inverted and the 'stock' is disposed within its expanse. Sometimes narrow tapes are attached from rib to rib of the umbrella, and within these tapes are placed the pictures, one resting tip on another. Sometimes a few pins are used to attach the larger prints to the cotton of the umbrella, the smaller ones being 'fitted in at the side' of the bigger. 'Pins is best, sir, in my opinion,' said a little old man, who used to have a 'print umbrella' in the New Cut; 'for the public has a more unbrokener display. I used werry fine pins, though they's dearer, for people as has a penny to spare likes to see things nice, and big pins makes big holes in the pictures.'

This trade is most pursued on still summer evenings, and the use of an inverted umbrella seems so far appropriate that it can only be so used, in the street, in *dry* weather. 'I used to keep a sharp look-out, sir,' said the same informant, 'for wind or rain, and many's the time them devils o' boys—God forgive me, they's on'y poor children—but they *is* devils—has come up to me and has said—one in particler, standin' afore the rest: "It'll thunder in five minutes, old bloke, so hup with yer humbereller, and go 'ome; hup with it jist as it is; it'll show stunnin; and sell as yer goes." O, they're a shocking torment, sir; nobody can feel it like people in the streets,—shocking.'

The engravings thus sold are of all descriptions. Some have evidently been the frontispieces of sixpenny or lower-priced works. These works sometimes fall into hands of the 'waste collectors', and any 'illustrations' are extracted from the letter-press and are disposed of by the collectors, by the gross or dozen, to those warehousemen who supply the small shopkeepers and the street-sellers. Sometimes, I was informed, a number of engravings, which had for a while appeared as 'frontispieces' were issued for sale separately. Many of these were and are found in the 'street umbrellas'; more especially the portraits of popular actors and actresses. 'Mr J. P. Kemble, as Hamlet'—'Mr Fawcett, as Captain Copp'—'Mr Young, as Iago'—'Mr Liston, as Paul Pry'—'Mrs Siddons, as Lady Macbeth'—'Miss O'Neil, as Belvidera', &c., &c. In the course of an inquiry into the subject nearly a year and a half ago, I learned from one 'umbrella man' that, six or seven years previously, he used to sell more portraits of 'Mr Edmund Kean,* as Richard III', than of anything else.

The following statement, from a middle-aged woman, further shows the nature of the trade, and the class of customers:

'I've sat with an umbrella,' she said, 'these seven or eight years, I suppose it is. My husband's a penny lot-seller, with just a middling pitch' [the vendor of a number of articles, sold at a penny 'a lot'] 'and in the summer I do a little in engravings, when I'm not minding my husband's "lots", for he has sometimes a day, and oftener a night, with portering and packing for a tradesman, that's known him long. Well, sir, I think I sell most "coloured". "Master Toms" wasn't bad last summer. "Master Toms" was pictures of cats, sir—you must have seen them—and I had them different colours. If a child looks on with its father, very likely, it'll want "pussy", and if the child cries for it, it's almost a sure sale, and more, I think, indeed I'm sure, with men than with women. Women knows the value of money better than men, for men never understand what housekeeping is. I have no children, thank God, or they might be pinched, poor things. "Miss Kitties" was the same sale. Toms is hes, and Kitties is she cats. I've sometimes sold to poor women who was tiresome; they must have just what would fit over their mantel-pieces, that was papered with pictures. I seldom venture on anything above 1*d.*, I mean to sell at 1*d.* I've had Toms and Kitties at 2*d.* though. "Fashions" isn't worth umbrella room; the poorest needlewoman won't be satisfied with them from an umbrella. "Queens" and "Alberts" and "Wales's" and the other children isn't near so good as they was. There's so many "fine portraits of Her Majesty", or the others, given away with the first number of this or of that, that people's overstocked. If a working-man can buy a newspaper or a number, why of course he may as well have a picture with it. They gave away glasses of gin at the opening of that baker's shop there, and it's the same doctrine' [The word she used]. 'I never offer penny theatres, or comic exhibitions, or anything big; they spoils the look of the umbrella, and makes better things look mean. I sell only to working people, I think; seldom to boys, and seldomer to girls; seldom to servant-maids and hardly ever to women of the town. I *have* taken 6*d.* from one of them though. I think boys buy pictures for picture books. I never had what I suppose was old pictures. To a few old people, I've known, "Children" sell fairly, when they're made plump, and red cheeked, and curly haired. They sees a resemblance of their grandchildren, perhaps, and buys. Young married people does so too, but not so oft, I think.'

STREET-SELLERS OF MANUFACTURED ARTICLES

Of the Street-Sellers of Manufactured Articles

The street-sellers of manufactured articles present, as a body, so many and often such varying characteristics, that I cannot offer to give a description of them as a whole, as I have been able to do with other and less diversified classes.

Among them are several distinct and peculiar street-characters, such as the pack-men, who carry their cotton or linen goods in packs on their backs, and are all itinerants. Then there are duffers, who vend pretended smuggled goods, handkerchiefs, silks, tobacco or cigars; also, the sellers of sham sovereigns and sham gold rings for wagers. The crockery-ware and glass-sellers (known in the street-trade as 'crocks'), are peculiar from their principle of *bartering*. They will sell to any one, but they *sell* very rarely, and always clamour in preference for an exchange of their wares for wearing-apparel of any kind. They state, if questioned, that their reason for doing this is—at least I heard the statement from some of the most intelligent among them —that they do so because, if they 'sold outright', they required a hawker's license, and could not sell or 'swop' so cheap.

Some of the street-sellers of manufactured articles are also patterers. Among these are the 'cheap Jacks', or 'cheap Johns'; the grease and stain removers; the corn-salve and plate-ball* vendors; the sellers of sovereigns and rings for wagers; a portion of the lot-sellers; and the men who vend poison for vermin and go about the streets with live rats clinging to, or running about, their persons.

This class of street-sellers also includes many of the very old and the very young; the diseased, crippled, maimed, and blind. These poor creatures sell, and sometimes obtain a charitable penny, by offering to sell such things as boxes of lucifer-matches; cakes of blacking;* boot, stay, and other laces; pins, and sewing and knitting-needles; tapes; cotton-bobbins; garters; pincushions; combs; nutmeg-graters; metal skewers and meat-hooks; hooks and eyes; and shirt-buttons.

The rest of the class may be described as merely street-sellers; toiling, struggling, plodding, itinerant tradesmen.

*Of the Cheap Johns, or Street Hansellers**

This class of street-salesmen, who are perhaps the largest dealers of all in hardware, are not so numerous as they were some few years ago—the Excise Laws having interfered with their business. The principal portion of those I have met are Irishmen, who, notwithstanding, generally 'hail' from Sheffield, and all their sales are effected in an attempt at the Yorkshire dialect, interspersed, however, with an unmistakeable brogue. The brogue is the more apparent when cheap John gets a little out of temper—if his sales are flat, for instance, he'll say, 'By J——s, I don't belaive you've any money with you, or that you've lift any at home, at all, at all. Bad cess to you!'*

There are, however, many English cheap Johns, but few of them are natives of Sheffield or Birmingham, from which towns they invariably 'hail'. Their system of selling is to attract a crowd of persons by an harangue after the following fashion: 'Here I am, the original cheap John from Sheffield. I've not come here to get money; not I; I've come here merely for the good of the public, and to let you see how you've been imposed upon by a parcel of pompous shopkeepers, who are not content with less than 100 per cent. for rubbish. They got up a petition—which I haven't time to read to you just now—offering me a large sum of money to keep away from here. But no, I had too much friendship for you to consent, and here I am, cheap John, born without a shirt, one day while my mother was out, in a haystack; consequently I've no parish, for the cows eat up mine, and therefore I've never no fear of going to the workhouse. I've more money than the parson of the parish—I've in this cart a cargo of useful and cheap goods; can supply you with anything, from a needle to an anchor. Nobody *can* sell as cheap as me, seeing that I gets all my goods upon credit, and never means to pay for them. Now then, what shall we begin with? Here's a beautiful guard-chain; if it isn't silver, it's the same colour—I don't say it isn't silver, nor I don't say it is—in that affair use your own judgment. Now, in the reg'lar way of trade, you shall go into any shop in town, and they will ask you 1*l.* 18*s.* 6*d.* for an article not half so good, so what will you say for this splendid chain? Eighteen and sixpence without the pound? What, that's too much!

Well, then say 17, 16, 15, 14, 13, 12, 11, 10 shillings; what, none of you give ten shillings for this beautiful article? See how it improves a man's appearance' (hanging the chain round his neck). 'Any young man here present wearing this chain will always be shown into the parlour instead of the tap-room;* into the best pew in church, when he and—but the advantages the purchaser of this chain will possess I haven't time to tell. What! no buyers? Why, what's the matter with ye? Have you no money, or no brains? But I'll ruin myself for your sakes. Say 9*s*. for this splendid piece of jewellery—8, 7, 6, 5, 4, 3, 2, 1—a shilling, will anybody give a shilling? Well, here 11*d*., 10*d*., 9*d*., 8*d*., 7*d*., 6½*d*., 6*d*.! Is there ever a buyer at sixpence? Now I'll ask no more and I'll take no less; sell it or never sell it.' The concluding words are spoken with peculiar emphasis, and after saying them the cheap John never takes any lower sum. A customer perhaps is soon obtained for the guard-chain, and then the vendor elevates his voice: 'Sold to a very respectable gentleman, with his mouth between his nose and chin, a most remarkable circumstance. I believe I've just one more—this is better than the last; I must have a shilling for this. Sixpence? To you, sir. Sold again, to a gentleman worth 30,000*l*. a year; only the right owner keeps him out of it. I believe I've just one more; yes, here it is; it's brighterer, longerer, strongerer, and betterer than the last. I must have at least tenpence for this. Well then, 9, 8, 7, 6; take this one for a sixpence. Sold again, to a gentleman, his father's pet and his mother's joy. Pray, sir, does your mother know you're out? Well, I don't think I've any more, but I'll look; yes, here is *one* more. Now this is better than all the rest. Sold again, to a most respectable gentleman, whose mother keeps a chandler's shop, and whose father turns the mangle.' In this manner the cheap John continues to sell his guard-chain, until he has drained his last customer for that particular commodity. He has always his remark to make relative to the purchaser. The cheap John always takes care to receive payment before he hazards his jokes, which I need scarcely remark are ready made, and most of them ancient and worn threadbare, the joint property of the whole fraternity of cheap Johns. After supplying his audience with one particular article, he introduces another: 'Here is a carving-knife and fork, none of your wasters, capital buck-horn handle, manufactured of the best steel, in a regular workmanlike manner; fit for carving in the best style, from a sparrow to a bullock. I don't ask 7*s*. 6*d*. for this—although go over to Mr——, the ironmonger, and he will have the impudence to ask you 15*s*. for a worse article.' (The cheap Johns always make comparisons as to their own prices and the shopkeepers, and sometimes mention their names.) 'I say 5*s*. for the carving-knife and fork. Why, it's an article that'll almost fill your children's bellies by looking at it, and will always make 1 lb. of beef go as far as 6 lb. carved by any other knife and fork. Well, 4*s*., 3*s*., 2*s*., 1*s*. 11*d*., 1*s*. 10*d*., 1*s*. 9*d*., 1*s*. 8*d*., 1*s*. 7*d*., 18*d*. I ask no more, nor I'll take no less.' The salesman throughout his variety of articles indulges in the same jokes, and holds out the same inducements. I give a few.

'*This* is the original teapot' (producing one), 'formerly invented by the Chinese; the first that ever was imported by those celebrated people—only two of them came over in three ships. If I do not sell this to-day, I intend presenting it to the British Museum or the Great Exhibition. It is mostly used for making tea,—sometimes by ladies, for keeping a little drop on the sly; it is an article constructed upon scientific principles, considered to require a lesser quantity of tea to manufacture the largest quantity of tea-water, than any other teapot now in use—largely patronised by the tea-totallers. Now, here's a fine pair of bellows! Any of you want to raise the wind? This is a capital opportunity, if you'll try. I'll tell you how; buy these of me for 3*s*. 6*d*., and go and pawn them for 7*s*. Will you buy 'em, sir? No! well, then, you be blowed! Let's see—I said 3*s*. 6*d*.; it's too little, but as I have said it, they must go; well—3*s*.,' &c. &c. 'Capital article to chastise the children or a drunken husband. Well, take 'em for 1*s*.—I ask no more, and I'll take no less.'

These men have several articles which they sell singly, such as tea-trays, copper kettles, fire-irons, guns, whips, to all of which they have some preamble; but their most attractive lot is a heap of miscellaneous articles:—'I have here a pair of scissors; I only want half-a-crown for them. What! you won't give 1*s*.? well, I'll add something else. Here's a most useful article—a knife with eight blades, and there's not a blade among you all that's more highly polished. This knife's a case of instruments in addition to the blades; here's a corkscrew, a button-hook, a file, and a picker.* For this capital knife and first-rate pair of scissors I ask 1*s*. Well, well, you've no more conscience than a lawyer; here's something else—a pocket-book. This book no gentleman should be without; it contains a diary for every day in the week, an almanack, a ready-reckoner,* a tablet for your own memorandums, pockets to keep your papers, and a splendid pencil with a silver top.

No buyers! I'm astonished; but I'll add another article. Here's a pocket-comb. No young man with any sense of decency should be without a pocket-comb. What looks worse than to see a man's head in an uproar? Some of you look as if your hair hadn't seen a comb for years. Surely I shall get a customer now. What! no buyers—well I never! Here, I'll add half-a-dozen of the very best Britannia metal tea-spoons; and if you don't buy, you must be spoons yourselves. Why, you perfectly astonish me! I really believe if I was to offer all in the shop, myself included, I should not draw 1*s*. out of you. Well, I'll try again. Here, I'll add a dozen of black-lead pencils. Now, then, look at these articles'—(he spreads them out, holding them between his fingers to the best advantage)—'here's a pair of first-rate scissors, that will almost cut of themselves,—this valuable knife, which comprises within itself almost a chest of tools,—a splendid pocket-book, which must add to the respectability and consequence of any man who wears it,—a pocket-comb which possesses the peculiar property of making the hair curl, and dyeing it any colour you wish,—a half-dozen spoons, nothing inferior to silver, and that do not require half the usual quantity of sugar to sweeten your tea,—and a dozen beautiful pencils, at least worth the money I ask for the whole lot. Now, a reasonable price for these articles would be at least 10*s*. 6*d*.; I'll sell them for 1*s*. I ask no more, I'll take no less. Sold again!'

A few of them are not over particular as to the respectability of their transactions. I recollect one purchasing a brick at Sheffield; the brick was packed up in paper, with a knife tied on the outside, it appeared like a package of knives, containing several dozens. The 'cheap John' made out that he bought them as stolen property; the biter was deservedly bitten.

The Crippled Street-Seller of Nutmeg-Graters

I now give an example of one of the classes *driven* to the streets by utter inability to labour. Many ingrained beggars certainly use the street *trade* as a cloak for alms-seeking, but as certainly many more, with every title to our assistance, use it as a means of redemption from beggary. That the nutmeg-grater seller is a noble example of the latter class, I have not the least doubt. His struggles to earn his own living (notwithstanding his physical incapacity even to put the victuals to his mouth after he has earned them), are instances of a nobility

THE STREET-SELLER OF NUTMEG-GRATERS.

[*From a Daguerreotype by* BEARD.]

of pride that are I believe without a parallel. The poor creature's legs and arms are completely withered; indeed he is scarcely more than head and trunk. His thigh is hardly thicker than a child's wrist. His hands are bent inward from contraction of the sinews, the fingers being curled up and almost as thin as the claws of a bird's foot. He is unable even to stand, and cannot move from place to place but on his knees, which are shod with leather caps, like the heels of a clog, strapped round the joint; the soles of his hoots are on the *upper* leathers, that being the part always turned towards the ground while he is crawling along. His countenance is rather handsome than otherwise; the intelligence indicated by his ample forehead* is fully borne out by the testimony as to his sagacity in his business, and the mild expression of his eye by the statements as to his feeling for all others in affliction.

'I sell nutmeg-graters and funnels,' said the cripple to me; 'I sell them at 1*d.* and 1½*d.* a piece. I get mine of the man in whose house I live. He is a tinman, and makes for the street-trade and shops and all. I pay 7*d.* a dozen for them, and I get 12*d.* or 18*d.* a dozen, if I can when I sell them, but I mostly get only a penny a piece—it's quite a chance if I have a customer at 1½*d.* Some days I sell only three—some days not one—though I'm out from ten o'clock till six. The most I ever took was 3*s.* 6*d.* in a day. Some weeks I hardly clear my expenses—and they're between 7*s.* and 8*s.* a week; for not being able to dress and ondress myself, I'm obligated to pay some one to do it for me—I think I don't clear more than 7*s.* a week take one week with another. When I don't make that much, I go without—sometimes friends who are kind to me give me a trifle, or else I should starve. As near as I can judge, I *take* about 15*s.* a week, and out of that I clear about 6*s.* or 7*s.* I pay for my meals as I have them—3*d.* or 4*d.* a meal. I pay every night for my lodging as I go in, if I can; but if not my landlady lets it run a night or two. I give her 1*s.* a week for my washing and looking after me, and 1*s.* 6*d.* for my lodging. When I do very well I have three meals a day, but it's oftener only two—breakfast and supper—unless of Sunday. On a wet day when I can't get out, I often go without food. I may have a bit of bread and butter give me, but that's all—then I lie a-bed. I feel miserable enough when I see the rain come down of a week day, I can tell you. Ah, it *is* very miserable indeed lying in bed all day, and in a lonely room, without perhaps a person to come near one—helpless as I am—and hear the rain beat against the windows, and all that without nothing to put in your lips. It's very hard work indeed is street-selling for such as me. I can't walk no distance. I suffer a great deal of pains in my back and knees. Sometimes I go in a barrow, when I'm travelling any great way. When I go only a short way I crawl along on my knees and toes. The most I've ever crawled is two miles. When I get home afterwards, I'm in great pain. My knees swell dreadfully, and they're all covered with blisters, and my toes ache awful. I've corns all on top of them.

'Often after I've been walking, my limbs and back ache so badly that I can get no sleep. Across my lines it feels as if I'd got some great weight, and my knees are in a heat, and throb, and feel as if a knife was running into them. When I go up-stairs I have to crawl upon the back of my hands and my knees. I can't lift nothing to my mouth. The sinews of my hands is all contracted. I am obliged to have things held to my lips for me to drink, like a child. I *can* use a knife and fork by leaning my arm on the table and then stooping my head to it. I can't wash nor ondress myself. Sometimes I think of my helplessness a great deal. The thoughts of it used to throw me into fits at one time—very bad. It's the Almighty's will that I am so, and I must abide by it. People says, as they passes me in the streets, "Poor fellow, it's a shocking thing"; but very seldom they does any more than pity me; some lays out a halfpenny or a penny with me, but the most of 'em goes on about their business. Persons looks at me a good bit when I go into a strange place. I *do* feel it very much, that I haven't the power to get my living or to do a thing for myself, but I never begged for nothing. I'd sooner starve than I'd do that.'

Of the Life of a Street-Seller of Dog-Collars

'I was born in Brewer-street, St James,' he said, in answer to my questions; 'I am 73 years of age. My father and mother were poor people; I never went to school; my father died while I was young; my mother used to go out charing, she couldn't afford to pay for schooling, and told me, I must look out and *yearn* my own living while I was a mere chick. At ten years of age I went to sea in the merchant sarvice. While I was in the merchant sarvice, I could get good wages, for I soon knowed my duty. I was always of an industrious turn, and never liked to be idle; don't you see what I mean. In '97 I was pressed* on board the INCONSTANT frigate; I was paid off six months arterwards, but hadn't much to take, and that, like all other young men who hadn't larned the dodges of life, I spent very soon; but I never got drunk—thank God!' said the old man, 'I never got drunk, or I shouldn't ha been what I am now at 73 years of age. I was drafted into the Woolwich 44-gun ship; from her to the OVERISAL.' I inquired how the name of the ship was spelt; 'Oh I am not scholard enough, for that there,' he replied, 'tho' I did larn to read and write when abord a man of war. I larned myself. But you must look into a *Dutch dictionary*, for it's a Dutch name. I then entered on board the AMPHINE frigate, and arter I had sarved some months in her, I entered the merchant sarvice again, and arter that I went to Greenland to the whale-fishery—they calls me here in the college' (he is now an inmate of Greenwich Hospital*) ' "*Whaler Ben*", but I ar'n't affronted—most on 'em here have nicknames. I went three voyages besides to the West Ingees. I never got drunk even there, though I was obliged to drink rum; it wouldn't ha done to ha drunk the water NEAT, there was so many insects in it. When my sailor's life was over I comes to Liverpool and marries a wife—aye and as good a wife as any poor man ever had in England. I had saved a goodish bit o' money, nearly 300*l.*, for I was not so foolish as some of the poor sailors, who yearns their money like horses and spends it like asses, I say. Well we sets up a shop—a chandler shop—in Liverpool: me and my old 'ooman does; and I also entered into the pig-dealing line. I used to get some of my pigs from Ireland, and some I used to breed myself, but I was very misfortunate. You recollect the year when the disease was among the cattle, in course you recollects that; well, sir, I lost 24 pigs and a horse in one year, and that was a good loss for a poor man, wer'n't it? I thought it werry hard, for I'd worked hard for my money at sea, and I was always werry careful, arter I knowed what life was. My poor wife too used to trust a good deal in the shop, and by-and-by, behold you, me and my old 'ooman was on our beam ends.* My wife was took ill too—and, for the purpose of getting the best adwice, I brings her to London, but her cable had run out, and she died, and I've been a poor forlorned creatur' ever since. You wouldn't think it, but arter that I never slept on a bed for seven years. I had blankets and my clothes—but what I means is that I never had a bed to lie on. I sold most of my bits o' things to bury my wife. I didn't relish applying to the parish. I kept a few sticks tho', for I don't like them ere lodging-houses. I can't be a werry bad kerackter, for I was seven years under one landlord, and

THE STREET-SELLER OF DOGS' COLLARS.

[*From a Daguerreotype by* BEARD.]

I warrant me if I wanted a room agin he would let me have one. Arter my wife died, knowing some'at about ropes I gets work at Maberley's, the great contractors—in course you knows *him*. I made rope traces* for the artillery; there's a good deal of leather-work about the traces, and stitching them, you see, puts me up to the making of dogs'-collars. I was always handy with my fingers, and can make shoes or anythink. I can work now as well as ever I could in my life, only my eyes isn't so good. Ain't it curious now, sir, that wot a man larns in his fingers he never forgets? Well being out o' work, I was knocking about for some time, and then I was adwised to apply for a board to carry at one of them cheap tailors, but I didn't get none; so I takes to hawking link buttons* and key rings, and buys some brass dog-collars; it was them brass collars as made me bethought myself as I could make some leather ones. Altho' I had been better off I didn't think it any disgrace to get a honest living. The leather collars is harder to make than the brass ones, only the brass ones wants more implements. There are about a dozen selling in the streets as makes brass-collars—there's not much profit on the brass ones. People says there's nothing like leather, and I thinks they are right. Well, sir, as I was a telling you, I commences the leather-collar making,—in course I didn't make 'em as well at first as I do now. It was werry hard lines at the best of times. I used to get up at 4 o'clock in the morning in the summer time, and make my collars; then I'd turn out about 9, and keep out until 7 or 8 at night. I seldom took more than 2*s*. per day. What profit did I get out of 2*s*.? Why, lor bless you, sir! if I hadn't made them myself, I shouldn't have got no profit at all. But as it was, if I took 2*s*., the profits was from 1*s*. to 1*s*. 6*d*.; howsomever, sometimes I didn't take 6*d*. Wet days too used to run me aground altogether; my rheumatics used to bore me always when the rain come down, and then I couldn't get out to sell. If I'd any leather at them times I used to make it up; but if I hadn't none, why I was obligated to make the best on it. Oh, sir! you little knows what I've suffered; many a banyan day* I've had in my little room—upon a wet day—aye, and other days too. Why, I think I'd a starved if it hadn't a been for the 'bus-men* about Hungerford-market. They are good lads them there 'bus lads to such as me; they used to buy my collars when they didn't want them. Ask any on 'em if they know anything about old Tom, the collar-maker, and see if they don't flare up and respect me. They used sometimes to raffle my collars and give 'em back to me. Mr Longstaff too, the landlord of the

Hungerford Arms—I believe it's called the Hungerford Hotel—has given me something to eat very often when I was hungry, and had nothing myself. There's what you call a hor'nary there every day. You knows what I mean—gentlemen has their grub there at so much a head, or so much a belly it should be, I says, I used to come in for the scraps, and werry thankful I was for them I can assure you. Yes, Mr Longstaff is what you may call a good man. He's what you calls a odd man, and a odd man's always a good man. All I got to say is, "God bless him!" he's fed me many time when I've been hungry. I used to light upon other friends too,—landlords of public-houses, where I used to hawk my collars; they seemed to take to me somehow; it wer'n't for what I spent in their houses I'm sure, seeing as how I'd nothing to spend. I had no pension for my sarvice, and so I was adwised to apply for admission to "the house here" (Greenwich Hospital). I goes to Somerset-House;* another poor fellow was making a application at the same time; but I didn't nothing till one very cold day, when I was standing quite miserable like with my collars. I'd been out several hours and hadn't taken a penny, when up comes the man as wanted to get into the house, running with all his might to me. I thought he was going to tell me he had got into the house, and I was glad on it, for, poor fellow, he was werry bad oft; howsomever he says to me, "Tom," says he, "they wants you at the Admirality." "Does they?" says I, and 'cordingly away I goes; and arter telling the admiral my sarvice, and answering a good many questions as he put to me, the admiral says, says he, "The order will be made out; you shall go into the house." I think the admiral knowed me or somethink about me, you see. I don't know his name, and it wouldn't ha' done to have axed. God bless him, whoever he is, I says, and shall say to my dying day; it seemed like Providence. I hadn't taken a ha'penny all that day; I was cold and hungry, and suffering great pain from my rheumatics. Thank God,' exclaimed the old man in conclusion, 'I am quite comfortable now. I've everythink I want except a little more tea and shuggar, but I'm quite content, and thank God for all his mercies.'

Of the Tally Packman

The pedlar tallyman is a hawker who supplies his customers with goods, receiving payment by weekly instalments, and derives his name from the tally or score he keeps with his customers. Linen drapery—or at least the general routine of linen-draper's stock, as silk-mercery,* hosiery, woollen cloths, &c.—is the most prevalent trade of the tallyman. There are a few shoemakers and some household furniture dealers who do business in the tally or 'score' system; but the great majority are linen-drapers, though some of them sell household furniture as well. The system is generally condemned as a bad one; as leading to improvidence in the buyer and rapacity in the seller. There are many who have incurred a tally debt, and have never been able to 'get a-head of it', but have been kept poor by it all their lives. Some few, however, may have been benefited by the system, and as an outfit for a young man or woman entering service is necessary—when the parties are too poor to pay ready money—it is an accommodation. I have never heard any of the tallyman's customers express an opinion upon the subject, other than that they wish they had done with the tallyman, or could do without him.

The system does not prevail to so great an extent as it did some years back. The pedlar or hawking tallyman travels for orders, and consequently is said not to require a hawker's licence. The great majority of the tally-packmen are Scotchmen. The children who are set to watch the arrival of the tallyman, and apprise the mother of his approach, when not convenient to pay, whisper instead of 'Mother, here's the Tallyman,' 'Mother, here's the Scotchman.' These men live in private houses, which they term their warehouse; they are many of them proprietors themselves in a small way, and conduct the whole of their business unassisted. Their mode of doing business is as follows:—they seldom knock at a door except they have a customer upon whom they call for the weekly instalment, but if a respectable-looking female happens to be standing at her door, she, in all probability, is accosted by the Scotchman, 'Do you require anything in my way to-day, ma'am?' This is often spoken in broad Scotch, the speaker trying to make it sound as much like English as possible. Without waiting for a reply, he then runs over a programme of the treasures he has to dispose of, emphasising all those articles which he considers likely to suit the taste of the person he addresses. She doesn't want perhaps any—she has no money to spare then. 'She may want something in his way another day, may-be,' says the tallyman. 'Will she grant him permission to exhibit some beautiful shawls—the last new fashion? or some new style of dress, just out, and an extraordinary bargain?' The man's importunities, and the curiosity of the lady, introduce him into the apartment,—an acquaintance is called in to pass her opinion upon the tallyman's stock. Should she still demur, he says, 'O, I'm sure your husband cannot object—he will not be so unreasonable; besides, consider the easy mode of payment, you'll only have to pay 1*s.* 6*d.* a week for every pound's worth of goods you take; why it's like nothing; you possess yourself of respectable clothing and pay for them in such an easy manner that you never miss it; well, I'll call next week. I shall leave you this paper.' The paper left is a blank form to be filled up by the husband, and runs thus:—'I agree on behalf of my wife to pay, by weekly instalments of 1*s.* 6*d.* upon every pound's worth of good she may purchase.' This proceeding is considered necessary by the tallymen, as the judges in the Court of Requests* now so frequently decide against him, where the husband is not cognisant of the transaction.

These preliminaries being settled, and the question having been asked what business the husband is—where he works—and (if it can be done without offence) what are his wages? The Scotchman takes stock of the furniture, &c.; the value of what the room contains gives him a sufficiently correct estimate of the circumstances of his customers. His next visit is to the nearest chandler's shop, and there as blandly as possible he inquires into the credit, &c., of Mr ——. If he deal, however, with the chandler, the tallyman accounts it a bad omen, as people in easy circumstances seldom resort to such places. 'It is unpleasant to me,' he says to the chandler, 'making these inquiries; 'but Mrs —— wishes to open an account with me, and I should like to oblige them if I thought my money was safe.' 'Do *you* trust them, and what sort of payers are they?' According to the reply—the tallyman determines upon his course. But he rarely stops here; he makes inquiries also at the greengrocer's, the beer shop, &c.

The persons who connect themselves with the tallyman, little know the inquisition they subject themselves to.

When the tallyman obtains a customer who pays regularly, he is as importunate for her to recommend him another customer, as he originally was to obtain her custom. Some tallymen who keep shops have 'travellers' in their employ, some of whom have salaries, while others receive a percentage upon all payments, and do not suffer any loss upon bad debts. Notwithstanding the caution of the tallyman, he is frequently 'victimised'. Many pawn the goods directly they have obtained them, and in some instances spend the money in drink. Their many losses, as a matter of course, *somebody* must make good. It therefore becomes necessary for them to charge a higher price for their commodities than the regular trader.

However charitably inclined the tallyman may be at first, he soon becomes, I am told, inured to scenes of misery, while the sole feeling in his mind at length is, 'I will have my money'; for he is often tricked, and in some cases most impudently victimised. I am told by a tallyman that he once supplied goods to the amount of 2*l*., and when he called for the first instalment, the woman said she didn't intend to pay, the goods didn't suit her, and she would return them. The tallyman expressed his willingness to receive them back, whereupon she presented him a pawnbroker's duplicate. She had pledged them an hour after obtaining them. This was done in a court in the presence of a dozen women, who all chuckled with delight at the joke.

The cases are not a few where ruin has followed a connection with the tallymen. I will particularize one instance related to me on good authority. A lawyer's clerk married, when young, a milliner; his salary was a guinea per week, and he and his wife had agreed to 'get on in the world'. They occupied furnished lodgings at first, but soon accumulated furniture of their own, and every week added some little useful article towards their household stock. 'At the end of a year,' said the individual in question, 'I had as comfortable a little home as any man would wish to possess; I was fond of it too, and would rather have been there than anywhere else. My wife frequently wished to obtain credit; "it would be so easy," said she, "to pay a trifling instalment, and then we could obtain immediately whatever we might want." I objected, and preferred supplying our wants gradually, knowing that for ready money I could purchase to much better advantage. Consequently we still kept progressing, and I was really happy. Judge my astonishment one day, when I came home, and found an execution was in the house. My wife had run in debt with the tallyman unknown to me. Summonses had been served, which by some means she had concealed from me. The goods which I had taken so much pains to procure were seized and sold. But this was not all. My wife grew so much alarmed at the misery she had caused that she fled from me, and I have never seen her but once since. This occurred seven years ago, and she has been for some time the companion of those who hold their virtue of little worth. For some time after this I cared not what became of me; I lost my situation, and sunk to be a supernumerary for 1*s.* a night at one of the theatres. Here, after being entrusted with a line to speak, I eventually rose to a "general utility man", at 12*s.* per week. With this and some copying, that I occasionally obtain from the law-stationers, I manage to live, but far from comfortably, for I never think of saving now, and only look out for copying when I stand in need of more money. I am always poor, and scarcely ever have a shilling to call my own.'

Of the 'Duffers' or Hawkers of Pretended Smuggled Goods

Of 'duffers' and 'lumpers', as regards the sale of textile fabrics, there are generally, I am informed, about twenty in London. At such times as Epsom, Ascot-heath, or Goodwood races, however, there is, perhaps, not one. All have departed to prey, if possible, upon the countrymen. Eight of them are Jews, and the majority of the others are Irishmen. They are generally dressed as sailors, and some wear either fur caps, or cloth ones, with gilt bands round them, as if they were the mates or stewards of ships. They look out for any likely victim at public-houses, and sometimes accost persons in the streets—first looking carefully about them, and hint that they are smugglers, and have the finest and cheapest 'Injy'* handkerchiefs ever seen. These goods are now sold in 'pieces' of three handkerchiefs. When times were better, I was told, they were in pieces of four, five, and six. One street-seller said to me, 'Yes, I know the "duffers"; all of them. They do more business than you might think. Everybody likes a smuggled thing; and I should say these men, each of the "duffers", tops his 1*l.* a week, clear profit.' I am assured that one of the classes most numerously victimised is a body who generally account themselves pretty sharp, viz. gentlemen's grooms, and coachmen at the several mews. Sailors are the best customers, and the vicinity of the docks the best locality for this trade; for the hawker of pretended smuggled goods always does most business among the 'tars'. The mock handkerchiefs are damped carefully with a fine sponge, before they are offered for sale; and they are often strongly perfumed, some of the Jews supplying cheap perfumes, or common 'scents'. When the 'duffer' thinks he may venture upon the assertion, he assures a customer that this is 'the smell the handkerchiefs brought with 'em from foreign parts, as they was smuggled in a bale of spices!' The trade however is not without its hazards; for I am informed that the 'duffers' sometimes, on attempting their impositions imprudently, and sometimes on being discovered before they can leave the house, get soundly thrashed. They have, of course, no remedy.

There is a peculiar style among the 'duffers'; they never fold their goods neatly—the same as drapers do, but thrust them into the pack, in a confused heap, as if they did not understand their value—or their business. There are other classes of 'duffers' whose calling is rather more hazardous than the licensed-hawker 'duffer'. 'I have often thought it strange', says a correspondent, 'that these men could induce any one to credit the fact of their being sailors, for, notwithstanding the showy manner in which they chew their quid,* and the jack-tar like fashion in which they suffer their whiskers to grow, there is such a fresh-waterfied appearance about them, that they look no more like a regular mariner than the supernumerary seamen in a nautical drama, at the Victoria Theatre. Yet they obtain victims readily. Their mode of proceeding in the streets is to accost their intended dupes, while walking by their side; they usually speak in a half whisper, as they keep pace with them and look mysteriously around to see if there be any of "them ere Custom-house sharks afloat". They address the simple-looking passers by thus: "Shipmate" (here they take off their fur-cap and spit their quid into it)—"shipmate, I've just come ashore arter a long voyage—and splice me but I've something in the locker that'll be of service to you; and, shiver my timbers" (they are very profuse in nautical terms), "you shall have it at your own price, for I'm determined to have a spree, and I haven't a shot in the locker; helm's a-lee;* just let's turn into this creek, and I'll show you what it is" (perhaps he persuades his dupe down a court, or to a neighbouring public-house). "Now here is a beautiful piece of *Ingy* handkerchiefs." (They are the coarsest description of spun not *thrown* silk, well stiffened into stoutness, and cost the 'duffer' perhaps 15*d*. each; but as business is always done on the sly, in a hurry, and to escape observation, an examination seldom or never takes place.) "I got 'em on shore in spite of those pirates, the Custom-house officers. You shall have 'em cheap, there's half a dozen on 'em, they cost me 30*s*. at Madras, you shall have 'em for the same money." (The victim, may be, is not inclined to purchase. The pretended tar, however, must have money.) "Will you give me 25*s*. for them?" he says; "d——n it, a pound? Shiver my topsails, you don't want them any cheaper than that, do you!" The "duffer" says this to make his dupe believe that he really does want the goods, or has offered a price for them. Perhaps if the "duffer" cannot extort more he takes 10*s*. for the half dozen "Ingy" handkerchiefs, the profit being thus about 2*s*. 6*d*.; but more frequently he gets 100 and even 200 per cent on his transactions according to the gullibility of his customers. The "duffer" deals also in cigars; he accosts his victim in the same style as when selling handkerchiefs, and gives himself the same sailor-like airs.

'Sometimes the "duffers" visit the obscure streets in London, where there are small chandlers' shops; one of them enters, leaving his mate outside to give him the signal in case the enemy heaves in sight. He requests to be served with some trifling article—when if he approve of the physiognomy of the shopkeeper, and consider him or her likely to be victimized—he ventures an observation as to how enormously everything is taxed (though to one less innocent it might appear unusual for a sailor to talk politics); "even this 'ere baccy", he says, taking out his quid, "I can't chew, without paying a tax; but", he adds, chuckling—"us sailor chaps sometimes shirks the Custom-house lubbers, sharp as they are." (Here his companion outside puts his head in at the door, and, to make the scene as natural as possible, says, "Come, Jack, don't stop there all night spinning your yarns; come, bear a hand, or I shall part convoy.") "Oh, heave to a bit longer, my hearty," replies the "duffer", "I will be with you in the twinkling of a marling spike.* I'll tell you what we've got, marm, and if you likes to buy it you shall have it cheap, for me and my mate are both short of rhino.* We've half-a-dozen pounds of tea—you can weigh it if you like—and you shall have the lot for 12*s*." Perhaps there is an immediate purchase, but if 12*s*. is refused, then 10*s*. 8*s*. or 6*s*. is asked, until a sale be effected, after which the sailors make their exit as quickly as possible. Then the chandler's-shop keeper begins to exult over the bargain he or she has made, and to examine more minutely the contents of the neatly packed, and tea-like looking packet thus bought. It proves to be lined with a profuse quantity of tea lead, and though some Chinese characters are marked on the outside, it is discovered on opening to contain only half-a-pound of tea, the remainder consisting principally of chopped hay. The "duffers" enact the same part, and if a purchaser buy 10 lbs. of the smuggled article, then 9 lbs. at least consist of the same chopped hay.

'Sometimes the "duffers" sell all their stock to one individual. No sooner do they dispose of the handkerchiefs to a dupe, than they introduce the smuggled tobacco to the notice of the unsuspecting customer; then they palm off their cigars, next their tea, and lastly, as the "duffer" is determined to raise as much money as he can "to have his spree", "why d——e," he exclaims to his victim—"I'll sell you my watch. It cost me 6*l.* at Portsmouth—give me 3*l.* for it and it's yours, shipmate. Well, then, 2*l.*—1*l.*" The watch, I need not state, is made solely for sale.

'It is really astonishing', adds my informant, 'how these men ever succeed, for their look denotes cunning and imposition, and their proceedings have been so often exposed in the newspapers that numbers are alive to their tricks, and warn others when they perceive the "duffers" endeavouring to victimise them; but, as the thimble-men* say, "There's a fool born every minute." '

The Blind Street-Seller of Boot-Laces

'I can't see the least light in the world—not the brightest sun that ever shone. I have pressed my eye-balls—they are quite decayed, you see; but I have pushed them in, and they have merely hurt me, and the water has run from them faster than ever. I have never seen any colours when I did so.' (This question was asked to discover whether the illusion called 'peacock's feathers'* could still be produced by pressure on the nerve.) 'I have been struck on the eye since I have been blind, and then I have seen a flash of fire like lightning. I know it's been like that, because I've seen the lightning sometimes, when it's been very vivid, even since I was stone blind. It was terrible pain when I was struck on the eye. A man one day was carrying some chairs along the street, and struck me right in the eye ball with the end of the leg of one of the chairs; and I fell to the ground with the pain. I thought my heart was coming out of my mouth; then I saw the brightest flash that ever I saw, either before or since I was blind.' (I irritated the ball of the eye with the object of discovering whether the nerve was decayed, but found it impossible to produce any luminous impression—though I suspect this arose principally from the difficulty of getting him to direct his eye in the proper direction.) 'I know the difference of colours, because I remember them; but I can't distinguish them by my touch, nor do I think that any blind man in the world ever could. I have heard of blind people playing at cards, but it's impossible they can do so any other way than by having them marked. I know many that plays cards that way.' He was given two similar substances, but of different colours, to feel, but could not distinguish between them—both were the same to him, he said, 'with the exception that one felt stiffer than the other. I know hundreds of people myself—and they know hundreds more—and none of us has ever heard of one that could tell colours by the feel. There's blind people in the school can tell the colours of their rods; but they do so by putting their tongue to them, and so they can distinguish them that's been dipped in copperas* from them that hasn't. I know blind people can take a clock to pieces, and put it together again, as well as any person that can see. Blind people gets angry when they hear people talk of persons seeing with their fingers. A man has told me that a blind person in St James's workhouse could read the newspaper with his fingers,* but that, the blind know, is quite impossible.'

Many blind men can, I am told, distinguish between the several kinds of wood by touch alone. Mahogany, oak, ash, elm, deal, they say, have all a different feel. They declare it is quite ridiculous, the common report, that blind people can discern colours by the touch. One of my informants, who assured me that he was considered to be one of the cleverest of blind people, told me that he had made several experiments on this subject, and never could distinguish the least difference between black or red, or white, or yellow, or blue, or, indeed, any of the mixed colours. 'My wife', said one, 'went blind so young, that she doesn't never remember having seen the light; and I am often sorry for her that she has no idea of what a beautiful thing light or colours is. We often talk about it together, and then she goes a little bit melancholy, because I can't make her understand what the daylight is like, or the great delight that there is in seeing it. I've often asked whether she knows that the daylight and the candlelight is of different colours, and she has told me she thinks they are the same; but then she has no notion of colours at all. Now, it's such people as these I pities.' I told the blind man of Saunderson's* wonderful effect of imagination in conceiving that the art of seeing was similar to that of a series of threads being drawn from the distant object to the eye; and he was delighted with the explanation, saying, 'he could hardly tell how a born blind man could come at such an idea'. On talking with this man, he told me he remembered having seen a looking-glass once—his mother was standing putting her cap on before it, and he thought he never saw anything so pretty as the reflection of the half-mourning gown she had on, and the white feathery pattern upon it (he was five years old then). He also remembered having seen his shadow, and following it across the street; these were the only two objects he can call to mind. He told me that he knew many blind men who could not comprehend how things could be seen, round or square, *all at once*; they are obliged, they say, to pass their fingers all over them; and how it is that the shape of a thing can be known in an instant, they cannot possibly imagine. I found out that this blind man fancied the looking-glass reflected only one object at once—only the object that was immediately in front of it; and when I told him that, looking in the glass, I could see everything in the room, and even himself, with my back turned towards him, he smiled with agreeable astonishment. He said, 'You see how little I have thought about the matter.' There was a blind woman of his acquaintance, he informed me, who could thread the smallest needle with the finest hair in a minute, and never miss once. 'She'll do it in a second. Many blind women thread their needles with their tongues: the woman who stitches by the Polytechnic* always does so.' My informant was very fond of music. One of the blind makes his own teeth, he told me; his front ones have all been replaced by one long bit of bone which he has fastened to the stumps of his two eye teeth: he makes them out of any old bit of bone he can pick up. He files them and drills a hole through them to fasten them into his head, and eats his food with them. He is obliged to have teeth because he plays the clarionet in the street. 'Music', he said, 'is our only enjoyment, we all like to listen to it and learn it.' It affects them greatly, they tell me, and if a lively tune is played, they can hardly help dancing. 'Many a tune I've danced to so that I could hardly walk the next day,' said one. Almost all of the blind men are clever at reckoning. It seems to come natural to them after the loss of their sight. By counting they say they spend many a dull hour—it appears to be all mental arithmetic with them, for they never aid their calculations by their fingers or any signs whatever. My informant knew a blind man who could reckon on what day it was new moon for a hundred years back, or when it will be new moon a century to come—he had never had a book read to him on the subject in his life—he was one of the blind wandering musicians. My informant told me he often sits for hours and calculates how many quarters of ounces there are in a ship-load of tea, and such like things. Many of the blind are very partial to the smell of flowers. My informant knew one blind man about the streets who always would have some kind of smelling flowers in his room.

'The blind are very ingenious; oh, very!' said one to me, 'they can do anything that they can feel. One blind man who kept a lodging-house at Manchester and had a wife fond of drink, made a little chest of drawers (about two feet high), in which he used to put his money, and so cleverly did he arrange it that neither his wife nor any one else could get at the money without breaking the drawers all to pieces. Once while her blind husband was on his travels, she opened every drawer by means of false keys, and though she took each one out, she could find no means to get at the money, which she could hear jingling inside when she shook it. At last she got so excited over it that she sent for a carpenter, and even he was obliged to confess that he could not get to it without taking the drawers to pieces. The same blind man had a great fancy for white mice, and made a little house for them out of pieces of wood cut into the shape of bricks: there were doors, windows, and all,' said my informant. The blind are remarkable for the quickness of their hearing—one man assured me he could hear the lamp-posts in the streets, and, indeed, any *substance* (any solid thing he said) that he passed in the street, provided it be as high as his ear; if it were below that he could not *hear* it so well.

'Do you know, I can hear any substance in the street as I pass it by, even the lamp-post or a dead wall—anything that's the height of my head, let it be ever so small, just as well, and tell what it is as well as you as can see. One night I was coming home—you'll be surprised to hear this—along Burlington-gardens, between twelve and one o'clock, and a gentleman was following me. I knew he was not a poor man by his walk, but I didn't consider he was watching me. I just heerd when I got between Sackville-street and Burlington-street. Oh, I knows every inch of the street, and I can go as quick as you can, and walk four mile an hour; know where I am all the while. I can tell the difference of the streets by the sound of my ear—a wide street and a narrow street—I can't tell a long street till I get to the bottom of it. I can tell when I come to an opening or a turning just by the click on the ear, without either my touching with hand or stick. Well, as I was saying, this gentleman was noticing me, and just as I come to turn up Cork-street, which, you know, is my road to go into Bond-street, on my way home; just as I come into Cork-street, and was going to turn round the corner, the sergeant of police was coming from Bond-street, at the opposite corner of Cork-street, I heerd him, and he just stopped to notice me, but didn't know the gentleman was noticing me too. I whipped round the corner as quick as any man that had his sight, and said, "Good night, policeman." I can tell a policeman's foot anywhere, when he comes straight along in his regular way while on his beat, and they all know it too. I can't tell it where there's a noise, but in the stillness of the night nothing would beat me.'

Many of the blind are very fond of keeping birds and animals; some of them keep pigeons in one of their rooms, others have cocks and hens, and others white mice and rabbits, and almost all have dogs, though all are not led about by them. Some blind men take delight in having nothing but bull-dogs, not to lead them, but solely for fancy. Nobody likes a dog so much as a blind man, I am told—'they can't—the blind man is so much beholden to his dog, he does him such favours and sarvices. With my dog I can go to any part of London as independent as any one who has got his sight. Yesterday afternoon when I left your house, sir, I was ashamed of going through the street. People was a saying, "Look'ee there, that's the man as says he's blind." I was going so quick, it was so late you know, they couldn't make it out, but without my dog I must have crawled along, and always be in great fear. The name of my present dog is "KEEPER"; he is a mongrel breed; I have had him nine years, and he is with me night and day, goes to church with me and all. If I go out without him, he misses me, and then he scampers all through the streets where I am in the habit of going, crying and howling after me, just as if he was fairly out of his mind. It's astonishing. Often, before my first blind wife died (for I've been married twice to blind women, and once to a seeing woman), I used to say I'd sooner lose my wife than my dog; but when I did lose her I was sorry that ever I did say so. I didn't know what it was. I'm sorry for it yet, and ever will be sorry for it; she was a very good woman, and had fine principles. I shall never get another that I liked so much as the first. My dog knows every word I say to him. Tell him to turn right or left, or cross over, and whip! round he goes in a moment. Where I go for my tobacco, at the shop in Piccadilly, close to the Arcades*—it's down six or seven steps, straight down—and when I tells Keeper to go to the baccy shop, off he is, and drags me down the steps, with the people after me, thinking he's going to break my neck down the place, and the people stands on top the steps making all kinds of remarks, while I'm below. If he was to lose me to-night or to-morrow, he'd come back here and rise the whole neighbourhood. He knows any public-house, no matter whether he was there before or not; just whisper to him, go to the public-house, and away he scampers and drags me right into the first he comes to. Directly I whisper to him, go to the public-house, he begins playing away with the basket he has in his mouth, throwing it up and laying it down—throwing it and laying it down for pleasure; he gets his rest there, and that's why he's so pleased. It's the only place I can go to in my rounds to sit down. Oh, he's a dear clever fellow. Now, only to show you how faithful he is, one night last week I was coming along Burlington-gardens, and I stopped to light my pipe as I was coming home, and I let him loose to play a bit and get a drink; and after I had lit my pipe I walked on, for I knew the street very well without any guide. I didn't take notice of the dog, for I thought he was following me. I was just turning into Clifford-street when I heard the cries of him in Burlington-gardens. I know his cry, let him be ever so far away; the screech that he set up was really quite dreadful; it would grieve anybody to hear him. So I puts my fingers in my mouth and gives a loud whistle; and at last he heard me, and then up he comes tearing along and panting away as if his heart was in his mouth; and when he gets up to me he jumped up to me right upon my back, and screams like—as if really he wanted to speak—you can't call it panting, because it's louder than that, and he does pant when he a'n't tired at all; all I can say is, it's for all the world like his speaking, and I understands it as such. If I say a cross word to him after he's lost—such as, ah, you rascal, you—he'll just stand of one side, and give a cry just like a Christian. I've known him break the windows up two story high when I've left him behind, and down he would have been after me only he durstn't jump out. I've had Keeper nine year. The dog I had before him was Blucher; he was a mongrel too; he had a tail like a wolf, an ear like a fox, and a face black like a monkey. I had him thirteen year. He was as clever as Keeper, but not so much loved as he is. At last he went blind; he was about two year losing his sight. When I found his eyes was getting bad I got Keeper. The way I first noticed him going blind was when I would come to cross a street on my way home; at nightfall the shade of the house on the opposite side, as we was crossing, would frighten him and drive him in the middle of the road; and he wouldn't draw to the pavement till he found he was wrong; and then after that he began to run again the lamp-posts in the dark; when he did this he'd cry out just like a Christian. I was sorry for him, and he knowed that, for I used to fret. I was sorry for him on account of my own affliction. At last I was obligated to take to Keeper. I got him of another blind man, but he had no larning in him when he come to me. I was a long time teaching him, for I didn't do it all at once. I could have teached him in a week, but I used to let the old dog have a run, while I put Keeper into the collar for a bit' (here the blind man was some time before he could proceed for his tears), 'and so he larnt all he knows, little by little. Now Keeper and Blucher used to agree pretty well; but I've got another dog now, named Dash, and Keeper's as jealous of him as a woman is of a man. If I say, "Come Keeper, come and have the collar on," I may call twenty times before he'll come; but if I say, "Dash, come and have the collar on," Keeper's there the first word, jumping up agin me, and doing anything but speak. At last my old Blucher went stone blind, as bad as his master; it was, poor thing; and then he used to fret so when I went out without him that I couldn't bear it, and so got at length to take him always with me, and then he used to follow the knock of my stick. He done so for about six months, and then I was one night going along Piccadilly and I stops speaking to a policeman, and Blucher misses me; he couldn't hear where I was for the noise of the carriages. He didn't catch the sound of my stick, and couldn't hear my voice for the carriages, so he went seeking me into the middle of the road, and there a buss run over him, poor thing. I heerd him scream out and I whistled to him, and he came howling dreadful on to the pavement again. I didn't think he was so much hurt then, for I puts the collar on him to take him safe back, and he led me home blind as he was. The next morning he couldn't rise up at all, his hind parts was useless to him. I took him in my arms and found he couldn't move. Well, he never eat nor drink nothing for a week, and got to be in such dreadful pain that I was forced to have him killed. I got a man to drown him in a bag. I couldn't have done it myself for all the world. It would have been as bad to me as killing a Christian. I used to grieve terribly after I'd lost him. I couldn't get him off my mind. I had had him so many years, and he had been with me night and day, my constant companion, and the most faithful friend I ever had, except Keeper: there's nothing in the world can beat Keeper for faithfulness—nothing.'

Of the Street-Sellers of Corn-Salve

The patter of these traders is always to the same purport (however differently expressed)—the long-tested efficacy and the unquestionable cheapness of their remedies. The vendors are glib and unhesitating; but some, owing, I imagine, to a repetition of the same words, as they move from one part of a thoroughfare to another, or occupy a pitch, have acquired a monotonous tone, little calculated to impress a street audience—to effect which a man must be, or appear to be, in earnest. The patter of one of these dealers, who sells corn-salve on fine evenings, and works the public-houses, 'with anything likely', on wet evenings, is, from his own account, in the following words:

'Here you have a speedy remedy for every sort of corn! Your hard corn, soft corn, blood corn, black corn, old corn, new corn, wart, or bunion, can be safely cured in three days! Nothing further to do but spread this salve on a piece of glove-leather, or wash-leather, and apply it to the place. Art and nature does the rest. Either corns, warts, or bunions, cured for one penny.'

This, however, is but as the announcement of the article on sale, and is followed by a recapitulation of the many virtues of that peculiar recipe; but, as regards the major part of these street-traders, the recapitulation is little more than a change of words, if that. There are, however, one and sometimes two patterers, of acknowledged powers, who every now and then sell corn-salve—for the restlessness of this class of people drives them to incessant changes in their pursuits—and their oratory is of a higher order. One of the men in question speaks to the following purport:

'Here you are! here you are! all that has to complain of corns. As fast as the shoemaker lames you, I'll cure you. If it wasn't for me he dursn't sing at his work; bless you, but he knows I'll make his pinching easy to you. Hard corn, soft corn, any corn—sold again! Thank you, sir, you'll not have to take a 'bus home when you've used my corn-salve, and you can wear your boots out then; you can't when you've corns. Now, in this little box you see a large corn which was drawn by this very salve from the honourable foot of the late lamented Sir Robert Peel. It's been in my possession three years and four months, and though I'm a poor man—hard corn, soft corn, or any corn—though I'm a poor man, the more's the pity, I wouldn't sell that corn for the newest sovereign coined. I call it the free-trade corn,* gen'l'men and leddis. No cutting and paring, and sharpening pen-knives, and venturing on razors to level your corns; this salve draws them out—only one penny—and without pain. But wonders can't be done in a moment. To draw out such a corn as I've shown you, the foot, the whole foot, must be soaked five minutes in warm soap and water. That makes the salve penetrate, and draw the corn, which then falls out, in three days, like a seed from a flower. Hard corn, soft corn, &c., &c.'

The corn from 'the honourable foot' of Sir Robert Peel, or from the foot of any one likely to interest the audience, has been scraped and trimmed from a cow's heel, and may safely be submitted to the inspection and handling of the incredulous. 'There it is,' the corn-seller will reiterate—'it speaks for itself.'

One practice—less common than it was, however,—of the corn-salve street-seller, is to get a friend to post a letter—expressive of delighted astonishment at the excellence and rapidity of the corn-cure—at some post-office not very contiguous. If the salve-seller be anxious to remove the corns of the citizens, he displays this letter, with the genuine post-mark of Piccadilly, St James's-street, Pall-mall, or any such quarter, to show how the fashionable world avails itself of his wares, cheap as they are, and fastidious as are the fashionable! If the street-professional be offering his corn-cures in a fashionable locality, he produces a letter from Cheapside, or Cornhill—'there it is, it speaks for itself'—to show how the shrewd city-people, who were never taken in by street-sellers in their lives, and couldn't be, appreciated that particular corn-salve! Occasionally, as the salve-seller is pattering, a man comes impetuously forward, and says loudly, 'Here, doctor, let me have a shilling's-worth. I bought a penn'orth, and it cured one corn by bringing it right out—here the d——d thing is, it troubled me seven year—and I've got other corns, and I'm determined I'll root out the whole family of them. Come, now, look sharp, and put up a shilling's-worth.' The shilling's-worth is gravely handed to the applicant as if it were not only a *boná fide*, but an ordinary occurrence in the way of business.

One corn-salve seller—who was not in town at the time of my inquiry into this curious matter—had, I was assured, 'and others might have' full faith in the efficacy of the salve he vended. One of his fellow-traders said to me, 'Ay, sir, and he has good reason for trusting to it for a cure; he cured *me* of my corns, that I'm sure of; so there can be no nonsense about it. He has a secret.' On my asking this informant if he had tried his own corn-salve, he laughed, and said 'No! I'm like the regular doctors that way, never tries my own things.' The same man, who had no great faith in what he sold being of any use in the cure of 'corn, wart, or bunion', assured me—and I have no doubt with truth—that he had sold his remedy to persons utter strangers to him, who had told him afterwards that it had cured their corns. 'False relics', says a Spanish proverb, 'have wrought true miracles', and to what cause these corn-cures were attributable, it is not my business to inquire.

Of the Street-Seller of Crackers and Detonating Balls

The trade is only known in the streets at holiday seasons, and is principally carried on for a few days before and after the 5th of November, and again at Christmas-tide. 'Last November was good for crackers,' said one man; 'it was either Guy Faux* day, or the day before, I'm not sure which now, that I took 15*s*., and nearly all of boys, for Waterloo crackers and ball crackers (the common trade names), "waterloo" being the "pulling crackers". At least three parts was ball crackers. I sold them from a barrow, wheeling it about as if it was hearthstone, and just saying quietly when I could, "Six a penny crackers." The boys soon tell one another. All sorts bought of me; doctors' boys, school boys, pages, boys as was dressed beautiful, and boys as hadn't neither shoes nor stockings. It's sport for them all.'

I inquired of a man who had carried on this street trade for a good many years, it might be ten or twelve, if he had noticed the uses to which his boy-customers put his not very innocent wares, and he entered readily into the subject.

'Why, sir,' he said, 'they're not all boy-customers, as you call them, but they're far the most. I've sold to men, and often to drunken men. What larks there is with the ball-crackers! One man lost his eye at Stepney Fair, but that's 6 or 7 years ago, from a lark with crackers. The rights of it I never exactly understood, but I know he lost his eye, from the dry gravel in the ball-cracker bouncing into it. But it's the boys as is fondest of crackers. I sold 'em all last Christmas, and made my 5*s*. and better on Boxing-day. I was sold out before 6 o'clock, as I had a regular run at last—just altogether. After that, I saw one lad go quietly behind a poor lame old woman and pull a Waterloo close behind her ear; he was a biggish boy and tidily dressed; and the old body screamed, "I'm shot." She turned about, and the boy says, says he, "Does your grandmother know you're out? It's a improper thing, so it is, for you to be walking out by yourself." You should have seen her passion! But as she was screaming out, "You saucy wagabone!* You boys is all wagabones. People can't pass for you. I'll give you in charge, I will," the lad was off like a shot.

'But one of the primest larks I ever saw that way was last winter, in a street by Shoreditch. An old snob* that had a bulk* was making it all right for the night, and a lad goes up. I don't know what he said to the old boy, but I saw him poke something, a last* I think it was, against the candle, put it out, and then run off. In a minute, three or four lads that was ready, let fly at the bulk with their ball-crackers, and there was a clatter as if the old snob had tumbled down, and knocked his lasts down; but he soon had his head out—he was Irish, I think—and he first set up a roar like a Smithfield* bull, and he shouts, "I'm kilt intirely wid the murthering pistols! Po–lice! Po–o–lice!" He seemed taken quite by surprise—for they was capital crackers—I think he couldn't have been used to bulks, or he would have been used to pelting; but how he did bellow, surely.

'I think it was that same night too, I saw a large old man, buttoned up, but seeming as if he was fine-dressed for a party, in a terrible way in the Commercial-road. I lived near there then. There was three boys afore me—and very well they did it—one of 'em throws a ball-cracker bang at the old gent's feet, just behind him, and makes him jump stunning, and the boy walks on with his hands in his pocket, as if he know'd nothing about it. Just after that another boy does the same, and then the t'other boy; and the old gent—Lord, how he swore! It was shocking in such a respectable man, as I told him, when he said, *I'd* crackered him! "Me cracker you," says I; "it'ud look better if you'd have offered to treat a poor fellow to a pint of beer with ginger in it, and the chill off, than talk such nonsense." As we was having this jaw, one of the boys comes back and lets fly again; and the old gent saw how it was, and he says, "Now, if you'll run after that lad, and give him a d——d good hiding, you shall have the beer." "Money down, sir," says I, "if you mean honour bright";* but he grumbled something, and walked away. I saw him soon after, talking to a Bobby, so I made a short cut home.'

At the fairs near London there is a considerable sale of these combustibles; and they are often displayed on large stalls in the fair. They furnish the means of practical jokes to the people on their return. 'After last Whitsun Greenwich Fair,' said a street-seller to me, 'I saw a gent in a white choker, like a parson, look in at a pastry-cook's shop, as is jist by the Elephant (and Castle), a-waiting for a 'bus, I s'pose. There was an old 'oman with a red face standing near him; and I saw a lad, very quick, pin something to one's coat and the t'other's gown. They turned jist arter, and bang goes a Waterloo, and they looks savage one at another; and hup comes that indentical boy, and he says to the red faced 'oman, a pointing to the white choker, "Marm, I seed him a twiddling with your gown. He done it for a lark arter the fair, and ought to stand something." So the parson, if he were a parson, walked away.'

Of the Street-Sellers of Dolls

The making of dolls, like that of many a thing required for a mere recreation, a toy, a pastime, is often carried on amidst squalor, wretchedness, or privation, or—to use the word I have frequently heard among the poor—'pinching'.

A vendor of dolls expresses an opinion that as long as ever there are children from two years old to ten, there will always be purchasers of dolls; 'but for all that,' said he, 'somehow or another 't is nothing of a trade to what it used to be. I've seen the time when I could turn out in the morning and earn a pound afore night; but it's different now there's so many bazaars, and so many toy shops that the doll hawker hasn't half the chance he used to have. Sartinly we gets a chance now and then—fine days is the best—and if we can get into the squares or where the children walks with their nurses, we can do tidy; but the police are so very particular there's not much of a livelihood to be got. Spoiled children are our best customers. Whenever we sees a likely customer approaching, we—that is, those who know their business—always throw ourselves in the way, and spread out our dolls to the best advantage. If we hears young miss say *she will* have one, and cries for it, we are almost sure of a customer, and if we see her kick and fight a bit with the nuss-maid we are sure of a good price. If a child *cries well* we never baits our price.

'When our 3*d*. dolls are made up, they cost about 1*s*. per dozen—so there is 2*d*. profit on every doll, which I thinks is little enough; but we often sells 'em at 2*d*.; we lays 'em out to the best advantage in a deep basket, all standing up, as it were, or leaning against the sides of the basket. The legs and bodies is carefully wrapped in tissue paper, not exactly to preserve the lower part of the doll, for that isn't so very valuable, but in reality to conceal the legs and body, which is rather the reverse of symmetrical; for, to tell the truth, every doll looks as if it were labouring under an attack of the gout. There are, however, some very neat articles exported from Germany, especially the jointed dolls, but they are too dear for the street-hawker, and would not show to such advantage. There is also the plaster dolls, with the match legs. I wonder how they keep their stand, for they are very old-fashioned; but they sell, for you never see a chandler's shop window without seeing one of these sticking in it, and a falling down as if it was drunk.'

I inquired of my informant whether he objected to relate a little of his history? He replied, 'not the least,' and recounted as follows:

'They call me *Dick the Dollman*. I was, I believe, the first as ever cried dolls three a shilling in the streets. Afore I began they al'ays stood still with 'em; but I cried 'em out same as they do mackrel; that is twenty years ago.

'The way I took to the dolls was this; I met a girl with a doll basket one day as I was standing at Somerset-house corner; she and I got a talking. "Will you go to the 'Delphy to night?" says I; she consented. They was a playing Tom and Jerry* at this time, all the street-sellers went to see it, and other people; and nice and crabbed some on 'em was. Well, we goes to the 'Delphy—and I sees her often arter that, and at last gets married. She used to buy her dolls ready made; I soon finds out where to get the heads—and the profits when we made them ourselves was much greater. We began to serve hawkers and shops; went to Bristol—saved 47*l*.—comes to London and spends it all; walks back to Bristol, and by the time we got there we had cleared more than 20*l*. We were about a month on the journey, and visited Cheltenham and other towns. We used to spend our money very foolishly; we were too fond of what was called getting on the spree. You see we might have done well if we had liked, but we hadn't the sense. My wife got very clever at the dolls and so did I. Then I tried my hand at the wax dolls, and got to make them very well. I paid a guinea to learn.

'I was selling wax-dolls one day in London, and a gentleman asked me if I could mend a wax figure whose face was broken. I replied yes, for I had made a few wax heads, large size, for some showmen, I had made some murderers who was hung; lately I made Rush and Mr and Mrs Manning;* but the showmen can't afford to get new heads now-a-days, so they generally makes one head do for all; sometimes they changes the dress. Well, as I was telling you, I went with this gentleman, and proposed that he should have a new head cast, for the face of the figure was so much broken. It was Androcles pulling the thorn out of the lion's foot,* and was to be exhibited. I got 20*s*. for making the new head. The gentleman asked me if I knew the story about Androcles. Now I had never heard on him afore, but I didn't like to confess my ignorance, so I says "yes"; then he offers me 30*s*. a week to describe it in the Flora Gardens, where it was to be exhibited. I at once accepted the engagement; but I was in a bit of a fix, for I didn't know what to say. I inquired of a good many people, but none on 'em could tell me; at last I was advised to go to Mr Charles Sloman—you know who I mean—him as makes a song and sings it directly; I was told he writes things for people. I went, and he wrote me out a patter. I asked him how much he charged; he said, "Nothing my man." Sartinly he wasn't long a-doing it, but it was very kind of him. I got what Mr Sloman wrote out for me printed, and this I stuck inside my hat; the people couldn't see it, though I dare say they wondered what I was looking in my hat about. However, in a week or so, I got it by heart, and could speak it well enough. After exhibiting Androcles I got an engagement with another waxwork show—named Biancis—and afterwards at other shows. I was considered a very good doors-man in time, but there's very little to be got by that now; so we keeps to the dolly business, and finds we can get a better living at that than anything else.'

Of the Street-Sellers of Poison for Rats

The rat-catcher's dress is usually a velveteen jacket, strong corduroy trowsers, and laced boots. Round his shoulder he wears an oil-skin belt, on which are painted the figures of huge rats, with fierce-looking eyes and formidable whiskers. His hat is usually glazed and sometimes painted after the manner of his belt. Occasionally—and in the country far more than in town—he carries in his hand an iron cage in which are ferrets, while two or three crop-eared rough terriers dog his footsteps. Sometimes a tamed rat runs about his shoulders and arms, or nestles in his bosom or in the large pockets of his coat. When a rat-catcher is thus accompanied, there is generally a strong aromatic odour about him, far from agreeable; this is owing to his clothes being rubbed with oil of thyme and oil of aniseed, mixed together. This composition is said to be so attractive to the sense of the rats (when used by a man who understands its due apportionment and proper application) that the vermin have left their holes and crawled to the master of the powerful spell. I heard of one man (not a ratcatcher professionally) who had in this way tamed a rat so effectually that the animal would eat out of his mouth, crawl upon his shoulder to be fed, and then 'smuggle into his bosom' (the words of my informant) 'and sleep there for hours'. The rat-catchers have many wonderful stories of the sagacity of the rat, and though in reciting their own feats, these men may not be the most trustworthy of narrators, any work on natural history will avouch that rats *are* sagacious, may be trained to be very docile, and are naturally animals of great resources in all straits and difficulties.

The rat-catchers are also rat-killers. They destroy the animals sometimes by giving them what is called in the trade 'an alluring poison'. Every professional destroyer, or capturer, of rats will pretend that as to poison he has his own particular method—his secret—his discovery. But there is no doubt that arsenic is the basis of all their poisons. Its being inodorous, and easily reducible to a soft fine powder, renders it the best adapted for mixing with anything of which rats are fond—toasted cheese, or bacon, or fried liver, or tallow, or oatmeal. Much as the poisoner may be able to tempt the animal's appetite, he must, and does, proceed cautiously. If the bait be placed in an unwonted spot, it is often untouched. If it be placed where rats have been accustomed to find their food, it is often devoured. But even then it is frequently accounted best to leave the bait un-poisoned for the first night; so that a hungry animal may attack it greedily the second. With oatmeal it is usual to mix for the first and even second nights a portion of pounded white sugar. If this be eaten it accustoms the jealous pest to the degree of sweetness communicated by arsenic. The 'oatmeal poison' is, I am told, the most effectual; but even when mixed only with sugar it is often refused; as 'rats is often better up to a dodge nor Kirstians' (Christians).

Another mode of killing rats is for the professional destroyer to slip a ferret into the rats' haunts wherever it is practicable. The ferret soon dislodges them, and as they emerge for safety they are seized by terriers, who, after watching the holes often a long time, and very patiently, and almost breathlessly, throttle them silently, excepting the short squeak, or half-squeak, of the rat, who, by a 'good dog', is seized unerringly by the part of the back where the terrier's gripe and shake is speedy death; if the rat still move, or shows signs of life, the well-trained rat-killer's dog cracks the vermin's skull between his teeth.

If the rats have to be taken alive, they are either trapped, so as not to injure them for a rat-hunt (or the procedure in the pit would be accounted 'foul'), or if driven out of their holes by ferrets, they can only run into some cask, or other contrivance, where they can be secured for the 'sportsman's' purposes. Although any visible injury to the body of the rat will prevent its reception into a pit, the creatures' teeth are often drawn, and with all the cruelty of a rough awkwardness, by means of pinchers,* so that they may be unable to bite the puppies being trained for the pit on the rats. If the vermin be not truly seized by the dog, the victim will twist round and inflict a tremendous bite on his worrier, generally on the lip. This often causes the terrier to drop his prey with a yell, and if a puppy he may not forget the lesson from the sharp nip of the rat. To prevent this it is that the rat-catchers play the dentist on their unfortunate captives.

I heard many accounts of the 'dodges' practised by, or imputed to, the rat-catchers: that it was not a very unusual thing to deposit here and there a dead rat, when those vermin were to be poisoned on any premises; it is then concluded that the good poison has done its good work, and the dead animal supplies an ocular demonstration of professional skill. These men, also, I am informed, let loose live rats in buildings adapted for the purpose, and afterwards apply for employment to destroy them.

The great sale of the rat-catchers is to the shops supplying 'private parties' with rats for the amusement of seeing them killed by dogs. With some 'fast' men, one of these shopkeepers told me, it was a favourite pastime in their own rooms on the Sunday mornings. It is, however, somewhat costly if earned on extensively, as the retail charge from the shops is 6*d*. per rat.

To show the nature of the sport of rat-catching, I print the following bill, of which I procured two copies. The words and type are precisely the same in each, but one bill is printed on good and the other on very indifferent paper, as if for distribution among distinct classes. The concluding announcement, as to the precise moment at which killing will commence, reads supremely businesslike:

RATTING FOR THE MILLION!

A SPORTING GENTLEMAN, Who is a Staunch Supporter of the destruction of these VERMIN

WILL GIVE A

GOLD REPEATER WATCH,

TO BE KILLED FOR BY

DOGS Under 13¾ *lbs. Wt.*

15 *RATS EACH!*

TO COME OFF AT JEMMY MASSEY'S,

KING'S HEAD,

COMPTON ST., SOHO,

On Tuesday, May 20, 1851

☞ To be Killed in a Large Wire Pit. A chalk Circle to be drawn in the centre for the Second.—Any Man touching Dog or Rats, or acting in any way unfair his dog will be disqualified.

TO GO TO SCALE AT Half past 7 KILLING TO COMMENCE At Half past 8 PRECISELY.

Of the Hawking of Tea

The branch of the tea trade closely connected with the street business is that in tea-leaves. The exhausted leaves of the tea-pot are purchased of servants or of poor women, and they are made into 'new' tea. One gentleman—to whose information, and to the care he took to test the accuracy of his every statement, I am bound to express my acknowledgments—told me that it would be fair to reckon that in London 1,500 lbs. of tea-leaves were weekly converted into new tea, or 78,000 lbs. in the year! One house is known to be very extensively and profitably concerned in this trade, or rather *manufacture*, and on my asking the gentleman who gave me the information if the house in question (he told me the name) was accounted respectable by their fellow-citizens, the answer was at once, '*Highly* respectable'.

The *old* tea-leaves, to be converted into *new*, are placed by the manufacturers on hot plates, and are re-dried and *re-dyed*. To give the 'green' hue, a preparation of copper is used. For the 'black' no dye is necessary in the generality of cases. This tea-manufacture is sold to 'cheap' or 'slop' shopkeepers, both in town and country, and especially for hawking in the country, and is almost always sold ready mixed.

The admixture of sloe-leaves, &c., which used to be gathered for the adulteration of tea, is now unknown, and has been unknown since tea became cheaper, but the old tea-leaf trade is, I am assured, carried on so quietly and cleverly, that the most vigilant excise-officers are completely in the dark; a smaller 'tea-maker' was, however, fined for tea-leaf conversion last year.

CHILDREN STREET-SELLERS

Of the Children Street-Sellers of London

Among the wares sold by the boys and girls of the streets are:—money-bags, lucifer-match boxes, leather straps, belts, firewood (common, and also 'patent', that is, dipped into an inflammable composition), fly-papers, a variety of fruits, especially nuts, oranges, and apples; onions, radishes, water-cresses, cut flowers and lavender (mostly sold by girls), sweet-briar, India rubber, garters, and other little articles of the same material, including elastic rings to encircle rolls of paper-music, toys of the smaller kinds, cakes, steel pens and penholders with glass handles, exhibition medals and cards, gelatine cards, glass and other cheap seals, brass watch-guards, chains, and rings; small tin ware, nutmeg-graters, and other articles of a similar description, such as are easily portable; iron skewers, fuzees,* shirt buttons, boot and stay-laces, pins (and more rarely needles), cotton bobbins, Christmasing (holly and other evergreens at Christmas-tide), May-flowers, coat-studs, toy-pottery, blackberries, groundsel and chickweed, and clothes'-pegs.

There are also other things which children sell temporarily, or rather in the season. This year I saw lads selling wild birds'-nests with their eggs, such as hedge-sparrows, minnows in small glass globes, roots of the wild Early Orchis (Orchis mascula*), and such like things found only out of town.

Independently of the vending of these articles, there are many other ways of earning a penny among the street boys: among them are found—tumblers, mud-larks, water-jacks,* Ethiopians,* ballad-singers, bagpipe boys, the variety of street musicians (especially Italian boys with organs), Billingsgate boys or young 'roughs', Covent Garden boys, porters, and shoeblacks (a class recently increased by the Ragged School Brigade*). A great many lads are employed also in giving away the cards and placards of advertising and puffing tradesmen, and around the theatres are children of both sexes (along with a few old people) offering play-bills for sale, but this is an occupation less pursued than formerly, as some managers sell their own bills inside the house and do not allow any to pass from the hands of the printer into those of the former vendors. Again: amid the employments of this class may be mentioned—the going on errands and carrying parcels for persons accidentally met with; holding horses; sweeping crossings (but the best crossings are usually in the possession of adults); carrying trunks for any railway traveller to or from the terminus, and carrying them from an omnibus when the passenger is not put down at his exact destination. During the frosty days of the winter and early spring, some of these little fellows used to run along the foot-path—Baker-street was a favourite place for this display—and keep pace with the omnibuses, not merely by using their legs briskly, but by throwing themselves every now and then on their hands and progressing a few steps (so to speak) with their feet in the air. This was done to attract attention and obtain the preference if a job were in prospect; done, too, in hopes of a halfpenny being given the urchin for his agility. I looked at the hands of one of these little fellows and the fleshy parts of the palm were as hard as soling-leather, as hard, indeed, as the soles of the child's feet, for he was bare-footed. At the doors of the theatres, and of public places generally, boys are always in waiting to secure a cab from the stand, their best harvest being when the night has 'turned out wet' after a fine day. Boys wait for the same purpose, lounging all night, and until the place closes, about the night-houses, casinos, saloons, &c., and sometimes without receiving a penny. There are, again, the very many ways in which street boys employed to 'help' other people, when temporary help is needed, as when a cabman must finish the cleaning of his vehicle in a hurry, or when a porter finds himself over-weighted in his truck. Boys are, moreover, the common custodians of the donkeys on which young ladies take invigorating exercise in such places as Hampstead-heath and Blackheath. At pigeon-shooting matches they are in readiness to pick up the dead birds, and secure the poor fluttering things which are 'hard hit' by the adventurous sportsman, without having been killed. They have their share again in the picking of currants and gooseberries, the pottling* of strawberries, in weeding, &c., &c., and though the younger children may be little employed in haymaking, or in the more important labours of the corn harvest, they have their shares, both with and without the company of their parents, in the 'hopping'. In fine there is no business carried on to any extent in the streets, or in the open air, but it will be found that boys have their portion. Thus they are brought into contact with all classes; another proof of what I have advanced touching the importance of this subject.

It will be perceived that, under this head, I have had to speak far more frequently of boys than of girls, for the boy is far more the child of the streets than is the girl. The female child can do little but *sell* (when a livelihood is to be gained without a recourse to immorality); the boy can not only sell, but *work*.

With many of these little traders a natural shrewdness compensates in some measure for the deficiency of education, and enables them to carry on their variety of trades with readiness and dexterity, and sometimes with exactness. One boy with whom I had a conversation, told me that he never made any mistake about the 'coppers', although, as I subsequently discovered, he had no notion at all of arithmetic beyond the capability of counting how many pieces of coin he had, and how much copper money was required to make a 'tanner' or a 'bob'.* This boy vended coat-studs: he had also some metal collars for dogs, or as he said, 'for cats aither'. These articles he purchased at the same shop in Houndsditch, where 'there was a wonderful lot of other things to be had, on'y some on 'em cost more money'.

In speaking of money, the slang phrases are constantly used by the street lads; thus a sixpence is a 'tanner'; a shilling a 'bob', or a 'hog'; a crown is 'a bull'; a half-crown 'a half bull', &c. Little, as a modern writer has remarked, do the persons using these phrases know of their remote and somewhat classical origin, which may, indeed, be traced to the period antecedent to that when monarchs monopolized the surface of coined money with their own images and superscriptions. They are identical with the very name of money among the early Romans, which was *pecunia*, from *pecus*, a flock. The collections of coin dealers amply show, that the figure of a hog was anciently placed on a small silver coin, and that that of a bull decorated larger ones of the same metal: these coins were frequently deeply crossed on the reverse: this was for the convenience of easily breaking them into two or more pieces, should the bargain for which they were employed require it, and the parties making it had no smaller change handy to complete the transaction. Thus we find that the 'half-bull' of the itinerant street-seller or 'traveller', so far from being a phrase of modern invention, as is generally supposed, is in point of fact referable to an era extremely remote. Numerous other instances might be given of the classical origin of many of the flash or slang words used by these people.

I now give the answers I received from two boys. The first, his mother told me, was the best scholar at his school when he was there, and before he had to help her in street sale. He was a pale, and not at all forward boy, of thirteen or fourteen, and did not appear much to admire being questioned. He had not been to a Ragged School, but to an 'academy' kept by an old man. He did not know what the weekly charge was, but when father was living (he died last autumn) the schoolmaster used to take it out in vegetables. Father was a costermonger; mother minded all about his schooling, and master often said she behaved to him like a lady. 'God', this child told me, 'was our Heavenly Father, and the maker of all things; he knew everything and everybody; he knew people's thoughts and every sin they committed if no one else knew it. His was the kingdom and the power, and the glory, for ever and ever, Amen.* Jesus Christ was our Lord and Saviour; he was the son of God, and was crucified for our sins. He was a God himself.' [The child understood next to nothing of the doctrine of the Trinity, and I did not press him.] 'The Scriptures, which were the Bible and Testament, were the Word of God, and contained nothing but what was good and true. If a boy lied, or stole, or committed sins,' he said, 'he would be punished in the next world, which endured for ever and ever, Amen. It was only after death, when it was too late to repent, that people went to the next world. He attended chapel, sometimes.'

As to mundane matters, the boy told me that Victoria was Queen of Great Britain and Ireland. She was born May 24, 1819, and succeeded his late Majesty, King William IV, July 20, 1837. She was married to his Royal Highness Prince Albert, &c., &c. France was a different country to this: he had heard there was no king or queen there, but didn't understand about it. You couldn't go to France by land, no more than you could to Ireland. Didn't know anything of the old times in history; hadn't been told. Had heard of the battle of Waterloo; the English licked. Had heard of the battle of Trafalgar, and of Lord Nelson; didn't know much about him; but there was his pillar at Charing-cross, just by the candlesticks (fountains). When I spoke of astronomy, the boy at once told me he knew nothing about it. He had heard that the earth went round the sun, but from what he'd noticed, shouldn't have thought it. He didn't think that the sun went round the earth, it seemed to go more sideways. Would like to read more, if he had time, but he had a few books, and there was hundreds not so well off as he was.

I am far from undervaluing, indeed I would not indulge in an approach to a scoff, at the extent of this boy's knowledge. Many a man who piques himself on the plenitude of his breeches' pocket, and who attributes his success in life to the fulness of his knowledge, knows no more of Nature, Man, and God, than this poor street child.

Another boy, perhaps a few months older, gave me his notions of men and things. He was a thick-limbed, red-cheeked fellow; answered very freely, and sometimes, when I could not help laughing at his replies, laughed loudly himself, as if he entered into the joke.

Yes, he had heer'd of God who made the world. Couldn't exactly recollec' when he'd heer'd on him, but he had, most sarten-ly. Didn't know when the world was made, or how anybody could do it. It must have taken a long time. It was afore his time, 'or yourn either, sir'. Knew there was a book called the Bible; didn't know what it was about; didn't mind to know; knew of such a book to a sartinty, because a young 'oman took one to pop (pawn) for an old 'oman what was on the spree—a bran new 'un—but the cove wouldn't have it, and the old 'oman said he might be d——d. Never heer'd tell on the deluge; of the world having been drownded; it couldn't, for there wasn't water enough to do it. He weren't a going to fret hisself for such things as that. Didn't know what happened to people after death, only that they was buried. Had seen a dead body laid out; was a little afeared at first; poor Dick looked so different, and when you touched his face, he was so cold! oh, so cold! Had heer'd on another world; wouldn't mind if he was there hisself, if he could do better, for things was often queer here. Had heered on it from a tailor—such a clever cove, a stunner—as went to 'Straliar (Australia), and heer'd him say he was going into another world. Had never heer'd of France, but had heer'd of Frenchmen; there wasn't half a quarter so many on 'em as of Italians, with their earrings like flash gals. Didn't dislike foreigners, for he never saw none. What was they? Had heer'd of Ireland. Didn't know where it was, but it couldn't be very far, or such lots wouldn't come from there to London. Should say they walked it, aye, every bit of the way, for he'd seen them come in, all covered with dust. Had heer'd of people going to sea, and had seen the ships in the river, but didn't know nothing about it, for he was very seldom that way. The sun was made of fire, or it wouldn't make you feel so warm. The stars was fire, too, or they wouldn't shine. They didn't make it warm, they was too small. Didn't know any use they was of. Didn't know how far they was off; a jolly lot higher than the gas lights some on 'em was. Was never in a church; had heer'd they worshipped God there; didn't know how it was done; had heer'd singing and playing inside when he'd passed; never was there, for he hadn't no togs to go in, and wouldn't be let in among such swells as he had seen coming out. Was a ignorant chap, for he'd never been to school, but was up to many a move, and didn't do bad. Mother said he would make his fortin yet.

Had heer'd of the Duke of Wellington; he was Old Nosey;* didn't think he ever seed him, but had seed his statty. Hadn't heer'd of the battle of Waterloo, nor who it was atween; once lived in Webber-row, Waterloo-road. Thought he had heerd speak of Buonaparte; didn't know what he was; thought he had heer'd of Shakespeare, but didn't know whether he was alive or dead, and didn't care. A man with something like that name kept a dolly and did stunning; but he was sich a hard cove that if *he* was dead it wouldn't matter. Had seen the Queen, but didn't recollec' her name just at the minute; oh! yes, Wictoria and Albert. Had no notion what the Queen had to do. Should think she hadn't such power [he had first to ask me what 'power' was] as the Lord Mayor, or as Mr Norton as was the Lambeth beak,* and perhaps is still. Was never once before a beak and didn't want to. Hated the crushers;* what business had they to interfere with him if he was only resting his basket in a street? Had been once to the Wick, and once to the Bower:* liked tumbling better; he meant to have a little pleasure when the peas came in.

The knowledge and the ignorance of these two striplings represent that of street children generally. Those who may have run away from a good school, or a better sort of home as far as means constitute such betterness, of course form exceptions. So do the utterly stupid.

VOLUME II

THE LONDON STREET-FOLK (CONTINUED)

STREET-SELLERS OF SECOND-HAND ARTICLES

Of the Street-Sellers of Second-Hand Articles

In London, where many, in order to live, struggle to extract a meal from the possession of an article which seems utterly worthless, nothing must be wasted. Many a thing which in a country town is kicked by the penniless out of their path even, or examined and left as meet only for the scavenger's cart, will in London be snatched up as a prize: it is money's worth. A crushed and torn bonnet, for instance, or, better still, an old hat, napless, shapeless, crownless, and brimless, will be picked up in the street, and carefully placed in a bag with similar things by one class of street-folk—the Street-Finders. And to tempt the well-to-do to *sell* their second-hand goods, the street-trader offers the barter of shapely china or shining glass vessels; or blooming fuchsias or fragrant geraniums for 'the rubbish', or else, in the spirit of the hero of the fairy tale,* he exchanges, 'new lamps for old'.

Of the Uses of Second-Hand Garments

Each 'left-off' garment has its peculiar after *uses*, according to its material and condition. The practised eye of the old clothes man at once embraces every capability of the apparel, and the amount which these capabilities will realize; whether they be woollen, linen, cotton, leathern, or silken goods; or whether they be articles which cannot be classed under any of those designations, such as macintoshes and furs.

A *surtout* coat is the most serviceable of any second-hand clothing, originally good. It can be re-cuffed, re-collared, or the skirts re-lined with new or old silk, or with a substitute for silk. It can be 'restored' if the seams be white and the general appearance what is best understood by the expressive word 'seedy'. This restoration is a sort of re-dyeing, or rather re-colouring, by the application of gall and logwood with a small portion of copperas.* If the under sleeve be worn, as it often is by those whose avocations are sedentary, it is renewed, and frequently with a second-hand piece of cloth 'to match', so that there is no perceptible difference between the renewal and the other parts. Many an honest artisan in this way becomes possessed of his Sunday frock-coat, as does many a smarter clerk or shopman, impressed with a regard to his personal appearance.

In the last century, I may here observe, and perhaps in the early part of the present, when woollen cloth was much dearer, much more substantial, and therefore much more durable, it was common for economists to have a good coat 'turned'. It was taken to pieces by the tailor and re-made, the inner part becoming the outer. This mode prevailed alike in France and England; for Molière makes his miser, *Harpagon*,* magnanimously resolve to incur the cost of his many-years'-old coat being 'turned', for the celebration of his expected marriage with a young and wealthy bride. This way of dealing with a second-hand garment is not so general now as it was formerly in London, nor is it in the country.

If the surtout be incapable of restoration to the appearance of a 'respectable' garment, the skirts are sold for the making of cloth caps; or for the material of boys' or 'youths'' waistcoats; or for 'poor country curates'' gaiters; but not so much now as they once were. 'The poor journeymen parsons,' I was told, 'now goes for the new slops; they're often green, and is had by 'vertisements, and bills, and them books about fashions which is all over both country and town. Do you know, sir, why them there books is always made so small? The leaves is about four inches square. That's to prevent their being any use as waste paper. I'll back a coat such as is sometimes sold by a gentleman's servant to wear out two new slops.'*

Cloaks are things of as ready sale as any kind of old garments. If good, or even reparable, they are in demand both for the home and foreign trades, as cloaks; if too far gone, which is but rarely the case, they are especially available for the same purposes as the surtout. The same may be said of the great-coat.

Dress-coats are far less useful, as if cleaned up and repaired they are not in demand among the working classes, and the clerks and shopmen on small salaries are often tempted by the price, I was told, to buy some wretched new slop thing rather than a superior coat second-hand. The dress-coats, however, are used for caps. Sometimes a coat, for which the collector may have given 9*d*., is cut up for the repairs of better garments.

Trousers are re-seated and repaired where the material is strong enough; and they are, I am informed, now about the only habiliment which is ever 'turned', and that but exceptionally. The repairs to trousers are more readily effected than those to coats, and trousers are freely bought by the collectors, and as freely re-bought by the public.

Waistcoats—I still speak of woollen fabrics—are sometimes used in cap-making, and were used in gaiter-making. But generally, at the present time, the worn edges are cut away, the buttons renewed or replaced by a new set, sometimes of glittering glass, the button-holes repaired or their jaggedness gummed down, and so the waistcoat is reproduced as a waistcoat, a size smaller. Sometimes a 'vest', as waistcoats are occasionally called, is used by the cheap boot-makers for the 'legs' of a woman's cloth boots, either laced or buttoned, but not a quarter as much, as they would be, I was told, if the buttons and button-holes of the waistcoat would 'do again' in the boot.

Nor is the woollen garment, if too thin, too worn, or too rotten to be devoted to any of the uses I have specified, flung away as worthless. To the traders in second-hand apparel, or in the remains of second-hand apparel, a dust-hole* is an unknown receptacle. The woollen rag, for so it is then considered, when unravelled can be made available for the manufacture of cheap yarns, being mixed with new wool. It is more probable, however, that the piece of woollen fabric which has been rejected by those who make or mend, and who must make or mend so cheaply that the veriest vagrant may be their customer, is formed not only into a new material, but into a material which sometimes is made into a new garment. These garments are inferior to those woven of new wool, both in look and wear; but in some articles the re-manufacture is beautiful. The fabric thus snatched, as it were, from the ruins of cloth, is known as shoddy, the chief seat of manufacture being in Dewsbury, a small town in Yorkshire.

At one time shoddy cloth was not good and firm enough to be used for other purposes than such as padding by tailors, and in the inner linings of carriages, by coach-builders. It was not used for purposes which would expose it to stress, but only to a moderate wear or friction. Now shoddy, which modern improvements have made susceptible of receiving a fine dye (it always looked a dead colour at one period), is made into cloth for soldiers' and sailors' uniforms and for pilot-coats;* into blanketing, drugget,* stair and other carpeting, and into those beautiful table-covers, with their rich woollen look, on which elegantly drawn and elaborately coloured designs are printed through the application of aquafortis.* Thus the rags which the beggar could no longer hang about him to cover his nakedness, may be a component of the soldier's or sailor's uniform, the carpet of a palace, or the library table-cover of a prime-minister.

There is yet another use for old woollen clothes. What is not good for shoddy is good for manure, and more especially for the manure prepared by the agriculturists in Kent, Sussex, and Herefordshire, for the culture of a difficult plant—hops. It is good also for corn land (judiciously used), so that we again have the remains of the old garment in our beer or our bread.

Of the Street-Sellers of Petticoat and Rosemary-Lanes

Immediately connected with the trade of the central mart for old clothes* are the adjoining streets of Petticoat-lane, and those of the not very distant Rosemary-lane. In these localities is a second-hand garment-seller at almost every step, but the whole stock of these traders, decent, frowsy, half-rotten, or smart and good habiliments, has first passed through the channel of the Exchange. The men who sell these goods have all bought them at the Exchange—the exceptions being insignificant—so that this street-sale is but an extension of the trade of the central mart, with the addition that the wares have been made ready for use.

A cursory observation might lead an inexperienced person to the conclusion, that these old clothes traders who are standing by the bundles of gowns, or lines of coats, hanging from their door-posts, or in the place from which the window has been removed, or at the sides of their houses, or piled in the street before them, are drowsy people, for they seem to sit among their property, lost in thought, or caring only for the fumes of a pipe. But let any one indicate, even by an approving glance, the likelihood of his becoming a customer, and see if there be any lack of diligence in business. Some, indeed, pertinaciously invite attention to their wares; some (and often well-dressed women) leave their premises a few yards to accost a stranger pointing to a 'good dress-coat' or 'an excellent frock' (coat). I am told that this practice is less pursued than it was, and it seems that the solicitations are now addressed chiefly to strangers. These strangers, persons

SCENE IN PETTICOAT-LANE.

happening to be passing, or visitors from curiosity, are at once recognised; for as in all not very extended localities, where the inhabitants pursue a similar calling, they are, as regards their knowledge of one another, as the members of one family. Thus a stranger is as easily recognised as he would be in a little rustic hamlet where a strange face is not seen once a quarter. Indeed so narrow are some of the streets and alleys in this quarter, and so little is there of privacy, owing to the removal, in warm weather, even of the casements, that the room is commanded in all its domestic details; and as among these details there is generally a further display of goods similar to the articles outside, the jammed-up places really look like a great family house with merely a sort of channel, dignified by the name of a street, between the right and left suites of apartments.

It must not be supposed that old clothes are more than the great staple of the traffic of this district. Wherever persons are assembled there are certain to be purveyors of provisions and of cool or hot drinks for warm or cold weather. The interior of the Old Clothes Exchange has its oyster-stall, its fountain of ginger-beer, its coffee-house, and ale-house, and a troop of peripatetic traders, boys principally, carrying trays. Outside the walls of the Exchange this trade is still thicker. A Jew boy thrusts a tin of highly-glazed cakes and pastry under the people's noses here; and on the other side a basket of oranges regales the same sense by its proximity. At the next step the thoroughfare is interrupted by a gaudy-looking ginger-beer, lemonade, raspberryade, and nectar fountain; 'a halfpenny a glass, a halfpenny a glass, sparkling lemonade!' shouts the vendor as you pass. The fountain and the glasses glitter in the sun, the varnish of the wood-work shines, the lemonade really does sparkle, and all looks clean—except the owner. Close by is a brawny young Irishman, his red beard unshorn for perhaps ten days, and his neck, where it had been exposed to the weather, a far deeper red than his beard, and he is carrying a small basket of nuts, and selling them as gravely as if they were articles suited to his strength. A little lower is the cry, in a woman's voice, 'Fish, fried fish! Ha'penny; fish, fried fish!' and so monotonously and mechanically is it ejaculated that one might think the seller's life was passed in uttering these few words, even as a rook's is in crying 'Caw, caw.' Here I saw a poor Irishwoman who had a child on her back buy a piece of this fish (which may be had 'hot' or 'cold'), and tear out a piece with her teeth, and this with all the eagerness and relish of appetite or hunger; first eating the brown outside and then *sucking* the bone. I never saw fish look firmer or whiter. That fried fish is to be procured is manifest to more senses than one, for you can hear the sound of its being fried, and smell the fumes from the oil. In an open window opposite frizzle on an old tray, small pieces of thinly-cut meat, with a mixture of onions, kept hot by being placed over an old pan containing charcoal. In another room a mess of batter is smoking over a grate. 'Penny a lot, oysters,' resounds from different parts. Some of the sellers command two streets by establishing their stalls or tubs at a corner. Lads pass, carrying sweet-stuff on trays. I observed one very dark-eyed Hebrew boy chewing the hard-bake he vended—if it were not a substitute—with an expression of great enjoyment. Heaped-up trays of fresh-looking sponge-cakes are carried in tempting pyramids. Youths have stocks of large hard-looking biscuits, and walk about crying, 'Ha'penny biscuits, ha'penny; three a penny, biscuits'; these, with a morsel of cheese, often supply a dinner or a luncheon. Dates and figs, as dry as they are cheap, constitute the stock in trade of other street-sellers. 'Coker-nuts'* are sold in pieces and entire; the Jew boy, when, he invites to the purchase of an entire nut, shaking it at the ear of the customer. I was told by a costermonger that these juveniles had a way of drumming with their fingers on the shell so as to satisfy a 'green' customer that the nut offered was a sound one.

Other street-sellers also abound. You meet one man who says mysteriously, and rather bluntly, 'Buy a good knife, governor.' His tone is remarkable, and if it attract attention, he may hint that he has smuggled goods which he *must* sell anyhow. Such men, I am told, look out mostly for seamen, who often resort to Petticoat-lane; for idle men like sailors on shore, and idle uncultivated men often love to lounge where there is bustle. Pocket and pen knives and scissors, 'Penny a piece, penny a pair', rubbed over with oil, both to hide and prevent rust, are carried on trays, and spread on stalls, some stalls consisting of merely a tea-chest lid on a stool. Another man, carrying perhaps a sponge in his hand, and well-dressed, asks you, in a subdued voice, if you want a good razor, as if he almost suspected that you meditated suicide, and were looking out for the means! This is another ruse to introduce smuggled (or 'duffer's') goods. Account-books are hawked. 'Penny-a-quire,' shouts the itinerant street stationer (who, if questioned, always declares he said 'Penny half quire'). 'Stockings, stockings, two pence a pair.' 'Here's your chewl-ry; penny, a penny; pick 'em and choose 'em.' [I may remark that outside the window of one shop, or rather parlour, if there be any such distinction here, I saw the handsomest, as far as I am able to judge, and the best cheap jewellery I ever saw in the streets.] 'Pencils, sir, pencils; steel-pens, steel-pens; ha'penny, penny; pencils, steel-pens; sealing-wax, wax, wax, wax!' shouts one, 'Green peas, ha'penny a pint!' cries another.

But Petticoat-lane is essentially the old clothes district. Embracing the streets and alleys adjacent to Petticoat-lane, and including the rows of old boots and shoes on the ground, there is perhaps between two and three miles of old clothes. Petticoat-lane proper is long and narrow, and to look down it is to look down a vista of many coloured garments, alike on the sides and on the ground. The effect sometimes is very striking, from the variety of hues, and the constant flitting, or gathering, of the crowd into little groups of bargainers. Gowns of every shade and every pattern are hanging up, but none, perhaps, look either bright or white; it is a vista of dinginess, but many coloured dinginess, as regards female attire. Dress coats, frock coats, great coats, livery and game-keepers' coats, paletots,* tunics, trowsers, knee-breeches, waistcoats, capes, pilot coats, working jackets, plaids, hats, dressing gowns, shirts, Guernsey frocks,* are all displayed. The predominant colours are black and blue, but there is every colour; the light drab of some aristocratic livery; the dull brown-green of velveteen; the deep blue of a pilot jacket; the variegated figures of the shawl dressing-gown; the glossy black of the restored garments; the shine of newly turpentined black satin waistcoats; the scarlet and green of some flaming tartan; these things—mixed with the hues of the women's garments, spotted and striped—certainly present a scene which, cannot be beheld in any other part of the greatest city of the world nor in any other portion of the world itself.

STREET-SELLERS OF MINERAL PRODUCTIONS AND NATURAL CURIOSITIES

Of the Street-Sellers of Coals

According to the returns of the coal market for the last few years, there has been imported into London, on an average, 3,500,000 tons of seaborne coal annually. Besides this immense supply, the various railways have lately poured in a continuous stream of the same commodity from the inland districts, which has found a ready sale without sensibly affecting the accustomed vend of the north country coals, long established on the Coal Exchange.*

The modes in which the coals imported into London are distributed to the various classes of consumers are worthy of observation, as they unmistakably exhibit not only the wealth of the few, but the poverty of the many. The inhabitants of Belgravia, the wealthy shopkeepers, and many others periodically see at their doors the well-loaded waggon of the coal merchant, with two or three swarthy 'coal-porters' bending beneath the black heavy sacks, in the act of laying in the 10 or 20 tons for yearly or half-yearly consumption. But this class is supplied from a very different quarter from that of the artizans, labourers, and many others, who, being unable to spare money sufficient to lay in at once a ton or two of coals, must have recourse to other means. To meet their limited resources, there may be found in every part, always in back streets, persons known as coal-shed men, who get the coals from the merchant in 7, 14, or 20 tons at a time, and retail them from ¼ cwt. upwards. The coal-shed men are a very numerous class, for there is not a low neighbourhood in any part of the city which contains not two or three of them in every street.

There is yet another class of purchasers of coals, however, which I have called the 'very poor',—the inhabitants of two pairs back*—the dwellers in garrets, &c. It seems to have been for the purpose of meeting the wants of this class that the street-sellers of coals have sprung into existence. Those who know nothing of the decent pride which often lingers among the famishing poor, can scarcely be expected to comprehend the great boon that the street-sellers of coals, if they could only be made honest and conscientious dealers, are calculated to confer on these people. 'I have seen', says a correspondent, 'the starveling child of misery, in the gloom of the evening, steal timidly into the shop of the coal-shed man, and in a tremulous voice ask, as if begging a great favour, for *seven pound of coals*. The coal-shed man has set down his pint of beer, taken the pipe from his mouth, blowing after it a cloud of smoke, and in a gruff voice, at which the little wretch has shrunk up (if it were possible) into a less space than famine had already reduced her to, and demanded—"Who told you as how I sarves seven pound o' coal?—Go to Bill C——, he may sarve you if he likes—I won't, and that's an end on 't—I wonders what people wants with seven pound o' coal." The coal-shed man, after delivering himself of this enlightened observation, has placidly resumed his pipe, while the poor child, gliding out into the drizzling sleet, disappeared in the darkness.'

The street-sellers vend any quantity at the very door of the purchaser, without rendering it necessary for them to expose their poverty to the prying eyes of the neighbourhood; and, as I have said were the street dealers only honest, they would be conferring a great boon upon the poorer portion of the people, but unhappily it is scarcely possible for them to be so, and realize a profit for themselves. The police reports of the last year show that many of the coal merchants, standing high in the estimation of the world, have been heavily fined for using false weights; and, did the present inquiry admit of it, there might be mentioned many other infamous practices by which the public are shamefully plundered in this commodity, and which go far to prove that the coal trade, *in toto*, is a gigantic fraud. May I ask how it is possible for the street-sellers, with such examples of barefaced dishonesty before their eyes, even to dream of acting honestly? If not actually certain, yet strongly suspecting, that they themselves are defrauded by the merchant, how can it be otherwise than that they should resort to every possible mode of defrauding their customers, and so add to the already almost unendurable burdens of the poorest of the poor, who by one means or other are made to bear all the burdens of the country?

I received the following statement from a person engaged in the street traffic:

'I kept a coal-shed and greengrocer's shop, and as I had a son grown up, I wanted to get something for him to do; so about six years ago, having a pony and cart, and seeing others selling coals through the street, I thought I'd make him try his hand at it. I went to Mr B——'s, at Whiting's wharf, and got the cart loaded, and sent my son round our own neighbourhood. I found that he soon disposed of them, and so he went on by degrees. People think we get a great deal of profit, but we don't get near as much as they think. I paid 16*s.* a ton all the winter for coals and sold them for a shilling a hundred, and when I came to feed the horse I found that he'll nearly eat it all up. A horse's belly is not so easy to fill. I don't think my son earns much more now, in summer, than feeds the horse. It's different in winter; he does not sell more nor half a ton a day now the weather's so warm. In winter he can always sell a ton at the least, and sometimes two, and on the Saturday he might sell three or four. My cart holds a ton; the vans hold from two to three tons. I can't exactly tell how many people are engaged in selling coals in the street, but there are a great many, that's certain. About eight o'clock what a number of carts and vans you'll see about the Regent's Canal! They like to get away before breakfast, because then they may have another turn after dinner. There's a great many go to other places for coals. The people who have vans do much better than those with the carts, because they carry so much that they save time. There are no great secrets in our business; we haven't the same chance of "doing the thing" as the merchants have. They can mix the coals up as they like for their customers, and sell them for best; all we can do is to buy a low quality; then we may lose our customers if we play any tricks. To be sure, after that we can go to parts where we're not known. I don't use light weights, but I know it's done by a good many, and they mix up small coals a good deal, and that of course helps their profits. My son generally goes four or five miles before he sells a ton of coals, and in summer weather a great deal farther. It's hard-earned money that's got at it, I can tell you. My cart is worth 12*l.*; I have a van worth 20*l.* I wouldn't take 20*l.* for my horse. My van holds two tons of coals, and the horse draws it easily. I send the van out in the winter when there's a good call, but in the summer I only send it out on the Saturday. I never calculated how much profit I made. I haven't the least idea how much is got by it, but I'm sure there's not near as much as you say. Why, if there was, I ought to have made a fortune by this time.' [It is right I should state that I received the foregoing account of the profits of the street trade in coals from one practically and eminently acquainted with it.] 'Some in the trade have done very well, but they were well enough off before. I know very well I'll never make a fortune at anything; I'll be satisfied if I keep moving along, so as to keep out of the Union.'

As to the habits of the street-sellers of coals, they are as various as their different circumstances will admit; but they closely resemble each other in one general characteristic—their provident and careful habits. Many of them have risen from struggling costermongers, to be men of substance, with carts, vans, and horses of their own. Some of the more wealthy of the class may be met with now and then in the parlours of respectable public houses, where they smoke their pipes, sip their brandy and water, and are remarkable for the shrewdness of their remarks. They mingle freely with the respectable tradesmen of their own localities, and may be seen, especially on the Sunday afternoons, with their wives and showily-dressed daughters in the gardens of the New Globe, or Green Dragon—the Cremorne and Vauxhall of the east.* I visited the house of one of those who I was told had originally been a costermonger. The front portion of the shop was almost filled with coals, he having added to his occupation of street-seller the business of a coal-shed man; this his wife and a little boy managed in his absence; while, true to his early training, the window-ledge and a bench before it were heaped up with cabbages, onions, and other vegetables. In an open space opposite his door, I observed a one-horse cart and two or three trucks with his name painted thereon. At his invitation, I passed through what may be termed the shop, and entered the parlour, a neat room nicely carpeted, with a round table in the centre, chairs ranged primly round the walls, and a long looking-glass reflecting the china shepherds and shepherdesses on the mantel-piece, while, framed and glazed, all around were highly-coloured prints, among which, Dick Turpin, in flash red coat, gallantly clearing the toll-gate in his celebrated ride to York,* and Jack Sheppard lowering himself down from the window of the lock-up house,* were most conspicuous. In the window lay a few books, and one or two old copies of *Bell's Life*.* Among the well-thumbed books, I picked out the *Newgate Calendar*,* and the '*Calendar of Orrers*',* as he called it, of which he expressed a very high opinion. 'Lor bless you,' he exclaimed, 'them there stories is the vonderfullest in the vorld! I'd never ha believed it, if I adn't seed it vith my own two hies, but there can't be no mistake ven I read it hout o' the book, can there, now? I jist asks yer that ere plain question.'

Of his career he gave me the following account:—'I vos at von time a coster, riglarly brought up to the business, the times vas good then; but lor, ve used to lush* at sich a rate! About ten year ago, I ses to meself, I say Bill, I'm blowed if this here game 'ill do any longer. I had a good moke (donkey), and a tidyish box ov a cart; so vot does I do, but goes and sees von o' my old pals that gits into the coal-line somehow. He and I goes to the Bell and Siven Mackerels* in the Mile End Road, and then he tells me all he knowed, and takes me along vith hisself, and from that time I sticks to the coals.

'I niver cared much about the lush myself, and ven I got avay from the old uns, I didn't mind it no how; but Jack my pal vos a awful lushy cove, he couldn't do no good at nothink, votsomever; he died they say of *lirium trumans*'* [not understanding what he meant, I inquired of what it was he died]; 'why, of *lirium trumans*, vich I takes to be too much of Trueman and Hanbury's heavy;* so I takes varnin by poor Jack, and cuts the lush; but if you thinks as ve don't enjoy ourselves sometimes, I tells you, you don't know nothink about it. I'm gittin on like a riglar house a fire.'

STREET-BUYERS

Of the Street-Buyers

The persons who traverse the streets, or call periodically at certain places to purchase articles which are usually sold at the door or within the house, are—according to the division I laid down in the first number of this work—STREET-BUYERS.

The principal things bought by the itinerant purchasers consist of waste-paper, hare and rabbit skins, old umbrellas and parasols, bottles and glass, broken metal, rags, dripping, grease, bones, tea-leaves, and old clothes.

With the exception of the buyers of waste-paper, among whom are many active, energetic, and intelligent men, the street-buyers are of the lower sort, both as to means and intelligence. The only further exception, perhaps, which I need notice here is, that among some umbrella-buyers, there is considerable smartness, and sometimes, in the repair or renewal of the ribs, &c. a slight degree of skill. The other street-purchasers—such as the hare-skin and old metal and rag buyers, are often old and infirm people of both sexes, of whom—perhaps by reason of their infirmities—not a few have been in the trade from their childhood, and are as well known by sight in their respective rounds, as was the 'long-remembered beggar'* in former times.

It is usually the lot of a poor person who has been driven to the streets, or has adopted such a life when an adult, to *sell* trifling things—such as are light to carry and require a small outlay—in advanced age. Old men and women totter about offering lucifer-matches, boot and stay-laces, penny memorandum books, and such like. But the elder portion of the street-folk I have now to speak of do not sell, but *buy*. The street-seller commends his wares, their cheapness, and excellence. The same sort of man, when a buyer, depreciates everything offered to him, in order to ensure a cheaper bargain, while many of the things thus obtained find their way into street-sale, and are then as much commended for cheapness and goodness, as if they were the stock-in-trade of an acute slop advertisement-monger, and this is done sometimes by the very man who, when a buyer, condemned them as utterly valueless. But this is common to all trades.

Of the Street-Buyers of Rags, Broken Metal, Bottles, Glass, and Bones

The traders in these things are not unprosperous men. The poor creatures who may be seen picking up rags in the street are 'street-finders', and not buyers. It is the same with the poor old men who may be seen bending under an unsavoury sack of bones. The bones have been found, or have been given for charity, and are not purchased. One feeble old man whom I met with, his eyes fixed on the middle of the carriage-way in the Old St Pancras-road, and with whom I had some conversation, told me that the best friend he had in the world was a gentleman who lived in a large house near the Regent's-park, and gave him the bones which his dogs had done with! 'If I can only see hisself, sir,' said the old man, 'he's sure to give me any coppers he has in his coat-pocket, and that's a very great thing to a poor man like me. O, yes, I'll buy bones, if I have any ha'pence, rather than go without them; but I pick them up, or have them given to me mostly.'

The street-buyers, who are only buyers, have barrows, sometimes even carts with donkeys, and, as they themselves describe it, they 'buy everything'. These men are little seen in London, for they 'work' the more secluded courts, streets, and alleys, when in town; but their most frequented rounds are the poorer parts of the populous suburbs. There are many in Croydon, Woolwich, Greenwich, and Deptford. 'It's no use', a man who had been in the trade said to me, 'such as us calling at fine houses to know if they've any old keys to sell! No, we trades with the poor.' Often, however, they deal with the servants of the wealthy; and their usual mode of business in such cases is to leave a bill at the house a few hours previous to their visit. This document has frequently the royal arms at the head of it, and asserts that the 'firm' has been established since the year ——, which is seldom less than half a century. The hand-bill usually consists of a short preface as to the increased demand for rags on the part of the paper-makers, and this is followed by a liberal offer to give the very best prices for any old linen, or old metal, bottles, rope, stair-rods, locks, keys, dripping, carpeting, &c., 'in fact, no rubbish or lumber, however worthless, will be refused'; and generally concludes with a request that this 'bill' may be shown to the mistress of the house and preserved, as it will be called for in a couple of hours.

A street-buyer of the class I have described, upon presenting himself at any house, offers to buy rags, broken metal, or glass, and for rags especially there is often a serious bargaining, and sometimes, I was told by an itinerant street-seller, who had been an ear-witness, a little joking not of the most delicate kind. For coloured rags these men give ½*d.* a pound, or 1*d.* for three pounds; for inferior white rags ½*d.* a pound, and up to 1½*d.*; for the best, 2*d.* the pound. It is common, however, and even more common, I am assured, among masters of the old rag and bottle shops, than among street-buyers, to announce 2*d.* or 3*d.*, or even as much as 6*d.*, for the *best* rags, but, somehow or other, the rags taken for sale to those buyers never are of the best. To offer 6*d.* a pound for rags is ridiculous, but such an offer may be seen at some rag-shops, the figure 6, perhaps, crowning a painting of a large plum-pudding, as a representation of what may be a Christmas result, merely from the thrifty preservation of rags, grease, and dripping. Some of the street-buyers, when working the suburbs or the country, attach a similar 'illustration' to their barrows or carts. I saw the winter placard of one of these men, which he was reserving for a country excursion as far as Rochester, 'when the plum-pudding time was a-coming'. In this pictorial advertisement a man and woman, very florid and full-faced, were on the point of enjoying a huge plum-pudding, the man flourishing a large knife, and looking very hospitable. On a scroll which issued from his mouth were the words: 'From our rags! The best prices given by —— ——, of London.' The woman in like manner exclaimed: 'From dripping and house fat! The best prices given by —— ——, of London.'

A little old man, who had been many years a street-buyer, gave me an account of his purchases of *bottles* and *glass*. This man had been a soldier in his youth; had known, as he said, 'many ups and downs'; and occasionally wheels a barrow, somewhat larger and shallower than those used by masons, from which he vends iron and tin wares, such as cheap gridirons, stands for hand-irons, dust-pans, dripping trays, &c. As he sold these wares, he offered to buy, or swop for, any second-hand commodities. 'As to the bottle and glass buying, sir,' he said, 'it's dead and buried in the streets, and in the country too. I've known the day when I've cleared 2*l.* in a week by buying old things in a country round. How long was that ago, do you say, sir? Why perhaps twenty years; yes, more than twenty. Now, I'd hardly pick up odd glass in the street.' [He called imperfect glass wares 'odd glass'.] 'O, I don't know what's brought about such a change, but everything changes. I can't say anything about the duty on glass. No, I never paid any duty on my glass; it ain't likely. I buy glass still, certainly I do, but I think if I depended on it I should be wishing myself in the East Injes* again, rather than such a poor consarn of a business—d——n me if I shouldn't. The last glass bargain I made about two months back, down Limehouse-way, and about the Commercial-road, I cleared 7*d*. by; and then I had to wheel what I bought—it was chiefly bottles—about five mile. It's a trade would starve a cat, the buying of old glass. I never bought glass by weight, but I've heard of some giving a halfpenny and a penny a pound. I always bought by the piece: from a halfpenny to a shilling (but that's long since) for a bottle; and farthings and halfpennies, and higher and sometimes lower, for wine and other glasses as was chipped or cracked, or damaged, for they could be sold in them days. People's got proud now, I fancy that's one thing, and must have everything slap.* O, I do middling: I live by one thing or other, and when I die there'll just be enough to bury the old man.' [This is the first street-trader I have met with who made such a statement as to having provided for his interment, though I have heard these men occasionally express repugnance at the thoughts of being buried by the parish.] 'I have a daughter, that's all my family now; she does well as a laundress, and is a real good sort; I have my dinner with her every Sunday. She's a widow without any young ones. I often go to church, both with my daughter and by myself, on Sunday evenings. It does one good. I'm fond of the music and singing too. The sermon I can very seldom make anything of, as I can't hear well if any one's a good way off me when he's saying anythink. I buy a little old metal sometimes, but it's coming to be all up with street glass-people; everybody seems to run with their things to the rag-and-bottle-shops.'

Of the 'Rag-and-Bottle', and the 'Marine-Store' Shops

The principal purchasers of any refuse or worn-out articles are the proprietors of the rag-and-bottle-shops. Some of these men make a good deal of money, and not unfrequently unite with the business the letting out of vans for the conveyance of furniture, or for pleasure excursions, to such places as Hampton Court. The stench in these shops is positively sickening. Here in a small apartment may be a pile of rags, a sack-full of bones, the many varieties of grease and 'kitchen-stuff', corrupting an atmosphere which, even without such accompaniments, would be too close. The windows are often crowded with bottles, which exclude the light; while the floor and shelves are thick with grease and dirt. The inmates seem unconscious of this foulness,—and one comparatively wealthy man, who showed me his horses, the stable being like a drawing-room compared to his shop, in speaking of the many deaths among his children, could not conjecture to what cause it could be owing. This indifference to dirt and stench is the more remarkable, as many of the shopkeepers have been gentlemen's servants, and were therefore once accustomed to cleanliness and order. The door-posts and windows of the rag-and-bottle-shops are often closely placarded, and the front of the house is sometimes one glaring colour, blue or red; so that the place may be at once recognised, even by the illiterate, as the 'red house', or the 'blue house'. If these men are not exactly street-buyers, they are street-billers, continually distributing hand-bills, but more especially before Christmas. The more aristocratic, however, now send round cards, and to the following purport: [*see opposite*]

Some content themselves with sending hand-bills to the houses in their neighbourhood, which many of the cheap printers keep in type, so that an alteration in the name and address is all which is necessary for any customer.

These shops are exceedingly numerous. Perhaps in the poorer and smaller streets they are more numerous even than the chandlers' or the beer-sellers' places. At the corner of a small street, both in town and the nearer suburbs, will frequently be found the chandler's shop, for the sale of small quantities of cheese, bacon, groceries, &c., to the poor. Lower down may be seen the beer-seller's; and in the same street there is certain to be one rag-and-bottle or marine-store shop, very often two, and not unfrequently another in some adjacent court.

The house I visited was an old one, and abounded in closets and recesses. The fire-place, which apparently had been large, was removed, and the space was occupied with a mass of old iron of every kind; all this was destined for the furnace of the iron-founder, wrought iron being preferred for several of the requirements of that trade. A chest or range of very old drawers, with defaced or worn-out labels—once a grocer's or a chemist's—was stuffed, in every drawer,

No. — No. —

THE —— HOUSE IS ——'S
RAG, BOTTLE, AND KITCHEN STUFF
WAREHOUSE,
—— STREET, —— TOWN,

Where you can obtain Gold and Silver to any amount.

ESTABLISHED ——.

THE HIGHEST PRICE GIVEN

For all the undermentioned articles, viz:

Wax and Sperm Pieces*	Old Copper, Brass, Pewter, &c.
Kitchen Stuff, &c.	Lead, Iron, Zinc, Steel, &c., &c.
Wine & Beer Bottles	Old Horse Hair, Mattresses, &c.
Eau de Cologne, Soda Water	Old Books, Waste Paper, &c.
Doctors' Bottles, &c.	All kinds of Coloured Rags
White Linen Rags	
Bones, Phials, & Broken Flint Glass	

The utmost value given for all kinds of Wearing Apparel.
Furniture and Lumber of every description bought, and full value given at his Miscellaneous Warehouse.
Articles sent for.

with old horse-shoe nails (valuable for steel manufacturers), and horse and donkey shoes; brass knobs; glass stoppers; small bottles (among them a number of the cheap cast 'hartshorn* bottles'); broken pieces of brass and copper; small tools (such as shoemakers' and harness-makers' awls*), punches, gimlets,* plane-irons,* hammer heads, &c.; odd dominoes, dice, and backgammon-men; lock escutcheons,* keys, and the smaller sort of locks, especially padlocks; in fine, any small thing which could be stowed away in such a place.

In one corner of the shop had been thrown, the evening before, a mass of old iron, then just bought. It consisted of a number of screws of different lengths and substance; of broken bars and rails; of the odds and ends of the cogged wheels of machinery, broken up or worn out; of odd-looking spikes, and rings, and links; all heaped together and scarcely distinguishable. These things had all to be assorted; some to be sold for re-use in their then form; the others to be sold that they might be melted and cast into other forms. The floor was intricate with hampers of bottles; heaps of old boots and shoes; old desks and work-boxes; pictures (all modern) with and without frames; waste-paper, the most of it of quarto,* and some larger sized, soiled or torn, and strung closely together in weights of from 2 to 7 lbs.; and a fire-proof safe, stuffed with old fringes, tassels, and other upholstery goods, worn and discoloured. The miscellaneous wares were carried out into the street, and ranged by the door-posts as well as in front of the house. In some small out-houses in the yard were piles of old iron and tin pans, and of the broken or separate parts of harness.

From the proprietor of this establishment I had the following account:

'I've been in the business more than a dozen years. Before that, I was an auctioneer's, and then a furniture broker's porter. I wasn't brought up to any regular trade, but just to jobbing about, and a bad trade it is, as all trades is that ain't regular employ for a man. I had some money when my father died—he kept a chandler's shop—and I bought a marine.' [An elliptical form of speech among these traders.] 'I gave 10*l.* for the stock, and 5*l.* for entrance and good-will, and agreed to pay what rents and rates was due. It was a smallish stock then, for the business had been neglected, but I have no reason to be sorry for my bargain, though it might have been better. There's lots taken in about good-wills, but perhaps not so many in my way of business, because we're rather "fly to a dodge".* It's a confined sort of life, but there's no help for that. Why, as to my way of trade, you'd be surprised, what different sorts of people come to my shop. I don't mean the regular hands; but the chance comers. I've had men dressed like gentlemen—and no doubt they was respectable when they was sober—bring two or three books, or a nice cigar case, or anythink that don't show in their pockets, and say, when as drunk as blazes, "Give me what you can for this; I want it sold for a particular purpose." That particular purpose was more drink, I should say; and I've known the same men come back in less than a week, and buy what they'd sold me at a little extra, and be glad if I had it by me still. O, we sees a deal of things in this way of life. Yes, poor people run to such as me. I've known them come with such things as teapots, and old hair mattresses, and flock beds, and *then* I'm sure they're hard up—reduced for a meal. I don't like buying big things like mattresses, though I do purchase 'em sometimes. Some of these sellers are as keen as Jews at a bargain; others seem only anxious to get rid of the things and have hold of some bit of money anyhow. Yes, sir, I've known their hands tremble to receive the money, and mostly the women's. They haven't been used to it, I know, when that's the case. Perhaps they comes to sell to me what the pawns* won't take in, and what they wouldn't like to be seen selling to any of the men that goes about buying things in the street.

'Why, I've bought everythink; at sales by auction there's often "lots" made up of different things, and they goes for very little. I buy of people, too, that come to me, and of the regular hands that supply such shops as mine. I sell retail, and I sell to hawkers. I sell to anybody, for gentlemen 'll come into my shop to buy anythink that's took their fancy in passing. Yes, I've bought old oil paintings. I've heard of some being bought by people in my way as have turned out stunners, and was sold for a hundred pounds or more, and cost, perhaps, half-a-crown or only a shilling. I never experienced such a thing myself. There's a good deal of gammon* about it. Well, it's hardly possible to say anything about a scale of prices. I give 2*d.* for an old tin or metal teapot, or an old saucepan, and sometimes, two days after I've bought such a thing, I've sold it for 3*d.* to the man or woman I've bought it of. I'll sell cheaper to them than to anybody else, because they come to me in two ways—both as sellers and buyers. For pictures I've given from 3*d.* to 1*s.* I fancy they're among the last things some sorts of poor people, which is a bit fanciful, parts with. I've bought them of hawkers, but often I refuse them, as they've given more than I could get. Pictures requires a judge. Some brought to me was published by newspapers and them sort of people. Waste-paper I buy as it comes. I can't read very much, and don't understand about books. I take the backs off and weighs them, and gives 1*d.*, and 1½*d.*, and 2*d.* a pound, and there's an end. I sell them at about ¼*d.* a pound profit, or sometimes less, to men as we calls "waste" men. It's a poor part of our business, but the books and paper takes up little room, and then it's clean and can be stowed anywhere, and is a sure sale. Well, the people as sells 'waste' to me is not such as can read, I think; I don't know what they is; perhaps they're such as obtains possession of the books and what-not after the death of old folks, and gets them out of the way as quick as they can. I know nothink about what they are. Last week, a man in black—he didn't seem rich—came into my shop and looked at some old books, and said "Have you any black lead?" He didn't speak plain, and I could hardly catch him. I said, "No, sir, I don't sell black lead, but you'll get it at No. 27," but he answered, "Not black lead, but black letter,"* speaking very pointed. I said, "No," and I haven't a notion what he meant.

'Metal (copper) that I give 5*d.* or 5½*d.* for, I can sell to the merchants from 6½*d.* to 8*d.* the pound. It's no great trade, for they'll often throw things out of the lot and say they're not metal. Sometimes, it would hardly be a farthing in a shilling, if it war'n't for the draught in the scales. When we buys metal, we don't notice the quarters of the pounds; all under a quarter goes for nothink. When we buys iron, all under half pounds counts nothink. So when we buys by the pound, and sells by the hundredweight, there's a little help from this, which we calls the draught.

'Glass bottles of all qualities I buys at three for a halfpenny, and sometimes four, up to 2*d.* a-piece for "good stouts" (bottled-porter vessels), but very seldom indeed 2*d.*, unless it's something very prime and big like the old quarts (quart bottles). I seldom meddles with decanters. It's very few decanters as is offered to me, either little or big, and I'm shy of them when they are. There's such a change in glass. Them as buys in the streets brings me next to nothing now to buy; they both brought and bought a lot ten year back and later. I never was in the street-trade in second-hand, but it's not what it was. I sell in the streets, when I put things outside, and know all about the trade.

'It ain't a fortnight back since a smart female servant, in slap-up black, sold me a basket-full of doctor's bottles. I knew her master, and he hadn't been buried a week before she come to me, and she said, "missus is glad to get rid of them, for they makes her cry." They often say their missusses sends things, and that they're not on no account to take less than so much. That's true at times, and at times it ain't. I gives from 1½*d.* to 3*d.* a dozen for good new bottles. I'm sure I can't say what I give for other odds and ends; just as they're good, bad, or indifferent. It's a queer trade.'

Of the Street-Buyers of Waste (Paper)

Beyond all others the street-purchase of waste paper is the most curious of any in the hands of the class I now treat of.

Every kind of paper is purchased by the 'waste-men'. One of these dealers said to me: 'I've often in my time "cleared out" a lawyer's office.

I've bought old briefs, and other law papers, and "forms" that weren't the regular forms then, and any d——d thing they had in my line. You'll excuse me, sir, but I couldn't help thinking what a lot of misery was caused, perhaps, by the cwts. of waste I've bought at such places. If my father hadn't got mixed up with law he wouldn't have been ruined, and his children wouldn't have had such a hard fight of it; so I hate law. All that happened when I was a child, and I never understood the rights or the wrongs of it, and don't like to think of people that's so foolish. I gave 1½*d.* a pound for all I bought at the lawyers, and done pretty well with it, but very likely that's the only good turn such paper ever did any one—unless it were the lawyers themselves.'

The waste-dealers do not confine their purchases to the tradesmen I have mentioned. They buy of any one, and sometimes act as middlemen or brokers. For instance, many small stationers and news-vendors, sometimes tobacconists in no extensive way of trade, sometimes chandlers, announce by a bill in their windows, 'Waste Paper Bought and Sold in any Quantity', while more frequently perhaps the trade is carried on, as an understood part of these small shopmen's business, without any announcement. Thus the shop-buyers have much miscellaneous waste brought to them, and perhaps for only some particular kind have they a demand by their retail customers. The regular itinerant waste dealer then calls and 'clears out everything', the 'everything' being not an unmeaning word. One man, who 'did largely in waste', at my request endeavoured to enumerate all the kinds of paper he had purchased as waste, and the packages of paper he showed me, ready for delivery to his customers on the following day, confirmed all he said as he opened them and showed me of what they were composed. He had dealt, he said—and he took great pains and great interest in the inquiry, as one very curious, and was a respectable and intelligent man—in 'books on *every* subject' [I give his own words] 'on which a book can be written.' After a little consideration he added: 'Well, perhaps *every* subject is a wide range; but if there are any exceptions, it's on subjects not known to a busy man like me, who is occupied from morning till night every week day. The only worldly labour I do on a Sunday is to take my family's dinner to the bake-house, bring it home after chapel, and read *Lloyd's Weekly*.* I've had Bibles—the backs are taken off in the waste trade, or it wouldn't be fair weight—Testaments, Prayer-books, Companions to the Altar, and Sermons and religious works. Yes, I've had the Roman Catholic books, as is used in their public worship—at least so I suppose, for I never was in a Roman Catholic chapel. Well, it's hard to say about proportions, but in my opinion, as far as it's good for anything, I've not had *them* in anything like the proportion that I've had Prayer-books, and Watts' and Wesley's hymns.* More shame; but you see, sir, perhaps a godly old man dies, and those that follow him care nothing for hymn-books, and so they come to such as me, for they're so cheap now they're not to be sold second-hand at all, I fancy. I've dealt in tragedies and comedies, old and new, cut and uncut*—they're best uncut, for you can make them into sheets then—and farces, and books of the opera. I've had scientific and medical works of every possible kind, and histories, and travels, and lives, and memoirs. I needn't go through them—everything, from a needle to an anchor, as the saying is. Poetry, ay, many a hundred weight; Latin and Greek (sometimes), and French, and other foreign languages. Well now, sir, as you mention it, I think I never *did* have a Hebrew work; I think not, and I know the Hebrew letters when I see them. Black letter, not once in a couple of years; no, nor in three or four years, when I think of it. I have met with it, but I always take anything I've got that way to Mr ——, the bookseller, who uses a poor man well. Don't you think, sir, I'm complaining of poverty; though I have been very poor, when I was recovering from cholera at the first break-out of it, and I'm anything but rich now. Pamphlets I've had by the ton, in my time; I think we should both be tired if I could go through all they were about. Very many were religious, more's the pity. I've heard of a page round a quarter of cheese, though, touching a man's heart.'*

In corroboration of my informant's statement, I may mention that in the course of my inquiry into the condition of the fancy cabinet-makers of the metropolis, one elderly and very intelligent man, a first-rate artisan in skill, told me he had been so reduced in the world by the underselling of slop-masters (called 'butchers' or 'slaughterers', by the workmen in the trade), that though in his youth he could take in the *News* and *Examiner* papers (each he believed 9*d*. at that time, but was not certain), he could afford, and enjoyed, no reading when I saw him last autumn, beyond the book-leaves in which he received his quarter of cheese, his small piece of bacon or fresh meat, or his saveloys; and his wife schemed to go to the shops who 'wrapped up their things from books', in order that he might have something to read after his day's work.

My informant went on with his specification: 'Missionary papers of all kinds. Parliamentary papers, but not so often new ones, very largely. Railway prospectuses, with plans to some of them, nice engravings; and the same with other joint-stock companies. Children's copy-books, and cyphering-books. Old account-books of every kind. A good many years ago, I had some that must have belonged to a West End perfumer, there was such French items for Lady this, or the Honourable Captain that. I remember there was an Hon. Capt. G., and almost at every second page was "100 tooth-picks, 3*s.* 6*d.*" I think it was 3*s.* 6*d.*; in arranging this sort of waste one now and then gives a glance to it. Dictionaries of every sort, I've had, but not so commonly. Music books, lots of them. Manuscripts, but only if they're rather old; well, 20 or 30 years or so: I call that old. Letters on every possible subject, but not, in my experience, any very modern ones. An old man dies, you see, and his papers are sold off, letters and all; that's the way; get rid of all the old rubbish, as soon as the old boy's pointing his toes to the sky. What's old letters worth, when the writers are dead and buried? why, perhaps 1½*d.* a pound, and it's a rattling big letter that will weigh half-an-ounce. O, it's a queer trade, but there's many worse.'

Of the Street-Buyers of Umbrellas and Parasols

The street-traders in old umbrellas and parasols are numerous, but the buying is but one part, and the least skilled part, of the business. Men, some tolerably well-dressed, some swarthy-looking, like gipsies, and some with a vagabond aspect, may be seen in all quarters of the town and suburbs, carrying a few ragged-looking umbrellas, or the sticks or ribs of umbrellas, under their arms, and crying 'Umbrellas to mend,' or 'Any old umbrellas to sell?' The traffickers in umbrellas are also the crockmen,* who are always glad to obtain them in barter, and who merely dispose of them at the Old Clothes Exchange, or in Petticoat-lane.

The umbrella-menders are known by an appellation of an appropriateness not uncommon in street language. They are *mushroom-fakers*. The form of the expanded umbrella resembles that of a mushroom, and it has the further characteristic of being rapidly or suddenly raised, the mushroom itself springing up and attaining its full size in a very brief space of time. The term, however, like all street or popular terms or phrases, has become very generally condensed among those who carry on the trade—they are now *mush-fakers*, a word which, to any one who has not heard the term in full, is as meaningless as any in the vocabulary of slang.

The mushroom-fakers will repair any umbrella on the owner's premises, and their work is often done adroitly, I am informed, and as often bunglingly, or, in the trade term, 'botched'. So far there is no traffic in the business, the mushroom-faker simply performing a piece of handicraft, and being paid for the job. But there is another class of street-folk who buy the old umbrellas in Petticoat-lane, or of the street buyer or collector, and 'sometimes', as one of these men said to me, 'we are our own buyers on a round'. They mend the umbrellas—some of their wives, I am assured, being adepts as well as themselves—and offer them for sale on the approaches to the bridges, and at the corners of streets.

The street umbrella trade is really curious. Not so very many years back the use of an umbrella by a man was regarded as partaking of effeminacy, but now they are sold in thousands in the streets, and in the second-hand shops of Monmouth-street and such places. One of these street-traders told me that he had lately sold, but not to an extent which might encourage him to proceed, old silk umbrellas in the street for gentlemen to protect themselves from the rays of the sun.

STREET-FINDERS OR COLLECTORS

Of the Street-Finders or Collectors

These men, for by far the great majority are men, may be divided, according to the nature of their occupations, into three classes:

1. The bone-grubbers and rag-gatherers, who are, indeed, the same individuals, the pure-finders, and the cigar-end and old wood collectors.
2. The dredgermen, the mud-larks, and the sewer-hunters.
3. The dustmen and nightmen, the sweeps and the scavengers.

The first class go abroad daily to *find* in the streets, and carry away with them such things as bones, rags, 'pure' (or dogs'-dung), which no one appropriates. These they sell, and on that sale support a wretched life. The second class of people are also as strictly *finders*; but their industry, or rather their labour, is confined to the river, or to that subterranean city of sewerage unto which the Thames supplies the great outlets. These persons may not be immediately connected with the *streets* of London, but their pursuits are carried on in the open air (if the sewer-air may be so included), and are all, at any rate, out-of-door avocations. The third class is distinct from either of these, as the labourers comprised in it are not finders, but *collectors* or *removers* of the dirt and tilth of our streets and houses, and of the soot of our chimneys.

The two first classes also differ from the third in the fact that the sweeps, dustmen, scavengers, &c., are paid (and often large sums) for the removal of the refuse they collect; whereas the bone-grubbers, and mud-larks, and pure-finders, and dredgermen, and sewer-hunters, get for their pains only the value of the articles they gather.

Bone-Grubbers and Rag-Gatherers

The habits of the bone-grubbers and rag-gatherers, the 'pure' or dogs'-dung collectors, and the cigar-end finders, are necessarily similar. All lead a wandering, unsettled sort of life, being compelled to be

THE BONE-GRUBBER.

[*From a Daguerreotype by* BEARD.]

continually on foot, and to travel many miles every day in search of the articles in which they deal. They seldom have any fixed place of abode, and are mostly to be found at night in one or other of the low lodging-houses throughout London. The majority are, moreover, persons who have been brought up to other employments, but who from some failing or mishap have been reduced to such a state of distress that they were obliged to take to their present occupation, and have never after been able to get away from it.

The bone-picker and rag-gatherer may be known at once by the greasy bag which he carries on his back. Usually he has a stick in his hand, and this is armed with a spike or hook, for the purpose of more easily turning over the heaps of ashes or dirt that are thrown out of the houses, and discovering whether they contain anything that is saleable at the rag-and-bottle or marine-store shop. The bone-grubber generally seeks out the narrow back streets, where dust and refuse are cast, or where any dust-bins are accessible. The articles for which he chiefly searches are rags and bones—rags he prefers—but waste metal, such as bits of lead, pewter, copper, brass, or old iron, he prizes above all. Whatever he meets with that he knows to be in any way saleable he puts into the bag at his back. He often finds large lumps of bread which have been thrown out as waste by the servants, and occasionally the housekeepers will give him some bones on which there is a little meat remaining; these constitute the morning meal of most of the class. One of my informants had a large rump of beef bone given to him a few days previous to my seeing him, on which 'there was not less than a pound of meat'.

The bone-pickers and rag-gatherers are all early risers. They have all their separate beats or districts, and it is most important to them that they should reach their district before any one else of the same class can go over the ground. Some of the beats lie as far as Peckham, Clapham, Hammersmith, Hampstead, Bow, Stratford, and indeed all parts within about five miles of London. In summer time they rise at two in the morning, and sometimes earlier. It is not quite light at this hour—but bones and rags can be discovered before daybreak. The 'grubbers' scour all quarters of London, but abound more particularly in the suburbs. In the neighbourhood of Petticoat-lane and Ragfair, however, they are the most numerous on account of the greater quantity of rags which the Jews have to throw out. It usually takes the bone-picker from seven to nine hours to go over his rounds, during which time he travels from 20 to 30 miles with a quarter to a half hundredweight on his back. In the summer he usually reaches home about eleven of the day, and in the winter about one or two. On his return home he proceeds to sort the contents of his bag. He separates the rags from the bones, and these again from the old metal (if he be lucky enough to have found any). He divides the rags into various lots, according as they are white or coloured; and if he have picked up any pieces of canvas or sacking, he makes these also into a separate parcel. When he has finished the sorting he takes his several lots to the rag-shop or the marine-store dealer, and realizes upon them whatever they may be worth.

Sometimes the bone-grubbers will pick up a stray sixpence or a shilling that has been dropped in the street. 'The handkerchief I have round my neck,' said one whom I saw, 'I picked up with 1*s.* in the corner. The greatest prize I ever found was the brass cap of the nave of a coach-wheel; and I *did* once find a quarter of a pound of tobacco in Sun-street, Bishopsgate. The best bit of luck of all that I ever had was finding a cheque for 12*l.* 15*s.* lying in the gateway of the mourning-coach yard in Titchborne-street, Haymarket. I was going to light my pipe with it, indeed I picked it up for that purpose, and then saw it was a cheque. It was on the London and County Bank, 21, Lombard-street. I took it there, and got 10*s.* for finding it. I went there in my rags, as I am now, and the cashier stared a bit at me. The cheque was drawn by a Mr Knibb, and payable to a Mr Cox. I *did* think I should have got the odd 15*s.* though.'

Between the London and St Katherine's Docks and Rosemary Lane, there is a large district interlaced with narrow lanes, courts, and alleys ramifying into each other in the most intricate and disorderly manner, insomuch that it would be no easy matter for a stranger to work his way through the interminable confusion without the aid of a guide, resident in and well conversant with, the locality. The houses are of the poorest description, and seem as if they tumbled into their places at random. Foul channels, huge dust-heaps,* and a variety of other unsightly objects, occupy every open space, and dabbling among these are crowds of ragged dirty children who grub and wallow, as if in their native element. None reside in these places but the poorest and most wretched of the population, and, as might almost be expected, this, the cheapest and filthiest locality of London, is the head-quarters of the bone-grubbers and other street-finders. I have ascertained on the best authority, that from the centre of this place, within a circle of a mile in diameter, there dwell not less than 200 persons of this class. In this quarter I found a bone-grubber who gave me the following account of himself:

'I don't go out before daylight to gather anything, because the police takes my bag and throws all I've gathered about the street to see if I have anything stolen in it. I never stole anything in all my life, indeed I'd do anything before I'd steal. Many a night I've slept under an arch of the railway when I hadn't a penny to pay for my bed; but whenever the police find me that way, they make me and the rest get up, and drive us on, and tell us to keep moving. I don't go out on wet days, there's no use in it, as the things won't be bought. I can't wash and dry them, because I'm in a lodging-house. There's a great deal more than a 100 bone-pickers about here, men, women, and children. The Jews in this lane and up in Petticoat-lane give a good deal of victuals away on the Saturday. They sometimes call one of us in from the street to light the fire for them, or take off the kettle, as they must not do anything themselves on the Sabbath; and then they put some food on the footpath, and throw rags and bones into the street for us, because they must not hand anything to us. There are some about here who get a couple of shillings' worth of goods, and go on board the ships in the Docks, and exchange them for bones and bits of old canvas among the sailors; I'd buy and do so too if I only had the money, but can't get it. The summer is the worst time for us, the winter is much better, for there is more meat used in winter, and then there are more bones.' (Others say differently.) 'I intend to go to the country this season, and try to get something to do at the hay-making and harvest. I make about 2*s.* 6*d.* a week, and the way I manage is this: sometimes I get a piece of bread about 12 o'clock, and I make my breakfast of that and cold water; very seldom I have any dinner,—unless I earn 6*d.* I can't get any,—and then I have a basin of nice soup, or a penn'orth of plum-pudding and a couple of baked 'tatoes. At night I get ¼*d.* worth of coffee, ½*d.* worth of sugar, and 1¼*d.* worth of bread, and then I have 2*d.* a night left for my lodging; I always try to manage that, for I'd do anything sooner than stop out all night. I'm always happy the day when I make 4*d.*, for then I know I won't have to sleep in the street. The winter before last, there was a straw-yard down in Black Jack's-alley, where we used to go after six o'clock in the evening, and get ½lb. of bread, and another ½lb. in the morning, and then we'd gather what we could in the daytime and buy victuals with what we got for it. We were well off then, but the straw-yard wasn't open at all last winter. There used to be 300 of us in there of a night, a great many of the dock-labourers and their families were there, for no work was to be got in the docks; so they weren't able to pay rent, and were obliged to go in. I've lost my health since I took to bone-picking, through the wet and cold in the winter, for I've scarcely any clothes, and the wet gets to my feet through the old shoes; this caused me last winter to be nine weeks in the hospital of the Whitechapel workhouse.'

The narrator of this tale seemed so dejected and broken in spirit, that it was with difficulty his story was elicited from him. He was evidently labouring under incipient consumption. I have every reason to believe that he made a truthful statement,—indeed, he did not appear to me to have sufficient intellect to invent a falsehood. It is a curious fact, indeed, with reference to the London street-finders generally, that they seem to possess less rational power than any other class. They appear utterly incapable of trading even in the most trifling commodities, probably from the fact that buying articles for the purpose of selling them at a profit, requires an exercise of the mind to which they feel themselves incapable. Begging, too, requires some ingenuity or tact, in order to move the sympathies of the well-to-do, and the street-finders being incompetent for this, they work on day after day as long as they are able to crawl about in pursuit of their unprofitable calling.

Of the Cigar-End Finders

There are, strictly speaking, none who make a living by picking up the ends of cigars thrown away as useless by the smokers in the streets, but there are very many who employ themselves from time to time in collecting them. Almost all the street-finders, when they meet with such things, pick them up, and keep them in a pocket set apart for that purpose. The men allow the ends to accumulate till they amount to two or three pounds weight, and then some dispose of them to a person residing in the neighbourhood of Rosemary-lane, who buys them all up at from 6*d.* to 10*d.* per pound, according to their length and quality. The long ends are considered the best, as I am told there is more sound tobacco in them, uninjured by the moisture of the mouth. The children of the poor Irish, in particular, scour Ratcliff-highway, the Commercial-road, Mile-end-road, and all the leading thoroughfares of the East, and every place where cigar smokers are likely to take an evening's promenade. The quantity that each of them collects is very trifling indeed—perhaps not more than a handful during a morning's search. I am informed, by an intelligent man living in the midst of them, that these children go out in the morning not only to gather cigar-ends, but to pick up out of dust bins, and from amongst rubbish in the streets, the smallest scraps and crusts of bread, no matter how hard or filthy they may be. These they put into a little bag which they carry for the purpose, and, after they have gone their rounds and collected whatever they can, they take the cigar-ends to the man who buys them—sometimes getting not more than a half-penny or a penny for their morning's collection. With this they buy a halfpenny or a penny-worth of oatmeal, which they mix up with a large quantity of water, and after washing and steeping the hard and dirty crusts, they put them into the pot or kettle and boil all together. Of this mass the whole family partake, and it often constitutes all the food they taste in the course of the day. I have often seen the bone-grubbers eat the black and soddened crusts they have picked up out of the gutter.

It would, indeed, be a hopeless task to make any attempt to get at the number of persons who occasionally or otherwise pick up cigar-ends with the view of selling them again. For this purpose almost all who ransack the streets of London for a living may be computed as belonging to the class; and to these should be added the children of the thousands of destitute Irish who have inundated the metropolis within the last few years, and who are to be found huddled together in all the low neighbourhoods in every suburb of the City. What quantity is collected, or the amount of money obtained for the ends, there are no means of ascertaining.

Let us, however, make a conjecture. There are in round numbers 300,000 inhabited houses in the metropolis; and allowing the married people living in apartments to be equal in number to the unmarried 'housekeepers', we may compute that the number of families in London is about the same as the inhabited houses. Assuming one young or old gentleman in every ten of these families to smoke one cigar per diem in the public thoroughfares, we have 30,000 cigar-ends daily, or 210,000 weekly cast away in the London streets. Now, reckoning

150 cigars to go to a pound, we may assume that each end so cast away weighs about the thousandth part of a pound; consequently the gross weight of the ends flung into the gutter will, in the course of the week, amount to about 2 cwt.; and calculating that only a sixth part of these are picked up by the finders, it follows that there is very nearly a ton of refuse tobacco collected annually in the metropolitan thoroughfares.

The aristocratic quarters of the City and the vicinity of theatres and casinos are the best for the cigar-end finders. In the Strand, Regent-street, and the more fashionable thoroughfares, I am told, there are many ends picked up; but even in these places they do not exclusively furnish a means of living to any of the finders. All the collectors sell them to some other person, who acts as middle-man in the business. How he disposes of the ends is unknown, but it is supposed that they are resold to some of the large manufacturers of cigars, and go to form the component part of a new stock of the 'best Havannahs'; or, in other words, they are worked up again to be again cast away, and again collected by the finders, and so on perhaps, till the millennium comes.

Of the Sewer-Hunters

The persons who are in the habit of searching the sewers, call themselves 'shore-men' or 'shore-workers'. They belong, in a certain degree, to the same class as the 'mud-larks', that is to say, they travel through the mud along shore in the neighbourhood of ship-building and ship-breaking yards, for the purpose of picking up copper nails, bolts, iron, and old rope. The shore-men, however, do not collect the lumps of coal and wood they meet with on their way, but leave them as the proper perquisites of the mud-larks. The sewer-hunters were formerly, and indeed are still, called by the name of 'Toshers', the articles which they pick up in the course of their wanderings along shore being known among themselves by the general term 'tosh', a word more particularly applied by them to anything made of copper. These 'Toshers' may be seen, especially on the Surrey side of the Thames, habited in long greasy velveteen coats, furnished with pockets of vast capacity, and their nether limbs encased in dirty canvas trowsers, and any old slops of shoes, that may be fit only for wading

THE SEWER-HUNTER.

[*From a Daguerreotype by* BEARD.]

through the mud. They carry a bag on their back, and in their hand a pole seven or eight feet long, on one end of which there is a large iron hoe. The uses of this instrument are various; with it they try the ground wherever it appears unsafe, before venturing on it, and, when assured of its safety, walk forward steadying their footsteps with the staff. Should they, as often happens, even to the most experienced, sink in some quagmire, they immediately throw out the long pole armed with the hoe, which is always held uppermost for this purpose, and with it seizing hold of any object within their reach, are thereby enabled to draw themselves out; without the pole, however, their danger would be greater, for the more they struggled to extricate themselves from such places, the deeper they would sink; and even with it, they might perish, I am told, in some part, if there were nobody at hand to render them assistance.

To enter the sewers and explore them to any considerable distance is considered, even by those acquainted with what is termed 'working the shores', an adventure of no small risk. There are a variety of perils to be encountered in such places. The brick-work in many parts—especially in the old sewers—has become rotten through the continual action of the putrefying matter and moisture, and parts have fallen down and choked up the passage with heaps of rubbish; over these obstructions, nevertheless, the sewer-hunters have to scramble 'in the best way they can'. In such parts they are careful not to touch the brick-work over head, for the slightest tap might bring down an avalanche of old bricks and earth, and severely injure them, if not bury them in the rubbish. Since the construction of the new sewers, the old ones are in general abandoned by the 'hunters'; but in many places the former channels cross and re-cross those recently constructed, and in the old sewers a person is very likely to lose his way. It is dangerous to venture far into any of the smaller sewers branching off from the main, for in this the 'hunters' have to stoop low down in order to proceed; and, from the confined space, there are often accumulated in such places, large quantities of foul air, which, as one of them stated, will 'cause instantious death'. Moreover, far from there being any romance in the tales told of the rats, these vermin are really numerous and formidable in the sewers, and have been known, I am assured, to attack men when alone, and even sometimes when accompanied by others, with such fury that the people have escaped from them with difficulty. They are particularly ferocious and dangerous, if they be driven into some corner whence they cannot escape, when they will immediately fly at any one that opposes their progress. I received a similar account to this from one of the London flushermen. There are moreover, in some quarters, ditches or trenches which are filled as the water rushes up the sewers with the tide; in these ditches the water is retained by a sluice, which is shut down at high tide, and lifted again at low tide, when it rushes down the sewers with all the violence of a mountain torrent, sweeping everything before it. If the sewer-hunter be not close to some branch sewer, so that he can run into it, whenever the opening of these sluices takes place, he must inevitably perish. The trenches or water reservoirs for the cleansing of the sewers are chiefly on the south side of the river, and, as a proof of the great danger to which the sewer-hunters are exposed in such cases, it may be stated, that not very long ago, a sewer on the south side of the Thames was opened to be repaired; a long ladder reached to the bottom of the sewer, down which the bricklayer's labourer was going with a hod of bricks, when the rush of water from the sluice, struck the bottom of the ladder, and instantly swept away ladder, labourer, and all. The bricklayer fortunately was enjoying his 'pint and pipe' at a neighbouring public-house. The labourer was found by my informant, a 'shore-worker', near the mouth of the sewer quite dead, battered, and disfigured in a frightful manner.

The shore-workers, when about to enter the sewers, provide themselves, in addition to the long hoe already described, with a canvas apron, which they tie round them, and a dark lantern* similar to a policeman's; this they strap before them on their right breast, in such a manner that on removing the shade, the bull's-eye* throws the light straight forward when they are in an erect position, and enables them to see everything in advance of them for some distance; but when they stoop, it throws the light directly under them, so that they can then distinctly see any object at their feet. The sewer-hunters usually go in gangs of three or four for the sake of company, and in order that they may be the better able to defend themselves from the rats. The old hands who have been often up (and every gang endeavours to include at least one experienced person), travel a long distance, not only through the main sewers, but also through many of the branches. Whenever the shore-men come near a street grating, they close their lanterns and watch their opportunity of gliding silently past unobserved, for otherwise a crowd might collect over head and intimate to the policeman on duty, that there were persons wandering in the sewers below. The shore-workers never take dogs with them, lest their barking when hunting the rats might excite attention. As the men go along they search the bottom of the sewer, raking away the mud with their hoe, and pick, from between the crevices of the brick-work, money, or anything else that may have lodged there. There are in many parts of the sewers holes where the brick-work has been worn away, and in these holes clusters of articles are found, which have been washed into them from time to time, and perhaps been collecting there for years; such as pieces of iron, nails, various scraps of metal, coins of every description, all rusted into a mass like a rock, and weighing from a half hundred to two hundred weight altogether. These 'conglomerates' of metal are too heavy for the men to take out of the sewers, so that if unable to break them up, they are compelled to leave them behind; and there are very many such masses, I am informed, lying in the sewers at this moment, of immense weight, and growing larger every day by continual additions. The shore-men find great quantities of money—of copper money especially; sometimes they dive their arm down to the elbow in the mud and filth and bring up shillings, sixpences, half-crowns, and occasionally half-sovereigns and sovereigns. They always find the coins standing edge uppermost between the bricks in the bottom, where the mortar has been worn away. The sewer-hunters occasionally find plate, such as spoons, ladles, silver-handled knives and forks, mugs and drinking cups, and now and then articles of jewellery; but even while thus 'in luck' as they call it, they do not omit to fill the bags on their backs with the more cumbrous articles they meet with—such as metals of every description, rope and bones. There is always a great quantity of these things to be met with in the sewers, they being continually washed down from the cesspools and drains of the houses. When the sewer-hunters consider they have searched long enough, or when they have found as much as they can conveniently take away, the gang leave the sewers and, adjourning to the nearest of their homes, count out the money they have picked up, and proceed to dispose of the old metal, bones, rope, &c.; this done, they then, as they term it, 'whack' the whole lot; that is, they divide it equally among all hands.

It might be supposed that the sewer-hunters (passing much of their time in the midst of the noisome vapours generated by the sewers, the odour of which, escaping upwards from the gratings in the streets, is dreaded and shunned by all as something pestilential) would exhibit in their pallid faces the unmistakable evidence of their unhealthy employment. But this is far from the fact. Strange to say, the sewer-hunters are strong, robust, and healthy men, generally florid in their complexion, while many of them know illness only by name. Some of the elder men, who head the gangs when exploring the sewers, are between 60 and 80 years of age, and have followed the employment during their whole lives. The men appear to have a fixed belief that the odour of the sewers contributes in a variety of ways to their general health; nevertheless, they admit that accidents occasionally occur from the air in some places being fully impregnated with mephitic gas.

I found one of these men, from whom I derived much information, and who is really an active intelligent man, in a court off Rosemary-lane. Access is gained to this court through a dark narrow entrance, scarcely wider than a doorway, running beneath the first floor of one of the houses in the adjoining street. The court itself is about 50 yards long, and not more than three yards wide, surrounded by lofty wooden houses, with jutting abutments in many of the upper stories that almost exclude the light, and give them the appearance of being about to tumble down upon the heads of the intruders.

In this court, up three flights of narrow stairs that creaked and trembled at every footstep, and in an ill-furnished garret, dwelt the shore-worker—a man who, had he been careful, according to his own account at least, might have money in the bank and be the proprietor of the house in which he lived. The sewer-hunters, like the street-people, are all known by some peculiar nickname, derived chiefly from some personal characteristic. It would be a waste of time to inquire for them by their right names, even if you were acquainted with them, for none else would know them, and no intelligence concerning them could be obtained; while under the title of Lanky Bill, Long Tom, One-eyed George, Short-armed Jack, they are known to every one.

My informant, who is also dignified with a title, or as he calls it a 'handle to his name', gave me the following account of himself: 'Bless your heart the smell's nothink; it's a roughish smell at first, but nothink near so bad as you thinks, 'cause, you see, there's sich lots o' water always a coming down the sewer, and the air gits in from the gratings, and that helps to sweeten it a bit. There's some places, 'specially in the old sewers, where they say there's foul air, and they tells me the foul air 'ill cause instantious death, but I niver met with anythink of the kind, and I think if there was sich a thing I should know somethink about it, for I've worked the sewers, off and on, for twenty year. When we comes to a narrow-place as we don't know, we takes the candle out of the lantern and fastens it on the hend of the o,* and then runs it up the sewer, and if the light stays in, we knows as there a'n't no danger. We used to go up the city sewer at Blackfriars-bridge, but that's stopped up now; it's boarded across inside. The city wouldn't let us up if they knew it, 'cause of the danger, they say, but they don't care if we hav'n't got nothink to eat nor a place to put our heads in, while there's plenty of money lying there and good for nobody. If you was caught up it and brought afore the Lord Mayor, he'd give you fourteen days on it, as safe as the bellows, so a good many on us now is afraid to wenture in. We don't wenture as we used to, but still it's done at times. There's a many places as I knows on where the bricks has fallen down, and that there's dangerous; it's so delaberated that if you touches it with your head or with the hend of the o, it 'ill all come down atop o' you. I've often seed as many as a hundred rats at once, and they're woppers in the sewers, I can tell you; them there water rats, too, is far more ferociouser than any other rats, and they'd think nothink of tackling a man, if they found they couldn't get away no how, but if they can why they runs by and gits out o' the road. I knows a chap as the rats tackled in the sewers; they bit him hawfully: you must ha' heard on it; it was him as the watermen went in arter when they heard him a shouting as they was a rowin' by. Only for the watermen the rats would ha' done for him, safe enough. Do you recollect hearing on the man as was found in the sewers about twelve year ago?—oh you must—the rats eat every bit of him, and left nothink but his bones. I knowed him well, he was a rig'lar shore-worker.'

There is a strange tale in existence among the shore-workers, of a race of wild hogs inhabiting the sewers in the neighbourhood of Hampstead. The story runs, that a sow in young, by some accident got down the sewer through an opening, and, wandering away from the spot, littered and reared her offspring in the drain, feeding on the offal and garbage washed into it continually. Here, it is alleged, the breed multiplied exceedingly, and have become almost as ferocious as they are numerous. This story, apocryphal as it seems, has nevertheless its believers, and it is ingeniously argued, that the reason why none of the subterranean animals have been able to make their way to the light of day is, that they could only do so by reaching the mouth of the sewer at the river-side, while, in order to arrive at that point, they must necessarily encounter the Fleet ditch, which runs towards the river with great rapidity, and as it is the obstinate nature of a pig to swim *against* the stream, the wild hogs of the sewers invariably work their way back to their original quarters, and are thus never to be seen. What seems strange in the matter is, that the inhabitants of Hampstead never have been known to see any of these animals pass beneath the gratings, nor to have been disturbed by their gruntings. The reader of course can believe as much of the story as he pleases, and it is right to inform him that the sewer-hunters themselves have never yet encountered any of the fabulous monsters of the Hampstead sewers.

Of the Mud-Larks

There is another class who may be termed river-finders, although their occupation is connected only with the shore; they are commonly known by the name of 'mud-larks', from being compelled, in order to obtain the articles they seek, to wade sometimes up to their middle through the mud left on the shore by the retiring tide. These poor creatures are certainly about the most deplorable in their appearance of any I have met with in the course of my inquiries. They may be seen of all ages, from mere childhood to positive decrepitude, crawling among the barges at the various wharfs along the river; it cannot be said that they are clad in rags, for they are scarcely half covered by the tattered indescribable things that serve them for clothing; their bodies are grimed with the foul soil of the river, and their torn garments stiffened up like boards with dirt of every possible description.

Among the mud-larks may be seen many old women, and it is indeed pitiable to behold them, especially during the winter, bent nearly double with age and infirmity, paddling and groping among the wet mud for small pieces of coal, chips of wood, or any sort of refuse washed up by the tide. These women always have with them an old basket or an old tin kettle, in which they put whatever they chance to find. It usually takes them a whole tide to fill this receptacle,

THE MUD-LARK.

[*From a Daguerreotype by* BEARD.]

but when filled, it is as much as the feeble old creatures are able to carry home.

The mud-larks generally live in some court or alley in the neighbourhood of the river, and, as the tide recedes, crowds of boys and little girls, some old men, and many old women, may be observed loitering about the various stairs, watching eagerly for the opportunity to commence their labours. When the tide is sufficiently low they scatter themselves along the shore, separating from each other, and soon disappear among the craft lying about in every direction. This is the case on both sides of the river, as high up as there is anything to be found, extending as far as Vauxhall-bridge, and as low down as Woolwich. The mud-larks themselves, however, know only those who reside near them, and whom they are accustomed to meet in their daily pursuits; indeed, with but few exceptions, these people are dull, and apparently stupid; this is observable particularly among the boys and girls, who, when engaged in searching the mud, hold but little converse one with another. The men and women may be passed and repassed, but they notice no one; they never speak, but with a stolid look of wretchedness they plash their way through the mire, their bodies bent down while they peer anxiously about, and occasionally stoop to pick up some paltry treasure that falls in their way.

The mud-larks collect whatever they happen to find, such as coals, bits of old-iron, rope, bones, and copper nails that drop from ships while lying or repairing along shore. Copper nails are the most valuable of all the articles they find, but these they seldom obtain, as they are always driven from the neighbourhood of a ship while being new-sheathed. Sometimes the younger and bolder mud-larks venture on sweeping some empty coal-barge, and one little fellow with whom I spoke, having been lately caught in the act of so doing, had to undergo for the offence seven days' imprisonment in the House of Correction: this, he says, he liked much better than mud-larking, for while he staid there he wore a coat and shoes and stockings, and though he had not over much to eat, he certainly was never afraid of going to bed without anything at all—as he often had to do when at liberty. He thought he would try it on again in the winter, he told me, saying, it would be so comfortable to have clothes and shoes and stockings then, and not be obliged to go into the cold wet mud of a morning.

At one of the stairs in the neighbourhood of the pool, I collected about a dozen of these unfortunate children; there was not one of them over twelve years of age, and many of them were but six. It would be almost impossible to describe the wretched group, so motley was their appearance, so extraordinary their dress, and so stolid and inexpressive their countenances. Some carried baskets, filled with the produce of their morning's work, and others old tin kettles with iron handles. Some, for want of these articles, had old hats filled with the bones and coals they had picked up; and others, more needy still, had actually taken the caps from their own heads, and filled them with what they had happened to find. The muddy slush was dripping from their clothes and utensils, and forming a puddle in which they stood. There did not appear to be among the whole group as many filthy cotton rags to their backs as, when stitched together, would have been sufficient to form the material of one shirt. There were the remnants of one or two jackets among them, but so begrimed and tattered that it would have been difficult to have determined either the original material or make of the garment. On questioning one, he said his father was a coal-backer; he had been dead eight years; the boy was nine years old. His mother was alive; she went out charing and washing when she could get any such work to do. She had 1*s*. a day when she could get employment, but that was not often; he remembered once to have had a pair of shoes, but it was a long time since. 'It is very cold in winter,' he said, 'to stand in the mud without shoes,' but he did not mind it in summer. He had been three years mud-larking, and supposed he should remain a mud-lark all his life. What else could he be? for there was nothing else that he knew *how* to do. Some days he earned 1*d*., and some days 4*d*.; he never earned 8*d*. in one day, that would have been a 'jolly lot of money'. He never found a saw or a hammer, he 'only wished' he could, they would be glad to get hold of them at the dolly's.* He had been one month at school before he went mud-larking. Some time ago he had gone to the ragged-school; but he no longer went there, for he forgot it. He could neither read nor write, and did not think he could learn if he tried 'ever so much'. He didn't know what religion his father and mother were, nor did know what religion meant. God was God, he said. He had heard he was good, but didn't know what good he was to him. He thought he was a Christian, but he didn't know what a Christian was. He had heard of Jesus Christ once, when he went to a Catholic chapel, but he never heard tell of who or what he was, and didn't 'particular care' about knowing. His father and mother were born in Aberdeen, but he didn't know where Aberdeen was. London was England, and England, he said, was in London, but he couldn't tell in what part. He could not tell where he would go to when he died, and didn't believe any one could tell *that*. Prayers, he told me, were what people said to themselves at night. *He* never said any, and didn't know any; his mother sometimes used to speak to him about them, but he could never learn any. His mother didn't go to church or to chapel, because she had no clothes. All the money he got he gave to his mother, and she bought bread with it, and when they had no money they lived the best way they could.

Such was the amount of intelligence manifested by this unfortunate child.

Of the Dustmen of London

Dust and rubbish accumulate in houses from a variety of causes, but principally from the residuum of fires, the white ash and cinders, or small fragments of unconsumed coke, giving rise to by far the greater quantity. Some notion of the vast amount of this refuse annually produced in London may be formed from the fact that the consumption of coal in the metropolis is, according to the official returns, 3,500,000 tons per annum, which is at the rate of a little more than 11 tons per house; the poorer families, it is true, do not burn more than 2 tons in the course of the year, but then many such families reside in the same house, and hence the average will appear in no way excessive. Now the ashes and cinders arising from this enormous consumption of coal would, it is evident, if allowed to lie scattered about in such a place as London, render, ere long, not only the back streets, but even the important thoroughfares, filthy and impassable. Upon the Officers of the various parishes, therefore, has devolved the duty of seeing that the refuse of the fuel consumed throughout London is removed almost as fast as produced; this they do by entering into an agreement for the clearance of the 'dustbins' of the parishioners as often as required, with some person who possesses all necessary appliances for the purpose—such as horses, carts, baskets, and shovels, together with a plot of waste ground whereon to deposit the refuse. The persons with whom this agreement is made are called 'dust-contractors', and are generally men of considerable wealth.

The collection of 'dust', is now, more properly speaking, the removal of it. The collection of an article implies the voluntary seeking after it, and this the dustmen can hardly be said to do; for though they parade the streets shouting for the dust as they go, they do so rather to fulfil a certain duty they have undertaken to perform than in any expectation of profit to be derived from the sale of the article.

Formerly the custom was otherwise; but then, as will be seen hereafter, the residuum of the London fuel was far more valuable. Not many years ago it was the practice for the various master dustmen to send in their tenders to the vestry, on a certain day appointed for the purpose, offering to pay a considerable sum yearly to the parish authorities for liberty to collect the dust from the several houses. The sum formerly paid to the parish of Shadwell, for instance, though not a very extensive one, amounted to between 400*l.* or 500*l.* per annum; but then there was an immense demand for the article, and the contractors were unable to furnish a sufficient supply from London; ships were frequently freighted with it from other parts, especially from Newcastle and the northern ports, and at that time it formed an article of considerable international commerce—the price being from 15*s.* to 1*l.* per chaldron.* Of late years, however, the demand has fallen off greatly, while the supply has been progressively increasing, owing to the extension of the metropolis, so that the Contractors have not only declined paying anything for liberty to collect it, but now stipulate to receive a certain sum for the removal of it.

The dust thus collected is used for two purposes, (1) as a manure for land of a peculiar quality; and (2) for making bricks.

But during the operation of sifting the dust, many things are found which are useless for either manure or brick-making, such as oyster shells, old bricks, old boots and shoes, old tin kettles, old rags and bones, &c. These are used for various purposes.

The bricks, &c., are sold for sinking beneath foundations, where a thick layer of concrete is spread over them. Many old bricks, too, are used in making new roads, especially where the land is low and marshy. The old tin goes to form the japanned* fastenings for the corners of trunks, as well as to other persons, who remanufacture it into a variety of articles. The old shoes are sold to the London shoemakers, who use them as stuffing between the in-sole and the outer one; but by far the greater quantity is sold to the manufacturers of Prussian blue,* that substance being formed out of refuse animal matter. The rags and bones are of course disposed of at the usual places—the marine-store shops.

A dust-heap, therefore, may be briefly said to be composed of the following things, which are severally applied to the following uses:

1. 'Soil', or fine dust, sold to brickmakers for making bricks, and to farmers for manure, especially for clover.
2. 'Brieze', or cinders, sold to brickmakers, for burning bricks.
3. Rags, bones, and old metal, sold to marine-store dealers.
4. Old tin and iron vessels, sold for 'clamps' to trunks, &c., and for making copperas.
5. Old bricks and oyster shells, sold to builders, for sinking foundations, and forming roads.
6. Old boots and shoes, sold to Prussian-blue manufacturers.
7. Money and jewellery, kept, or sold to Jews.

The dust-yards, or places where the dust is collected and sifted, are generally situated in the suburbs, and they may be found all round London, sometimes occupying open spaces adjoining back streets and lanes, and surrounded by the low mean houses of the poor; frequently, however, they cover a large extent of ground in the fields, and there the dust is piled up to a great height in a conical heap, and having much the appearance of a volcanic mountain. Some time since there was an immense dust-heap in the neighbourhood of Gray's-inn-lane, which sold for 20,000*l.*; but that was in the days when 15*s.* and 1*l.* per chaldron could easily be procured for the dust. According to the present rate, not a tithe of that amount could have been realized upon it.

A visit to any of the large metropolitan dust-yards is far from uninteresting. Near the centre of the yard rises the highest heap, composed of what is called the 'soil', or finer portion of the dust used for manure. Around this heap are numerous lesser heaps, consisting of the mixed dust and rubbish carted in and shot down previous to sifting. Among these heaps are many women and old men with sieves made of iron, all busily engaged in separating the 'brieze' from the 'soil'. There is likewise another large heap in some other part of the yard, composed of the cinders or 'brieze 'waiting to be shipped off to the brickfields. The whole yard seems alive, some sifting and others shovelling the sifted soil on to the heap, while every now and then the dustcarts return to discharge their loads, and proceed again on

VIEW OF A DUST YARD.

(From a Sketch taken on the spot.)

their rounds for a fresh supply. Cocks and hens keep up a continual scratching and cackling among the heaps, and numerous pigs seem to find great delight in rooting incessantly about after the garbage and offal collected from the houses and markets.

In a dust-yard lately visited the sifters formed a curious sight; they were almost up to their middle in dust, ranged in a semicircle in front of that part of the heap which was being 'worked'; each had before her a small mound of soil which had fallen through her sieve and formed a sort of embankment, behind which she stood. The appearance of the entire group at their work was most peculiar. Their coarse dirty cotton gowns were tucked up behind them, their arms were bared above their elbows, their black bonnets crushed and battered like those of fish-women; over their gowns they wore a strong leathern apron, extending from their necks to the extremities of their petticoats, while over this, again, was another leathern apron, shorter, thickly padded, and fastened by a stout string or strap round the waist. In the process of their work they pushed the sieve from them and drew it back again with apparent violence, striking it against the outer leathern apron with such force that it produced each time a hollow sound, like a blow on the tenor drum. All the women present were middle aged, with the exception of one who was very old—68 years of age she told me—and had been at the business from a girl. She was the daughter of a dustman, the wife, or woman of a dustman, and the mother of several young dustmen—sons and grandsons—all at work at the dust-yards at the east end of the metropolis.

CHIMNEY-SWEEPERS

Of the General Characteristics of the Working Chimney-Sweepers

There are many reasons why the chimney-sweepers have ever been a distinct and peculiar class. They have long been looked down upon as the lowest order of workers, and treated with contumely by those who were but little better than themselves. The peculiar nature of their work giving them not only a filthy appearance, but an offensive smell, of itself, in a manner, prohibited them from associating with other working men; and the natural effect of such proscription has been to compel them to herd together apart from others, and to acquire habits and peculiarities of their own widely differing from the characteristics of the rest of the labouring classes.

When such men are met with, perhaps the class cannot be looked upon as utterly cast away, although the need of reformation in the habits of the working sweepers is extreme, and especially in respect of drinking, gambling, and dirt. The journeymen (who have often a good deal of leisure) and the single-handed men are—in the great majority of cases at least—addicted to drinking, beer being their favourite beverage, either because it is the cheapest or that they fancy it the most suitable for washing away the sooty particles which find their way to their throats. These men gamble also, but with this proviso—they seldom play for money; but when they meet in their usual houses of resort—two famous ones are in Back C—— lane and S—— street, White-chapel—they spend their time and what money they may have in tossing for beer, till they are either drunk or penniless. Such men present the appearance of having just come out of a chimney. There seems never to have been any attempt made by them to wash the soot off their faces. I am informed that there is scarcely one of them who has a second shirt or any change of clothes, and that they wear their garments night and day till they literally rot, and drop in fragments from their backs. Those who are not employed as journeymen by the masters are frequently whole days without food, especially in summer, when the work is slack; and it usually happens that those who are what is called 'knocking about on their own account' seldom or never have a farthing in their pockets in the morning, and may, perhaps, have to travel till evening before they get a threepenny or sixpenny chimney to sweep. When night comes, and they meet their companions, the tossing and drinking again commences; they again get drunk; roll home to wherever it may be, to go through the same routine on the morrow; and this is the usual tenour of their lives, whether earning 5*s*. or 20*s*. a week.

The chimney-sweepers generally are fond of drink; indeed their calling, like that of dustmen, is one of those which naturally lead to it. The men declare they are ordered to drink gin and smoke as much as they can, in order to rid the stomach of the soot they may have swallowed during their work.

Washing among chimney-sweepers seems to be much more frequent than it was. In the evidence before Parliament* it was stated that some of the climbing-boys were washed once in six months, some once a week, some once in two or three months. I do not find it anywhere stated that any of these children were never washed at all; but from the tenour of the evidence it may be reasonably concluded that such was the case.

A master sweeper, who was in the habit of bathing at the Marylebone baths* once and sometimes twice a week, assured me that, although many now eat and drink and sleep sooty, washing is more common among his class than when he himself was a climbing-boy. He used then to be stripped, and compelled to step into a tub, and into water sometimes too hot and sometimes too cold, while his mistress, to use his own word, *scoured* him. Judging from what he had seen and heard, my informant was satisfied that, from 30 to 40 years ago, climbing-boys, with a very few exceptions, were but seldom washed; and then it was looked upon by them as a most disagreeable operation, often, indeed, as a species of punishment. Some of the climbing-boys used to be taken by their masters to bathe in the Serpentine many years ago; but one boy was unfortunately drowned, so that the children could hardly be coerced to go into the water afterwards.

The washing among the chimney-sweepers of the present day, when there are scarcely any climbing-boys, is so much an individual matter that it is not possible to speak with any great degree of certainty on the subject, but that it increases may be concluded from the fact that the number of sweeps who resort to the public baths increases.

The *diet of the journeymen sweepers and the apprentices*, and sometimes of their working employer, was described to me as generally after the following fashion. My informant, a journeyman, calculated what his food 'stood his master', as he had once 'kept hisself'.

	Daily	
	s.	*d.*
Bread and butter and coffee for breakfast	0	2
A saveloy and potatoes, or cabbage; or a 'fagot',* with the same vegetables; or fried fish (but not often); or pudding, from a pudding shop; or soup (a twopenny plate) from a cheap eating-house; average from 2*d.* to 3*d.*	0	2½
Tea, same as breakfast	0	2
	0	6½

On Sundays the fare was better. They then sometimes had a bit of 'prime fat mutton' taken to the oven, with 'taturs to bake along with it'; or a 'fry of liver, if the old 'oman was in a good humour', and always a pint of beer apiece.

They are considered *a short-lived people*, and among the journeymen, the masters 'on their own hook', &c., few old men are to be met with. In one of the reports of the Board of Health, out of 4,312 deaths among males, of the age of 15 and upwards, the mortality among the sweepers, masters and men, was 9, or one in 109 of the whole trade. As the calculation was formed, however, from data supplied by the census of 1841, and on the Post Office Directory, it supplies no reliable information. Many of these men still suffer, I am told, from the chimney-sweeper's cancer,* which is said to arise mainly from uncleanly habits. Some sweepers assure me that they have vomited balls of soot.

The localities in which many of the sweepers reside are the 'lowest' places in the district. Many of the houses in which I found the lower class of sweepers were in a ruinous and filthy condition.

The 'high-class' sweepers, on the other hand, live in respectable localities, often having back premises sufficiently large to stow away their soot.

I had occasion to visit the house of one of the persons from whom I obtained much information. He is a master in a small way, a sensible man, and was one of the few who are teetotallers. His habitation, though small—being a low house only one story high—was substantially furnished with massive mahogany chairs, table, chests of drawers, &c., while on each side of the fire-place, which was distinctly visible from the street over a hall door, were two buffets, with glass doors, well filled with glass and china vessels. It was a wet night, and a fire burned brightly in the stove, by the light of which might be seen the master of the establishment sitting on one side, while his wife and daughter occupied the other; a neighbour sat before the fire with his back to the door, and altogether it struck me as a comfortable-looking evening party. They were resting and chatting quietly together after the labour of the day, and everything betokened the comfortable circumstances in which the man, by sobriety and industry, had been able to place himself. Yet this man had been a climbing-boy, and one of the unfortunates who had lost his parents when a child, and was apprenticed by the parish to this business.* From him I learned that his was not a solitary instance of teetotalism; that, in fact, there were some more, and one in particular, named Brown, who was a good speaker, and devoted himself during his leisure hours at night in advocating the principles which by experience he had found to effect such great good to himself; but he also informed me that the majority of the others were a drunken and dissipated crew, sunk to the lowest degree of misery, yet recklessly spending every farthing they could earn in the public-house.

Different in every respect was another house which I visited in the course of my inquiries, in the neighbourhood of H—— street, Bethnal-green. The house was rented by a sweeper, a master on his own account, and every room in the place was let to sweepers and their wives or women, which, with these men, often signify one and the same thing. The inside of the house looked as dark as a coal-pit; there was an insufferable smell of soot, always offensive to those unaccustomed to it; and every person and every thing which met the eye, even to the caps and gowns of the women, seemed as if they had just been steeped in Indian ink. In one room was a sweep and his woman quarrelling. As I opened the door I caught the words, 'I'm d——d if I has it any longer. I'd see you b——y well d——d first, and you knows it.' The savage was intoxicated, for his red eyes flashed through his sooty mask with drunken excitement, and his matted hair, which looked as if it had never known a comb, stood out from his head like the whalebone ribs of his own machine. 'B——y Bet', as he called her, did not seem a whit more sober than her man; and the shrill treble of her voice was distinctly audible till I turned the corner of the street, whither I was accompanied by the master of the house, to whom I had been recommended by one of the fraternity as an intelligent man, and one who knew 'a thing or two'. 'You see,' he said, as we turned the corner, 'there isn't no use a talkin' to them ere fellows—they're all tosticated now, and they doesn't care nothink for nobody; but they'll be quiet enough to-morrow, 'cept they yarns somethink, and if they do then they'll be just as bad to-morrow night. They're a awful lot, and nobody ill niver do anythink with them.' This man was not by any means in such easy circumstances as the master first mentioned. He was merely a man working for himself, and unable to employ any one else in the business; as is customary with some of these people, he had taken the house he had shown me to let to lodgers of his own class, making something by so doing; though, if his own account be correct, I'm at a loss to imagine how he contrived even to get his rent. From him I obtained the following statement:

'Yes, I was a climbing-boy, and sarved a rigler printiceship for seven years, I was out on my printiceship when I was fourteen. Father was a silk-weaver, and did all he knew to keep me from being a sweep, but I would be a sweep, and nothink else.' [This is not so very uncommon a predilection, strange as it may seem.] 'So father, when he saw it was no use, got me bound printice. Father's alive now, and near 90 years of age. I don't know why I wished to be a sweep, 'cept it was this—there was sweeps always lived about here, and I used to see the boys with lots of money a tossin' and gamblin', and wished to have money too. You see they got money where they swept the chimneys; they used to get 2*d*. or 3*d*. for theirselves in a day, and sometimes 6*d*. from the people of the house, and that's the way they always had plenty of money. I niver thought anythink of the climbing; it wasn't so bad at all as some people would make you believe. There are two or three ways of climbing. In wide flues you climb with your elbows and your legs spread out, your feet pressing against the sides of the flue; but in narrow flues, such as nine-inch ones, you must slant it; you must have your sides in the angles, it's wider there, and go up just that way.' [Here he threw himself into position—placing one arm close to his side, with the palm of the hand turned outwards, as if pressing the side of the flue, and extending the other arm high above his head, the hand apparently pressing in the same manner.] 'There,' he continued, 'that's slantin'. You just put yourself in that way, and see how small you make yourself. I niver got to say stuck myself, but a many of them did; yes, and were taken out dead. They were smothered for want of air, and the fright, and a stayin' so long in the flue; you see the waistband of their trowsers sometimes got turned down in the climbing, and in narrow flues, when not able to get it up, then they stuck. I had a boy once—we were called to sweep a chimney down at Poplar. When we went in he looked up the flues, "Well, what is it like?" I said. "Very narrow," says he, "don't think I can get up there"; so after some time we gets on top of the house, and takes off the chimney-pot, and has a look down—it was wider a' top, and I thought as how he could go down. "You had better buff it, Jim," says I. I suppose you know what that means; but Jim wouldn't do it, and kept his trowsers on. So down he goes, and gets on very well till he comes to the shoulder of the flue, and then he couldn't stir. He shouts down, "I'm stuck." I shouts up and tells him what to do. "Can't move," says he, "I'm stuck hard and fast." Well, the people of the house got fretted like, but I says to them, "Now my boy's stuck, but for Heaven's sake don't make a word of noise; don't say a word, good or bad, and I'll see what I can do." So I locks the door, and buffs it, and forces myself up till I could reach him with my hand, and as soon as he got his foot on my hand he begins to prize himself up, and gets loosened, and comes out at the top again. I was stuck myself, but I was stronger nor he, and I manages to get out again. Now I'll be bound to say if there was another master there as would kick up a row and a-worrited, that ere boy 'ud a niver come out o' that ere flue alive. There was a many o' them lost their lives in that way. Most all the printices used to come from the "House" (workhouse.) There was nobody to care for them, and some masters used them very bad. I was out of my time at fourteen, and began to get too stout to go up the flues; so after knockin' about for a year or so, as I could do nothink else, I goes to sea on board a man-o'-war, and was away four year. Many of the boys, when they

THE LONDON SWEEP.

[*From a Daguerreotype by* BEARD.]

got too big and useless, used to go to sea in them days—they couldn't do nothink else. Yes, many of them went for sodgers;* and I know some who went for Gipsies, and others who went for play actors, and a many who got on to be swell-mobsmen,* and thieves, and house-breakers, and the like o' that ere. There ain't nothink o' that sort a-goin' on now since the Ack of Parliament. When I got back from sea father asked me to larn his business; so I takes to the silk-weaving and larned it, and then married a weaveress, and worked with father for a long time. Father was very well off—well off and comfortable for a poor man—but trade was good then. But it got bad afterwards, and none on us was able to live at it; so I takes to the chimney-sweeping again.'

Some years back the sweepers' houses were often indicated by an elaborate sign, highly coloured. A sweeper, accompanied by a 'chummy' (once a common name for the climbing-boy, being a corruption of chimney), was depicted on his way to a red brick house, from the chimneys of which bright yellow flames were streaming. Below was the detail of the things undertaken by the sweep, such as the extinction of fires in chimneys, the cleaning of smoke-jacks,* &c., &c. A few of these signs, greatly faded, may be seen still. A sweeper, who is settled in what is accounted a 'genteel neighbourhood', has now another way of making his calling known. He leaves a card whenever he hears of a new coiner, a tape being attached, so that it can be hung up in the kitchen, and thus the servants are always in possession of his address. The following is a customary style:

'Chimneys swept by the improved machine, much patronized by the Humane Society.

'W. H., Chimney Sweeper and Nightman, 1, —— Mews, in returning thanks to the inhabitants of the surrounding neighbourhood for the patronage he has hitherto received, begs to inform them that he sweeps all kinds of chimneys and flues in the best manner.

'W. H., attending to the business himself, cleans smoke-jacks, cures smoky coppers,* and extinguishes chimneys when on fire, with the greatest care and safety; and, by giving the strictest personal attendance to business, performs what he undertakes with cleanliness and punctuality, whereby he hopes to ensure a continuance of their favours and recommendations.

'Clean cloths for upper apartments. Soot-doors to any size fixed. Observe the address. 1, —— Mews, near ——.'

At the top of this card is an engraving of the machine; at the foot a rude sketch of a nightman's cart, with men at work. All the cards I saw reiterated the address, so that no mistake might lead the customer to a rival tradesman.

*The Quantity of Refuse Bought, Collected, or Found, in the Streets of London**

Perhaps the most curious trade is that in waste paper, or as it is called by the street collectors, in 'waste', comprising every kind of used or useless periodical, and books in all tongues. I may call the attention of my readers, by way of illustrating the extent of this business in what is proverbially refuse 'waste paper', to their experience of the penny postage.* Three or four sheets of note paper, according to the stouter or thinner texture, and an envelope with a seal or a glutinous and stamped fastening, will not exceed half-an-ounce, and is conveyed to the Orkneys and the further isles of Shetland, the Hebrides, the Scilly and Channel Islands, the isles of Achill and Cape Clear, off the western and southern coasts of Ireland, or indeed to and from the most extreme points of the United Kingdom, and no matter what distance, provided the letter be posted within the United Kingdom, for a penny. The weight of waste or refuse paper annually disposed of to the street collectors, or rather buyers, is 1,397,760 lbs. Were this tonnage, as I may call it, for it comprises 12,480 tons yearly, to be distributed in half-ounce letters, it would supply material, as respects weight, for *forty-four millions, seven hundred and twenty-eight thousand, four hundred and thirty* letters on business, love, or friendship.

I will next direct attention to what may be, by perhaps not over-straining a figure of speech, called 'the crumbs which fall from the rich man's table'; or, according to the quality of the commodity of refuse, of the tables of the *comparatively* rich, and that down to a low degree of the scale. These are not, however, unappropriated crumbs, to be swept away uncared for; but are objects of keen traffic and bargains between the possessors or their servants and the indefatigable street-folk. Among them are such things as champagne and other wine bottles, porter and ale bottles, and, including the establishments of all the rich and the comparative rich, kitchen-stuff, dripping, hog-wash, hare-skins, and tea-leaves. Lastly come the very lowest grades of the street-folk—the *finders*; men who will quarrel, and have been seen to quarrel, with a hungry cur for a street-found bone; not to pick or gnaw, although Eugène Sue* has seen that done in Paris; and I once, very early on a summer's morning, saw some apparently houseless Irish children contend with a dog and with each other for bones thrown out of a house in King William-street, City—as if after a very late supper—not to pick or gnaw, I was saying, but to *sell* for manure. Some of these finders have 'seen better days'; others, in intellect, are little elevated above the animals whose bones they gather, or whose ordure ('pure'), they scrape into their baskets.

The gross total, or average yearly money value, is 1,406,592*l.* for the second-hand commodities I have described in the foregoing pages; or as something like a minimum is given, both as to the number of the goods and the price, we may fairly put this total at a million and a half of pounds sterling!

CROSSING-SWEEPERS*

That portion of the London street-folk who earn a scanty living by sweeping crossings constitute a large class of the Metropolitan poor. We can scarcely walk along a street of any extent, or pass through a square of the least pretensions to 'gentility', without meeting one or more of these private scavengers. Crossing-sweeping seems to be one of those occupations which are resorted to as an excuse for begging; and, indeed, as many expressed it to me, 'it was the last chance left of obtaining an honest crust.'

The advantages of crossing-sweeping as a means of livelihood seem to be:

1st, the smallness of the capital required in order to commence the business;

2ndly, the excuse the apparent occupation it affords for soliciting gratuities without being considered in the light of a street-beggar;

And 3rdly, the benefits arising from being constantly seen in the same place, and thus exciting the sympathy of the neighbouring householders, till small weekly allowances or 'pensions' are obtained.

Concerning the *causes which lead or drive* people to this occupation, they are various. People take to crossing-sweeping either on account of their bodily afflictions, depriving them of the power of performing ruder work, or because the occupation is the last resource left open to them of earning a living, and they considered even the scanty subsistence it yields preferable to that of the workhouse. The greater proportion of crossing-sweepers are those who, from some bodily infirmity or injury, are prevented from a more laborious mode of obtaining their living. Among the bodily infirmities the chief are old age, asthma, and rheumatism; and the injuries mostly consist of loss of limbs. Many of the rheumatic sweepers have been bricklayers' labourers.

The classification of crossing-sweepers is not very complex. They may be divided into the *casual* and the *regular*.

By the casual I mean such as pursue the occupation only on certain days in the week, as, for instance, those who make their appearance on the Sunday morning, as well as the boys who, broom in hand, travel about the streets, sweeping before the foot-passengers or stopping an hour at one place, and then, if not fortunate, moving on to another.

The regular crossing-sweepers are those who have taken up their posts at the corners of streets or squares; and I have met with some who have kept to the same spot for more than forty years.

The Negro Crossing-Sweeper, who had lost both his Legs

This man sweeps a crossing in a principal and central thoroughfare when the weather is cold enough to let him walk; the colder the better, he says, as it 'numbs his stumps like'. He is unable to follow this occupation in warm weather, as his legs feel 'just like corns', and he cannot walk more than a mile a day. Under these circumstances he takes to begging, which he thinks he has a perfect right to do, as he has been left destitute in what is to him almost a strange country, and has been denied what he terms 'his rights'. He generally sits while begging dressed in a sailor shirt and trousers, with a black neckerchief round his neck, tied in the usual nautical knot. He places before him the placard which is given beneath, and never moves a muscle for the purpose of soliciting charity. He always appears scrupulously clean.

I went to see him at his home early one morning—in fact, at half-past eight, but he was not then up. I went again at nine, and found him prepared for my visit in a little parlour, in a dirty and rather disreputable alley running out of a court in a street near Brunswick-square. The negro's parlour was scantily furnished with two chairs, a turn-up bedstead, and a sea-chest. A few odds and ends of crockery stood on the sideboard, and a kettle was singing over a cheerful bit of fire. The little man was seated on a chair, with his stumps of legs sticking straight out. He showed some amount of intelligence in answering my questions. We were quite alone, for he sent his wife and child—the former a pleasant-looking 'half-caste', and the latter the cheeriest little crowing, smiling 'piccaninny'* I have ever seen—he sent them out into the alley, while I conversed with himself.

His life is embittered by the idea that he has never yet had 'his rights'—that the owners of the ship in which his legs were burnt off have not paid him his wages (of which, indeed, he says, he never received any but the five pounds which he had in advance before starting), and that he has been robbed of 42*l.* by a grocer in Glasgow. How true these statements may be it is almost impossible to say, but from what he says, some injustice seems to have been done him by the canny Scotchman, who refuses him his 'pay', without which he is determined 'never to leave the country'.

'I was on that crossing', he said, 'almost the whole of last winter. It was very cold, and I had nothing at all to do; so, as I passed there, I asked the gentleman at the baccer-shop, as well as the gentleman at the office, and I asked at the boot-shop, too, if they would let me sweep there. The policeman wanted to turn me away, but I went to the gentleman inside the office, and he told the policeman to leave me alone. The policeman said first, "You must go away," but I said, "I couldn't do anything else, and he ought to think it a charity to let me stop."

'I don't stop in London very long, though, at a time; I go to Glasgow, in Scotland, where the owners of the ship in which my legs were burnt off live. I served nine years in the merchant service and the navy. I was born in Kingston, in Jamaica; it is an English place, sir, so I am counted as not a foreigner. I'm different from them Lascars.* I went to sea when I was only nine years old. The owners is in London who had that ship. I was cabin-boy; and after I had served my time I became cook, or when I couldn't get the place of cook I went before the mast. I went as head cook in 1851, in the *Madeira* barque; she used to be a West Indy trader, and to trade out when I belonged to her. We got down to 69 south of Cape Horn; and there we got almost froze and perished to death. That is the book what I sell.'

The 'Book' (as he calls it) consists of eight pages, printed on paper the size of a sheet of note paper; it is entitled—

'BRIEF SKETCH OF THE LIFE OF

EDWARD ALBERT!

A native of Kingston, Jamaica.

Showing the hardships he underwent and the sufferings he endured in having both legs amputated.

HULL:

W. HOWE, PRINTER.'

It is embellished with a portrait of a black man, which has evidently been in its time a comic 'nigger' of the Jim-Crow* tobacco-paper kind, as is evidenced by the traces of a tobacco-pipe, which has been unskilfully erased.

The 'Book' itself is concocted from an affidavit made by Edward Albert before 'P. Mackinlay, Esq., one of Her Majesty's Justices of the Peace for the country (so it is printed) of Lanark'.

I have seen the affidavit, and it is almost identical with the statement in the 'book', excepting in the matter of grammar, which has rather suffered on its road to Mr Howe, the printer.

The following will give an idea of the matter of which it is composed:

'In February, 1851, I engaged to serve as cook on board the barque *Madeira*, of Glasgow, Captain J. Douglas, on her voyage from Glasgow to California, thence to China, and thence home to a port of discharge in the United Kingdom. I signed articles, and delivered up my register-ticket as a British seaman, as required by law. I entered the service on board the said vessel, under the said engagement, and sailed with that vessel on the 18th of February, 1851. I discharged my duty as cook on board the said vessel, from the date of its having left the Clyde, until June the same year, in which month the vessed rounded Cape Horne, at that time my legs became frost bitten, and I became in consequence unfit for duty.

'In the course of the next day after my limbs became affected, the master of the vessel, and mate, took me to the ship's oven, in order, as they said, to cure me; the oven was hot at the time, a fowl that was roasting therein having been removed in order to make room for my feet, which was put into the oven; in consequence of the treatment, my feet burst through the intense swelling, and mortification ensued.

'The vessel called, six weeks after, at Valpariso, and I was there taken to an hospital, where I remained five months and a half. Both my legs were amputated three inches below my knees soon after I went to the hospital at Valpariso. I asked my master for my wages due to me, for my service on board the vessel, and demanded my register-ticket; when the captain told me I should not recover, that the vessel could not wait for me, and that I was a dead man, and that he could not discharge a dead man; and that he also said, that as I had no friends there to get my money, he would only put a little money into the hands of the consul, which would be applied in burying me. On being discharged from the hospital I called on the consul, and was informed by him that master had not left any money.

'I was afterwards taken on board one of her Majesty's ships, the *Driver*, Captain Charles Johnston, and landed at Portsmouth; from thence I got a passage to Glasgow, ware I remained three months. Upon supplication to the register-office for seamen, in London, my register-ticket has been forwarded to the Collector of Customs, Glasgow; and he is ready to deliver it to me upon obtaining the authority of the Justices of the Peace, and I recovered the same under the 22nd section of the General Merchant Seaman's Act. Declares I cannot write.

'(Signed) DAVID MACKINLAY, J.P.

'The Justices having considered the foregoing information and declaration, finds that Edward Albert, therein named the last-register ticket, sought to be covered under circumstances which, so far as he was concerned, were unavoidable, and that no fraud was intended or committed by him in reference thereto, therefore authorised the Collector and Comptroller of Customs at the port of Glasgow to deliver to the said Edward Albert the register-ticket, sought to be recovered by him all in terms of 22nd section of the General Merchant Seamen's Act.

'(Signed) DAVID MACKINLAY, J.P.

'Glasgow, Oct. 6th, 1852.
'Register Ticket, No. 512, 652, age 25 years.'

'I could make a large book of my sufferings, sir, if I liked,' he said, 'and I will disgrace the owners of that ship as long as they don't give me what they owe me.

'I will never leave England or Scotland until I get my rights; but they says money makes money, and if I had money I could get it. If they would only give me what they owe me, I wouldn't ask anybody for a farthing, God knows, sir. I don't know why the master put my feet in the oven; he said to cure me: the agony of pain I was in was such, he said, that it must be done.

'The loss of my limbs is bad enough, but it's still worse when you can't get what is your rights, nor anything for the sweat that they worked out of me.

'After I went down to Glasgow for my money I opened a little coffee-house; it was called "Uncle Tom's Cabin".* I did very well. The man who sold me tea and coffee said he would get me on, and I had better give my money to him to keep safe, and he used to put it away in a tin box which I had given four-and-sixpence for. He advertised my place in the papers, and I did a good business. I had the place open a month, when he kept all my savings—two-and-forty pounds—and shut up the place, and denied me of it, and I never got a farthing.

'I declare to you I can't describe the agony I felt when my legs were burst; I fainted away over and over again. There was four men came; I was lying in my hammock, and they moved the fowl that was roasting, and put my legs in the oven. There they held me for ten minutes. They said it would take the cold out; but after I came out the cold caught 'em again, and the next day they swole up as big round as a pillar, and burst, and then like water come out. No man but God knows what I have suffered and went through.

'When I got back to London, I commenced sweeping the crossin', sir. I only sweep it in the winter, because I can't stand in the summer. Oh, yes, I feel my feet still: it is just as if I had them sitting on the floor, now. I feel my toes moving, like as if I had 'em. I could count them, the whole ten, whenever I work my knees. I had a corn on one of my toes, and I can feel it still, particularly at the change of weather.'

The following is a verbatim copy of the placard which the poor fellow places before him when he begs. He carries it, when not in use, in a little calico bag which hangs round his neck:

KIND CHRISTIAN FRIENDS

THE UNFORTUNATE

EDWARD ALBERT

WAS COOK ON BOARD THE BARQUE MADEIRA OF GLASGOW CAPTAIN J. DOUGLAS IN FEBRUARY 1851 WHEN AFTER ROUNDING CAPE HORNE HE HAD HIS LEGS AND FEET FROST BITTEN when in that state the master and mate put my Legs and Feet into the Oven as they said to cure me the Oven being hot at the time a fowl was roasting was took away to make room for my feet and legs in consequence of this my feet and legs swelled and burst——Mortification then Ensued after which my legs were amputated Three Inches below the knees soon after my entering the Hospital at Valpariso.

AS I HAVE NO OTHER MEANS TO GET A LIVELYHOOD BUT BY APPEALING TO

A GENEROUS PUBLIC

YOUR KIND DONATIONS WILL BE MOST THANKFULLY RECEIVED.

Boy Crossing-Sweepers and Tumblers

A remarkably intelligent lad, who, on being spoken to, at once consented to give all the information in his power, told me the following story of his life.

It will be seen from this boy's account, and the one or two following, that a kind of partnership exists among some of these young sweepers. They have associated themselves together, appropriated several crossings to their use, and appointed a captain over them. They have their forms of trial, and 'jury-house' for the settlement of disputes; laws have been framed, which govern their commercial proceedings, and a kind of language adopted by the society for its better protection from its arch-enemy, the policeman.

I found the lad who first gave me an insight into the proceedings of the associated crossing-sweepers crouched on the stone steps of a door in Adelaide-street, Strand; and when I spoke to him he was preparing to settle down in a corner and go to sleep—his legs and body being curled round almost as closely as those of a cat on a hearth.

The moment he heard my voice he was upon his feet, asking me to 'give a halfpenny to poor little Jack'.

He was a good-looking lad, with a pair of large mild eyes, which he took good care to turn up with an expression of supplication as he moaned for his halfpenny.

A cap, or more properly a stuff bag, covered a crop of hair which had matted itself into the form of so many paint-brushes, while his face, from its roundness of feature and the complexion of dirt, had an almost Indian look about it; the colour of his hands, too, was such that you could imagine he had been shelling walnuts.

He ran before me, treading cautiously with his naked feet, until I reached a convenient spot to take down his statement, which was as follows:

'I was fifteen the 24th of last May, sir, and I've been sweeping crossings now near upon two years. There's a party of six of us, and we have the crossings from St Martin's Church as far as Pall Mall. I always go along with them as lodges in the same place as I do. In the daytime, if it's dry, we do anythink what we can—open cabs, or anythink; but if it's wet, we separate, and I and another gets a crossing—those who gets on it first, keeps it,—and we stand on each side and take our chance.

'We do it in this way:—if I was to see two gentlemen coming, I should cry out, "Two toffs": and then they are mine; and whether they give me anythink or not they are mine, and my mate is bound not to follow them; for if he did he would get a hiding from the whole lot of us. If we both cry out together, then we share. If it's a lady and gentleman, then we cries, "A toff and a doll!" Sometimes we are caught out in this way. Perhaps it is a lady and gentleman and a child; and if I was to see them, and only say, "A toff and a doll," and leave out the child, then my mate can add the child; and as he is right and I wrong, then it's his party.

'If there's a policeman close at hand we mustn't ask for money; but we are always on the look-out for the policemen, and if we see one, then we calls out "Phillup!" for that's our signal. One of the policemen at St Martin's Church—Bandy, we calls him—knows what Phillup means, for he's up to us; so we had to change the word. (At the request of the young crossing-sweeper the present signal is omitted.)

'When we see the rain we say together, "Oh! there's a jolly good rain! we'll have a good day to-morrow." If a shower comes on, and we are at our room, which we general are about three o'clock, to get somethink to eat—besides, we general go there to see how much each other's taken in the day—why, out we run with our brooms.

'We're always sure to make money if there's mud—that's to say, if we look for our money, and ask; of course, if we stand still we don't. Now, there's Lord Fitzhardinge,* he's a good gentleman, what lives in Spring-gardens, in a large house. He's got a lot of servants and carriages. Every time he crosses the Charing-cross crossing he always gives the girl half a sovereign.' (This statement was taken in June 1856.) 'He doesn't cross often, because, hang it, he's got such a lot of carriages, but when he's on foot he always does. If they asks him he doesn't give nothink, but if they touches their caps he does. The housekeeper at his house is very kind to us. We run errands for her, and when she wants any of her own letters taken to the post then she calls, and if we are on the crossing we takes them for her. She's a very nice lady, and gives us broken victuals. I've got a share in that crossing,—there are three of us, and when he gives the half sovereign he always gives it to the girl, and those that are in it shares it. She would do us out of it if she could, but we all takes good care of that, for we are all cheats.

THE BOY CROSSING-SWEEPERS.

[*From a Daguerreotype by* BEARD.]

'At night-time we tumbles—that is, if the policemen ain't nigh. We goes general to Waterloo-place when the Opera's on. We sends on one of us ahead, as a looker-out, to look for the policeman, and then we follows. It's no good tumbling to gentlemen *going* to the Opera; it's when they're coming back they gives us money. When they've got a young lady on their arm they laugh at us tumbling; some will give us a penny, others threepence, sometimes a sixpence or a shilling, and sometimes a halfpenny. We either do the cat'un-wheel,* or else we keep before the gentleman and lady, turning head-over-heels, putting our broom on the ground and then turning over it.

'I work a good deal fetching cabs after the Opera is over; we general open the doors of those what draw up at the side of the pavement for people to get into as have walked a little down the Haymarket looking for a cab. We gets a month in prison if we touch the others by the columns. I once had half a sovereign give me by a gentleman; it was raining awful, and I run all about for a cab, and at last I got one. The gentleman knew it was half a sovereign, because he said—"Here, my little man, here's half a sovereign for your trouble." He had three ladies with him, beautiful ones, with nothink on their heads, and only capes on their bare shoulders; and he had white kids on, and his regular Opera togs, too. I liked him very much, and as he was going to give me somethink the ladies says—"Oh, give him somethink extra!" It was pouring with rain, and they couldn't get a cab; they were all engaged, but I jumped on the box of one as was driving along the line. Last Saturday Opera night I made fifteen pence by the gentlemen coming from the Opera.

'After the Opera we go into the Haymarket, where all the women are who walk the streets all night. They don't give us no money, but they tell the gentlemen to. Sometimes, when they are talking to the gentlemen, they say, "Go away, you young rascal!" and if they are saucy, then we say to them, "We're not talking to you, my doxy,* we're talking to the gentleman,"—but that's only if they're rude, for if they speak civil we always goes. They knows what "doxy" means. What is it? Why that they are no better than us! If we are on the crossing, and we says to them as they go by, "Good luck to you!" they always give us somethink either that night or the next. There are two with bloomer bonnets, who always give us somethink if we says "Good luck." Sometimes a gentleman will tell us to go and get them a young lady, and then we goes, and they general gives us sixpence for that. If the gents is dressed finely we gets them a handsome girl; if they're dressed middling, then we gets them a middling-dressed one; but we usual prefers giving a turn to girls that have been kind to us, and they are sure to give us somethink the next night. If we don't find any girls walking, we knows where to get them in the houses in the streets round about.

'When we gets home at half-past three in the morning, whoever cries out "first wash" has it. First of all we washes our feet, and we all uses the same water. Then we washes our faces and hands, and necks, and whoever fetches the fresh water up has first wash; and if the second don't like to go and get fresh, why he uses the dirty. Whenever we come in the landlady makes us wash our feet. Very often the stones cuts our feet and makes them bleed; then we bind a bit of rag round them. We like to put on boots and shoes in the day-time, but at night-time we can't, because it stops the tumbling.

'When we are talking together we always talk in a kind of slang. Each policeman we gives a regular name—there's "Bull's Head", "Bandy Shanks", and "Old Cherry Legs", and "Dot-and-carry-one"; they all knows their names as well as us. We never talks of crossings, but "fakes". We don't make no slang of our own, but uses the regular one.

'A broom doesn't last us more than a week in wet weather, and they costs us twopence halfpenny each; but in dry weather they are good for a fortnight.'

The 'King' of the Tumbling-Boy Crossing-Sweepers

The young sweeper who had been styled by his companions the 'King' was a pretty-looking boy, only tall enough to rest his chin comfortably on the mantel-piece as he talked to me, and with a pair of grey eyes that were as bright and clear as drops of sea-water. He was clad in a style in no way agreeing with his royal title; for he had on a kind of dirt-coloured shooting-coat of tweed, which was fraying into a kind of cobweb at the edges and elbows. His trousers too, were rather faulty, for there was a pink-wrinkled dot of flesh at one of the knees; while their length was too great for his majesty's short legs, so that they had to be rolled up at the end like a washerwoman's sleeves.

His royal highness was of a restless disposition, and, whilst talking, lifted up, one after another, the different ornaments on the mantelpiece, frowning and looking at them sideways, as he pondered over the replies he should make to my questions.

When I arrived at the grandmother's apartment the 'king' was absent, his majesty having been sent with a pitcher to fetch some spring-water.

The 'king' also was kind enough to favour me with samples of his wondrous tumbling powers. He could bend his little legs round till they curved like the long German sausages we see in the ham-and-beef shops; and when he turned head over heels, he curled up his tiny body as closely as a wood-louse, and then rolled along, wabbling like an egg.

'The boys call me Johnny,' he said; 'and I'm getting on for eleven, and I goes along with the Goose and Harry, a-sweeping at St Martin's Church, and about there. I used, too, to go to the crossing where the statute is, sir, at the bottom of the Haymarket. I went along with the others; sometimes there were three or four of us, or sometimes one, sir. I never used to sweep unless it was wet. I don't go out not before twelve or one in the day; it ain't no use going before that; and beside, I couldn't get up before that, I'm too sleepy. I don't stop out so late as the other boys; they sometimes stop all night, but I don't like that. The Goose was out all night along with Martin; they went all along up Piccirilly, and there they climbed over the Park railings and went a birding all by themselves, and then they went to sleep for an hour on the grass—so they says. I likes better to come home to my bed. It kills me for the next day when I do stop out all night. The Goose is always out all night; he likes it.

'Neither father nor mother's alive, sir, but I lives along with grandmother and aunt, as owns this room, and I always gives them all I gets.

'Sometimes I makes a shilling, sometimes sixpence, and sometimes less. I can never take nothink of a day, only of a night, because I can't tumble of a day, and I can of a night.

'The Gander taught me tumbling, and he was the first as did it along the crossings. I can tumble quite as well as the Goose; I can turn a caten-wheel,* and he can't, and I can go further on forards than him, but I can't tumble backards as he can. I can't do a handspring, though. Why, a handspring's pitching yourself forards on both hands, turning over in front, and lighting on your feet; that's very difficult, and very few can do it. There's one little chap, but he's very clever, and can tie himself up in a knot a'most. I'm best at caten-wheels; I can do 'em twelve or fourteen times running—keep on at it. It just *does* tire you, that's all. When I gets up I feels quite giddy. I can tumble about forty times over head and heels. I does the most of that, and I thinks it's the most difficult, but I can't say which gentlemen likes best. You see they are anigh sick of the head-and-heels tumbling, and then werry few of the boys can do caten-wheels on the crossings—only two or three besides me.

'When I see anybody coming, I says, "Please, sir, give me a half-penny," and touches my hair, and then I throws a caten-wheel, and has a look at 'em, and if I sees they are laughing, then I goes on and throws more of 'em. Perhaps one in ten will give a chap something. Some of 'em will give you a threepenny-bit or p'rhaps sixpence, and others only give you a kick. Well, sir, I should say they likes tumbling over head and heels; if you can keep it up twenty times then they begins laughing, but if you only does it once, some of 'em will say, "Oh, I could do that myself," and then they don't give nothink.

'Goose can stand on his nose as well as me; we puts the face flat down on the ground, instead of standing on our heads. There's Duckey Dunnovan, and the Stuttering Baboon, too, and two others as well, as can do it; but the Stuttering Baboon's getting too big and fat to do it well; he's a very awkward tumbler. It don't hurt, only at larn-ing; cos you bears more on your hands than your nose.

'Sometimes they says—"Well, let us see you do it," and then p'raps they'll search in their pockets, and say—"O, I haven't got any cop-pers": so then we'll force 'em, and p'raps they'll pull out their purse and gives us a little bit of silver.

'Ah, we works hard for what we gets, and then there's the police-men birching us. Some of 'em is so spiteful, they takes up their belt what they uses round the waist to keep their coat tight, and 'll hit us with the buckle; but we generally gives 'em the lucky dodge and gets out of their way.

'One night, two gentlemen, officers they was, was standing in the Haymarket, and a drunken man passed by. There was snow on the ground, and we'd been begging of 'em, and says one of them—"I'll give you a shilling if you'll knock that drunken man over." We was three of us; so we set on him, and soon had him down. After he got up he went and told the policemen, but we all cut round different ways and got off, and then met again. We didn't get the shilling, though, cos a boy crabbed us. He went up to the gentleman, and says he—"Give it me, sir, I'm the boy"; and then we says—"No, sir, it's us." So, says the officer—"I sharn't give it to none of you," and puts it back again in his pockets. We broke a broom over the boy as crabbed us, and then we cut down Waterloo-place, and afterwards we come up to the Haymarket again, and there we met the officers, again. I did a caten-wheel, and then says I—"Then won't you give me un now?" and they says—"Go and sweep some mud on that woman." So I went and did it, and then they takes me in a pastry-shop at the corner, and they tells me to tumble on the tables in the shop. I nearly broke one of 'em, they were so delicate. They gived me a fourpenny meat-pie and two penny sponge-cakes, which I puts in my pocket, cos there was another sharing with me. The lady of the shop kept on screaming—"Go and fetch me a police—take the dirty boy out," cos I was standing on the tables in my muddy feet, and the officers was a bursting their sides with laughing; and says they, "No, he sharn't stir."

'I was frightened, cos if the police had come they'd been safe and sure to have took me. They made me tumble from the door to the end of the shop, and back again, and then I turned 'em a caten-wheel, and was near knocking down all the things as was on the counter.

'They didn't give me no money, only pies; but I got a shilling another time for tumbling to some French ladies and gentlemen in a pastry-cook's shop under the Colonnade. I often goes into a shop like that; I've done it a good many times.

'I've been sweeping the crossings getting on for two years. Before that I used to go caten-wheeling after the busses. I don't like the sweeping, and I don't think there's e'er a one of us wot likes it. In the winter we has to be out in the cold, and then in summer we have to sleep out all night, or go asleep on the church-steps, reg'lar tired out.

'One of us 'll say at night—"Oh, I'm sleepy now, who's game for a doss? I'm for a doss";—and then we go eight or ten of us into a door-way of the church, where they keep the dead in a kind of airy-like underneath, and there we go to sleep. The most of the boys has got no homes. Perhaps they've got the price of a lodging, but they're hungry, and they eats the money, and then they must lay out. There's some of 'em will stop out in the wet for perhaps the sake of a halfpenny, and get themselves sopping wet. I think all our chaps would like to get out of the work if they could; I'm sure Goose would, and so would I.

'All the boys call me the King, because I tumbles so well, and some calls me "Pluck", and some "Judy". I'm called "Pluck", cause I'm so plucked a going at the gentlemen! Tommy Dunnovan—"Tipperty Tight"—we calls him, cos his trousers is so tight he can hardly move in them sometimes,—he was the first as called me "Judy". Dunnovan once swallowed a pill for a shilling. A gentleman in the Haymarket says—"If you'll swallow this here pill I'll give you a shilling"; and Jimmy says, "All right, sir"; and he puts it in his mouth, and went to the water-pails near the cab-stand and swallowed it.

'All the chaps in our gang likes me, and we all likes one another. We always shows what we gets given to us to eat.

'Sometimes we gets one another up wild, and then that fetches up a fight, but that isn't often. When two of us fights, the others stands round and sees fair play. There was a fight last night between "Broke his Bones"—as we calls Antony Hones—and Neddy Hall—the "Sparrow", or "Spider", we calls him,—something about the root of a pineapple, as we was aiming with at one another, and that called up a fight. We all stood round and saw them at it, but neither of 'em licked, for they gived in for to-day, and they're to finish it to-night. We makes 'em fight fair. We all of us likes to see a fight, but not to fight ourselves. Hones is sure to beat, as Spider is as thin as a wafer, and all bones. I can lick the Spider, though he's twice my size.'

VOLUME III

THE LONDON STREET-FOLK (CONCLUDED)

DESTROYERS OF VERMIN

The Rat-Killer

In 'the Brill', or rather in Brill-place, Somers'-town, there is a variety of courts branching out into Chapel-street, and in one of the most angular and obscure of these is to be found a perfect nest of rat-catchers—not altogether professional rat-catchers, but for the most part sporting mechanics and costermongers. The court is not easily to be found, being inhabited by men not so well known in the immediate neighbourhood as perhaps a mile or two away, and only to be discovered by the aid and direction of the little girl at the neighbouring cat's-meat shop.

My first experience of this court was the usual disturbance at the entrance. I found one end or branch of it filled with a mob of eager listeners, principally women, all attracted to a particular house by the sounds of quarrelling. One man gave it as his opinion that the disturbers must have earned too much money yesterday; and a woman, speaking to another who had just come out, lifting up both her hands and laughing, said, 'Here they are—*at it* again!'

The rat-killer whom we were in search of was out at his stall in Chapel-street when we called, but his wife soon fetched him. He was a strong, sturdy-looking man, rather above the middle height, with light hair, ending in sandy whiskers, reaching under his chin, sharp deep-set eyes, a tight-skinned nose that looked as if the cuticle had been stretched to its utmost on its bridge. He was dressed in the ordinary corduroy costermonger habit, having, in addition, a dark blue Guernsey drawn over his waistcoat.

After I had satisfied him that I was not a collector of dog-tax, trying to find out how many animals he kept, he gave me what he evidently thought was 'a treat'—a peep at his bull-dog, which he fetched from upstairs, and let it jump about the room with a most unpleasant liberty, informing me the while how he had given five pound for him, and that one of the first pups he got by a bull he had got five pounds for, and that cleared him. 'That Punch' (the bull-dog's name), he said, 'is as quiet as a lamb—wouldn't hurt nobody; I frequently takes him through the streets without a lead. Sartainly he killed a cat the t'other afternoon, but he couldn't help that, 'cause the cat flew at him; though he took it as quietly as a man would a woman in a passion, and only went at her just to save his eyes. But you couldn't easy get him off, master, when he once got a holt. He was a good one for rats, and, he believed, the stanchest and tricksiest dog in London.

'All my lifetime I've been a-dealing a little in rats; but it was not till I come to London that I turned my mind fully to that sort of thing. My father always had a great notion of the same. We all like the sport. When any on us was in the country, and the farmers wanted us to, we'd do it. If anybody heerd tell of my being an activish chap like, in that sort of way, they'd get me to come for a day or so.

'If anybody has a place that's eaten up with rats, I goes and gets some ferruts,* and takes a dog, if I've got one, and manages to kill 'em. Sometimes I keep my own ferruts, but mostly I borrows them. This young man that's with me, he'll sometimes have an order to go fifty or sixty mile into the country, and then he buys his ferruts, or gets them the best way he can. They charges a good sum for the loan of 'em—sometimes as much as you get for the job.

'You can buy ferruts at Leadenhall-market for 5*s.* or 7*s.*—it all depends; you can't get them all at one price, some of 'em is real cowards to what others is; some won't even kill a rat. The way we tries 'em is, we puts 'em down anywhere, in a room maybe, with a rat, and if they smell about and won't go up to it, why they won't do; 'cause you see, sometimes the ferrut has to go up a hole, and at the end there may be a dozen or sixteen rats, and if he hasn't got the heart to tackle one on 'em, why he ain't worth a farden.

'I have kept ferruts for four or five months at a time, but they're nasty stinking things. I've had them get loose; but, bless you, they do no harm, they're as hinnocent as cats; they won't hurt nothink; you can play with them like a kitten. Some puts things down to ketch rats—sorts of pison, which is their secret—but I don't. I relies upon my dogs and ferruts, and nothink else.'

A Night at Rat-Killing

Considering the immense number of rats which form an article of commerce with many of the lower orders, whose business it is to keep them for the purpose of rat matches, I thought it necessary, for the full elucidation of my subject, to visit the well-known public-house in London, where, on a certain night in the week, a pit is built up, and regular rat-killing matches take place, and where those who have sporting dogs, and are anxious to test their qualities, can, after such matches are finished, purchase half a dozen or a dozen rats for them to practise upon, and judge for themselves of their dogs' 'performances'.

To quote the words printed on the proprietor's card, 'he is always at his old house at home, as usual, to discuss the FANCY* generally.'

I arrived at about eight o'clock at the tavern where the performances were to take place. I was too early, but there was plenty to occupy my leisure in looking at the curious scene around me, and taking notes of the habits and conversation of the customers who were flocking in.

The front of the long bar was crowded with men of every grade of society, all smoking, drinking, and talking about dogs. Many of them had brought with them their 'fancy' animals, so that a kind of 'canine exhibition' was going on; some carried under their arm small bull-dogs, whose flat pink noses rubbed against my arm as I passed; others had Skye-terriers, curled up like balls of hair, and sleeping like children, as they were nursed by their owners. The only animals that seemed awake, and under continual excitement, were the little brown English terriers, who, despite the neat black leathern collars by which they were held, struggled to get loose, as if they smelt the rats in the room above, and were impatient to begin the fray.

There is a business-like look about this tavern which at once lets you into the character of the person who owns it. The drinking seems to have been a secondary notion in its formation, for it is a low-roofed room without any of those adornments which are now generally considered so necessary to render a public-house attractive. The tubs where the spirits are kept are blistered with the heat of the gas, and so dirty that the once brilliant gilt hoops are now quite black.

Sleeping on an old hall-chair lay an enormous white bulldog, 'a great beauty', as I was informed, with a head as round and smooth as a clenched boxing-glove, and seemingly too large for the body. Its forehead appeared to protrude in a manner significant of water on the brain, and almost overhung the short nose, through which the animal breathed heavily. When this dog, which was the admiration of all beholders, rose up, its legs were as bowed as a tailor's, leaving a peculiar pear-shaped opening between them, which, I was informed, was one of its points of beauty. It was a white dog, with a sore look, from its being peculiarly pink round the eyes, nose, and indeed at all the edges of its body.

On the other side of the fire-place was a white bull-terrier dog, with a black patch over the eye, which gave him rather a disreputable look. This animal was watching the movements of the customers in front, and occasionally, when the entrance-door was swung back, would give a growl of inquiry as to what the fresh-comer wanted. The proprietor was kind enough to inform me, as he patted this animal's ribs, which showed like the hoops on a butter-firkin,* that he considered there had been a 'little of the greyhound in some of his back generations'.

About the walls were hung clusters of black leather collars, adorned with brass rings and clasps, and pre-eminent was a silver dog-collar, which, from the conversation of those about me, I learnt was to be the prize in a rat-match to be 'killed for' in a fortnight's time.

As the visitors poured in, they, at the request of the proprietor 'not to block up the bar', took their seats in the parlour, and, accompanied by a waiter, who kept shouting, 'Give your orders, gentlemen,' I entered the room.

I found that, like the bar, no pains had been taken to render the room attractive to the customers, for, with the exception of the sporting pictures hung against the dingy paper, it was devoid of all adornment. Over the fireplace were square glazed boxes, in which were the stuffed forms of dogs famous in their day. Pre-eminent among the prints was that representing the 'Wonder' Tiny, 'five pounds and a half in weight', as he appeared lulling 200 rats. This engraving had a singular look, from, its having been printed upon a silk handkerchief. Tiny had been a great favourite with the proprietor, and used to wear a lady's bracelet as a collar.

Among the stuffed heads was one of a white bull-dog, with tremendous glass eyes sticking out, as if it had died of strangulation. The proprietor's son was kind enough to explain to me the qualities that had once belonged to this favourite. 'They've spoilt her in stuffing, sir,' he said; 'made her so short in the head; but she was the wonder of her day. There wasn't a dog in England as would come nigh her. There's her daughter,' he added, pointing to another head, something like that of a seal, 'but she wasn't reckoned half as handsome as her mother, though she was very much admired in her time.

'That there *is* a dog,' he continued, pointing to one represented with a rat in its mouth, 'it was as good as any in England, though it's so small. I've seen her kill a dozen rats almost as big as herself, though they killed *her* at last; for sewer-rats are dreadful for giving dogs canker in the mouth, and she wore herself out with continually killing them, though we always rinsed her mouth out well with peppermint and water while she were at work. When rats bite they are pisonous, and an ulcer is formed, which we are obleeged to lance; that's what killed her.'

The company assembled in 'the parlour' consisted of sporting men, or those who, from curiosity, had come to witness what a rat-match was like. Seated at the same table, talking together, were those dressed in the costermonger's suit of corduroy, soldiers with their uniforms carelessly unbuttoned, coachmen in their livery, and tradesmen who had slipped on their evening frock-coats, and run out from the shop to see the sport.

The dogs belonging to the company were standing on the different tables, or tied to the legs of the forms, or sleeping in their owners' arms, and were in turn minutely criticised—their limbs being stretched out as if they were being felt for fractures, and their mouths looked into, as if a dentist were examining their teeth. Nearly all the little animals were marked with scars from bites. 'Pity to bring him up to rat-killing,' said one, who had been admiring a fierce-looking bull-terrier, although he did not mention at the same time what line in life the little animal ought to pursue.

At another table one man was declaring that his pet animal was the exact image of the celebrated rat-killing dog 'Billy', at the same time pointing to the picture against the wall of that famous animal, 'as he performed his wonderful feat of killing 500 rats in five minutes and a half'.

There were amongst the visitors some French gentlemen, who had evidently witnessed nothing of the kind before; and whilst they endeavoured to drink their hot gin and water, they made their interpreter translate to them the contents of a large placard hung upon a hatpeg, and headed—

'Every Man has his Fancy.
Ratting Sports in Reality.'

About nine o'clock the proprietor took the chair in the parlour, at the same time giving the order to 'shut up the shutters in the room above, and light up the pit'. This announcement seemed to rouse the spirits of the impatient assembly, and even the dogs tied to the legs of the tables ran out to the length of their leathern thongs, and their tails curled like eels, as if they understood the meaning of the words.

'Why, that's the little champion,' said the proprietor, patting a dog with thighs like a grasshopper, and whose mouth opened back to its ears. 'Well, it *is* a beauty! I wish I could gammon* you to take a "fiver" for it.' Then looking round the room, he added, 'Well, gents, I'm glad to see you look so comfortable.'

The performances of the evening were somewhat hurried on by the entering of a young gentleman, whom the waiters called 'Cap'an'.

'Now, Jem, when is this match coming off?' the Captain asked impatiently; and despite the assurance that they were getting ready, he threatened to leave the place if kept waiting much longer. This young officer seemed to be a great 'fancier' of dogs, for he made the round of the room, handling each animal in its turn, feeling and squeezing its feet, and scrutinising its eyes and limbs with such minuteness, that the French gentlemen were forced to inquire who he was.

There was no announcement that the room above was ready, though everybody seemed to understand it; for all rose at once, and mounting the broad wooden staircase, which led to what was once the 'drawing-room', dropped their shillings into the hand of the proprietor, and entered the rat-killing apartment.

'The pit', as it is called, consists of a small circus, some six feet in diameter. It is about as large as a centre flower-bed, and is fitted with a high wooden rim that reaches to elbow height. Over it the branches of a gas lamp are arranged, which light up the white painted floor, and every part of the little arena. On one side of the room is a recess, which the proprietor calls his 'private box', and this apartment the Captain and his friend soon took possession of, whilst the audience generally clambered upon the tables and forms, or hung over the sides of the pit itself.

All the little dogs which the visitors had brought up with them were now squalling and barking, and struggling in their masters' arms, as if they were thoroughly acquainted with the uses of the pit; and when a rusty wire cage of rats, filled with the dark moving mass, was brought forward, the noise of the dogs was so great that the proprietor was obliged to shout out—'Now, you that have dogs *do* make 'em shut up.'

The Captain was the first to jump into the pit. A man wanted to sell him a bull-terrier, spotted like a fancy rabbit, and a dozen of rats was the consequent order.

The Captain preferred pulling the rats out of the cage himself, laying hold of them by their tails and jerking them into the arena. He was cautioned by one of the men not to let them bite him, for 'believe me,' were the words, 'you'll never forget, Cap'an; these 'ere are none of the cleanest.'

Whilst the rats were being counted out, some of those that had been taken from the cage ran about the painted floor and climbed up the young officer's legs, making him shake them off and exclaim, 'Get out, you varmint!' whilst others of the ugly little animals sat upon their hind legs, cleaning their faces with their paws.

When the dog in question was brought forth and shown the dozen rats, he grew excited, and stretched himself in his owner's arms, whilst all the other animals joined in a full chorus of whining.

'Chuck him in,' said the Captain, and over went the dog; and in a second the rats were running round the circus, or trying to hide themselves between the small openings in the boards round the pit.

Although the proprietor of the dog endeavoured to speak up for it, by declaring 'it was a good 'un, and a very pretty performer,' still it was evidently not worth much in a rat-killing sense; and if it had not been for his 'second', who beat the sides of the pit with his hand, and shouted 'Hi! hi! at 'em!' in a most bewildering manner, we doubt if the terrier would not have preferred leaving the rats to themselves, to enjoy their lives. Some of the rats, when the dog advanced towards them, sprang up in his face, making him draw back with astonishment. Others, as he bit them, curled round in his mouth and fastened on his nose, so that he had to carry them as a cat does its kittens. It also required many shouts of 'Drop it—dead 'un,' before he would leave those he had killed.

We cannot say whether the dog was eventually bought; but from its owner's exclaiming, in a kind of apologetic tone, 'Why, he never saw a rat before in all his life,' we fancy no dealings took place.

The Captain seemed anxious to see as much sport as he could, for he frequently asked those who carried dogs in their arms whether 'his little 'un would kill', and appeared sorry when such answers were given as—'My dog's mouth's a little out of order, Cap'an,' or 'I've only tried him at very small 'uns.'

One little dog was put in the pit to amuse himself with the dead bodies. He seized hold of one almost as big as himself, shook it furiously till the head thumped the floor like a drumstick, making those around shout with laughter, and causing one man to exclaim, 'He's a good 'un at shaking heads and tails, ain't he?'

Preparations now began for the grand match of the evening, in which fifty rats were to be killed. The 'dead 'uns' were gathered up by their tails and flung into the corner. The floor was swept, and a big flat basket produced, like those in which chickens are brought to market, and under whose iron wire top could be seen small mounds of closely packed rats.

This match seemed to be between the proprietor and his son, and the stake to be gained was only a bottle of lemonade, of which the father stipulated he should have first drink.

It was strange to observe the daring manner in which the lad introduced his hand into the rat cage, sometimes keeping it there for more than a minute at a time, as he fumbled about and stirred up with his fingers the living mass, picking out, as he had been requested, 'only the big 'uns'.

When the fifty animals had been flung into the pit, they gathered themselves together into a mound which reached one-third up the sides, and which reminded one of the heap of hair-sweepings in a barber's shop after a heavy day's cutting. These were all sewer and water-ditch rats, and the smell that rose from them was like that from a hot drain.

The Captain amused himself by flicking at them with his pocket handkerchief, and offering them the lighted end of his cigar, which the little creatures tamely snuffed at, and drew back from, as they singed their noses.

It was also a favourite amusement to blow on the mound of rats, for they seemed to dislike the cold wind, which sent them fluttering

nd
ies as
up.
like a few
to drinking'
he epilogue of

r collar to be killed
they must be novice
*hee*nomenons. We shall
will be loads of rat-killing.
rgetting your dogs, likewise;
over, who had good trouble to
re they didn't come to life again.
ur down-stairs, where we meets for

ch-'em-Alive' Sellers

of 'catch-'em-alive' boys residing in Pheasant-
ane.
sing title given to this alley, one might almost be led
as a very delightful spot, though it is only necessary to
e little bricken archway that marks its entrance, and see
s—dirty as the sides of a dust-bin, and with the patched
panes and yellow sheets hanging from the windows—to feel
ed that it is one of the most squalid of the many wretched courts
t branch out from Gray's-inn-lane.

I found the lads playing at 'pitch and toss'* in the middle of the paved yard. They were all willing enough to give me their statements; indeed, the only difficulty I had was in making my choice among the youths.

'Please, sir, I've been at it longer than him,' cried one with teeth ribbed like celery.

about like so many feathers; indeed, whilst the match was going on, whenever the little animals collected together, and formed a barricade as it were to the dog, the cry of 'Blow on 'em! blow on 'em!' was given by the spectators, and the dog's second puffed at them as if extinguishing a fire, when they would dart off like so many sparks.

The company was kept waiting so long for the match to begin that the impatient Captain again threatened to leave the house, and was only quieted by the proprietor's reply of 'My dear friend, be easy, the boy's on the stairs with the dog'; and true enough we shortly heard a wheezing and a screaming in the passage without, as if some strong-winded animal were being strangled, and presently a boy entered, carrying in his arms a bull-terrier in a perfect fit of excitement, foaming at the mouth and stretching its neck forward, so that the collar which held it back seemed to be cutting its throat in two.

The animal was nearly mad with rage—scratching and struggling to get loose. 'Lay hold a little closer up to the head or he'll turn round and nip yer,' said the proprietor to his son.

Whilst the gasping dog was fastened up in a corner to writhe its impatience away, the landlord made inquiries for a stop-watch, and also for an umpire to decide, as he added, 'whether the rats were dead or alive when they're "killed", as Paddy says'.

When all the arrangements had been made the 'second' and the dog jumped into the pit, and after 'letting him see 'em a bit', the terrier was let loose.

The moment the dog was 'free', he became quiet in a most business-like manner, and rushed at the rats, burying his nose in the mound till he brought out one in his mouth. In a short time a dozen rats with wetted necks were lying bleeding on the floor, and the white paint of the pit became grained with blood.

In a little time the terrier had a rat hanging to his nose, which, despite his tossing, still held on. He dashed up against the sides, leaving a patch of blood as if a strawberry had been smashed there.

'He doesn't squeal, that's one good thing,' said one of the lookers-on.

As the rats fell on their sides after a bite they were collected together in the centre, where they lay quivering in their death-gasps!

'Hi, Butcher! hi, Butcher!' shouted the second, 'good dog! bur-r-r-r-h!' and he beat the sides of the pit like a drum till the dog flew about with new life.

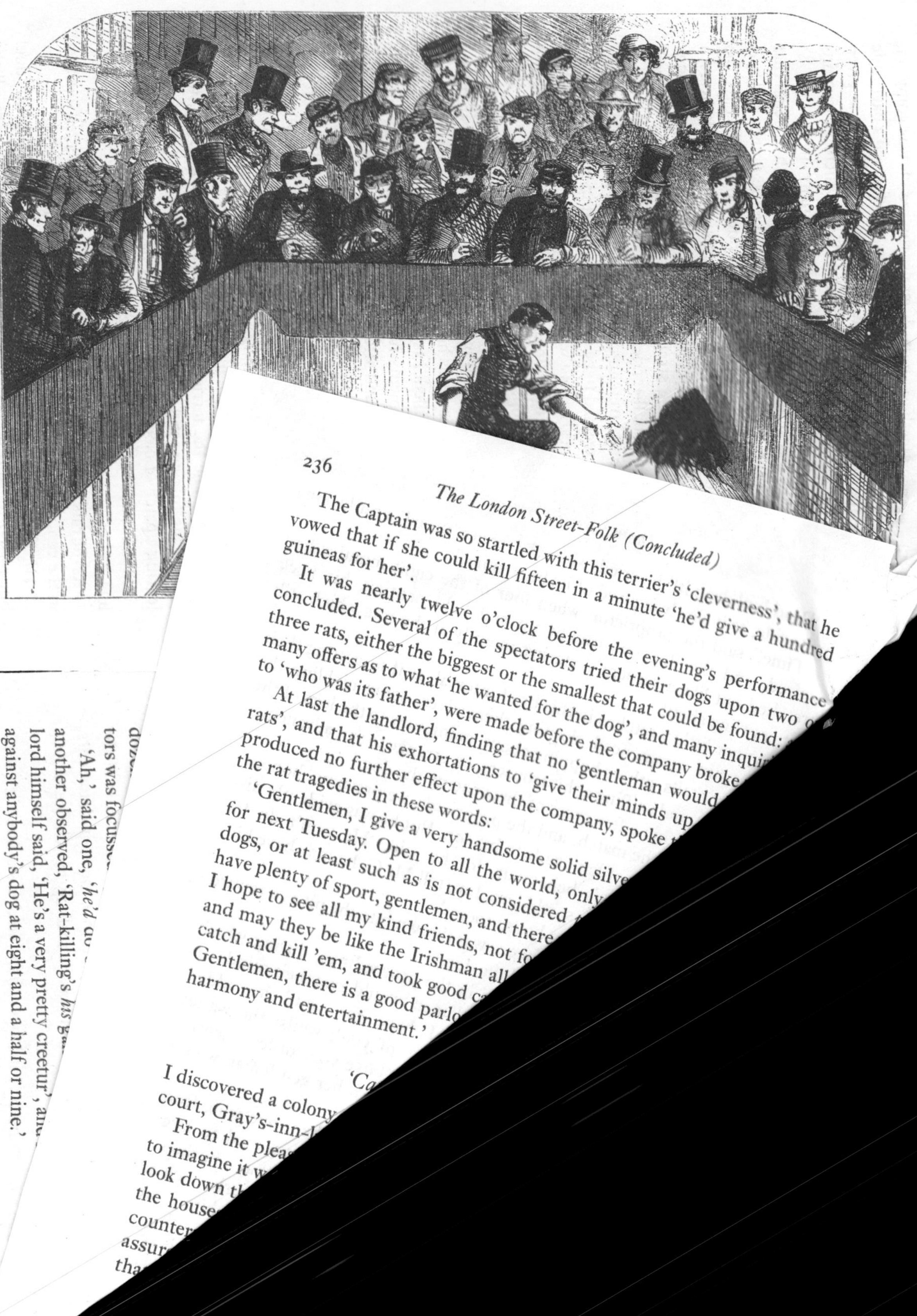

The Captain was so startled with this terrier's 'cleverness', that he vowed that if she could kill fifteen in a minute 'he'd give a hundred guineas for her'.

It was nearly twelve o'clock before the evening's performance concluded. Several of the spectators tried their dogs upon two o… three rats, either the biggest or the smallest that could be found: … many offers as to what 'he wanted for the dog', and many inqui… to 'who was its father', were made before the company broke…

At last the landlord, finding that no 'gentleman would… rats', and that his exhortations to 'give their minds up… produced no further effect upon the company, spoke… the rat tragedies in these words:

'Gentlemen, I give a very handsome solid silve… for next Tuesday. Open to all the world, only… dogs, or at least such as is not considered… have plenty of sport, gentlemen, and there… I hope to see all my kind friends, not fo… and may they be like the Irishman all… catch and kill 'em, and took good c… Gentlemen, there is a good parlo… harmony and entertainment.'

'Ca…

I discovered a colony… court, Gray's-inn-…

From the plea… to imagine it w… look down th… the house… counte… assur… tha…

doz… tors was focusse…

'Ah,' said one, '*he'd* do … another observed, 'Rat-killing's *his* ga… lord himself said, 'He's a very pretty creetur', and … against anybody's dog at eight and a half or nine.'

'Please, sir, he ain't been out this year with the papers,' said another, who was hiding a handful of buttons behind his back.

'He's been at shoe-blacking, sir; I'm the only reg'lar fly-boy,' shouted a third, eating a piece of bread as dirty as London snow.

A big lad with a dirty face, and hair like hemp, was the first of the 'catch-'em-alive' boys who gave me his account of the trade. He was a swarthy-featured boy, with a broad nose like a negro's, and on his temple was a big half-healed scar, which he accounted for by saying that 'he had been runned over' by a cab, though, judging from the blackness of one eye, it seemed to have been the result of some street-fight. He said:

'I'm an Irish boy, and near turned sixteen, and I've been silling fly-papers for between eight and nine year. I must have begun to sill them when they first come out. Another boy first tould me of them, and he'd been silling them about three weeks before me. He used to buy them of a party as lives in a back-room near Drury-lane, what buys paper and makes the catch 'em alive himself. When they first came out they used to charge sixpence a-dozen for 'em, but now they've got 'em to twopence ha'penny. When I first took to silling 'em, there was a tidy lot of boys at the business, but not so many as now, for all the boys seem at it. In our court alone I should think there was above twenty boys silling the things.

'At first, when there was a good time, we used to buy three or four gross together, but now we don't do more than half a gross. As we go along the streets we call out different cries. Some of us says, "Fly-papers, flypapers, ketch 'em all alive." Others make a kind of song of it, singing out, "Fly-paper, ketch 'em all alive, the nasty flies, tormenting the baby's eyes. Who'd be fly-blow'd, by all the nasty blue-bottles, beetles, and flies?"

'People likes to buy of a boy as sings out well, 'cos it makes 'em laugh.

'I don't think I sell so many in town as I do in the borders of the country, about Highbury, Croydon, and Brentford. I've got some regular customers in town about the City-prison and the Caledonian-road; and after I've served them and the town custom begins to fall off, then I goes to the country.

'We goes two of us together, and we takes about three gross. We keep on silling before us all the way, and we comes back the same road. Last year we sould very well in Croydon, and it was the best place for gitting a price for them; they'd give a penny a-piece for 'em there, for they didn't know nothing about them. I went off one day at tin o'clock and didn't come home till two in the morning. I sould eighteen dozen out in that d'rection the other day, and got rid of them before I had got half-way.

'But flies are very scarce at Croydon this year, and we haven't done so well. There ain't half as many flies this summer as last.

'Some people says the papers draws more flies than they ketches, and that when one gets in, there's twenty others will come to see him.

'It's according to the weather as the flies is about. If we have a fine day it fetches them out, but a cold day kills more than our papers.

'We sills the most papers to little cook-shops and sweetmeat-shops. We don't sill so many at private-houses. The public-houses is pretty good customers, 'cos the beer draws the flies. I sould nine dozen at one house—a school—at Highgate, the other day. I sould 'em two for three-ha'pence. That was a good hit, but then t'other days we loses. If we can make a ha'penny each we thinks we does well.

'The stuff as they puts on the paper is made out of boiled oil and turpentine and resin. It's seldom as a fly lives more than five minutes after it gets on the paper, and then it's as dead as a house. The blue-bottles is tougher, but they don't last long, though they keeps on fizzing as if they was trying to make a hole in the paper. The stuff is only p'isonous for flies, though I never heard of any body as ever eat a fly-paper.'

STREET EXHIBITORS

Punch

The performer of Punch that I saw was a short, dark, pleasant-looking man, dressed in a very greasy and very shiny green shooting-jacket. This was fastened together by one button in front, all the other button-holes having been burst through. Protruding from his bosom, a corner of the pandean pipes* was just visible, and as he told me the story of his adventures, he kept playing with the band of his very limp and very rusty old beaver hat. He had formerly been a gentleman's servant, and was especially civil in his manners. He came to me with his hair tidily brushed for the occasion, but apologised for his appearance on entering the room. He was very communicative, and took great delight in talking like Punch, with his call in his mouth, while some young children were in the room, and who, hearing the well-known sound of Punch's voice, looked all about for the figure. Not seeing the show, they fancied the man had the figure in his pocket, and that the sounds came from it. The change from Punch's voice to the man's natural tone was managed without an effort, and instantaneously. It had a very peculiar effect.

'I am the proprietor of a Punch's show,' he said. 'I goes about with it myself, and performs inside the frame behind the green baize. I have a pardner what plays the music—the pipes and drum; him as you see'd with me. I have been five-and-twenty year now at the business. I wish I'd never seen it, though it's *been* a money-making business—indeed, the best of all the street hexhibitions I may say. I am fifty years old. I took to it for money gains—that was what I done it for. I formerly lived in service—was a footman in a gentleman's family. When I first took to it, I could make two and three pounds a-day—I could so. You see, the way in which I took first to the business was this here—there was a party used to come and "cheer" for us at my master's house, and her son having a hexhibition of his own, and being in want of a pardner, axed me if so be I'd go out, which was a thing that I degraded at the time. He gave me information as to what the money-taking was, and it seemed to me that good, that it would pay me better nor service. I had twenty pounds a-year in my place, and my board and lodging, and two suits of clothes, but the young man told me as how I could make one pound a-day at the Punch-and-Judy business, after a little practice. I took a deal of persuasion, though, before I'd join him—it was beneath my dignity to fall from a footman to a showman. But, you see, the French gennelman as I lived with (he were a merchant in the city, and had fourteen clerks working for him) went back to his own country to reside, and left me with a written kerrackter; but that was no use to me: though I'd fine recommendations at the back of it, no one would look at it; so I was five months out of employment, knocking about—living first on my wages and then on my clothes, till all was gone but the few rags on my back. So I began to think that the Punch-and-Judy business was better than starving after all. Yes, I should think anything was better than that, though it's a business that, after you've once took to, you never can get out of—people fancies you know too much, and won't have nothing to say to you. If I got a situation at a tradesman's, why the boys would be sure to recognise me behind the counter, and begin a shouting into the shop (they *must* shout, you know): "Oh, there's Punch and Judy—there's Punch a-sarving out the customers!" Ah, it's a great annoyance being a public kerrackter, I can assure you, sir; go where you will, it's "Punchy, Punchy!" As for the boys, they'll never leave me alone till I die, I know; and I suppose in my old age I shall have to take to the parish broom. All our forefathers died in the workhouse. I don't know a Punch's showman that hasn't. One of my pardners was buried by the workhouse; and even old Pike, the most noted showman as ever was, died in the workhouse—Pike and Porsini.* Porsini was the first original street Punch, and Pike was his apprentice; their names is handed down to posterity among the noblemen and footmen of the land. They both died in the workhouse, and, in course, I shall do the same. Something else *might* turn up, to be sure. We can't say what this luck of the world is. I'm obliged to strive very hard—very hard indeed, sir, now, to get a living; and then not to get it after all—at times, compelled to go short, often.

'Punch, you know, sir, is a dramatic performance in two hacts. It's a play, you may say. I don't think it can be called a tragedy hexactly; a drama is what we names it. There is tragic parts, and comic and sentimental parts, too. Some families where I performs will have it most sentimental—in the original style; them families is generally sentimental theirselves. Others is all for the comic, and then I has to kick up all the games I can. To the sentimental folk I am obliged to perform werry steady and werry slow, and leave out all comic words and business. They won't have no ghost, no coffin, and no devil; and that's what I call spiling the performance entirely. It's the march of hintellect* wot's a doing all this—it is, sir.

'The best pitch of all in London is Leicester-square; there's all sorts of classes, you see, passing there. Then comes Regent-street (the corner of Burlington-street is uncommon good, and there's a good publican there besides). Bond-street ain't no good now. Oxford-street, up by Old Cavendish-street, or Oxford-market, or Wells-street, are all favourite pitches for Punch. We don't do much in the City. People has their heads all full of business there, and them as is greedy arter the money ain't no friend of Punch's. Tottenham-court-road, the New-road, and all the henvirons of London, is pretty good. Hampstead, tho', ain't no good; they've got too poor there. I'd sooner not go out at all than to Hampstead. Belgrave-square, and all about that part, is uncommon good; but where there's many chapels Punch won't do at all. I did once, though, strike up hopposition to a street preacher wot was a holding forth in the New-road, and did uncommon well. All his flock, as he called 'em, left him, and come over to look at me. Punch and preaching is two different creeds—hopposition parties, I may say. We in generally walks from twelve to twenty mile every day, and carries the show, which weighs a good half-hundred, at the least. Arter great exertion, our woice werry often fails us; for speaking all day through the "call" is werry trying, 'specially when we are chirruping up so as to bring the children to the vinders. The boys is the greatest nuisances we has to contend with. Wherever we goes we are sure of plenty of boys for a hindrance; but they've got no money, bother 'em! and they'll follow us for miles, so that we're often compelled to go miles to awoid 'em. Many parts is swarming with boys, such as Vitechapel. Spitalfields, that's the worst place for boys I ever come a-near; they're like flies in summer there, only much more thicker. I never shows my face within miles of them parts. Chelsea, again, has an uncommon lot of boys; and wherever we know the children swarm, there's the spots we makes a point of awoiding. Why, the boys is such a hobstruction to our performance, that often we are obliged to drop the curtain for 'em. They'll throw one another's caps into the frame while I'm inside on it, and do what we will, we can't

PUNCH'S SHOWMEN.

[*From a Photograph.*]

keep 'em from poking their fingers through the baize and making holes to peep through. Then they *will* keep tapping the drum; but the worst of all is, the most of 'em ain't got a farthing to bless themselves with, and they *will* shove into the best places.'

Exhibitor of Mechanical Figures

'I am the only man in London—and in England, I think—who is exhibiting the figuer of méchanique; that is to say, leetle figuers, that move their limbs by wheels and springs, as if they was de living cretures. I am a native of Parma in Italy, where I was born; that is, you understand, I was born in the Duchy of Parma, not in the town of Parma—in the campagne, where my father is a farmer; not a large farmer, but a little farmer, with just enough land for living. I used to work for my father in his fields. I was married when I have 20 years of age, and I have a child aged 10 years. I have only 30 years of age, though I have the air of 40. Pardon, Monsieur! all my friends say I have the air of 40, and you say that to make me pleasure.

'It is two months since I have my new figuers. I did have them sent from Germany to me. They have cost a great deal of money to me; as much as 35*l.* without duty. They have been made in Germany, and are very clever figures. I will show them to you. They perform on the round table, which must be level or they will not turn round. This is the Impératrice of the French—Eugénie* —at least I call her so, for it is not like her, because her cheveleure* is not arranged in the style of the Impératrice. The infants like better to see the Impératrice than a common lady, that is why I call her the Impératrice. She holds one arm in the air, and you will see she turns round like a person waltzing. The noise you hear is from the wheels of the méchanique, which is under her petticoats. You shall notice her eyes do move as she waltz. The next figure is the carriage of the Emperor of the French, with the Queen and Prince Albert and the King de Sardaigne* inside. It will run round the table, and the horses will move as if they gallop. It is a very clever méchanique. I attache this wire from the front wheel to the centre of the table, or it would not make the round of the table, but it would run off the side and break itself. My most clever méchanique is the elephant. It does move its trunk, and its tail, and its legs, as if walking, and all the time it roll its eyes from side to side like a real elephant. It is the cleverest elephant of méchanique in the world.

The leetle Indian on the neck, who is the driver, lift his arm, and in the pavilion on the back the chieftain of the Indians lift his bow and arrow to take aim, and put it down again. That méchanique cost me very much money. The elephant is worth much more than the Impératrice of the French. I could buy two—three—Impératrice for my elephant. I would like sooner lose the Impératrice than any malheur arrive to my elephant. There are plenty more Impératrice, but the elephant is very rare. I have also a figuer of Tyrolese peasant. She go round the table a short distance and then turn, like a dancer. I must get her repaired. She is so weak in her wheels and springs, which wind up under her petticoats, like the Impératrice. She has been cleaned twice, and yet her méchanique is very bad. Oh, I have oiled her; but it is no good, she must be taken to pieces.

'I exhibit my leetle figuers in the street. The leetle children like to see my figuers méchanique dance round the table, and the carriage, with the horses which gallop; but over all they like my elephant, with the trunk which curls up in front, like those in the Jardin des Plantes, or what you call it Zoological Gardens.*

'It is not only the leetle children that admire my méchanique, but persons of a ripe age. I often have gentlemen and ladies stand round my table, and they say "Very clever!" to see the lady figuers valtz, but above all when my elephant lift his trunk. The leetle children will follow me a long way to see my figuers, for they know we cannot carry the box far without exhibiting, on account of its weight. But my table is too high for them, unless they are at a distance to see the figuers perform. If my table was not high, the leetle children would want to take hold of my figuers. I always carry a small stick with me; and when the leetle children, who are being carried by other leetle children, put their hand to my figuers, I touch them with stick, not for to hurt them, but to make them take their hand away and prevent them from doing hurt to my méchanique.

'When the costume of my Impératrice is destroyed by time and wear, my wife makes new clothes for her. Yes, as you say, she is the dress-maker of the Impératrice of the French, but it is not the Emperor who pays the bill, but myself. The Impératrice—the one I have, not that of the Emperor—does not want more than half a yard of silk for a petticoat. In the present style of fashion I make her petticoat very large and full, not for the style, but to hide the méchanique in her inside.'

Exhibitor of the Microscope

'My microscope contains six objects, which are placed on a wheel at the back, which I turn round in succession. The objects are in cell-boxes of glass. The objects are all of them familiar to the public, and are as follows:—1. The flea. 2. The human hair, or the hair of the head. 3. A section of the old oak tree. 4. The animalculae* in water. 5. Cheese-mites. And 6. The transverse section of cane used by school-masters for the correction of boys.

'I always take up my stand in the day-time in Whitechapel, facing the London Hospital, being a large open space, and favourable for the solar rays—for I light up the instrument by the direct rays of the sun. At night-time I am mostly to be found on Westminster-bridge, and then I light up with the best sperm oil* there is. I am never interfered with by the police; on the contrary, they come and have a look, and admire and recommend, such is the interest excited.

'The first I exhibit is the flea, and I commence a short lecture as follows:—"Gentlemen," I says, "the first object I have to present to your notice is that of a flea. I wish to direct your attention especially to the head of this object. Here you may distinctly perceive its proboscis or dart. It is that which perforates the cuticle or human skin, after which the blood ascends by suction from our body into that of the flea. Thousands of persons in London have seen a flea, have felt a flea, but have never yet been able by the human eye to discover that instrument which made them sensible of the flea about their person, although they could not catch the old gentleman. This flea, gentlemen, by Dr Lardner's micrometer,* measures accurate 24 inches in length, and 11 across the back. My instrument, mark you, being of high magnifying power, will not show you the whole of the object at once. Mark you, gentlemen, this is not the flea of the dog or the cat, but the human flea, for each differ in their formation, as clearly proved by this powerful instrument. For they all differ in their form and shape, and will only feed upon the animal on which they are bred. Having shown you the head and shoulders, with its dart, I shall now proceed to show you the posterior view of this object, in which you may clearly discover every artery, vein, muscle and nerve, exact like a lobster in shape, and quite as large as one at 2*s.* 6*d.*" That pleases them, you know; and sometimes I add, to amuse them, "An object of that size would make an excellent supper for half-a-dozen persons." That pleases them.

'One Irishwoman, after seeing the flea, threw up her arms and screamed out, "O J——! and I've had hundreds of them in my bed at once." She got me a great many customers from her exclamations. You see, my lecture entices those listening to have a look. Many listeners say, "Ain't that true, and philosophical, and correct?" I've had many give me 6*d*. and say, "Never mind the change, your lecture is alone worth the money."

'I'll now proceed to No. 2. "The next object I have to present to your notice, gentlemen, is that of the hair of the human head. You perceive that it is nearly as large as yonder scaffolding poles of the House of Lords."* I say this when I am on Westminster-bridge, because it refers to the locality, and is a striking figure, and excites the listeners. "But mark you, it is not, like them, solid matter, through which no ray of light can pass." That's where I please the gentlemen, you know, for they say, "How philosophical!" "You can readily perceive, mark you, that they are all tubes, like tubes of glass; a proof of which fact you have before you, from the light of the lamp shining direct through the body of the object, and that light direct portrayed in the lens of your eye, called the retina, on which all external objects are painted." "Beautiful!" says a gentleman. "Now, if the hair of the head be a hollow tube, as you perceive it is, then what caution you ought to exercise when you place your head in the hands of the hairdresser, by keeping your hat on, or else you may be susceptible to catch cold; for that which we breathe, the atmosphere, passing down these tubes, suddenly shuts to the doors, if I may be allowed such an expression, or, in other words, closes the pores of the skin and thereby checks the insensible perspiration, and colds are the result. Powdering the head is quite out of date now, but if a little was used on those occasions referred to, cold in the head would not be so frequent." What do you think of that? I never had an individual complain of my lecture yet.

'Now comes No. 3. "This, gentlemen, is the brave old oak, a section of it not larger than the head of a pin. Looking at it through this powerful instrument, you may accurately perceive millions of perforations, or pores, through which the moisture of the earth rises, in order to aid its growth. Of all the trees of the forest, none is so splendid as the brave old oak. This is the tree that braves the battle and the breeze, and is said to be in its perfection at 100 years. Who that looks at it would not exclaim, in the language of the song,* 'Woodman, spare that tree, and cut it not down?' Such is the analogy existing between vegetable and animal physiology, that a small portion of the cuticle or human skin would present the same appearance, for there are millions of pores in the human skin which a grain of sand is said to cover; and here are millions of perforations through which the moisture of the earth is said to rise to aid the growth of the tree. See the similitude between the vegetable and animal physiology. Here is the exhibition of nature—see how it surpasses that of art. See the ladies at the Great Exhibition admiring the shawls that came from India:* yet they, though truly deserving, could not compare with this bit of bark from the brave old oak. Here is a pattern richer and more deserving than any on any shawl, however wonderful. Where is the linendraper in this locality that can produce anything so beautiful as that on this bit of bark? Such are the works of art as compared with those of nature."

'No. 4 is the animalculae in water. "Gentlemen, the object now before you is a drop of water, that may be suspended on a needle's point, teeming with millions of living objects. This one drop of water contains more inhabitants than the globe on which I stand. See the velocity of their motion, the action of their stomachs! the vertebrae is elegantly marked, like the boa-constrictor in the Zoological Gardens. They are all moving with perfect ease in this one drop, like the mighty monsters of the vast deep."

'The next object is the cheese-mite—No. 5. I always begin in this way,—"Those who are unacquainted with the study of entomology declare that these mites are beetles, and not mites; but could I procure a beetle with eight legs, I should present it to the British Museum as a curiosity." This is the way I clench up the mouths of those sceptics who would try to ridicule me, by showing that I am philosophic. "Just look at them. Notice, for instance, their head, how it represents the form of an hedgehog. The body presents that of the beetle shape. They have eight legs and eight joints. They have four legs forward and four legs back; and they can move with the same velocity forwards as they can back, such is their construction. They are said to be moving with the velocity of five hundred steps in one minute. Read Blair's 'Preceptor',* where you may see a drawing of the mite accurately given, as well as read the description just given." A cheesemonger in

Whitechapel brought me a few of these objects for me to place in my microscope. He invited his friends, which were taking supper with him, to come out and have a glance at the same objects. He gave me sixpence for exhibiting them to him, and was highly gratified at the sight of them. I asked him how he could have the impudence to sell them for a lady's supper at 10*d*. a-pound. The answer he gave me was,—"What the eye cannot see the heart never grieves." Then I go on,—"Whilst this lady is extending her hand to the poor, and doing all the relief in her power, she is slaying more living creatures with her jaw-bone than ever Samson* did with his." If it's a boy looking through, I say, "Now, Jack, when you are eating bread and cheese don't let it be said that you slay the mites with the jaw-bone of an ass. Cultivate the intellectual and moral powers superior to the passions, and then you will rise superior to that animal in intellect." "Good," says a gentleman, "good; here's sixpence for you"; and another says, "Here's twopence for you, and I'm blessed if I want to see anything after hearing your lecture." Then I continue to point out the affection of the mite for its young. "You see fathers looking after their daughters, and mothers after their sons, when they are taking their walks; and such is their love for their young, that when the young ones are fatigued with their journey the parents take them up on their backs. Do you not see it?" And then some will say, "I'll give a penny to see that"; and I've had four pennies put in my hand at once to see it. Excitement is everything in this world, sir.

'Next comes the cane—No. 6. "The object before you, gentlemen, is a transverse section of cane,—common cane,—such, mark you, as is used by schoolmasters for the correction of boys who neglect their tasks, or play the wag." I make it comic, you know. "This I call the tree of knowledge, for it has done more for to learn us the rules of arithmetic than all the vegetable kingdom combined. To it we may attribute the rule of three, from its influence on the mind,"—that always causes a smile,—"just look at it for one moment. Notice, in the first place, its perforations. Where the human hand has failed to construct a micrometer for microscopic or telescopic purposes, the spider has lent its web in one case, and the cane in the other. Through the instrumentality of its perforations, we may accurately infer the magnifying power of other objects, showing the law of analogy. The perforations of this cane, apart from this instrument, would hardly admit a needle's point, but seem now large enough for your arm to enter.

This cane somewhat represents a telescopic view of the moon at the full, when in conjunction with the sun, for instance. Here I could represent inverted rocks and mountains. You may perceive them yourself, just as they would be represented in the moon's disc through a powerful telescope of 250 times, such as I have exhibited to a thousand persons in St Paul's Churchyard. On the right of this piece of cane, if you are acquainted with the science of astronomy, you may depicture very accurately Mount Tycho; for instance, representing a beautiful burning mountain, like Mount Vesuvius or Etany, near the fields of Naples. You might discover accurately all the diverging streaks of light emanating from the crater. Further on to the right you may perceive Mount St Catherine, like the blaze of a candle rushing through the atmosphere. On the left you may discover Mount Ptolemy.* Such is a similar appearance of the moon's mountainous aspect. I ask you, if the school-boy had but an opportunity of glancing at so splendid an object as the cane, should he ever be seen to shed a tear at its weight?" '

The Strong Man

'I have been in the profession for about thirteen years, and I am thirty-two next birthday. Excepting four years that I was at sea, I've been solely by the profession. I'm what is termed a strong man, and perform feats of strength and posturing. What is meant by posturing is the distortion of the limbs, such as doing the splits, and putting your leg over your head and pulling it down your back, a skipping over your leg, and such-like business. Tumbling is different from posturing, and means throwing summersets* and walking on your hands; and acrobating means the two together, with mounting three stories high, and balancing each other. These are the definitions I make.

'The first thing I did was at a little beer-shop, corner of Southwark-bridge-road and Union-street. I had seen Herbert do the Grecian statues* at the Vic., in "Hercules, King of Clubs", and it struck me I could do 'em. So I knew this beer-shop, and I bought half-a-crown's worth of tickets to be allowed to do these statues. It was on a boxing-night, I remember. I did them, but they were dreadful bad. The people did certainly applaud, but what for, I don't know, for I kept shaking and wabbling so, that my marble statue was rather ricketty;

and there was a strong man in the room, who had been performing them, and he came up to me and said that I was a complete duffer, and that I knew nothing about it at all. So I replied, that he knew nothing about his feats of strength, and that I'd go and beat him. So I set to work at it; for I was determined to lick him. I got five quarter-of-hundred weights, and used to practice throwing them at a friend's back-yard in the Waterloo-road. I used to make myself all over mud at it, besides having a knock of the head sometimes. At last I got perfect chucking the quarter hundred, and then I tied a fourteen pound weight on to them, and at last I got up half-hundreds. I learnt to hold up one of them at arm's length, and even then I was obliged to push it up with the other hand. I also threw them over my head, as well as catching them by the ring.

'I went to this beer-shop as soon as I could do, and came out. I wasn't so good as he was at lifting, but that was all he could do; and I did posturing with the weights as well, and that licked him. He was awfully jealous, and I had been revenged. I had learnt to do a split, holding a half-hundred in my teeth, and rising with it, without touching the ground with my hands. Now I can lift five, for I've had more practice. I had tremendous success at this beer-shop.

'It hurt me awfully when I learnt to do the split with the weight on my teeth. It strained me all to pieces. I couldn't put my heels to the ground not nicely, for it physicked* my thighs dreadful. When I was hot I didn't feel it; but as I cooled, I was cramped all to bits. It took me nine months before I could do it without feeling any pain.

'Another thing I learnt to do at this beer-shop was, to break the stone on the chest. This man used to do it as well, only in a very slight way—with thin bits and a cobbler's hammer. Now mine is regular flagstones. I've seen as many as twenty women faint seeing me do it. At this beer-shop, when I first did it, the stone weighed about three quarters of a hundred, and was an inch thick. I laid down on the ground, and the stone was put on my chest, and a man with a sledge hammer, twenty-eight pounds weight, struck it and smashed it. The way it is done is this. You rest on your heels and hands and throw your chest up. There you are, like a stool, with the weight on you. When you see the blow coming, you have to give, or it would knock you all to bits.

'When I was learning to do this, I practised for nine months. I got a friend of mine to hit the stone. One day I cut my chest open doing it.

I wasn't paying attention to the stone, and never noticed that it was hollow; so then when the blow came down, the sharp edges of the stone, from my having nothing but a fleshing suit on, cut right into the flesh, and made two deep incisions. I had to leave it off for about a month. Strange to say, this stone-breaking never hurt my chest or my breaking; I rather think it has done me good, for I'm strong and hearty, and never have illness of any sort.

'When I'm engaged for a full performance I do this. All the weights, and the stone and the hammer, are ranged in front of the stage. Then I come on dressed in silk tights with a spangled trunk. Then I enter at the back of the stage, and first do several feats of posturing, such as skipping through my leg or passing it down my back, or splits. Then I take a ladder and mount to the top, and stand up on it, and hold one leg in my hand, shouldering it; and then I give a spring with the other leg, and shoot off to the other side of the stage and squash down with both legs open, doing a split. It's a very good trick, and always gets a round. Then I do a trick with a chair standing on the seat, and I take one foot in my hand and make a hoop of the leg, and then hop with one leg through the hoop of the other, and spring over the back and come down in a split on the other side. I never miss this trick, though, if the chair happens to be ricketty, I may catch the toe, but it doesn't matter much.

'Then I begin my weight business. I take one half-hundred weight and hold it up at arm's-length; and I also hold it out perpendicularly, and bring it up again and swing it two or three times round the head, and then throw it up in the air and catch it four or five times running; not by the ring, as others do, but in the open hand.

'The next trick is doing the same thing with both hands instead of one, that is with two weights at the same time; and then, after that, I take up a half-hundred by the teeth, and shouldering the leg at the same, and in that style I fall down into the splits. Then I raise myself up gradually, till I'm upright again. After I'm upright I place the weight on my forehead, and lay down flat on my back with it, without touching with the hands. I take it off when I'm down and place it in my mouth, and walk round the stage like a Greenwich-pensioner, with my feet tucked up like crossing the arms, and only using my knees. Then I tie three together, and hold them in the mouth, and I put one in each hand. Then I stand up with them and support them. It's an awful weight, and you can't do much exhibiting with them.

'When I was at Vauxhall, Yarmouth, last year, I hurt my neck very badly in lifting those weights in the mouth. It pulled out the back of my neck, and I was obliged to give over work for months. It forced my head over one shoulder, and then it sunk, as if I'd got a stiff neck. I did nothing to it, and only went to a doctor-chap, who made me bathe the neck in hot water. That's all.

'One of my most curious tricks is what I call the braces trick. It's a thing just like a pair of braces, only, instead of a button, there's a half-hundred weight at each end, so that there are two behind and two in front. Then I mount on two swinging ropes with a noose at the end, and I stretch out my legs into a split, and put a half-hundred on each thigh, and take up another in my mouth. You may imagine how heavy the weight is, when I tell you that I pulled the roof of a place in once at Chelsea. It was a exhibition then. The tiles and all come down, and near smothered me. You must understand, that in these tricks I have to put the weights on myself, and raise them from the ground, and that makes it so difficult.

'The next, and the best, and most difficult trick of all is, I have a noose close to the ceiling, in which I place one of my ankles, and I've another loose noose with a hook at the end, and I place that on the other ankle. Two half-hundreds are placed on this hook, and one in each hand. The moment these weights are put on this ankle, it pulls my legs right apart, so that they form a straight line from the ceiling, like a plumb-line, and my body sticks out at the side horizontally, like a T-square sideways. I strike an attitude when I have the other weights in my hand, and then another half-hundred is put in my mouth, and I am swung backwards and forwards for about eight or twelve times. It don't hurt the ankle, because the sling is padded. At first it pulls you about, and gives you a tremendous ricking. After this rope-performance I take a half-hundred and swing it round about fifty times. It goes as rapidly as a wheel, and if I was to miss my aim I should knock my brains out. I have done it seventy times, but that was to take the shine out of an opposition fellow.

'I always wind up with breaking the stone, and I don't mind how thick it is, so long as it isn't heavy enough to crush me. A common curb-stone, or a Yorkshire-flag, is nothing to me, and I've got so accustomed to this trick, that once it took thirty blows with a twenty-eight pound sledge-hammer to break the stone, and I asked for a cigar and smoked it all the while.'

The Street Fire-King, or Salamander

This person came to me recommended by one of my street acquaintances as the 'pluckiest fire-eater going', and that as he was a little 'down at heel', he should be happy for a consideration to give me any information I might require in the 'Salamander line'.

He was a tall, gaunt man, with an absent-looking face, and so pale that his dark eyes looked positively wild.

I could not help thinking, as I looked at his bony form, that fire was not the most nutritious food in the world, until the poor fellow explained to me that he had not broken his fast for two days.

He gave the following account of himself:

'When I perform I usually have a decanter of ale and two glasses upon the table, and after every trick I sit down whilst an overture is being done and wash my mouth out, for it gets very hot. You're obliged to pause a little, for after tasting one thing, if the palate doesn't recover, you can't tell when the smoke is coming.

'I wore a regular dress, a kind of scale-armour costume, with a red lion on the breast. I do up my moustache with cork, and rouge a bit. My tights is brown, with black enamel jack-boots. On my head I wears a king's coronet and a ringlet wig, bracelets on my wrists, and a red twill petticoat under the armour dress, where it opens on the limps.

'For my performances I begin with eating the lighted link,* an ordinary one as purchased at oil-shops. There's no trick in it, only confidence. It won't burn you in the inside, but if the pitch falls on the outside, of course it will hurt you. If you hold your breath the moment the lighted piece is put in your mouth, the flame goes out on the instant. Then we squench the flame with spittle. As we takes a bit of link in the mouth, we tucks it on one side of the cheek, as a monkey do with nuts in his pouch. After I have eaten sufficient fire I take hold of the link, and extinguish the lot by putting the burning end in my mouth. Sometimes, when I makes a slip, and don't put it in careful, it makes your moustache fiz up. I must also mind how I opens my mouth, 'cos the tar sticks to the lip wherever it touches, and pains sadly. This sore on my hand is caused by the melted pitch dropping on my fingers, and the sores is liable to be bad for a week or eight days. I don't spit out my bits of link; I always swallow them. I never did spit 'em out, for they are very wholesome, and keeps you from having any sickness. Whilst I'm getting the next trick ready I chews them up and eats them. It tastes rather roughish, but not nasty when you're accustomed to it. It's only like having a mouthful of dust, and very wholesome.

'My next trick is with a piece of tow* with a piece of tape rolled up in the interior. I begin to eat a portion of this tow—plain, not a-light—till I find a fitting opportunity to place the tape in the mouth. Then I pause for a time, and in the meantime I'm doing a little pantomime business—just like love business, serious—till I get the end of this tape between my teeth, and then I draws it out, supposed to be manufactured in the pit of the stomach. After that—which always goes immensely—I eat some more tow, and inside this tow there is what I call the fire-ball—that is, a lighted fusee bound round with tow and placed in the centre of the tow I'm eating—which I introduce at a fitting opportunity. Then I blows out with my breath, and that sends out smoke and fire. That there is a very hard trick, for it's according how this here fire-ball bustes.* Sometimes it bustes on the side, and then it burns all the inside of the mouth, and the next morning you can take out pretty well the inside of your mouth with your finger; but if it bustes near the teeth, then it's all right, for there's vent for it. I also makes the smoke and flame—that is, sparks—come down my nose, the same as coming out of a blacksmith's chimney. It makes the eyes water, and there's a tingling; but it don't burn or make you giddy.

'My next trick is with the brimstone. I have a plate of lighted sulphur, and first inhale the fumes, and then devour it with a fork and swallow it. As a costermonger said when he saw me do it, "I say, old boy, your game ain't all brandy." There's a kind of a acid, nasty, sour taste in this feat, and at first it used to make me feel sick; but now I'm used to it, and it don't. When I puts it in my mouth it clings just like sealing-wax, and forms a kind of a dead ash. Of a morning, if I haven't got my breakfast by a certain time, there's a kind of a retching in my stomach, and that's the only inconvenience I feel from swallowing the sulphur for that there feat.

'The next is, with two sticks of sealing-wax and the same plate. They are lit by the gas and dropped on one another till they are bodily a-light. Then I borrow either a ring of the company, or a pencil-case, or a seal. I set the sealing-wax a-light with a fork, and I press the impression of whatever article I can get with the tongue, and the seal is passed round to the company. Then I finish eating the burning wax. I always spits that out after, when no one's looking. The sealing-wax is all right if you get it into the interior of the mouth, but if it is stringy, and it falls, you can't get it off, without it takes away skin and all. It has a very pleasant taste, and I always prefer the red, as its flavour is the best. Hold your breath and it goes out, but still the heat remains, and you can't get along with that so fast as the sulphur. I often burn myself, especially when I'm bothered in my entertainment; such as any person talking about me close by, then I listen to 'em perhaps, and I'm liable to burn myself. I haven't been able to perform for three weeks after some of my burnings. I never let any of the audience know anything of it, but smother up the pain, and go on with my other tricks.

'The other trick is a feat which I make known to the public as one of Ramo Samee's,* which he used to perform in public-houses and tap-rooms, and made a deal of money out of. With the same plate and a piece of dry tow placed in it, I have a pepper-box, with ground rosin and sulphur together. I light the tow, and with a knife and fork I set down to it and eat it, and exclaim, "This is my light supper." There isn't no holding the breath so much in this trick as in the others, but you must get it into the mouth any how. It's like eating a hot beef-steak when you are ravenous. The rosin is apt to drop on the flesh and cause a long blister. You see, we have to eat it with the head up, full-faced; and really, without it's seen, nobody would believe what I do.

'There's another feat, of exploding the gunpowder. There's two ways of exploding it. This is my way of doing it, though I only does it for my own benefits and on grand occasions, for it's very dangerous indeed to the frame, for it's sure to destroy the hair of the head; or if anything smothers it, it's liable to shatter a thumb or a limb.

'I have a man to wait on me for this trick, and he unloops my dress and takes it off, leaving the bare back and arms. Then I gets a quarter of a pound of powder, and I has an ounce put on the back part of the neck, in the hollow, and I holds out each arm with an orange in the palm of each hand, with a train along the arms, leading up to the neck. Then I turns my back to the audience, and my man fires the gunpowder, and it blew up in a minute, and ran down the train and blew up that in my hands. I've been pretty lucky with this trick, for it's only been when the powder's got under my bracelets, and then it hurts me. I'm obliged to hold the hand up, for if it hangs down it hurts awful. It looks like a scurvy, and as the new skin forms, the old one falls off.

'That's the whole of my general performance for concert business, when I go busking at free concerts or outside of shows (I generally gets a crown a-day at fairs). I never do the gunpowder, but only the tow and the link.

'I have been engaged at the Flora Gardens, and at St Helena Gardens,* Rotherhithe, and then I was Signor Salamander, the great fire-king from the East-end theatres. At the Eel-pie-house, Peckham, I did the "terrific flight through the air", coming down a wire surrounded by fire-works. I was called Herr Alma, the flying fiend. There was four scaffold-poles placed at the top of the house to form a tower, just large enough for me to lie down on my belly, for the swivels on the rope to be screwed into the cradle round my body. A wire is the best, but they had a rope. On this cradle were places for the fireworks to be put in it. I had a helmet of fire on my head, and the three spark cases (they are made with steel-filings, and throw out sparks) made of Prince of Wales feathers. I had a sceptre in my hand of two serpents, and in their open mouths they put fire-balls, and they looked as if they was spitting fiery venom. I had wings, too, formed from the ankle to the waist. They was netting, and spangled, and well sized to throw off the fire. I only did this two nights, and I had ten shillings each performance. It's a momentary feeling coming down, a kind of suffocation like, so that you must hold your breath. I had two men to cast me off. There was a gong first of all, knocked to attract the attention, and then I made my appearance. First, a painted pigeon, made of lead, is sent down the wire as a pilot. It has moveable wings. Then all the fire-works are lighted up, and I come down right through the thickest of 'em. There's a trap-door set in the scene at the end, and two men is there to look after it. As soon as I have passed it, the men shut it, and I dart up against a feather-bed. The speed I come down at regularly jams me up against it, but you see I throw away this sceptre and save myself with my hands a little. I feel fagged for want of breath. It seems like a sudden fright, you know. I sit down for a few minutes, and then I'm all right.

'I'm never afraid of fire. There was a turner's place that took fire, and I saved that house from being burned. He was a friend of mine, the turner was, and when I was there, the wife thought she heard the children crying, and asked me to go up and see what it was. As I went up I could smell fire worse and worse, and when I got in the room it was full of smoke, and all the carpet, and bed-hangings, and curtains smouldering. I opened the window, and the fire burst out, so I ups with the carpet and throw'd it out of window, together with the blazing chairs, and I rolled the linen and drapery up and throw'd them out. I was as near suffocated as possible. I went and felt the bed, and there was two children near dead from the smoke; I brought them down, and a medical man was called, and he brought them round.

'I was very hard up at one time—when I was living in Friar-street—and I used to frequent a house kept by a betting-man, near the St George's Surrey Riding-school. A man I knew used to supply this betting-man with rats. I was at this public-house one night when this rat-man comes up to me, and says he, "Hallo! my pippin; here, I want you: I want to make a match. Will you kill thirty rats against my dog?" So I said, "Let me see the dog first"; and I looked at his mouth, and he was an old dog; so I says, "No, I won't go in for thirty; but I don't mind trying at twenty." He wanted to make it twenty-four, but I wouldn't. They put the twenty in the rat-pit, and the dog went in first and killed his, and he took a quarter of an hour and two minutes. Then a fresh lot were put in the pit, and I began; my hands were tied behind me. They always make an allowance for a man, so the pit was made closer, for you see a man can't turn round like a dog; I had half the space of the dog. The rats lay in a cluster, and then I picked them off where I wanted 'em, and bit 'em between the shoulders. It was when they came to one or two that I had the work, for they cut about. The last one made me remember him, for he gave me a bite, of which I've got the scar now. It festered, and I was obliged to have it cut out. I took Dutch drops for it, and poulticed it by day, and I was bad for three weeks. They made a subscription in the room of fifteen shillings for killing these rats. I won the match, and beat the dog by four minutes. The wager was five shillings, which I had. I was at the time so hard up, I'd do anything for some money; though, as far as that's concerned, I'd go into a pit now, if anybody would make it worth my while.'

The Snake, Sword, and Knife-Swallower

He was quite a young man, and, judging from his countenance, there was nothing that could account for his having taken up so strange a method of gaining his livelihood as that of swallowing snakes.

He was very simple in his talk and manner. He readily confessed that the idea did not originate with him, and prided himself only on being the second to take it up. There is no doubt that it was from his being startled by the strangeness and daringness of the act that he was induced to make the essay. He said he saw nothing disgusting in it; that people liked it; that it served him well in his 'professional' engagements; and spoke of the snake in general as a reptile capable of affection, not unpleasant to the eye, and very cleanly in its habits.

'I swallow snakes, swords, and knives; but, of course, when I'm engaged at a penny theatre I'm expected to do more than this, for it would only take a quarter of an hour, and that isn't long enough for them. They call me in the perfession a "Sallementro",* and that is what I term myself; though p'raps it's easier to say I'm a "swallower".

'It was a mate of mine that I was with that first put me up to sword-and-snake swallowing. I copied off him, and it took me about three months to learn it. I began with a sword first—of course not a sharp sword, but one blunt-pointed—and I didn't exactly know how to do it, for there's a trick in it. I see him, and I said, "Oh, I shall set up master for myself, and practise until I can do it."

'At first it turned me, putting it down my throat past my swallow, right down—about eighteen inches. It made my swallow sore—very sore, and I used lemon and sugar to cure it. It was tight at first, and I kept pushing it down further and further. There's one thing, you mustn't cough, and until you're used to it you want to very bad, and then you must pull it up again. My sword was about three-quarters of an inch wide.

'At first I didn't know the trick of doing it, but I found it out this way. You see the trick is, you must oil the sword—the best sweet oil, worth fourteen pence a pint—and you put it on with a sponge. Then, you understand, if the sword scratches the swallow it don't make it sore, 'cos the oil heals it up again. When first I put the sword down, before I oiled it, it used to come up quite slimy, but after the oil it slips down quite easy, is as clean when it comes up as before it went down.

'As I told you, we are called at concert-rooms where I perform the "Sallementro". I think it's French, but I don't know what it is exactly; but that's what I'm called amongst us.

'The knives are easier to do than the sword because they are shorter. We puts them right down till the handle rests on the mouth. The sword is about eighteen inches long, and the knives about eight inches in the blade. People run away with the idea that you slip the blades down your breast, but I always hold mine right up with the neck bare, and they see it go into the mouth atween the teeth. They also fancy it hurts you; but it don't, or what a fool I should be to do it. I don't mean to say it don't hurt you at first, 'cos it do, for my swallow was very bad, and I couldn't eat anything but liquids for two months whilst I was learning. I cured my swallow whilst I was stretching it with lemon and sugar.

'I was the second one that ever swallowed a snake. I was about seventeen or eighteen years old when I learnt it. The first was Clarke as did it. He done very well with it, but he wasn't out no more than two years before me, so he wasn't known much. In the country there is some places where, when you do it, they swear you are the devil, and won't have it nohow.

'The snakes I use are about eighteen inches long, and you must first cut the stingers out, 'cos it might hurt you. I always keep two or three by me for my performances. I keep them warm, but the winter kills 'em. I give them nothing to eat but worms or gentles.* I generally keep them in flannel, or hay, in a box. I've three at home now.

'When first I began swallowing snakes they tasted queer like. They draw'd the roof of the mouth a bit. It's a roughish taste. The scales rough you a bit when you draw them up. You see, a snake will go into ever such a little hole, and they are smooth one way.

'The head of the snake goes about an inch and a half down the throat, and the rest of it continues in the mouth, curled round like. I hold him by the tail, and when I pinch it he goes right in. You must cut the stinger out or he'll injure you. The tail is slippery, but you nip it with the nails like pinchers. If you was to let him go, he'd go right down; but most snakes will stop at two inches down the swallow, and then they bind like a ball in the mouth.

'I in general get my snakes by giving little boys ha'pence to go and catch 'em in the woods. I get them when I'm pitching in the country. I'll get as many as I can get, and bring 'em up to London for my engagements.

'When first caught the snake is slimy, and I have to clean him by scraping him off with the finger-nail as clean as I can, and then wiping him with a cloth, and then with another, until he's nice and clean. I have put 'em down slimy, on purpose to taste what it was like. It had a nasty taste with it—very nasty.

'I give a man a shilling always to cut the stinger out—one that knows all about it, for the stinger is under the tongue. It was this Clarke I first see swallow a snake. He swallowed it as it was when he caught it, slimy. He said it was nasty. Then he scraped it with his nail and let it crawl atween his hands, cleaning itself. When once they are cleaned of the slime they have no taste. Upon my word they are clean things, a'most like metal. They only lives on worms, and that ain't so nasty; besides, they never makes no mess in the box, only frothing in the mouth at morning and evening: but I don't know what comes from 'em, for I ain't a doctor.

'When I exhibit, I first holds the snake up in the air and pinches the tail, to make it curl about and twist round my arm, to show that he is alive. Then I holds it above my mouth, and as soon as he sees the hole in he goes. He goes wavy-like, as a ship goes,—that's the comparison. You see, a snake will go in at any hole. I always hold my breath whilst his head is in my swallow. When he moves in the swallow, it tickles a little, but it don't make you want to retch. In my opinion he is more glad to come up than to go down, for it seems to be too hot for him. I keep him down about two minutes. If I breathe or cough, he draws out and curls back again. I think there's artfulness in some of them big snakes, for they seem to know which is the master. I was at Wombwell's menagerie* of wild beasts for three months, and I had the care of a big snake, as thick round as my arm. I wouldn't attempt to put that one down my throat, I can tell you, for I think I might easier have gone down his'n. I had to show it to the people in front of the carriages to draw 'em in, at fair time. I used to hold it up in both hands, with my arms in the air. Many a time it curled itself three or four times round my neck and about my body, and it never even so much as squeeged me the least bit. I had the feeding on it, and I used to give it the largest worms I could find. Mr Wombwell has often said to me, "It's a dangerous game you're after, and if you don't give the snake plenty of worms and make it like you, it'll nip you some of these times." I'm sure the snake know'd me. I was very partial to it, too. It was a furren snake, over spots, called a boa-constructor. It never injured me, though I'm told it is uncommon powerful, and can squeege a man up like a sheet of paper, and crack his bones as easy as a lark's. I'm tremendous courageous, nothing frightens me; indeed, I don't know what it is to be afraid.'

Street Clown

He was a melancholy-looking man, with the sunken eyes and other characteristics of semi-starvation, whilst his face was scored with lines and wrinkles, telling of paint and premature age.

I saw him performing in the streets with a school of acrobats soon after I had been questioning him, and the readiness and business-like way with which he resumed his professional buffoonery was not a little remarkable. His story was more pathetic than comic, and proved that the life of a street clown is, perhaps, the most wretched of all existence. Jest as he may in the street, his life is literally no joke at home.

'I have been a clown for sixteen years,' he said, 'having lived totally by it for that time. I was left motherless at two years of age, and my father died when I was nine. He was a carman,* and his master took me as a stable-boy, and I stayed with him until he failed in business. I was then left destitute again, and got employed as a supernumerary at Astley's,* at one shilling a-night. I was a "super"* some time, and got an insight into theatrical life, I got acquainted, too, with singing people, and could sing a good song, and came out at last on my own account in the streets, in the Jim Crow line. My necessities forced me into a public line, which I am far from liking. I'd pull trucks at one shilling a-day, rather than get twelve shillings a-week at my business. I've tried to get out of the line. I've got a friend to advertise for me for any situation as groom. I've tried to get into the police, and I've tried other things, but somehow there seems an impossibility to get quit of the street business. Many times I have to play the clown, and indulge in all kinds of buffoonery, with a terrible heavy heart. I have travelled very much, too, but I never did over-well in the profession. At races I may have made ten shillings for two or three days, but that was only occasional; and what is ten shillings to keep a wife and family on, for a month maybe? I have three children, one now only eight weeks old. You can't imagine, sir, what a curse the street business often becomes, with its insults and starvations. The day before my wife was confined, I jumped and labour'd doing Jim Crow for twelve hours—in the wet, too—and earned one shilling and threepence; with this I returned to a home without a bit of coal, and with only half-a-quartern loaf in it.

'I dare say', continued the man, 'that no persons think more of their dignity than such as are in my way of life. I would rather starve than ask for parochial relief. Many a time I have gone to my labour without breaking my fast, and played clown until I could raise dinner. I have to make jokes as clown, and could fill a volume with all I knows.'

He told me several of his jests; they were all of the most venerable kind, as for instance:—'A horse has ten legs: he has two fore legs and two hind ones. Two fores are eight, and two others are ten.' The other jokes were equally puerile, as, 'Why is the City of Rome' (he would have it Rome) 'like a candle wick? Because it's in the midst of Greece.' 'Old and young are both of one age: your son at twenty is young, and your horse at twenty is old: and so old and young are the same.' 'The dress', he continued, 'that I wear in the streets consists of red striped cotton stockings, with full trunks, dotted red and black. The body, which is dotted like the trunks, fits tight like a woman's gown, and has full sleeves and frills. The wig or scalp is made of horse-hair, which is sewn on to a white cap, and is in the shape of a cock's comb. My face is painted with dry white lead. I grease my skin first and then dab the white paint on (flake-white is too dear for us street clowns); after that I colour my cheeks and mouth with vermilion. I never dress at home; we all dress at public-houses. In the street where I lodge, only a very few know what I do for a living. I and my wife both strive to keep the business a secret from our neighbours. My wife does a little washing when able, and often works eight hours for sixpence. I go out at eight in the morning and return at dark. My children hardly know what I do. They see my dresses lying about, but that is all. My eldest is a girl of thirteen. She has seen me dressed at Stepney fair, where she brought me my tea (I live near there); she laughs when she sees me in my clown's dress, and wants to stay with me: but I would rather see her lay dead before me (and I had two dead in my place at one time, last Whitsun Monday was a twelvemonth) than she should ever belong to my profession.'

I could see the tears start from the man's eyes as he said this.

'Frequently when I am playing the fool in the streets, I feel very sad at heart. I can't help thinking of the bare cupboards at home; but what's that to the world? I've often and often been at home all day

CIRCUS CLOWN AT FAIR.

when it has been wet, with no food at all, either to give my children or take myself, and have gone out at night to the public-houses to sing a comic song or play the funnyman for a meal—you may imagine with what feelings for the part—and when I've come home I've call'd my children up from their beds to share the loaf I had brought back with me. I know three or more clowns as miserable and bad off as myself. The way in which our profession is ruined is by the stragglers or outsiders, who are often men who are good tradesmen. They take to the clown's business only at holiday or fair time, when there is a little money to be picked up at it, and after that they go back to their own trades; so that, you see, we, who are obliged to continue at it the year through, are deprived of even the little bit of luck we should otherwise have. I know only of another regular street clown in London besides myself. Some schools of acrobats, to be sure, will have a comic character of some kind or other, to keep the pitch up; that is, to amuse the people while the money is being collected: but these, in general, are not regular clowns. They are mostly dressed and got up for the occasion. They certainly don't do anything else but the street comic business, but they are not pantomimists by profession. The street clowns generally go out with dancers and tumblers. There are some street clowns to be seen with the Jacks-in-the-greens; but they are mostly sweeps, who have hired their dress for the two or three days, as the case may be. I think there are three regular clowns in the metropolis, and one of these is not a professional: he never smelt the sawdust, I know, sir. The most that I have known have been shoemakers before taking to the business. When I go out as a street clown, the first thing I do is a comic medley dance; and then, after that I crack a few jokes, and that is the whole of my entertainment. The first part of the medley dance is called 'the good St Anthony' (I was the first that ever danced the polka in the streets); then I do a waltz, and wind up with a hornpipe. After that I go through a little burlesque business. I fan myself, and one of the school asks me whether I am out of breath? I answer, "No, the breath is out of me." The leading questions for the jokes are all regularly prepared beforehand. The old jokes always go best with our audiences. The older they are, the better for the streets. I know, indeed, of nothing new in the joking way; but even if there was, and it was in any way deep, it would not do for the public thorough-fares. I have read a great deal of "Punch",* but the jokes are nearly all too high there; indeed, I can't say I think very much of them myself. The principal way in which I've got up my jokes is through associating with other clowns. We don't make our jokes ourselves; in fact, I never knew one clown who did. I must own that the street clowns like a little drop of spirits, and occasionally a good deal. They are in a measure obligated to it. I can't fancy a clown being funny on small beer;* and I never in all my life knew one who was a teetotaller. I think such a person would be a curious character, indeed. Most of the street clowns die in the workhouses. In their old age they are generally very wretched and poverty-stricken. I can't say what I think will be the end of me. I daren't think of it, sir.'

A few minutes afterwards I saw this man dressed as Jim Crow, with his face blackened, dancing and singing in the streets as if he was the lightest-hearted fellow in all London.

Strolling Actors

What are called strolling actors are those who go about the country and play at the various fairs and towns. As long as they are acting in a booth they are called canvas actors; but supposing they stop in a town a few days after a fair, or build up in a town where there is no fair, that constitutes what is termed private business.

'We call strolling acting "mumming", and the actors "mummers". All spouting is mumming. A strolling actor is supposed to know something of everything. He doesn't always get a part given to him to learn, but he's more often told what character he's to take, and what he's to do, and he's supposed to be able to find words capable of illustrating the character; in fact, he has to "gag", that is, make up words.

'The mummers have got a slang of their own, which parties connected with the perfession generally use. It is called "mummers' slang", and I have been told that it's a compound of broken Italian and French. Some of the Romanee* is also mixed up with it. This, for instance, is the slang for "Give me a glass of beer,"—"Your nabs sparkle my nabs," "a drop of beware". "I have got no money" is, "My nabs has nanti dinali." I'll give you a few sentences.

'"Parni" is rain; and "toba" is ground.

'"Nanti numgare" is—No food.

'"Nanti fogare" is—No tobacco.

'"Is his nabs a bona pross?"—Is he good for something to drink?

'"Nanti, his nabs is a keteva homer"—No, he's a bad sort.

'"The casa will parker our nabs multi" means,—This house will tumble down.

'"Vada the glaze" is—Look at the window.

'These are nearly all the mummers' slang words we use; but they apply to different meanings. We call breakfast, dinner, tea, supper, all of them "numgare"; and all beer, brandy, water, or soup, are "beware". We call everybody "his nabs", or "her nabs". I went among the penny-ice men, who are Italian chaps, and I found that they were speaking a lot of mummers' slang. It is a good deal Italian. We think it must have originated from Italians who went about doing pantomimes.

'Now, the way we count money is nearly all of it Italian; from one farthing up to a shilling is this:

'"Patina, nadsa, oni soldi, duey soldi, tray soldi, quatro soldi, chinqui soldi, say soldi, seter soldi, otter soldi, novra soldi, deshra soldi, lettra soldi, and a biouk." A half-crown is a "metsa carroon"; a "carroon" is a crown; "metsa punta" is half-a-sovereign; a "punta" is a pound. Even with these few words, by mixing them up with a few English ones, we can talk away as fast as if we was using our own language.

'Mumming at fairs is harder than private business, because you have to perform so many times. You only wear one dress, and all the actor is expected to do is to stand up to the dances outside and act in. He'll have to dance perhaps sixteen quadrilles in the course of the day, and act about as often inside. The company generally work in shares, or if they pay by the day, it's about four or five shillings a-day. When you go to get engaged, the first question is, "What can you do?" and the next, "Do you find your own properties, such as russet boots,* your dress, hat and feathers, &c.?" Of course they like your dress the better if it's a showy one; and it don't much matter about its corresponding with the piece. For instance, Henry the Second, in "Fair Rosamond",* always comes on with a cavalier's dress, and nobody notices the difference of costume. In fact, the same dresses are used over and over again for the same pieces. The general dress for the ladies is a velvet skirt with a satin stomacher, with a gold band round the waist and a pearl band on the forehead. They, too, wear the same dresses for all the pieces. A regular fair show has only a small compass of dresses, for they only goes to the same places once in a year, and of course their costumes ain't remembered.

'It's a very jolly life strolling, and I wouldn't leave it for any other if I had my choice. At times it's hard lines; but for my part I prefer it to any other. It's about fifteen shillings a-week for certain. If you can make up your mind to sleep in the booth, it ain't such bad pay. But the most of the men go to lodgings, and they don't forget to boast of it. "Where do you lodge?" one 'll ask. "Oh, I lodged at such a place," says another; for we're all first-rate fellows, if you can get anybody to believe us.

'Mummers' feed is a herring, which we call a pheasant. After performance we generally disperse, and those who have lodgings go to 'em; but if any sleep in the booth, turn in. Perhaps there's a batch of coffee brought forwards, a subscription supper of three. The coffee and sugar is put in a kettle and boiled up, and then served up in what we can get: either a saucepan lid, or a cocoa-nut shell, or a publican's pot, or whatever they can get. Mummers is the poorest, flashest, and most independent race of men going. If you was to offer some of them a shilling they'd refuse it, though the most of them would take it. The generality of them is cobblers' lads, and tailors' apprentices, and clerks, and they do account for that by their having so much time to study over their work.

'Private business is a better sort of acting. There we do nearly the entire piece, with only the difficult parts cut out. We only do the outline of the story, and gag it up. We've done various plays of Shakspeare in this way, such as "Hamlet" or "Othello", but only on benefit occasions. Then we go as near as memory will let us, but we must never appear to be stuck for words.

'Our rehearsals for a piece are the funniest things in the world. Perhaps we are going to play "The Floating Beacon, or The Weird Woman of the Wreck".* The manager will, when the night's performance is over, call the company together, and he'll say to the low-comedyman, "Now, you play Jack Junk, and this is your part: you're supposed to fetch Frederick for to go to sea. Frederick gets capsized in the boat, and gets aboard of the floating beacon. You go to search for him, and the smugglers tell you he's not aboard, and they give you the lie; then you say, 'What, the lie to a English sailor!' and you chuck your quid in his eye, saying, 'I've had it for the last fourteen days, and now I scud it with a full sail into your lubberly eye.' Then you have to get Frederick off."

'Then the manager will turn to the juvenile, and say, "Now, sir, you'll play Frederick. Now then, Frederick, you're in love with a girl, and old Winslade, the father, is very fond of you. You get into the boat to go to the ship, and you're wrecked and get on to the beacon. You're very faint, and stagger on, and do a back fall. You're picked up by the weird woman, and have some dialogue with her; and then you have some dialogue with the two smugglers, Ormaloff and Augerstoff. You pretend to sleep, and they're going to stab you, when the wild woman screams, and you awake and have some more dialogue. Then they bring a bottle, and you begin drinking. You change the cups. Then there's more dialogue, and you tackle Ormaloff. Then you discover your mother and embrace. Jack Junk saves you. Form a picture with your mother, the girl, and old Winslade, and Jack Junk over you."

'That's his part, and he's got to put it together and do the talk.

'Then the manager turns to Ormaloff and Augerstoff, and says: "Now, you two play the smugglers, do you hear? You're to try and poison the young fellow, and you're defeated."

'Then he say to the wild woman: "You're kept as a prisoner aboard the beacon, where your husband has been murdered. You have refused to become the wife of Ormaloff. Your child has been thrown overboard. You discover him in Frederick, and you scream when they are about to stab him, and also when he's about to drink. Make as much of it as you can, please; and don't forget the scream."

' "Winslade, you know your part. You've only got to follow Junk."

' "You're to play the lady, you Miss. You're in love with Frederick. You know the old business:* 'What! to part thus? Alas! alas! never to this moment have I confessed I love you!' "

'That's a true picture of a mumming rehearsal, whether it's fair or private business. Some of the young chaps, stick in their parts. They get the stage-fever* and knocking in the knees. We've had to shove them on to the scene. They keep on asking what they're to say. "Oh, say anything!" we tell 'em, and push 'em on to the stage.

'If a man's not gifted with the gab, he's no good at a booth. I've been with a chap acting "Mary Woodbine",* and he hasn't known a word of his part. Then, when he's stuck, he has seized me by the throat, and said, "Caitiff! dog! be sure thou provest my wife unfaithful to me." Then I saw his dodge, and I said, "Oh, my lord!"

and he continued—"Give me the proof, or thou hadst best been born a dog." Then I answered, "My lord, you wrong your wife, and torture me"; and he said, "Forward, then, liar! dog!" and we both rushed off.'

Gun-Exercise Exhibitor—One-Legged Italian

'I was wounded at the bataille de Pescare,* against the Austrians. We gained the battle and entered the town. The General Radetzky was against us. He is a good general, but Ferdinando Marmora beat him. Ferdinando was wounded by a ball in the cheek. It passed from left to right. He has the mark now. Ah, he is a good general. I was wounded. Pardon! I cannot say if it was a bal de canon or a bal de fusil.* I was on the ground like one dead. I fell with my leg bent behind me, because they found me so. They tell me, that as I fell I cried, "My God! my God!" but that is not in my memory. After they had finished the battle they took up the wounded. Perhaps I was on the ground twelve hours, but I do not know exactly. I was picked up with others and taken to the hospital, and then one day after my leg decomposed, and it was cut directly. All the bone was fracassé, vairy beaucoup.* I was in the hospital for forty days. Ah! it was terrible. To cut the nerves was terrible. They correspond with the head. Ah, horrible! They gave me no chloroform. Rien! rien! No, nor any dormitore, as we call it in Italian, you know,—something in a glass to drink and make you sleep. Rien! rien!

'I have been very unfortunate. I have a tumour come under the arm where I rest on my crutch. It is a tumour, as they call it in France, but I do not know what it is named in English. I went to the hospital of San Bartolommeo* and they cut it for me. Then I have hurt my stomach, from the force of calling out the differing orders of commanding, whilst I am doing my gun exercises in the streets. I was two months in my bed with my arm and my stomach being bad. Some days I cannot go out, I am so ill. I cannot drink beer, it is too hot for me, and gets to my head, and it is bad for my stomach. I eat fish: that is good for the voice and the stomach. Now I am better, and my side does not hurt me when I cry out my commanding orders. If I do it for a long time it is painful.

'When I do my exercise, this what I do. I first of all stand still on one leg, in the position of a militaire, with my crutch shouldered like a gun. That is how I accumulate the persons. Then I have to do all. It makes me laugh, for I have to be the general, the capitaines, the drums, the soldiers, and all. Pauvre diable!* I must live. It is curious, and makes me laugh.

'I first begin my exercises by doing the drums. I beat my hands together, and make a noise like this—"hum, hum! hum, hum, hum! hum, hum! hum, hum! hu-u-u-m!" and then the drums go away and I do them in the distance. You see I am the drummers then. Next I become the army, and make a noise with my foot, resembling soldiers on a march, and I go from side to side to imitate an army marching. Then I become the trumpeters, but instead of doing the trumpets I whistle their music, and the sound comes nearer and nearer, and gets louder and louder, and then gradually dies away in the distance, as if a bataillon was marching in front of its general. I make a stamping with my foot, like men marching past. After that I become the officiers, the capitaines and the lieutenants, as if the general was passing before them, and my crutch becomes my sword instead of my gun. Then I draw it from my side, and present it with the handle pointed to my breast. Then I become the general, and I gives this order: "Separate bataillons three steps behind—un, deux, trois!" and I instantly turn to the army again and give three hops to the side, so that the general may walk up and down before me and see how the soldiers are looking. Then I in turn become the officier who gives the commands, and the soldiers who execute them. It hurts my voice when I cry out these commands. They must be very loud, or all the army would not hear them. I can be heard a long way off when I call them out. I begin with "PORTEZ AR-R-R-MES!" that is, "Carry arms," in England. Then I lift my crutch up on my left side and hold it there. Then comes "PRESENT AR-R-RMES!" and then I hold the gun—my crutch, you know—in front of me, straight up. The next is, "REPOSE AR-R-RMES!" and I put to my hip, with the barrel leaning forwards. When I say, barrel, it's only my crutch, you understand. Then I shout, "Un, deux, trois! GROUND AR-R-RMS!" and let the top of my crutch slide on to the road, and I stamp with my toes to resemble the noise. Afterwards I give the command, "PORTEZ AR-R-RMES!" and then I carry my arms again in my left hand, and slap my other hand hard down by my right side, like a veritable soldier, and stand upright in position. Whilst I am so I shout, "SEPARATE THE COLUMNS! UN, DEUX, TR-R-ROIS!" and instantly I hop on my one leg three times backwards, so as to let the general once more walk down the ranks and inspect the men. As soon as he is supposed to be near to me, I shout "PRÉSENT AR-R-RMES!" and then I hold my gun—the crutch, you comprehend—in front of me. Then, as soon as the general is supposed to have passed, I shout out, "REPOSE AR-R-RMES!" and I let the crutch slant from the right hip, waiting until I cry again "GROUND AR-R-R-RMS! UN, DEUX, TR-R-ROIS!" and then down slides the crutch to the ground.

'Next I do the other part of the review. I do the firing now, only, you comprehend, I don't fire, but only imitate it with my crutch. I call out "GROUND AR-R-RMS!" and let the top of my crutch fall to the earth. After that I shout, "LOAD AR-R-RMS! UN, DEUX, TR-R-ROIS!" and I pretend to take a cartouche from my side, and bite off the end, and slip it down the barrel of my crutch. Next I give the command, "Draw RAMRODS! UN, DEUX, TR-R-ROIS!" and then I begin to ram the cartridge home to the breech of the barrel. Afterwards I give the command, "COCK AR-R-RMS!" and then I pretend to take a percussion cap from my side-pocket, and I place it on the nipple and draw back the hammer. Afterwards I shout, "POINT AR-R-RMS!" and I pretend to take aim. Next I shout, "RECOVER AR-R-RMS!" that is, to hold the gun up in the air, and not to fire. Then I give orders, such as "POINT TO THE LEFT," or "Point to the right," and whichever way it is, I have to twist myself round on my one leg, and take an aim that way. Then I give myself the order to "FIRE!" and I imitate it by a loud shout, and then rattling my tongue as if the whole line was firing. As quickly as I can call out I shout, "RECOVER AR-R-RMS!" and I put up my gun before me to resist with my bayonet any charge that may be made. Then I shout out, "DRAW UP THE RANKS AND RECEIVE THE CAVALRY!" and then I work myself along on my one foot, but not by hopping; and there I am waiting for the enemy's horse, and ready to receive them. Often, after I have fired, I call out "CHAR-R-RGE!" and then I hop forwards as fast as I can, as if I was rushing down upon the enemy, like this. Ah! I was nearly charging through your window; I only stopped in time, or I should have broken the squares in reality. Such a victory would have cost me too dear. After I have charged the enemy and put them to flight, then I draw myself up again, and give the order to "FORM COLUMNS!" And next I "CARRY AR-R-RMS," and then

"PRESENT AR-R-RMS," and finish by "GROUNDING AR-R-RMS, UN, DEUX, TR-R-ROIS."

'Oh, I have forgotten one part. I do it after the charging. When I have returned from putting the enemy to flight, I become the general calling his troops together. I shout, "AR-R-RMS on the SHOULDER!" and then I become the soldier, and let my gun rest on my shoulder, the same as when I am marching. Then I shout, "MARCH!" and I hop round on my poor leg, for I cannot march, you comprehend, and I suppose myself to be defiling before the general. Next comes the order "Halt!" and I stop still.

'It does not fatigue me to hop about on one leg. It is strong as iron. It is never fatigued. I have walked miles on it with my crutch. It only hurts my chest to holloa out the commands, for if I do not do it with all my force it is not heard far off. Besides, I am supposed to be ordering an army, and you must shout out to be heard by all the men; and although I am the only one, to be sure, still I wish to make the audience believe I am an army.'

STREET MUSICIANS

Concerning street musicians, they are of multifarious classes. As a general rule, they may almost be divided into the tolerable and the intolerable performers, some of them trusting to their skill in music for the reward for their exertions, others only making a *noise*, so that whatever money they obtain is given them merely as an inducement for them to depart. The well-known engraving by Hogarth, of 'the enraged musician',* is an illustration of the persecutions inflicted in olden times by this class of street performers; and in the illustrations by modern caricaturists we have had numerous proofs, that up to the present time the nuisance has not abated. Indeed, many of these people carry with them musical instruments, merely as a means of avoiding the officers of the Mendicity Society,* or in some few cases as a signal of their coming to the persons in the neighbourhood, who are in the habit of giving them a small weekly pension.

These are a more numerous class than any other of the street performers I have yet dealt with. The musicians are estimated at 1,000, and the ballad singers at 250.

The street musicians are of two kinds, the skilful and the blind. The former obtain their money by the agreeableness of their performance, and the latter, in pity for their affliction rather than admiration of their harmony. The blind street musicians, it must be confessed, belong generally to the rudest class of performers. Music is not used by them as a means of pleasing, but rather as a mode of soliciting attention. Such individuals are known in the 'profession' by the name of 'pensioners'; they have their regular rounds to make, and particular houses at which to call on certain days of the week, and from which they generally obtain a 'small trifle'. They form, however, a most peculiar class of individuals. They are mostly well-known characters, and many of them have been performing in the streets of London for many years. They are also remarkable for the religious cast of their thoughts, and the comparative refinement of their tastes and feelings.

'Old Sarah'

One of the most deserving and peculiar of the street musicians was an old lady who played upon a hurdy-gurdy. She had been about the streets of London for upwards of forty years, and being blind, had had during that period four guides, and worn out three instruments. Her cheerfulness, considering her privation and precarious mode of life, was extraordinary. Her love of truth, and the extreme simplicity of her nature, were almost childlike. Like the generality of blind people, she had a deep sense of religion, and her charity for a woman in her station of life was something marvellous; for, though living on alms, she herself had, I was told, two or three little pensioners. When questioned on this subject, she laughed the matter off as a jest, though I was assured of the truth of the fact. Her attention to her guide was most marked. If a cup of tea was given to her after her day's rounds, she would be sure to turn to the poor creature who led her about, and ask, 'You comfortable, Liza?' or 'Is your tea to your liking, Liza?'

When conveyed to Mr Beard's establishment to have her daguerreotype* taken, she for the first time in her life rode in a cab; and then her fear at being pulled 'back'ards' as she termed it (for she sat with her back to the horse), was almost painful. She felt about for something to lay hold of, and did not appear comfortable until she had a firm grasp of the pocket. After her alarm had in a measure subsided, she turned to her guide and said, 'We must put up with those trials, Liza.' In a short time, however, she began to find the ride pleasant enough. 'Very nice, ain't it Liza?' she said; 'but I shouldn't like to ride on them steamboats, they say they're shocking dangerous; and as for them railways, I've heard tell they're dreadful; but these cabs, Liza, is very nice.' On the road she was continually asking 'Liza' where they were, and wondering at the rapidity at which they travelled. 'Ah!' she said, laughing, 'if I had one of these here cabs, my "rounds" would soon be over.' Whilst ascending the high flight of stairs that led to the portrait-rooms, she laughed at every proposal made to her to rest. 'There's twice as many stairs as these to our church, ain't there, Liza?' she replied when pressed. When the portrait was finished she expressed a wish to feel it.

The following is the history of her life, as she herself related it, answering to the variety of questions put to her on the subject:

'I was born the 4th April, 1786 (it was Good Friday that year), at a small chandler's shop, facing the White Horse, Stuart's-rents,

"OLD SARAH," THE WELL-KNOWN HURDY-GURDY PLAYER.

[*From a Daguerreotype by* BEARD.]

Drury-lane. Father was a hatter, and mother an artificial-flower maker and feather finisher. When I was but a day old, the nurse took me out of the warm bed and carried me to the window, to show some people how like I was to father. The cold flew to my eyes and I caught inflammation in them. Owing to mother being forced to be from home all day at her work, I was put out to dry-nurse when I was three weeks old. My eyes were then very bad, by all accounts, and some neighbours told the woman I was with, that Turner's cerate* would do them good. She got some and put it on my eyes, and when poor mother came to suckle me at her dinner-hour, my eyes was all "a gore of blood". From that time I never see afterwards. She did it, poor woman, for the best; it was no fault of her'n, and I'm sure I bears her no malice for it. I stayed at home with mother until I was thirteen, when I was put to the Blind-school, but I only kept there nine months; they turned me out because I was not clever with my hands, and I could not learn to spin or make sash-lines;* my hands was ocker'd* like. I had not been used at home to do anything for myself—not even to dress myself. Mother was always out at her work, so she could not learn me, and no one else would, so that's how it was I was turned out. I then went back to my mother, and kept with her till her death. I well remember that; I heard her last. When she died I was just sixteen year old. I was sent to the Union*—"Pancridge" Union it was—and father with me (for he was ill at the time). He died too, and left me, in seven weeks after mother. When they was both gone, I felt I had lost my only friends, and that I was all alone in the world and blind. But, take it altogether, the world has been very good to me, and I have much to thank God for and the good woman I am with. I missed mother the most, she was so kind to me; there was no one like her; no, not even father. I was kept in the Union until I was twenty; the parish paid for my learning the "cymbal":* God bless them for it, I say. A poor woman in the workhouse first asked me to learn music; she said it would always be a bit of bread for me; I did as she told me, and I thank her to this day for it. It took me just five months to learn the—cymbal, if you please—the hurdy-gurdy ain't its right name. The first tune I ever played was "God save the King", the Queen as is now; then "Harlequin Hamlet", that took me a long time to get off; it was three weeks before they put me on a new one. I then learnt "Moll Brook"; then I did the "Turnpike-gate" and "Patrick's day in the morning": all of them I learnt in the Union. I got a poor man to teach me the "New-rigged ship". I soon learnt it, because it was an easy tune. Two-and-forty years ago I played "The Gal *I* left behind me". A woman learnt it me; she played my cymbal and I listened, and so got it. "Oh, Susannah!" I learnt myself by hearing it on the horgan. I always try and listen to a new tune when I am in the street, and get it off if I can: it's my bread. I waited to hear one to-day, quite a new one, but I didn't like it, so I went on. "Hasten to the Wedding" is my favourite; I played it years ago, and play it still. I like "Where have you been all the night?" it's a Scotch tune. The woman as persuaded me to learn the cymbal took me out of the Union with her; I lived with her, and she led me about the streets. When she died I took her daughter for my guide. She walked with me for more than five-and-twenty year, and she might have been with me to this day, but she took to drinking and killed herself with it. She behaved very bad to me at last, for as soon as we got a few halfpence she used to go into the public and spend it all; and many a time I'm sure she's been too tipsy to take me home. One night I remember she rolled into the road at Kensington, and as near pulled me with her. We was both locked up in the station-house, for she couldn't stand for liquor, and I was obligated to wait till she could lead me home. It was very cruel of her to treat me so, but, poor creature, she's gone, and I forgive her I'm sure. I'd many guides arter her, but none of them was honest like Liza is: I don't think she'd rob me of a farden. Would you, Liza? Yes, I've my reg'lar rounds, and I've kept to 'em for near upon fifty year. All the children like to hear me coming along, for I always plays my cymbal as I goes. At Kentish-town they calls me Mrs Tuesday, and at Kensington I'm Mrs Friday, and so on. At some places they likes polkas, but at one house I plays at in Kensington they always ask me for "Haste to the Wedding". No, the cymbal isn't very hard to play; the only thing is, you must be very particular that the works is covered up, or the halfpence is apt to drop in. King David, they say, played on one of those here instruments.* We're very tired by night-time; ain't we, Liza? but when I gets home the good woman I lodges with has always a bit of something for me to eat with my cup of tea. She's a good soul, and keeps me tidy and clean. I helps her all I can; when I come in, I carries her a pail of water up-stairs, and such-like. Many ladies as has known me since they was children allows me a trifle. One maiden lady near Brunswick-square has given me sixpence a week for many a year, and another allows me eighteenpence a fortnight; so that, one way and another, I am very comfortable, and I've much to be thankful for.'

It was during one of old Sarah's journeys that an accident occurred, which ultimately deprived London of the well-known old hurdy-gurdy woman. In crossing Seymour-street, she and her guide Liza were knocked down by a cab, as it suddenly turned a corner. They were picked up and placed in the vehicle (the poor guide dead, and Sarah with her limbs broken), and carried to the University Hospital. Old Sarah's description of that ride is more terrible and tragic than I can hope to make out to you. The poor blind creature was ignorant of the fate of her guide, she afterwards told us, and kept begging and praying to Liza to speak to her as the vehicle conveyed them to the asylum. She shook her, she said, and intreated her to say if she was hurt, but not a word was spoken in answer, and then she felt how terrible a privation was her blindness; and it was not until they reached the hospital, and they were lifted from the cab, that she knew, as she heard the people whisper to one another, that her faithful attendant was dead. In telling us this, the good old soul forgot her own sufferings for the time, as she lay with both her legs broken beneath the hooped bed-clothes of the hospital bed; and when, after many long weeks, she left the medical asylum, she was unable to continue her playing on the hurdy-gurdy, her hand being now needed for the crutch that was requisite to bear her on her rounds.

The shock, however, had been too much for the poor old creature's feeble nature to rally against, and though she continued to hobble round to the houses of the kind people who had for years allowed her a few pence per week, and went limping along music-less through the streets for some months after she left the hospital, yet her little remaining strength at length failed her, and she took to her bed in a room in Bell-court, Gray's-inn-lane, never to rise from it again.

'Farm-Yard' Player

A quiet-looking man, half-blind, and wrapped in a large, old, faded black-cotton great-coat, made the following statement, having first given me some specimens of his art:

'I imitate all the animals of the farm-yard on my fiddle: I imitate the bull, the calf, the dog, the cock, the hen when she's laid an egg, the peacock, and the ass. I have done this in the streets for nearly twelve years. I was brought up as a musician at my own desire. When a young man (I am now 53) I used to go out to play at parties, doing middling until my sight failed me; I then did the farm-yard on the fiddle for a living. Though I had never heard of such a thing before, by constant practice I made myself perfect. I studied from nature, I never was in a farm-yard in my life, but I went and listened to the poultry, anywhere in town that I could meet with them, and I then imitated them on my instrument. The Smithfield* cattle gave me the study for the bull and the calf. My peacock I got at the Belvidere-gardens* in Islington. The ass is common, and so is the dog; and them I studied anywhere. It took me a month, not more, if so much, to acquire what I thought a sufficient skill in my undertaking, and then I started it in the streets. It was liked the very first time I tried it. I never say what animal I am going to give; I leave that to the judgment of the listeners. They could always tell what it was. I could make 12*s*. a week the year through. I play it in public-houses as well as in the streets. My pitches are all over London, and I don't know that one is better than another. Working-people are my best friends. Thursday and Friday are my worst days; Monday and Saturday my best, when I reckon 2*s*. 6*d*. a handsome taking. I am the only man who does the farm-yard.'

The Dancing Dogs

I received the following narrative from the old man who has been so long known about the streets of London with a troop of performing dogs. He was especially picturesque in his appearance. His hair, which was grizzled rather than grey, was parted down the middle, and hung long and straight over his shoulders. He was dressed in a coachman's blue greatcoat with many capes. His left hand was in a sling made out of a dirty pocket-handkerchief, and in his other he held a stick, by means of which he could just manage to hobble along. He was very ill, and very poor, not having been out with his dogs for nearly two months. He appeared to speak in great pain. The civility, if not politeness of his manner, threw an air of refinement about him, that struck me more forcibly from its contrast with the manners of the English belonging to the same class. He began:

'I have de dancing dogs for de street—now I have nothing else. I have tree dogs—One is called Finette, anoder von Favorite, that is her nomme, an de oder von Ozor. Ah!' he said, with a shrug of the shoulders, in answer to my inquiry as to what the dogs did, 'un danse, un valse, un jomp a de stick and troo de hoop—non, noting else. Sometime I had de four dogs—I did lose de von. Ah! she had beaucoup d'esprit—plenty of vit, you say—she did jomp a de hoop better dan all. Her nomme was Taborine!—she is dead dare is long time. All ma dogs have des habillements*—the dress and de leetle hat. Dey have a leetel jackette in divers colours en étoffe*—some de red, and some de green, and some de bleu. Deir hats is de rouge et noir—red and black, wit a leetle plume—fedder, you say. Dere is some 10 or 11 year I have been in dis country. I come from Italie—Italie—Oui, Monsieur, oui. I did live in a leetle ville, trento miglia, dirty mile, de Parma. Je travaille dans le campagne, I vork out in de countrie—je ne sais comment vous appellez la campagne.* There is no commerce in de montagne.* I am come in dis country here. I have leetel business to come. I thought to gagner ma vie—to gain my life wid my leetel dogs in dis countrie. I have dem déjà* when I have come here from Parma—j'en avait dix. I did have de ten dogs—je les apporte. I have carried all de ten from Italie. I did learn—yes—yes—de dogs to danse in ma own countrie. It did make de cold in de montagne in winter, and I had not no vork dere, and I must look for to gain my life some oder place. Après ça,* I have instruct my dogs to danse. Yes, ils learn to danse; I play de music, and dey do jomp. Non, non—pas du tout.* I did not never beat ma dogs; dare is a way to learn de dogs without no vip. Premièrement,* ven I am come here I have gained a leetel monnaie—plus que now—beaucoup d'avantage—plenty more. I am left ma logement—my lodging, you say, at 9 hours in de morning, and am stay away vid ma dogs till 7 or 8 hours in de evening. Oh! I cannot count how many times de leetel dogs have danse in de day—twenty—dirty—forty peut-être*—all depends: sometimes I would gain de tree shilling—sometime de couple—sometime not nothing—all depend. Ven it did make bad time, I could not vork; I could not danse. I could not gain my life den. If it make cold de dogs are ill—like tout de monde.* I did pay plenty for de nouriture* of de dogs. Sometime dey did get du pain de leetel dogs (de bread) in de street—sometime I give dem de meat, and make de soup for dem. Ma dogs danse comme les chiens, mais dey valtz comme les dames, and dey stand on dare back-legs like les gentilhommes.* After I am come here to dis countrie two day, am terrible malade,* I am gone to hospital, to St Bartolomé,* de veek before de Jour de Noël (Christmas-day). In dat moment I have de fevre. I have rested in l'hospital quatre semaine—four veek. Ma dogs vere at libertie all de time. Von compagnon of mine have promised me to take de care of ma dogs, and he have lose dem all—tout les dix. After dat I have bought tree oder dogs—one espanol, anoder von appellé "Grifon",* and de oder vas de dog ordinaire,—non! non! not one "pull dog". He no good. I must have one month, or sis semaine, to instruite ma dogs. I have rested in a logement Italien at Saffron-hill, ven I am come here to London. Dare vas plenty of Italiens dare. It was tout plein—quite full of strangers. All come dare—dey come from France, from Germany, from Italie. I have paid two shillings per semaine each veek—only pour le lit, for de bed. Every von make de kitchen for himself. Vot number vas dare, you say? Sometime dare is 20 person dere, and sometime dere is dirty person in de logement, sometime more dan dat. It is very petite maison.* Dare is von dozen beds—dat is all—and two sleep demselves in each bed. Sometimes, ven dere arrive plenty, dey sleep demselves tree in von bed—but ordinairement dere is only two. Dey is all musicians dere—one play de organ, de piano, de guitar, de flute, yes, dare vos some vot played it, and de viol too. De great part vas Italiens. Some of dem have des monkeys, de oders des mice white, and des pigs d'Indes (guinea-pigs), and encore oders have des dolls vid two heads, and des puppets vot danse vid de foot on de boards. Des animals are in an appartement apart vid de moosick. Dare vos sometime tree dancing dogs, one dozen of mice, five or six pigs d'Indes, and ma monkey, altogether vid de moosick, by demselves.

'Dare is all de actors vot vas dare. Ma tree dogs gained me sometime two shillan, sometime von shillan, and sometime I would rest on my feet all day, and not gain two sous.* Sometimes de boys would ensault ma dogs vid de stones. Dare is long time I have rested in London. Dare is short time I vas in de campagne de countree here, not much. London is better dan de campagne for ma dogs—dare is always de vorld in London—de city is large—yes! I am always rested* at Saffron-hill for 10, 11 years. I am malade at present, since the 15th of Mars;* in ma arms, ma legs, ma tighs have de douleure—I have plenty of pains to march. Ma dogs are in de logement now. It is since the 15th of Mars dat I have not vent out vid ma dogs—yes, since de 15th of Mars I have done no vork. Since dat time I have not paid no money for ma logement—it is due encore. Non! non! I have not gained my life since the 15th of Mars. Plenty of time I have been vitout noting to eat. Des Italiens at de logement dey have given me pieces of bread and bouilli.* Ah! it is very miserable to be poor, like me. I have sixty and tirteen years. I cannot march now but vith plenty of pains. Von doctor have give to me a letter for to present to de poor-house. He did give me my medicine for nothing—gratis. He is obliged, he is de doctor of de paroisse.* He is a very brave and honest man, dat doctor dare. At de poor-house day have give to me a bread and six sous on Friday of de veek dat is past, and told me to come de Vednesday next. But I am arrive dere too late, and dey give me noting, and tell me to come de Vednesday next encore. Ma dogs dey march now in de street, and eat something dare. Oh! ma God, non! dey eat noting but what dey find in de street ven it makes good times; but ven it makes bad times dey have noting at all, poor dogs! ven I have it, dey have it,—but ven dere is noting for me to eat, dare is noting for dem, and dey must go out in de streets and get de nouriture for themselves. Des enfans vot know ma dogs vill give to dem to eat sometimes. Oh! yes, if I had de means, I would return to Italie, ma countree. But I have not no silver, and not no legs to walk. Vot can I do? Oh! yes, I am very sick at present. All my limbs have great douleur—Oh, yes! plenty of pain.'

STREET ARTISTS

Street Photography

Within the last few years photographic portraits have gradually been diminishing in price, until at the present time they have become a regular article of street commerce. Those living at the west-end of London have but little idea of the number of persons who gain a livelihood by street photography.

There may be one or two 'galleries' in the New-road, or in Tottenham-court-road, but these supply mostly shilling portraits. In the eastern and southern districts of London, however, such as in Bermondsey, the New-cut, and the Whitechapel-road, one cannot walk fifty yards without passing some photographic establishment, where for sixpence persons can have their portrait taken, and framed and glazed as well.

It was in Bermondsey that I met with the first instance of what may be called pure street photography. Here a Mr F——l was taking sixpenny portraits in a booth built up out of old canvas, and erected on a piece of spare ground in a furniture-broker's yard.

Mr F——l had been a travelling showman, but finding that photography was attracting more attention than giants and dwarfs, he relinquished the wonders of Nature for those of Science.

Into this yard he had driven his yellow caravan, where it stood like an enormous Noah's ark, and in front of the caravan (by means of clothes-horses and posts, over which were spread out the large sail-like paintings (show-cloths), which were used at fairs to decorate the fronts of booths), he had erected his operating-room, which is about as long and as broad as a knife-house, and only just tall enough to allow a not particularly tall customer to stand up with his hat off: whilst by means of two window-sashes a glazed roof had been arranged for letting light into this little tent.

On the day of my visit Mr F——l was, despite the cloudy state of the atmosphere, doing a large business. A crowd in front of his tent was admiring the photographic specimens, which, of all sizes and in all kinds of frames, were stuck up against the canvas-wall, as irregularly as if a bill-sticker had placed them there. Others were gazing up at the chalky-looking paintings over the door-way, and on which a lady was represented photographing an officer, in the full costume of the 11th Hussars.

Inside the operating room we found a crowd of women and children was assembled, all of them waiting their turn to be taken. Mr F——l remarked, as I entered, that 'It was wonderful the sight of children that had been took'; and he added, 'when *one* girl comes for her portrait, there's a *dozen* comes along with her to see it took.'

The portraits I discovered were taken by Mrs F——l, who, with the sleeves of her dress tucked up to the elbows, was engaged at the moment of my visit in pointing the camera at a lady and her little boy, who, from his wild nervous expression, seemed to have an idea that the operatress was taking her aim previous to shooting him.* Mr F——l explained to me the reason why his wife officiated. 'You see,' said he, 'people prefers more to be took by a woman than by a man. Many's a time a lady tells us to send that man away, and let the missis come. It's quite natural,' he continued; 'for a lady don't mind taking her bonnet off and tucking up her hair, or sticking a pin in here and there before one of her own sect, which before a man proves objectionable.'

After the portrait had been taken I found that the little square piece of glass on which it was impressed was scarcely larger than a visiting card, and this being handed over to a youth, was carried into the caravan at the back, where the process was completed. I was invited to follow the lad to the dwelling on wheels.

The outside of the caravan was very remarkable, and of that peculiar class of architecture which is a mixture of coach-and-ship building. In the centre of the front of the show were little folding-doors with miniature brass knockers, and glass let into the upper panels. On each side of the door were long windows, almost big enough for a shop-front, whilst the white curtains, festooned at their sides, gave them a pleasant appearance. The entire erection was coloured yellow, and the numerous little wooden joists and tie-beams, which framed and strengthened the vehicle, conferred upon it a singular plaid-like appearance.

I mounted the broad step-ladder and entered. The room reminded me of a ship's cabin, for it was panelled and had cross-beams to the arched roof, whilst the bolts and fastenings, were of bright brass.

If the windows had not been so large, or the roof so high, it would have resembled the fore-cabin of a Gravesend steamer. There were tables and chairs, as in an ordinary cottage room. At one end was the family bed, concealed during the day by chintz curtains, which hung down like a drop-scene before a miniature theatre; and between the openings of these curtains I could catch sight of some gaudily attired wax figures stowed away there for want of room, but standing there like a group of actors behind the scenes.

Along one of the beams a blunderbuss and a pistol rested on hooks, and the showman's speaking trumpet (as large as the funnel to a grocer's coffee-mill) hung against the wall, whilst in one corner was a kind of cabin stove of polished brass, before which a boy was drying some of the portraits that had been recently taken.

'So you've took him at last,' said the proprietor, who accompanied us as he snatched the portrait from the boy's hand. 'Well, the eyes ain't no great things, but as it's the third attempt it must do.'

On inspecting the portrait I found it to be one of those drab-looking portraits with a light back-ground, where the figure rises from the bottom of the plate as straight as a post, and is in the cramped, nervous attitude of a patient in a dentist's chair.

After a time I left Mr F——l's, and went to another establishment close by, which had originally formed part of a shop in the penny-ice-and-bull's-eye line—for the name-board over 'Photographic Depôt' was still the property of the confectioner—so that the portraits displayed in the window were surmounted by an announcement of 'Ginger beer 1*d*. and 2*d*.'.

A touter at the door was crying out 'Hi! hi!—walk inside! walk inside! and have your c'rect likeness took, frame and glass complete, and only 6*d*.!—time of sitting only four seconds!'

A rough-looking, red-faced tanner, who had been staring at some coloured French lithographs which decorated the upper panes, and who, no doubt, imagined that they had been taken by the photographic process, entered, saying, 'Let me have my likeness took.'

The touter instantly called out, 'Here, a shilling likeness for this here gent.'

The tanner observed that he wanted only a sixpenny.

'Ah, very good, sir!' and raising his voice, the touter shouted louder than before—'A sixpenny one first, and a shilling one afterwards.'

'I tell yer I don't want only sixpennorth,' angrily returned the customer, as he entered.

At this establishment the portraits were taken in a little alley adjoining the premises, where the light was so insufficient, that even the blanket hung up at the end of it looked black from the deep shadows cast by the walls.

When the tanner's portrait was completed it was nearly black; and, indeed, the only thing visible was a slight light on one side of the face, and which, doubtlessly, accounted for the short speech which the operator thought fit to make as he presented the likeness to his customer.

'There,' he said, 'there is your likeness, if you like! look at it yourself; and only eightpence'—'Only sixpence,' observed the man.—'Ah! continued the proprietor, 'but you've got a patent American preserver, and that's twopence more.'

Then followed a discussion, in which the artist insisted that he lost by every sixpenny portrait he took, and the tanner as strongly protesting that he couldn't believe that, for they must get *some* profit any how. 'You don't tumble to the rig,' said the artist; 'it's the half-guinea ones, you see, that pays us.'

The touter, finding that this discussion was likely to continue, entered and joined the argument. 'Why, it's cheap as dirt,' he exclaimed indignantly; 'the fact is, our governor's a friend of the people, and don't mind losing a little money. He's determined that everybody shall have a portrait, from the highest to the lowest. Indeed, next Sunday, he *do* talk of taking them for threepence-ha'penny, and if that ain't philandery,* what is?'

After the touter's oration the tanner seemed somewhat contented, and paying his eightpence left the shop, looking at his picture in all lights, and repeatedly polishing it up with the cuff of his coat-sleeve, as if he were trying to brighten it into something like distinctness.

Whilst I was in this establishment a customer was induced to pay twopence for having the theory of photography explained to him. The lecture was to the effect, that the brass tube of the 'camerer' was filled with clockwork, which carried the image from the lens to the ground glass at the back. To give what the lecturer called 'hockeylar proof' of this, the camera was carried to the shop-door, and a boy who was passing by ordered to stand still for a minute.

'Now, then,' continued the lecturer to the knowledge-seeker, 'look behind here; there's the himage, you see'; and then addressing the boy, he added, 'Just open your mouth, youngster'; and when the lad did so, the student was asked, 'Are you looking down the young un's throat?' and on his nodding assent, he was informed, 'Well, that's the way portraits is took.'

Statement of a Photographic Man

'Sunday is the best day for shilling portraits; in fact, the majority is shilling ones, because then, you see, people have got their wages, and don't mind spending. Nobody knows about men's ways better than we do. Sunday and Monday is the Derby-day* like, and then after that they are about cracked up and done. The largest amount I've taken at Southwark on a Sunday is 80—over 4*l.* worth, but then in the week-days it's different; Sunday's 15*s.* we think that very tidy, some days only 3*s.* or 4*s.*

'You see we are obliged to resort to all sort of dodges to make sixpenny portraits pay. It's a very neat little picture our sixpenny ones is; with a little brass rim round them, and a neat metal inside, and a front glass; so how can that pay if you do the legitimate business? The glass will cost you 2*d.* a-dozen—this small size—and you give two with every picture; then the chemicals will cost quite a halfpenny, and varnish, and frame, and fittings, about 2*d.* We reckon 3*d.* out of each portrait. And then you see there's house-rent and a man at the door, and boy at the table, and the operator, all to pay their wages out of this 6*d.*; so you may guess where the profit is.

'One of our dodges is what we term "An American Air-Preserver"; which is nothing more than a card,—old benefit tickets, or, if we are hard up, even brown paper, or anythink,—soap wrappings, just varnished on one side. Between our private residence and our shop, no piece of card or old paper escapes us. Supposing a party come in, and says "I should like a portrait"; then I inquire which they'll have, a shilling or a sixpenny one. If they prefer a sixpenny one, I then make them one up, and I show them one of the air-preservers,—which we keep ready made up,—and I tell them that they are all chemicalized, and come from America, and that without them their picture will fade. I also tell them that I make nothing out of them, for that they are only 2*d.* and cost all the money; and that makes 'em buy one directly.

They always bite at them; and we've actually had people come to us to have our preservers put upon other persons' portraits, saying they've been everywhere for them and can't get them. I charge 3*d*. if it's not one of our pictures. I'm the original inventor of the "Patent American Air-Preserver". We first called them the "London Air-Preservers"; but they didn't go so well as since they've been the Americans.

'Another dodge is, I always take the portrait on a shilling size; and after they are done, I show them what they can have for a shilling,—the full size, with the knees; and table and a vase on it,—and let them understand that for sixpence they have all the back-ground and legs cut off; so as many take the shilling portraits as sixpenny ones.

'Talking of them preservers, it is astonishing how they go. We've actually had photographers themselves come to us to buy our "American Air-Preservers". We tells them it's a secret, and we manufacture them ourselves. People won't use their eyes. Why, I've actually cut up an old band-box afore the people's eyes, and varnished it and dried it on the hob before their eyes, and yet they still fancy they come from America! Why, we picks up the old paper from the shop-sweeping, and they make first-rate "Patent American Air-Preservers". Actually, when we've been short, I've torn off a bit of old sugar-paper, and stuck it on without any varnish at all, and the party has gone away quite happy and contented. But you must remember it is really a useful thing, for it does do good and do preserve the picture.

'Another of our dodges,—and it is a splendid dodge, though it wants a nerve to do it,—is the brightening solution, which is nothing more than aqua distilled, or pure water. When we take a portrait, Jim, my mate, who stops in the room, hollows to me, "Is it bona?" That is,—Is it good? If it is, I say, "Say." That is,—Yes. If not, I say "Nanti." If it is a good one he takes care to publicly expose that one, that all may see it, as a recommendation to others. If I say "Nanti," then Jim takes it and finishes it up, drying it and putting it up in its frame. Then he wraps it up in a large piece of paper, so that it will take some time to unroll it, at the same time crying out "Take sixpence from this lady, if you please." Sometimes she says, "O let me see it first"; but he always answers, "Money first, if you please ma'am; pay for it first, and then you can do what you like with it. Here, take sixpence from this lady." When she sees it, if it is a black one, she'll say, "Why this ain't like me; there's no picture at all." Then Jim says, "It will become better as it dries, and come to your natural complexion." If she still grumbles, he tells her that if she likes to have it passed through the brightening solution, it will come out lighter in an hour or two. They in general have it brightened; and then, before their face, we dip it into some water. We then dry it on and replace it in the frame, wrap it up carefully, and tell them not to expose it to the air, but put it in their bosom, and in an hour or two it will be all right. This is only done when the portrait come out black, as it doesn't pay to take two for sixpence. Sometimes they brings them back the next day, and says, "It's not dried out as you told us"; and then we take another portrait, and charge them 3*d*. more.

'We also do what we call the "bathing",—another dodge. Now to-day a party came in during a shower of rain, when it was so dark it was impossible to take a portrait; or they will come in, sometimes, just as we are shutting up, and when the gas is lighted, to have their portraits taken; then we do this. We never turn business away, and yet it's impossible to take a portrait; so we ask them to sit down, and then we go through the whole process of taking a portrait, only we don't put any plate in the camera. We always make 'em sit a long time, to make 'em think it's all right,—I've had them for two-and-a-half minutes, till their eyes run down with water. We then tell them that we've taken the portrait, but that we shall have to keep it all night in the chemical bath to bring it out, because the weather's so bad. We always take the money as a deposit, and give them a written paper as an order for the picture. If in the morning they come themselves we get them to sit again, and then we do really take a portrait of them; but if they send anybody, we either say that the bath was too strong and eat the picture out, or that it was too weak and didn't bring it out; or else I blow up Jim, and pretend he has upset the bath and broke the picture. We have had as many as ten pictures to bathe in one afternoon.

'If the eyes in a portrait are not seen, and they complain, we take a pin and dot them; and that brings the eye out, and they like it. If the hair, too, is not visible we takes the pin again, and soon puts in a beautiful head of hair. It requires a deal of nerve to do it; but if they still grumble I say, "It's a beautiful picture, and worth half-a-crown, at the least"; and in the end they generally go off contented and happy.

'When we are not busy, we always fill up the time taking specimens for the window. Anybody who'll "sit we take him; or we do one another, and the young woman in the shop who colours. Specimens are very useful things to us, for this reason,—if anybody comes in a hurry, and won't give us time to do the picture, then, as we can't afford to let her go, we sit her and goes through all the business, and I says to Jim, "Get one from the window," and then he takes the first specimen that comes to hand. Then we fold it up in paper, and don't allow her to see it until she pays for it, and tell her not to expose it to the air for three days, and that if then she doesn't approve of it and will call again we will take her another. Of course they in general comes back. We have made some queer mistakes doing this. One day a young lady came in, and wouldn't wait, so Jim takes a specimen from the window, and, as luck would have it, it was the portrait of a widow in her cap. She insisted upon opening, and then she said, "This isn't me; it's got a widow's cap, and I was never married in all my life!" Jim answers, "Oh, miss! why it's a beautiful picture, and a correct likeness,"—and so it was, and no lies, but it wasn't of her.—Jim talked to her, and says he, "Why this ain't a cap, it's the shadow of the hair,"—for she had ringlets,—and she positively took it away believing that such was the case; and even promised to send us customers, which she did.

'There was another lady that came in a hurry, and would stop if we were not more than a minute; so Jim ups with a specimen, without looking at it, and it was the picture of a woman and her child. We went through the business of focussing the camera, and then gave her the portrait and took the 6*d*. When she saw it she cries out, "Bless me! there's a child: I haven't ne'er a child!" Jim looked at her, and then at the picture, as if comparing, and says he, "It is certainly a wonderful likeness, miss, and one of the best we ever took. It's the way you sat; and what has occasioned it was a child passing through the yard." She said she supposed it must be so, and took the portrait away highly delighted.

'Once a sailor came in, and as he was in haste, I shoved on to him the picture of a carpenter, who was to call in the afternoon for his portrait. The jacket was dark, but there was a white waistcoat; still I persuaded him that it was his blue Guernsey which had come up very light, and he was so pleased that he gave us 9*d*. instead of 6*d*. The fact is, people don't know their own faces. Half of 'em have never looked in a glass half a dozen times in their life, and directly they see a pair of eyes and a nose, they fancy they are their own.

'The only time we were done was with an old woman. We had only one specimen left, and that was a sailor man, very dark—one of our black pictures. But she put on her spectacles, and she looked at it up

PHOTOGRAPHIC SALOON, EAST END OF LONDON.

[*From a Sketch.*]

and down, and says, "Eh?" I said, "Did you speak, ma'am?" and she cries, "Why, this is a man! here's the whiskers." I left, and Jim tried to humbug her, for I was bursting with laughing. Jim said, "It's you ma'am; and a very excellent likeness, I assure you." But she kept on saying, "Nonsense, I ain't a man," and wouldn't have it. Jim wanted her to leave a deposit, and come next day, but she never called. It was a little too strong.

'People seem to think the camera will do anything. We actually persuade them that it will mesmerise* them. After their portrait is taken, we ask them if they would like to be mesmerised by the camera, and the charge is only *2d*. We then focus the camera, and tell them to look firm at the tube; and they stop there for two or three minutes staring, till their eyes begin to water, and then they complain of a dizziness in the head, and give it up, saying they "can't stand it". I always tell them the operation was beginning, and they were just going off, only they didn't stay long enough. They always remark, "Well, it certainly is a wonderful machine, and a most curious invention." Once a coal-heaver came in to be mesmerised, but he got into a rage after five or six minutes, and said, "Strike me dead, ain't you keeping me a while!" He wouldn't stop still, so Jim told him his sensitive nerves was too powerful, and sent him off cursing and swearing because he couldn't be mesmerised. We don't have many of these mesmerism customers, not more than four in these five months; hut it's a curious circumstance, proving what fools people is. Jim says he only introduces these games when business is dull, to keep my spirits up—and they certainly are most laughable.

'I also profess to remove warts, which I do by touching them with nitric acid. My price is a penny a wart, or a shilling for the job; for some of the hands is pretty well smothered with them. You see, we never turn money away, for it's hard work to make a living at sixpenny portraits. My wart patients seldom come twice, for they screams out ten thousand blue murders when the acid bites them.'

EXHIBITORS OF TRAINED ANIMALS

The Happy Family Exhibitor

'Happy Families', or assemblages of animals of diverse habits and propensities living amicably, or at least quietly, in one cage, are so well known as to need no further description here. Concerning them I received the following account:

'I have been three years connected with happy families, living by such connexion. These exhibitions were first started at Coventry, sixteen years ago, by a man who was my teacher. He was a stocking-weaver, and a fancier of animals and birds, having a good many in his place—hawks, owls, pigeons, starlings, cats, dogs, rats, mice, guinea-pigs, jackdaws, fowls, ravens, and monkeys. He used to keep them separate and for his own amusement, or would train them for sale, teaching the dogs tricks, and such-like. He found his animals agree so well together, that he had a notion—and a snake-charmer, an old Indian, used to advise him on the subject—that he could show in public animals and birds, supposed to be one another's enemies and victims, living in quiet together. He did show them in public, beginning with cats, rats, and pigeons in one cage; and then kept adding by degrees all the other creatures I have mentioned. He did very well at Coventry, but I don't know what he took. His way of training the animals is a secret, which he has taught to me. It's principally done, however, I may tell you, by continued kindness and petting, and studying the nature of the creatures. Hundreds have tried their hands at happy families, and have failed. The cat has killed the mice, the hawks have killed the birds, the dogs the rats, and even the cats, the rats, the birds, and even one another; indeed, it was anything but a happy family. By our system we never have a mishap; and have had animals eight or nine years in the cage—until they've died of age, indeed. In our present cage we have 54 birds and animals, and of 17 different kinds; 3 cats, 2 dogs (a terrier and a spaniel), 2 monkeys, 2 magpies, 2 jackdaws, 2 jays, 10 starlings (some of them talk), 6 pigeons, 2 hawks, 2 barn fowls, 1 screech owl, 5 common sewer-rats, 5 white rats (a novelty), 8 guinea-pigs, 2 rabbits (1 wild and 1 tame),

1 hedgehog, and 1 tortoise. Of all these, the rat is the most difficult to make a member of a happy family: among birds, the hawk. The easiest trained animal is a monkey, and the easiest trained bird a pigeon. They live together in their cages all night, and sleep in a stable, unattended by any one. They were once thirty-six hours, as a trial, without food—that was in Cambridge; and no creature was injured; but they were very peckish, especially the birds of prey. I wouldn't allow it to be tried (it was for a scientific gentleman) any longer, and I fed them well to begin upon. There are now in London five happy families, all belonging to two families of men. Mine, that is the one I have the care of, is the strongest—fifty-four creatures: the others will average forty each, or 214 birds and beasts in happy families. Our only regular places now are Waterloo-bridge and the National Gallery. The expense of keeping my fifty-four is 12*s.* a-week; and in a good week—indeed, the best week—we take 30*s.*; and in a bad week sometimes not 8*s.* It's only a poor trade, though there are more good weeks than bad: but the weather has so much to do with it. The middle class of society are our best supporters. When the happy family—only one—was first in London, fourteen years ago, the proprietor took 1*l.* a-day on Waterloo-bridge; and only showed in the summer. The second happy family was started eight years ago, and did as well for a short time as the first. Now there are too many happy families. There are none in the country.'

SKILLED AND UNSKILLED LABOUR

The Doll's-Eye Maker

A curious part of the street toy business is the sale of dolls, and especially that odd branch of it, doll's-eye making. There are only two persons following this business in London, and by the most intelligent of these I was furnished with the following curious information:

'I make all kinds of eyes,' the eye-manufacturer said, 'both dolls' and human eyes; birds' eyes are mostly manufactured in Birmingham, and as you say, sir, bulls' eyes* at the confectioner's. Of dolls' eyes there are two sorts, the common and the natural, as we call it. The common are simply small hollow glass spheres, made of white enamel, and coloured either black or blue, for only two colours of these are made. The bettermost dolls' eyes, or the natural ones, are made in a superior manner, but after a similar fashion to the commoner sort. The price of the common black and blue dolls' eyes is five shillings for twelve dozen pair. We make very few of the bettermost kind, or natural eyes for dolls, for the price of those is about fourpence a pair, but they are only for the very best dolls. Average it throughout the year, a journeyman doll's-eye maker earns about thirty shillings a-week. The common dolls' eyes were twelve shillings the twelve dozen pairs twenty-five years ago, but now they are only five shillings. The decrease of the price is owing to competition, for though there are only two of us in the trade in London, still the other party is always pushing his eyes and underselling our'n. Immediately the demand ceases at all, he goes round the trade with his eyes in a box, and offers them at a lower figure than in the regular season, and so the prices have been falling every year. There is a brisk and a slack season in our business, as well as in most others. After the Christmas holidays up to March we have generally little to do, but from that time eyes begin to look up a bit, and the business remains pretty good till the end of October. Where we make one pair of eyes for home consumption, we make ten for exportation; a great many eyes go abroad. Yes, I suppose we should be soon over-populated with dolls if a great number of them were not to emigrate every year.* The annual increase of dolls goes on at an alarming rate. As you say, sir, the yearly rate of mortality must be very high, to be sure, but still it's nothing to the rate at which they are brought into the world. They can't make wax dolls in America, sir, so we ship off a great many there. The reason why they can't produce dolls in America is owing to the climate. The wax won't set in very hot weather, and it cracks in extreme cold. I knew a party who went out to the United States to start as doll-maker. He took several gross of my eyes with him, but he couldn't succeed. The eyes that we make for Spanish America are all black. A blue-eyed doll wouldn't sell at all there. Here, however, nothing but blue eyes goes down; that's because it's the colour of the Queen's eyes, and she sets the fashion in our eyes as in other things. We make the same kind of eyes for the gutta-percha* dolls as for the wax. It is true, the gutta-percha complexion isn't particularly clear; nevertheless, the eyes I make for the washable faces are all of the natural tint, and if the gutta-percha dolls look rather bilious, why I ain't a going to make my eyes look bilious to match.

'I also make human eyes. These are two cases; in the one I have black and hazel, and in the other blue and grey.' [Here the man took the lids off a couple of boxes, about as big as binnacles,* that stood on the table: they each contained 190 different eyes, and so like nature, that the effect produced upon a person unaccustomed to the sight was most peculiar, and far from pleasant. The whole of the 380 optics all seemed to be staring directly at the spectator, and occasioned a feeling somewhat similar to the bewilderment one experiences on suddenly becoming an object of general notice; as if the eyes, indeed, of a whole lecture-room were crammed into a few square inches, and all turned full upon you. The eyes of the whole world, as we say, literally appeared to be fixed upon one, and it was almost impossible at first to look at them without instinctively averting the head. The hundred eyes of Argus* were positively insignificant in comparison to the 380 belonging to the human eye-maker.] 'Here you see are the ladies' eyes,' he continued, taking one from the blue-eye tray. 'You see there's more sparkle and brilliance about them than the gentlemen's. Here's two different ladies' eyes; they belong to fine-looking young women, both of them. When a lady or gentleman comes to us for an eye, we are obliged to have a sitting just like a portrait-painter. We take no sketch, but study the tints of the perfect eye. There are a number of eyes come over from France, but these are generally what we call misfits; they are sold cheap, and seldom match the other eye. Again, from not fitting tight over the ball like those that are made expressly for the person, they seldom move "consentaneously", as it is termed, with the natural eye, and have therefore a very unpleasant and fixed stare, worse almost than the defective eye itself. Now, the eyes we make move so freely, and have such a natural appearance, that I can assure you a gentleman who had one of his from me passed nine doctors without the deception being detected.

'There is a lady customer of mine who has been married three years to her husband, and I believe he doesn't know that she has a false eye to this day.

'The generality of persons whom we serve take out their eyes when they go to bed, and sleep with them either under their pillow, or else in a tumbler of water on the toilet-table at their side. Most married ladies, however, never take their eyes out at all.

'Some people wear out a false eye in half the time of others. This doesn't arise from the greater use of them, or rolling them about, but from the increased secretion of the tears, which act on the false eye like acid on metal, and so corrodes and roughens the surface. This roughness produces inflammation, and then a new eye becomes necessary. The Scotch lose a great many eyes, why I cannot say; and the men in this country lose more eyes, nearly two to one. We generally make only one eye, but I did once make two false eyes for a widow lady. She lost one first, and we repaired the loss so well, that on her losing the other eye she got us to make her a second.

'False eyes are a great charity to servants. If they lose an eye no one will engage them. In Paris there is a charitable institution for the supply of false eyes to the poor; and I really think, if there was a similar establishment in this country for furnishing artificial eyes to those whose bread depends on their looks, like servants, it would do a great deal of good. We always supplies eyes to such people at half-price. My usual price is *2l. 2s.* for one of my best eyes. That eye is a couple of guineas, and as fine an eye as you would wish to see in any young woman's head.

'I suppose we make from 300 to 400 false eyes every year. The great art in making a false eye is in polishing the edges quite smooth.

Of dolls' eyes we make about 6,000 dozen pairs of the common ones every year. I take it that there are near upon 24,000 dozen, or more than a quarter of a million, pairs of all sorts of dolls' eyes made annually in London.'

CHEAP LODGING-HOUSES

I now come to the class of cheap lodging-houses usually frequented by the casual labourers at the docks.

On my first visit, the want and misery that I saw were such, that, in consulting with the gentleman who led me to the spot, it was arranged that a dinner should be given on the following Sunday to all those who were present on the evening of my first interview; and, accordingly, enough beef, potatoes, and materials for a suet-pudding, were sent in from the neighbouring market to feed them every one. I parted with my guide, arranging to be with him the next Sunday at half-past one. We met at the time appointed, and set out on our way to the cheap lodging-house. The streets were alive with sailors, and bonnetless and capless women. The Jews' shops and public-houses were all open, and parties of 'jolly tars' reeled past us, singing and bawling on their way. Had it not been that here and there a stray shop was closed, it would have been impossible to have guessed it was Sunday. We dived down a narrow court, at the entrance of which lolled Irish labourers smoking short pipes. Across the court hung lines, from which dangled dirty-white clothes to dry; and as we walked on, ragged, unwashed, shoeless children scampered past us, chasing one another. At length we reached a large open yard. In the centre of it stood several empty costermongers' trucks and turned-up carts, with their shafts high in the air. At the bottom of these lay two young girls huddled together, asleep. Their bare heads told their mode of life, while it was evident, from their muddy Adelaide boots,* that they had walked the streets all night. My companion tried to see if he knew them, but they slept too soundly to be roused by gentle means. We passed on, and a few paces further on there sat grouped on a door-step four women, of the same character as the last two. One had her head covered up in an old brown shawl, and was sleeping in the lap of the one next to her. The other two were eating walnuts; and a coarse-featured man in knee-breeches and 'ankle-jacks'* was stretched on the ground close beside them.

At length we reached the lodging-house. It was night when I had first visited the place, and all now was new to me. The entrance was through a pair of large green gates, which gave it somewhat the appearance of a stable-yard. Over the kitchen door there hung a clothes-line, on which were a wet shirt and a pair of ragged canvas trousers, brown with tar. Entering the kitchen, we found it so full of smoke that the sun's rays, which shot slanting down through a broken tile in the roof, looked like a shaft of light cut through the fog. The flue of the chimney stood out from the bare brick wall like a buttress, and was black all the way up with the smoke; the beams, which hung down from the roof, and ran from wall to wall, were of the same colour; and in the centre, to light the room, was a rude iron gas-pipe, such as are used at night when the streets are turned up. The floor was unboarded, and a wooden seat projected from the wall all round the room. In front of this was ranged a series of tables, on which lolled dozing men. A number of the inmates were grouped around the fire; some kneeling toasting herrings, of which the place smelt strongly; others, without shirts, seated on the ground close beside it for warmth; and others drying the ends of cigars they had picked up in the streets. As we entered the men rose, and never was so motley and so ragged an assemblage seen. Their hair was matted like flocks of wool, and their chins were grimy with their unshorn beards. Some were in dirty smock-frocks; others in old red plush waistcoats, with long sleeves. One was dressed in an old shooting-jacket, with large wooden buttons; a second in a blue flannel sailor's shirt; and a third, a mere boy, wore a long camlet coat* reaching to his heels, and with the ends of the sleeves hanging over his hands. The features of the lodgers wore every kind of expression: one lad was positively handsome, and there was a frankness in his face and a straightforward look in his eye that strongly impressed me with a sense of his honesty, even although I was assured he was a confirmed pickpocket. The young thief who had brought back the 11½*d* change out of the shilling that had been entrusted to him on the preceding evening,* was far from prepossessing, now that I could see him better. His cheek-bones were high, while his hair, cut close on the top, with a valance of locks, as it were, left hanging in front, made me look upon him with no slight suspicion. On the form at the end of the kitchen was one whose squalor and wretchedness produced a feeling approaching to awe. His eyes were sunk deep in his head, his cheeks were drawn in, and his nostrils pinched with evident want, while his dark stubbly beard gave a grimness to his appearance that was almost demoniac; and yet there was a patience in his look that was almost pitiable. His clothes were black and shiny at every fold with grease, and his coarse shirt was so brown with long wearing, that it was only with close inspection you could see that it had once been a checked one: on his feet he had a pair of lady's side-laced boots, the toes of which had been cut off so that he might get them on. I never beheld so gaunt a picture of famine. To this day the figure of the man haunts me.

The dinner had been provided for thirty, but the news of the treat had spread, and there was a muster of fifty. We hardly knew how to act. It was, however, left to those whose names had been taken down as being present on the previous evening to say what should be done; and the answer from one and all was that the new-comers were to share the feast with them. The dinner was then half-portioned out in an adjoining outhouse into twenty-five platefuls—the entire stock of crockery belonging to the establishment numbering no more—and afterwards handed into the kitchen through a small window to each party, as his name was called out. As he hurried to the seat behind the bare table, he commenced tearing the meat asunder with his fingers, for knives and forks were unknown there. Some, it is true, used bits of wood like skewers, but this seemed almost like affectation in such a place: others sat on the ground with the plate of meat and pudding on their laps; while the beggar-boy, immediately on receiving his portion, danced along the room, whirling the plate round on his thumb as he went, and then, dipping his nose in the plate, seized a potato in his mouth. I must confess the sight of the hungry crowd gnawing their food was far from pleasant to contemplate; so, while the dinner was being discussed, I sought to learn from those who remained to be helped, how they had fallen to so degraded a state. A sailor lad assured me he had been robbed of his mariner's ticket;* that he could not procure another under 13*s*.; and not having as many pence, he was unable to obtain another ship. What could he do? he said. He knew no trade: he could only get employment occasionally as a labourer at the docks; and this was so seldom, that if it had not been for the few things he had, he must have starved outright. The good-looking youth I have before spoken of wanted but 3*l*. 10*s*. to get back to America. He had worked his passage over here; had fallen into bad company; been imprisoned three times for picking pockets; and was heartily wearied of his present course. He could get no work. In America he would be happy, and among his friends again. I spoke to the gentleman who had brought me to the spot, and who knew them all well. His answers, however, gave me little hope. The boy, whose face seemed beaming with innate frankness and honesty, had been apprenticed by him to a shoe-stitcher. But, no! he preferred vagrancy to work. I could have sworn he was a trustworthy lad, and shall never believe in 'looks' again.*

The lodging-house makes up as many as 84 'bunks', or beds, for which 2*d*. per night is charged. For this sum the parties lodging there for the night are entitled to the use of the kitchen for the following day. In this a fire is kept all day long, at which they are allowed to cook their food. The kitchen opens at 5 in the morning, and closes at about 11 at night, after which hour no fresh lodger is taken in, and all those who slept in the house the night before, but who have not sufficient money to pay for their bed at that time, are turned out. Strangers who arrive in the course of the day must procure a tin ticket, by paying 2*d*. at the wicket in the office, previously to being allowed to enter the kitchen. The kitchen is about 40 feet long by about 40 wide. The 'bunks' are each about 7 feet long, and 1 foot 10 inches wide, and the grating on which the straw mattrass is placed is about 12 inches from the ground. The wooden partitions between the 'bunks' are about 4 feet high. The coverings are a leather or a rug, but leathers are generally preferred. Of these 'bunks' there are five rows, of about 24 deep; two rows being placed head to head, with a gangway between each of such two rows, and the other row against the wall. The average number of persons sleeping in this house of a night is 60. Of these there are generally about 30 pickpockets, 10 street-beggars, a few infirm old people who subsist occasionally upon parish relief and occasionally upon charity, 10 or 15 dock-labourers, about the same number of low and precarious callings, such as the neighbourhood affords, and a few persons who have been in good circumstances, but who have been reduced from a variety of causes. At one time there were as many as 9 persons lodging in this house who subsisted by picking up dogs' dung out of the streets, getting about 5*s*. for every basketful. The earnings of one of these men were known to average 9*s*. per week. There are generally lodging in the house a few bone-grubbers, who pick up bones, rags, iron, &c., out of the streets. Their average earnings are about 1*s*. per day. There are several mud-larks, or youths who go down to the water-side when the tide is out, to see whether any article of value has been left upon the bank of the river. The person supplying this information to me, who was for some time resident in the house, has seen brought home by these persons a drum of figs at one time, and a Dutch cheese at another. These were sold in small lots or slices to the other lodgers.

The pickpockets generally lodging in the house consist of handkerchief-stealers, shoplifters—including those who rob the till as well as steal articles from the doors of shops. Legs and breasts of mutton are frequently brought in by this class of persons. There are seldom any housebreakers lodging in such places, because they require a room of their own, and mostly live with prostitutes. Besides pickpockets, there are also lodging in the house speculators in stolen goods. These may be dock-labourers or Billingsgate* porters, having a few shillings in their pockets. With these they purchase the booty of the juvenile thieves. 'I have known', says my informant, 'these speculators wait in the kitchen, walking about with their hands in their pockets, till a little fellow would come in with such a thing as a cap, a piece of bacon, or a piece of mutton. They would purchase it, and then either retail it amongst the other lodgers in the kitchen or take it to some "fence", where they would receive a profit upon it.' The general feeling of the kitchen—excepting with four or five individuals—is to encourage theft. The encouragement to the 'gonaff' (a Hebrew word signifying a young thief, probably learnt from the Jew 'fences' in the neighbourhood) consists in laughing at and applauding his dexterity in thieving; and whenever anything is brought in, the 'gonaff' is greeted for his good luck, and a general rush is made towards him to see the produce of his thievery. The 'gonaffs' are generally young boys; about 20 out of 30 of these lads are under 21 years of age. They almost all of them love idleness, and will only work for one or two days together, but then they will work very hard. It is a singular fact that, as a body, the pickpockets are generally very sparing of drink. They are mostly libidinous, indeed universally so, and spend whatever money they can spare upon the low prostitutes round about the neighbourhood. Burglars and smashers generally rank above this class of thieves. A burglar would not condescend to sit among pickpockets. My informant has known a housebreaker to say with a sneer, when requested to sit down with the 'gonaffs', 'No, no! I may be a thief, sir; but, thank God, at least I'm a respectable one.' The beggars who frequent these houses go about different markets and streets asking charity of the people that pass by. They generally go out in couples; the business of one of the two being to look out and give warning when the policeman is approaching, and of the other to stand 'shallow'; that is to say, to stand with very little clothing on, shivering and shaking, sometimes with bandages round his legs, and sometimes with his arm in a sling. Others beg 'scran' (broken victuals) of the servants at respectable houses, and bring it home to the lodging-house, where they sell it. You may see, I am told, the men who lodge in the place, and obtain an honest living, watch for these beggars coming in, as if they were the best victuals in the City. My informant knew an instance of a lad who seemed to be a very fine little fellow, and promised to have been possessed of excellent mental capabilities if properly directed, who came to the lodging-house when out of a situation as an errand-boy. He stayed there a month or six weeks, during which time he was tampered with by the others, and ultimately became a confirmed 'gonaff'. The conversation among the lodgers relates chiefly to thieving and the best manner of stealing. By way of practice, a boy will often pick the pocket of one of the lodgers walking about the room, and if detected declare he did not mean it.

The sanitary state of these houses is very bad. Not only do the lodgers generally swarm with vermin, but there is little or no ventilation to the sleeping-rooms, in which 60 persons, of the foulest habits, usually sleep every night. There are no proper washing utensils, neither towels nor basins, nor wooden bowls. There are one or two buckets, but these are not meant for the use of the lodgers, but for cleaning the rooms. The lodgers never think of washing themselves. The cleanliest among them will do so in the bucket, and then wipe themselves with their pocket-handkerchiefs, or the tails of their shirts.

A large sum to be made by two beggars in one week is 20*s*.; or 10*s*. a-piece, one for looking out, and the other for 'standing shallow'. The average earnings of such persons are certainly below 8*s*. per week. If the Report of the Constabulary Force Commissioners* states that 20*s*. per week is the average sum earned, I am told the statement must have been furnished by parties who had either some object in overrating the amount, or else who had no means of obtaining correct information on the subject. From all my informant has seen as to the earnings of those who make a trade of picking pockets and begging, he is convinced that the amount is far below what is generally believed to be the case. Indeed, nothing but the idle, roving life that is connected with the business, could compensate the thieves or beggars for the privations they frequently undergo.

LONDON OMNIBUS-DRIVERS AND CONDUCTORS

Omnibus Drivers

The omnibus drivers have been butchers, farmers, horsebreakers, cheesemongers, old stage-coachmen, broken-down gentlemen, turfmen, gentlemen's servants, grooms, and a very small sprinkling of mechanics. Nearly all can read and write, the exception being described to me as a singularity; but there are such exceptions, and all must have produced good characters before their appointment. The majority of them are married men with families; their residences being in all parts, and on both sides of the Thames. I did not hear of any of the wives of coachmen in regular employ working for the slop-tailors.* 'We can keep our wives too respectable for that,' one of them said, in answer to my inquiry. Their children, too, are generally sent to school; frequently to the national schools. Their work is exceedingly hard, their lives being almost literally spent on the coach-box. The most of them must enter 'the yard' at a quarter to eight in the morning, and must see that the horses and carriages are in a proper condition for work; and at half-past eight they start on their long day's labour. They perform (I speak of the most frequented lines), twelve journeys during the day, and are so engaged until a quarter-past eleven at night. Some are on their box till past midnight. During these hours of labour they have twelve 'stops'; half of ten and half of fifteen minutes' duration. They generally breakfast at home, or at a coffee-shop, if unmarried men, before they start; and dine at the inn, where the omnibus almost invariably stops, at one or other of its destinations. If the driver be distant from his home at his dinner hour, or be unmarried, he arranges to dine at the public-house; if near, his wife, or one of his children, brings him his dinner in a covered basin, some of them being provided with hot-water plates to keep the contents properly warm, and that is usually eaten at the public-house, with a pint of beer for the accompanying beverage. The relish with which a man who has been employed several hours in the open air enjoys his dinner can easily be understood. But if his dinner is brought to him on one of his shorter trips, he often hears the cry before he has completed his meal, 'Time's up!' and he carries the remains of his repast to be consumed at his next resting-place. His tea, if brought to him by his family, he often drinks within the omnibus, if there be an opportunity. Some carry their dinners with them, and eat them cold. All these men live 'well'; that is, they have sufficient dinners of animal food every day, with beer. They are strong and healthy men, for their calling requires both strength and health. Each driver (as well as the time-keeper and conductor) is licensed, at a yearly cost to him of 5*s*. From a driver I had the following statement:

'I have been a driver fourteen years. I was brought up as a builder, but had friends that was using horses, and I sometimes assisted them in driving and grooming when I was out of work. I got to like that sort of work, and thought it would be better than my own business if I could get to be connected with a 'bus; and I had friends, and first got employed as a time-keeper; but I've been a driver for fourteen years. I'm now paid by the week, and not by the box. It's a fair payment, but we must live well. It's hard work is mine; for I never have any rest but a few minutes, except every other Sunday, and then only two hours; that's the time of a journey there and back. If I was to ask leave to go to church, and then go to work again, I know what answer there would be—"You can go to church as often as you like, and we can get a man who doesn't want to go there." The cattle I drive are equal to gentlemen's carriage-horses. One I've driven five years, and I believe she was worked five years before I drove her. It's very hard work for the horses, but I don't know that they are overworked in 'busses. The starting after stopping is the hardest work for them; it's such a terrible strain. I've felt for the poor things on a wet night, with a 'bus full of big people. I must keep exact time at every place where a time-keeper's stationed. Not a minute's excused—there's a fine for the least delay. I can't say that it's often levied; but still we are liable to it. If I've been blocked,* I must make up for the block by galloping; and if I'm seen to gallop, and anybody tells our people, I'm called over the coals. I must drive as quick with a thunder-rain pelting in my face, and the roads in a muddle, and the horses starting—I can't call it shying, I have 'em too well in hand,—at every flash, just as quick as if it was a fine hard road, and fine weather. It's not easy to drive a 'bus; but I can drive, and must drive, to an inch: yes, sir, to half an inch. I know if I can get my horses' heads through a space, I can get my splinter-bar through. I drive by my pole, making it my centre. If I keep it fair in the centre, a carriage must follow, unless it's slippery weather, and then there's no calculating. I saw the first 'bus start in 1829. I heard the first 'bus called a Punch-and-Judy carriage, 'cause you could see the people inside without a frame. The shape was about the same as it is now, but bigger and heavier. A 'bus changes horses four or five times a-day, according to the distance. There's no cruelty to the horses, not a bit, it wouldn't be allowed. I fancy that 'busses now pay the proprietors well. The duty was 2½*d*. a-mile, and now it's 1½*d*. Some companies save twelve guineas a-week by the doing away of toll-gates. The 'stablishing the threepennies—the short uns—has put money in their pockets. I'm an unmarried man. A 'bus driver never has time to look out for a wife. Every horse in our stables has one day's rest in every four; but it's no rest for the driver.'

LONDON VAGRANTS

The evils consequent upon the uncertainty of labour I have already been at considerable pains to point out. There is still one other mischief attendant upon it that remains to be exposed, and which, if possible, is greater than any other yet adduced. Many classes of labour are necessarily uncertain or fitful in their character. Some work can be pursued only at certain seasons; some depends upon the winds, as, for instance, dock labour; some on fashion; and nearly all on the general prosperity of the country. Now, the labourer who is deprived of his usual employment by any of the above causes, must, unless he has laid by a portion of his earnings while engaged, become a burden to his parish, or the state, or else he must seek work, either of another kind or in another place. The mere fact of a man's seeking work in different parts of the country, may be taken as evidence that he is indisposed to live on the charity or labour of others; and this feeling should be encouraged in every rational manner. Hence the greatest facility should be afforded to all labourers who may be unable to obtain work in one locality, to pass to another part of the country where there may be a demand for their labour. In fine, it is expedient that every means should be given for extending the labour-market for the working classes; that is to say, for allowing them as wide a field for the exercise of their calling as possible. To do this involves the establishment of what are called the 'casual wards' of the different unions throughout the country. These are, strictly speaking, the free hostelries of the unemployed workpeople, where they may be lodged and fed, on their way to find work in some more active district. But the establishment of these gratuitous hotels has called into existence a large class of wayfarers, for whom they were never contemplated. They have been the means of affording great encouragement to those vagabond or erratic spirits who find continuity of application to any task specially irksome to them, and who are physically unable or mentally unwilling to remain for any length of time in the same place, or at the same work—creatures who are vagrants in disposition and principle; the wandering tribe of this country; the nomads of the present day.*

The causes and encouragements of vagrancy are two-fold,— *direct* and *indirect*. The roving disposition to which, as I have shown, vagrancy is *directly* ascribable, proceeds (as I have said) partly from a certain physical conformation or temperament, but mainly from a non-inculcation of industrial habits and moral purposes in youth. The causes from which the vagabondism of the young *indirectly* proceeds are:

1. The neglect or tyranny of parents or masters. (This appears to be a most prolific source.)
2. Bad companions.
3. Bad books, which act like the bad companions in depraving the taste, and teaching the youth to consider that approvable which to all rightly constituted minds is morally loathsome.
4. Bad amusements—as penny-theatres, where the scenes and characters described in the bad books are represented in a still more, attractive form. Mr Ainsworth's 'Rookwood',* with Dick Turpin 'in his habit as he lived in', is now in the course of being performed nightly at one of the East-end saloons.
5. Bad institutions—as, for instance, the different refuges scattered throughout the country, and which, enabling persons to live without labour, are the means of attracting large numbers of the most idle and dissolute classes to the several cities where the charities are dispensed. Captain Carroll, C.B., R.N., chief of police, speaking of the Refuges for the Destitute in Bath, and of a kindred institution which distributes bread and soup, says,—'I consider those institutions an attraction to this city for vagrants.' At Liverpool, Mr Henry Simpson said of a Night Asylum, supported by voluntary contributions, and established for several years in this town—'This charity was used by quite a different class of persons from those for whom it was designed. A vast number of abandoned characters, known thieves and prostitutes, found nightly shelter there.' 'The chief inducement to vagrancy in the town,' says another Report, speaking of a certain part of the North Riding of York, 'is the relief given by mistaken but benevolent individuals, more particularly by the poorer class. Instances have occurred where the names of such benevolent persons have been found in the possession of vagrants, obtained, no doubt, from their fellow-travellers.'
6. Vagrancy is largely due to, and, indeed, chiefly maintained by the low lodging-houses.

Statements of Vagrants

The first vagrant was one who had the thorough look of a 'professional'. He was literally a mass of rags and filth. He was, indeed, exactly what in the Act of Henry VIII is denominated a 'valiant beggar'.* He stood near upon six feet high, was not more than twenty-five, and had altogether the frame and constitution of a stalwart labouring man. His clothes, which were of fustian and corduroy, tied close to his body with pieces of string, were black and shiny with filth, which looked more like pitch than grease. He had no shirt, as was plain from the fact that, where his clothes were torn, his bare skin was seen. The ragged sleeves of his fustian jacket were tied like the other parts of his dress, close to his wrists, with string. This was clearly to keep the bleak air from his body. His cap was an old, brimless 'wide-awake',* and when on his head gave the man a most unprepossessing appearance. His story was as follows:

'I am a carpet-weaver by trade. I served my time to it. My father was a clerk in a shoe-thread manufactory at ——. He got 35*s.* a-week, and his house, coals, and candles found him. He lived very comfortably; indeed, I was very happy. Before I left home, I knew none of the cares of the world that I have known since I left him. My father and mother are living still. He is still as well off as when I was at home. I know this, because I have heard from him twice, and seen him once. He won't do anything to assist me. I have transgressed so many times, that he won't take me in hand any more. I will tell you the truth, you may depend upon it; yes, indeed, I would, even if it were to injure myself. He has tried me many times, but now he has given me up. At the age of twenty-one he told me to go from home and seek a living for myself. He said he had given me a home ever since I was a child, but now I had come to manhood I was able to provide for myself. He gave me a good education, and I might have been a better scholar at the present time, had I not neglected my studies. He put me to a day-school in the town when I was eight years old, and I continued there till I was between twelve and thirteen. I learnt reading, writing, and ciphering. I was taught the catechism, the history of England, geography, and drawing. My father was a very harsh man when he was put out of his way. He was a very violent temper when he was vexed, but kind to us all when he was pleased. I have five brothers and six sisters. He never beat me more than twice, to my remembrance.

VAGRANT FROM THE REFUGE IN PLAYHOUSE YARD, CRIPPLEGATE.

[From a Photograph.]

The first time he thrashed me with a cane, and the last with a horsewhip. I had stopped out late at night. I was then just rising sixteen, and had left school. I am sure those thrashings did me no good, but made me rather worse than before. I was a self-willed lad, and determined, if I couldn't get my will in one way, I would have it another. After the last thrashing he told me he would give me some trade, and after that he would set me off and get rid of me. Then I was bound apprentice as a carpet-weaver for three years. My master was a very kind one. I runned away once. The cause of my going off was a quarrel with one of the workmen that was put over me. He was very harsh, and I scarce could do anything to please him; so I made up my mind to leave. The first place I went when I bolted was to Crewkerne, in Somersetshire. There I asked for employment at carpet-weaving. I got some, and remained there three days, when my father found out where I was, and sent my brother and a special constable after me. They took me from the shop where I was at work, and brought me back to ——, and would have sent me to prison had I not promised to behave myself, and serve my time out as I ought. I went to work again; and when the expiration of my apprenticeship occurred, my father said to me, "Sam, you have a trade at your fingers' ends: you are able to provide for yourself." So then I left home. I was twenty-one years of age. He gave me money, 3*l.* 10*s.*, to take me into Wales, where I told him I should go. I was up for going about through the country. I made my father believe I was going into Wales to get work; but all I wanted was, to go and see the place. After I had runned away once from my apprenticeship, I found it very hard to stop at home. I couldn't bring myself to work somehow. While I sat at the work, I thought I should like to be away in the country: work seemed a burden to me. I found it very difficult to stick to anything for a long time; so I made up my mind, when my time was out, that I'd be off roving, and see a little of life. I went by the packet from Bristol to Newport. After being there three weeks, I had spent all the money that I had brought from home. I spent it in drinking—most of it, and idling about. After that I was obliged to sell my clothes, &c. The first thing I sold was my watch; I got 2*l.* 5*s.* for that. Then I was obliged to part with my suit of clothes. For these I got 1*l.* 5*s.* With this I started from Newport to go farther up over the hills. I liked this kind of life much better than working, while the money lasted. I was in the public-house three parts of my time out of four. I was a great slave to drink. I began to like drink when I was between thirteen and fourteen. At that time my uncle was keeping a public-house, and I used to go there, backwards and forward, more or less every week. Whenever I went to see my uncle he gave me some beer. I very soon got to like it so much, that, while an apprentice, I would spend all I could get in liquor. This was the cause of my quarrels with my father, and when I went away to Newport I did so to be my own master, and drink as much as I pleased, without anybody saying anything to me about it. I got up to Nant-y-glô, and there I sought for work at the iron-foundry, but I could not get it. I stopped at this place three weeks, still drinking. The last day of the three weeks I sold the boots off my feet to get food, for all my money and clothes were now gone. I was sorry then that I had ever left my father's house; but, alas! I found it too late. I didn't write home to tell them how I was off; my stubborn temper would not allow me. I then started off barefoot, begging my way from Nant-y-glô to Monmouth. I told the people that I was a carpet-weaver by trade, who could not get any employment, and that I was obliged to travel the country against my own wish. I didn't say a word about the drink—that would never have done. I only took 2½*d.* on the road, 19 miles long; and I'm sure I must have asked assistance from more than a hundred people. They said, some of them, that they had "nout" for me; and others did give me a bit of "bara caws", or "bara minny" (that is, bread and cheese, or bread and butter). Money is very scarce among the Welsh, and what they have they are very fond of. They don't mind giving food; if you wanted a bagful you might have it there of the working people. I inquired for a night's lodging at the union in Monmouth. That was the first time I ever asked for shelter in a workhouse in my life. I was admitted into the tramp-room. Oh, I felt then that I would much rather be in prison than in such a place, though I never knew what the inside of a prison was—no, not then. I thought of the kindness of my father and mother. I would have been better, but I knew that, as I had been carrying on, I never could expect shelter under my father's roof any more; I knew he would not have taken me in had I gone back, or I would have returned. Oh, I was off from home, and I didn't much trouble my head about it after a few minutes; I plucked up my spirits and soon forgot where I was. I made no male friends in the union; I was savage that I had so hard a bed to lie upon; it was nothing more than the bare boards, and a rug to cover me. I knew very well it wasn't my bed, but still I thought I ought to have a better.

I merely felt annoyed at its being so bad a place, and didn't think much about the rights of it. In the morning I was turned out, and after I had left I picked up with a young woman, who had slept in the union over-night. I said I was going on the road across country to Birmingham, and I axed* her to go with me. I had never seen her before. She consented, and we went along together, begging our way. We passed as man and wife, and I was a carpet-weaver out of employment. We slept in unions and lodging-houses by the way. In the lodging-houses we lived together as man and wife, and in the unions we were separated. I never stole anything during all this time. After I got to Birmingham I made my way to Wolverhampton. My reason for going to Wolverhampton was, that there was a good many weavers there, and I thought I should make a good bit of money by begging of them. Oh, yes, I have found that I could always get more money out of my own trade than any other people. I did so well at Wolverhampton, begging, that I stopped there three weeks. I never troubled my head whether I was doing right or wrong by asking my brother-weavers for a portion of their hard earnings to keep me in idleness. Many a time I have given part of my wages to others myself. I can't say that I would have given it to them if I had known they wouldn't work like me. I wouldn't have worked sometimes if I could have got it. I can't tell why, but somehow it was painful to me to stick long at anything. To tell the truth, I loved a roving, idle life. I would much rather have been on the road than at my home. I drank away all I got, and feared and cared for nothing. When I got drunk overnight, it would have been impossible for me to have gone to work in the morning, even if I could have got it. The drink seemed to take all the work out of me. This oftentimes led me to think of what my father used to tell me, that "the bird that can sing and won't sing ought to be made to sing." During my stay in Wolverhampton I lived at a tramper's house,* and there I fell in with two men well acquainted with the town, and they asked me to join them in breaking open a shop. No, sir, no, I didn't give a thought whether I was doing right or wrong at it. I didn't think my father would ever know anything at all about it, so I didn't care. I liked my mother best, much the best. She had always been a kind, good soul to me, often kept me from my father's blows, and helped me to things unknown to my father. But when I was away on the road I gave no heed to her. I didn't think of either father or mother till after I was taken into custody for that same job. Well, I agreed to go with the other two; they were old hands at the business—regular house-breakers. We went away between twelve and one at night. It was pitch dark. My two pals broke into the back part of the house, and I stopped outside to keep watch. After watching for about a quarter of an hour, a policeman came up to me and asked what I was stopping there for. I told him I was waiting for a man that was in a public-house at the corner. This led him to suspect me, it being so late at night. He went to the public-house to see whether it was open, and found it shut, and then came back to me. As he was returning he saw my two comrades coming through the back window (that was the way they had got in). He took us all three in custody; some of the passers by assisted him in seizing us. The other two had six months' imprisonment each, and I, being a stranger, had only fourteen days. When I was sent to prison, I thought of my mother. I would have written to her, but couldn't get leave. Being the first time I ever was nailed, I was very downhearted at it. I didn't say I'd give it up. While I was locked up, I thought I'd go to work again, and be a sober man, when I got out. These thoughts used to come over me when I was "on the stepper", that is, on the wheel.* But I concealed all them thoughts in my breast. I said nothing to no one. My mother was the only one that I ever thought upon. When I got out of prison, all these thoughts went away from me, and I went again at my old tricks. From Wolverhampton I went to Manchester, and from Manchester I came to London, begging and stealing wherever I had a chance. This is not my first year in London. I tell you the truth, because I am known here; and if I tell you a lie, you'll say "You spoke an untruth in one thing, and you'll do so in another." The first time I was in London, I was put in prison fourteen days for begging, and after I had a month at Westminster Bridewell,* for begging and abusing the policeman. Sometimes I'd think I'd rather go anywhere, and do anything, than continue as I was; but then I had no clothes, no friends, no house, no home, no means of doing better. I had made myself what I was. I had made my father and mother turn their backs upon me, and what could I do, but go on? I was as bad off then as I am now, and I couldn't have got work then if I would. I should have spent all I got in drink then, I know. I wrote home twice. I told my mother I was hard up; had neither a shoe to my foot, a coat to my back, nor a roof over my head. I had no answer to my first letter, because it fell into the hands of my brother, and he tore it up, fearing that my mother might see it. To the second letter that

I sent home my mother sent me an answer herself. She sent me a sovereign. She told me that my father was the same as when I first left home, and it was no use my coming back. She sent me the money, bidding me get some clothes and seek for work. I didn't do as she bade. I spent the money—most part in drink. I didn't give any heed whether it was wrong or right. Soon got, soon gone; and I know they could have sent me much more than that if they had pleased. It was last June twelvemonth when I first came to London, and I stopped till the 10th of last March. I lost the young woman when I was put in prison in Manchester. She never came to see me in quod.* She cared nothing for me. She only kept company with me to have some one on the road along with her; and I didn't care for her, not I. One half of my time last winter I stopped at the "Strawyards", that is, in the asylums for the houseless poor here and at Glasshouse. When I could get money I had a lodging. After March I started off through Somersetshire. I went to my father's house then. I didn't go in. I saw my father at the door, and he wouldn't let me in. I was a little better dressed than I am now. He said he had enough children at home without me, and gave me 10*s*. to go. He could not have been kind to me, or else he would not have turned me from his roof. My mother came out to the garden in front of the house, after my father had gone to his work, and spoke to me. She wished me to reform my character. I could not make any rash promises then. I had but very little to say to her. I felt myself at that same time, for the very first time in my life, that I was doing wrong. I thought, if I could hurt my mother so, it must be wrong to go on as I did. I had never had such thoughts before. My father's harsh words always drove such thoughts out of my head; but when I saw my mother's tears, it was more than I could stand. I was wanting to get away as fast as I could from the house. After that I stopped knocking about the country, sleeping in unions, up to November. Then I came to London again, and remained up to this time. Since I have been in town I have sought for work at the floorcloth and carpet manufactory in the Borough, and they wouldn't even look at me in my present state. I am heartily tired of my life now altogether, and would like to get out of it if I could. I hope at least I have given up my love of drink, and I am sure, if I could once again lay my hand on some work, I should be quite a reformed character. Well, I am altogether tired of carrying on like this. I haven't made 6*d*. a-day ever since I have been in London this time. I go tramping it across the country just to pass the time, and see a little of new places. When the summer comes I want to be off. I am sure I have seen enough of this country now, and I should like to have a look at some foreign land. Old England has nothing new in it now for me. I think a beggar's life is the worst kind of life that a man can lead. A beggar is no more thought upon than a dog in the street, and there are too many at the trade. I wasn't brought up to a bad life. You can see that by little things—by my handwriting; and, indeed, I should like to have a chance at something else. I have had the feelings of a vagabond for full ten years. I know, and now I am sure, I'm getting a different man. I begin to have thoughts and ideas I never had before. Once I never feared nor cared for anything, and I wouldn't have altered if I could; but now I'm tired out, and if I haven't a chance of going right, why I must go wrong.'

Statement of a Returned Convict

I shall now give the statement of a man who was selected at random from amongst a number such as himself, congregated in one of the most respectable lodging-houses. He proved, on examination, to be a returned convict, and one who had gone through the severest bodily and mental agony. He had lived in the bush, and been tried for his life. He was an elderly-looking man, whose hair was just turning grey, and in whose appearance there was nothing remarkable, except that his cheek-bones were unusually high, and that his face presented that collected and composed expression which is common to men exposed to habitual watchfulness from constant danger. He gave me the following statement. His dress was bad, but differed in nothing from that of a long-distressed mechanic. He said:

'I am now 43 (he looked much older), and had respectable parents, and a respectable education. I am a native of London. When I was young I was fond of a roving life, but cared nothing about drink. I liked to see "life", as it was called, and was fond of the company of women. Money was no object in those days; it was like picking up dirt in the streets. I ran away from home. My parents were very kind to me; indeed, I think I was used too well, I was petted so, when I was between 12 and 13. I got acquainted with some boys at Bartlemy-fair a little before that, and saw them spending lots of money and throwing at cock-shies,* and such-like; and one of them said, "Why don't you come out like us?" So afterwards I ran away and joined them. I was not kept shorter of money than other boys like me, but I couldn't settle. I couldn't fix my mind to any regular business but a waterman's, and my friends wouldn't hear of that. There was nine boys of us among the lot that I joined, but we didn't all work together. All of 'em came to be sent to Van Dieman's Lands* as transports except one, and he was sent to Sydney. While we were in London it was a merry life, with change of scene, for we travelled about. We were successful in nearly all our plans for several months. I worked in Fleet Street, and could make 3*l.* a-week at handkerchiefs alone, sometimes falling across a pocket-book. The best handkerchiefs then brought 4*s.* in Field-lane. Our chief enjoyments were at the "Free and Easy",* where all the thieves and young women went, and sang and danced. I had a young woman for a partner then; she went out to Van Dieman's Land. She went on the lift in London (shopping and stealing from the counter). She was clever at it. I carried on in this way for about 15 months, when I was grabbed for an attempt on a gentleman's pocket by St Paul's Cathedral, on a grand charity procession day. I had two months in the Old Horse (Bridewell). I never thought of my parents at this time—I wouldn't. I was two years and a half at this same trade. One week was very like another,—successes and escapes, and free-and-easies, and games of all sorts, made up the life. At the end of the two years and a half I got into the way of forged Bank-of-England notes. A man I knew in the course of business, said, "I would cut that game of 'smatter-hauling', (stealing handkerchiefs), and do a little soft" (pass bad notes). So I did, and was very successful at first. I had a mate. He afterwards went out to Sydney, too, for 14 years. I went stylishly dressed as a gentleman, with a watch in my pocket, to pass my notes. I passed a good many in drapers' shops, also at tailors' shops. I never tried jewellers, they're reckoned too good judges. The notes were all finnies (5*l.* notes), and a good imitation. I made more money at this game, but lived as before, and had my partner still. I was fond of her; she was a nice girl, and I never found that she wronged me in any way. I thought at four months' end of retiring into the country with gambling-tables, as the risk was becoming considerable. They hung them for it in them days, but that never daunted me the least in life. I saw Cashman* hung for that gunsmith's shop on Snow-hill, and I saw Fauntleroy* hung, and a good many others, but it gave me no uneasiness and no fear. The gallows had no terror for people in my way of life. I started into the country with another man and his wife—his lawful wife—for I had a few words with my own young woman, or I shouldn't have left her behind me, or, indeed, have started at all. We carried gambling on in different parts of the country for six months. We made most at the E. O. tables,* —not those played with a ball, they weren't in vogue then, but throwing dice for prizes marked on a table. The highest prize was ten guineas, but the dice were so made that no prize could be thrown; the numbers were not regular as in good dice, and they were loaded as well. If anybody asked to see them, we had good dice ready to show. All sorts played with us. London men and all were taken in. We made most at the races. My mate and his wife told me that at the last Newmarket meeting we attended, 65*l.* was made, but they rowed in the same boat. I know they got a deal more. The 65*l.* was shared in three equal portions, but I had to maintain the horse and cart out of my own share. We used to go out into the roads (highway robbery) between races, and if we met an "old bloke" (man) we "propped him" (knocked him down), and robbed him. We did good stakes that way, and were never found out. We lived as well as any gentleman in the land. Our E. O. table was in a tilted cart.* I stayed with this man and his wife two months. She was good-looking, so as to attract people. I thought they didn't use me altogether right, so at Braintree I gave another man in the same way of business 25*l.* for his kit—horse, harness, tilted cart, and table. I gave him two good 5*l.* notes and three bad ones, for I worked that way still, not throwing much of a chance away. I came to London for a hawker's stock, braces and such-like, to sell on the road, just to take the down off (remove suspicion). In the meantime, the man that I bought the horse, &c., of, had been nailed passing a bad note, and he stated who he got it from, and I was traced. He was in a terrible rage to find himself done, particularly as he used to do the same to other people himself. He got acquitted for that there note after he had me "pinched" (arrested). I got "fullied" (fully committed). I was tried at the "Start" (Old Bailey*), and pleaded guilty to the minor offence (that of utterance, not knowing the note to be forged), or I should have been hanged for it then. It was a favourable sessions when I was tried. Thirty-six were cast for death, and only one was "topped" (hanged), the very one that expected to be "turned up" (acquitted) for highway robbery. I was sentenced to 14 years' transportation. I was ten weeks in the Bellerophon hulk* at Sheerness, and was then taken to Hobart Town,*

Van Dieman's Land, in the Sir Godfrey Webster. At Hobart Town sixty of us were picked out to go to Launceston.* There (at Launceston) we lay for four days in an old church, guarded by constables; and then the settlers came there from all parts, and picked their men out. I got a very bad master. He put me to harvest work that I had never even seen done before, and I had the care of pigs as wild as wild boars. After that I was sent to Launceston with two letters from my master to the superintendent, and the other servants thought I had luck to get away from Red Barks to Launceston, which was 16 miles off. I then worked in a Government potato-field; in the Government charcoal-works for about 11 months; and then was in the Marine department, going by water from Launceston to George Town,* taking Government officers down in gigs, provisions in boats, and such-like. There was a crew of six (convicts) in the gigs, and four in the watering-boats. All the time I consider I was very hardly treated. I hadn't clothes half the time, being allowed only two slop-suits* in a year, and no bed to lie on when we had to stay out all night with the boats by the river Tamar. With 12 years' service at this my time was up, but I had incurred several punishments before it was up. The first was 25 lashes, because a bag of flour had been burst, and I picked up a capfull. The flogging is dreadfully severe, a soldier's is nothing to it. I once had 50 lashes, for taking a hat in a joke when I was tipsy; and a soldier had 300 the same morning. I was flogged as a convict, and he as a soldier; and when we were both at the same hospital after the flogging, and saw each other's backs, the other convicts said to me, "D—— it, you've got it this time"; and the soldier said, when he saw my back, "You've got it twice as bad I have." "No," said the doctor, "ten times as bad—he's been flogged; but you, in comparison, have only had a child's whipping." The cats the convicts were then flogged with were each six feet long, made out of the log-line of a ship of 500 tons burden; nine over-end knots were in each tail, and nine tails whipped at each end with wax-end. With this we had half-minute lashes; a quick lashing would have been certain death. One convict who had 75 lashes was taken from the triangles* to the watch-house in Launceston, and was asked if he would have some tea,—he was found to be dead. The military surgeon kept on saying in this case, "Go on, do your duty." I was mustered there, as was every hand belonging to the Government, and saw it, and heard the doctor. When I was first flogged, there was inquiry among my fellow-convicts, as to

"How did D—— (meaning me) stand it—did he sing?" The answer was, "He was a pebble"; that is, I never once said, "Oh!" or gave out any expression of the pain I suffered. I took my flogging like a stone. If I had sung, some of the convicts would have given me some lush with a locust in it (laudanum hocussing), and when I was asleep would have given me a crack on the head that would have laid me straight. That first flogging made me ripe. I said to myself, "I can take it like a bullock." I could have taken the flogger's life at the time, I felt such revenge. Flogging always gives that feeling; I know it does, from what I've heard others say who had been flogged like myself. In all I had 875 lashes at my different punishments. I used to boast of it at last. I would say, "I don't care, I can take it till they see my backbone." After a flogging, I've rubbed my back against a wall, just to show my bravery like, and squeezed the congealed blood out of it. Once I would not let them dress my back after a flogging, and I had 25 additional for that. At last I bolted to Hobart Town, 120 miles off. There I was taken before Mr H——, the magistrate, himself a convict formerly, I believe from the Irish Rebellion;* but he was a good man to a prisoner. He ordered me 50, and sent me back to Launceston. At Launceston I was "fullied" by a bench of magistrates, and had 100. Seven years before my time was up I took to the bush. I could stand it no longer, of course not. In the bush I met men with whom, if I had been seen associating, I should have been hanged on any slight charge, such as Brittan* was and his pals.'

I am not at liberty to continue this man's statement at present: it would be a breach of the trust reposed in me. Suffice it, he was in after days tried for his life. Altogether it was a most extraordinary statement; and, from confirmations I received, was altogether truthful. He declared that he was so sick of the life he was now leading, that he would, as a probation, work on any kind of land anywhere for nothing, just to get out of it. He pronounced the lodging-houses the grand encouragements and concealments of crime, though he might be speaking against himself, he said, as he had always hidden safely there during the hottest search. A policeman once walked through the ward in search of him, and he was in bed. He knew the policeman well, and was as well known to the officer, but he was not recognised. He attributed his escape to the thick, bad atmosphere of the place giving his features a different look, and to his having shaved off his whiskers, and pulled his nightcap over his head. The officer, too, seemed half-sick, he said.

*Description of the Asylum for the Houseless**

The Asylum for the Houseless Poor of London is opened only when the thermometer reaches freezing-point, and offers nothing but dry bread and warm shelter to such as avail themselves of its charity.

To this place swarm, as the bitter winter's night comes on, some half-thousand penniless and homeless wanderers. The poverty-stricken from every quarter of the globe are found within its wards; from the haggard American seaman to the lank Polish refugee, the pale German 'out-wanderer',* the tearful black sea-cock,* the shivering Lascar, crossing-sweeper, the helpless Chinese beggar, and the half-torpid Italian organ-boy. It is, indeed, a ragged congress of nations—a convocation of squalor and misery—of destitution, degradation, and suffering, from all the corners of the earth.

Nearly every shade and grade of misery, misfortune, vice, and even guilt, are to be found in the place; for characters are not demanded previous to admission, want being the sole qualification required of the applicants. The Asylum for the Houseless is at once the beggar's hotel, the tramp's town-house, the outcast's haven of refuge—the last dwelling, indeed, on the road to ruin.

It is impossible to mistake the Asylum if you go there at dark, just as the lamp in the wire cage over the entrance-door is being lighted. This is the hour for opening; and ranged along the kerb is a kind of ragged regiment, drawn up four deep, and stretching far up and down the narrow lane, until the crowd is like a hedge to the roadway. Nowhere in the world can a similar sight be witnessed.

It is a terrible thing, indeed, to look down upon that squalid crowd from one of the upper windows of the institution. There they stand shivering in the snow, with their thin, cobwebby garments hanging in tatters about them. Many are without shirts; with their bare skin showing through the rents and gaps of their clothes, like the hide of a dog with the mange. Some have their greasy coats and trousers tied round their wrists and ankles with string, to prevent the piercing wind from blowing up them. A few are without shoes; and these keep one foot only to the ground, while the bare flesh that has had to tramp through the snow is blue and livid-looking as half-cooked meat.

It is a sullenly silent crowd, without any of the riot and rude frolic which generally ensue upon any gathering in the London streets; for the only sounds heard are the squealing of the beggar infants, or the wrangling of the vagrant boys for the front ranks, together with a continued succession of hoarse coughs, that seem to answer each other like the bleating of a flock of sheep.

To each person is given half-a-pound of the best bread on coming in at night, and a like quantity on going out in the morning; and children, even if they be at the breast, have the same, which goes to swell the mother's allowance. A clerk enters in a thick ledger the name, age, trade, and place of birth of the applicants, as well as where they slept the night before.

As the eye glances down the column of the register, indicating where each applicant has passed the previous night, it is startled to find how often the clerk has had to write down, 'in the streets'; so that 'ditto', 'ditto', continually repeated under the same head, sounded as an ideal chorus of terrible want in the mind's ear.

The sleeping-wards at the Asylum are utterly unlike all preconceived notions of a dormitory. There is not a bedstead to be seen, nor is even so much as a sheet or blanket visible. The ward itself is a long, bare, whitewashed apartment, with square post-like pillars supporting the flat-beamed roof, and reminding the visitor of a large unoccupied store-room—such as are occasionally seen in the neighbourhood of Thames-street and the Docks. Along the floor are ranged what appear at first sight to be endless rows of large empty orange chests, packed closely side by side, so that the boards are divided off into some two hundred shallow tanpit-like* compartments. These are the berths, or, to speak technically, the 'bunks' of the institution. In each of them is a black mattress, made of some shiny waterproof material, like tarpauling stuffed with straw. At the head of every bunk, hanging against the wall, is a leather—a big 'basil'* covering—that looks more like a wine-cooper's apron than a counterpane. These 'basils' are used as coverlids,* not only because they are strong and durable, but for a more cogent reason—they do not retain vermin.

Around the fierce stove, in the centre of the ward, there is generally gathered a group of the houseless wanderers, the crimson rays tinting the cluster of haggard faces with a bright lurid light that colours the skin as red as wine. One and all are stretching forth their hands, as if to let the delicious heat soak into their half-numbed limbs. They seem positively greedy of the warmth, drawing up their sleeves and trousers so that their naked legs and arms may present a larger surface to the fire.

Not a laugh nor sound is heard, but the men stand still, munching their bread, their teeth champing like horses in a manger. One poor wretch, at the time of my visit, had been allowed to sit on a form inside the railings round the stove, for he had the ague; and there he crouched, with his legs near as a roasting-joint to the burning coals, as if he were trying to thaw his very marrow.

Then how fearful it is to hear the continued coughing of the wretched inmates! It seems to pass round the room from one to another, now sharp and hoarse as a bark, then deep and hollow as a lowing, or—with the old—feeble and trembling as a bleat.

In an hour after the opening the men have quitted the warm fire and crept one after another to their berths, where they lie rolled round in their leathers—the rows of tightly-bound figures, brown and stiff as mummies, suggesting the idea of some large catacomb.

The stillness is broken only by the snoring of the sounder sleepers and the coughing of the more restless.

It is a marvellously pathetic scene. Here is a herd of the most wretched and friendless people in the world, lying down close to the earth as sheep; here are some two centuries of outcasts, whose days are an unvarying round of suffering, enjoying the only moments when they are free from pain and care—life being to them but one long painful operation as it were, and sleep the chloroform which, for the time being, renders them insensible.

The sight sets the mind speculating on the beggars' and the outcasts' dreams. The ship's company, starving at the North Pole, dreamt, every man of them, each night, of feasting; and are those who compose this miserable, frozen-out beggar crew, now regaling themselves, in their sleep, with visions of imaginary banquets?—are they smacking their mental lips over ideal beef and pudding? Is that poor wretch yonder, whose rheumatic limbs rack him each step he takes—is *he* tripping over green fields with an elastic and joyous bound, that in his waking moments he can never know again? Do that man's restlessness and heavy moaning come from nightmare terrors of policemen and treadwheels?—and which among those runaway boys is fancying that he is back home again, with his mother and sisters weeping on his neck?

The next moment the thoughts shift, and the heart is overcome with a sense of the vast heap of social refuse—the mere human street-sweepings—the great living mixen* —that is destined, as soon as the spring returns, to be strewn far and near over the land, and serve as manure to the future crime-crops of the country.

Then come the self-congratulations and the self-questionings! and as a man, sound in health and limb, walking through a hospital, thanks God that he has been spared the bodily ailments, the mere sight of which sickens him, so in this refuge for the starving and the homeless, the first instinct of the well-to-do visitor is to breathe a thanksgiving (like the Pharisee in the parable*) that 'he is not as one of these'.

But the vain conceit has scarcely risen to the tongue before the better nature whispers in the mind's ear, 'By what special virtue of your own are you different from them? How comes it that you are well clothed and well fed, whilst so many go naked and hungry?' And if you in your arrogance, ignoring all the accidents that have helped to build up your worldly prosperity, assert that you have been the 'architect of your own fortune', who, let us ask, gave you the genius or energy for the work?

Then get down from your moral stilts, and confess it honestly to yourself, that you are what you are by that inscrutable grace which decreed your birthplace to be a mansion or a cottage rather than a 'padding-ken',* or which granted you brains and strength, instead of sending you into the world, like many of these, a cripple or an idiot.

It is hard for smug-faced respectability to acknowledge these dirt-caked, erring wretches as brothers, and yet, if from those to whom little is given little is expected, surely, after the atonement of their long suffering, they will make as good angels as the best of us.

VOLUME IV

THOSE THAT WILL NOT WORK

INTRODUCTION AND CLASSIFICATION

Of the Workers and Non-Workers

THE essential quality of an animal is that it seeks its own living, whereas a vegetable has its living brought to it. An animal cannot stick its feet in the ground and suck up the inorganic elements of its body from the soil, nor drink in the organic elements from the atmosphere. The leaves of plants are not only their lungs but their stomachs. As *they* breathe they acquire food and strength, but as animals breathe *they* gradually waste away. The carbon which is *secreted* by the process of respiration in the vegetable is excreted by the very same process in the animal. Hence a fresh supply of *carbonaceous* matter must be sought after and obtained at frequent intervals, in order to repair the continual waste of animal life.

But in the act of seeking for substances fitted to replace that which is lost in respiration, nerves must be excited and muscles moved; and recent discoveries have shown that such excitation and motion are attended with decomposition of the organs in which they occur. Muscular action gives rise to the destruction of muscular tissue, nervous action to a change in the nervous matter; and this destruction and decomposition necessarily involve a fresh supply of *nitrogenous* matter, in order that the loss may be repaired.

Now a tree, being inactive, has little or no waste. All the food that it obtains goes to the invigoration of its frame; not one atom is destroyed in seeking more: but the essential condition of animal life is muscular action; the essential condition of muscular action is the destruction of muscular tissue; and the essential condition of the destruction of muscular tissue is a supply of food fitted for the reformation of it, or—*death*. It is impossible for an animal—like a vegetable—to stand still and not destroy. If the limbs are not moving, the heart is beating, the lungs playing, the bosom heaving. Hence an animal, in order to continue its existence, must obtain its subsistence either by its own exertions or by those of others—in a word, it must be *autobious* or *allobious*.

The procuration of sustenance, then, is the necessary condition of animal life, and constitutes the sole apparent reason for the addition of the locomotive apparatus to the vegetative functions of sentient nature; but the faculties of comparison and volition have been further added to the animal nature of Man, in order to enable him, among other things, the better to gratify his wants—to give him such a mastery over the elements of material nature, that he may force the external world the more readily to contribute to his support. Hence the derangement of either one of those functions must degrade the human being—as regards his means of sustenance—to the level of the brute. If his intellect be impaired, and the faculty of perceiving 'the fitness of things' be consequently lost to him—or, this being sound, if the power of moving his muscles in compliance with his will be deficient—then the individual becomes no longer capable, like his fellows, of continuing his existence by his *own* exertions.

Hence, in every state, we have two extensive causes of allobiism, or living by the labour of others; the one intellectual, as in the case of lunatics and idiots, and the other physical, as in the case of the infirm, the crippled, and the maimed—the old and the young.

But a third, and a more extensive class, still remains to be particularized. The members of every community may be divided into the *energetic* and the *an-ergetic*; that is to say, into the hardworking and the non-working, the industrious and the indolent classes; the distinguishing characteristic of the *anergetic* being the extreme irksomeness of all labour to them, and their consequent indisposition to work for their subsistence. Now, in the circumstances above enumerated, we have three capital causes why, in every State, a certain portion of the community must derive their subsistence from the exertions of the rest; the first proceeds from some *physical* defect, as in the case of the old and the young, the super-annuated and the sub-annuated, the crippled and the maimed; the second from some *intellectual* defect, as in the case of lunatics and idiots; and the third from some *moral* defect, as in the case of the indolent, the vagrant, the professional mendicant, and the criminal. In all civilized countries, there will necessarily be a greater or less number of human parasites living on the sustenance of their fellows. The industrious must labour to support the lazy, and the sane to keep the insane, and the able-bodied to maintain the infirm.

Still, to complete the social fabric, another class requires to be specified. As yet, regard has been paid only to those who must needs labour for their living, or who, in default of so doing, must prey on the proceeds of the industry of their more active or more stalwart brethren. There is, however, in all civilized society, a farther portion of the people distinct from either of those above mentioned, who, being already provided—no matter how—with a sufficient stock of sustenance, or what will exchange for such, have no occasion to toil for an additional supply.

Hence all society would appear to arrange itself into four different classes:

I. Those that Will Work.
II. Those that Cannot Work.
III. Those that Will Not Work.
IV. Those that Need Not Work.

Under one or other section of this quadruple division, every member, not only of our community, but of every other civilized State, must necessarily be included; the rich, the poor, the industrious, the idle, the honest, the dishonest, the virtuous, and the vicious—each and all must be comprised therein.

PROSTITUTION IN LONDON

Seclusives, or Those that Live in Private Houses and Apartments

It is frequently a matter of surprise amongst the friends of a gentleman of position and connection that he exhibits an invincible distaste to marriage. If they were acquainted with his private affairs their astonishment would speedily vanish, for they would find him already to all intents and purposes united to one who possesses charms, talents, and accomplishments, and who will in all probability exercise the same influence over him as long as the former continue to exist. The prevalence of this custom, and the extent of its ramifications is hardly dreamed of, although its effects are felt, and severely. The torch of Hymen* burns less brightly than of yore, and even were the blacksmith of Gretna* still exercising his vocation, he would find his business diminishing with startling rapidity year by year.

It is a great mistake to suppose that kept mistresses are without friends and without society; on the contrary, their acquaintance, if not select, is numerous, and it is their custom to order their broughams* or their pony carriages, and at the fashionable hour pay visits and leave cards on one another.

They possess no great sense of honour, although they are generally more or less religious. If they take a fancy to a man they do not hesitate to admit him to their favour. Most kept women have several lovers who are in the habit of calling upon them at different times, and as they are extremely careful in conducting these amours they perpetrate infidelity with impunity, and in ninety-nine cases out of a hundred escape detection. When they are unmasked, the process, unless the man is very much infatuated, is of course summary in the extreme. They are dismissed probably with a handsome douceur* and sent once more adrift. They do not remain long, however, in the majority of cases, without finding another protector.

A woman who called herself Lady —— met her admirer at a house in Bolton Row that she was in the habit of frequenting. At first sight Lord —— became enamoured, and proposed *sur le champ*,* after a little preliminary conversation, that she should live with him.

The proposal with equal rapidity and eagerness was accepted, and without further deliberation his lordship took a house for her in one of the terraces overlooking the Regent's Park, allowed her four thousand a year, and came as frequently as he could, to pass his time in her society. She immediately set up a carriage and a stud, took a box at the opera on the pit tier, and lived, as she very well could, in excellent style. The munificence of her friend did not decrease by the lapse of time. She frequently received presents of jewelry from him, and his marks of attention were constant as they were various. The continual contemplation of her charms instead of producing satiety added fuel to the fire, and he was never happy when out of her sight. This continued until one day he met a young man in her *loge** at the opera, whom she introduced as her cousin. This incident aroused his suspicions, and he determined to watch her more closely. She was surrounded by spies, and in reality did not possess one confidential attendant, for they were all bribed to betray her. For a time, more by accident than precaution or care on her part, she succeeded in eluding their vigilance, but at last the catastrophe happened; she was surprised with her paramour in a position that placed doubt out of the question, and the next day his lordship, with a few sarcastic remarks, gave her her *congé** and five hundred pounds.

These women are rarely possessed of education, although they undeniably have ability. If they appear accomplished you may rely that it is entirely superficial. Their disposition is volatile and thoughtless, which qualities are of course at variance with the existence of respectability. Their ranks too are recruited from a class where education is not much in vogue. The fallacies about clergymen's daughters and girls from the middle classes forming the majority of such women are long ago exploded; there may be some amongst them, but they are few and far between. They are not, as a rule, disgusted with their way of living; most of them consider it a means to an end, and in no measure degrading or polluting. One and all look forward to marriage and a certain state in society as their ultimate lot. This is their bourne, and they do all in their power to travel towards it.

'I am not tired of what I am doing,' a woman once answered me, 'I rather like it. I have all I want, and my friend loves me to excess. I am the daughter of a tradesman at Yarmouth. I learned to play the piano a little, and I have naturally a good voice. Yes, I find these accomplishments of great use to me; they are, perhaps, as you say, the only ones that could be of use to a girl like myself. I am three and twenty, I was seduced four years ago. I tell you candidly I was as much to blame as my seducer; I wished to escape from the drudgery of my father's shop. I have told you they partially educated me; I could cypher a little as well, and I knew something about the globes; so I thought I was qualified for something better than minding the shop occasionally, or sewing, or helping my mother in the kitchen and other domestic matters. I was very fond of dress, and I could not at home gratify my love of display. My parents were stupid, easy-going old people, and extremely uninteresting to me. All these causes combined induced me to encourage the addresses of a young gentleman of property in the neighbourhood, and without much demur I yielded to his desires. We then went to London, and I have since that time lived with four different men. We got tired of one another in six months, and I was as eager to leave him as he was to get rid of me, so we mutually accommodated one another by separating. Well, my father and mother don't exactly know where I am or what I am doing, although if they had any penetration they might very well guess. Oh, yes! they know I am alive, for I keep them pleasantly aware of my existence by occasionally sending them money. What do I think will become of me? What an absurd question. I could marry to-morrow if I liked.'

Board Lodgers

Board lodgers are those who give a portion of what they receive to the mistress of the brothel in return for their board and lodging. During the progress of these researches, we met a girl residing at a house in a street running out of Langham Place. Externally the house looked respectable enough; there was no indication of the profession or mode of life of the inmates, except that, from the fact of some of the blinds being down in the bed rooms, you might have thought the house contained an invalid. The rooms, when you were ushered in, were well, though cheaply furnished; there were coburg chairs and sofas, glass chandeliers, and handsome green curtains. The girl with whom we were brought into conversation was not more than twenty-three; she told us her age was twenty, but statements of a similar nature, when made by this class, are never to be relied on. At first she treated our inquiries with some levity, and jocularly inquired what we were inclined to stand, which we justly interpreted into a desire for something to drink; we accordingly 'stood' a bottle of wine, which had the effect of making our informant more communicative. What she told us was briefly this. Her life was a life of perfect slavery, she was seldom if ever allowed to go out, and then not without being watched. Why was this? Because she would 'cut it' if she got a chance, they knew that very well, and took very good care she shouldn't have much opportunity. Their house was rather popular, and they had lots of visitors; she had some particular friends who always came to see her. They paid her well, but she hardly ever got any of the money. Where was the odds, she couldn't go out to spend it? What did she want with money, except now and then for a train of white satin. What was white satin? Where had I been all my life to ask such a question? Was I a dodger? She meant a parson. No; she was glad of that, for she hadn't much idea of them, they were a canting lot. Well, white satin, if I must know, was gin, and I couldn't say she never taught me anything. Where was she born? Somewhere in Stepney. What did it matter where; she could tell me all about it if she liked, but she didn't care. It touched her on the raw—made her feel too much. She was 'ticed when she was young, that is, she was decoyed by the mistress of the house some years ago. She met Mrs —— in the street, and the woman began talking to her in a friendly way. Asked her who her father was (he was a journeyman carpenter), where he lived, extracted all about her family, and finally asked her to come home to tea with her. The child, delighted at the making the acquaintance of so kind and so well-dressed a lady, willingly acquiesced, without making any demur, as she never dreamt of anything wrong, and had not been cautioned by her father. She had lost her mother some years ago. She was not brought direct to the house where I found her? Oh! no. There was a branch establishment over the water, where they were broken in as it were. How long did she remain there? Oh! perhaps two months, maybe three; she didn't keep much account how time went. When she was conquered and her spirit broken, she was transported from the first house to a more aristocratic neighbourhood. How did they tame her? Oh! they made her drunk and sign some papers, which she knew gave them great power over her, although she didn't exactly know in what the said power consisted, or how it might be exercised. Then they clothed her and fed her well, and gradually inured her to that sort of life. And now, was there anything else I'd like to know particularly, because if there was, I'd better look sharp about asking it, as she was getting tired of talking, she could tell me. Did she expect to lead this life till she died? Well she never did, if I wasn't going to preachify. She couldn't stand that—anything but that.

I really begged to apologize if I had wounded her sensibility; I wasn't inquiring from a religious point of view, or with any particular motive. I merely wished to know, to satisfy my own curiosity.

Well, she thought me a very inquisitive old party, anyhow. At any rate, as I was so polite she did not mind answering my questions. Would she stick to it till she was a stiff un? She supposed she would; what else was there for her? Perhaps something might turn up; how was she to know? She never thought she would go mad; if she did, she lived in the present, and never went blubbering about as some did. She tried to be as jolly as she could; where was the fun of being miserable?

Men frequent the houses in which women board and lodge for many reasons, the chief of which is secrecy; they also feel sure that the women are free from disease, if they know the house, and it bears an average reputation for being well conducted. Men in a certain position avoid publicity in their amours beyond all things, and dread being seen in the neighbourhood of the Haymarket or the Burlington Arcade at certain hours, as their professional reputation might be compromised. Many serious, demure people conceal the iniquities of their private lives in this way.

If Asmodeus* were loquacious, how interesting and anecdotical a scandal-monger he might become!

Thieves' Women

Several showily-dressed, if not actually well-attired women, who are to be found walking about the Haymarket, live in St Giles's and about Drury Lane. But the lowest class of women, who prostitute themselves for a shilling or less, are the most curious and remarkable class in this part. One of them, a woman over forty, shabbily dressed, and with a disreputable, unprepossessing appearance, volunteered the following statement for a consideration of a spirituous nature.

'Times is altered, sir, since I come on the town. I can remember when all the swells used to come down here-away, instead of going to the Market; but those times is past, they is, worse luck, but, like myself, nothing lasts for ever, although I've stood my share of wear

THE HAYMARKET—MIDNIGHT.

and tear, I have. Years ago Fleet Street and the Strand, and Catherine Street, and all round there was famous for women and houses.* Ah! those were the times. Wish they might come again, but wishing's no use, it ain't. It only makes one miserable a thinking of it. I come up from the country when I was quite a gal, not above sixteen I dessay. I come from Dorsetshire, near Lyme Regis, to see a aunt of mine. Father was a farmer in Dorset, but only in a small way—tenant farmer, as you would say. I was mighty pleased, you may swear, with London, and liked being out at night when I could get the chance. One night I went up the area and stood looking through the railing, when a man passed by, but seeing me he returned and spoke to me something about the weather. I, like a child, answered him unsuspectingly enough, and he went on talking about town and country, asking me, among other things, if I had long been in London, or if I was born there. I not thinking told him all about myself; and he went away apparently very much pleased with me, saying before he went that he was very glad to have made such an agreeable acquaintance, and if I would say nothing about it he would call for me about the same time, or a little earlier, if I liked, the next night, and take me out for a walk. I was, as you may well suppose, delighted, and never said a word. The next evening I met him as he appointed, and two or three times subsequently. One night we walked longer than usual, and I pressed him to return, as I feared my aunt would find me out; but he said he was so fatigued with walking so far, he would like to rest a little before he went back again; but if I was very anxious he would put me in a cab. Frightened about him, for I thought he might be ill, I preferred risking being found out; and when he proposed that we should go into some house and sit down I agreed. He said all at once, as if he had just remembered something, that a very old friend of his lived near there, and we couldn't go to a better place, for she would give us everything we could wish. We found the door half open when we arrived. "How careless," said my friend, "to leave the street-door open, any one might get in." We entered without knocking, and seeing a door in the passage standing ajar we went in. My friend shook hands with an old lady who was talking to several girls dispersed over different parts of the room, who, she said, were her daughters. At this announcement some of them laughed, when she got very angry and ordered them out of the room. Somehow I didn't like the place, and not feeling all right I asked to be put in a cab and sent home. My friend made no objection and a cab was sent for. He, however, pressed me to have something to drink before I started. I refused to touch any wine, so I asked for some coffee, which I drank. It made me feel very sleepy, so sleepy indeed that I begged to be allowed to sit down on the sofa. They accordingly placed me on the sofa, and advised me to rest a little while, promising, in order to allay my anxiety, to send a messenger to my aunt. Of course I was drugged, and so heavily I did not regain my consciousness till the next morning. I was horrified to discover that I had been ruined,* and for some days I was inconsolable, and cried like a child to be killed or sent back to my aunt.

'When I became quiet I received a visit from my seducer, in whom I had placed so much silly confidence. He talked very kindly to me, but I would not listen to him for some time. He came several times to see me, and at last said he would take me away if I liked, and give me a house of my own. Finally, finding how hopeless all was I agreed to his proposal, and he allowed me four pounds a week. This went on for some months, till he was tired of me, when he threw me over for some one else. There is always as good fish in the sea as ever came out of it, and this I soon discovered.

'Then for some years—ten years, till I was six-and-twenty,—I went through all the changes of a gay* lady's life, and they're not a few, I can tell you. I don't leave off this sort of life because I'm in a manner used to it, and what could I do if I did? I've no character; I've never been used to do anything, and I don't see what employment I stand a chance of getting. Then if I had to sit hours and hours all day long, and part of the night too, sewing or anything like that, I should get tired. It would worrit me so; never having been accustomed, you see, I couldn't stand it. I lodge in Charles Street, Drury Lane, now. I did live in Nottingham Court once, and Earls Street. But, Lord, I've lived in a many places you wouldn't think, and I don't imagine you'd believe one half. I'm always a-chopping and a-changing like the wind as you may say. I pay half-a-crown a week for my bed-room; it's clean and comfortable, good enough for such as me. I don't think much of my way of life. You folks as has honour, and character, and feelings, and such, can't understand how all that's been beaten out of people like me. I don't feel. *I'm used to it.* I did once, more especial when mother died. I heard on it through a friend of mine, who told me her last words was of me. I did cry and go on then ever so, but Lor', where's the good of fretting? I arn't happy either. It isn't happiness, but I get enough money to keep me in victuals and drink, and it's the drink mostly that keeps me going. You've no idea how I look forward to my drop of gin. It's everything to me. I don't suppose I'll live much longer, and that's another thing that pleases me. I don't want to live, and yet I don't care enough about dying to make away with myself. I arn't got that amount af feeling that some has, and that's where it is I'm kinder 'fraid of it.'

THIEVES AND SWINDLERS

The Sneaks, or Common Thieves

The common thief is not distinguished for manual dexterity and accomplishment, like the pickpocket or mobsman, nor for courage, ingenuity, and skill, like the burglar, but is characterized by low cunning and stealth—hence he is termed the *Sneak*, and is despised by the higher classes of thieves.

There are various orders of Sneaks—from the urchin stealing an apple at a stall, to the man who enters a dwelling by the area or an attic window and carries off the silver plate.

Street-stalls.—In wandering along Whitechapel we see ranges of stalls on both sides of the street, extending from the neighbourhood of the Minories to Whitechapel church. Various kinds of merchandize are exposed to sale. There are stalls for fruit, vegetables, and oysters. There are also stalls where fancy goods are exposed for sale—combs, brushes, chimney-ornaments, children's toys, and common articles of jewellery. We find middle-aged women standing with baskets of firewood, and Cheap Johns* selling various kinds of Sheffield cutlery, stationery, and plated goods.

It is an interesting sight to saunter along the New Cut, Lambeth, and to observe the street stalls of that locality. Here you see some old Irish woman, with apples and pears exposed on a small board placed on the top of a barrel, while she is seated on an upturned bushel basket smoking her pipe.

Alongside you notice a deal board on the top of a tressel, and an Irish girl of 18 years of age seated on a small three-legged stool, shouting in shrill tones 'Apples, fine apples, ha'penny a lot!'

You find another stall on the top of two tressels, with a larger quantity of apples and pears, kept by a woman who sits by with a child at her breast.

In another place you see a costermonger's barrow, with large green and yellow piles of fruit of better quality than the others, and a group of boys and girls assembled around him as he smartly disposes of pennyworths to the persons passing along the street.

Outside a public-house you see a young man, humpbacked, with a basket of herrings and haddocks standing on the pavement, calling 'Yarmouth herrings—three a-penny!' and at the door of a beershop with the sign of the 'Pear Tree' we find a miserable looking old woman selling cresses, seated on a stool with her feet in an old basket.

As we wander along the New Cut during the day, we do not see so many young thieves loitering about; but in the evening when the lamps are lit, they steal forth from their haunts, with keen roguish eye, looking out for booty. We then see them loitering about the stalls or mingling among the throng of people in the street, looking wistfully on the tempting fruit displayed on the stalls.

These young Arabs* of the city have a very strange and motley appearance. Many of them are only 6 or 7 years of age, others 8 or 10. Some have no jacket, cap, or shoes, and wander about London with their ragged trowsers hung by one brace; some have an old tattered coat, much too large for them, without shoes and stockings, and with one leg of the trowsers rolled up to the knee; others have on an old greasy grey or black cap, with an old jacket rent at the elbows, and strips of the lining hanging down behind; others have on an old dirty pinafore; while some have petticoats. They are generally in a squalid and unwashed condition, with their hair clustered in wild disorder like a mop, or hanging down in dishevelled locks,—in some cases cropped close to the head.

Groups of these ragged urchins may be seen standing at the corners of the streets and in public thoroughfares, with blacking-boxes slung on their back by a leathern belt, or crouching in groups on the pavement; or we may occasionally see them running alongside of omnibuses, cabs, and hansoms, nimbly turning somersaults on the pavement as they scamper along, and occasionally walking on their hands with their feet in the air in our fashionable streets, to the merriment of the passers-by. Most of them are Irish cockneys, which we can observe in their features and accent—to which class most of the London thieves belong. They are generally very acute and ready-witted, and have a knowing twinkle in their eye which exhibits the precocity of their minds.

As we ramble along the New Cut in the dusk, mingled in the throng on the crowded street, chiefly composed of working people, the young ragged thieves may be seen stealing forth: their keen eye readily recognizes the police-officers proceeding in their rounds, as well as the detective officers in their quiet and cautious movements. They seldom steal from costermongers, but frequently from the old women's stalls. One will push an old woman off her seat—perhaps a bushel basket, while the others will steal her fruit or the few coppers lying on her stall. This is done by day as well as by night, but chiefly in the dusk of the evening.

They generally go in a party of three or four, sometimes as many as eight together. Watching their opportunity, they make a sudden snatch at the apples or pears, or oranges or nuts, or walnuts, as the case may be, then run off, with the cry of 'stop thief!' ringing in their ears from the passers-by. These petty thefts are often done from a love of mischief rather than from a desire for plunder.

When overtaken by a police-officer, they in general readily go with him to the police-station. Sometimes the urchin will lie down in the street and cry 'let me go!' and the bystanders will take his part. This is of frequent occurrence in the neighbourhood of the New-cut and the Waterloo-road—a well-known rookery* of young thieves in London.

By the petty thefts at the fruit-stalls they do not gain much money—seldom so much as to get admittance to the gallery of the Victoria Theatre, which they delight to frequent. They are particularly interested in the plays of robberies, burglaries, and murders performed there, which are done in melodramatic style. There are similar fruit-stalls in the other densely populated districts of the metropolis.

In the Mile-end-road, and New North-road, and occasionally in other streets in different localities of London, common jewellery is exposed for sale, consisting of brooches, rings, bracelets, breast-pins, watch-chains, eye-glasses, ear-rings and studs, &c. There are also stalls for the sale of china, looking-glasses, combs, and chimney-ornaments. The thefts from these are generally managed in this way:

One goes up and looks at some trifling article in company with his associates. The party in charge of the stall—generally a woman—knowing their thieving propensity, tells them to go away; which they decline to do. When the woman goes to remove him, another boy darts forward at the other end of the stall and steals some article of jewellery, or otherwise, while her attention is thus distracted.

Stealing from the Tills.—This is done by the same class of boys, generally by two or three, or more, associated together. It is committed at any hour of the day, principally in the evening, and generally in the following way: One of the boys throws his cap into the shop of some greengrocer or other small dealer, in the absence of the person in charge; another boy, often without shoes or stockings, creeps in on his hands and knees as if to fetch it, being possibly covered from without by some of the boys standing beside the shop-door, who is also on the look-out. Any passer-by seeing the cap thrown in would take no particular notice in most cases, as it merely appears to be a thoughtless boyish frolic. Meantime the young rogue within the shop crawls round the counter to the till, and rifles its contents.

If detected, he possibly says, 'Let me go; I have done nothing. That boy who is standing outside and has just run away threw in my bonnet, and I came to fetch it.' When discovered by the shopkeeper, the boy will occasionally be allowed to get away, as the loss may not be known till afterwards.

Sometimes one of these ragged urchins watches a favourable opportunity and steals from the till while his comrade is observing the movements of the people passing by and the police, without resorting to the ingenious expedient of throwing in the cap.

The shop tills are generally rifled by boys, in most cases by two or more in company; this is only done occasionally. It is confined chiefly to the districts where the working classes reside.

In some cases, though rarely, a lad of 17 or 19 years of age or upwards, will reach his hand over the counter to the till, in the absence of the person in charge of the shop.

These robberies are not very numerous, and are of small collective value.

Stealing from the Doors and Windows of Shops.—In various shopping districts of London we see a great variety of goods displayed for sale at the different shop-doors and windows, and on the pavement in front of the shops of brokers, butchers, grocers, milliners, &c.

Let us take a picture from the New-cut, Lambeth. We observe many brokers' shops along the street, with a heterogenous assortment of household furniture, tables, chairs, looking-glasses, plain and ornamental, cupboards, fire-screens, &c., ranged along the broad pavement; while on tables are stores of carpenters' tools in great variety, copper-kettles, brushes, and bright tin pannikins,* and other articles.

We see the dealer standing before his door, with blue apron, hailing the passer-by to make a purchase. Upon stands on the pavement at each side of his shop-door are cheeses of various kinds and of different qualities, cut up into quarters and slices, and rashers of bacon lying in piles in the open windows, or laid out on marble slabs. On deal racks are boxes of eggs, 'fresh from the country', and white as snow, and large pieces of bacon, ticketed as of 'fine flavour', and 'very mild'.

Alongside is a milliner's shop with the milliner, a smart young woman, seated knitting beneath an awning in front of her door. On iron and wooden rods, suspended on each side of the door-way, are black and white straw bonnets and crinolines, swinging in the wind; while on the tables in front are exposed boxes of gay feathers, and flowers of every tint, and fronts of shirts of various styles, with stacks of gown-pieces of various patterns.

A green-grocer stands by his shop with a young girl of 17 by his side. On each side of the door are baskets of apples, with large boxes of onions and peas. Cabbages are heaped at the front of the shop, with piles of white turnips and red carrots.

Over the street is a furniture wareroom. Beneath the canvas awning before the shop are chairs of various kinds, straw-bottomed and seated with green or puce-coloured leather, fancy looking-glasses in gilt frames, parrots in cages, a brass-mounted portmanteau, and other miscellaneous articles. An active young shopman is seated by the shop-door, in a light cap and dark apron—with newspaper in hand.

Near the Victoria Theatre we notice a second-hand clothes store. On iron rods suspended over the doorway we find trowsers, vests, and coats of all patterns and sizes, and of every quality dangling in the wind; and on small wooden stands along the pavement are jackets and coats of various descriptions. Here are corduroy jackets, ticketed '15*s*. and 16*s*. made to order'. Corduroy trowsers warranted 'first rate', at 7*s*. 6*d*. Fustian trowsers to order for 8*s*. 6*d*.; while dummies are ranged on the pavement with coats buttoned upon them, inviting us to enter the shop.

In the vicinity we see stalls of workmen's iron tools of various kinds—some old and rusty, others bright and new.

Thefts are often committed from the doors and windows of these shops during the day, in the temporary absence of the person in charge. They are often seen by passers-by, who take no notice, not wishing to attend the police court, as they consider they are insufficiently paid for it.

The coat is usually stolen from the dummy in this way: one boy is posted on the opposite side of the street to see if a police-officer is in sight, or a policeman in plain clothes, who might detect the depredation. Another stands two or three yards from the shop. The third comes up to the dummy, and pretends to look at the quality of the coat to throw off the suspicion of any bystander or passer-by. He then unfastens the button, and if the shopkeeper or any of his assistants come out, he walks away. If he finds that he is not seen by the people in the shop, he takes the coat off the dummy and runs away with it.

If seen, he will not return at that time, but watches some other convenient opportunity. When the young thief is chased by the shopkeeper, his two associates run and jostle him, and try to trip him up, so as to give their companion an opportunity of escaping. This is generally done at dusk, in the winter time, when thieving is most prevalent in those localities.

In stealing a piece of bacon from the shop-doors or windows, they wait till the shopman turns his back, when they take a piece of bacon or cheese in the same way as in the case alluded to. This is commonly done by two or more boys in company.

Handkerchiefs at shop-doors are generally stolen by one of the boys and passed to another who runs off with it. When hotly chased, they drop the handkerchief and run away.

These young thieves are the ragged boys formerly noticed, varying from 9 to 14 years of age, without shoes or stockings. Their parents are of the lowest order of Irish cockneys, or they live in low lodging-houses, where they get a bed for *2d.* or *3d.* a night, with crowds of others as destitute as themselves.

There are numbers of young women of 18 years of age and upwards, Irish cockneys, belonging to the same class, who steal from these shop-doors. They are poorly dressed, and live in some of the lowest streets in Surrey and Middlesex, but chiefly in the Borough and the East end. Some of them are dressed in a clean cotton dress, shabby bonnet and faded shawl, and are accompanied by one or more men, costermongers in appearance. They steal rolls of printed cotton from the outside of linen drapers' shops, rolls of flannel, and of coarse calico, hearthrugs and rolls of oilskin and table-covers; and from brokers' shops they carry off rolls of carpet, fenders, fire-irons, and other articles, exposed in and around the shop-door. The thefts of these women are of greater value than those committed by the boys. They belong to the felon-class and are generally expert thieves.

The mode in which they commit these thefts is by taking advantage of the absence of the person in charge of the shop, or when his back is turned. It is done very quickly and dexterously, and they are often successful in carrying away articles such as those named without any one observing them.

Another class of Sneaks, who steal from the outsides of shops, are women more advanced in life than those referred to,—some middle-aged and others elderly. Some of them are thieves, or the companions of thieves, and others are the wives of honest, hard-working mechanics and labouring men, who spend their money in gin and beer at various public-houses.

These persons go and look over some pieces of bacon or meat outside of butchers' shops; they ask the price of it, sometimes buy a small piece and steal a large one, but more frequently buy none. They watch the opportunity of taking a large piece which they slip into their basket and carry to some small chandler's shop in a low neighbourhood, where they dispose of it at about a fourth of its value.

We have met some thieves of this order, basket in hand, returning from Drury Lane, who were pointed out to us by a detective officer.

The mechanics' and labourers' wives in many cases leave their homes in the morning for the purpose of purchasing their husband's dinner. They meet with other women fond of drink like themselves. They meet, for example, outside the 'Plumb Tree', or such-like public-house, and join their money together to buy beer or gin. After partaking of it, they leave the house, and remain for some time outside conversing together. They again join their money and return to the public-house, and have some additional liquor: leave the house and separate. Some of them join with other parties fond of liquor as they did with the former. One says to the other: 'I have no money, otherwise we would have a drop of gin. I have just met Mrs So-and-so, and spent nearly all my money.' The other may reply: 'I have not much to get the old man's dinner, but we can have a quartern of gin.' After getting the liquor, they separate. The tradesman's wife, finding that she has spent nearly the whole of her money, goes to a cheesemonger's or butcher's shop, and steals a piece of meat, or bacon, for the purpose of placing it before her husband for dinner, perhaps selling the remainder of the booty at shops in low neighbourhoods, or to lodging-houses.

Such cases frequently occur, and are brought before the police-courts.

Small articles are occasionally taken from shop windows in the winter evenings, by means of breaking a pane of glass in a very ingenious way. These thefts are committed at the shops of confectioners, tobacconists, and watchmakers, &c., in the quiet by-streets.

Sometimes they are done by the younger ragged-boys, but in most cases by lads of 14 and upwards, belonging to the fraternity of London thieves.

In the dark winter evenings we may sometimes see groups of these ragged boys, assembled around the windows of a small grocery-shop, looking greedily at the almond-rock, lollipops, sugar-candy, barley-sugar, brandy-balls, pies, and tarts, displayed in all their tempting sweetness and in all their gaudy tints. They insert the point of a knife or other sharp instrument into the corner or side of the pane, then give it a wrench, when the pane cracks in a semicircular starlike form around the part punctured. Should a piece of glass large enough to admit the hand not be sufficiently loosened, they apply the sharp instrument at another place in the pane, when the new cracks communicate with the rents already made; on applying a sticking-plaster to the pane, the piece readily adheres to it, and is abstracted. The thief inserts his hand through an opening in the window, seizes a handful of sweets or other goods, and runs away, perhaps followed by the shopman in full chase. These thieves are termed star-glazers.

Such petty robberies are often committed by elder lads at the windows of tobacconists, when cigars and pipes are frequently stolen.

They cut the pane in the manner described, and sometimes get a younger boy to commit the theft, while they get the chief share of the plunder, without having exposed themselves to the danger of being arrested stealing the property.

A Visit to the Rookery of St Giles and its Neighbourhood

In company with a police officer we proceeded to the Seven Dials,* one of the most remarkable localities in London, inhabited by bird-fanciers, keepers of stores of old clothes and old shoes, costermongers,

BOYS EXERCISING AT TOTHILL FIELDS PRISON.

patterers, and a motley assemblage of others, chiefly of the lower classes. As we stood at one of the angles in the centre of the Dials we saw three young men—burglars—loitering at an opposite corner of an adjoining dial. One of them had a gentlemanly appearance, and was dressed in superfine black cloth and beaver hat. The other two were attired as mechanics or tradesmen. One of them had recently returned from penal servitude, and another had undergone a long imprisonment.

Leaving the Seven Dials and its dingy neighbourhoood, we went to Oxford Street, one of the first commercial streets in London, and one of the finest in the world. It reminded us a good deal of the celebrated Broadway, New York, although the buildings of the latter are in some places more costly and splendid, and some of the shops more magnificent. Oxford Street is one of the main streets of London, and is ever resounding with the din of vehicles, carts, cabs, hansoms, broughams, and omnibuses driving along. Many of the shops are spacious and crowded with costly goods, and the large windows of plate-glass, set in massive brass frames, are gaily furnished with their various articles of merchandise.

On the opposite side of the street we observed a jolly, comfortable-looking, elderly man, like a farmer in appearance, not at all like a London sharper.* He was standing looking along the street as though he were waiting for some one. He was a magsman (a skittle-sharp), and no doubt other members of the gang were hovering near. He appeared to be as cunning as an old fox in his movements, admirably fitted to entrap the unwary.

A little farther along the street we saw a fashionably-dressed man coming towards us, arm in arm with his companion, among the throng of people. They were in the prime of life, and had a respectable, and even opulent appearance. One of them was good-humoured and social, as though he were on good terms with himself and society in general; the other was more callous and reserved, and more suspicious in his aspect. Both were bedecked with glittering watch chains and gold rings. They passed by a few paces, when the more social of the two, looking over his shoulder, met our eye directed towards him, turned back and accosted us, and was even so generous as to invite us into a gin-palace near by, which we courteously declined. The two magsmen (card-sharpers) strutted off, like fine gentlemen, along the street on the outlook for their victims.

Here we saw another young man, a burglar, pass by. He had an engaging appearance, and was very tasteful in his dress, very unlike the rough burglars we met at Whitechapel, the Borough, and Lambeth.

Leaving Oxford Street we went along Holborn to Chancery Lane, chiefly frequented by barristers and attorneys, and entered Fleet Street, one of the main arteries of the metropolis, reminding us of London in the olden feudal times, when the streets were crowded together in dense masses, flanked with innumerable dingy alleys, courts, and by-streets, like a great rabbit-warren. Fleet Street, though a narrow, business street, with its traffic often choked with vehicles, is interesting from its antique, historical, and literary associations. Elbowing our way through the throng of people, we pass through one of the gloomy arches of Temple Bar, and issue into the Strand, where we saw two pickpockets, young, tall, gentlemanly men, cross the street from St Clement's Church and enter a restaurant. They were attired in a suit of superfine black cloth, cut in fashionable style. They entered an elegant dining-room, and probably sat down to costly viands and wines.

Leaving the Strand, we went up St Martin's Lane, a narrow street leading from the Strand to the Seven Dials. We here saw a young man, an expert burglar, of about twenty-four years of age and dark complexion, standing at the corner of the street. He was well dressed, in a dark cloth suit, with a billicock* hat. One of his comrades was taken from his side about three weeks ago on a charge of burglary.

Entering a beershop in the neighbourhood of St Giles, close by the Seven Dials, we saw a band of coiners and ringers of changes.* One of them, a genteel-looking, slim youth is a notorious coiner, and has been convicted. He was sitting quietly by the door over a glass of beer, with his companion by his side. One of them is a moulder; another was sentenced to ten years' penal servitude for coining and selling base coin. A modest-looking young man, one of the gang, was seated by the bar, also respectably dressed. He is generally supposed to be a subordinate connected with this coining band, looking out, while they are coining, that no officers of justice are near, and carrying the bag of base money* for them when they go out to sell it to base wretches in small quantities at low prices. Five shillings' worth of base money is generally sold for tenpence. '*Ringing the changes*' is effected in this way:—A person offers a good sovereign to a shopkeeper to be changed. The gold piece is chinked on the counter, or otherwise tested, and is proved to be good. The man hastily asks back and gets the sovereign, and pretends that he has some silver, so that he does not require to change it. On feeling his pocket he finds he does not have it, and returns a base piece of money resembling it, instead of the genuine gold piece.

We returned to Bow Street, and saw three young pickpockets proceeding along in company, like three well-dressed costermongers, in dark cloth frock-coats and caps.

Being desirous of having a more thorough knowledge of the people residing in the rookery of St Giles, we visited it with Mr Hunt, inspector of police. We first went to a lodging-house in George Street, Oxford Street, called the Hampshire-Hog Yard. Most of the lodgers were then out. On visiting a room in the garret we saw a man, in mature years, making artificial flowers; he appeared to be very ingenious, and made several roses before us with marvellous rapidity. He had suspended along the ceiling bundles of dyed grasses of various hues, crimson, yellow, green, brown, and other colours to furnish cases of stuffed birds. He was a very intelligent man and a natural genius. He told us strong drink had brought him to this humble position in the garret, and that he once had the opportunity of making a fortune in the service of a nobleman. We felt, as we looked on his countenance, and listened to his conversation, he was capable of moving in a higher sphere of life. Yet he was wonderfully contented with his humble lot.

We visited Dyott House, George Street, the ancient manor-house of St Giles-in-the-fields, now fitted up as a lodging-house for single men. The kitchen, an apartment about fifteen feet square, is surrounded with massive and tasteful panelling in the olden style. A large fire blazing in the grate—with two boilers on each side—was kept burning night and day to supply the lodgers with hot water for their tea and coffee. Some rashers of bacon were suspended before the fire, with a plate underneath. There was a gas-light in the centre of the apartment, and a dial on the back wall. The kitchen was furnished with two long deal tables and a dresser, with forms to serve as seats. There were about fifteen labouring men present, most of them busy at supper on fish, and bread, and tea. They were a very mixed company, such as we would expect at a London lodging-house, men working in cab-yards assisting cabmen, some distributing bills in the streets, one man carrying advertizing boards, and others jobbing at anything they can find to do in the neighbourhood. This house was clean and comfortable, and had the appearance of being truly a comfortable poor man's home. It was cheerful to look around us and to see the social air of the inmates. One man sat with his coat off, enjoying the warmth of the kitchen; a boy was at his tea, cutting up dried fish and discussing his bread and butter. A young man of about nineteen sat at the back of the apartment, with a very sinister countenance, very unlike the others. There was something about him that indicated a troubled mind. We also observed a number of elderly men among the party, some in jackets, and others in velvet coats, with an honest look about them.

When the house was a brothel, about fifteen years ago, an unfortunate prostitute, named Mary Brothers, was murdered in this kitchen by a man named Connell, who was afterwards executed at Newgate for the deed. He had carnal connexion with this woman some time before, and he suspected that she had communicated to him the venereal disease with which he was afflicted. In revenge he took her life, having purchased a knife at a neighbouring cutler's shop.

We were introduced to the landlady, a very stout woman, who came up to meet us, candle in hand, as we stood on the staircase. Here we saw the profile of the ancient proprietor of the house, carved over the paneling, set, as it were, in an oval frame. In another part of the staircase we saw a similar frame, but the profile had been removed or destroyed. Over the window that overlooks the staircase there are three figures, possibly likenesses of his daughters; such is the tradition. The balustrade along the staircase is very massive and tastefully carved and ornamented. The bed-rooms were also clean and comfortable.

The beds are furnished with a bed-cover and flock* bed, with sufficient warm and clean bedding, for the low charge of *2s.* a week, or *4d.* a night. The first proprietor of the house is said to have been a magistrate of the city, and a knight or baronet.

Leaving George Street we passed on to Church Lane, a by-street in the rear of New Oxford Street, containing twenty-eight houses. It was dark as we passed along. We saw the street lamps lighted in Oxford Street, and the shop-windows brilliantly illumined, while the thunder of vehicles in the street broke on our ear, rolling in perpetual stream. Here a very curious scene presented itself to our view. From the windows of the three-storied houses in Church Lane were suspended wooden rods with clothes to dry across the narrow street,—cotton gowns, sheets, trousers, drawers, and vests, some ragged and patched, and others old and faded, giving a more picturesque aspect to the scene, which was enhanced by the dim lights in the windows, and the groups of the lower orders of all ages assembled below, clustered around the doorways, and in front of the houses, or indulging in merriment in the street. Altogether the appearance of the inhabitants was much more clean and orderly than might be expected in such a low locality. Many women of the lower orders, chiefly of the Irish cockneys, were seated, crouching with their knees almost touching their chin, beside the open windows. Some men were smoking their pipes as they stood leaning against the walls of their houses, whom from their appearance we took to be evidently out-door labourers. Another labouring man was seated on the sill of his window, in corduroy trousers, light-gray coat and cap, with an honest look of good-humour and industry. Numbers of young women, the wives of costermongers, sat in front of their houses in the manner we have described, clad in cotton gowns, with a general aspect of personal cleanliness and contentment. At the corners of the streets, and at many of the doorways, were groups of young costermongers, who had finished their hard day's work, and were contentedly chatting and smoking. They generally stood with their hands in their breeches pockets. Most of these people are Irish, or the children of Irish parents. The darkness of the street was lighted up by the street lamps as well as by the lights in the windows of two chandlers' shops and one public-house. At one of the chandlers' shops the proprietor was standing by his door with folded arms as he looked good-humouredly on his neighbours around his shop-door. We also saw some of the young Arabs bareheaded and barefooted, with their little hands in their pockets, or squatted on the street, having the usual restless, artful look peculiar to their tribe.

Here a house was pointed out to us, No. 21, which was formerly let at a rent of 25*l.* per annum to a publican that resided in the neighbourhood. He let the same in rooms for 90*l.* a year, and these again receive from parties residing in them upwards of 120*l.* The house is still let in rooms, but they are occupied, like all others in the neighbourhood, by one family only.

At one house as we passed along we saw a woman selling potatoes, at the window, to persons in the street. On looking into the interior we saw a cheerful fire burning in the grate and some women sitting around it. We also observed several bushel baskets and sacks placed round the room, filled with potatoes, of which they sell a large quantity.

In Church Lane we found two lodging-houses, the kitchens of which are entered from the street by a descent of a few steps leading underground to the basement. Here we found numbers of people clustered together around several tables, some reading the newspapers, others supping on fish, bread, tea, and potatoes, and some lying half asleep on the tables in all imaginable positions. These, we were told, had just returned from hopping* in Kent, had walked long distances, and were fatigued.

On entering some of these kitchens, the ceiling being very low, we found a large fire burning in the grate, and a general air of comfort, cleanliness, and order. Such scenes as these were very homely and picturesque, and reminded us very forcibly of localities of London in the olden time. In some of them the inmates were only half dressed, and yet appeared to be very comfortable from the warmth of the apartment. Here we saw a number of the poorest imbeciles we had noticed in the course of our rambles through the great metropolis. Many of them were middle-aged men, others more elderly, very shabbily dressed, and some half naked. There was little manliness left in the poor wretches as they squatted drearily on the benches. The inspector told us they were chiefly vagrants, and were sunk in profound ignorance and debasement, from which they were utterly unable to rise.

The next kitchen of this description we entered was occupied by females. It was about fifteen feet square, and belongs to a house with ten rooms, part of which is occupied as a low lodging-house. Here we found five women seated around a table, most of them young, but one more advanced in life. Some of them were good-looking, as though they had been respectable servants. They were busy at their tea, bread, and butcher's meat. On the table stood a candle on a small candlestick. They sat in curious positions round the table, some of them with an ample crinoline. One sat by the fire with her gown drawn over her knees, displaying her white petticoat. As we stood beside them they burst out in a titter which they could not suppress. On looking round we observed a plate-rack at the back of the kitchen, and, as usual in these lodging-houses, a glorious fire burning brightly in the grate. An old chest of drawers, surmounted with shelves, stood against the wall. The girls were all prostitutes and thieves, but had no appearance of shame. They were apparently very merry. The old woman sat very thoughtful, looking observant on, and no doubt wondering what errand could have brought us into the house.

We then entered another dwelling-house. On looking down the stairs we saw a company of young women, from seventeen to twenty-five years of age. A rope was hung over the fireplace, with stockings and shirts suspended over it, and clothes were drying on a screen. A young woman, with her hair netted and ornamented, sat beside the fire with a green jacket and striped petticoat with crinoline. Another good-looking young woman sat by the table dressed in a cotton gown and striped apron, with coffeepot in hand, and tea-cups before her. Some pleasant-looking girls sat by the table with their chins leaning on their hands, smiling cheerfully, looking at us with curiosity. Another coarser featured dame lolled by the end of the table with her gown drawn over her head, smirking in our countenance; and one sat by, her shawl drawn over her head. Another apparently modest girl sat by cutting her nails with a knife. On the walls around the apartment were suspended a goodly assortment of bonnets, cloaks, gowns, and petticoats.

Meantime an elderly little man came in with a cap on his head and a long staff in his hand, and stood looking on with curiosity. On the table lay a pack of cards beside the bowls, cups, and other crockery-ware. Some of the girls appeared as if they had lately been servants in respectable situations, and one was like a quiet genteel shop girl. They were all prostitutes, and most of them prowl about at night to plunder drunken men. As we looked on the more interesting girls, especially two of them, we saw the sad consequences of one wrong step, which may launch the young and thoughtless into a criminal career, and drive them into the dismal companionship of the most lewd and debased.

We then went to Short's Gardens, and entered a house there. On the basement underground we saw a company of men, women, and children of various ages, seated around the tables, and by the fire. The men and women had mostly been engaged in hopping, and appeared to be healthy, industrious, and orderly. Until lately thieves used to lodge in these premises.

As we entered Queen Street we saw three thieves, lads of about fourteen years of age, standing in the middle of the street as if on the outlook for booty. They were dressed in black frock-coats, corduroy, and fustian trousers, and black caps. Passing along Queen Street, which is one of the wings of the Dials, we went up to the central space between the Seven Dials. Here a very lively scene presented itself to our view; clusters of labouring men, and a few men of doubtful character, in dark shabby dress, loitered by the corners of the surrounding streets. We also saw groups of elderly women standing at some of the angles, most of them ragged and drunken, their very countenances the pictures of abject misery. The numerous public-houses in the locality were driving a busy traffic, and were thronged with motley groups of people of various grades, from the respectable merchant and tradesman to the thief and the beggar.

Bands of boys and girls were gamboling in the street in wild frolic, tumbling on their head with their heels in the air, and shouting in merriment, while the policeman was quietly looking on in good humour.

Around the centre of the Dials were bakers' shops with large illuminated fronts, the shelves being covered with loaves, and the baker busy attending to his customers. In the window was a large printed notice advertising the 'best wheaten bread at 6*d.*' a loaf. A druggist's shop was invitingly adorned with beautiful green and purple jars, but no customers entered during the time of our stay.

At the corner of an opposite dial was an old clothes store, with a large assortment of second-hand garments, chiefly for men, of various kinds, qualities, and styles, suspended around the front of the shop. There were also provision shops, which were well attended with customers. The whole neighbourhood presented an appearance of bustle and animation, and omnibuses and other vehicles were passing along in a perpetual stream.

Pickpockets and Shoplifters

In tracing the pickpocket from the beginning of his career, in most cases we must turn our attention to the little ragged boys living by a felon's hearth, or herding with other young criminals in a low lodging-house, or dwelling in the cold and comfortless home of drunken and improvident parents. The great majority of the pickpockets of the metropolis, with few exceptions, have sprung from the dregs of society—from the hearths and homes of London thieves—so that they have no reason to be proud of their lineage. Fifteen or twenty years ago many of those accomplished pickpockets, dressed in the highest style of fashion, and glittering in gold chains, studs, and rings, who walk around the Bank of England and along Cheapside, and our busy thoroughfares, were poor ragged boys walking barefooted among the dark and dirty slums and alleys of Westminster and the Seven Dials, or loitering among the thieves' dens of the Borough and Whitechapel.

Step by step they have emerged from their rags and squalor to a higher position of physical comfort, and have risen to higher dexterity and accomplishment in their base and ignoble profession.

The chief sources whence our pickpockets spring are from the low lodging-houses—from those dwellings in low neighbourhoods, where their parents are thieves, and where improvident and drunken people neglect their children, such as Whitechapel, Shoreditch, Spitalfields, New Cut, Lambeth, the Borough, Clerkenwell, Drury Lane, and other localities. Many of them are the children of Irish parents, costermongers, bricklayers' labourers, and others. They often begin to steal at six or seven years of age, sometimes as early as five years, and commit petty sneaking thefts, as well as pick handkerchiefs from gentlemen's pockets. Many of these ragged urchins are taught to steal by their companions, others are taught by trainers of thieves, young men and women, and some middle-aged convicted thieves. They are learned to be expert in this way. A coat is suspended on the wall with a bell attached to it, and the boy attempts to take the handkerchief from the pocket without the bell ringing. Until he is able to do this with proficiency he is not considered well trained. Another way in which they are trained is this: The trainer—if a man—walks up and down the room with a handkerchief in the tail of his coat, and the ragged boys amuse themselves abstracting it until they learn to do it in an adroit manner.* We could point our finger to three of these execrable wretches, who are well known to train schools of juvenile thieves—one of them, a young man at Whitechapel; another, a young woman at Clerkenwell; and a third, a middle-aged man residing about Lambeth Walk. These base wretches buy the stolen handkerchiefs from the boys at a paltry sum. We have also heard of some being taught to pick pockets by means of an effigy; but this is not so well authenticated.

Great numbers of these ragged pickpockets may be seen loitering about our principal streets, ready to steal from a stall or shop-door when they find an opportunity. During the day they generally pick pockets two or three in a little band, but at dusk a single one can sometimes do it with success. They not only steal handkerchiefs of various kinds, but also pocket-books from the tails of gentlemen's coats. We may see them occasionally engaged at this work on Blackfriars Bridge and London Bridge, also along Bishopsgate, Shoreditch, Whitechapel, Drury Lane, and similar localities. They may be seen at any hour of the day, but chiefly from 10 to 2 o'clock. They are generally actively on the look-out on Saturday evening in the shopping streets where the labouring people get their provisions in for the Sunday. At this early stage the boys occasionally pick pockets, and go about cadging and sneaking (begging and committing petty felonies).

The next stage commences—we shall say—about fourteen years of age, when the stripling lays aside his rags, and dresses in a more decent way, though rather shabby. Perhaps in a dark or gray frock-coat, dark or dirty tweed trousers, and a cap with peak, and shoes. At this time many of them go to low neighbourhoods, or to those quieter localities where the labouring people reside, and pick the pockets of the wives and daughters of this class of persons; others steal from gentlemen passing along thoroughfares, while a few adroit lads are employed by men to steal from ladies' pockets in the fashionable streets of the metropolis.

These young thieves seldom commit their depredations in the localities where they are known, but prowl in different parts of the metropolis. They are of a wandering character, changing from one district to another, and living in different lodging-houses—often leaving their parents' houses as early as ten years of age. Sometimes they are driven by drunken loafing parents to steal, though in most cases they leave their comfortless homes and live in lodging-houses.

When they have booty, they generally bring it to some person to dispose of, as suspicion would be aroused if they went to sell or pawn it themselves. In some cases they give it to the trainer of thieves, or they take it to some low receiving house, where wretches encourage them in stealing; sometimes to low coffee-houses, low hairdressers or tailors, who act as middlemen to dispose of the property, generally giving them but a small part of the value.

In the event of their rambling to a distant part of London, they sometimes arrange to get one of their number to convey the stolen goods to these parties. At other times they dispose of them to low wretches connected with the lodging-houses, or other persons in disreputable neighbourhoods.

At this time many of them cohabit with girls in low lodging-houses; many of whom are older than themselves, and generally of the felon class.

These lads frequently steal at the 'tail' of gentlemen's coats, and learn the other modes of picking pockets.

Stealing the handkerchief from the 'tail' of a gentleman's coat in the street is generally effected in this way, Three or four usually go together. They see an old gentleman passing by. One remains behind, while the other two follow up close beside him, but a little behind. The one walking by himself behind is the looker out to see if there are any police or detectives near, or if any one passing by or hovering around is taking notice of them. One of the two walking close by the gentleman adroitly picks his pocket, and coils the handkerchief up in his hand so as not to be seen, while the other brings his body close to him, so as not to let his arm be seen by any passer by.

If the party feel him taking the handkerchief from his pocket, the thief passes it quickly to his companion, who runs off with it. The looker-out walks quietly on as if nothing had occurred, or sometimes walks up to the gentleman and asks him what is the matter, or pretends to tell him in what direction the thief has run, pointing him to a very different direction from the one he has taken.

They not only abstract handkerchiefs but also pocket-books from the tail of gentlemen's coats, or any other article they can lay their fingers on.

This is the common way in which the coat-pocket is picked when the person is proceeding along the street. Sometimes it happens that one thief will work by himself, but this is very seldom. In the case of a person standing, the coat-tail pocket is picked much in the same manner.

These boys in most cases confine themselves to stealing from the coat-pocket on the streets, but in the event of a crowd on any occasion, they are so bold as to steal watches from the vest-pocket. This is done in a different style, and generally in the company of two or three in this manner: One of them folds his arms across his breast in such a way that his right hand is covered with his left arm. This enables him to use his hand in an unobserved way, so that he is thereby able to abstract the watch from the vest-pocket of the gentleman standing by his side.

A police-officer informed us, that when at Cremorne about a fortnight ago, a large concourse of people was assembled to see the female acrobat, termed the 'Female Blondin',* cross the Thames on a rope suspended over the river, he observed two young men of about twenty-four years of age, and about the middle height, respectably dressed, whom he suspected to be pickpockets. They went up to a smart gentlemanly man standing at the riverside looking eagerly at the Female Blondin, then walking the rope over the middle of the river. As his attention was thus absorbed, the detective saw these two men go up to him. One of them placed himself close on the right hand side of him, and putting his right arm under his left, thus covered his right hand, and took the watch gently from the pocket of the gentleman's vest. The thief made two attempts to break the ring attached to the watch, termed the 'bowl' or swivel, with his finger and thumb.

After two ineffective endeavours he bent it completely round, and yet it would not break. He then left the watch hanging down in front of the vest, the gentleman meanwhile being unaware of the attempted felony. The detective officer took both the thieves into custody. They were brought before the Westminster police-court and sentenced each to three months' imprisonment for an attempt to steal from the person.

The same officer informed us that about a month or six weeks ago, in the same place, on a similar occasion, he observed three persons, a man, a boy, and a woman, whom he suspected to be picking pockets. The man was about twenty-eight years of age, rather under the middle size. The woman hovered by his side. She was very good-looking, about twenty-four years of age, dressed in a green coloured gown, Paisley shawl, and straw bonnet trimmed with red velvet and red flowers. The man was dressed in a black frock-coat, brown trousers, and black hat. The boy, who happened to be his brother, was about fourteen years old, dressed in a brown shooting-coat, corduroy trousers, and black cap with peak. The boy had an engaging countenance, with sharp features and smart manner. The officer observed the man touch the boy on the shoulder and point him towards an old lady. The boy placed himself on her right side, and the man and woman kept behind. The former put his left hand into the pocket of the lady's gown and drew nothing from it, then left her and went about two yards farther; there he placed himself by other two ladies, tried both their pockets and left them again. He followed another lady and succeeded in picking her pocket of a small sum of money and a handkerchief. The officer took them all to the police station with the assistance of another detective officer, when they were committed for trial at Clerkenwell sessions. The man was sentenced to ten years' penal servitude, the boy to two months' hard labour, and three months in a reformatory, and the woman was sentenced to two years' imprisonment, with hard labour, in the House of Correction at Westminster.

It appeared, in the course of the evidence at the trial, that this man had previously been four years in penal servitude, and since his return had decoyed his little brother from a situation he held, for the purpose of training him to pick pockets, having induced him to rob his employer before leaving service.

The *scarf pin* is generally taken from the breast in this way. The thief generally has a handkerchief in his hand, pretending to wipe his nose, as he walks along the street. He then places his right hand across the breast of the person he intends to rob, bringing his left hand stealthily under his arm. This conceals his movements from the eyes of the person. With the latter hand he snatches out the pin from the scarf. It is sometimes done with the right hand, at other times with the left, according to the position of the person, and is generally done in the company of one or more. The person robbed is rarely aware of the theft. Should he be aware, or should any one passing by have observed the movement, the pin got from the scarf is suddenly passed into the hands of the other parties, when all of them suddenly make off in different directions soon to meet again in some neighbouring locality.

At other times the thief drives the person with a push, in the street, bringing his hands to his breast as if he had stumbled against him, at the same time adroitly laying hold of the pin. This is done in such a way that the person is seldom aware of the robbery until he afterwards finds out the loss of the article.

The *trousers pocket* is seldom picked on the public street, as this is an operation of considerable difficulty and danger. It is not easy to slip the hand into the trousers pocket without being felt by the person attempted to be robbed. This is generally done in crowds where people are squeezed together, when they contrive to do it in this way: They cut up the trousers with a knife or other sharp instrument, lay open the pocket, and adroitly rifle the money from it; or they insert the fingers or hand into it in a push, often without being observed, while the person's attention is distracted, possibly by some of the accomplices or stalls. They often occasion a disturbance in crowds, and create a quarrel with people near them, or have sham fights with each other, or set violently on the person they intend to rob. Many rough expedients are occasionally had recourse to, to effect this object.

Sometimes the pocket is picked in a crowd by means of laying hold of the party by the middle as if they had jostled against him, or by pressing on his back from behind, while the fingers or hand are inserted into the pocket of his trousers to snatch any valuables, money or otherwise, contained therein.

This mode of stealing is sometimes done by one person, at other times by the aid of accomplices. It is most commonly done in the manner now described.

By dint of long experience and natural skill, some attain great perfection in this difficult job, and accomplish their object in the most clever and effective manner. They are so nimble and accomplished that they will accost a gentleman in the street, and while speaking to him, and looking him in the face, will quietly insert their hand into his vest pocket and steal his watch.

Statement of a Young Pickpocket

He wore a ragged, dirty, and very thin great coat, of some dark jean or linen, under which was another thin coat, so arranged that what appeared rents—and, indeed, were rents, but designedly made—in the outer garment, were slits through which the hand readily reached the pockets of the inner garment, and could there deposit any booty. He was a slim, agile lad, with a sharp but not vulgar expression, and small features. His hands were of singular delicacy and beauty. His fingers were very long, and no lady's could have been more taper. A burglar told me that with such a hand he ought to have made his fortune. He was worth 20*l.* a week, he said, as a '*wire*', that is, a picker of ladies' pockets. When engaged 'for a turn', as he told me he once was by an old pickpocket, the man looked minutely at his fingers, and approved of them highly. His hands, the boy said, were hardly serviceable to him when very cold. His feet were formed in the same symmetrical and beautiful mould as his hands. 'I am 15,' he said. 'My father was a potter, and I can't recollect my mother' (many of the thieves are orphans or motherless). 'My father has been dead about five years. I was then working at the pottery in High-street, Lambeth, earning about 4*s*. a week; in good weeks, 4*s*. 6*d*. I was in work eight months after my father died; but one day I broke three bottles by accident, and the foreman said "I shan't want you any more"; and I took that as meant for a discharge; but I found afterwards that he didn't so mean it. I had 2*s*. and a suit of clothes then, and tried for work at all the potteries; but I couldn't get any. It was about the time Smithfield fair was on. I went, but it was a very poor concern. I fell asleep in a pen in the afternoon, and had my shoes stolen off my feet. When I woke up, I began crying. A fellow named Gyp then came along (I knew his name afterwards), and he said, "What are you crying for?" and I told him, and he said, "Pull off your stockings, and come with me, and I'll show you where to sleep." So I did, and he took me to St Olave's workhouse, having first sold my stockings. I had never stolen anything until then. There I slept in the casual ward,* and Gyp slept there too. In the morning we started together for Smithfield, where he said he had a job to sweep the pens, but he couldn't sweep them without pulling off his coat, and it would look so queer if he hadn't a shirt—and he hadn't one. He promised to teach me how to make a living in the country if I would lend him mine, and I was persuaded—for I was an innocent lad then—and went up a gateway and stripped off my shirt and gave it to him, and soon after he went into a public-house to get half a pint of beer; he went in at one door and out at another, and I didn't see him for six months afterwards. That afternoon I went into Billingsgate market and met some boys, and one said, "Mate, how long have you been knocking about; where did you doss?" I didn't know what they meant, and when they'd told me they meant where did I sleep? I told them how I'd been served. And they said, "Oh! you must expect that, until you learn something," and they laughed. They all know'd Gyp; he was like the head of a Billingsgate gang once. I became a pal with these boys at Billingsgate, and we went about stealing fish and meat. Some boys have made 2*s*. in a morning, when fish is dear—those that had pluck and luck; they sold it at half-price. Billingsgate market is a good place to sell it; plenty of costermongers are there who will buy it, rather than of the salesmen. I soon grew as bad as the rest at this work. At first I sold it to other boys, who would get 3*d*. for what they bought at 1*d*. Now they can't do me. If I can get a thing cheap where I lodge, and have the money, and can sell it dear, that's the chance. I carried on this fish rig* for about two years, and went begging a little, too. I used to try a little thieving sometimes in Petticoat-lane. They say the "fliest" is easy to take in sometimes—that's the artfullest; but I could do no good there. At these two years' end, I was often as happy as could be; that is, when I had made money. Then I met B——, whom I had often heard of as an uncommon clever pickpocket; he could do it about as well as I can now, so as people won't feel it. Three of his mates were transported for stealing silver plate. He and I became pals, and started for the country with 1*d*. We went through Foot's Cray, and passed a farm where a man's buried at the top of a house; there's something about money while a man's above ground; I don't understand it, but it's something like that. A baker, about thirty miles from London, offended us about some bread; and B—— said "I'll serve him out." We watched him out, and B—— tried at his pocket, saying, "I'll show you how to do a handkerchief"; but the baker looked round, and B—— stopped; and just after that I flared it (whisked the handkerchief out); and that's the first I did. It brought 1*s*. 3*d*. We travelled across country, and got to Maidstone, and did two handkerchiefs. One I wore round my neck, and the other the lodging-housekeeper pawned for us for 1*s*. 6*d*. In Maidstone, next morning, I was nailed, and had three months of it. I didn't mind it so much then, but Maidstone's far worse now, I've heard. I have been in prison three times in Brixton, three times in the Old Horse (Bridewell), three times in the Compter, once in the Steel, and once in Maidstone—thirteen times in all, including twice I was remanded, and got off; but I don't reckon that prison. Every time I came out harder than I went in. I've had four floggings; it was bad enough—a flogging was—while it lasted; but when I got out I soon forgot it. At a week's end I never thought again about it. If I had been better treated I should have been a better lad. I could leave off thieving now as if I had never thieved, if I could live without,' [I am inclined to doubt this part of the statement.] 'I have carried on this sort of life until now. I didn't often make a very good thing of it. I saw Manning and his wife hung. Mrs Manning was dressed beautiful when she came up. She screeched when Jack Ketch* pulled the bolt away. She was harder than Manning, they all said; without her there would have been no murder. It was a great deal talked about, and Manning was pitied. It was a punishment to her to come on the scaffold and see Manning with the rope about his neck, if people takes it in the right light. I did 4*s*. 6*d*. at the hanging—two handkerchiefs, and a purse with 2*s*. in it—the best purse I ever had; but I've only done three or four purses. The reason is, because I've never been well dressed. If I went near a lady, she would say, "Tush, tush, you ragged fellow!" and would shrink away. But I would rather rob the rich than the poor; they miss it less. But 1*s*. honest goes further than 5*s*. stolen. Some call that only a saying, but it's true. All the money I got soon went—most of it a-gambling. Picking pockets, when any one comes to think on it, is the daringest thing that a boy can do. It didn't in the least frighten me to see Manning and Mrs Manning hanged. I never thought I should come to the gallows, and I never shall—I'm not high-tempered enough for that. The only thing that frightens me when I'm in prison is sleeping in a cell by myself—you do in the Old Horse and the Steel* —because I think things may appear. You can't imagine how one dreams when in trouble. I've often started up in a fright from a dream. I don't know what might appear. I've heard people talk about ghosts and that. Once, in the County, a tin had been left under a tap that went drip—drip—drip. And all in the ward were shocking frightened; and weren't we glad when we found out what it was! Boys tell stories about haunted castles, and cats that are devils; and that frightens one. At the fire in Monument-yard I did 5*s*. 7*d*.—3*s*. in silver and 2*s*. 3*d*. in handkerchiefs, and 4*d*. for three pairs of gloves. I sell my handkerchiefs in the Lane (Petticoat-lane). I carry on this trade still. Most times I've got in prison is when I've been desperate from hunger, and have said to B——, "Now I'll have money, nailed or not nailed." I can pick a woman's pocket as easy as a man's, though you wouldn't think it. If one's in prison for begging, one's laughed at. The others say, "Begging! Oh, you cadger!" So a boy is partly forced to steal for his character.'

Housebreakers and Burglars

Breaking into houses, *shops*, *and warehouses* is accomplished in various ways, such as picking the locks with skeleton keys; inserting a thin instrument between the sashes and undoing the catch of the windows, which enables the thieves to lift up the under sash; getting over the walls at the back, and breaking open a door or window which is out of sight of the street, or other public place; lifting the cellar-flap or area-grating; getting into an empty house next door, or a few doors off, and passing from the roof to that of the house they intend to rob; entering by an attic-window, or trap-door, and if there are neither window nor door on the roof, taking off some of the tiles and entering the house. Sometimes the thieves will make an entry through a brick wall in an adjoining building, or climb the waterspout to get in at the window. These are the general modes of breaking into houses.

Sometimes when doors are fastened with a padlock outside, and no other lock on the door, thieves will get a padlock as near like it as possible. They will then break off the proper lock, one of them will enter the house, and an accomplice will put on a lock as like it as possible to deceive the police, while one or more inside will meantime pack up the goods. Sometimes a well-dressed thief waylays a servant-girl going out on errands in the evening, professes to fall in love with her, and gets into her confidence, till she perhaps admits him into the house when her master and mistress are out. Having confidence in him she shows him over the house, and informs him where the valuables are kept. If the house is well secured, so that there will be difficulty of breaking in by night, he manages to get an accomplice inside to secrete himself till the family has gone to bed, when he admits one or more of his companions into the house. They pack up all they can lay hold of, such as valuables and jewels. On such occasions there is generally one on the outlook outside, who follows the policeman unobserved, and gives the signal to the parties inside when it is safe to come out.

In warehouses one of the thieves frequently slips in at closing-time, when only a few servants are left behind, and are busy shutting up. He secretes himself behind goods in the warehouse, and when all have retired for the night, and the door locked, he opens it and lets in his companions to pack up the booty. Should it consist of heavy goods, they generally have a cart to take it away. They are sometimes afraid to engage a cabman unless they can get him to connive at the theft, and besides, the number of the cab can be taken. They get the goods away in the following manner. If consisting of bulky articles, such as cloth, silks, &c., they fill large bags, similar to sacks, and get as much as they think the cart can conveniently hold, placed near the door. When the policeman has passed by on his round, the watch stationed outside gives the signal; the door is opened, the cart drives up, and four or five sacks are handed into it by two thieves in about a minute, when the vehicle retires. It is loaded and goes off sooner than a gentleman would take his carpet-bag and portmanteau into a cab when going to a railway-station. The cart proceeds with the driver in one way, while the thieves walk off in a different direction. They close the outer door after them when they enter a shop or warehouse, most of which have spring locks. When the policeman comes round on his beat he finds the door shut, and there is nothing to excite his suspicion. The cart is never seen loitering at the door above a couple of minutes, and does not make its appearance on the spot till the robbery is about to be committed, when the signal is given.

Lighter goods, such as jewellery, or goods of less bulk, are generally taken away in carpet bags in time to catch an early train, often about five or six o'clock, and the robbers being respectably-dressed, and in a neighbourhood where they are not known, pass on in most cases unmolested. Sometimes they pack up the goods in hampers, as if they were going off to some railway-station. When there is no one sleeping on the premises, and when they have come to learn where the party lives who keeps the keys, they watch him home at night after locking up, and set a watch on his house, that their confederates may not be disturbed when rifling the premises. If they are to remove the goods in the morning they do it about an hour before the warehouse is usually opened, so that the neighbours are taken off their guard, supposing the premises are opened a little earlier than usual in consequence of being busy. Sometimes they stand and see the goods taken out, and pay no particular attention to it. In the event of the person who keeps the keys coming up sooner than usual, the man keeping watch hastens forward and gives the signal to his companions, if they have not left the warehouse.

It often happens when they have got an entry into a house, they have to break their way into the apartments in the interior to reach the desired booty, such as wrenching open an inner door with a small crowbar they term a jemmy, cutting a panel out of a door, or a partition, with a cutter similar to a centrebit, which works with two or three knives; this is done very adroitly in a short space of time, and with very little noise. At other times, when on the floor above, they cut through one or more boards in the flooring, and frequently cut panes of glass in the windows with a knife or awl.

They get information as to the property in warehouses from porters and others unwittingly by leading them into conversation regarding the goods on the premises, the silks they have got, &c., and find out the part of the premises where they are to be found. Sometimes they go in to inspect them on the pretence of looking at some articles of merchandise.

It occasionally happens servants are in league with thieves, and give them information as to the hour when to come, and the easiest way to break in. Sometimes servants basely admit the thieves into the premises to steal, and give them impressions of the keys, which enables them to make other keys to enter the house. Thieves sometimes take a blank key without wards, cover it with wax, work it in the keyhole against the wards of the lock, and by that means the impression is left in the wax. They then take it home and make a similar key. When looking into the lock they frequently strike a match on the doorway, and pretend to be lighting a pipe or cigar, which prevents passers by suspecting their object.

Burglaries in the working districts of the metropolis are effected in various ways—by one man mounting the shoulders of another and getting into a first-floor window, similar to acrobats, by climbing over walls leading to the rear of premises, cutting or breaking a pane of glass, and then unfastening the catch; or by pushing back the catch of the window with a sharp instrument, or by cutting a panel of a door with a sharp tool, such as an American 'auger'. Frequently they force the lock of the door with a jemmy. The lower class of burglars who have not proper tools sometimes use a screw-driver instead of a jemmy. In the forcing of the locks of drawers or boxes, in search of property, they use a small chisel with a fine edge, and occasionally an old knife.

There are frequently three persons employed in these burglaries—two to enter a house, and one to keep watch outside, to see that there is no person passing likely to detect. This man is generally termed a 'crow'. Sometimes a woman, called a 'canary', carries the tools, and watches outside.

If the burglars cannot enter by the back of the premises, they go to the first-floor window in front, where there are no shutters. It matters not whether it be public or not; they will enter in a couple of minutes the premises by cutting the glass and undoing the catch.

The dwelling-houses in the West-end have often been entered by the first-floor window; and servants have many times been wrongfully charged with these burglaries, and lost their places in consequence.

Burglars generally leave their haunts to plunder about twelve o'clock at midnight, often driving up in a cab to a short distance from the spot where the burglary is to be attempted; but they frequently do not enter the house till one or two in the morning. In general, they take some liquor, such as gin and brandy, to keep up their spirits, as they call it. The one who is to watch outside generally takes up his position first, and the others follow. This is arranged so that the persons who enter—generally two, sometimes three—should not be seen by the policeman or others near the house.

When the latter come up, and find their companion at his post, and see the coast clear, they instantly proceed to enter the house, in front or behind, by the door or windows. Expert burglars go separate, to avoid suspicion.

On entering the house, they go about the work very cautiously and quietly, taking off their shoes, some walking in their stockings, and others with India-rubber overalls. If disturbed they very seldom leave their shoes or boots behind them.

Their chief object is to get plate, jewellery, cash, and other valuables. The drawing-room is usually on the first-floor in front; sometimes the whole of the first-floor is a drawing-room. They often find valuables in the drawing-room. They search parlour, kitchen, and pantry, and even open the servant's workbox for her small savings.

When they cannot get enough jewellery and plate they carry off wearing apparel. They often take money in the drawing-room from writing-desks and ladies' work-boxes. Experienced burglars do not spare time and trouble to look well for their plunder.

This is the general course adopted on entering a dwelling-house. In entering a shop, if they can find sufficient money to satisfy them, they do not carry off bulky property, but if there is no money in the desk or tills they rifle the goods, if they are of value.

In West-end robberies there are often two good cracksmen, one to keep watch outside, while another is busy at his work of plunder within. The person outside has to be on the alert, as he has generally to keep watch over an experienced officer, and to let his companions know when it is safe for them to work or to come out.

When a catch is in the centre of the window it is opened with a knife. If there should be one on each side they will cut a pane of glass in less than fifteen seconds, and undo them. The burglars seldom think of carrying a diamond with them, but generally cut the glass with a knife, as the starglazers do.

The shutters behind the window frame are often cut with what the burglars term a cutter. It cuts with two knives, with a centrebit stock, and makes a hole sufficiently large to admit the burglar's arm.

When the shutters are opened there are often iron bars to guard the window. The burglars tie a piece of strong cord or rope about two of the bars, and insert a piece of wood about a foot in length between this rope, and twist the wood. The bar is thereby bent sufficient to allow them to enter, or it gives way in the socket. These bars are sometimes forced asunder by a small instrument called a jack, by which a worm worked by a small handle displaces them. The rope and stick are used when they have not a jack. The latter can be conveniently carried in the trousers pocket.

Woodwork, such as shutters, doors, and partitions, is often cut in late years with the cutter, instead of the jemmy, as the former is a more effective tool, and makes an opening more expeditiously. With this instrument a door or shutter can be pierced sufficiently large to admit the arm in a few minutes.

A brick wall requires more time. If there are no persons within hearing, an opening can be made sufficiently large for a man to pass through, in an hour. If there are people near the apartment, it requires to be more softly done, and frequently occupies two or three hours, even when done by an expert burglar. They generally pierce one brick with an auger, and displace it; after the first brick is out, they work with a jemmy, and take the mortar out, then pierce a brick on the other side of the wall.

Expert burglars are generally equipped with good tools. They have a jemmy, a cutter, a dozen of betties, better known as picklocks, a jack to remove iron bars, a dark lantern or a taper and some silent lights, and a life-preserver,* and sometimes have a cord or rope with them, which can be easily converted into a rope ladder. A knife is often used in place of a chisel for opening locks, drawers, or desks. They often carry masks on their face, so that they might not be identified. The dark lantern is very small, with oil and cotton wick, and sometimes only shows a light about the size of a shilling, so that the reflection is not seen on the street without. Burglars often use the jemmy in place of picklocks. When they go out with their tools, they usually carry them wrapped up with list, so that they can throw them away without making a noise, should a policeman stop them, or attempt to arrest them. These are easily carried in the coat pocket, as they are not bulky.

There are parties—sometimes old convicts—who lend tools out on hire.

When discovered by the inmates they are generally disposed to make their escape rather than to fight, and try to avoid violence unless hotly pursued. If driven to extremity, they are ready to use the life-preserver, jemmy, or other weapon.

Sometimes they carry a life-preserver of a peculiar style, consisting of a small ball attached to a piece of gut, that fastens round the wrist. With this instrument, easily carried in the palm of the hand, they can strike the persons who oppose them senseless, and severely injure them.

In going up and down stairs, they often creep up not in the centre but the side of the stair, to avoid being heard, as it is apt to creak beneath the footstep, and they generally take off their shoes to move more stealthily along.

If experienced burglars, they listen at the doors of the apartments, and know by the breathing in general if the inmates are sound asleep. They sometimes begin their operations by going up to the highest floor, and work their way down, carrying off the plunder. After having finished what they call their work, they await the signal from the 'watch' set outside. These signals are sometimes given by one or more coughs; some give a whistle, or sing a certain song, or tap on the door or shutter, or make a particular cry, understood between the parties.

Should the plunder be bulky, they will have a cart or a cab, or a costermonger's barrow, ready on a given signal to carry it away. They in general wait for the time when the police are changed, if the inmates are not getting up, sometimes coming out at the front door, but oftener at the back.

Some burglars, after they have secured valuable booty, do not attempt another burglary for a time. Others go out the very next night, and commit other depredations, as they are avaricious for money. Some of them lose it by keeping it loosely in the house, or placing it in the bank, when the women they cohabit with reap the benefit. These females often try to induce them to save money and place it in their name in the bank, so that if their paramour gets apprehended, they have the pleasure of spending his ill-gotten wealth.

Some cracksmen succeed occasionally in rifling large quantities of valuable property or money. In such instances they live luxuriously, and spend large sums on pleasure, women, wine, and gambling. Some of them keep their females in splendid style, and live in furnished apartments in quiet respectable streets. Others are afraid to keep women, as the latter are frequently the cause of their being brought to justice.

There are some old burglars at present, keeping cabs, omnibuses, and public houses, whose wealth has been secured chiefly from plunder they have rifled from premises with their own hands, or received from burglars since they have abandoned their midnight work. They had the self-command to abandon their criminal courses after a time, while the most of the others have been more shortsighted. Some of these persons, though abounding in wealth, receive stolen goods, and are ready to open their houses at any hour of the night.

The burglars in our day are not in general such desperate men as those in former times. They are better known to the police than formerly, and are kept under more strict surveillance. Many of the cracksmen have been repeatedly subjected to prison discipline, and have their spirits in a great measure subdued. The crime of our country is not so bold and open as in the days of the redoubtable men whose dark deeds are recorded in the Newgate Calendar. It has assumed more subtle forms, instead of bold swagger and defiance—and has more of the secret, restless, and deceitful character of our great arch-enemy.

Narrative of a Burglar

The following narrative was given us by an expert burglar and returned convict we met one evening in the West-end of the metropolis. For a considerable number of years he had been engaged in a long series of burglaries connected with several gangs of thieves, and had been so singularly cunning and adroit in his movements he had never been caught in the act of plunder; but was at last betrayed into the hands of the police by one of his confederates, who had quarrelled with him while indulging rather freely in liquor. He was often employed as a putter up of burglaries in various parts of the metropolis, and was generally an outsider on the watch while some of his pals were rifling the house. We visited him at his house in one of the gloomiest lanes in a very low neighbourhood, inhabited chiefly by thieves and prostitutes, and took down from his lips the following recital. In the first part of his autobiography he was very frank and candid, but as he proceeded became more slow and calculating in his disclosures. We hinted to him he was 'timid'. 'No,' he replied, 'I am not timid, but I am cautious, which you need not be surprised at.' He was then seated by the fire beside his paramour, a very clever woman, whose history is perhaps as wild and romantic as his own. He is a slim-made man, beneath the middle size, with a keen dark intelligent eye, and about thirty-six years of age. He is good-looking, and very smart in his movements, and was in the attire of a well-dressed mechanic.

'I was born in the city of London in the year 1825. My father was foreman to a coach and harness-maker in Oxford Street. My mother, before her marriage, was a milliner. They had eleven children, and I was the youngest but two. I had six brothers and four sisters. My father had a good salary coming in to support his family, and we lived in comfort and respectability up to his death. He died when I was only about eight years old. My mother was left with eleven children, with very scanty means. Having to support so large a family she soon after became reduced in circumstances. My eldest brother was subject to fits, and died at the age of twenty-four years. He occupied my father's place while he lived. My second brother went to work at the same shop, but got into idle and dissipated habits, and was thrown out of employment. He afterwards got a situation in a lacemaker's shop, and had to leave for misconduct. He then went to a druggist's, and had to leave for the same cause. After this he got a situation as potman to a public-house, which completed his ruin. He took every opportunity to lead his younger brothers astray instead of setting us a good example.

'My brother next to him in age did not follow his bad courses, but I was not so fortunate. I went to school at Mr Low's, Harp Alley, Farringdon Street, but I did not stay there long. At nine years of age I was sent out to work, to help to support myself. I went to work at cotton-winding, and only got 3*s*. a week. I sometimes worked all night, and had 9*d*. for it, in addition to my 3*s*., and often gained 3*s*. a week besides the six days' wages. I was very happy then to think I could earn so much money, being so young. At this time I was only nine years of age. My brother tried to tempt me to pilfer from my master, but he failed then. I afterwards got a better situation at a trunkmaker's in the City. There my mistress and young master took a liking to me.

I was earning 7*s*. a week, and was only ten years of age. At this time my brother succeeded in tempting me to rob my employers after I had been two months in their service. I carried off wearing apparel and silver plate to the value of several pounds, which my brother disposed of, while he only gave me a few halfpence. I was suspected to be the thief, and was discharged in consequence. I got another situation in a bookbinder's shop, and was not eleven years old then. My brother did not succeed for two or three months to get me to plunder my master, although he often tried to prevail on me to do so. My master had no plate to lose.

'I used to take out hoards of books; one night my brother met me coming from the binder's with a truck loaded with books, stopt me, and pretended to be very kind by giving me money to go and buy a pie at a pie-shop. When I came out I found the books were gone and the truck empty. My brother was standing at the door waiting me, but he had companions who meantime emptied the truck of the whole of the contents. I told him he must know who had taken them, but he told me he did not. He desired me to say to my master that a strange man had sent me to get a pie for him and one for myself, and when I came back the books and the man had both disappeared. He told me if I did not say this I would get myself into trouble and him too. I went and told my master the tale my brother had told me. He sent for a policeman, and tried to frighten me to tell the truth. I would not alter from what I had told him, though he tried very hard to get me to do so. He kept me till Saturday night and discharged me, but endeavoured in the meanwhile to get me to unfold the truth, so I was thrown out of employment again.

'I then went to work at the blacking trade, and had a kinder master than ever. My wages were 7*s*. a week. I then made up my mind that my brother should not tempt me to steal another time. I was in this situation a year and nine months before my brother succeeded in inducing me to commit another robbery. My master was very kind and generous to me, increased my wages from 7*s*. to 16*s*. a week as I was becoming of more service to him.

'We made the blacking with sugar-candy and other ingredients. I was the only lad introduced into the apartment where the blacking was made and the sugar-candy was kept. My brother tempted me to bring him a small quantity of sugar-candy at first. I did so, and he threatened to let my mother know if I did not fetch more. At first

I took home 7 lbs. of candy, and at last would carry off a larger quantity. I used to get a trifle of money from my brother for this. Being strongly attached to him, up to this time he had great influence over me.

'One day, after bringing him a quantity of sugar-candy, I watched him to see where he sold it. He went into a shop in the City where the person retailed sweets. After he came out of the shop I went in and asked the man in the shop if he would buy some from me, as I was the brother of the young man who had just called in, and had got him the sugar-candy. He told me he would buy as much as I liked to bring.

'I used to bring large quantities to him, generally in the evening, and carried it in a bag. The sugar-candy I should have mixed in the blacking I laid aside till I had an opportunity of carrying it to the receiver. My master continued to be very fond of me, and had strong confidence in me until I got a young lad into the shop beside me, who knew what I had been doing, and informed him of my conduct. He wanted to get me discharged, as he thought he would get my situation, which he did. He told my master I was plundering him; but my master would not believe him until he pointed out a low coffee-house where I used to go, which was frequented by bad characters. My master came into this den of infamy one evening when I was there, and persuaded me to come away with him, which I did. He told me he would forget all I was guilty of, if I would keep better company and behave myself properly in future. I conducted myself better for about a week, but I had got inveigled into bad company through my brother. These lads waited about my employer's premises for me at meal-times and at night. At last they prevailed on me again to go to the same coffee-house. The young lad I had got into the shop beside me soon found means to acquaint my master. He came to see me in the coffee-house again; but I had been prevailed on to drink that evening, and was the worse of intoxicating liquor, although I was not fourteen years of age. My master tried all manner of kind means to persuade me to leave that house, but I would not do so, and insulted him for his kindness.

'On the following morning he paid a visit to my mother's house while I was at breakfast. My mother and he tried to persuade me to go back and finish my week's work, but I was too proud, and would not go back. He then paid my mother my fortnight's wages, and said if I would attend church twice each week he would again take me back into his service. I never attended any church at all, for I had then got into bad habits, and cared no more about work.

'I lived at home with my mother for a short time, and she was very kind to me, and gave me great indulgence. She wished me to remain at home with her to assist in her business as a greengrocer, and used to allow me from 1*s.* to 1*s.* 3*d.* of pocket-money a day. My old companions still followed me about, and prevailed on me to go to the Victoria Theatre. On one of these occasions I was much struck with the play of Oliver Twist.* I also saw Jack Sheppard* performed there, and was much impressed with it.

'Soon after this I left my mother's house, and took lodgings at the coffee-house, where my master found me, and engaged in an open criminal career. About this time ladies generally carried reticules* on their arm. My companions were in the habit of following them and cutting the strings, and carrying them off. They sometimes contained a purse with money and other property. I occasionally engaged in these robberies for about three months. Sometimes I succeeded in getting a considerable sum of money; at other times only a few shillings.

'I was afterwards prevailed on to join another gang of thieves, expert shoplifters. They generally confined themselves to the stationers' shops, and carried off silver pencil-cases, silver and gold mounted scent-bottles, and other articles, and I was engaged for a month at this.

'Being well-dressed, I would go into a shop and price an article of jewellery, or such like valuable, and after getting it in my hand would dart out of the shop with it. I carried on this system occasionally, and was never apprehended, and became very venturesome in robbery.

'I was then about sixteen years of age. A young man came from sea of the name of Philip Scott, who had in former years been a playmate of mine. He requested me to go to one of the theatres with him, when Jack Sheppard was again performed. We were both remarkably pleased with the play, and soon after determined to try our hand at housebreaking.

'He knew of a place in the City where some plate could be got at. We went out one night with a screw-driver and a knife to plunder it. I assisted him in getting over a wall at the back of the house. He entered from a back-window by pushing the catch back with a knife. He had not been in above three quarters of an hour when he handed me a silver pot and cream-jug from the wall. I conveyed these to the coffee-shop in which we lodged, when we afterwards disposed of them. The young man was well acquainted with this house, as his father was often employed jobbing about it.

'After this I cohabited with a female, but my "pal" did not, although we lived in the same house.

'Soon after we committed another burglary in the south-side of the metropolis, by entering the kitchen window of a private house at the back. I watched while my comrade entered the house. He cut a pane of glass out, and drew the catch back. After gathering what plate he could find lying about, he went up-stairs and got some more plate. We sold this to a receiver in Clerkenwell for about 9*l.* 18*s.* From this house we also carried off some wearing apparel. Each of us took three shirts, two coats and an umbrella.

'Some time after this we made up our minds to try another burglary in the city. We secreted ourselves in a brewer's yard beside the house we intended to plunder, about eight o'clock in the evening, before it was shut up. We cut a panel out of a shutter in the dining-room window on the first floor, but were disturbed when attempting this robbery. I ran off and got away. My companion was not so fortunate; he was captured, and got several months' imprisonment.

'A week after I joined two other burglars. We resolved to attempt a burglary in a certain shop in the East-end of the metropolis. There happened to be a dog in the shop. As usual I kept watch outside, while the other two entered from the first-floor window, which had no shutters. So soon as they got in the dog barked. They cut the dog's throat with a knife, and began to plunder the shop of pencil cases, scent-bottles, postage-stamps, &c., and went up-stairs, and carried off pieces of plate. The inmates of the house slept in the upper part of the house. The property when brought to the receiver sold for about 42*l.*

'Another burglary was committed by us at a haberdasher's shop in the West-end. While I kept watch, the other two climbed to the top of a warehouse at the back of the shop, wrenched open the window on the roof, and having tied a rope to an iron bar, they lowered themselves down, broke open the desks and till, and got a considerable sum of money, nearly all in silver. They then went to the first-floor drawing-room window over the shop, and entered. The door of this room being locked, they cut out a panel, put their arm through and forced back the lock. They found only a small quantity of plate along with a handsome gold watch and chain. The few articles of plate sold for 38*s*., and the watch and chain for 7*l*. 15*s*.

'The thieves entered about one o'clock at midnight, and went out about a quarter past five in the morning.

'These are the only jobs I did with these two men, until my comrade came out of prison, when we commenced again. We committed burglaries in different parts of London, at silk-mercers,* stationers' shops, and dwelling-houses* —some of considerable value; in others the booty was small.

'In these burglaries numbers of other parties were engaged with us—some of them belonging to the Borough, others to St Giles's, Golden Lane, St Luke's, and other localities.

'In 1850 I took a part in a burglary in a shop in the south-side of the metropolis along with two other parties. One went inside, and the others were on the watch without. We got access to the shop by the back-yard of a neighbouring public-house, which is usually effected in this way. One person goes to the bar, and gets into conversation with the barmaid, while one or more of their "pals" takes a favourable opportunity of slipping back into the yard or court behind the house. This is often done about a quarter of an hour, or half an hour, before the house is shut up. The party who kept the barmaid in conversation, would go to the back of the house, and assist the other burglar who was to enter the house in getting over the wall. So soon as this is effected, his other "pal" comes out again. If the wall can be easily climbed, the party who enters lurks concealed in the water-closet, or some of the outhouses, till the time of effecting the burglary.

'The house intended to be entered is sometimes five or six houses away from this public-house, and sometimes the next house to it.

'When all is ready, the outside man gives the signal. The signal given from the front, such as a cough or otherwise, can be heard by his confederate behind the house. On hearing it the latter begins his work. In this instance the burglar entered the premises by cutting open the shutters of a window in the first floor to the back. He then cut a pane of glass, and removed the catch, and went down stairs into the shop, and took from a desk about 60*l*. in money, with several valuable snuff-boxes and other articles. He had to wait till the morning before he could get out. The police seemed to have a suspicion that all was not right, but he got out of the shop about the time when the police were changed.

'I was connected with another burglary, committed in the same year in the West-end in a linendraper's shop. It was entered from a public-house in the same manner as in the one described. The same person was engaged inside, while the others were stationed outside. The signal to begin work was given about one o'clock. He had first to remove an iron bar at the first floor landing window to the back, which he did with his jack. (The bars had been seen in the day-time, and we bought this instrument to remove them.) He removed the bar in ten minutes, cut a pane of glass, and removed the two catches. By this means he effected an entry into the house, and to his surprise found the drawing-room was left unlocked. He proceeded there, and got nearly a whole service of plate. After he had gathered the plate up, he made his way toward the shop, cutting through the door which intercepted him. He went to the desk and found 72*l.* in silver money, and 12*l.* in gold. He also packed up half a dozen of new shirts and half a dozen of silk handkerchiefs.

'He was ready to come out of the house, but a coffee-stall being opposite, and the policeman taking his coffee there, the outside man could not give him the signal for some time. To the great surprise of the burglar in the shop, he heard the servant coming down stairs, when he opened the door, and rushed suddenly out, while the policeman was on the kerb near by. He bade the policeman good morning as he passed along with two large bundles in his hands.

'He had not gone fifty yards round the corner of the street, before the servant appeared at the door and asked the policeman as to the person who had just come out. Along with other two constables he gave chase to the burglar, but, being an active, athletic man, he effected his escape.

'I was engaged with two others in another burglary in the West-end soon afterwards. Three persons were engaged in it: one to enter, and other two "pals" to keep watch. We got access to the house by a mews, and got on the top of a wall, when I gave the end of a rope to my companion to hold by while he slid down on the other side. The house was entered at the kitchen window by removing two narrow bars with the jack, and sliding back the catch. There was no booty to be found in the kitchen. On going up-stairs our "pal" got several pieces of plate, and other articles. On coming down into the shop, he got a quantity of receipt-stamps* with a few postage-stamps.

'The putter up of this robbery was a connection of the people of the house.

'I was connected with another burglary in the south-side of the metropolis. A man who frequented a public-house there put up a burglary in a stationer's shop. Two persons were engaged in it, and got access to the premises to be plundered from the public-house. He then climbed several walls, and got access to the shop by a fanlight from behind. Here we found a large sum of money in gold and silver, which had been deposited in a bureau, some plate, and other articles. His "pal" went to him at half past three, and gave him the signal. He came out soon after, and had only gone a short distance off when he heard a call for the police, and the rattle* of the policeman was sprung.

'After a desperate struggle with two constables, he was arrested and taken to the station, with the stolen property in his possession. He was tried and found guilty of committing the burglary, and for assaulting the constables by cutting and wounding them, and was sentenced to fourteen years' transportation, having been four times previously convicted.

'I have been engaged in many depredations from 1840 to 1851, many of which were "put up" by myself.

'In the year 1851 I was transported several years for burglary. I returned home on a ticket of leave* in 1854, and was sent back in the following year for harbouring an escaped convict. I returned home in 1858, at the expiry of my sentence, and since that time have abandoned my former criminal life.'

Swindlers

Swindling is carried on very extensively in the metropolis in different classes of society, from the young man who strolls into a coffeehouse in Shoreditch or Bishops-gate, and decamps without paying his night's lodging, to the fashionable rogue who attends the brilliant assemblies in the West-end. It occurs in private life and in the commercial world in different departments of business. Large quantities of goods are sent from the provinces to parties in London, who give orders and are entirely unknown to those who send them, and fictitious references are given, or references to confederates in town connected with them.

We select a few illustrations of various modes of swindling which prevail over the metropolis.

A young man calls at a coffeehouse, or hotel, or a private lodging, and represents that he is the son of a gentleman in good position, or that he is in possession of certain property, left him by his friends, or that he has a situation in the neighbourhood, and after a few days or weeks decamps without paying his bill, perhaps leaving behind him an empty carpet bag, or a trunk, containing a few articles of no value.

An ingenious case of swindling occurred in the City some time since. A fashionably attired young man occupied a small office in White Lion Court, Cornhill, London. It contained no furniture, except two chairs and a desk. He obtained a number of bracelets from different jewellers, and quantities of goods from different tradesmen to a considerable amount, under false pretences. He was apprehended and tried before the police court, and sentenced to twelve months' imprisonment with hard labour.

At the time of his arrest he had obtained possession of a handsome residence at Abbey Wood, Kent, which was evidently intended as a place of reference, where no doubt he purposed to carry on a profitable system of swindling.

Swindlers have many ingenious modes of obtaining goods, sometimes to a very considerable amount, from credulous tradesmen, who are too often ready to be duped by their unprincipled devices. For example, some of them of respectable or fashionable appearance may pretend they are about to be married, and wish to have their house furnished. They give their name and address, and to avoid suspicion may even arrange particulars as to the manner in which the money is to be paid. A case of this kind occurred in Grove Terrace, where a furniture-dealer was requested to call on a swindler by a person who pretended to be his servant, and received directions to send him various articles of furniture. The goods were accordingly sent to the house. On a subsequent day the servant called on him at his premises, with a well-dressed young lady, whom she introduced as the intended wife of her employer, and said they had called to select some more goods. They selected a variety of articles, and desired they should be added to the account. One day the tradesman called for payment, and was told the gentleman was then out of town, but would call on him as soon as he returned. Soon after he made another call at the house, which he found closed up, and that he had been heartlessly duped. The value of the goods amounted to 58*l*. 18*s*. 4*d*.

Swindling is occasionally carried on in the West-end in a bold and brilliant style by persons of fashionable appearance and elegant address. A lady-like person who assumed the name of Mrs Gordon, and sometimes Mrs Major Gordon, and who represented her husband to be in India, succeeded in obtaining goods from different tradesmen and mercantile establishments at the West-end to a great amount, and gave references to a respectable firm as her agents. Possessing a lady-like appearance and address, she easily succeeded in obtaining a furnished residence at St John's Wood, and applied to a livery stable-keeper for the loan of a brougham, hired a coachman, and got a suit of livery for him, and appeared in West-end assemblies as a lady of fashion. After staying about a fortnight at St John's Wood she left suddenly, without settling with any of her creditors. She addressed a letter to each of them, requesting that their account should be sent to her agents, and payment would be made as soon as Captain Gordon's affairs were settled. She expressed regret that she had been called away so abruptly on urgent business.

She was usually accompanied by a little girl, about eleven years of age, her daughter, and by an elderly woman, who attended to domestic duties.

She was afterwards convicted at Marylebone police court, under the name of Mrs Helen Murray, charged with obtaining large quantities of goods from West-end tradesmen by fraudulent means.

A considerable traffic in commercial swindling in various forms is carried on in London. Sometimes fraudulently under the name of another well-known firm; at other times under the name of a fictitious firm.

A case of this kind was tried at the Liverpool assizes, which illustrates the fraudulent system we refer to. Charles Howard and John Owen were indicted for obtaining goods on false pretences. In other counts of their indictment they were charged with having conspired with another man named Bonar Russell—not in custody—with obtaining goods under false pretences. The prosecutor Thomas Parkenson Luthwaite, a currier at Barton in Westmoreland, received an order by letter from John Howard and Co. of Droylesden, near Manchester, desiring him to send them a certain quantity of leather, and reference was given as to their respectability. The prosecutor sent the leather and a letter by post containing the invoice. The leather duly arrived at Droylesden; but the police having received information gave notice to the railway officials to detain it, until they got further knowledge concerning them. Howard and Russell went to the station, but were told they could not get the leather, as there was no such firm as Howard and Co. at Droylesden. Howard replied that there was—that he lived there. It was subsequently arranged that the goods should be delivered, on the party producing a formal order. On the next day, Owen came with a horse and cart to Droylesden station, and asked for the goods, at the same time producing his order.

They were delivered to him, when he put them in his cart and drove off. Two officers of police in plain clothes accosted him, and asked for a ride in his cart which he refused. The officers followed him, and found he did not go to Droylesden, but to a house at Hulme near Manchester, as he had been directed. This house was searched, and Howard and Russell were arrested. Howard having been admitted to bail, did not appear at the trial.

On farther inquiries it was found there was no such firm as John Howard and Co. at Droylesden, but that Howard and Russell had taken a house there which was not furnished, and where they went occasionally to receive letters addressed to Howard and Co., Droylesden. Owen was acquitted; Howard was found guilty of conspiracy with intent to defraud.

A number of cases occur where swindlers attempt to cheat different societies in various ways. Two men were tried at the police court a few days ago for unlawfully attempting to cheat and defraud a loan society to obtain 5*l*. The prisoners formed part of a gang of swindlers, who operated in this way:—Some of them took a house for the purpose of giving references to others, who applied to loan societies for an advance of money, and produced false receipts for rent and taxes. They had carried on this system for years, and many of them had been convicted. Some of the gang formerly had an office in Holborn, where they defrauded young men in search of situations by getting them to leave a sum of money as security. They were tried and convicted on this charge.

There is another heartless system of base swindling perpetrated by a class of cheats, who pretend to assist parties in getting situations, and hold out flaming inducements through advertisements in the newspapers to working men, servants, clerks, teachers, clergymen, and others; and contrive to get a large income by duping the public.

A swindler contrived to obtain sums of 5*s*. each in postage stamps, or post-office orders, from a large number of people, under pretence of obtaining situations for them as farm bailiffs. An advertisement was inserted in the newspaper, and in reply to the several applicants, a letter was returned, stating that although the applicant was among the leading competitors another party had secured the place. At the same time another attempt was made to inveigle the dupe, under the pretence of paying another fee of 5*s*., with the hope of obtaining a similar situation in prospect. The swindler intimated that the only interest he had in the matter was the agent's fee, charged alike to the employer and the employed, and generally paid in advance. He desired that letters addressed to him should be directed to 42, Sydney Street, Chorlton-upon-Medlock. He had an empty house there, taken for the purpose, with the convenience of a letter-box in the door into which the postman dropped letters twice a day. A woman came immediately after each post and took them away.

On arresting the woman, the officers found in her basket 87 letters, 44 of them containing 5*s*. in postage stamps, or a post-office order payable to the swindler himself. Nearly all the others were letters from persons at a distance from a post office, who were unable to remit the 5*s*., but promised to send the money when they got an opportunity.

On a subsequent day, 120 letters were taken out of the letter-box, most of them containing a remittance, This system had been in operation for a month. One day 190 letters were delivered by one post. It was estimated that no fewer than 3,000 letters had come in during the month, most of them enclosing 5*s*.; and it is supposed the swindler had received about 700*l*., a handsome return for the price of a few advertisements in newspapers, a few lithographed circulars, a few postage-stamps, and a quarter of a year's rent of an empty house.

Another case of a similar kind, occurred at the Maidstone assizes. Henry Moreton, aged 43, a tall gentlemanly man, and a young woman aged 19 years, were indicted for conspiring to obtain goods and money by false pretences. The name given by the male prisoner was known to be an assumed one. It was stated that he was well connected and formerly in a good position in society.

At the trial, a witness deposed that an advertisement had appeared in a Cornish newspaper, addressed to Cornish miners, stating they could be sent out to Australia by an English gold-mining company, and would be paid 20*l.* of wages per month, to commence on their arrival at the mines. The advertisement also stated that if 1*s.* or twelve postage stamps were sent to Mr Henry Moreton, Chatham, a copy of the stamped agreement and full particulars as to the company, would be given.

The prisoner was arrested, and 41 letters found in his possession, addressed to 'Mr H. Moreton, Chatham': 25 of the letters contained twelve postage stamps each and some of them had 1*s.* inside. It was ascertained the female cohabited with him. It appeared that he had pawned 482 stamps on the 14th February, for 1*l.* 15*s.*, 289 on the 21st, for 1*l.*, and 744 on another day.

Eighty-two letters came in one day chiefly from Ireland and Cornwall.

On searching a box in his room they found a large quantity of Irish and Cornish newspapers, many of them containing the advertisement referred to.

He was found guilty, and was sentenced to hard labour for fifteen months. The young woman was acquitted.

The judge, in passing sentence, observed that the prisoner had been convicted of swindling poor people, and his being respectably connected aggravated the case.

We give the following illustration of an English swindler's adventures on the Continent.

A married couple were tried at Pau, on a charge of swindling. The husband represented himself to be the son of a colonel in the English army and of a Neapolitan princess. His wife pretended to be the daughter of an English general. They said they were allied to the families of the Dukes of Norfolk, Leinster, and Devonshire. They came in a post-chaise* to the Hotel de France, accompanied by several servants, lived in the style of persons of the highest rank, and ran up a bill of 6,000 francs. As the landlord declined to give credit for more, they took a château, which they got fitted up in a costly way. They paid 2,500 francs for rent, and were largely in debt to the butcher, tailor, grocer, and others. The lady affected to be very pious, and gave 895 francs to the abbé for masses.

An English lady who came from Brussels to give evidence, stated that her husband had paid 50,000 francs to release them from a debtors' prison at Cologne, as he believed them to be what they represented. It was shown at the trial that they had received letters from Lord Grey,* the King of Holland, and other distinguished personages. They were convicted of swindling, and condemned to one year's imprisonment, or to pay a fine of 200 francs.

On hearing the sentence the woman uttered a piercing cry and fainted in her husband's arms, but soon recovered. They were then removed to prison.

The assumption of a variety of names, some of them of a high-sounding and pretentious character, is resorted to by swindlers giving orders for goods by letter from a distance—an address is also assumed of a nature well calculated to deceive: as an instance, we may mention that an individual has for a long period of time fared sumptuously upon the plunder obtained by his fraudulent transactions, of whose aliases and pseudo residences the following are but a few:

Creighton Beauchamp Harper; the Russets, near Edenbridge.
Beauchamp Harper; Albion House, Rye.
Charles Creighton Beauchamp Harper; ditto.
Neanberrie Harper, M. N. I.; The Broadlands, Winchelsea.
Beauchamp Harper; Halden House, Lewes.
R. E. Beresford; The Oaklands, Chelmsford.

The majority of these residencies existed only in the imagination of this indefatigable cosmopolite. In some cases he had christened a paltry tenement let at the rent of a few shillings per week 'House'; a small cottage in Albion Place, Rye, being magnified into 'Albion House'. When an address is assumed having no existence, his plan is to request the postmaster of the district to send the letters, &c., to his real address—generally some little distance off—a similar notice also being given at the nearest railway station. The goods ordered are generally of such a nature as to lull suspicion, viz., a gun, as 'I am going to a friend's grounds to shoot and I want one immediately'; 'a silver cornet'; 'two umbrellas, one for me and one for Mrs Harper'; 'a fashionable bonnet with extra strings, young looking, for Mrs Harper'; 'white lace frock for Miss Harper, immediately'; 'a violet-coloured velvet bonnet for my sister', &c., &c., &c., ad infinitum.

A person, pretending to be a German baron, some time ago ordered and received goods to a large amount from merchants in Glasgow. It was ascertained he was a swindler. He was a man of about forty years of age, 5 feet 8 inches high, and was accompanied by a lady about twenty-five years of age. They were both well-educated people, and could speak the English language fluently.

A fellow, assuming the name of the Rev. Mr Williams, pursued a romantic and adventurous career of swindling in different positions in society, and was an adept in deception. On one occasion, by means of forged credentials, he obtained an appointment as curate in Northamptonshire, where he conducted himself for some time with a most sanctimonious air. Several marriages were celebrated by him, which were apparently satisfactorily performed. He obtained many articles of jewellery from firms in London, who were deceived by his appearance and position. He wrote several modes of handwriting, and had a plausible manner of insinuating himself into the good graces of his victims.

He died a very tragical death. Having been arrested for swindling he was taken to Northampton. On his arrival at the railway station there, he threw himself cross the rails and was crushed to death by the train.

BEGGARS AND CHEATS

Begging-Letter Writers

Foremost among beggars, by right of pretension to blighted prospects and correct penmanship, stands the Begging-Letter Writer. He is the connecting link between mendicity and the observance of external respectability. He affects white cravats, soft hands, and filbert nails.* He oils his hair, cleans his boots, and wears a portentous stick-up collar. The light of other days of gentility and comfort casts a halo of 'deportment' over his well-brushed, white-seamed coat, his carefully darned black-cloth gloves, and pudgy gaiters. He invariably carries an umbrella, and wears a hat with an enormous brim. His once raven hair is turning grey, and his well-shaved whiskerless cheeks are blue as with gunpowder tattoo.* He uses the plainest and most respectable of cotton pocket-handkerchiefs, and keeps his references as to character in the most irreproachable of shabby leather pocket-books. His mouth is heavy, his under-lip thick, sensual, and lowering, and his general expression of pious resignation contradicted by restless, bloodshot eyes, that flash from side to side, quick to perceive the approach of a compassionate-looking clergyman, a female devotee, or a keen-scented member of the Society for the Suppression of Mendicity.*

Among the many varieties of mendacious beggars, there is none so detestable as this hypocritical scoundrel, who, with an ostentatiously-submissive air, and false pretence of faded fortunes, tells his plausible tale of undeserved suffering, and extracts from the hearts and pockets of the superficially good-hearted their sympathy and coin. His calling is a special one, and requires study, perseverance, and some personal advantages. The begging-letter writer must write a good hand, speak grammatically, and have that shrewd perception of character peculiar to fortune-tellers, horoscopists, cheap-jacks, and pedlars. He 'must read and write, and cast accounts'; have an intuitive knowledge of the 'nobility and landed gentry'; be a keen physiognomist, and an adept at imitation of handwritings, old documents, quaint ancient orthography, and the like. He must possess an artistic eye for costume, an unfaltering courage, and have tears and hysterics at immediate command.

His great stock-in-trade is his register. There he carefully notes down the names, addresses, and mental peculiarities of his victims, and the character and pretence under which he robbed them of their bounty. It would not do to tell the same person the same story *twice*, as once happened to an unusually audacious member of the fraternity, who had obtained money from an old lady for the purpose of burying his wife, for whose loss he, of course, expressed the deepest grief. Confident in the old lady's kindness of heart and weakness of memory, three months after his bereavement he again posted himself before the lady's door, and gave vent to violent emotion.

'Dear me!' thought the old lady, 'there's that poor man who lost his wife some time ago.' She opened the window, and, bidding the vagabond draw nearer, asked him what trouble he was in at present.

After repeated questioning the fellow gurgled out, 'That the wife of his bosom, the mother of his children, had left him for that bourne from which no traveller returns,* and that owing to a series of unprecedented and unexpected misfortunes he had not sufficient money to defray the funeral expenses, and—'

'Oh, nonsense!' interrupted the old lady. 'You lost your wife a quarter of a year ago. You couldn't lose her twice; and as to marrying again, and losing again in that short time, it is quite impossible!'

I subjoin some extracts from a Register kept by a begging-letter writer, and who was detected and punished:

Cheltenham. *May* 14, 1842

REV. JOHN FURBY.—Springwood Villa.—Low Church.—Fond of architecture—Dugdale's Monastica*—Son of architect—Lost his life in the 'Charon', U.S. packet—£2, and suit of clothes—Got reference.

MRS BRANXHOLME.—Clematis Cottage—Widow—Through Rev. Furby, £3 and prayer-book.

Gloucester. *May* 30

MRS CAPTAIN DANIELS.— —— Street.—Widow—Son drowned off Cape, as purser of same ship, 'The Thetis'—£5 and old sea-chest. N.B.: Vamosed* next day—Captain returned from London—Gaff blown* in county paper. Mem.: Not to visit neighbourhood for four years.

Lincoln. *June* 19

ANDREW TAGGART.— —— street.—Gentleman—Great abolitionist of slave trade—As tradesman from U.S., who had lost his custom by aiding slope* of fugitive female slave—By name Naomi Brown—£5. N.B.: To work him again, for he is good.

Grantham. *July* 1

Charles James Campion.—Westby House.—Gentleman—Literary—Writes plays and novels—As distant relative of George Frederick Cooke, and burnt-out bookseller—£2 2s. N.B.: Gave me some of his own books to read—Such trash— Cadger* in one—No more like cadger than I'm like Bobby Peel*—Went to him again on 5th—Told him thought it wonderful, and the best thing out since Vicar of Wakefield*—Gave me £1 more—Very good man—To be seen to for the future.

Huntingdon. *July* 15

Mrs Siddick.— —— Street.—Widow—Cranky—Baptist—As member of persuasion from persecution of worldly-minded relatives—£10—Gave her address in London—Good for a £5 every year—Recognized inspector—Leave to-night.

There are, of course, many varieties of the begging-letter writer; but although each and all of them have the same pretensions to former respectability, their mode of levying contributions is entirely different. There are but few who possess the versatility of their great master—Bampfylde Moore Carew; and it is usual for every member of the fraternity to chalk out for himself a particular 'line' of imposition—a course of conduct that renders him perfect in the part he plays, makes his references and certificates continually available, and prevents him from 'jostling' or coming into collision with others of his calling who might be 'on the same lay as himself, and spoil his game!'*

Among the begging-letter fraternity there are not a few persons who affect to be literary men. They have at one time or another been able to publish a pamphlet, a poem, or a song—generally a patriotic one, and copies of these works—they always call them 'works'—they constantly carry about with them to be ready for any customer who may turn up. I have known a notable member of this class of beggars for some years. He was introduced to me as a literary man by an innocent friend who really believed in his talent. He greeted me as a brother craftsman, and immediately took from the breast-pocket of his threadbare surtout a copy of one of his works. 'Allow me', he said, 'to present you with my latest work; it is dedicated, you will perceive, to the Right Honourable the Earl of Derby*—here is a letter from his lordship complimenting me in the most handsome terms'; and before I could look into the book, the author produced from a well-worn black pocket-book a dirty letter distinguished by a large red seal. Sure enough it was a genuine letter beginning

'The Earl of Derby presents his compliments', and going on to acknowledge the receipt of a copy of Mr Driver's work. Mr Driver—I will call my author by that name—produced a great many other letters, all from persons of distinction, and the polite terms in which they were expressed astonished me not a little. I soon, however, discovered the key to all this condescension. The work was a political one, glorifying the Conservative party, and abounding with all sorts of old-fashioned Tory sentiments. The letters Mr Driver showed me were of course all from tories. The 'work' was quite a curiosity. It was called a political novel. It had for its motto, 'Pro Rege, Lege, Aris et Focis',* and the dedication to the Eight Honourable the Earl of Derby was displayed over a whole page in epitaph fashion. At the close of our interview Mr Driver pointed out to me that the price of the work was two shillings. Understanding the hint, I gave him that amount, when he called for pen and ink, and wrote on the fly leaf of the work, 'To —— ——, Esq., with the sincere regards of the author.—J. Fitzharding Driver.' On looking over the book—it was a mere paper-covered pamphlet of some hundred pages—I found that the story was not completed. I mentioned this to Mr Driver the next time I met him, and he explained that he meant to go to press—that was a favourite expression of his—to go to press with the second volume shortly. Ten years, however, have elapsed since then, and Mr Driver has not yet gone to press with his second volume. The last time I met him he offered me the original volume as his 'last new work', which he presumed I had never seen. He also informed me that he was about to publish a patriotic song in honour of the Queen. Would I subscribe for a copy—only three-and-sixpence—and he would leave it for me? Mr Driver had forgotten that I had subscribed for this very song eight years previously. He showed me the selfsame MS of the new national anthem, which I had perused so long ago. The paper had become as soft and limp and dingy as a Scotch one-pound note, but it had been worth a good many one-pound notes to Mr Fitzharding Driver. Mr Driver has lived upon this as yet unpublished song, and that unfinished political novel, for ten years and more. I have seen him often enough to know exactly his *modus operandi*.* Though practically a beggar Mr Driver is no great rogue. Were you to dress him well, he might pass for a nobleman. As it is, in his shabby genteel clothes he looks a broken-down swell.* And so in fact he is. In his young days he had plenty of money, and went the pace among the young bloods of Bond Street. Mr Driver's young days were the days of the Regent.* He drove a dashing phaeton-and-four* then, and lounged and gambled, and lived the life of a man about town. He tells you all that with great pride, and also how he came to grief, though this part of the story is not so clear. There is no doubt that he had considerable acquaintance among great people in his prosperous days. He lives now upon his works, and the public-house parlours of the purlieus of the west-end serve him as publishing houses. He is a great political disputant, and his company is not unwelcome in those quarters. He enters, takes his seat, drinks his glass, joins in the conversation, and, as he says himself, shows that he is a man of parts.* In this way he makes friends among the tradesmen who visit these resorts. They soon find out that he is poor, and an author, and moved both to pity and admiration, each member of the company purchases a copy of that unfinished political novel, or subscribes for that new patriotic song, which I expect will yet be in the womb of the press* when the crack of doom* comes. I think Mr Driver has pretty well used up all the quiet parlours of W. district by this time. Not long ago I had a letter from him enclosing a prospectus of a new work to be entitled 'Whiggery, or the Decline of England', and soliciting a subscription to enable him to go to press with the first edition. I have no doubt that every conservative member of both houses of Parliament has had a copy of that prospectus. Mr Fitzharding Driver will call at their houses for an answer, and some entirely out of easy charity, and others from a party feeling of delight at the prospect of the Whigs being abused in a book even by this poor beggar, will send him down half-crowns, and enable the poor wretch to eat and drink for a few months longer. On more than one occasion while I have known him, Mr Driver has been on the point of 'being well off again', to use his own expression. His behaviour under the prospect was characteristic of the man, his antecedents, and his mode of life. He touched up his seedy clothes, had some cotton-velvet facings put to his threadbare surtout, revived his hat, mounted a pair of shabby patent-leather boots, provided himself with a penny cane, adorned with an old silk tassel, and appeared each day with a flower in his button-hole. In addition to these he had sewn into the breast of his surtout a bit of parti-coloured ribbon to look like a decoration. In this guise he came up to me at the Crystal Palace* one day, and appeared to be in great glee. His ogling and mysterious manner puzzled me. Judge of my astonishment when this hoary, old, tottering, toothless beggar informed me, with many self-satisfied chuckles, that a rich widow, 'a fine dashing woman, sir', had fallen in love with him, and was going to marry him. The marriage did not come off, the pile is worn away from the velvet facings, the patent-leather boots have become mere shapeless flaps of leather, the old broad-brimmed hat is past the power of reviver, and the Bond Street buck of the days of the Regent now wanders from public-house to public-house selling lucifer-matches. He still however carries with him a copy of his 'work', the limp and worn MS of his anthem, and the prospectus of 'Whiggery, or the Decline of England'. These and the letters from distinguished personages stand him in better stead than the lucifer-matches, when he lights upon persons of congenial sympathies.

Ashamed Beggars

By the above title I mean those tall, lanthorn-jawed men, in seedy well-brushed clothes, who, with a ticket on their breasts, on which a short but piteous tale is written in the most respectable of large-hand, and with a few boxes of lucifer-matches in their hands, make no appeal by word of mouth but invoke the charity of passers-by by meek glances and imploring looks—fellows who, having no talent for 'patter', are gifted with great powers of facial pathos, and make expression of feature stand in lieu of vocal supplication. For some years I have watched a specimen of this class, who has a regular 'beat' at the west end of London. He is a tall man, with thin legs and arms, and a slightly-protuberant stomach. His 'costume' (I use the word advisedly, for he is really a great actor of pantomime) consists of an old black dress-coat, carefully buttoned, but left sufficiently open at the top to show a spotlessly white shirt, and at the bottom, to exhibit an old grey waistcoat; and a snowy apron, which he wears after the fashion of a Freemason, forgetting that real tradesmen are never seen in their aprons except behind the counter. A pair of tight, dark, shabby trousers, black gaiters without an absent button, and heavy shoes of the severest thickness, cover his nether man. Round his neck is a red worsted comforter, which neatly tied at the throat, descends straight and formally beneath his coat, and exhibits two fringed ends, which fall, in agreeable contrast of colour, over the before-mentioned apron. I never remember seeing a beggar of this class without an apron and a worsted comforter—they would appear to be his stock-in-trade, a necessary portion of his outfit; the white apron to relieve the sombre hue of his habiliments, and show up their well-brushed shabbiness; the scarlet comforter to contrast with the cadaverous complexion which he owes to art or nature. In winter the comforter also serves as an advertisement that his great-coat is gone.

The man I am describing wears a 'pad' round his neck, on which is written—

> Kind Friends and Christian Brethren!
> I was once a
> Respectable Tradesman,
> doing a Good Business;
> till Misfortune reduced me to this Pass!
> Be kind enough to Buy
> some of the Articles I offer,
> and you will confer a
> Real Charity!

In his hands, on which he wears scrupulously-darned mittens, he carries a box or two of matches, or a few quires of note-paper or envelopes, and half-a-dozen small sticks of sealing-wax. He is also furnished with a shabby-genteel looking boy of about nine years old, who wears a Shakesperian collar, and the regulation worsted comforter, the ends of which nearly trail upon the ground. The poor child, whose features do not in the least resemble the man's, and who, too young to be his son, is too old to be his grandson, keeps his little hands in his large pockets, and tries to look as unhappy and half-starved as he can.

But the face of the beggar is a marvellous exhibition! His acting is admirable! Christian resignation and its consequent fortitude are written on his brow. His eyes roll imploringly, but no sound escapes him. The expression of his features almost pronounces, 'Christian friend, purchase my humble wares, for *I scorn to beg*. I am starving, but tortures shall not wring the humiliating secret from my lips.' He exercises a singular fascination over old ladies, who slide coppers into his hand quickly, as if afraid that they shall hurt his feelings. He pockets the money, heaves a sigh, and darts an abashed and grateful look at them that makes them feel how keenly he appreciates their delicacy. When the snow is on the ground he now and then introduces a little shiver, and with a well-worn pocket-handkerchief stifles a cough that he intimates, by a despairing dropping of his eyelids, is slowly killing him.

Naval and Military Beggars

are most frequently met with in towns situated at some distance from a seaport or a garrison. As they are distinct specimens of the same tribe, they must be separately classified. The more familiar nuisance is the

Turnpike Sailor

This sort of vagabond has two lays,* the 'merchant' lay, and the 'R'yal Navy' lay. He adopts either one or the other according to the exigencies of his wardrobe, his locality, or the person he is addressing. He is generally the offspring of some inhabitant of the most notorious haunts of a seaport town, and has seldom been at sea, or when he has, has run away after the first voyage. His slang of seamanship has been picked up at the lowest public-houses in the filthiest slums that offer diversion to the genuine sailor.

When on the 'merchant lay' his attire consists of a pair of tattered trousers, an old guernsey-shirt, and a torn straw-hat. One of his principal points of 'costume' is his bare feet. His black silk handkerchief is knotted jauntily round his throat after the most approved models at the heads of penny ballads, and the outsides of songs. He wears small gold earrings, and has short curly hair in the highest and most offensive state of glossy greasiness. His hands and arms are carefully tattooed—a foul anchor, or a long-haired mermaid sitting on her tail and making her toilette, being the favourite cartoons. In his gait he endeavours to counterfeit the roll of a true seaman, but his hard feet, knock-knees, and imperceptibly acquired turnpike-trot betray him. His face bears the stamp of diabolically low cunning, and it is impossible to look at him without an association with a police-court. His complexion is coarse and tallowy, and has none of the manly bronze that exposure to the weather, and watching the horizon give to the real tar.

I was once walking with a gentleman who had spent the earlier portion of his life at sea, when a turnpike sailor shuffled on before us. We had just been conversing on nautical affairs, and I said to him—

'Now, there is a brother sailor in distress; of course you will give him something?'

'*He* a sailor!' said my friend, with great disgust. 'Did you see him spit?'

The fellow had that moment expectorated.

I answered that I had.

'He spit to wind'ard!' said my friend.

'What of that?' said I.

'A regular landsman's trick,' observed my friend. 'A real sailor never spits to wind'ard. *Why, he couldn't*.'

We soon passed the fellow, who pulled at a curl upon his forehead, and began in a gruff voice, intended to convey the idea of hardships, storms, shipwrecks, battles, and privations. 'God—bless—your—'onors—give—a—copper—to—a—poor—sailor—as—hasn't—spliced—the—main—jaw*—since—the—day—'fore—yesterday—at—eight—bells*—God—love—yer—'onors—do!—I—avent—tasted—sin'—the—day—'fore—yesterday—so—drop—a—cop— poor—seaman—do.'

My friend turned round and looked the beggar full in the face.

'What ship?' he asked, quickly.

The fellow answered glibly.

'What captain?' pursued my friend.

The fellow again replied boldly, though his eyes wandered uneasily.

'What cargo?' asked my inexorable companion.

The beggar was not at fault, but answered correctly.

The name of the port, the reason of his discharge, and other questions were asked and answered; but the man was evidently beginning to be embarrassed. My friend pulled out his purse as if to give him something.

'What are you doing here?' continued the indefatigable inquirer. 'Did you leave the coast for the purpose of trying to find a ship *here?*' (We were in Leicester.)

The man stammered and pulled at his useful forelock to get time to collect his thoughts and invent a good lie.

'He had a friend in them parts as he thought could help him.'

'How long since you were up the Baltic?'

'Year—and—a—arf,—yer—'onor.'

'Do you know Kiel?'

'Yes,—yer—'onor.'

'D'ye know the "British flag" on the quay there?'

'Yes,—yer—'onor.'

'Been there often?'

'Yes,—yer—'onor.'

'Does Nick Johnson still keep it?'

'Yes,—yer—'onor.'

'Then,' said my friend, after giving vent to a strong opinion as to the beggar's veracity, 'I'd advise you to be off quickly, for there's a policeman, and if I get within hail of him I shall tell him you're an impostor. There's no such house on the quay. Get out, you scoundrel!'

The fellow shuffled off, looking curses, but not daring to express them.

On the 'R'yal Navy' lay, the turnpike sailor assumes different habiliments, and altogether a smarter trim. He wears coarse blue trousers symmetrically cut about the hips, and baggy over the foot. A 'jumper', or loose shirt of the same material, a tarpaulin hat, with the name of a vessel in letters of faded gold, is struck on the back of his neck, and he has a piece of whipcord, or 'lanyard' round his waist, to which is suspended a jack-knife, which if of but little service in fighting the battles of his country has stood him in good stead in silencing the cackling of any stray poultry that crossed his road, or in frightening into liberality the female tenant of a solitary cottage. This 'patter', or 'blob', is of Plymouth, Portsmouth, Cawsen' Bay, Hamoaze—ships paid off, prize-money, the bo'sen and the first le'tenant. He is always an able-bodied, never an ordinary seaman, and cannot get a ship 'becos orders is at the Hadmiralty as no more isn't to be put into commission'. Like the fictitious merchant-sailor he calls every landsman 'your honour', in accordance with the conventional rule observed by the jack tars in nautical dramas.* He exhibits a stale plug of tobacco, and replaces it in his jaw with ostentatious gusto. His chief victims are imaginative boys fresh from 'Robinson Crusoe'* and 'Tales of the Ocean',* and old ladies who have relatives at sea. For many months after a naval battle he is in full force, and in inland towns tells highly-spiced narratives of the adventures of his own ship and its gallant crew in action. He is profuse in references to 'the cap'en', and interlards his account with, 'and the cap'en turns round, and he says to me, he says—' He feels the pulse of his listener's credulity through their eyes, and throws the hatchet with the enthusiasm of an artist. 'When we boarded 'em,' I heard one of these vagabonds say—'oh, when we boarded 'em!' but it is beyond the power of my feeble pen to relate the deeds of the turnpike true blue, and his ship and its gallant, gallant crew, when they boarded 'em. I let him run out his yarn, and then said, 'I saw the account of the action in the papers, but they said nothing of boarding, As I read it, the enemy were in too shallow water to render that manoeuvre possible; but that till they struck their flag, and the boats went out to take possession, the vessels were more than half a mile apart.'

This would have posed an ordinary humbug, but the able-bodied liar immediately, and with great apparent disgust, said, 'The papers! the noo—o—o—s—papers! d——n the noo—o—o—s—papers. You don't believe what they says, surely. Look how they sarved out old Charley Napier.* Why, sir, *I was there*, *and I ought to know*.'

At times the turnpike sailor roars out a song in praise of British valour by sea; but of late this 'lay' has been unfrequent. At others he borrows an interesting-looking little girl, and tying his arm up in a sling, adds his wounds and a motherless infant to his other claims upon the public sympathy. After a heavy gale and the loss of several vessels, he appears with a fresh tale and a new suit of carefully chosen rags. When all these resources fail him he is compelled to turn merchant, or 'duffer', and invests a small capital in a few hundred of the worst, and a dozen or two of the very best, cigars. If he be possessed of no capital he steals them. He allows his whiskers to grow round his face, and lubricates them in the same liberal manner as his shining hair. He buys a pea-coat,* smart waistcoat, and voluminous trousers, discards his black neckerchief for a scarlet one, the ends of which run through a massive ring. He wears a large pair of braces over his waistcoat, and assumes a half-foreign air, as of a mariner just returned from distant climes. He accosts you in the streets mysteriously, and asks you if you want 'a few good cigars?' He tells you they are smuggled, that he 'run' them himself, and that the 'Custom-'us horficers'* are after him. I need hardly inform my reader that the cigar he offers as a sample is excellent, and that, should he be weak enough to purchase a few boxes he will not find them 'according to sample'. Not unfrequently, the cigar-'duffer' lures his victim to some low tavern to receive his goods, where in lieu of tobacco, shawls, and laces, he finds a number of cut-throat-looking confederates, who plunder and ill-treat him.

It must not be forgotten that at times a begging sailor may be met, who has really been a seaman, and who is a proper object of benevolence. When it is so, he is invariably a man past middle age, and offers for sale or exhibition a model of a man-of-war or a few toy yachts. He has but little to say for himself, and is too glad for the gift of a pair of landsmen's trousers to trouble himself about their anti-nautical cut. In fact, the real seaman does not care for costume, and is as frequently seen in an old shooting-coat as a torn jacket; but despite his habiliments, the true salt oozes out in the broad hands that dangle heavily from the wrists, as if wanting to grip a rope or a handspike;* in the tender feet accustomed to the smooth planks of the deck, and in the settled, far-off look of the weather-beaten head,* with its fixed expression of the aristocracy of subordination.

In conclusion, a real sailor is seldom or never seen inland, where he can have no chance of employment, and is removed from the sight of the sea, docks, shipmates, and all things dear and familiar to him. He carries his papers about him in a small tin box, addresses those who speak to him as 'sir' and 'marm', and never as 'your honour' or 'my lady'; is rather taciturn than talkative, and rarely brags of what he has seen, or done, or seen done. In these and all other respects he is the exact opposite of the turnpike sailor.

Street Campaigners

Soldier beggars may be divided into three classes: those who really have been soldiers and are reduced to mendicancy, those who have been ejected from the army for misconduct, and those with whom the military dress and bearing are pure assumptions.

The difference between these varieties is so distinct as to be easily detected. The first, or soldier proper, has all the evidence of drill and barrack life about him; the eye that always 'fronts' the person he addresses; the spare habit, high cheekbones, regulation whisker, stiff chin, and deeply-marked line beneath from ear to ear. He carries his papers about him, and when he has been wounded or seen service, is modest and retiring as to his share of glory. He can give little information as to the incidents of an engagement, except as regards the deeds of his own company, and in conversation speaks more of the personal qualities of his officers and comrades than of their feats of valour. Try him which way you will he never will confess that he has killed a man.

He compensates himself for his silence on the subject of fighting by excessive grumbling as to the provisions, quarters, &c., to which he has been forced to submit in the course of his career. He generally has a wife marching by his side—a tall strapping woman, who looks as if a long course of washing at the barracks had made her half a soldier. Ragged though he be, there is a certain smartness about the soldier proper, observable in the polish of his boots, the cock of his cap, and the disposition of the leather strap under his lower lip. He invariably carries a stick, and when a soldier passes him, casts on him an odd sort of look, half envying, half pitying, as if he said, 'Though you are better fed than I, you are not so free!'

The soldier proper has various occupations. He does not pass all his time in begging: he will hold a horse, clean knives and boots, sit as a model to an artist, and occasionally take a turn at the wash-tub. Begging he abhors, and is only driven to it as a last resource.

If my readers would inquire why a man so ready to work should not be able to obtain employment, he will receive the answer that universally applies to all questions of hardship among the humbler classes—the vice of the discharged soldier is intemperance.

The second sort of soldier-beggar is one of the most dangerous and violent of mendicants. Untamable even by regimental discipline, insubordinate by nature, he has been thrust out from the army to prey upon society. He begs but seldom, and is dangerous to meet with after dark upon a lonely road, or in a sequestered lane. Indeed, though he has every right to be classed among those who will not work, he is not thoroughly a beggar, but will be met with again, and receive fuller justice at our hands, in the, to him, more congenial catalogue of thieves.

The third sort of street campaigner is a perfect impostor, who being endowed, either by accident or art, with a broken limb or damaged feature, puts on an old military coat, as he would assume the dress of a frozen-out gardener, distressed dock-yard labourer, burnt-out tradesman, or scalded mechanic. He is imitative, and in his time plays many parts.* He 'gets up' his costume with the same attention to detail as the turnpike sailor. In crowded busy streets he 'stands pad', that is, with a written statement of his hard case slung round his neck, like a label round a decanter. His bearing is most military; he keeps his neck straight, his chin in, and his thumbs to the outside seams of his trousers; he is stiff as an embalmed preparation, for which, but for the motion of his eyes, you might mistake him. In quiet streets and in the country he discards his 'pad' and begs 'on the blob', that is, he 'patters' to the passers-by, and invites their sympathy by word of mouth. He is an ingenious and fertile liar, and seizes occasions such as the late war in the Crimea* and the mutiny in India* as good distant grounds on which to build his fictions.

I was walking in a high-road, when I was accosted by a fellow dressed in an old military tunic, a forage-cap like a charity boy's, and tattered trousers, who limped along barefoot by the aid of a stick. His right sleeve was empty, and tied up to a button-hole at his breast, *à la* Nelson.*

'Please your honour,' he began, in a doleful exhausted voice, 'bestow your charity on a poor soldier which lost his right arm at the glorious battle of Inkermann.'*

I looked at him, and having considerable experience in this kind of imposition, could at once detect that he was 'acting'.

'To what regiment did you belong?' I asked.

'The Thirty ——, sir.'

I looked at his button and read Thirty ——.

'I haven't tasted bit o' food, sir, since yesterday at half-past four, and then a lady give me a cruster bread,' he continued.

'The Thirty ——!' I repeated. 'I knew the Thirty ——. Let me see—who was the colonel?'

The man gave me a name, with which I suppose he was provided.

'How long were you in the Thirty ——?' I inquired.

'Five year, sir.'

'I had a schoolfellow in that regiment, Captain Thorpe, a tall man with red whiskers—did you know him?'

'There was a captain, sir, with large red whiskers, and I think his name was Thorpe; but he warn't captain of my company, so I didn't know for certain,' replied the man, after an affected hesitation.

'The Thirty —— was one of the first of our regiments that landed, I think?' I remarked.

'Yes, your honour, it were.'

'You impudent impostor!' I said; 'the Thirty —— did not go out till the spring of '55. How dare you tell me you belonged to it?'

The fellow blenched for a moment, but rallied and said, 'I didn't like to contradict your honour for fear you should be angry and wouldn't give me nothing.'

'That's very polite of you,' I said, 'but still I have a great mind to give you into custody. Stay; tell me who and what you are, and I will give you a shilling and let you go.'

He looked up and down the road, measured me with his eye, abandoned the idea of resistance, and replied:

'Well, your honour, if you won't be too hard on a poor man which finds it hard to get a crust anyhow or way, I don't mind telling you I never was a soldier.' I give his narrative as he related it to me.

'I don't know who my parents ever was. The fust thing as I remember was the river side (the Thames), and running in low tide to find things. I used to beg, hold hosses, and sleep under dry arches. I don't remember how I got any clothes. I never had a pair of shoes or stockings till I was almost a man. I fancy I am now nearly forty years of age.

'An old woman as kep a rag and iron shop by the water-side give me a lodging once for two years. We used to call her "Nanny"; but she turned me out when she caught me taking some old nails and a brass cock out of her shop; I was hungry when I done it, for the old gal gi' me no grub, nothing but the bare floor for a bed.

'I have been a beggar all my life, and begged in all sorts o' ways and all sorts o' lays. I don't mean to say that if I see anything laying about handy that I don't mouch it (*i. e.* steal it). Once a gentleman took me into his house as his servant. He was a very kind man; I had a good place, swell clothes, and beef and beer as much as I liked; but I couldn't stand the life, and I run away.

'The loss o' my arm, sir, was the best thing as ever happen'd to me: it's been a living to me; I turn out with it on all sorts o' lays, and it's as good as a pension. I lost it poaching; my mate's gun went off by accident, and the shot went into my arm, I neglected it, and at last was obliged to go to a orspital and have it off. The surgeon as ampitated it said that a little longer and it would ha' mortified.

'The Crimea's been a good dodge to a many, but it's getting stale; all dodges are getting stale; square coves (*i. e.* honest folks) are so wide awake.'

'Don't you think you would have found it more profitable, had you taken to labour or some honester calling than your present one?' I asked.

'Well, sir, p'raps I might,' he replied; 'but going on the square is so dreadfully confining.'

Disaster Beggars

This class of street beggars includes shipwrecked mariners, blown-up miners, burnt-out tradesmen, and lucifer droppers. The majority of them are impostors, as is the case with all beggars who pursue begging pertinaciously and systematically. There are no doubt genuine cases to be met with, but they are very few, and they rarely obtrude themselves. Of the shipwrecked mariners I have already given examples under the head of Naval and Military Beggars. Another class of them, to which I have not referred, is familiar to the London public in connection with rudely executed paintings representing either a shipwreck, or more commonly the destruction of a boat by a whale in the North Seas. This painting they spread upon the pavement, fixing it at the corners, if the day be windy, with stones. There are generally two men in attendance, and in most cases one of the two has lost an arm or a leg. Occasionally both of them have the advantage of being deprived of either one or two limbs. Their misfortune so far is not to be questioned. A man who has lost both arms, or even one, is scarcely in a position to earn his living by labour, and is therefore a fit object for charity. It is found, however, that in most instances the stories of their misfortunes printed underneath their pictures are simply inventions, and very often the pretended sailor has never been to sea at all. In one case which I specially investigated, the man had been a bricklayer and had broken both his arms by falling from a scaffold. He received some little compensation at the time, but when that was spent he went into the streets to beg, carrying a paper on his breast describing the cause of his misfortune. His first efforts were not successful. His appearance (dressed as he was in workman's clothes) was not sufficiently picturesque to attract attention, and his story was of too ordinary a kind to excite much interest. He had a very hard life of it for some length of time; for, in addition to the drawback arising from the uninteresting nature of his case, he had had no experience in the art of begging, and his takings were barely sufficient to procure bread. From this point I will let him tell his own story:

A Shipwrecked Mariner

'I had only taken a penny all day, and I had had no breakfast, and I spent the penny in a loaf. I was three nights behind for my lodging, and I knew the door would be shut in my face if I did not take home sixpence. I thought I would go to the workhouse, and perhaps I might get a supper and a lodging for that night. I was in Tottenham Court-road by the chapel, and it was past ten o'clock. The people were thinning away, and there seemed no chance of anything. So says I to myself I'll start down the New Road to the work'ouse. I knew there was a work'ouse down that way, for I worked at a 'ouse next it once, and I used to think the old paupers looked comfortable like. It came across me all at once, that I one time said to one of my mates, as we was sitting on the scaffold, smoking our pipes, and looking over the work'ouse wall, "Jem, them old chaps there seems to do it pretty tidy; they have their soup and bread, and a bed to lie on, and their bit o' baccy, and they comes out o' a afternoon and baskes in the sun, and has their chat, and don't seem to do no work to hurt 'em." And Jem he says, "it's a great hinstitooshin, Enery," says he, for you see Jem was a bit of a scollard, and could talk just like a book. "I don't know about a hinstitooshin, Jem," says I, "but what I does know is that a man might do wuss nor goe in there and have his grub and his baccy regular, without nought to stress him, like them old chaps." Somehow or other that 'ere conversation came across me, and off I started to the work'ouse. When I came to the gate I saw a lot of poor women and children sitting on the pavement round it. They couldn't have been hungrier than me, but they were awful ragged, and their case looked wuss. I didn't like to go in among them, and I watched a while a little way off. One woman kep on ringing the bell for a long time, and nobody came, and then she got desperate, and kep a-pulling and ringing like she was mad, and at last a fat man came out and swore at her and drove them all away. I didn't think there was much chance for me if they druv away women and kids, and such as them, but I thought I would try as I was a cripple, and had lost both my arms. So I stepped across the road, and was just agoing to try and pull the bell with my two poor stumps when some one tapped me on the shoulder. I turned round and saw it was a sailor-like man, without ne'er an arm like myself, only his were cut off short at the shoulder. "What are you agoing to do?" says he. "I was agoing to try and ring the work'ouse bell," says I. "What for?" says he. "To ask to be took in," says I. And then the sailor man looks at me in a steady kind of way, and says, "Want to get into the work'ouse, and you got ne'er an arm? You're a infant," says he. "If you had only lost one on 'em now, I could forgive you, but—" "But surely," says I, "it's a greater misfortune to lose two nor one; half a loaf's better nor no bread, they say." "You're a infant," says he again. "One off ain't no good; both on 'em's the thing. Have you a mind to earn a honest living," says he, quite sharp. "I have," says I; "anything for a honest crust." "Then," says he, "come along o' me." So I went with the sailor man to his lodging in Whitechapel, and a very tidy place it was, and we had beef-steaks and half a gallon o' beer, and a pipe, and then he told me what he wanted me to do. I was to dress like him in a sailor's jacket and trousers and a straw 'at, and stand o' one side of a picture of a shipwreck, vile he stood on the 'tother. And I consented, and he learned me some sailors' patter, and at the end of the week he got me the togs, and then I went out with him. We did only middlin the first day, but after a bit the coppers tumbled in like winkin'. It was so affectin' to see two mariners without ne'er an arm between them, and we had crowds round us. At the end of the week we shared two pound and seven shillings, which was more or a pound than my mate ever did by his self. He always said it was pilin' the hagony to have two without ne'er an arm. My mate used to say to me, "Enery, if your stumps had only been a trifle shorter, we might ha' made a fortun by this time; but you waggle them, you see, and that frightens the old ladies." I did well when Trafalgar Jack was alive. That was my mate, sir; but he died of the cholera, and I joined another pal who had a wooden leg; but he was rough to the kids, and got us both into trouble. How do I mean rough to the kids? Why, you see, the kids used to swarm round us to look at the pictur just like flies round a sugar-cask, and that crabbed the business. My mate got savage with them sometimes, and clouted their heads, and one day the mother o' one o' the brats came up a-screaming awful and give Timber Bill, as we called him, into custody, and he was committed for a rogue and vagabond.* Timber Bill went into the nigger line* arterwards and did well. You may have seen him, sir. He plays the tambourine, and dances, and the folks laugh at his wooden leg, and the coppers come in in style. Yes, I'm still in the old line, but it's a bad business now.'

Lucifer Droppers

The lucifer droppers are impostors to a man—to a boy—to a girl. Men seldom, if ever, practise this 'dodge'. It is children's work; and the artful way in which boys and girls of tender years pursue it, shows how systematically the seeds of mendicancy and crime are implanted in the hearts of the young Arab tribes of London. The artfulness of this device is of the most diabolical kind; for it trades not alone upon deception, but upon exciting sympathy with the guilty at the expense of the innocent. A boy or a girl takes up a position on the pavement of a busy street, such as Cheapside or the Strand. He, or she—it is generally a girl—carries a box or two of lucifer matches, which she offers for sale. In passing to and fro she artfully contrives to get in the way of some gentleman who is hurrying along. He knocks against her and upsets the matches which fall in the mud. The girl immediately begins to cry and howl. The bystanders, who are ignorant of the trick, exclaim in indignation against the gentleman who has caused a poor girl such serious loss, and the result is that either the gentleman, to escape being hooted, or the ignorant passers by, in false compassion, give the girl money. White peppermint lozenges are more often used than lucifers. It looks a hopeless case, indeed, when a trayful of white lozenges fall in the mud.

Bodily Afflicted Beggars

Beggars who excite charity by exhibiting sores and bodily deformities are not so commonly to be met with in London as they were some years ago. The officers of the Mendicity Society have cleared the streets of nearly all the impostors, and the few who remain are blind men and cripples. Many of the blind men are under the protection of a Society, which furnishes them with books printed in raised type which they decipher by the touch.* Others provide their own books, and are allowed to sit on door steps or in the recesses of the bridges without molestation from the police. It has been found on inquiry that these afflicted persons are really what they appear to be—poor, helpless, blind creatures, who are totally incapacitated from earning a living, and whom it would be heartless cruelty to drive into the workhouse, where no provision is made for their peculiar wants.

The bodily afflicted beggars of London exhibit seven varieties. 1. Those having real or pretended sores, vulgarly known as the 'Scaldrum Dodge'. 2. Having swollen legs. 3. Being crippled, deformed, maimed, or paralyzed. 4. Being blind. 5. Being subject to fits. 6. Being in a decline. 7. 'Shallow Coves', or those who exhibit themselves in the streets, half-clad, especially in cold weather.

First, then, as to those having real or pretended sores. As I have said, there are few beggars of this class left. When the officers of the Mendicity Society first directed their attention to the suppression of this form of mendicancy, it was found that the great majority of those who exhibit sores were unmitigated impostors. In nearly all the cases investigated the sores did not proceed from natural causes, but were either wilfully produced or simulated. A few had lacerated their flesh in reality; but the majority had resorted to the less painful operation known as the 'Scaldrum Dodge'. This consists in covering a portion of the leg or arm with soap to the thickness of a plaister, and then saturating the whole with vinegar. The vinegar causes the soap to blister and assume a festering appearance, and thus the passer-by is led to believe that the beggar is suffering from a real sore. So well does this simple device simulate a sore that the deception is not to be detected even by close inspection. The 'Scaldrum Dodge' is a trick of very recent introduction among the London beggars. It is a concomitant of the advance of science and the progress of the art of adulteration. It came in with penny postage, daguerreotypes, and other modern innovations of a like description. In less scientific periods within the present century it was wholly unknown; and sores were produced by burns and lacerations which the mendicants inflicted upon themselves with a ruthless hand. An old man who has been a beggar all his life, informed me that he had known a man prick the flesh of his leg all over, in order to produce blood and give the appearance of an ulcerous disease. This man is a cripple and walks about upon crutches, selling stay laces. He is now upwards of seventy years of age. At my solicitation he made the following statement without any apparent reserve.

Seventy Years a Beggar

'I have been a beggar ever since I was that high—ever since I could walk. No, I was not born a cripple. I was thirty years of age before I broke my leg. That was an accident. A horse and cart drove over me in Westminster. Well; yes I was drunk. I was able-bodied enough before that. I was turned out to beg by my mother. My father, I've heard, was a soldier; he went to Egypt, or some foreign part, and never came back. I never was learnt any trade but begging, and I couldn't turn my hand to nothing else. I might have been learnt the shoemaking; but what was the use? Begging was a better trade then; it isn't now though. There was fine times when the French war was on. I lived in Westminster then. A man as they called Copenhagen Jack, took a fancy to me, and made me his valet. I waited upon, fetched his drink, and so forth. Copenhagen Jack was a captain; no not in the army, nor in the navy neither. He was the captain of the Pye-Street beggars. There was nigh two hundred of them lived in two large houses, and Jack directed them. Jack's word was law, I assure you. The boys—Jack called them his boys, but there was old men among them, and old women too—used to come up before the captain every morning before starting out for the day, to get their orders. The captain divided out the districts for them, and each man took his beat according to his directions. It was share and share alike, with an extra for the captain. There was all manner of "lays"; yes, cripples and darkies. We called them as did the blind dodge, darkies,—and "shakers" them as had fits,—and shipwrecked mariners, and—the scaldrum dodge, no; that's new; but I know what you mean. They did the real thing then—scrape the skin off their feet with a bit of glass until the blood came. Those were fine times for beggars. I've known many of 'em bring in as much as thirty shillings a day, some twenty, some fifteen. If a man brought home no more than five or six shillings, the captain would enter him, make a note of him, and change his beat. Yes, we lived well. I've known fifty sit down to a splendid supper, geese and turkeys, and all that, and keep it up until daylight, with songs and toasts. No; I didn't beg then; but I did before, and I did after. I begged after, when the captain came to misfortune. He went a walking one day in his best clothes, and got pressed,* and never came back, and there was a mutiny among them in Pye-Street, and I nearly got murdered. You see, they were jealous of me, because the captain petted me. I used to dress in top-boots and a red coat when I waited on the captain. It was his fancy. Romancing? I don't know what you mean. Telling lies, oh! It's true by ——. There's nothing like it nowadays. The new police and this b—— Mendicity Society has spoilt it all. Well, they skinned me; took off my fine coat and boots, and sent me out on the orphan lay in tatters. I sat and cried all day on the door steps, for I was really miserable now my friend was gone, and I got lots of halfpence, and silver too, and when I took home the swag, they danced round me and swore that they would elect me captain if I went on like that; but there was a new captain made, and when they had their fun out, he came and took the money away, and kicked me under the table. I ran away the next day, and went to a house in St Giles's, where I was better treated. There was no captain there; the landlord managed the house, and nobody was master but him. There was nigh a hundred beggars in that house, and some two or three hundred more in the houses next it. The houses are not standing now. They were taken down when New Oxford-street was built; they stood on the north side. Yes; we lived well in St Giles's—as well as we did in Westminster. I have earned 8, 10, 15, ay, 30 shillings a day, and more nor that sometimes. I can't earn one shilling now. The folks don't give as they did. They think every body an imposture now. And then the police won't let you alone. No; I told you before, I never was anything else but a beggar. How could I? It was the trade I was brought up to. A man must follow his trade. No doubt I shall die a beggar, and the parish will bury me.'

Beggars Subject to Fits

are impostors, I may say, wholly without exception. Some of them are the associates and agents of thieves, and fall down in the street in assumed fits in order to collect a crowd and afford a favourable opportunity to the pickpockets, with whom they are in league. The simulation of fits is no mean branch of the beggar's art of deception. The various symptoms—the agitation of the muscles, the turning up of the whites of the eyes, the pallor of the face and the rigidity of the mouth and jaw—are imitated to a nicety; and these symptoms are sometimes accompanied by copious frothing at the mouth. I asked Mr Horsford, of the Mendicity Society, how this was done, and received the laconic answer—'Soap'. And this brought to my memory that I had once seen an actor charge his mouth with a small piece of soap to give due *vraissemblance* to the last scene of *Sir Giles Overreach*.* I was shown an old woman who was in the habit of falling down in assumed fits simply to get brandy. She looked very aged and poor, and I was told she generally had her fits when some well-dressed gentleman was passing with a lady on his arm. She generally chose the scene of her performance close to the door of a public-house, into which some compassionate person might conveniently carry her. She was never heard to speak in her fits except to groan and mutter 'brandy', when that remedy did not appear to suggest itself to those who came to her aid. An officer said to me, 'I have known that old woman have so many fits in the course of the day that she has been found lying in the gutter dead drunk from the effect of repeated restoratives. She has been apprehended and punished over and over again, but she returns to the old dodge the minute she gets out. She is on the parish; but she gets money as well as brandy by her shamming.'

I have heard that there are persons who purposely fall into the Serpentine in order to be taken to the receiving-house of the Humane Society,* and recovered with brandy. One man repeated the trick so often that at last the Society's men refused to go to his aid. It is needless to say that he soon found his way out of the water unaided, when he saw that his dodge was detected.

Petty Trading Beggars

This is perhaps the most numerous class of beggars in London. Their trading in such articles as lucifers, boot-laces, cabbage-nets, tapes, cottons, shirt-buttons, and the like, is in most cases a mere 'blind' to evade the law applying to mendicants and vagrants. There are very few of the street vendors of such petty articles as lucifers and shirt-buttons who can make a living from the profits of their trade. Indeed they do not calculate upon doing so. The box of matches, or the little deal box of cottons, is used simply as a passport to the resorts of the charitable. The police are obliged to respect the trader, though they know very well that under the disguise of the itinerant merchant there lurks a beggar.

Beggars of this class use their trade to excite compassion and obtain a gift rather than to effect a sale. A poor half-clad wretch stands by the kerb exposing for sale a single box of matches, the price being 'only a halfpenny'. A charitable person passes by and drops a halfpenny or a penny into the poor man's hand, and disdains to take the matches. In this way a single box will be sufficient for a whole evening's trading, unless some person should insist upon an actual 'transaction', when the beggar is obliged to procure another box at the nearest oilman's. There are very few articles upon which an actual profit is made by legitimate sale. Porcelain shirt-buttons, a favourite commodity of the petty trading beggars, would not yield the price of a single meal unless the seller could dispose of at least twenty dozen in a day. Cottons, stay-laces, and the like, can now be obtained so cheaply at the shops, that no one thinks of buying these articles in the streets unless it be in a charitable mood. Almost the only commodities in which a legitimate trade is carried on by the petty traders of the streets are flowers, songs, knives, combs, braces, purses, portmonnaies.* The sellers of knives, combs, &c., are to a certain extent legitimate traders, and do not calculate upon charity. They are cheats, perhaps, but not beggars. The vendors of flowers and songs, though they really make an effort to sell their goods, and often realize a tolerable profit, are nevertheless beggars, and trust to increase their earnings by obtaining money without giving an equivalent. A great many children are sent out by their parents to sell flowers during the summer and autumn. They find their best market in the bars of public-houses, and especially those frequented by prostitutes. If none else give prostitutes a good character, the very poor do. 'I don't know what we should do but for them,' said an old beggar-woman to me one day. 'They are good-hearted souls—always kind to the poor. I hope God will forgive them.' I have had many examples of this sympathy for misfortune and poverty on the part of the fallen women of the streets. A fellow feeling no doubt makes them wondrous kind. They know what it is to be cast off, and spurned, and despised; they know, too, what it is to starve, and, like the beggars, they are subject to the stern 'move on' of the policeman.

The relations which subsist between the prostitutes and the beggars reveal some curious traits. Beggars will enter a public-house because they see some women at the bar who will assist their suit. They offer their little wares to some gentlemen at the bar, and the women will say, 'Give the poor devil something,' or 'buy bouquets for us,' or if the commodity should be laces or buttons, they say, 'Don't take the poor old woman's things; give her the money.' And the gentlemen, just to show off, and appear liberal, do as they are told. Possibly, but for the pleading of their gay companions, they would have answered the appeal with a curse and gruff command to begone. I once saw an old woman kiss a bedizened prostitute's hand, in real gratitude for a service of this kind. I don't know that I ever witnessed anything more touching in my life. The woman, who a few minutes before had been flaunting about the bar in the reckless manner peculiar to her class, was quite moved by the old beggar's act, and I saw a tear mount in her eye and slowly trickle down her painted cheek, making a white channel through the rouge as it fell. But in a moment she dashed it away, and the next was flaunting and singing as before. Prostitutes are afraid to remain long under the influence of good thoughts. They recal their days of innocence, and overpower them with an intolerable sadness—a sadness which springs of remorse. The gay women assume airs of patronage towards the beggars, and as such are looked up to; but a beggar-woman, however poor, and however miserable, if she is conscious of being virtuous, is always sensible of her superiority in that respect. She is thankful for the kindness of the 'gay lady', and extols her goodness of heart; but she pities while she admires, and mutters as a last word, 'May God forgive her.' Thus does one touch of nature make all the world akin,* and thus does virtue survive all the buffets of evil fortune to raise even a beggar to the level of the most worthy, and be a treasure dearer and brighter than all the pleasures of the world.

The sellers of flowers and songs are chiefly boys, and young girls. They buy their flowers in Covent Garden, when the refuse of the market is cleared out, and make them up into small bouquets, which they sell for a penny. When the flower season is over they sell songs—those familiar productions of Ryle, Catnach and company,* which, it is said, the great Lord Macaulay* was wont to collect and treasure up as collateral evidences of history. Some of the boys who pursue this traffic are masters of all the trades that appertain to begging. I have traced one boy, by the identifying mark of a most villanous squint, through a career of ten years. When I first saw him he was a mere child of about four years of age. His mother sent him with a ragged little girl (his sister) into public-house bars to beg. Their diminutive size attracted attention and excited charity. By-and-by, possibly in consequence of the interference of the police, they carried pennyworths of flowers with them, at other times matches, and at others halfpenny sheets of songs. After this the boy and the girl appeared dressed in sailor's costume, (both as boys), and sung duets. I remember that one of the duets, which had a spoken part, was not very decent; the poor children evidently did not understand what they said; but the thoughtless people at the bar laughed and gave them money. By-and-by the boy became too big for this kind of work, and I next met him selling fuzees. After the lapse of about a year he started in the shoe-black line. His station was at the end of Endell Street, near the baths; but as he did not belong to one of the regularly organized brigades, he was hunted about by the police, and could not make a living. On the death of the crossing-sweeper at the corner he succeeded to that functionary's broom, and in his new capacity was regarded by the police as a useful member of society. The last time I saw him he was in possession of a costermonger's barrow selling mackerel. He had grown a big strong fellow, but I had no difficulty in identifying the little squinting child, who begged, and sold flowers and songs in public-house bars, with the strong loud-lunged vendor of mackerel. I suppose this young beggar may be said to have pursued an honourable career, and raised himself in the world. Many who have such an introduction to life finish their course in a penal settlement.

There are not a few who assume the appearance of petty traders for the purpose of committing thefts, such as picking a gentleman's pocket when he is intoxicated, and slinking into parlours to steal bagatelle* balls. Police spies occasionally disguise themselves as petty traders. There is a well-known man who goes about with a bag of nuts, betting that he will tell within two how many you take up in your hand. This man is said to be a police spy. I have not been able to ascertain whether this is true or not; but I am satisfied that the man does not get his living by his nut trick. In the day-time he appears without his nuts, dressed in a suit of black, and looking certainly not unlike a policeman in mufti.*

Among the petty trading beggars there are a good many idiots and half-witted creatures, who obtain a living—and a very good one too—by dancing in a grotesque and idiotic manner on the pavement to amuse children. Some of them are not such idiots as they appear, but assume a half-witted appearance to give oddness to their performance, and excite compassion for their misfortune. The street boys are the avengers of this imposition upon society.

The idiot performer has a sad life of it when the boys gather about him. They pull his clothes, knock off his hat, and pelt him with lime and mud. But this persecution sometimes redounds to his advantage; for when the grown-up folks see him treated thus, they pity him the more. These beggars always take care to carry something to offer for sale. Halfpenny songs are most commonly the merchandise.

The little half-witted Italian man who used to go about grinding an organ that 'had no inside to it', as the boys said, was a beggar of this class, and I really think he traded on his constant persecution by the *gamins*.* Music, of course, he made none, for there was only one string left in his battered organ; but he always acted so as to convey the idea that the boys had destroyed his instrument. He would turn away at the handle in a desperate way, as if he were determined to spare no effort to please his patrons; but nothing ever came of it but a feeble tink-a-tink at long intervals. If his organ could at any time have been spoiled, certainly the boys might have done it; for their great delight was to put stones in it, and batter in its deal back with sticks. I am informed that this man had a good deal more of the rogue than of the fool in his composition. A gentleman offered to have his organ repaired for him; but he declined; and at length when the one remaining string gave way he would only have that one mended. It was his 'dodge' to grind the air, and appear to be unconscious that he was not discoursing most eloquent music.*

Tract-selling in the streets is a line peculiar to the Hindoos. I find that the tracts are given to them by religious people, and that they are bought by religious people, who are not unfrequently the very same persons who provided the tracts. Very few petty trading beggars take to tract-selling from their own inspiration; for in good sooth it does not pay, except when conducted on the principle I have just indicated. Some find it convenient to exhibit tracts simply to evade the law applying to beggars and vagrants; but they do not use them if they can procure a more popular article. In these remarks it is very far from my intention to speak of 'religious people' with any disrespect. I merely use the expression 'religious people' to denote those who employ themselves actively and constantly in disseminating religious publications among the people. Their motives and their efforts are most praiseworthy, and my only regret is that their labours are not rewarded by a larger measure of success.

APPENDIX 1
MONEY AND THE COST OF LIVING

MUCH of Mayhew's account is concerned with money: how it is earned, saved and spent. Pre-decimal currency has the following values:

£1 (1*l.*) = 20 shillings (20*s.*) (a guinea was worth £1 1*s.*)
1 half-sovereign = 10 shillings
1 crown = 5 shillings
1 shilling = 12 pence (12*d.*)
1 penny = 4 farthings

As the cost of living varied from year to year,[1] the protracted publication history of *London Labour and the London Poor* makes it hard to draw firm conclusions from Mayhew's figures or compare them with other accounts from the period covered by his investigations. In 1857 David A. Wells provided the following comparison of prices between 1810 and 1851 as part of an argument about 'the great social progress which has been made in defiance of all obstacles within the last forty years':

> The price of a hat in 1810 was 20*s.*, and in 1851 it had fallen to 7*s.*;—or if a labourer's weekly wage had been paid for in hats, he would have had three times as great a supply in the present year as he had forty years ago. A gown cost 21*s.* in 1810, and only 6*s.* in 1851. Calico was 2*s.* 6*d.* a yard against 6*d.* at present. Tea was 8*s.* per lb. against 4*s.* now. Brown sugar was 10*d.*, now 4*d.* Salt was 18*s.* per bushel, and has fallen to 1*s.* A bushel of flour was 20*s.* in 1810, and 5*s.* in 1851. In reply to these facts, it may be said that the rate of money wages has fallen with money prices. This assertion is difficult of proof. In some few cases money wages have declined; but as a general result, they have not declined in the same ratio as money prices. Therefore the condition of the people is materially improved, inasmuch as the real or commodity price of labour of the English working classes is probably as much as one-half or three-fourths better than it was in 1810.[2]

[1] See John Burnett, *A History of the Cost of Living* (Harmondsworth: Penguin, 1969), chs. 4 and 5.

[2] *Things Not Generally Known: A Popular Hand-Book of Facts Not Readily Accessible in Literature, History and Science* (New York: D. Appleton & Co., 1857), 192–3; Wells's work is based on John Timbs's *Things Not Generally Known, Familiarly Explained* (1856).

Wells's figures might have raised some eyebrows among Mayhew's interviewees, not because he was altogether wrong about the relative fall in prices,[3] but because in dealing with neat lines of statistics he wholly ignored the more unruly trajectories of individual lives. The same is true of John Aikin and Anna Letitia Barbauld's *Evenings at Home* (1851), which provides some additional information on the cost of living at the time of Mayhew's interviews. Although the tone of this children's story is bluntly moralistic, it reveals a broader sense of the choices over how money could be spent which many middle-class readers assumed—falsely—were equally open to the poor. In a chapter entitled 'Half a Crown's Worth', a 13-year-old boy at public school writes to ask his father for some pocket money, casually mentioning that other boys in his class receive half a crown per week. His father replies with a letter that briskly explains 'what sort of sum half a crown was, and to how many more important uses it might be put':

> It is calculated (said he) that a grown man may be kept in health and fit for labour upon a pound and a half of good bread a day. Suppose the value of this to be two pence halfpenny, and add a penny for a quart of milk, which will greatly improve his diet. Half a crown will keep him, eight or nine days in this manner.
>
> A common labourer's wages in our country are seven shillings per week, and if you add somewhat extraordinary for harvest work, this will not make it amount to three half crowns on an average the year round. Suppose his wife and children to earn another half crown. For this ten shilling per week he will maintain himself, his wife, and half a dozen children, in food, lodging, clothes, and fuel. A half a crown, then, may be reckoned the full weekly maintenance of two human creatures in every thing necessary.
>
> Where potatoes are much cultivated, two bushels, weighing eighty pounds apiece, may be purchased for a half a crown. Here is one hundred and sixty pounds of solid food; of which, allowing for the waste in dressing, you may reckon two pounds and a half sufficient for the sole daily nourishment of one person. At this rate, nine people might be fed a week for a half a crown; poorly indeed, but so as many thousands are fed, with the addition of a little salt or buttermilk.[4]

[3] The tables reproduced in *English Historical Documents 1783–1832*, ed. A. Aspinall, Anthony Smith, and David Charles Douglas, 2nd edn. (London: Routledge, 1996), 612, show the working-class cost-of-living index falling more rapidly than industrial wages in the period between 1810 and 1850.

[4] *Evenings at Home: or, the Juvenile Budget Opened … For the Instruction and Amusement of Young Persons*, 2 vols. (Philadelphia: Troutman & Hayes, 1851), i.228–30.

Such calculations about how far half a crown might be stretched are intended to be exemplary—a crash-course in thrift—but Mayhew makes it clear that many of the street folk never possessed such a large sum. Seasonal factors and sickness meant that their earnings were subject to unpredictable fluctuations, a fact which made a nonsense of the standard advice, captured in Aikin and Barbauld's breezy calculation about purchasing 160 *lb* of potatoes, that they could save money by careful budgeting and buying in bulk.[5] The same problem helped to explain why the poor seemed to develop habits, particularly drink, they could not always afford. 'Were the income of the casual labourer at the docks 5*s*. per week from one year's end to another,' Mayhew points out, 'the workman would know exactly how much he had to subsist upon, and might therefore be expected to display some little providence and temperance in the expenditure of his wages. But where the means of subsistence occasionally rise to 15*s*. a-week, and occasionally sink to nothing, it is absurd to look for prudence, economy, or moderation. Regularity of habits are incompatible with irregularity of income' (*LLLP*, iii.309). Despite this, some of the workers Mayhew interviewed clearly tried to live on tight budgets, and when these are reproduced in *LLLP* they provide a good deal of information about what things cost and what could be afforded on an average weekly wage. At the relatively comfortable end of the scale, an unmarried scavenger working for a large contractor might have enough money left over each week for some 'Amusements':

[5] An article in Mayhew's *Figaro in London* (1 April 1837) sardonically compares a Poor Law Commissioner's daily expenses of one guinea, paid 'as a just compensation for their trouble in estimating how much, or rather how little, a poor man can live upon', with their estimate of what an able-bodied man needed each day: 11*d*., comprising half a loaf (4*d*.), half a pound of cheese (4*d*.), tea and sugar (2*d*.) and milk (1*d*.), but allowing nothing for rent, coals, meat, candles, clothes, soap, washing, or any of the other expenses the Commissioners would have taken for granted in their own lives. Mayhew's own research concluded that even skilled workers, such as tailors and dress-makers, sometimes had to live on half of that sum or less.

WEEKLY INCOME				WEEKLY EXPENDITURE			
Constant Wages	£	*s.*	*d.*		£	*s.*	*d.*
Nominal weekly wages	0	16	0	Rent	0	2	0
Perquisites	0	2	0	Washing and mending	0	0	10
				Clothes, and repairing ditto.	0	0	10
Actual weekly wages	0	18	0	Butcher's meat	0	3	6
				Bacon	0	0	8
				Vegetables	0	0	4
				Cheese	0	0	4
				Beer	0	3	0
				Spirits	0	1	0
				Tobacco	0	0	10½
				Butter	0	0	7½
				Sugar	0	0	4
				Tea	0	0	3
				Coffee	0	0	3
				Fish	0	0	4
				Soap	0	0	2
				Shaving	0	0	1
				Fruit	0	0	4
				Keep of 2 dogs	0	0	6
				Amusements, as skittles, &c.	0	1	9
					0	18	0

Source: LLLP, ii.231.

On the other hand, many of Mayhew's subjects—particularly the costermongers—were unable to provide him with such detailed breakdowns, because their incomes depended on factors largely beyond their control: competition, fashion, their health, the weather, luck. Unable to forecast how much they would have to spend on their stock and on themselves at the end of each week, they merely struggled on from day to day, their lives permanently shadowed by the twin threats of eviction and starvation. ('I keeps no account', another scavenger told him: 'money comes and it goes, and it goes a damned sight faster than it comes.') But even a budget of 18 shillings per week comes into clearer focus if it is compared with middle-class alternatives. The first edition of Mrs Beeton's *Book of Household Management* (1861) is full of money-saving tips for the frugal housewife; it also provides a list, 'supplied by Messrs. Richard & John Slack, 336, Strand', intended to show 'the articles required for the kitchen of a family in the middle class of life'. From '1 Tea-kettle' (6*s.* 6*d.*) to '1 Wood Meat-screen' (30*s.*), the list comprises 37 items, at a total cost of £8 11*s.* 1*d.*, with the reminder that Messrs. Slack publish 'a useful illustrated catalogue ... which it will be found advantageous to consult by those about to furnish'.[6] It is enough to put the most ambitious of wedding-lists to shame. Possibly some of Mayhew's readers, too.

[6] Mrs Isabella Beeton (ed.), *The Book of Household Management* (London: S. O. Beeton, 1861), 31.

APPENDIX 2

LONDON *c*.1848

MAP ENGRAVED IN GERMANY

Lower Holloway
Kentish Town
Belle Isle
Tunnel
Eisenbahn von Birmingham
ISLINGTON
CAMDEN TOWN
PORTLAND TOWN
Thiergarten
Regents P.
Pancras
Hyde Park
Serpentine
Green Park
Themse Strom
Battersea Newtown
Battersea
South Lambeth
Eisenbahn v. Southampton
Wandsworth
NORTH BRIXTON

Homerton
Hackney Marshes
Hackney Brook
Hackney Cut
KINGSLAND
Canal
Oltford
GLOBE TOWN
Bow
Counties
Eisenbahn
Eastern
Bromley Newtown
Canal
Bromley
Eisenbahn v. Blackwall
West India
Docks
Blackwall
Collier
Docks
Hunds Insel
Themse
Strom
Eisenbahn
Eisenbahn
Surrey
Canal
Peckham Newtown
Greenwich
Croydon
DEPTFORD
Hatcham

APPENDIX 3

'A TABLE SHOWING THE QUANTITY OF REFUSE BOUGHT, COLLECTED, OR FOUND, IN THE STREETS OF LONDON'

MAYHEW's love of order and statistical evidence can be seen at its sharpest, or possibly its bluntest, in the many tables of data he added to Vols. I–III of *London Labour and the London Poor.* (Vol. IV of the work, largely written by other hands, continued in the same spirit, eventually petering out into an appendix of thirty-three items that attempted to interpret England and Wales's criminal statistics in 1851, ranging from a predictable 'Map showing the Density of the Population' to a more quirky 'Map showing Committals for Bigamy'.) He was enthusiastic in retrieving this data but comparatively amateurish in analysing it, and Mayhew's facts and figures probably do not give an accurate picture of what his subjects spent their lives doing or avoiding,[1] but they serve as valuable snapshots of his own investigative priorities and blind-spots. The following table was part of Mayhew's survey of refuse collection, added to the work in 1856; his commentary appears on p. 206 above.

[1] Mayhew seems not to have corrected the errors in his text, even when he was willing to acknowledge them. (The long list of errata at the end of Vol. I is mostly taken up by inaccurate calculations.) E. P. Thompson's conclusion seems reasonable: 'Every single table and set of statistical data in Mayhew must be scrutinised, not for dishonesty or manipulation, but for sheer slipshod technique and haste in getting to press', 'The Political Education of Henry Mayhew', *Victorian Studies*, 11 (September 1967); 41–62 (p. 58).

A TABLE SHOWING THE QUANTITY OF REFUSE BOUGHT, COLLECTED, OR FOUND, IN THE STREETS OF LONDON.

Articles bought, collected, or found.	Annual gross quantity.	Average Number of Buyers, and quantity sold Daily or Weekly.	Obtained of the Street Buyers.	Price per pound weight, &c.	Average Yearly Money Value. £ s. d.	Parties to whom sold.
Refuse Metal.						
Copper	291,600 lbs.	200 buyers ¼ cwt. each weekly	1-500th	6d. per lb.	7,290 0 0	Sold to brass-founders and pewterers.
Brass	291,600 „	200 do. ¼ „ do.	„	4d. „	4,860 6 8	Do. do.
Iron	2,329,600 „	200 do. 2 „ do.	1-200th	¼d. „	2,426 13 4	Do. to iron-founders and manufacturers.
Steel	62,400 „	200 do. 6 lbs. do.	none	1d. „	260 0 0	Do. to manufacturers.
Lead	1,164,800 „	200 do. 1 cwt. do.	1-500th	1½d. „	7,280 0 0	Do. to brass-founders and pewterers.
Pewter	291,600 „	200 do. ¼ „ do.	„	5d. „	6,075 13 4	Do. do.
					28,192 13 4	
Horse & Carriage Furniture.						
Carriages	120 „	4 do. 30 sets yearly	none	11l. each	1,320 0 0	Sold to Jew dealers.
Wheels (4, from coach-builders)	600 sets	100 do. 8 do.	„	25s. a set	750 0 0	Do. to costers and small tradesmen.
Wheels, in pairs for carts & trucks	600 pairs	50 do. 12 pairs yearly	„	7s. a pair	210 0 0	Do. do.
Springs for trucks and small carts	780 „	5 do. 3 „ weekly	„	6s. per pair	234 0 0	Do. to costers and others.
Lace, from coach-builders	1,344 lbs.	12 do. 112 lbs. yearly	„	1d. per lb.	5 12 0	Do. to cab-masters and to Jews.
Fringe and tassels, from ditto	2,688 „	12 do. 224 „ do.	„	½d. „	5 12 0	Do. to Jews.
Coach & carriage linings, singly	156	12 do. 13 yearly	„	25s. each	195 0 0	Do. to cab-masters.
Harness (carriage pairs)	60 pairs	10 do. 6 pairs do.	„	3l. per pair	180 0 0	Do. to omnibus proprietors.
Ditto (single sets)	144 sets	12 do. 12 sets do.	„	30s. per set	216 0 0	Do, to cab-masters.
Ditto (sets of donkey and pony)	41,600 „	100 do. 8 sets weekly	harness makers	4s. a set	8,320 0 0	Do. to little master harness-makers.
Saddles	1,040 „	10 do. 2 „ do.	none	4s. „	203 0 0	Do. do.
Collars	2,080 „	10 do. 4 „ do.	„	9d. „	78 0 0	Do. do. and marine stores.
Bridles	4,160 „	10 do. 6 „ do.	„	8d. „	138 13 4	Do. do. do.
Pads	2,080 „	10 do. 4 „ do.	„	6d. „	52 0 0	Do. do.
Bits	4,160 „	10 do. 3 „ do.	„	2d. „	34 13 4	Do. do. do.
Leather (new cuttings from coach-builders)	58,136 lbs.	24 do. 22 cwt. yearly	„	4d. „	985 12 0	Do. to Jews and also to gunsmiths.
Ditto (morocco cuttings from do.)	960 „	20 do. 48 „ do.	„	1s. 6d. „	72 0 0	Do. to tailors' trimming-sellers.
Old leather (waste from ditto)	53,760 „	12 do. 20 „ do.	„	2½d. „	560 0 0	Do. to Jews.
					13,560 2 8	
Refuse Linen, Cotton, &c.						
Rags (woollen, consisting of tailors' shreds, old flannel drugget, carpet, and moreen)	4,659,200 lbs.	200 do. 4 „ weekly	1-1000th	½d. per lb.	9,706 13 4	Sold for manure and to nail up fruit-trees.
Ditto (coloured cotton)	2,912,000 „	200 do. 2½ „ do.	1-500th	½d. „	6,066 13 4	Do. to paper-makers and for quilts.
Ditto (white)	1,164,800 „	200 do. 1 „ do.	1-1000th	2d. „	9,706 13 4	Do. to paper-makers.
Canvas	44,800 „	200 do. 2 „ yearly	none	1d. „	186 13 4	Do. to chance customers.
Rope and sacking	291,200 „	200 do. ¼ „ weekly	1-500th	½d. „	606 13 4	Do. for oakum and sacking to mend old sacks.
					36,898 13 4	
Paper.						
Waste paper	1,397,760 „	60 colls. each disposing of 4 cwt. weekly	all	18s. per cwt.	11,232 0 0	Do. to shopkeepers.
Glass and Crockeryware.						
Bottles (common and doctors')	62,400 doz.	200 buyers, 24 weekly	1-100th	2d. per doz.	520 0 0	Do. to doctors and chemists.
Ditto (wine)	31,200 „	200 do. 12 do.	1-200th	6d. „	780 0 0	Do. to Brit. wine merchants & ale stores.
Ditto (porter and stout)	4,800 „	200 do. 24 dozen yearly	none	6d. „	120 0 0	Do. to ale and porter stores.
Flint glass	15,600 lbs.	200 do. 1½ lbs. weekly	1-1000th	¼d. per lb.	16 5 0	Do. to glass manufacturers.
Pickling jars	7,200 „	200 do. 36 yearly	none	¾d. each	22 10 0	Do. to Italian warehouses, &c.
Gallipots	20,800 doz.	200 do. 24 weekly	„	2d. per doz.	173 6 8	Do. do.
					1,632 1 8	

Article	Quantity	Collectors	How obtained	Price	£	s.	d.	How disposed of
Refuse Apparel.								
Coats	624,000	300 colls each. purchasing 8 coats daily	bt. of old clo' men	6s. each	187,200	0	0	Sold to old clo' men and wholesale dealers.
Trousers	312,000 pairs	300 do. do. 4 pr. trousers do.	,,	3s. 3d. per pr.	50,700	0	0	Do. do.
Waistcoats	312,000	300 do. do. 3 waistcoats do.	,,	7d. each	9,100	0	0	Do. do.
Under-waistcoats	46,800	300 do. do. 3 weekly	,,	2d. ,,	390	0	0	Do. to wholesale and wardrobe dealers.
Breeches and gaiters	15,600 pairs	300 do. do. 1 pair weekly	,,	2s. per pair	1,560	0	0	Do. to old clo' men and wholesale dealers.
Dressing-gowns	3,000	100 do. do. 30 yearly	,,	4s. 2d. each	625	0	0	Do. to wholesale and wardrobe dealers.
Cloaks (men's)	1,000	100 do. do. 10 cloaks yearly	,,	10s. ,,	500	0	0	Do. to wholesale dealers.
Boots and shoes	1,560,000 pairs	100 do. do. 60 pairs daily	,,	7d. per pair	45,500	0	0	Do. to wardrobe dealers and second-hand boot and shoe makers.
Boot and shoe soles	648,000 dz. pr	100 do. each collecting 30 dz. pr. daily	none	1s. per dz. pr.	32,400	0	0	Do. to Jews and gunsmiths to temper gun-barrels.
Boot legs	520,000 ,, ,,	200 do. do. 50 ,, weekly	,,	5s. ,,	130,000	0	0	Do. to translators.
Hats	1,879,000	300 colls. each purchasing 24 hats daily	bt. of old clo' men	4d. each	31,200	0	0	Do. to dealers and master hatters.
Boys' suits	3,600	300 do. do. 12 suits yearly	,,	3s. a suit	540	0	0	Do. Jew dealers.
Shirts and chemises	626,400	300 do. do. 8 daily	,,	4d. each	10,400	0	0	Do. to old clo' men and wholesale dealers.
Stockings of all kinds	783,000 pairs	100 do. do. 30 pair daily	,,	1d. per pair	3,272	10	0	Do. to wholesale and wardrobe dealers.
Drawers (men's and women's)	93,600 ,,	300 do. do. 6 ,, weekly	,,	3d. ,,	1,170	0	0	Do. do.
Women's dresses of all kinds	496,800	300 do. do. 6 dresses daily	,,	1s. 9d. each	41,107	10	0	Do. do.
Petticoats	939,600	300 do. do. 12 daily	,,	7d. ,,	27,405	0	0	Do. do.
Women's stays	261,000 pairs	100 do. do. 10 pair do.	,,	5d. per pair	5,437	10	0	Do. do.
Children's shirts	187,920	60 do. do. 12 daily	,,	3d. a doz.	195	15	0	Do. do.
Ditto petticoats	261,000	200 do. do. 5 do.	,,	1½d. each	1,639	11	8	Do. do.
Ditto frocks	522,000	200 do. do. 10 do.	,,	4d. ,,	8,700	0	0	Do. do.
Cloaks (women's), capes, visites, &c	5,200	20 do. do. 5 cloaks weekly	,,	4s. ,,	1,040	0	0	Do. to wholesale dealers.
Bonnets	1,409,400	150 do. do. 3 doz. daily	,,	6d. ,,	35,235	0	0	Do. do.
Shawls of all kinds	469,800	300 do. do. 6 daily	,,	1s. 2d. ,,	27,405	0	0	Do. to wholesale and wardrobe dealers.
Fur boas and victorines	261,000	100 do. do. 10 do.	,,	1s. 2d. ,,	15,220	0	0	Do. do.
Fur tippets and muffs	130,500	100 do. do. 5 do.	,,	1s. 2d. ,,	7,612	10	0	Do. do.
Umbrella and parasol frames	518,400	200 do., each collecting 12 daily	all	5d. ,,	10,300	0	0	Do. to Jews and old umbrella menders.
					675,555	6	8	
Household Refuse.								
Tea-leaves	78,000 lbs.	... ...	,,	2½d. per lb.	812	10	0	Do. to merchants to re-make into tea.
Fish-skins	3,900 ,,	25 do. do. 2 lbs. weekly for 6 months.	costers and fishmongers	1d. ,,	16	5	0	Do. to brewers to fine their ale.
Hare-skins	80,000	50 do. do. 50 weekly	all	1s. a doz.	333	6	8	Do. to Jews, hatters, and furriers.
Kitchen-stuff	62,400 lbs.	200 do. do. 6 lbs. weekly	none	1½d. per lb.	390	0	0	Do. at marine stores.
Dripping	52,000 ,,	200 do. do. 5 ,, do.	,,	3d. ,,	650	0	0	Do. do.
Bones	3,494,400 ,,	200 buyers 3 cwt. weekly	1-1000th	¾d. ,,	105,625	0	0	Do. for manure, knife-handles, &c.
Hogwash	2,504,000 gals.	200 do., each purchasing 40 gal. daily	all	1d. per gallon	10,433	6	8	Do. to pig-dealers.
Dust (from houses)	900,000 loads	... ...	none	2s. 6d. per ld.	112,500	0	0	Do. for manure and to brickmakers.
Soot	800,000 bush.	800 colls. each collectg. 19 bush. weekly	,,	5d. per bushel	16,666	13	4	Do. to farmers, graziers, and gardeners.
Soil (from cesspools)	750,000 loads	... .	,,	10s. per load	375,000	0	0	Do. for manure.
					622,427	1	8	
Street Refuse.								
Street sweepings (scavengers')	140,983 ,,	444 do. the whole ,, 452 lds. daily	,,	3s. ,,	21,147	9	0	Do. do.
Ditto (street orderlies')	2,817 ,,	546 do. do. ,, 9 ,, do.	,,	2s. 6d. ,,	2,352	2	6	Do. do.
Coal and coke (mudlarks')	64,656 cwt.	550 do., each collecting 42 lbs. do.	,,	8d. per cwt.	2,151	17	4	Do. to the poor.
"Pure"	52,000 pails	200 do. do. 5 pails weekly	,,	1s. per pail	2,600	0	0	Do. to tanners and leather-dressers.
Cigar ends	2,240 lbs.	50 do. do. 8½ lbs. do.	street-finders	8d. per lb.	74	13	4	Do. to Jews in Rosemary-lane.
					28,326	2	2	
				Gross Total	1,406,592	1	6	

APPENDIX 4

'A VISIT TO THE CHOLERA DISTRICTS OF BERMONDSEY'[1]

THERE is an Eastern fable which tells us that a certain city was infested by poisonous serpents that killed all they fastened upon; and the citizens, thinking them sent from Heaven as a scourge for their sins, kept praying that the visitation might be removed from them, until scarcely a house remained unsmitten. At length, however, concludes the parable, the eyes of the people were opened; for, after all their prayers and fastings, they found that the eggs of the poisonous serpents were hatched in the muck-heaps that surrounded their own dwellings.

The history of the late epidemic, which now seems to have almost spent its fatal fury upon us, has taught us that the masses of filth and corruption round the metropolis are, as it were, the nauseous nests of plague and pestilence. Indeed, so well known are the localities of fever and disease, that London would almost admit of being mapped out pathologically, and divided into its morbid districts and deadly cantons. We might lay our fingers on the Ordnance map, and say here is the typhoid parish, and there the ward of cholera; for as truly as the West-end rejoices in the title of Belgravia, might the southern shores of the Thames be christened Pestilentia. As season follows season, so does disease follow disease in the quarters that may be more literally than metaphorically styled the plague-spots of London. If the seasons are favourable, and typhus does not bring death to almost every door, then influenza and scarlatina fill the workhouses with the families of the sick. So certain and regular are the diseases in their returns, that each epidemic, as it comes back summer after summer, breaks out in the self-same streets as it appeared on its former visit, with but this slight difference, that if at its last visitation it began at the top of the street, and killed its way down, this time it begins at the bottom, and kills its way as surely up the lines of houses.

Out of the 12,800 deaths which, within the last three months, have arisen from cholera, 6,500 have occurred on the southern shores of the Thames; and to this awful number no localities have contributed so largely as Lambeth, Southwark, and Bermondsey, each, at the height of the disease, adding its hundred victims a week to the fearful catalogue of mortality. Any one who has ventured a visit to the last-named of these places in particular, will not wonder at the ravages of the pestilence in this malarious quarter, for it is bounded on the north and east by filth and fever, and on the south

[1] This was the first of Mayhew's *Morning Chronicle* articles, published on 24 September 1849 (see Introduction, p. xviii).

and west by want, squalor, rags and pestilence. Here stands, as it were, the very capital of cholera, the Jessore* of London—JACOB'S ISLAND, a patch of ground insulated by the common sewer. Spared by the fire of London, the houses and comforts of the people in this loathsome place have scarcely known any improvement since that time. The place is a century behind even the low and squalid districts that surround it.

In the days of Henry II, the foul stagnant ditch that now makes an island of this pestilential spot, was a running stream, supplied with the waters which poured down from the hills about Sydenham and Nunhead, and was used for the working of the mills that then stood on its banks. These had been granted by charter to the monks of St Mary and St John, to grind their flour, and were dependencies upon the Priory of Bermondsey. Tradition tells us that what is now a straw yard skirting the river, was once the City Ranelagh, called 'Cupid's Gardens', and that the trees, which are now black with mud, were the bowers under which the citizens loved, on the sultry summer evenings, to sit beside the stream drinking their sack and ale. But now the running brook is changed into a tidal sewer, in whose putrid filth staves are laid to season; and where the ancient summer-houses stood, nothing but hovels, sties, and muck-heaps are now to be seen.

Not far from the Tunnel there is a creek opening into the Thames. The entrance to this is screened by the tiers of colliers which lie before it. This creek bears the name of the Dock Head. Sometimes it is called St Saviour's, or, in jocular allusion to the odour for which it is celebrated, Savory Dock. The walls of the warehouses on each side of this muddy stream are green and slimy, and barges lie beside them, above which sacks of corn are continually dangling from the cranes aloft. This creek was once supplied by the streams from the Surrey hills, but now nothing but the drains and refuse of the houses that have grown up round about it thickens and swells its waters.

On entering the precincts of the pest island, the air has literally the smell of a graveyard, and a feeling of nausea and heaviness comes over any one unaccustomed to imbibe the musty atmosphere. It is not only the nose, but the stomach, that tells how heavily the air is loaded with sulphuretted hydrogen; and as soon as you cross one of the crazy and rotting bridges over the reeking ditch, you know, as surely as if you had chemically tested it, by the black colour of what was once the white-lead paint upon the door-posts and window-sills, that the air is thickly charged with this deadly gas. The heavy bubbles which now and then rise up in the water show you whence at least a portion of the mephitic compound comes, while the open doorless privies that hang over the water side on one of the banks, and the dark streaks of filth down the walls where the drains from each house discharge themselves into the ditch on the opposite side, tell you how the pollution of the ditch is supplied.

The water is covered with a scum almost like a cobweb, and prismatic with grease. In it float large masses of green rotting weed, and against the posts of the bridges are swollen carcasses of dead animals, almost bursting with the gases of putrefaction. Along its shores are heaps of indescribable filth, the phosphoretted smell from which tells you of the rotting fish there, while the oyster shells are like pieces of slate from their coating of mud and filth. In some parts the fluid is almost as red as blood from the colouring matter that pours into it from the reeking leather-dressers' close by.

The striking peculiarity of Jacob's Island consists in the wooden galleries and sleeping-rooms at the back of the houses which overhang the dark flood, and are built upon piles, so that the place has positively the air of a Flemish street, flanking a sewer instead of a canal; while the little ricketty bridges that span the ditches and connect court with court, give it the appearance of the Venice of drains, where channels before and behind the houses do duty for the ocean. Across some parts of the stream whole rooms have been built, so that house adjoins house; and here, with the very stench of death rising through the boards, human beings sleep night after night, until the last sleep of all comes upon them years before its time. Scarce a house but yellow linen is hanging to dry over the balustrade of staves, or else run out on a long oar where the sulphur-coloured clothes hang over the waters, and you are almost wonderstruck to see their form and colour unreflected in the putrid ditch beneath.

At the back of nearly every house that boasts a square foot or two of outlet—and the majority have none at all—are pig-sties. In front waddle ducks, while cocks and hens scratch at the cinder-heaps. Indeed, the creatures that fatten on offal are the only living things that seem to flourish here.

The inhabitants themselves show in their faces the poisonous influence of the mephitic air they breathe. Either their skins are white, like parchment, telling of the impaired digestion, the languid circulation, and the coldness of the skin peculiar to persons suffering from chronic poisoning, or else their cheeks are flushed hectically, and their eyes are glassy, showing the wasting fever and general decline of the bodily functions. The brown, earthlike complexion of some, and their sunk eyes, with the dark areolae round them, tell you that the sulphuretted hydrogen of the atmosphere in which they live has been absorbed into the blood; while others are remarkable for the watery eye exhibiting the increased secretion of tears so peculiar to those who are exposed to the exhalations of hydro-sulphate of ammonia.

Scarcely a girl that has not suffusion and soreness of the eyes, so that you would almost fancy she had been swallowing small doses of arsenic; while it is evident from the irritation and discharge from the mucous membranes of the nose and eyes for which all the children are distinguished, that the poor emaciated things are suffering from continual inhalation of the vapour of carbonate of ammonia and other deleterious gases.

Nor was this to be wondered at, when the whole air reeked with the stench of rotting animal and vegetable matter; for the experiment of Professor Donovan has shown that a rabbit, with only its body enclosed in a bladder filled with sulphuretted hydrogen, and allowed to breathe freely, will die in ten minutes. Thenard also has proved that one eight hundredth part of this gas in the atmosphere is sufficient to destroy a dog, and one two hundred and fiftieth will kill a horse; while Mr Taylor, in his book on poisons, assures us that the men who were engaged in excavating the Thames Tunnel suffered severely during the work from the presence of this gas in the atmosphere in which they were obliged to labour. 'The air, as well as the water which trickled through the roof', he tells us, 'was found to contain sulphuretted hydrogen. This was probably derived from the action of the iron pyrites in the clay. By respiring this atmosphere the strongest and most robust men were, in the course of a few months, reduced to a state of extreme exhaustion and died. They became emaciated, and fell into a state of low fever, accompanied with delirium. In one case which I saw,' he adds, 'the face of the man was pale, the lips of a violet hue, the eyes sunk and dark all round, and the whole muscular system flabby and emaciated.' To give the reader some idea as to the extent with which the air in Jacob's Island is charged with this most deadly compound, it will be sufficient to say that a silver spoon of which we caught sight in one of the least wretched dwellings was positively chocolate-coloured by the action of the sulphur on the metal.

On approaching the tidal ditch from the Neckinger-road, the shutters of the house at the corner were shut from top to bottom. Our intelligent and obliging guide, Dr Martin, informed us that a girl was then lying dead there from cholera, and that but very recently another victim had fallen in the house adjoining it. This was the beginning of the tale of death, for the tidal ditch was filled up to this very point. Here, however, its putrefying waters were left to mingle their poison with the 267 cubic feet of air that each man daily takes into his lungs, and this was the point whence the pestilence commenced its ravages. As we walked down George-row, our informant told us that at the corner of London-street he could see, a short time back, as many as nine houses in which there were one or two persons lying dead of the cholera at the same time; and yet there could not have been more than a dozen tenements visible from the spot.

We crossed the bridge, and spoke to one of the inmates. In answer to our questions, she told us she was never well. Indeed, the signs of the deadly influence of the place were painted in the earthy complexion of the poor woman. 'Neither I nor my children know what health is,' said she. 'But what is one to do? We must live where our bread is. I've tried to let the house, and put a bill up, but cannot get any one to take it.' From this spot we were led to narrow close courts, where the sun never shone, and the air seemed almost as stagnant and putrid as the ditch we had left. The blanched cheeks of the people that now came out to stare at us, were white as vegetables grown in the dark, and as we stopped to look down the alley, our informant told us that the place teemed with children, and that if a horn was blown they would swarm like bees at the sound of a gong. The houses were mostly inhabited by 'cornrunners', coal-porters, and 'longshore-men', getting a precarious living—earning sometimes as much as 12*s.* a day, and then for weeks doing nothing. Fevers prevailed in these courts we were told more than at the side of the ditch.

By this way we reached a dismal stack of hovels called, by a strange incongruity, Pleasant-row. Inquiring of one of the inmates, we were informed that they were quite comfortable now! The stench had been all removed, said the woman, and we were invited to pass to the back-yard as evidence of the fact. We did so; the boards bent under our feet, and the air in the cellar-like yard was foetid to positive nausea. As we left the house a child sat nursing a dying half-comatose baby on a door step. The skin of its little arms, instead of being plumped out with health, was loose and shrivelled, like an old crone's, and had a flabby monkey-like appearance more than the character of human cuticle. The almost jaundiced colour of the child's skin, its half paralyzed limbs, and state of stupor, told it was suffering from some slow poison; indeed the symptoms might readily have been mistaken for those of chronic poisoning from acetate of lead. At the end of this row our friend informed us that the last house on either side was *never* free from fever.

Continuing our course we reached 'The Folly', another street so narrow that the names and trades of the shopmen were painted on boards that stretched, across the street, from the roof of their own house to that of their neighbour's. We were here stopped by our companion in front of a house 'to let'. The building was as narrow and as unlike a human habitation as the wooden houses in a child's box of toys. 'In this house,' said our friend, 'when the scarlet fever was raging in the neighbourhood, the barber who was living here suffered fearfully from it; and no sooner did the man get well of this than he was seized with typhus, and scarcely had he recovered from the first attack than he was struck down a second time with the same terrible disease. Since then he has lost his child with cholera, and at this moment his wife is in the workhouse suffering from the same affliction. The only wonder is that they are not all dead, for as the man sat at his meals in his small shop, if he put his hand against the wall behind him, it would be covered with the soil of his neighbour's privy, sopping through the wall.

At the back of the house was an open sewer, and the privies were full to the seal.'

One fact, says an eminent writer in toxicology, is worthy of the attention of medical jurists, namely, that the respiration of an atmosphere only slightly impregnated with the gases emanating from drains and sewers, may, if long continued, seriously affect an individual and cause death. M. D'Arcet had to examine a lodging in Paris, in which three young and vigorous men had died successively in the course of a few years, under similar symptoms. The lodging consisted of a bed-room with a chimney, and an ill-ventilated ante-room. The pipe of a privy passed down one side of the room, by the head of the bed, and the wall in this part was damp from infiltration. At the time of the examination there was no perceptible smell in the room, though it was small and low. M. D'Arcet attributed the mortality in the lodging to the slow and long-continued action of the emanations from the pipe (Ann. d'Hyg., Juillet 1836).

We then journeyed on to London-street, down which the tidal ditch continues its course. In No. 1 of this street the cholera first appeared seventeen years ago, and spread up it with fearful virulence; but this year it appeared at the opposite end, and ran down it with like severity. As we passed along the reeking banks of the sewer the sun shone upon a narrow slip of the water. In the bright light it appeared the colour of strong green tea, and positively looked as solid as black marble in the shadow—indeed it was more like watery mud than muddy water; and yet we were assured this was the only water the wretched inhabitants had to drink. As we gazed in horror at it, we saw drains and sewers emptying their filthy contents into it; we saw a whole tier of doorless privies in the open road, common to men and women, built over it; we heard bucket after bucket of filth splash into it, and the limbs of the vagrant boys bathing in it seemed, by pure force of contrast, white as Parian marble. And yet, as we stood doubting the fearful statement, we saw a little child, from one of the galleries opposite, lower a tin can with a rope to fill a large bucket that stood beside her. In each of the balconies that hung over the stream the self-same tub was to be seen in which the inhabitants put the mucky liquid to stand, so that they may, after it has rested for a day or two, skim the fluid from the solid particles of filth, pollution, and disease. As the little thing dangled her tin cup as gently as possible into the stream, a bucket of night-soil was poured down from the next gallery.

In this wretched place we were taken to a house where an infant lay dead of the cholera. We asked if they *really did* drink the water? The answer was, 'They were obliged to drink the ditch, without they could beg a pailfull or thieve a pailfull of water.' 'But have you spoken to your landlord about having it laid on for you?' 'Yes, sir; and he says he'll do it, and do it, but we know him better than to believe him.' 'Why, sir,' cried another woman, who had shot out from an adjoining room, 'he won't even give us a little whitewash, though we tell him we'll willingly do the work ourselves: and look here, sir,' she added, 'all the tiles have fallen off, and the rain pours in wholesale.'

We had scarcely left the house when a bill caught our eye, announcing that 'this valuable estate' was to be sold!

From this spot we crossed the little shaky bridge into Providence-buildings—a narrow neck of land set in sewers. Here, in front of the houses, were small gardens that a table-cloth would have covered. Still the one dahlia that here raised its round red head made it a happier and brighter place. Never was colour so grateful to the eye. All we had looked at had been so black and dingy, and had smelt so much of churchyard clay, that this little patch of beauty was brighter and greener than ever was oasis in the desert. Here a herd of children came out, and stared at us like sheep. One child our guide singled out from the rest. She had the complexion of tawed leather, and her bright, glassy eyes were sunk so far back in her head, that they looked more like lights shining through the hollow sockets of a skull than a living head, and her bones seemed ready to start through the thin layer of skin. We were told she had had the cholera twice. Her father was dead of it. 'But she, sir,' said a woman addressing us, 'won't die. Ah! if she'd had plenty of victuals and been brought up less hardy she would have been dead and buried long ago, like many more. And here's another,' she added, pushing forward a long thin woman in rusty black. 'Why, I've know'd her eat as much as a quartern loaf at a meal. and you can't fatten her no how.' Upon this there was a laugh, but in the woman's bloodless cheeks and blue lips we saw that she like the rest was wasting away from the influence of the charnel-like atmosphere around her.

The last place we went to was in Joiner's-court, with four wooden houses in it, in which there had lately been as many as five cases of cholera. In front, the poor souls, as if knowing by an instinct that plants were given to purify the atmosphere, had pulled up the paving-stones before their dwellings, and planted a few stocks here and there in the rich black mould beneath. The first house we went to, a wild ragged-headed boy shot out in answer to our knock, and putting his hands across the doorway, stood there to prevent our entrance. Our friend asked whether he could enter, and see the state of the drainage? 'No; t'ain't convenient,' was the answer, given so quickly and sharply, that the lad forced some ugly and uncharitable suspicion upon us. In the next house, the poor inmate was too glad to meet with any one ready to sympathise with her sufferings. We were taken up into a room, where we were told she had positively lived for nine years. The window was within four feet of a high wall, at the foot of which, until very recently, ran the open common sewer. The room was so dark that it was several minutes before we could see anything within it, and there was a smell of must and dry rot that told of damp and imperfect ventilation, and the unnatural size of the pupils of the wretched woman's eyes convinced us how much too long she had dwelt in this gloomy place.

Here, as usual, we heard stories that made one's blood curdle, of the cruelty of those from whom they rented the sties called dwellings. They had begged for pure water to be laid on, and the rain to be shut out; and the answer for eighteen years had been, that the lease was just out. 'They knows it's handy for a man's work,' said one and all, 'and that's the reason why they impose on a body.' This, indeed, seems to us to be the great evil. Out of these wretches' health, comfort, and even lives, small capitalists reap a petty independence; and until the poor are rescued from the fangs of these mercenary men, there is but little hope either for their physical or moral welfare.

The extreme lassitude and deficient energy of both body and mind induced by the mephitic vapours they continually inhale leads them—we may say, *forces* them to seek an unnatural stimulus in the gin-shop; indeed, the publicans of Jacob's Island drive even a more profitable trade than the landlords themselves. What wonder, then, since debility is one of the predisposing conditions of cholera, that—even if these stenches of the foul tidal ditch be not the *direct* cause of the disease—that the impaired digestive functions, the languid circulation, the depression of mind produced by the continued inhalation of the noxious gases of the tidal ditch, together with the intemperance that it induces—the cold, damp houses—and, above all, the quenching of the thirst and cooking of the food with water saturated with the very excrements of their fellow creatures, should make Jacob's Island notorious as the Jessore of England.

EXPLANATORY NOTES

No attempt is made here to offer a full glossary of the street slang which peppers Mayhew's prose, although words and phrases are explained where their sense is unclear, or where it has altered significantly since the date of original publication. Where appropriate, these explanations draw on specialized studies from the period such as J. C. Hotton's *The Slang Dictionary, Etymological, Historical, and Anecdotal* (rev. edn., 1874), and Albert Barrère and Charles G. Leland's *A Dictionary of Slang, Jargon and Cant* (2 vols., 1889). The only exceptions to this rule are terms which Mayhew himself glosses, as in his description of an encounter between two 'patterers' on p. 75. Biblical references are to the King James Bible (1611).

3 *'blue book'*: Royal Commission and Select Committee reports on sanitation, housing, health, and other social concerns, which were issued with a blue cover and often referred to in the press.

Bruce: James Bruce (1730–94), Scottish traveller and travel-writer who was the first to trace the origins of the Blue Nile; although his account of his adventures met with disbelief upon his return to London in 1774, it was subsequently proven to be accurate.

4 *Mr HENRY WOOD and Mr RICHARD KNIGHT*: members of the London City Mission, founded in 1835 by David Nasmith (1799–1839) with the aim of 'evangelization of the vast mass of heathenism in our midst, commencing with the very poorest and most neglected portions of London. It seeks to effect this object by a system of visitation of the poor at their own dwellings' (R. W. Vanderkiste, *Notes and Narratives of a Six Years Mission, Principally Among the Dens of London*, 1852).

5 *Costermongers*: men and women who sold fruit, vegetables, fish, etc. in the street from a barrow.

Patterers: Mayhew defines this class in the section on street-sellers of stationery, literature, and the fine arts: see p. 76.

9 *grun'sel*: i.e. groundsel, a common weed used for medicinal purposes or fed to caged birds; in *Oliver Twist* (1838), there is a reference to 'Fresh groundsel . . . for Miss Maylie's birds' (ch. 32).

plum 'duff': a rich pudding made with raisins, currants and spices; 'duff' is a dialect version of 'dough'. The dish, or at least the word for it, was relatively new: the *OED*'s first citation is from 1838. (Mayhew's later reference to 'plum duffers'—i.e. street-sellers of plum duff—is the only one recorded in the *OED*.)

10 *gelatine poetry cards*: thin sheets of gelatine were applied to cards as a form of varnish. An 1854 article in *Household Words* describes how a skilled 'gelatineur' can apply it to 'address cards, visiting cards, or *images*

réligieuses, which may be either coloured or colourless' ('Done to a Jelly'); later in *LLLP* Mayhew adds that 'Some of the gelatine cards contain pieces of poetry, in letters of gold, always . . . of a religious or sentimental character.'

10 *lucifers*: matches that worked when struck against a rough surface were invented in 1827 and sold as 'Lucifers' from 1829.

corn-salves: ointment for softening and (supposedly) removing corns and bunions on the feet; see p. 130.

plating-balls: chemical compound designed to give metal surfaces a newly polished appearance.

detonating-balls: small firecrackers designed to explode when trodden on or thrown; Joseph Fitzgerald Molloy's biography of King William IV (1765–1837), *The Sailor King* (1903), describes how Lord Melbourne was 'startled and irritated' by the naughty antics of a page boy who 'delighted in flinging detonating balls into the fire' (ch. 5).

cigar-lights: tapers or matches.

Dutch ovens: cast-iron cooking pots with tight-fitting lids.

stay-laces: the strings or cords used to draw together a woman's stays or bodice.

'lots': sets of small articles sold together for a penny.

wash-leather: a soft kind of leather, usually sheepskin.

Bristol toys: cheap toys, many of which were sold for a penny or less.

spar ornaments: ornaments made from fragments of 'spar', a form of natural crystal.

11 *fantoccini*: dancing marionettes, from the Italian *fantoccio* (puppet); they had been a popular London street attraction since at least the eighteenth century—Boswell mentions them in his *Life of Samuel Johnson* (1791).

Chinese shades: according to John Times's *Curiosities of London* (rev. edn., 1868), 'the Chinese Shades consist of a frame like Punch's, with a transparent curtain and moveable figures; shown only at night, with much dialogue'.

sapient pigs: during the eighteenth and early nineteenth centuries there was a fashion for 'learned pigs' trained to do tricks; in 1820 Nicholas Hoare published *The Life and Adventures of Toby, the Sapient Pig . . . Written by Himself*, a tongue-in-cheek work which included 'An Elegant Frontispiece, Descriptive of a Literary Pig Sty, with the Author in Deep Study'. Surviving advertising bills show that in 1817 Toby's owner was claiming that in each performance 'THIS MOST EXTRAORDINARY CREATURE Will Spell and Read, Cast Accounts, PLAY AT CARDS; Tell any Person what o'Clock it is to a Minute BY THEIR OWN WATCH; ALSO TELL THE AGE OF ANY ONE IN COMPANY, And what is more Astonishing he will Discover a Person's Thoughts.'

'Billy Barlows': 'Billy Barlow' is described by Mayhew elsewhere in *LLLP* as a 'supposed comic character that usually accompanies either the street dancers or acrobats in their peregrinations. The dress consists of a cocked hat and red feather, a soldier's coat (generally a sergeant's, with sash), white trousers with the bottoms tucked into wellington boots, a large tin eyeglass, and an old broken and ragged umbrella. The nose and cheeks are coloured bright red with vermilion. The "comic business" consists of the songs of the "Merry month of May", and "Billy Barlow", together with a few old conundrums and jokes, and sometimes ("where the halfpence are very plentiful") a "comic dance".'

'Jim Crows': a character made popular by the American 'blackface' minstrel Tomas D. Rice (1806–60), depicting a ragged, charismatic slave singing and dancing with madcap energy; the original and most popular version of the song associated with the character was 'Jump Jim Crow'.

happy families: see p. 293 on these 'assemblages of animals of diverse habits and propensities living amicably, or at least quietly, in one cage'.

thaumascope: a scientific toy which combined two or more images into one, e.g. by spinning a piece of card that has an image printed on each side.

12 *improvisatori*: described in Tobias Smollett's *Travels Through France and Italy* (1766) as 'the name given to certain individuals, who have the surprising talent of reciting verses extempore, on any subject you propose'. They later became a wider European fad: fictional versions appear in Madame de Staël's *Corinne, or Italy* (1807) and Hans Christian Andersen's *The Improvisatore* (1830), while Thackeray's *The Newcomes* (1855) includes the figure of 'little Nadab the Improvisatore' (ch. 1).

Chinese roarers: a toy consisting of a strip of wood or bone which is whirled around by means of a string to produce a loud hum or 'roar'; more commonly known as a 'bull-roarer'.

Dutch dolls: jointed wooden dolls.

buy-a-brooms: girls or young women who sold brooms on the streets; they were often Dutch and quaintly dressed. Here Mayhew is referring to the dolls made in their image; William Hone's *Every Day Book* (1825–6) describes how 'Their figures are exactly miniatured in an unpainted penny doll of turnery ware . . . sold in the toyshops for the amusement of infancy.'

gutta-percha heads: 'small coloured models of the human face, usually with projecting nose and chin, and wide or distorted mouth, which admit of being squeezed into a different form of features, their elasticity causing them to return to the original caste' (*LLLP*, i.434). Gutta-percha—a form of tropical rubber—was a relatively new manufacturing material: a visit to the 'Gutta Percha Company's Works' recorded in David W. Bartlett's *London by Day and Night* (1852) suggests that the first shipment of raw materials was sent in 1843. It was soft and pliable, so gave the illusion of lifelike flesh when used in the manufacture of dolls; *Chamber's Journal* reported in 1856 that, although wax and china dolls had become impressively detailed in design, 'the introduction of gutta-percha has given a new element; and crying dolls, walking dolls, and talking dolls, make grandmothers feel that they lived a century too early' ('Children's Playthings'). Mayhew goes on to suggest that these cheap novelty heads were in fact made from a mixture of glue and treacle rather than genuine gutta-percha (i.434).

13 *night-shades*: screens designed to protect the flame of a candle or lamp.

hassocks: firm cushions, often stuffed with straw, used to rest the feet on.

flushermen: workers employed to flush out the sewers.

'street-orderlies': road-sweepers.

watering-carts: used since the start of the eighteenth century to clean the city's streets and damp down their dust.

turn-cocks: officials employed by the waterworks.

link-men: 'links' were torches made of cloth dipped in pitch or tar; 'link-men' or 'links' hired themselves out to light the way of travellers along the streets.

14 *New-cut . . . Brill*: streets in, respectively, Lambeth and Somers Town, well known for their markets; in one of his original *Morning Chronicle* letters (27 November 1849) Mayhew observed that 'These are both about half a mile in length, and each of them is frequented by as nearly as possible 300 hucksters.'

self-generating gas-lamp: a lamp, patented in the 1820s, which produced its own gas by dripping oil onto a heated plate.

cheapen: bid or bargain for.

15 *a skin, blacking*: 'blacking' was a form of liquid shoe polish, usually sold in earthenware bottles but sometimes in 'skins' (slang), containers made from animal hide.

Half-quire: about a dozen sheets of paper (a quire is 24 or 25 sheets).

ha'p'orths: sweets costing a halfpenny.

toasters: toasting-forks, or perhaps here meaning fish ready to be broiled.

Chesterfields: the 'Chesterfield' is a style of overcoat which first appeared in the 1840s. Named after the well-known socialite George Stanhope, 6th earl of Chesterfield (1805–66), it was usually a long double-breasted coat with a velvet collar.

fustian jackets: made from a coarse cotton cloth and usually dyed a dark colour.

16 *Mazeppa*: Ivan Stepanovych Mazepa (popularly spelled Mazeppa) (1639–1709), Hetman (military commander) of the Hetmanate, a state in the Ukraine, in 1687–1708, who led his Cossacks against the Russian Empire, and is still viewed accordingly as either a national hero or a

traitor. His life inspired poems by Lord Byron, Alexander Pushkin, and Victor Hugo.

Paul Jones the pirate: born in Scotland, the former slave-trader and merchant seaman John Paul Jones (1747–92) joined the new Continental Navy soon after he arrived in America in 1774. He became notorious during the American War of Independence for his sudden and bloody attacks on British ships, and was accordingly celebrated in his adopted country as a patriot while being viewed in Britain as a ruthless pirate in the vein of Blackbeard. His exploits featured in many blood-curdling chapbooks and caricatures.

16 *Leather-lane . . . Whitecross-street*: venues of popular London street markets.

17 *the language of the class*: see p. 30 below.

usual games: all-fours: a card game in which four different items count towards the score; all-fives: like 'all-fours' with the addition of an extra scoring item; cribbage: another scoring game, in which points are awarded for particular card combinations; put: a tavern card game, castigated by seventeenth-century moralists as one of particularly ill repute, in which bluff plays a major part; whist: a more genteel card game, which generated elaborate rules and forms of etiquette during the nineteenth century.

18 *'Skittles'*: an early version of bowling, with many regional variations such as 'ninepins' (a popular pub game) in London.

20 *tanners*: men who converted hides into leather by tanning.

'a lark': a joke, or a bit of fun; hence Joe Gargery's catchphrase 'what larks' in Dickens's *Great Expectations* (1860–1).

'the art of self-defence': boxing; many books and articles were published with this title during the nineteenth century.

'Twopenny hops': dancing rooms, costing twopence for admission; 'The clog hornpipe, the pipe dance, flash jigs, and hornpipes in fetters, *à la* Jack Sheppard, are the favourite movements, all entered into with great gusto' (Hotten, *Slang Dictionary*).

professor: a grandiose and often mocking title applied to professional teachers of dancing (also called 'dancing masters') and other pastimes.

'Jack Sheppard': Jack Sheppard (1702–24) was a notorious thief who became a folk hero among the poor after escaping from prison four times, but was eventually recaptured and hanged at Tyburn. In the nineteenth century his life inspired William Ainsworth Harrison's novel *Jack Sheppard* (1839), which was adapted for the stage by John Buckstone and frequently pirated. Widespread public fear that Sheppard might inspire others to follow his example led to the Lord Chamberlain banning the licensing of any play in London with 'Jack Sheppard' in the title for forty years.

21 *cornopean*: another name for the *cornet à piston*, a brass musical instrument in the trumpet class.

21 *the Surrey-side*: the south side of the Thames.

neither end nor side: i.e. neither head nor tail.

can't tumble to that barrikin: i.e. don't understand that language (slang).

Flash: showy, smart, knowing; also counterfeit or deceptive (slang).

22 *Marshal Haynau*: Julius Jacob von Haynau (1786–1853), who rose to the rank of field marshal lieutenant in the Austrian army, had a reputation for brutality (in Italy he ordered that any women who showed sympathy for insurgents should be whipped) that led to him being beaten up by two draymen at Barclay, Perkins & Co.'s Bankside brewery in 1850. The event inspired several popular songs celebrating the men as chivalrous and patriotic heroes. When the Italian leader Giuseppe Garibaldi visited England in 1864, he insisted on visiting the brewery to thank 'the men who flogged Haynau'.

'Britons . . . slaves': part of the chorus to 'Rule, Britannia!', a poem by James Thomson which was set to music by Thomas Arne in 1740 and rapidly established itself as an unofficial alternative to the National Anthem. The line 'Britannia, rule the waves' was often rendered as 'Britannia rules the waves' in the nineteenth century, once it became clear that what had originally been intended as a patriotic exhortation was now largely a matter of fact.

court: one of the small, crowded courtyards off the main streets of London, here punning on the sense of a royal court.

23 *Red-house*: the Red House was an old tavern, demolished in 1853, which had become notorious for theft, brawling, and debauchery. The surrounding area of Battersea Fields was used for racing, gambling, and shooting until it was cleaned up and landscaped as Battersea Park.

bobbies: policemen (slang), named after Sir Robert Peel, who was Home Secretary when the Metropolitan Police Act was passed in 1828.

24 *pad*: an open wickerwork basket used as a measure for fish.

Coburg: the Coburg Theatre was built in 1818; in 1833 it was renamed the Royal Victorian Theatre after the heir to the throne Princess Victoria, and is now popularly known as the Old Vic.

25 *terrible results*: perhaps a reference to the collapse of a staircase at The Polytechnic in January 1859 as a crowd of between 700 and 1,000 was leaving: a 10-year old girl was killed and thirty other people injured.

return checks: a type of theatre ticket designed to prevent fraud; a sketch published in *Punch* describes how 'words, selected at random, were printed on them, and changed every night to prevent cheating by the class . . . who haunt the plebian part of the theatre' ('The Naggletons and the Bishop', 25 April 1863).

26 *'the gods'*: spectators in the upper gallery of a theatre, so named because of the height and the fact that the ceiling was often painted blue.

'a-larning the pynanney': i.e. learning the piano, widely seen as a social accomplishment of women of the middle and upper classes.

27 *microscopic eels in paste*: see p. 245 for Mayhew's description of the street-exhibitor of the microscope. Through popular exhibitions and publications, the microscope revealed a world of minute creatures hidden from everyday sight; on a visit to London in 1833, Tennyson looked through microscopes at 'moths' wings, gnats' heads, and at all the lions and tigers which lie perdus in a drop of spring water' (Hallam Tennyson, *Tennyson, a Memoir*, 1897).

'The Child of the Storm's' declaration: D. W. Osbaldiston's (1794–1850) play *Catharine of Russia; or, The Child of the Storm* (1850), performed at the Victoria Theatre in September 1850 with Eliza Vincent (d. 1856) as Catharine.

split in the hornpipe: an athletic dance move.

'dummestic dreamer': i.e. domestic drama, a form of melodrama with clear moral lessons that was especially popular among working-class audiences.

'Port-a-a-a-r': i.e. porter, a dark-brown or black bitter beer.

28 *Exeter Hall*: built between 1829 and 1831 on the north side of the Strand, on a site formerly part of Exeter House, the main auditorium could hold more than 4,000 people, and was used for holding meetings of religious and philanthropic associations, including the Protestant Association and the Anti-Slavery Society. It became a byword for noisy audiences: 'When such an assembly rises, for prayer or praise . . . the degree of sound they are to produce, in the way of cheering or singing, is almost incredible' (*Random Recollections of Exeter Hall, in 1834–1837; by One of The Protestant Party*, 1838).

'angcore': i.e. encore.

"Duck-legged Dick": see p. 22.

29 *plasket*: i.e. basket.

Euston-square: Euston station, which opened as the terminus of the London and Birmingham Railway in 1837.

Billingsgate: London's largest fish market; in 1849 it moved to its own riverside building, which was subsequently demolished in 1873 and replaced by an arcaded market hall designed by Horace Jones.

30 *tap-room*: a room in a tavern, in which liquors are kept on tap.

redeem . . . uncle's: i.e. buy back my best clothes from the pawnbroker (slang); Dickens's *Martin Chuzzlewit* (1843–4) has fun at the expense of a character who is 'constantly making reference to an uncle, in respect of whom he would seem to have entertained great expectations, as he was in the habit of seeking to propitiate his favour by presents of plate, jewels, books, watches, and other valuable articles' (ch. 1).

Malthus: the Revd Thomas Malthus (1766–1834), who argued in the second edition of his *Essay on the Principles of Population* (1803) that any child unable to be supported by his parents, and whose labour was not wanted by society, 'has no claim of *right* to the smallest portion of food, and, in fact, has no business to be where he is'. Mayhew had raised the subject in one of his 'Answers to Correspondents' printed on the wrapper of *LLLP*, sarcastically (and erroneously) arguing that Thomas Carlyle had advocated the policy that 'all children of working people, after the third, be disposed of by "painless extinction"' (no. 58, 17 January 1852).

34 *tol-de-rol*: a nonsense word, like 'fol-de-rol', used in the choruses of many popular songs.

'Gaffy': from a 'gaff' (slang), a place of popular entertainment.

35 *M. Jullien*: Louis Antoine Jullien (1812–60), French orchestral conductor and showman, who became famous for his portly, gorgeously waistcoated appearance, and his 'monster concerts', which included special effects such as a garden-roller being dragged across sheets of iron to simulate the roar of artillery. He was still being recalled many years after his death: W. S. Gilbert's libretto for *Patience* (1881) includes a reference to 'Jullien, the eminent musico'.

36 *Dutch clock*: a cheap German ('Deutsch') clock from the Black Forest area.

37 *band-boxes*: cheap and flimsy cardboard boxes for storing collars, hats, and millinery; originally made for 'bands' or ruffs.

38 *twelfth-cake day*: Twelfth Night (6 January), when large decorated cakes were traditionally eaten to mark the end of Christmas festivities.

tick: the cover for a mattress or pillow, made from tough linen or cotton.

39 *jacketing*: thrashing (slang), probably derived from the phrase 'to dust one's jacket'.

Ing-uns: onions. 'Among the costermongers I heard this useful root . . . called ing-guns, ing-ans, injens, injyens, inions, innons, almost everything but onions' (*LLLP*, i.94).

40 *Prince Halbert*: i.e. Prince Albert of Saxe-Coburg and Gothe (1819–61), the Prince Consort and husband of Queen Victoria.

42 *pottles*: small containers, often conical in shape, used for holding strawberries or other soft fruit.

43 *excursion-van*: a large horse-drawn vehicle which could be hired for day trips within or beyond the city; a popular song describes how 'We 'ad a jolly outing larst Sunday arternoon; | And such a jolly lark it was, I shan't forget it soon! | We borrered an excursion van to take us down to Kew, | And oh, we did enjoy ourselves! I don't mind telling you' ('The Poor Old 'Orse', in *Mr Punch's Model Music-Hall Songs and Dramas*, 1892).

45 *Hibernians*: Irish people.

49 *mechanics*: manual workers.

52 *heart-cakes*: heart-shaped cakes.

hard-bakes: almond toffees.

horehound: an extract of the plant *Marrubium vulgare*, manufactured into candy drops or lozenges as a cough remedy.

sherbet: a fizzy drink made with water, bicarbonate of soda, cream of tartar, sugar, and flavouring; 'Persian Sherbet' was one of several different trade-names for drinks which resembled lemonade 'in a slightly different colour or fashion' (*LLLP*, i.188).

53 *surtout*: an overcoat.

peck: a quarter of a bushel, roughly equivalent to two gallons (UK) or eight quarts (US).

54 *Jim Crow*: see note to p. 11.

55 *both the great theatres*: until the Theatre Regulation Act of 1843, the only two officially licensed London theatres (or 'patent theatres') were at Drury Lane and Covent Garden, which together had a monopoly on spoken drama; the minor theatres staged mainly burlettas, burlesques, and farces such as Mayhew's *The Wandering Minstrel* (1834).

56 *Ashley's, the Surrey, and the Vic.*: three popular theatres; 'Ashley's' may be the speaker's version of Astley's, a theatre built in 1841 which contained a circus ring and was famous for its spectacular equestrian performances (see note to p. 261). For the Vic., see note to p. 24.

the Standard: a large theatre in Shoreditch, built in 1835.

stays: a laced bodice or corset, stiffened by strips of whalebone.

57 *'Lympic . . . 'Delphi*: the Olympic Theatre on Drury Lane, rebuilt in 1849 after a fire, was famous for its comedies and melodramas; the Adelphi Theatre on the Strand was originally called 'The Sans Pareil' when it opened in 1806, and was rebuilt as the New Adelphi in 1858.

Vauxhall: Vauxhall Gardens, situated on the Surrey side of the Thames, was a popular place of entertainment from the reign of Charles II to the mid-nineteenth century, finally closing in 1859. Once famous for their elegance and gentility (entertainments included illuminated fountains, fireworks, and balloon ascents), towards the end of their life Vauxhall's pleasure gardens were better known as the haunt of seedy characters and over-priced refreshments: one popular rhyme on 'Vauxhall slices' (meat that was sliced so thinly it was practically see-through) explains that 'The purse, and not the throat, to cram, | Was why the measure first was taken; | For by that way you save your ham, | And that's the way to "save your bacon"' (Anon., *Vauxhall Papers*, 1841).

58 *the parish*: the workhouse. The Poor Law Amendment Act of 1834 grouped parishes together into 'poor law unions' that established workhouses (popularly known as 'Unions') to house the destitute.

59 *cram-bones*: small bones.

lights: lungs.

60 *saloop*: a once-fashionable hot drink made from dried salep (a kind of orchid), milk, and sugar.

61 *cheap adulteration*: the adulteration of common foodstuffs was a matter of increasing concern. A. H. Hassall wrote a series of outraged pieces in the *Lancet* (1851–4) which were later turned into a book; the matter was also discussed at a special conference in Birmingham in 1854, which led to articles such as 'The Poisoners of the Present Century' (*Punch*, 9 December 1854) and a number of literary echoes: the speaker of Tennyson's *Maud* (1855) describes how 'chalk and alum and plaster are sold to the poor for bread'. Elsewhere in this volume of *LLLP* Mayhew reports that 'I was assured, by a leading grocer, that he could not mention twenty shops in the city, of which he could say: "you can go in and buy a pound of ground coffee there, and it will not be adulterated"' (i.184).

62 *rushlight*: a cheap candle made by dipping a rush in tallow or other grease.

65 *Annette Myers*: a lady's maid, condemned to death in 1848 for shooting a soldier in St James's Park who had seduced her by promising marriage and then, after extracting money from her to spend on gambling and carousing, abandoned her; she was saved from the gallows by an outpouring of public sympathy which included an editorial in the respectable *Morning Post* accusing her seducer of being 'the vilest of the vile'.

66 *Great Exhibition*: an international exhibition (also called the Great Exposition, from the French Industrial Exposition of 1844), which took place in a specially constructed 'Crystal Palace' in Hyde Park from 1 May to 15 October 1851. It was the first and most famous of a series of World's Fair exhibitions of culture and industry that were to become a regular feature of the nineteenth century. Mayhew's novel *1851; or the Adventures of Mr and Mrs Sandboys* (illustrated by George Cruikshank) was one of many literary attempts to cash in on the Exhibition's success.

69 *street-crier of gingerbread*: Mayhew's original introduction to the section on 'Street-Sellers of Eatables and Drinkables' includes a correspondent's recollection of an earlier street-cry: 'Hot spiced gingerbread nuts, nuts, nuts! If *one*'ll warm you, *wha-at*'ll a pound do?—*Wha-a-a-at*'ll a pound do?'

Greenwich Fair: a fair held in May that was famous for its hawkers and entertainment (everything from circus acts to prize fights), attracting up to 200,000 people each year before, following a drunken riot in 1850, it was finally suppressed in 1857. Dickens devotes one of his *Sketches by Boz* to Greenwich Fair, describing it as 'a sort of spring-rash: a three days' fever which cools the blood for six months afterwards' (ch. 12).

71 *Sir Robert Peel*: (1788–1850), Conservative Prime Minister in 1834–5 and 1841–6, who as Home Secretary was responsible for the formation of the Metropolitan Police Force in 1829.

mock turtle: either a calf's head prepared to resemble turtle, or a soup made from the same main ingredient in imitation of genuine turtle soup.

73 *horrid horn*: fool (slang).

bad scran: bad luck (slang).

74 *Bosjesman, Carib, or Thug*: three foreign bogeymen: the African bushman (Afrikaans *boschjeman*), Amerindian (popularly thought to practise cannibalism), and member of the Thuggee cult (notorious for robbing and murdering travellers in India).

75 *telegraphic dispatch*: the first commercial electric telegraph came into operation in 1839, running for 13 miles between Paddington station and West Drayton. By the time of Mayhew's work telegraph wires criss-crossed the country, and had become a popular metaphor for the speedy and accurate transmission of information.

quod: jail (an abbreviated form of quadrangle, a reference to being kept within four walls).

76 *Rush*: James Blomfield Rush (1800–49), sentenced to death for the murder of the judge Isaac Preston and his son at Stanfield Hall in 1848; the trial attracted a great deal of publicity, and a wax death mask of Rush was displayed in Madame Tussaud's for many years afterwards. See also p. 80 below.

77 *crim.-cons.*: criminal conversation, i.e. adultery.

'cocks': glossed by Mayhew elsewhere in *LLLP* as 'a fictitious statement or even a pretended fictitious statement'; examples given earlier in the work include love letters such as 'The Husband caught in a Trap' and 'Letters from a Lady in this neighbourhood to a Gentleman not 100 miles off'.

78 *William Corder*: the perpetrator of the notorious 'Murder in the Red Barn'. Corder killed Maria Marten in 1826 shortly after eloping with her, and the trial attracted special attention after Maria's stepmother claimed to have had visions of the spot where her daughter was buried. After Corder was hanged on 11 August 1828 his body was dissected by surgeons, his skull examined by phrenologists (who announced that it was especially developed in the areas of 'secretiveness, acquisitiveness, [and] destructiveness'), and his skin used to bind an account of the murder. The case provoked dozens of plays, penny dreadfuls, and popular ballads.

Steinburgh's little job: Nicholas Steinberg, who cut the throats of his wife and four children, and then committed suicide, on 8 September 1834. There is an extant ballad, 'The Pentonville Tragedy', published as a single sheet in 1834 by a printer on Tooley Street, which begins 'Here is a dreadful tragedy most horrid to unfold . . .'

Pegsworth: John Pegsworth, who contracted a debt of £1 to a tailor, John Holliday Ready of Ratcliff Highway, for making his son a coat. Faced with a court order to pay by monthly instalments of 4*s*., on 9 January 1837 he stabbed Ready with a large knife bought especially for the purpose, and then sat down to wait for the police.

Greenacre: James Greenacre, who killed and dismembered his fiancée Hannah Brown in 1836; her body parts were found scattered around London. Known as the 'Edgware Murder', versions of the story were popular in penny dreadful publications and cheap theatres for many months after his execution in 1837.

78 *Wilson Gleeson*: i.e. John Gleeson Wilson, convicted of bludgeoning to death a woman, her two sons, and a servant, who was hanged at Liverpool's Kirkdale Gaol on 15 September 1849. A huge crowd of spectators attended his execution, many of them arriving by special excursion trains.

80 *Madam Toosow*: i.e. Marie Tussaud (b. Marie Grosholtz, 1761–1850), whose museum of waxworks in Baker Street included a 'Chamber of Horrors' that exhibited death masks and other paraphernalia associated with executions; the patterer's complaint is corroborated by *Punch*, which reported in 1849 that at Wilson's hanging 'MADAME TUSSAUD had a representative present to obtain the clothes of the wretch' ('Horrid Murder in Baker Street').

Hocker: Thomas Hocker, hanged on 28 April 1845 for the murder of his friend James Delarue. It was claimed during the trial that after Delarue's body had been discovered, Hocker approached the policeman guarding it and volunteered to check the corpse's pulse. Charles Dickens wrote a scathing piece about Hocker as a 'miserable wretch' whose only motive for murder was a 'mad self-conceit' that meant he would do anything to 'make a noise in the papers' ('The Effect of Capital Punishment on the Commission of Murder', *Daily News*, 9 March 1846).

Courvoisier: François Benjamin Courvoisier (d. 1840), valet to Lord William Russell, who murdered his employer while he slept; some newspaper reports implied that he had been directly influenced by Ainsworth's novel *Jack Sheppard* (see note to p. 20). One of the crowd who attended his execution in 1840 was W. M. Thackeray, who responded with an essay, 'Going to See a Man Hanged' (*Fraser's Magazine*, August 1840), which concludes by describing his disgust at '*the murder I saw done*'.

Jones in the Palace: Edward Jones, also known as 'Boy Jones', a pauper who was caught inside Buckingham Palace in December 1840, and claimed to have spent weeks living there unobserved by the palace staff; he was eventually transported.

Oxford: Edward Oxford (b. 1822) was tried for high treason after attempting to assassinate Queen Victoria in 1840; he was acquitted on the grounds of insanity and sent to Bethlem Royal Hospital (popularly known as Bedlam).

Francis: John Francis, sentenced to death (later commuted to transportation) for treason after firing a pistol at Queen Victoria on 29 May 1842 as she rode in her carriage through St James's Park.

Bean: John William Bean fired at Queen Victoria, using a pistol loaded with paper and tobacco, on 3 July 1842, just two days after John Francis's sentence was commuted; he was sentenced to eighteen months' imprisonment.

81 *Sun*: a daily London newspaper with a reputation for politically progressive views; in the 1830s its contributors included a young Charles Dickens.

whale of tears: i.e. 'vale of tears', a phrase common in Christian prayers; from Psalm 23 ('Yea, though I walk through the valley of the shadow of death, I will fear no evil'), used in the funeral service of the Book of Common Prayer. Mayhew may be recalling Mrs Gamp in Dickens's *Martin Chuzzlewit* sighing over the 'wale of grief' into which we are born.

82 *Duke of Wellington*: Arthur Wellesley, 1st duke of Wellington (1769–1852), the soldier and statesman who became a national hero after defeating Napoleon at the Battle of Waterloo in 1815.

Louis Phillipe: i.e. Louis Philippe (1773–1850), king of France from 1830 to 1848.

Feargus O'Connor: (1794–1855), Irish MP and Chartist leader who was frequently imprisoned for his views.

Marshal Haynau: see note to p. 22.

Jane Wilbred: a servant girl who was admitted to the Royal Free Hospital in 1850 after neighbours raised the alarm about her treatment—starved and beaten—at the hand of her employers, Mr and Mrs George Sloane. Her case attracted much sympathy, and in February 1851 the Sloanes were convicted and sentenced to two years' hard labour.

Mrs Sloane: the version of events given here is a melodramatic fiction designed to sell copies.

83 *Emily Sandford*: the mistress of James Blomfield Rush and an important witness at his trial.

84 *Manning . . . Good*: Frederick and Maria Manning were executed in 1849 for the murder of Patrick O'Connor, Maria's former lover, who was shot in the head and then bludgeoned to death; the combination of brutality and sexual intrigue made the case especially notorious. Daniel Good, a coachman, was convicted of murder in 1842 after a woman's torso was discovered hidden in his stable; the head and limbs had been cut off and burned in the harness-room fireplace.

Duc de Praslin: French nobleman (1804–47) who stabbed and bludgeoned his wife to death in August 1847; he committed suicide while awaiting trial.

85 *Jack Straw*: described by Mayhew in an earlier section as 'the original strawer'; his name may be a pseudonym (Jack Straw was one of the leaders of the 1381 Peasants' Revolt).

86 *the Strand . . . Holywell-street*: areas of London known for bookselling; Holywell Street was notorious for its real and sham trade in pornography.

89 *Allan Bane*: the bard in Sir Walter Scott's narrative poem *The Lady of the Lake* (1810); in canto 6 he witnesses the death of the clan chief Roderick Dhu, and 'when he saw that life was fled, | He poured his wailing o'er the dead'.

90 *marriage of the Queen*: Queen Victoria married Prince Albert on 10 February 1840 in the Chapel Royal of St James's Palace in London.

91 *Scott or Moore*: the poet and novelist Sir Walter Scott (1771–1832); the poet and songwriter Thomas Moore (1779–1852).

93 *reading of the poor . . . criminals*: in his comic novel *The Greatest Plague of Life* (1847, co-written with his brother Augustus), Mayhew describes a servant 'sitting for hours . . . crying her eyes out, over "THE MURDER AT THE OLD SMITHY", or "THE HEADS OF THE HEADLESS" . . . I declare, there wasn't a single murder or last dying speech and confession, cried out in the streets, but she must rush up, all haste, to the door just to have another pen'orth of horrors' (ch. 12).

97 *"though his sins ... white as snow"*: Isaiah 1: 18: 'though your sins be as scarlet, they shall be as white as snow'.

98 *the law . . . was passed*: the repeal of the 1752 Murder Act in 1836 introduced a period of 14–27 days between sentence and execution, 'more effectually to preserve from an irrecoverable Punishment any Persons who may hereafter be convicted upon erroneous or perjured Evidence'.

Eliza Grimwood: a prostitute found murdered in Lambeth in May 1838. Although her pimp was arrested he was later released, leading to speculation (which was later the subject of a libel action) that the real culprit had been the duke of Brunswick. In addition to many 'street papers', the case provoked an anonymous novel, *Eliza Grimwood*, published in 1839.

Thomas Hopkins: contemporary reports do not mention anyone called Thomas Hopkins in relation to Eliza Grimwood's murder; the pimp's name was George Hubbard.

William Game: newspaper reports suggest that Lucy Game was only 4 years old when she was battered to death by her 9-year-old brother in 1848.

99 *Calcraft*: probably William Calcraft (1800–79), the most famous hangman of the nineteenth century, who between 1829 and 1874 executed around 450 criminals, usually by the 'short drop' method which left them strangling for several minutes.

Courvoisier: see note to p. 80.

Joseph Carr: although this case claims to be 'founded on facts', there are no contemporary reports matching its details.

'Wonderful Picture': a pictorial illusion.

101 *'Conundrums'*: riddles which brought together logic and play were popular not only in children's books, such as Lewis Carroll's *Alice's Adventures in Wonderland* (1865), but also in adult conversation: Edward Clodd's 1892 diary records that when Tennyson met Hardy he asked him to name the first person mentioned in the Bible, 'to which the required answer was Chap. 1'.

103 *Kemble . . . Kean*: celebrated nineteenth-century actors. Edmund Kean (1789–1833) was widely regarded at the time as the finest actor of all time; his performance as Richard III was captured in numerous works of art,

including a painting by John James Halls (1814) that is now in the Victoria and Albert Museum.

105 *corn-salve and plate-ball*: see notes to p. 10.

blacking: see note to p. 15.

106 *Hansellers*: a 'hansel' is the first of something, such as the first money taken in the morning (slang), hence hawkers who sell goods on a first-come, first-served basis.

Bad cess to you!: may evil befall you (Irish slang).

107 *parlour . . . tap-room*: different areas in a public house; the parlour was the more refined of the two.

108 *picker*: a pointed tool, here probably meaning a toothpick.

ready-reckoner: a book or table listing standard numerical calculations.

111 *intelligence . . . forehead*: according to the Victorian pseudo-science of phrenology, personal qualities were determined by the shape of the skull, which phrenologists divided up into forty sections or 'organs', each of which was supposed to govern one particular mental or moral faculty.

112 *pressed*: 'impressed', or conscripted into military or naval service.

113 *Greenwich Hospital*: founded in 1694 as the Royal Naval Hospital, it was established as a residential home for injured sailors on the model of Les Invalides in Paris and Chelsea Hospital (home of the Chelsea pensioners) in London. It occupied the same site until it closed in 1869.

on our beam ends: in great need (nautical slang).

115 *traces*: ropes attached to a horse for pulling a weight (here, a gun).

link buttons: cufflinks.

banyan day: one on which no meat is issued to sailors on board a ship (nautical slang).

'bus-men: omnibus-drivers.

116 *Somerset-House*: a large neo-classical building constructed on the Strand between 1776 and 1796; the Admiralty had its main offices here in the first half of the nineteenth century.

117 *silk-mercery*: silk cloth sold by a mercer.

118 *Court of Requests*: a minor court for dealing with debts under 40 shillings.

120 *'Injy'*: i.e. Indian.

121 *chew their quid*: a 'quid' (a variant form of 'cud') is a lump of tobacco for chewing (slang).

helm's a-lee: turn the wheel leeward, towards shelter (nautical slang).

122 *marling spike*: a pointed tool used to splice strands of rope.

rhino: money (slang).

123 *thimble-men*: or thimble-riggers, conmen who play a game which involves asking spectators to choose which of three thimbles hides a pea.

123 *'peacock's feathers'*: refers to Newton's account in *Opticks* (1704) of forms of vision that can be produced 'when we see Fire by striking the Eye, or see Colours like the Eye of a Peacock's Feather, by pressing our Eyes in either corner while we look the other way'.

124 *copperas*: ferrous sulphate, a chemical used in dyeing, tanning, and making ink.

read ... with his fingers: possibly a reference to the Braille system of raised dots on paper, devised by Louis Braille (1809–52) in 1821 to allow the blind to read and write; by the time this interview took place his system had started to spread around the world, although the reference here may be to one of the rival systems being promoted in the mid-nineteenth century: Boston Line Type, Moon Type, British Braille, and others.

Saunderson's: Nicholas Saunderson (1682–1739), the blind scientist and mathematician who developed a device that employed threads connecting pins to make geometric constructions; his was one of the lives celebrated in James Wilson's *Biography of the Blind* (1838).

125 *Polytechnic*: the Royal Polytechnic Institution on Regent Street, which opened in 1838 and was dedicated to the advancement and public understanding of science. It became a major tourist attraction, thanks to exhibits that included state of the art machinery and spectacular shows in the Polytechnic Theatre.

127 *the Arcades*: the Burlington Arcade, a set of fashionable shops in a covered pedestrian arcade that runs between Piccadilly and Burlington Gardens; it opened in 1819.

130 *free-trade corn*: punning on the debates that surrounded the repeal of the Corn Laws in 1846, an event that marked a significant step towards free trade.

132 *Guy Faux*: i.e. Guy (or Guido) Fawkes (1570–1606), one of the conspirators behind the Roman Catholic plot to blow up the Houses of Parliament on 5 November 1605. The events are commemorated each year in Britain by fireworks and bonfires that feature a 'Guy'; they were also the subject of more sympathetic treatment in William Ainsworth Harrison's 1842 novel *Guy Fawkes: A Historical Romance*.

133 *wagabone*: vagabond.

snob: in mid-nineteenth-century usage, a vulgar or common person who is keen to associate with, or be regarded as, someone of rank or importance. There was a fad for poking fun at 'snobs', epitomized in Thackeray's sketches for *Punch* that were later collected as *The Book of Snobs* (1848).

bulk: a street prostitute.

last: a wooden model of the foot, used by cobblers.

Smithfield: the principal live cattle and horse market in London until it was relocated to Islington in 1855.

honour bright: by your honour, truthfully (slang).

135 *Tom and Jerry*: the heroes of Pierce Egan's *Life in London* (1821), which recounted the adventures of young Regency bucks drinking, fighting and having fun in the capital; it was adapted for the theatre by William Moncrieff as *Tom and Jerry, or Life in London*, and ran at the Adelphi Theatre between 1821 and 1823.

136 *Mr and Mrs Manning*: see note to p. 84.

Androcles . . . lion's foot: the story of Androcles, first told by Apion (d. AD45), recounts how a runaway slave pulls a thorn out of a lion's paw, and is rewarded by the lion's devotion. When he is later thrown to the lions in Rome, the most fearsome of these beasts turns out to be his old friend and refuses to attack him; overcome by feeling, the emperor pardons Androcles on the spot.

138 *pinchers*: pincers.

141 *fuzees*: matches.

Orchis mascula: the early purple orchid, also known as 'dead men's fingers' or 'long purples' (as referred to by Gertrude in *Hamlet*, IV. vii).

water-jacks: waterman's attendants, who helped passengers on and off boats.

Ethiopians: blackface minstrels, many of whom were trying to cash in on the success of the Ethiopian Serenaders, an American troupe that toured Britain to great acclaim in 1846–7.

Ragged School Brigade: the ragged schools were charity schools established to provide a free education—and often food, clothing, and lodging too—for children too poor to pay. One offshoot of this movement was the London Shoe-Black Brigade, established in 1851 by John MacGregor and Lord Shaftesbury to offer regular employment and free evening school to children who made a living cleaning shoes; by 1869 the various London Shoe-Black Societies employed more than 350 boys.

142 *pottling*: putting strawberries in containers.

143 *'tanner' . . . 'bob'*: a sixpence; a shilling.

144 *His was the kingdom . . . Amen*: an adaptation of the Lord's Prayer (Matthew 6: 9–13 and Luke 11: 2–4).

146 *Old Nosey*: nickname for the Duke of Wellington, because of a nose which, as Rosamund Waite's *Life of the Duke of Wellington* (1884) tactfully put it, was 'the most prominent feature of the whole countenance'.

beak: magistrate (slang).

crushers: policemen (slang).

Wick . . . Bower: two British prisons.

149 *fairy tale*: in 'Aladdin', one of the tales in *The Arabian Nights*, Aladdin's wife is tricked into giving up his magic lamp by a sorcerer offering to exchange 'new lamps for old'.

gall . . . logwood . . . copperas: three ingredients used in dyeing; gall: an excrescence on oak trees produced by the action of insects; logwood: extract of the American tree *Haematoxylon Campechianum*, imported in the form of logs; for copperas, see note to p. 124.

150 *Harpagon*: the moneylender at the heart of Molière's 1688 comedy *L'Avare* (*The Miser*).

slops: an outer garment such as a loose jacket or smock.

151 *dust-hole*: a dustbin or other container for collecting dust and refuse.

pilot-coats: large coats of the sort worn by pilots (navigators taken on board to guide ships in and out of harbour).

drugget: matting of coarse woollen cloth.

152 *aquafortis*: the popular name for nitric acid, a powerful solvent and corrosive.

central mart for old clothes: the Old Clothes Exchange, a regulated market in Houndsditch described by Mayhew in an earlier section of *LLLP*.

155 *'Coker-nuts'*: i.e. coconuts. Earlier in *LLLP* Mayhew observes that 'Coker-nuts are now used at fairs to "top" the sticks . . . The interior is sold in halfpenny-worths and penny-worths' (i.89).

156 *paletots*: loose coats, cloaks or other outer garments.

Guernsey frocks: woollen jumpers or 'jerseys'.

157 *Coal Exchange*: an elaborate Italianate building on Lower Thames Street that opened in 1849.

two pairs back: poor-quality housing.

160 *New Globe, or Green Dragon . . . of the east*: pleasure gardens: the New Globe Pleasure-Grounds (Mile End Road) and Green Dragon Gardens (Stepney) were East End rivals to the Cremorne Gardens (Chelsea) and Vauxhall Gardens (Kennington).

Dick Turpin . . . York: the highwayman Dick Turpin (1705–39) is said to have escaped justice by riding the 200 miles from London to York in less than fifteen hours; the feat is celebrated in William Harrison Ainsworth's novel *Rookwood* (1834).

Jack Sheppard . . . house: see note to p. 20. In 1724 Sheppard escaped from St Giles's Roundhouse (a London prison) by breaking through the timber ceiling and lowering himself to the ground with a rope fashioned from bedclothes.

Bell's Life: *Bell's Life in London, and Sporting Chronicle*, a weekly newspaper published between 1822 and 1886.

Newgate Calendar: subtitled 'the Malefactors' Bloody Register', the Newgate Calendar was the generic title of a series of volumes, published during the eighteenth and nineteenth centuries, which contained gory accounts of notorious crimes and criminals.

'Calendar of Orrers': *The Calendar of Horrors: A Series of Romantic Legends, Terrific Tales, Awful Narrations, and Supernatural Adventures* (1835–6), a

'penny dreadful' edited by Thomas Peckett Prest which featured stories such as 'Geraldina the Demon Nun'.

161 *lush*: drink (slang).

Bell and Siven Mackerels: possibly a mistake; the only recorded public house on the Mile End Road which comes close to this name is the Old Three Mackerels.

lirium trumans: i.e. delirium tremens, the hallucinations and uncontrollable shaking associated with alcoholics.

Trueman and Hanbury's heavy: porter or stout; 'heavy wet' was a slang term for strong beer, also called 'treble X'.

162 *'long-remembered beggar'*: from Oliver Goldsmith's *The Deserted Village* (1770): 'The long-remembered beggar was his guest, | Whose beard descending swept his aged breast.'

165 *East Injes*: i.e. the East Indies.

slap: first-rate or fashionable (slang).

Sperm Pieces: ornaments made from sperm whale bone or ivory.

167 *hartshorn*: smelling-salts containing ammonium chloride, traditionally derived from the antlers of a hart.

awls: small tools used for piercing holes in leather.

gimlets: tools used for boring holes.

plane-irons: the cutting blades of a plane.

lock escutcheons: key-hole plates.

168 *quarto*: a size of paper, obtained by folding a whole sheet twice to form four leaves; depending on the size of the original sheet, quarto paper can range from *c.*19.7 cm × 15.2 cm. ('pot quarto') up to *c.*38 cm × 28 cm ('imperial quarto').

"fly to a dodge": quick to recognize a trick (slang); a popular song of the period boasts that 'when they try their games with me, I let them see | That I am fly to all their tricks' ('That's a Game Best Left Alone').

169 *pawns*: pawnbrokers (slang).

gammon: nonsense; humbug (slang).

170 *black letter*: a form of type used by early printers, as opposed to later 'Roman' type; a variant is still used in Germany. Here, it could refer either to old or foreign books.

171 *Lloyd's Weekly*: the short name for *Lloyd's Penny Weekly Miscellany*, a popular newspaper founded by Edward Lloyd (1815–90) in 1842.

172 *Watts' and Wesley's hymns*: Methodist hymn books containing hymns written by Isaac Watts (1674–1748) and Charles Wesley (1707–88).

cut and uncut: with pages that have been cut or left uncut; many Victorian publishers retained the older style of leaving readers to cut their own pages.

172 *page . . . a man's heart*: sheets of printed matter were sometimes used to wrap food for sale, a tradition that continued into the twentieth century with fish and chips being wrapped in old newspapers.

173 *crockmen*: sellers of crockery.

178 *dust-heaps*: piles of dust and refuse collected from houses by dust-collectors; famed for their value (although Mayhew denies the 'popular notion' that any dustman ever got rich from his work), and used as a potent symbol of waste and redemption, they form one of the central features of Dickens's fictional landscape in his last completed novel, *Our Mutual Friend* (1864–5).

185 *dark lantern*: a lamp with a slide or other means of hiding the light.

bull's-eye: a lantern with a glass lens on one side to concentrate the light.

188 *the hend of the o*: i.e. 'the end of the hoe'.

192 *dolly's*: cheap pawnbroker's (slang).

194 *chaldron*: a standard measure of coals, equivalent to 36 bushels.

japanned: varnished or lacquered.

Prussian blue: a deep blue pigment used in dyeing and painting.

199 *evidence before Parliament*: the debate leading to the passage of the Chimney Sweeps Act (1840), which prohibited any child under 16 from being apprenticed to a chimney-sweep, and anyone under 21 from being forced to climb a chimney.

Marylebone baths: the Marylebone Public Baths and Wash-houses opened in 1849, the first in London following the passing of an Act in 1846 empowering local authorities to provide public washing facilities for the poor.

200 *'fagot'*: defined elsewhere in *LLLP* as 'a sort of cake, roll or ball . . . made of chopped liver and lights [lungs], mixed with gravy, and wrapped in pieces of pig's caul'.

chimney-sweeper's cancer: cancer of the testicles or scrotum.

201 *lost his parents . . . this business*: parishes which apprenticed orphans as climbing-boys were coming under increasing attack in the first half of the nineteenth century, as reflected in Dickens's *Oliver Twist* (1838), which introduces the sinister figure of Gamfield offering to take Oliver off the parish's hands: '"If the parish would like him to learn a right pleasant trade, in a good 'spectable chimbley-sweepin' bisness . . . I wants a prentis, and I am ready to take him"' (ch. 3).

205 *sodgers*: i.e. soldiers.

swell-mobsmen: swindlers dressed as gentlemen.

smoke-jacks: machines powered by the rising column of smoke produced by a fire, often used to turn a cooking spit.

coppers: large metal containers used for cooking and cleaning.

206 *Quantity . . . London*: the table that accompanies this section is reproduced as Appendix 3 on pp. 424–5.

penny postage: the Uniform Penny Post, established in 1840, allowed letters no heavier than half an ounce to be sent anywhere within the UK with a prepaid penny stamp (the Penny Black).

207 *Eugène Sue*: Joseph Marie Eugène Sue (1804–57), French novelist whose most famous work, *Les Mystères de Paris* (1842–3), has been credited with helping to prepare the ground for the 1848 Revolution.

208 *Crossing-Sweepers*: tipped small coins to sweep horse manure and other filth out of the way on pedestrian crossings so that prosperous men and, especially, women (whose dresses touched the ground) would not be dirtied as they stepped off the pavement. Competition for the best pitches and customers was fierce: a cartoon from *Punch* for 26 January 1856 ('The Crossing-Sweeper Nuisance') shows a top-hatted gentleman being swept up by a crowd of more than a dozen ragged children brandishing their little brooms. Mayhew returned to the topic in his novel (co-authored with his brother Augustus) *Paved with Gold* (1857), which reprinted material from his earlier investigations into the lives of crossing-sweeper boys.

209 *'piccaninny'*: a black child.

210 *Lascars*: sailors from Asia employed on European ships. The British East India Company recruited seamen from Bengal, Assam, Gujarat, and Yemen; by 1855 there were around 12,000 visiting Britain annually.

211 *Jim-Crow*: see note to p. 11.

212 *"Uncle Tom's Cabin"*: the title of an anti-slavery novel by Harriet Beecher Stowe (1811–1986) published in 1852. It was the best-selling novel of the nineteenth century and often adapted for the stage.

215 *Lord Fitzhardinge*: i.e. William Fitzhardinge Berkeley, 1st Baron Segrave (1786–1857), whose London residence was Berkeley House, Spring Gardens.

217 *cat'un-wheel*: i.e. cartwheel.

doxy: the female companion of a thief or a beggar, but also used more loosely as an endearment (cf. 'darling' or 'love').

219 *caten-wheel*: i.e. cartwheel.

226 *ferruts*: i.e. ferrets.

227 *FANCY*: sport or breeding animals (cf. pigeon-fanciers).

228 *butter-firkin*: a small, hooped cask for storing butter.

230 *gammon*: deceive (slang).

236 *'pitch and toss'*: a street gambling game in which coins are tossed at a target, and the player whose coin lands nearest is allowed to throw all the remaining coins up in the air and claim those that land face up.

239 *pandean pipes*: pan pipes.

240 *Pike and Porsini*: 'Porsini and Pike were celebrated Punch exhibitors; the former is said to have frequently taken 10*l.* a day; but he died in St. Giles' workhouse' (John Timbs, *Curiosities of London*, 1855).

241 *march of hintellect*: the 'march of intellect' was a popular catchphrase among those wanting to celebrate (or satirize) Britain's material and moral progress: see e.g. Williams Heath's picture *March of Intellect* (1829), showing flying machines and other fantastic inventions, William Moncrieff and Robert Cruikshank's *The March of Intellect: A Comic Poem* (1830), and Catherine Sinclair's book *Modern Accomplishments, or The March of Intellect* (1838).

243 *Eugénie*: Eugénie de Montijo (1826–1920), wife of Napoleon III and the last empress consort of France (1853–71).

cheveleure: i.e. chevelure, hairstyle.

King de Sardaigne: probably Victor Emmanuel II (1820–78), King of Sardinia 1849–61.

244 *Zoological Gardens*: popularly known as London Zoo, situated in Regent's Park; created in 1828 by the Zoological Society of London, it opened to the public in 1847 and soon became one of the city's most popular tourist attractions.

245 *animalculae*: animals so tiny as to be visible only through a microscope; micro-organisms.

sperm oil: from sperm whales, used for making high-quality candles and lamp oil.

micrometer: a device for measuring small objects viewed under a microscope.

246 *scaffolding . . . House of Lords*: the design of the present Houses of Parliament, by Sir Charles Barry (1795–1860), was chosen by a Royal Commission in 1836 to replace the previous building destroyed by fire in 1834. Although most of the work had been completed by 1860, construction continued for another decade.

247 *the song*: a parlour song written by Henry Russell in 1837 to words originally published as a poem by George Pope Morris in 1830: 'Woodman, spare that tree! | Touch not a single bough! | In youth it sheltered me, | And I'll protect it now.'

Great Exhibition . . . India: the opulent Indian Court at the 1851 Great Exhibition included fabrics and clothing, in addition to more exotic exhibits such as the Koh-i-noor diamond and a stuffed elephant.

Blair's 'Preceptor': 'David Blair' (pseud.), *The Universal Preceptor* (1811, and often reprinted during the nineteenth century), a 'General grammar of arts, sciences and useful knowledge', was a collection of facts and figures often drawn on by teachers and others seeking to educate themselves; it is one of two books chosen by the governess for some last-minute cramming in George Sala's *Twice Around the Clock, Or, The Hours of the*

Day and Night in London (1862), 'though she would, perhaps, prefer shutting herself up in her own room and having a good cry' ('Nine O'Clock A.M.').

248 *Samson*: the biblical strongman famed for slaying one thousand Philistines armed only with the jawbone of an ass (Judges 15).

249 *Mount Tycho . . . Mount Ptolemy*: famous mountains. Tycho: a landmass on the moon; Mount Vesuvius and 'Etany' (i.e. Etna): volcanoes in Italy; St Catherine: a volcano in Grenada; Ptolemy (named after the Roman astronomer who wrote about Africa's 'Mountains of the Moon'): in Canada.

summersets: i.e. somersaults.

the Grecian statues: 'poses plastiques' involved performers standing motionless in imitation of famous paintings or statues; although they were sometimes (as in the case of the celebrated *fin de siècle* Prussian strongman Eugen Sandow) intended to show off a muscular physique, they also offered the opportunity—usually for scantily dressed female performers—for more titillating entertainment under the guise of classical learning.

250 *physicked*: punished, hurt (slang).

253 *link*: torch.

254 *tow*: rope.

bustes: bursts, explodes.

255 *Ramo Samee's*: Ramo Samee (d. 1852) came to England *c.*1819 and quickly established himself as one of the nation's most celebrated entertainers. His skill at juggling and sword-swallowing is the subject of William Hazlitt's essay 'The Indian Jugglers', in *Table Talk* (1828); W. M. Thackeray's *The Book of Snobs* describes how 'I have seen . . . the Hereditary Princess of Poptztausend-Donnerwetter . . . use her knife in lieu of a fork or spoon; I have seen her almost swallow it, by Jove! like Ramo Samee, the Indian juggler.'

256 *Flora Gardens . . . St Helena Gardens*: smaller, less fashionable rivals to Vauxhall Gardens in south London.

258 *"Sallementro"*: a phoney Italian stage name.

259 *gentles*: maggots.

260 *Wombwell's menagerie*: Wombwell's Travelling Menagerie, founded by George Wombwell (1777–1850) in 1810, toured the fairs of Britain with animals including the first lion ('William') to be bred in captivity.

261 *carman*: a carter, carrier.

Astley's: Astley's Royal Amphitheatre, founded by Philip Astley (1742–1814) in 1777 and subsequently rebuilt and expanded, incorporated a circus ring and was renowned for its spectacular 'feats of horsemanship'.

"super": supernumerary, or theatrical 'extra' (slang).

264 *"Punch"*: influential weekly satirical magazine. Mayhew was one of the founding members in 1841, and briefly co-editor with Mark Lemon;

he was then 'suggestor in chief' until he severed his links with the magazine in 1845.

265 *small beer*: weak beer.

Romanee: Romany, or gypsy slang.

266 *russet boots*: old-fashioned brown leather boots, much used in theatrical costume dramas.

"Fair Rosamond": probably Tom Taylor's 1838 burlesque *Fair Rosamund: According to the History of England*.

267 *"The Floating . . . Wreck"*: Edward Fitzball's melodrama *The Floating Beacon: Or, the Wild Woman of the Wreck* was first published in 1824 (when the subtitle was *Or, the Norwegian Wreckers*) and remained a firm favourite throughout the century.

268 *old business*: conventional stage business.

stage-fever: stage fright.

"Mary Woodbine": presumably a theatrical adaptation of the novel *The Village Coquette* (1822) in which Mary Woodbine is a leading character; the novel itself is based on Charles Rivière Dufresny's 1715 comedy *La Coquette du village*, which produced many imitators, including Dickens's 1836 comic opera *The Village Coquettes*.

269 *bataille de Pescare*: the siege of Peschiera in March 1848, a key battle in the first Italian War of Independence.

a bal de canon or a bal de fusil: a cannon ball or a rifle bullet.

fracassé, vairy beaucoup: very badly shattered.

hospital of San Bartolommeo: St Bartholomew's Hospital in Smithfield.

270 *Pauvre diable!*: poor devil.

273 *'the enraged musician'*: a 1741 engraving by William Hogarth (1697–1764) depicting a violinist driven to distraction by the noise of street performers and traders outside his window.

Mendicity Society: the Society for the Suppression of Mendicity was founded in 1818 to apprehend vagrants and impostors while helping the 'deserving poor'. Members could direct begging-letter writers to the Society's office, where their claims would be investigated and help offered if they were found to be in genuine need.

274 *daguerreotype*: an early photographic process invented by Louis Daguerre (1787–1851), in which the image was exposed onto a polished metal surface; although Daguerre attempted to patent his process, in 1839 the French government announced that it was a gift 'Free to the World'. Mayhew describes how street photographers worked on p. 283.

276 *Turner's cerate*: a form of ointment; according to John F. South's *Household Surgery; or, Hints on Emergencies* (4th edition 1852; cover motto: 'Go thou and do likewise') it 'Consists of one half a pound of yellow wax and a pint of olive oil, which are to be melted together; this being done, half a pound

of calamine powder is to be sifted in, and stirred till the whole be completely mixed'.

sash-lines: strong cords used in sash windows.

ocker'd: i.e. awkward.

the Union: i.e. the workhouse; see note on *the parish*, p. 58.

"cymbal": a word incorrectly applied to many different kinds of musical instrument.

277 *King David . . . instruments*: 2 Samuel 6: 5 describes how 'David and all the house of Israel played before the Lord on all manner of instruments made of fir wood, even on harps, and on psalteries, and on timbrels, and on cornets, and on cymbals'.

279 *Smithfield*: see note to p. 133.

Belvidere-gardens: the Belvidere Tavern and Tea Gardens on the Pentonville Road.

280 *habillements*: clothing; notes on other French words in this section are given only where the sense is not clear from the context. Mayhew does not explain why an Italian should speak in French.

en étoffe: made of cloth.

je ne sais . . . campagne: I don't know what you call the countryside.

commerce . . . montagne: business in the mountains.

déjà: already.

Après ça: after that.

pas du tout: not at all.

Premièrement: firstly.

peut-être: perhaps.

tout de monde: for 'tout le monde', everybody.

nouriture: food.

gentilhommes: gentlemen.

malade: sick.

St Bartolomé: St Bartolomew's.

281 *appellé "Grifon"*: called 'Grifon'.

petite maison: little house.

sous: small coins.

I am . . . rested: that is, I have stayed (from the French *rester*).

Mars: March.

282 *bouilli*: boiled beef.

paroisse: parish.

284 *shooting him*: a popular anxiety: 'It is no uncommon thing for persons to resist the importunities of friends for years and come at last to the photographic

studio as to a place of execution' (James Mudd, 'Portraiture: The Management of the Sitter', *Year-Book of Photography*, 1867); the *OED* gives 1890 as the first recorded use of 'shooting' to mean 'photographing'.

286 *philandery*: philanthropy.

287 *Derby-day*: the annual Epsom Derby, inaugurated by the 12th Earl of Derby in 1780, which takes place on the first weekend in June and is a highlight of the horse-racing season; it was the subject of William Powell Frith's oil painting *The Derby Day* (1856–8), which featured many of the character types described in *LLLP*, including a thimble-rigger, flower-girl, pickpocket, and acrobat.

292 *mesmerise*: hypnotize; named after Franz Anton Mesmer (1734–1815), who launched a Europe-wide craze in the late eighteenth century, mesmerism was a much debated Victorian medical fad.

295 *bulls' eyes*: boiled sweets.

296 *over-populated . . . emigrate every year*: a joke about one popular solution to over-population in Britain. Mayhew himself had been involved in the founding of the Female Emigration Society in 1849, following his *Morning Chronicle* revelations about the terrible pay and working conditions of needlewomen. By mid-January 1850, £17,000 had been pledged; the first group of women set off for the colonies on 25 February. By the time the last ship sailed in January 1852, around 700 women had left Britain with the Society's help.

gutta-percha: see note to p. 12.

binnacles: a binnacle is a box on board ship in which the compass is kept.

Argus: a mythological creature fabled to have a hundred eyes; after his death, the eyes were transferred by the goddess Hera to the tail of the peacock.

299 *Adelaide boots*: women's boots, named after the queen consort of King William IV (1765–1837); introduced in the 1830s, they covered the ankle as well as the foot, and versions were made for indoor (silk) or outdoor (leather) use.

'ankle-jacks': stout boots reaching above the ankle.

300 *camlet coat*: a coat made of wool and cotton or silk.

young thief . . . preceding evening: the event parallels 'A Meeting of Thieves' (*LLLP*, i.418–23), during which Mayhew entrusts a sovereign to a boy to get it changed; the thieves wait with keen anticipation, and break into loud applause when the boy returns with the money in full. Mayhew had originally told the story in Letter V of his *Morning Chronicle* series, and in 1851 he published a comic account in the *Comic Almanac* of the domestic disasters that occurred when he brought the boy to his home, concluding that 'the bosom of a quiet family is not exactly the place in which to foster and reclaim a London pickpocket' ('Our Pet Thief').

301 *mariner's ticket*: sailing licence.

302 *never believe in 'looks' again*: a reference to the pseudo-science of physiognomy, which claimed to be able to determine character by facial appearance alone. The ideas were often applied to criminals: as late as 1890, Havelock Ellis published a study that overlaid the images of dozens of convicted criminals to produce the blurred image of a single 'criminal type' (*The Criminal*). Mayhew was more uncertain: in one footnote to *The Criminal Prisons of London* (1862), he claimed that 'the generality' of violent criminals were distinguished by thick necks and a 'peculiar lascivious look', while denying that such men 'in general' had their characters 'stamped on their faces'.

303 *Billingsgate*: see note to p. 29.

304 *Report . . . Commissioners*: the published report of the Royal Commission into a constabulary force in England and Wales (1839), which painted an alarming picture of the country being overwhelmed by thieves, vagrants and beggars.

306 *slop-tailors*: makers of cheap clothes, whose dreadful working conditions had been highlighted by works such as Charles Kingsley's *Cheap Clothes and Nasty* (1850), a pamphlet which drew extensively on Mayhew's articles in the *Morning Chronicle*.

307 *blocked*: caught in a traffic jam.

309 *nomads of the present day*: a reference back to Mayhew's Preface, in which he discusses 'the nomadic races of England . . . from the habitual vagrant . . . to the mechanic on tramp'.

310 *'Rookwood'*: see note to p. 160.

311 *Act . . . 'valiant beggar'*: the Vagrancy Act of 1531, amended in 1535–6, laid down tough penalties for 'valiant beggars and sturdy vagabonds', i.e. vagrants who were 'whole and mighty in body, and able to labour'.

'wide-awake': a soft felt hat with a broad brim and low crown, said to have been punningly named for not having a 'nap'.

315 *axed*: asked (slang).

tramper's house: a low lodging-house.

316 *the wheel*: the treadwheel, one of the punishments associated with imprisonment with hard labour, was introduced in the second decade of the nineteenth century; Mayhew describes its operation in *The Criminal Prisons of London*, concluding that the 'excessive' nature of the labour is proven by the fact that a prisoner sentenced to a standard day of 4¾ hours climbs the equivalent of 7,200 feet, or the same as a hod-carrier working flat out.

Bridewell: built as a palace for Henry VIII, the original Bridewell later became a poorhouse and prison for 'disorderly women' in London; the name was subsequently adopted by other institutions, including Tothill Fields Bridewell (also known as Westminster Bridewell), which was rebuilt in 1834 and accommodated up to 900 prisoners.

317 *quod*: see note to p. 75.

318 *cock-shies*: a throwing game, originally with the object of knocking over a cock, and subsequently applied to any other game that involves throwing balls at a target.

319 *Van Dieman's Lands*: i.e. Van Diemen's Land, the original European name for Tasmania; it became a penal colony in 1803.

"Free and Easy": a place for drinking and entertainment; William Shaw's *The Land of Promise; Or, My Impressions of Australia* (1855) describes one such place in Adelaide, where 'rapturous applause greeted each melodist, and the entertainment was what it professed to be, a very "Free and Easy" one' (ch. 7).

Cashman: a young sailor who joined rioters in looting a gunsmith's shop in 1816, and was hanged in 1817. The case attracted much public sympathy, and Cashman's bravery on the scaffold was still being celebrated fifty years later (see e.g. 'Old Stories Re-told: The Spafields Riots', *All the Year Round*, 22 December 1866).

Fauntleroy: Henry Fauntleroy, a banker who funded his lavish lifestyle through forgery, and was hanged in 1824.

320 *E. O. tables*: 'Even-Odd', a game like roulette, popular towards the end of the eighteenth century.

tilted cart: a covered cart.

Old Bailey: originally a court for trying offences committed in the City and Middlesex, but after 1856 the Central Criminal Court.

hulk: old warships, moored in rivers and harbours around the south-east coast of England, were first used as temporary prisons in the 1770s, when the War of Independence put a stop to transportation to the American colonies. Most of those on board had been sentenced to short terms of imprisonment; from the 1780s onwards convicts sentenced to longer terms (over fourteen years) or life imprisonment were usually sent on to New South Wales. The hulks remained in service until 1857; the practice of transporting convicts was finally abolished in 1867.

Hobart Town: the main town of Tasmania, founded as a penal colony in 1803.

321 *Launceston*: a settlement and trading centre in the north of Tasmania.

George Town: founded in 1804, the original settlement in northern Tasmania before the main site was moved to Launceston.

slop-suits: the loose trousers and short woollen jacket worn by seamen.

triangles: soldiers ordered to be flogged were bound to a tripod, originally made from three halberds stuck in the ground.

322 *Irish Rebellion*: an uprising lasting several months in 1798; it led to the 1801 Act of Union, bringing Ireland more tightly under British control.

Brittan: no record of this individual has been traced.

323 *Asylum for the Houseless*: established in 1822 to provide shelter to the destitute during winter. Mayhew visited the Cripplegate asylum in 1849 for the *Morning Chronicle*. The account here largely reprints his 1849 article, and was reprinted again in his novel (co-authored with his brother Augustus) *Paved with Gold*, where the scene was illustrated by Hablot K. Browne ('Phiz').

'out-wanderer': emigrant.

sea-cock: sailor.

324 *tanpit-like*: like the pits in which hides are laid for tanning.

'basil': sheepskin.

coverlids: counterpanes or coverings for a bed.

325 *mixen*: dunghill or compost heap.

326 *Pharisee in the parable*: Luke 18: 9–14.

'padding-ken': a lodging-house for tramps or itinerants (slang).

332 *Hymen*: the Greek god of marriage ceremonies.

blacksmith of Gretna: the blacksmith of Gretna Green (a small village just over the Scottish border) was rumoured to marry eloping couples wishing to take advantage of more lenient Scottish marriage laws. He is the subject of a musical farce by William Collier (*The Blacksmith, or A Day at Gretna Green*, 1834) and a comic poem by James Smith ('The Gretna Green Blacksmith') repr. in *Rejected Addresses and Other Poems* (1840); he is also suggested as a solution to one character's problems in Wilkie Collins's novel *Armadale* (1866): '"Lots of people in our situation have tried the blacksmith, and found him quite as good as a clergyman, and a most amiable man I believe, into the bargain"' (ch. 11).

broughams: small closed carriages pulled by one horse.

douceur: a gift or tip; a bribe.

sur le champ: without delay.

333 *loge*: a 'box' at the theatre.

gave her her congé: dismissed her.

336 *Asmodeus*: a demon. In Alain-René Lesage's novel *Le Diable boiteux* (1707) Asmodeus takes Don Cleofas for a night flight, and through magic removes the roofs from a village's houses to reveal what is going on inside. The story became a popular reference point for writers imagining people's secret lives: in *Dombey and Son* (1846–8), Dickens appeals for a 'good spirit' to lift off the London roofs and reveal the evil lurking within (ch. 47).

338 *houses*: i.e. brothels.

339 *ruined*: robbed of one's virginity, raped.

gay: living by prostitution.

341 *Cheap Johns*: see p. 106 above.

342 *Arabs*: street children, described by Lord Shaftesbury in 1848 as 'City Arabs . . . [who] are like tribes of lawless freebooters, bound by no obligations, and utterly ignorant or utterly regardless of social duties' (cited in *OED*).

343 *rookery*: a densely populated area of poor housing.

344 *pannikins*: small tin pans or drinking vessels.

348 *Seven Dials*: an area near Covent Garden where seven streets converge. By the mid-nineteenth century it had become one of the most notorious slums in London; in *Sketches by Boz* (1836) Dickens claimed that 'The stranger who finds himself in the Dials for the first time . . . at the entrance of Seven obscure passages, uncertain which to take, will see enough around him to keep his curiosity awake for no inconsiderable time' ('Seven Dials').

350 *sharper*: a cheat or swindler, especially in cards and other games.

351 *billicock*: a low-crowned felt hat.

coiners and ringers of changes: forgers and fraudsters; the procedure for 'ringing the changes' is explained later in the paragraph.

base money: counterfeit money.

353 *flock*: stuffed with scraps of wool or cotton.

355 *hopping*: picking hops, to be used in brewing beer.

358 *The trainer . . . adroit manner*: the pickpocket's training methods were fictionalized in *Oliver Twist* (1838), ch. 9.

361 *"Female Blondin"*: Selina Young (b. 1840/41), a tightrope walker who attempted to cross the Thames from Battersea to Cremorne on 24 August 1861. She was forced to abandon her attempt when the rope slackened and started to sway 'like a garden swing'; after dangling by her hands for some time she was eventually rescued by a boat, at which point the spectators, 'relieved from the dreadful feelings of suspense which until now had weighed heavily upon them, gave vent to their admiration . . . in long and continued bursts of applause' (George Linnaeus Banks, *Blondin: His Life and Performances*, 1862).

364 *casual ward*: part of a workhouse designed to accommodate vagrants; established in the 1830s, the casual ward was designed to be off-puttingly uncomfortable, and able-bodied inmates were obliged to perform a certain amount of work—chopping logs, breaking stones, or picking oakum—to earn their keep.

365 *rig*: lark or game.

Jack Ketch: the original Jack Ketch (d. 1686) was an executioner renowned for his clumsy (or sadistic) technique when beheading his victims; 'Jack Ketch' later became a nickname applied to any executioner, including the hangman in Punch and Judy shows.

366 *Old Horse . . . Steel*: nicknames for, respectively, the prisons at Horsemonger Lane and Cold Bath Fields.

371 *life-preserver*: a stick or truncheon weighted with lead at one end, designed for self-defence.

377 *Oliver Twist*: Dickens's novel was widely adapted for the stage, starting with a version by Gilbert À Beckett at St James's Theatre on 27 March 1838 when only half the novel had been serialized; at least five different versions were running by the end of the year.

Jack Sheppard: see note to p. 20.

reticules: small bags or handbags.

379 *silk-mercers*: tradesmen who deal in silk.

dwelling-houses: residences, as distinguished from places of business.

380 *receipt-stamps*: the 1694 Stamp Act established a tax on the transfer of legal documents; it was paid by the purchase of official stamps.

381 *rattle*: issued to police for attracting attention; it was replaced by a whistle towards the end of the nineteenth century.

ticket of leave: an 'order of licence' giving a convict his liberty (under certain restrictions) as a reward for good behaviour before the term of his sentence had formally expired—a form of parole.

386 *post-chaise*: a closed horse-drawn carriage for carrying mail and passengers.

387 *Lord Grey*: probably Henry Grey, 3rd Earl Grey (1802–94), statesman and son of the Prime Minister at the time of the 1832 Reform Bill.

389 *filbert nails*: i.e. elegantly manicured.

gunpowder tattoo: burns caused by gunpowder exploding close to the skin.

Society for the Suppression of Mendicity: see note to p. 273.

390 *that bourne . . . returns*: the allusion is to Hamlet's 'To be or not to be' soliloquy: 'the dread of something after death, | The undiscovered country from whose bourn | No traveller returns, puzzles the will' (*Hamlet*, III. i).

Dugdale's Monastica: Sir William Dugdale's work of medieval English ecclesiastical history *Monasticon Anglicanum* (1655–73); a 'new edition' was published 1817–30.

Vamosed: ran away (slang).

Gaff blown: secret revealed (slang).

slope: sneaking off, escape (slang).

391 *Cadger*: beggar or trickster (slang).

Bobby Peel: i.e. Sir Robert Peel: see note to p. 71.

Vicar of Wakefield: a novel (published in 1766) by Oliver Goldsmith. It retained its popularity throughout the nineteenth century, and is mentioned in works including Charles Dickens's *A Tale of Two Cities* (1859) and *David Copperfield* (1850), Charlotte Brontë's *Villette* (1853) and *The Professor* (1857), and George Eliot's *Middlemarch* (1871–2).

391 *"on the same lay . . . spoil his game!"*: i.e. trying the same swindle and interfering with his targets.

Earl of Derby: as the work glorifies the Tory party, the dedicatee is presumably Edward Stanley, the 14th earl of Derby (1799–1869), who entered government in 1827 as a Whig, but after defecting to the Tories headed two brief ministries in 1852 and 1858–9.

392 *"Pro Rege . . . Focis"*: for the king, the law, our altars and our hearths [i.e. religion and family]; an adaptation of Cicero's phrase 'Pro aris et focis' in *De natura deorum*.

modus operandi: way of working.

swell: a flashily dressed man about town (slang).

393 *the Regent*: George IV (1762–1830), who was Prince Regent from 1811 until his accession in 1820 during his father's relapse into insanity.

phaeton-and-four: a light open carriage, with four horses.

man of parts: a man of many talents, a man of the world.

womb of the press: a playful allusion to Shakespeare, *Othello*, I. iii. 369–70: 'There are many events in the womb of time which will be delivered.'

crack of doom: Shakespeare, *Macbeth*, IV. i. 117: 'What, will the line stretch out to the crack of doom?'

Crystal Palace: a large steel-and-glass construction in Hyde Park designed by Joseph Paxton (1803–65) to house the 1851 Great Exhibition (see note to p. 66).

396 *lays*: schemes or lines of business.

397 *spliced . . . jaw*: a slightly confused version of nautical slang; 'splice the main brace' was naval shorthand for 'give every sailor an extra tot of rum', so the beggar seems to mean that he hasn't had a drink for two days.

eight—bells: a nautical term for noon, traditionally the time for changing the ship's watch.

398 *jack tars in nautical dramas*: 'Jack Tar' was a common term for a sailor; melodramas with a nautical theme, such as Douglas William Jerrold's potpoiler *Black-Ey'd Susan* (1829), which features a sailor hero and a great deal of nautical slang, were especially popular in the 1820s and 1830s.

"Robinson Crusoe": a novel by Daniel Defoe first published in 1719 which extended its influence across the nineteenth century—see e.g. Wilkie Collins's *The Moonstone* (1868), which features a character, Gabriel Betteredge, who uses the novel as a practical guide to life.

"Tales of the Ocean": sea stories by John Sherburne Sleeper (1794–1878), first published in 1842 and often reprinted.

399 *Charley Napier*: Admiral Sir Charles John Napier (1786–1860), a senior naval officer who refused to attack the great naval bases of Sveaborg

and Kronstadt during the Crimean War, having (accurately) judged that they were impregnable against the forces at his command, and was subsequently subjected to an outcry in the press, led by *The Times*, for his lack of gung-ho spirit.

pea-coat: a double-breasted woollen coat commonly worn by sailors.

"Custom-'us horficers": i.e. Custom House officers, government officials employed to collect duties on imported goods.

400 *handspike*: a lever or crowbar used on board ship.

far-off look . . . head: a popular pose for old sailors in Victorian art; see e.g. the grizzled sea-dog who sits in his study gazing off into the distance in John Everett Millais's *The North-West Passage* (1874).

401 *in his time . . . parts*: an allusion to Jaques's 'All the world's a stage' speech in Shakespeare's *As You Like It*: 'And one man in his time plays many parts, | His acts being seven ages' (II. vii).

402 *late war in the Crimea*: the Crimean War (October 1853–February 1856), in which the Russian Empire fought an alliance of France, Britain, Sardinia, and the Ottoman Empire.

mutiny in India: known by a number of different names, including the Indian Mutiny, the Great Rebellion, and India's First War of Independence, this began as a local mutiny in the town of Meerut by sepoys in the British East India Company's army on 10 May 1857, and rapidly developed into a brutal conflict that spread across much of the British-occupied territory; it was finally suppressed in 1858.

Nelson: Vice-Admiral Horatio Nelson (1758–1805), a naval officer during the Napoleonic Wars who was killed during his victory at the Battle of Trafalgar (1805). Wounded during the Battle of Santa Cruz de Tenerife (1797) he instructed the ship's surgeon to amputate his right arm, declaring that 'the sooner it was off the better', and was issuing orders again within half an hour.

battle of Inkermann: a battle of the Crimean War, fought on 5 November 1854, which resulted in a victory for British and French forces, commanded by General Pierce Bosquet, against the Russian army led by General Menshikov.

406 *rogue and vagabond*: the 1824 Vagrancy Act made offences such as begging punishable by fines or imprisonment up to a month; the phrase 'rogue and vagabond' had been retained from Elizabethan vagrancy laws.

nigger line: i.e. a blackface minstrel.

407 *books . . . touch*: see note to p. 124.

409 *pressed*: see note to p. 112.

410 *Sir Giles Overreach*: i.e. Philip Massinger's play *A New Way to Pay Old Debts* (1633). The central character, Sir Giles Overreach, who loses his sanity in the final scene, was one of the most popular villains on the nineteenth-century stage.

411 *Humane Society*: founded in 1774 by William Hawes (1736–1808) and Thomas Cogan (1736–1818) as the 'Society for the Recovery of Persons Apparently Drowned', to promote the resuscitation of people wrongly thought to be dead.

412 *portmonnaies*: wallets or purses.

413 *Thus does one touch of nature make all the world akin*: from *Troilus and Cressida*, III. iii. 175.

Ryle, Catnach and company: publishers of ballads, songs and scandal sheets: founded by James Catnatch in 1813, it was later taken on by his sister, Anne Ryle.

Macaulay: Thomas Babington Macaulay (1800–59), Whig MP and historian, who drew on what he called 'the lighter literature of the age' (chapbooks, ballads, and popular songs) when composing his *History of England* (1848–59).

414 *bagatelle*: a game similar to billiards, played on a board with nine holes at one end.

in mufti: in civilian's clothes; out of uniform.

415 *gamins*: boys left to roam the streets.

discoursing . . . music: an allusion to *Hamlet*: 'give it [the recorder] breath with your mouth, and it will discourse most eloquent music' (III. ii).

427 *Jessore*: a district in India renowned for its poverty and one of the areas thought to be a source of Asiatic cholera.

The Oxford World's Classics Website

www.worldsclassics.co.uk

- Browse the full range of Oxford World's Classics online
- Sign up for our monthly e-alert to receive information on new titles
- Read extracts from the Introductions
- Listen to our editors and translators talk about the world's greatest literature with our Oxford World's Classics audio guides
- Join the conversation, follow us on Twitter at OWC_Oxford
- Teachers and lecturers can order inspection copies quickly and simply via our website

www.worldsclassics.co.uk

MORE ABOUT **OXFORD WORLD'S CLASSICS**

American Literature
British and Irish Literature
Children's Literature
Classics and Ancient Literature
Colonial Literature
Eastern Literature
European Literature
Gothic Literature
History
Medieval Literature
Oxford English Drama
Philosophy
Poetry
Politics
Religion
The Oxford Shakespeare

A complete list of Oxford World's Classics, including Authors in Context, Oxford English Drama, and the Oxford Shakespeare, is available in the UK from the Marketing Services Department, Oxford University Press, Great Clarendon Street, Oxford OX2 6DP, or visit the website at www.oup.com/uk/worldsclassics.

In the USA, visit www.oup.com/us/owc for a complete title list.

Oxford World's Classics are available from all good bookshops. In case of difficulty, customers in the UK should contact Oxford University Press Bookshop, 116 High Street, Oxford OX1 4BR.